P9-DTC-771

Western Garden Annual

2001 EDITION

By the Editors of *Sunset Magazine* and Sunset Books

A bouquet of winning long-stemmed zinnias *(page 191)*

Sunset Publishing Corporation ■ Menlo Park, California

TERRENCE MOORE

SUNSET BOOKS

VP and General Manager
Richard A. Smeby
VP, Editorial Director
Bob Doyle
Production Director
Lory Day
Art Director
Vasken Guiragossian

STAFF FOR THIS BOOK

Managing Editor
Suzanne Normand Eyre
Contributing Editors
Philip Edinger
Helen Sweetland
Indexer
Pamela Evans
Production Coordinator
Patricia S. Williams

SUNSET PUBLISHING CORPORATION

Senior Vice President
Kevin Lynch
VP, Publisher
Christopher D. Kevorkian
VP, Manufacturing Director
Lorinda Reichert
VP, Editor-in-Chief, Sunset Magazine
Rosalie Muller Wright
Consumer Marketing Director
Christina Olsen
Managing Editor
Carol Hoffman
Art Director
James H. McCann
Senior Editor, Gardening
Kathleen Norris Brenzel
Designers
Dennis W. Leong
Laura H. Martin
Keith Whitney

A Yearly Tradition

The dawn of a new century coincides with the eighth *Western Garden Annual,* by now a familiar and anticipated accompaniment to the new year. Just as previous editions did, this volume encompasses every gardening and outdoor living article from the past year's regional issues of *Sunset Magazine.* In these 402 pages you'll find informative, thought-provoking articles and clippings covering the broad spectrum of gardening and garden-related activities—from hands-in-dirt guidance to regional display sites to newly published books on specific topics. No part of the West is unaddressed, from midnight-sun Alaska to sun-drenched Arizona, from windswept Colorado plains to balmy California shores.

Each chapter encompasses one month and has a consistent format. It begins with the Garden Guide's points of information relevant to the month—a smorgasbord of material on plants, tools, books, events, places to visit, and garden tips. The Checklists follow: a page for each of the West's gardening regions, detailing the tasks to tackle that month. Concluding the chapter are all of the month's feature-length illustrated articles.

Throughout these pages, plants and gardening activities are keyed to the climate zones mapped and described in the *Sunset Western Garden Book.*

Front cover: 'Orange Julius' dahlias, grown at Swan Island Dahlias, Canby, Oregon. Photographer: Stephen Cridland.

Back cover: Container plantings with a Southwestern theme (see page 152). Photographer: Norman A. Plate.

Endpapers (hardcover edition): *Lysimachia nummularia.* Photographer: David McDonald.

First printing: February 2001

ISSN 1073-5089
Hardcover edition: ISBN 0376-03894-2
Softcover edition: ISBN 0376-03897-7
Printed in the United States.

All material in this book originally appeared in the 2000 issues of *Sunset Magazine*.

Sunset Western Garden Annual was produced by Sunset Books. If you have comments or suggestions, please let us hear from you. Write us at:

Sunset Books
Garden Book Editorial
80 Willow Road
Menlo Park, CA 94025
or visit our website at
www.sunsetbooks.com

Contents

LEFT TO RIGHT: 'Bonnie B' hibiscus, cool-season vegetable garden, New Generation lupines

Guide to the New Century

In a year when the calendar has rolled over to three zeros, the French expression *Plus ça change, plus c'est la même chose* (roughly, "The more things change, the more they stay the same") offers reassurance. And one reassuring element is *Sunset*'s guiding hand extended to Western gardeners—there for the better part of the last century and ready to lead us through the next with the same sound yet innovative advice that millions of readers have come to expect. Thus the year 2000, the dawn of a new century, found *Sunset Magazine* full of forward-looking articles.

What's new? For those looking for dazzling new plants, nothing could be more exciting than "The New Hibiscus," displayed in vibrant color in July's chapter. And gardeners who have worshiped Russell hybrid lupines from afar can try the less fussy New Generation lupines with renewed hope. "Roses for the 21st Century" traces the trend toward mass-flowering roses as landscape shrubs. Devotees of homegrown fruit will appreciate the bolt-upright pillar apples that offer the promise of fruit in a fraction of the space a traditional, even dwarf, tree occupies. And to amaze your friends, slice up the new, pink-fleshed 'Cara Cara' orange! For easing garden maintenance tasks, there are now superior pruning tools of Japanese steel as well as lightweight pruners. A preview of more finely tuned climate zones for Mountain states (as they appear in the 2001 revised edition of the *Sunset Western Garden Book)* reflects that region's increase in population and gardening interest.

What's innovative? Would you believe a "tree" constructed from a giant umbrella frame draped with a vine? Or a fountain spilling blossoms rather than water? Or recycled trees dripping with annuals in long cascades? Other innovative ideas include university-designed "compost factories" and mirrors employed in the garden for special illusions. And conserving both muscle and money are synthetic containers that mimic terra-cotta and stone.

What's popular? Photo essays of garden designs and makeovers continue to inspire readers. Among the noteworthy features were a showstopper spring garden, a desert garden combining plants with art and architecture, and small gardens you can replicate in as little as a weekend's time. Clever designs for vase and container are welcome solutions to gift-giving and entertaining puzzles. Ever-popular plants featured are impatiens, Japanese maples, orchids, ornamental grasses, succulents, and zinnias.

What's tasty? Mouthwatering articles focus on specific fruits and vegetables, from both slicing and cluster tomatoes to exotic tropical fruits for milder climes. Onions receive close scrutiny in a guide to the entire clan. Northwest gardeners are introduced to the best seedless table grapes for the region as well as to a luscious hardy kiwi. Vegetable gardens are explored in depth, from choosing appropriate varieties to timing, preparation, planting, and harvest.

What's technical? Because much of the West is moisture challenged, water conservation is paramount. Two California gardens model year-round strategies in "Water Wisdom," while a feature on summer irrigation demonstrates how another scheme accommodates plants of diverse water needs. Common garden pests are dealt with in a gentle (nontoxic) manner, and fertilizers are demystified in an all-you-need-to-know piece. In the construction field, greenhouses get dollars-and-sense coverage, and fences are hailed as more than just barriers.

What's traditional? Modern sweet peas go back to the 18th century; we remind you of the sweetest smelling ones. Climbing roses have been around even longer—a good reason to showcase those that dependably deliver both vigor and bloom. And the classic rock garden is alive and evolving, as evidenced in all Western climes.

What's next? Miteproof fuchsias, frostproof tomatoes, blue cannas? Who knows? But this prediction is certain: whatever it is and whenever it appears, you're sure to read about it in *Sunset.*

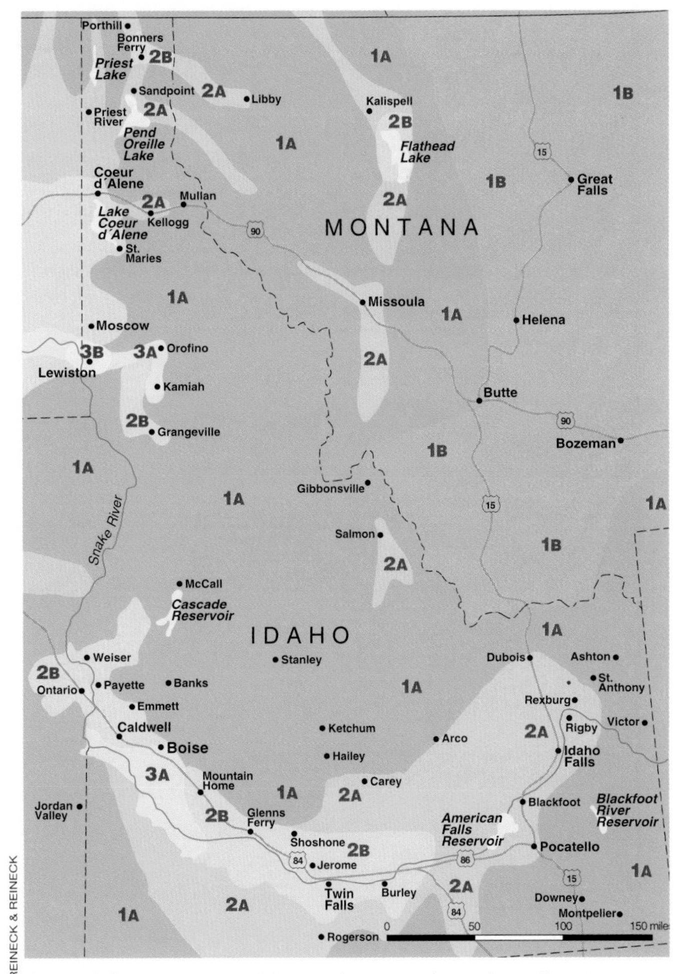

One of Sunset's new Mountain states' garden climate zone maps (see pages 388–389)

NORMAN A PLATE

ARRANGE January-blooming branches for a spring-fresh bouquet. For details on these cuttings and other good bouquet choices, see page 13.

January

gardenguide

PAUL AND MARY SCHWEIKHER (2)

NEWLY INSTALLED landscape (left) took three years to fill out.

Makeover for a Phoenix front yard

The owners lost a lawn, but gained a landscape with outdoor living space

■ Paul and Mary Schweikher approached Phoenix landscape architect Christy Ten Eyck about a front-yard transformation with high hopes and modest means. For starters, they asked for an outdoor living room. Instead of a water-hogging lawn, they wanted a mostly native garden that would attract birds and butterflies. And they needed a sound buffer against traffic noise. Their budget: $7,000 to $8,000.

Ten Eyck spent most of that amount removing the turf and asphalt driveway that dominated the front yard, then repositioning the carport entrance away from the front door. To create living space, she built a circular patio of recycled bricks near the entrance, and to help mask street noise, she installed a seating wall with an aqueduct-like chute that splashes water into a small basin. A curved walkway of decomposed granite leads to the patio.

Next, Ten Eyck brought in trees in 24-inch boxes, including a mesquite to shade the patio, as well as the palo verde in bloom in the photo above. Plants in 1-gallon containers, including brittlebush, hop bush, and *Salvia greggii,* were used elsewhere. For extra spring color, the yard was liberally seeded with African daisies and wildflowers.

— *Sharon Cohoon*

Fiery orange cosmos, pretty sweet corn

■ Last spring in *Sunset's* garden, we set out seedlings of the nine plants named as All-America Selections for 2000. After watching them all grow to maturity, our garden staff was particularly impressed with two plants. Look for seedlings in nurseries this spring, or order seed now from the sources listed at right. Plant in full sun.

'Cosmic Orange' cosmos. Its incandescent orange flowers seem to glow with heat. Waves of the 2-inch-wide, semidouble blooms with ruffled petals appear over a long season on compact plants 1 to 2½ feet tall.

'Indian Summer' sweet corn. With kernels in shades of rusty red, deep plum, sunny yellow, and pearly white, it looks just like old-fashioned Indian

corn. But nibble a freshly cooked ear and you discover 'Indian Summer' isn't merely ornamental; it's a delicious supersweet variety. The multicolored kernels form along 8-inch ears on stalks 6½ to 7 feet tall. You can start harvesting about 80 days after sowing.

Seed sources

Nichols Garden Nursery, Albany, OR; (541) 928-9280.
Park Seed Company, Greenwood, SC; (800) 845-3369.
W. Atlee Burpee, Warminster, PA; (800) 888-1447.

— Dick Bushnell

NORMAN A. PLATE (3)

Long-armed lightweights

■ Like star bantamweight boxers, these new garden tools—from the YardShark line by Shark Corporation—are at the top of their game. Each weighs in at less than 2½ pounds, but all are sturdy enough to tackle heavyweight pruning chores that usually strain arms and backs. Their oval handles are made from extruded aluminum with comfortable, nonslip, impact-absorbing grips. Razor-sharp blades are made of double-tempered high-carbon Japanese steel.

A: The Bypass Lopper ($34.99) is good for cutting live growth up to 1½ inches thick. **B:** The Telescopic Hedger/Pruner ($36.99) has adjustable handles that extend the tool's length from 30 to 46 inches; its 6-inch cutting blades are useful for trimming hedges or small tree branches. **C:** The Anvil Lopper ($32.99) is designed for pruning dry or dead wood.

For details, call (800) 891-7855 or visit www.sharkcorp.com.

— Peter O. Whiteley

NORMAN A. PLATE

COMPACT COLONNADE apple tree fits well into a small space between shrubs in this Los Altos garden.

Apple pillars

■ Meet the rising new stars among apple trees. Colonnade apples, introduced into the United States in the mid '90s, grow upright and narrow (see photo above). Instead of developing horizontal branches like standard apple trees do, these trees form fruit on short spurs that develop along the main trunk. They fit easily into the smallest gardens; you can plant several along a fence or deck, in a side yard, or even in containers on a sunny porch.

One Green World (503/651-3005 or www.onegreenworld.com) in Molalla, Oregon, sells scab-resistant varieties developed in Canada. Trees grow 10 to 12 feet tall, 3 feet wide. They include **'Golden Sentinel'**, yellow, sweet, juicy fruit; **'Northpole'**, crisp, juicy, McIntosh-type fruit; and **'Scarlet Sentinel'**, large, sweet, green-yellow fruit with red blush.

Stark Brothers (800/325-4180; www.starkbros.com) and Monrovia Nursery (wholesale only; ask your nursery to order for you) sell English varieties. Trees grow about 8 feet tall and 2 feet wide. Varieties are **'Crimson Spire'**, tart sweet red apple with white flesh; **'Emerald Spire'**, mellow, sweet green apple with gold blush; **'Scarlet Spire'**, juicy red-and-green eating apple; and **'Ultra Spire'**, tart, tangy red apple with a yellowish blush (trees are more compact than the other varieties).

Colonnade apple trees need little maintenance. Water them regularly and fertilize them two to three times a year (more often for plants in containers). In summer, prune only to shape the tree and cut back wayward growth, if it develops; prune long stems back to three leaves.

Pick the apples in September when they taste ripe.

— Lauren Bonar Swezey

ALLAN MANDELL

Silktassel dangles its charms

■ When *Garrya* blooms in winter or early spring, you immediately see how this genus of native Western shrubs earned its nickname, silktassel. Chains of silky flower clusters called catkins dangle from branches clad with evergreen leaves. Yet as showy and easy to grow as these shrubs are, they're still not very common in Western gardens.

Several species and varieties are available. The most well-known of these is coast silktassel (*Garrya elliptica*), which can be grown in *Sunset* climate zones 4–9 and 14–21. This plant normally grows 4 to 8 feet tall with an equal spread, and can be pruned as a small tree or trained up a wall. Its wavy-edged leaves are green on top with woolly gray undersides. The color and length of the tassels vary according to the sex of the plant: Females of *G. elliptica* bear pale green ones 2 to 3½ inches long; males bear chartreuse or yellowish catkins 3 to 8 inches long (the male variety *G.e.* 'Evie' has 10-inch catkins).

Two close cousins are Fremont silktassel (*G. fremontii*), which bears somewhat shorter yellowish or purple catkins and glossy green leaves with smooth edges (grows in zones 2–10, 12, 14–17), and the hybrid *G. issaquahensis* 'Pat Ballard' (zones 4–7 and 14–17), which bears 8-inch catkins.

Garrya can take full sun or partial shade. In the landscape, it works well as a screen or informal hedge. Look for blooming silktassels in nurseries later this month; plant immediately. One good mail-order source is Forest Farm (990 Tetherow Rd., Williams, OR 97544; 541/846-7269), which sells 1-gallon plants for $8 to $9, plus shipping.

— Steven R. Lorton

Spare the shears

For roses in February, prune lightly now

■ Cutting rose canes back to hardwood makes sense in areas where winters are frigid; there the practice protects plants from frost damage. But in Southern California gardens, that precaution is unnecessary and even counterproductive, says Jan Smithen, gardening instructor at the Arboretum of Los Angeles County. "All it does is delay the next bloom cycle," she says.

"Roses need to grow to their genetic height before they put out blooms. So, if you cut them back hard, they have to regain that height before they form flowers." Why waste the energy? "Prune back lightly now, and you'll get blooms again in about six weeks," Smithen says.

Carrie Davich, a graduate of Smithen's class, never hard-prunes her roses. The border of hybrid teas in her Pasadena garden, shown here, was photographed in February. — *S.C.*

STEVEN GUNTHER

LOOSELY PRUNED 'Helen Traubel', a hybrid tea rose, has a carefree look against the precision of the ivy lattice (trained on wires) on the wall.

Winter pruning à la Smithen

Remove unproductive wood. Cut out all dead and damaged wood.

Open up the center. To improve air circulation, remove branches that cross through the center.

Lightly prune the remaining canes. Cut back long, gangly canes to correspond to the general outline of the shrub. Prune the rest of the canes minimally. Make all cuts back to an outward-facing bud.

Remove foliage and apply dormant oil. Strip off all rose leaves and rake up and dispose of the foliage underneath the shrubs. Apply dormant horticultural oil to the stripped canes. "Yes, the dormant season spray is a nuisance," admits Smithen, "but it pays off." The flip side to rose gardening in a Mediterranean climate, she says, is that all those sucking insects that love rose foliage never stop reproducing. But dormant oil smothers their eggs, putting at least a temporary dent in the population. It's easiest to apply the oil when the canes are defoliated.

CHARLES MANN

BROMELIADS (front right), pink-flowered anthuriums, bamboo, and papyrus flourish around a pond.

Tropical paradise in Grand Junction

Rendezvous with more than 600 species of exotic plants in this rain-forest exhibit

■ On a frigid winter day, visitors to the Western Colorado Botanical Society in Grand Junction receive a balmy surprise when they step into the Rainforest Rendezvous. In this 4,000-square-foot greenhouse, they're enveloped in a warm (the air temperature is constantly 80° to 85°), humid (50 to 60 percent) environment. Designed to recreate a tropical rain forest, the exhibit is threaded with boardwalks that lead visitors through gardens and over ponds providing habitat for more than 600 species of plants. Orchids grow from a wall cloaked with Spanish moss (*Tillandsia usneoides*). Many of the plants can be grown at home, from flamingo flower (*Anthurium scherzeranum*) to weeping fig (*Ficus* species).

In the adjacent Butterfly House, winged beauties drift through the air like exotic snowflakes. An enclosed glass "birthing room" (called a puparium) offers a fascinating view of fledgling butterflies emerging from the chrysalides that protect them during metamorphosis.

Enter the Rainforest Rendezvous—the first phase of a long-range plan that calls for construction of several outdoor theme gardens—through the Botanica gift shop, 655 Struthers Avenue. Hours are 10 to 5 Wednesdays through Sundays. Admission costs $3, $2 ages 62 and over and students with ID, $1.50 ages 5 through 12. For information on docent-led tours or membership, contact the Western Colorado Botanical Society at (970) 245-3288 or www.wcbotanic.org.

— Pamela Cornelison

Budding branches

■ In winter, many plants in Western gardens are as eager to charge into spring as huskies frolicking at the starting gate of a dogsled race. Festooned with flowers that range from the softest pink to vibrant yellow, their branches are perfect for bouquets.

When cut and placed in water-filled vases, branches of deciduous trees such as flowering plum continue to unfurl as they would on the tree. Evergreens such as camellias make handsome teammates.

In addition to the cuttings pictured on page 6 and described here, good choices for bouquets include flowering quince (*Chaenomeles*, flowers in shades of coral, orange, and many shades of pink, red, and white), forsythia (fragrant yellow flowers), and many fruit trees, including apple, apricot, cherry, and peach. If you don't already have a few of these plants in your garden, January is a good month to set them out.

For longest-lasting bloom, snip a few small branches either when the first buds are showing color or when they have just opened. Follow proper pruning practices when cutting off the branches: Prune to thin or shape the plant, and always prune back to a side branch (never leave stubs).

Our winter bouquet contains cuttings from the following plants:

• **Acacia.** Yellow blossoms last about a week in vases. Trees grow well in milder-winter areas of California and Arizona.

• **Camellia.** Glossy green leaves, pale pink flowers. Zones 4–9, 12, 14–24.

• **Flowering plum.** Rose pink blooms are followed by deep maroon leaves. In bouquets, the flowers last five to seven days if you cut branches before buds open. Most species grow well throughout most of the West.

• **Almond.** White blossoms. All zones.

• **Polyanthus jasmine** (*Jasminum polyanthum*). Fast-climbing evergreen vine (to 20 feet) with lacy leaflets and fragrant white flowers. Cut branches drape beautifully over vase edges. Zones 5–9, 12–24.

DESIGN: Bud Stuckey

— *Kathleen N. Brenzel*

BACK TO BASICS

NORMAN A. PLATE

How to rewet peat moss

Place dry peat moss in a wheelbarrow. Fill a gallon-size watering can with water, then add two or three drops of liquid dish soap (such as Ivory Liquid); stir with a stick. Slowly pour the water over the peat moss, stirring as you pour. Use only enough water to moisten but not soak the peat moss. Once moist, it can absorb additional water more easily.

— *Lauren Bonar Swezey*

Glittering city on a fencetop

■ When the days are short and winter's gloom seems endless, Barbara Parker and William Nichols need only look out from their house to enjoy a panoramic view of the Seattle skyline that glitters on their garden fence. This whimsical piece of garden art always lifts their spirits.

Parker sketched the actual skyline as it would appear from their home, then transferred the drawing to cardboard templates. She turned the templates over to a carpenter to cut into cedar lattice silhouettes of landmark structures. To illuminate the skyline, a 150-foot string of minilights was stapled atop the lath-capped silhouettes.

The fence is built of 4-by-4 posts with 2-by-4 stringers and cedar slats in between. From spring through autumn, a handsome border of shrubs, perennials, and annuals flourishes at the foot of the fencetop city, while vines scramble up the buildings.

— *S.R.L.*

BEN WOOLSEY

FROM THE SPACE NEEDLE to Smith Tower (far right), lattice and lights re-create Seattle's skyline.

PROJECT

A foolproof system for starting seeds

C

NORMAN A. PLATE (4)

■ Seeds of summer vegetables, including tomatoes and peppers, need warm soil to germinate and light to grow. The compact seed-starting system pictured here satisfies both needs.

When it was time to start tomato seeds early last spring, I used the Green Thumb Grow Light System ($90). Consisting of two 4-foot-long fluorescent lights mounted on a stand, it accommodates two flats of 2-inch cells—100 seedlings—at a time. Under the flats, I put two heating mats ($23 each) that are preset to keep the soil 15° to 20° above room temperature. I sowed seeds in pairs to ensure that I'd get at least one viable seedling per cell.

This system delivered the best results I've had with tomatoes—from seedling to harvest, I didn't lose a single plant.

To find out where to buy the Grow Light System and heating mats, contact Hydrofarm at (800) 634-9990 or www.hydrofarm.com. Free catalog.

STEP-BY-STEP

1. To sow the seeds, wet the tip of a wood chopstick **(A)**, touch it to two dry seeds, poke them into the potting soil, and release the seeds by twisting the chopstick as you pull it out. Most seeds germinate well if you sow them about ¼ inch deep; cover seeds and firm soil over them. Water the seed flats and keep the soil moist. Turn on the heating mats and keep them on until transplant time.

2. When seedlings break the surface, turn on the lights **(B)**. Hang the lights in their low position, about 7 inches above the flats; keep them on from breakfast to bedtime. Once seedlings are 1 to 2 inches tall **(C)**, use scissors to nip off the weaker one in each cell.

3. When seedlings develop two sets of true leaves **(D)**, they're ready to transplant. You can move them into 4-inch pots for a few weeks to develop sturdier stems. Or if you prefer to set them directly in the garden, first harden off plants by moving the flat outdoors to a spot where they'll get filtered sun and be protected from cold at night. After four days, plant them in the ground. Be prepared to protect them against nighttime frosts with hot caps or row covers. About two months after transplanting, the first ripe fruits will be ready to harvest. — *Jim McCausland*

WHAT TO DO IN YOUR GARDEN IN JANUARY

Pacific Northwest Checklist

PLANTING

✔ BARE-ROOT STOCK. Zones 4–7: This month, nurseries offer bare-root berries, grapes, fruit and shade trees, ornamental shrubs (including roses), vines, and perennial vegetables such as asparagus, horseradish, and rhubarb. Plant as soon as you get them home. Zones 2–3: Plant as soon as stock is available and your garden soil becomes workable.

✔ PERENNIALS. To get a jump on spring, sow seeds of aster, delphinium, hellebore, Shasta daisy, veronica, and viola in a coldframe or greenhouse. Transplant into the garden about a month before the last spring frost.

✔ WINTER-BLOOMING TREES AND SHRUBS. Zones 4–7: Shop nurseries for Sasanqua camellias, *Viburnum bodnantense*, wintersweet (*Chimonanthus praecox*), and witch hazel.

✔ WINTER COLOR. Set out English daisies, pansies, and primroses whenever the soil is dry enough to work.

MAINTENANCE

✔ APPLY DORMANT OIL. On a calm, dry day, spray dormant fruit trees and roses with horticultural oil to kill overwintering eggs and larvae.

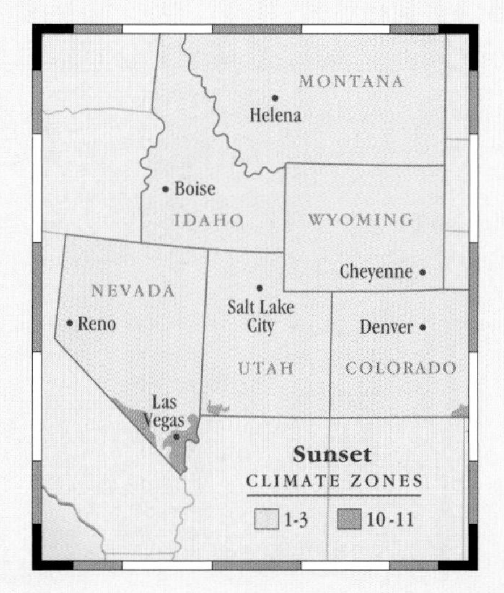

✔ CARE FOR HOUSE PLANTS. Start the grooming process by rinsing foliage off in lukewarm shower water. Then nip off dead or weak leaves and branches, and feed plants that are flowering or fruiting now (wait until spring growth begins to feed other plants). If the soil is crusty, scoop off the top ½ inch or so and replace it with fresh potting soil.

✔ FEED ASPARAGUS, RHUBARB. Spread a 2-inch layer of composted manure atop established beds of asparagus and rhubarb.

✔ FIGHT SLUGS. During spells of mild weather, slugs appear out of nowhere. When you spot them, cut them in half with a knife or machete, or set out bait in a place where birds and pets can't get at it, such as under a board that's propped up on bricks.

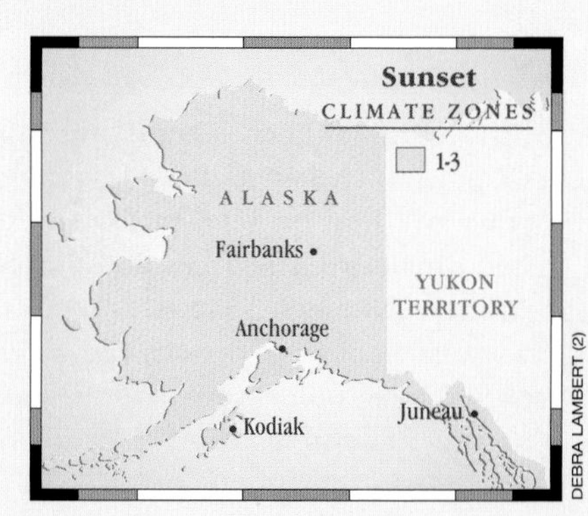

DEBRA LAMBERT (2)

✔ PRUNE FRUIT TREES. Zones 4–7: First cut out branches that are dead, diseased, or injured. Then remove closely parallel, rubbing, or crossing branches. Finally, prune for shape. Zones 1–3: Hold off pruning until mild weather comes.

✔ PRUNE HYBRID TEA ROSES. Cut them back to three to five of the most vigorous canes, removing diseased and injured ones along the way.

✔ WEED. Even in winter, weeds like dandelions grow surprisingly quickly. Pull them up, roots and all, or they'll come back to haunt you in spring. ◆

WHAT TO DO IN YOUR GARDEN IN JANUARY

Northern California Checklist

PLANNING

✔ ORDER SEEDS. Thumb through catalogs to choose and order varieties you can't find on seed racks. Several good mail-order sources are Nichols Garden Nursery (541/928-9280 or www.gardennursery.com), Ornamental Edibles (408/946-7333 or www.ornamentaledibles.com), Redwood City Seed Company (650/325-7333 or www.ecoseeds.com), and Renee's Garden (www.reneesgarden.com).

PLANTING

✔ BERRIES. Zones 7–9, 14–17: Blackberries, raspberries, and strawberries are all available bare-root this month. For a treat, try 'Olallie' blackberry. The huge 1½-inch-long berries are sweet and succulent, and the plant is well adapted to Northern California. For strawberries, it's hard to beat the flavor of 'Sequoia'.

✔ WINTER BLOOMERS. Zones 7–9, 14–17: For midwinter bloom, purchase 4-inch pots of calendula, candytuft, cineraria, dianthus, English daisy, English and fairy primrose, Iceland poppy, pansy, snapdragon, stock, and viola. Plant in containers or in flower beds. Smaller plants will just sit until spring.

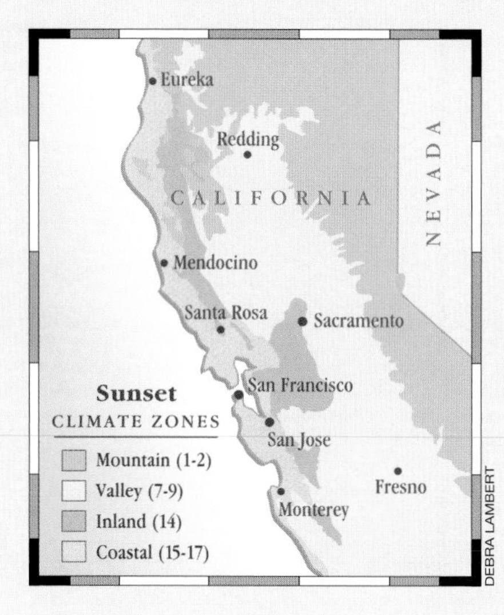

✔ TREES. Zones 7–9: The following trees are recommended for the Central Valley's hot, dry climate by the City of Modesto Urban Forestry Division: Chinese pistache (*Pistacia chinensis*), European ash (*Fraxinus excelsior*), ginkgo (*Ginkgo biloba* 'Autumn Gold' or 'Fairmount'), Hesse ash (*Fraxinus excelsior* 'Hessei'), holly oak (*Quercus ilex*), and sawleaf zelkova (*Zelkova serrata*).

✔ VEGETABLE SEEDS. Zones 7–9, 14–17: Sow seeds of cool-season vegetables such as chard, lettuce, and spinach indoors for planting in February. For crunchy, semi-heading lettuces, try Batavia types, such as red 'Cardinale', green 'Loma', or green 'Nevada' (from Ornamental Edibles; 408/946-7333).

MAINTENANCE

✔ CARE FOR GIFT PLANTS. Snip spent blossoms from blooming plants; move hardier types such as azaleas, cinerarias, cyclamen, cymbidiums, and miniature Christmas trees to protected spots outdoors. Keep tender plants such as amaryllis and kalanchoe indoors in a well-lighted spot. Water regularly. Repot if plants are rootbound and dry out quickly. Fertilize amaryllis and azaleas after bloom finishes. Fertilize cymbidiums with half-strength fertilizer every week or so; other plants should be fertilized every two to four weeks. Zones 1–2: Keep all plants indoors until after the last hard freeze.

✔ CARE FOR LIVING CHRISTMAS TREES. If you haven't done so already, move your living Christmas tree outdoors. Check the roots. If they're coming out the drain hole, transplant the tree into a larger container, or trim off some of the rootball and replant it in the same container with fresh potting mix. Water thoroughly. Give the tree part sun to begin with, then move it into full sun after a week or two. Rinse off the foliage and thoroughly soak the soil. ◆

WHAT TO DO IN YOUR GARDEN IN JANUARY

Southern California Checklist

PLANTING

✔ANNUALS. It's still possible to plant annuals, especially in mild coastal areas. Choices include calendula, dianthus, Iceland poppy, larkspur, nemesia, pansy, primrose, snapdragon, and stock. Low-desert gardeners (zone 13) can also plant petunias.

✔BARE-ROOT PLANTS. Bare-root plants are a bargain, and they're also fun: Watching a twiggy stick turn into a leafy plant is always a kick. You have plenty of opportunity to plant this month. Nurseries will still be well stocked with roses, and they will also have stone fruit trees, cane berries, grape and kiwi vines, strawberries, artichokes, and asparagus. Some may also have deciduous ornamental trees. Plant immediately if possible. If soil is too soggy, cover roots with moist soil or plant temporarily in containers.

✔WINTER COLOR. In Southern California, a surprising number of plants bloom in the middle of winter. To add sparkle to the garden during this season, consider a winter-flowering tree such as *Acacia baileyana,* Hong Kong orchid tree (*Bauhinia blakeana*), or feathery cassia (*Cassia artemisioides*). Tuck a winter-blooming shrub like Christmas heather (*Erica canaliculata*), Geraldton waxflower, or euryops into the flower border, and add bergenia, hellebores, or yellow flax (*Reinwardtia indica*) to your perennial beds. Train flame vine (*Pyrostegia venusta*) or *Jasminum polyanthum* up a trellis. Use aloes or other flowering succulents as accents.

DEBRA LAMBERT

✔WINTER VEGETABLES. Germination will be slow, but it's still possible to start cool-season crops from seed. Lettuces and other greens, flat-leaf parsley, peas and radishes, and green and bulb onions are the safest bets. You can also set out transplants of broccoli and cabbage.

MAINTENANCE

✔BEGIN DORMANT-SEASON PRUNING. Start with roses. (See page 11 for pruning tips.) Deciduous fruit trees need pruning too; plums, apricots, and peaches each require a different technique. If in doubt, attend a pruning demonstration at an arboretum or consult a good reference book before proceeding. Don't prune spring-flowering plants now—wait until after bloom. Also wait for spring before removing frost-damaged branches. The damaged portion protects tender interior growth.

✔GROOM CAMELLIAS. If camellia blight is a problem (petals turn brown and flowers rot in the center), pick infected flowers from plants and remove fallen flowers and leaves promptly from ground beneath plants.

PEST CONTROL

✔APPLY DORMANT SPRAY. After pruning, spray roses and deciduous flowering and fruit trees with horticultural oil to smother overwintering insects such as mites, scale, and sawfly larvae. For fungal diseases such as peach leaf curl, mix lime sulfur or fixed copper into the oil. Spray the branches, crotches, trunk, and ground beneath the tree's drip line. If rain occurs within 48 hours, repeat. ◆

Mountain Checklist

PLANNING AND PLANTING

✔ ORDER SEEDS, PLANTS. Place seed orders early for best selection. Most companies will hold plants for shipping at the proper planting time in your area. Check out the catalog offerings of these regional sources. Montana-based ***Garden City Seeds*** (778 U.S. 93 N., Hamilton, MT 59840; 406/961-4837 or www.gardencityseeds.com) specializes in short-season vegetables. Idaho-based ***Seeds Trust/High Altitude Gardens*** (Box 1048, Hailey, ID 83333; 208/788-4363 or www.seedsave.org) carries wildflower seeds and open-pollinated vegetables. Colorado-based ***Sun Chaser Seeds*** (14290 W. 54th Ave., Arvada, CO 80002; 303/666-0911) offers a large selection of seeds of wildflowers and shrubs native to the Rocky Mountains.

✔ SOW HARDY PERENNIALS. Seeds of most hardy perennials, including bleeding hearts, columbines, phlox, and primulas, require a period of chilling to germinate. Sow seeds now in soil-filled pots and place them outdoors out of direct sun. Whenever snow is available, pile it atop the pots. After six weeks of chilling, bring the pots into a greenhouse or set them on a sunny windowsill to sprout. When seedlings have two sets of true leaves, transplant them into individual containers and continue growing them indoors until spring, then set them out in the garden.

MAINTENANCE

✔ CHECK STORED BULBS. Examine bulbs, corms, and tubers for shriveling and rot. If bulbs are shriveling, sprinkle on a little water to rehydrate them. Discard any that show decay except dahlia tubers: You can cut the bad spots out of those, dust with sulfur, and store them apart from the rest.

✔ MULCH FLOWER BEDS. Overlap Christmas tree boughs and evergreen prunings atop beds to protect newly planted and tender perennials and bulbs. Hay, straw, and pine needles also work.

✔ PRUNE TREES, SHRUBS. Winter is the ideal time to prune—you can easily see the branch structure of deciduous trees and shrubs. Cut out dead, diseased, crossing, and closely parallel branches. Don't prune lilacs or other early-spring bloomers or you could cut off this year's flowers. Hire a tree service to remove dead trees or to prune big shade trees.

✔ WATCH FOR FROST-HEAVED PLANTS. When soil freezes and thaws in recurrent cycles, it can heave fall-planted perennials and small shrubs out of the ground. If this happens, add soil around the base of the plant to cover the exposed roots.

✔ WATER. Dry winter conditions can seriously dehydrate plants. When snow or rain has not fallen for a few weeks and the soil is dry several inches beneath the surface (use a trowel to check), set out a sprinkler to soak all plantings and lawns thoroughly. Irrigate when the temperature is above freezing, and water at midday when the surface of the soil is not frozen solid.

— *Marcia Tatroe* ◆

WHAT TO DO IN YOUR GARDEN IN JANUARY

Southwest Checklist

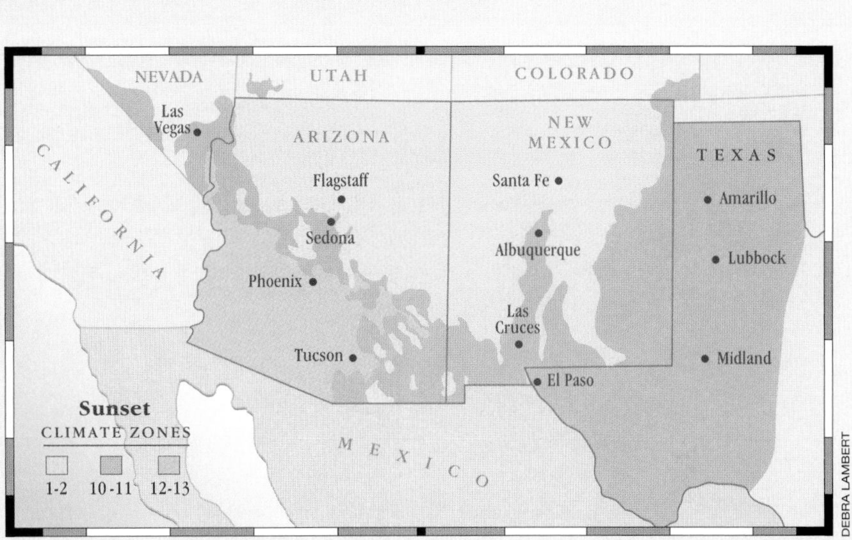

PLANTING

✔ BARE-ROOT STOCK. Buy and plant berries, cane fruits, fruit and shade trees, roses, and perennial vegetables such as Jerusalem artichoke. Ask the nursery staff to pack the bare roots in damp peat moss or sawdust for the trip home. Plant them immediately.

✔ CHILLED BULBS. If you refrigerated your bulbs to provide pre-planting chill, take them out after 6 to 10 weeks. Plant them in well-amended soil and water well; bulbs should emerge in a month or two.

✔ VEGETABLES. Zones 12–13: Sow seeds of warm-season crops including eggplant, melons, peppers, and tomatoes indoors now for transplanting outside after the danger of frost is past. Set out short-day onions.

✔ WINTER COLOR. Zones 10–13: Set out bachelor's buttons, calendulas, cinerarias, cyclamens, English daisies, pansies, petunias, primroses, snapdragons, stock, sweet alyssum, and wallflowers.

MAINTENANCE

✔ CARE FOR INDOOR PLANTS. Examine house plants regularly for aphids, scale insects, spider mites, and mealy bugs. Sometimes the first sign is sticky honeydew on pot rims and leaves; it's exuded by feeding insects. Rinse infested plants with lukewarm water from the shower, then spray with insecticidal soap.

✔ FEED AND PROTECT CITRUS. Water trees deeply one day, then spread ammonium sulfate the next day at the following rates for mature trees: 2½ pounds for grapefruit, 4 pounds for oranges and tangerines, and 5 pounds for lemon trees. Water again after feeding.

When night temperatures below 28° are predicted, cover trees with old sheets, uncovering them in the morning. If fruit is damaged (common at 25° or below), pick and juice it within 24 hours.

✔ IRRIGATE. Zones 12–13: Deep-water trees and shrubs every two to three weeks if sporadic winter rain doesn't do it for you. Deep-water conifers at least monthly. The best test: Stab a trowel or spade into the ground; water when the soil is dry an inch down.

✔ PRUNE HYBRID TEA ROSES. Cut plants back to three to five strongest canes. Cut top growth back by a third.

✔ SPRAY DORMANT TREES, SHRUBS. After pruning dormant deciduous trees and shrubs, spray horticultural oil to kill overwintering insects, eggs, and larvae. ◆

THREE MOTH ORCHIDS (phalaenopsis), each growing in a plastic pot nestled inside the large stoneware container, show off their winglike petals in this living bouquet. Maidenhair fern, sprays of lacy dendrobium orchids in water-filled tubes, and palm leaves complete the arrangement.

Winter

orchids

These four orchids are elegant, easy to grow, and in bloom now

BY SHARON COHOON
PHOTOGRAPHS BY NORMAN A. PLATE

■ GIVEN THEIR GLAMOROUS APPEARANCE AND CONSIDERABLE CACHET, ORCHIDS make impressive gifts. Their thick, waxy flowers last four to six weeks, often longer. Their length of bloom makes them a good value for the price—$28 to $45 for a 4- to 6-inch pot is typical. But that's not the end of it. The orchids described here and on page 22 make good house or patio plants—no steamy hothouse environment is necessary to keep them happy. With reasonable care, they'll bloom again next winter and for years to come. Oncidiums, cymbidiums, phalaenopsis, and zygopetalums are widely available now in nurseries, florist shops, and even supermarkets.

GENEROUS FLOWER SPRAYS and chocolate-vanilla scent make *Oncidium Sharry Baby* 'Sweet Fragrance' a top seller.

Oncidium

Florists call oncidiums "spray orchids" for obvious reasons. These beautiful plants produce tall, branching flower stems that dance with dozens of dainty, ruffle-edged blossoms. A few species and varieties are also fragrant: *O. Sharry Baby* 'Sweet Fragrance', for instance, exudes a powerful chocolate and vanilla scent. Oncidiums need more light than some of the other orchids, but when the right conditions are provided, they are contented house plants. BLOOM TIME: Varies. LIGHT: Bright, indirect light all day or direct light mornings only. TEMPERATURE: 70°–80° (day), 55°–65° (night). POTTING MIX: A commercial orchid mix, or medium-grade fir bark with or without perlite. WATERING: Keep potting mix moist during growing and bloom season. After bloom, allow the soil to dry out somewhat for two to three weeks. To provide the extra humidity this orchid likes, place the pot on an inverted saucer in a pan filled with pebbles and water. Keep water level below top of pebbles. Morning misting is also helpful. FEEDING: Fertilize with high-nitrogen fertilizer at least once a month for the first six months after bloom. Switch to low-nitrogen fertilizer for next six months.

MINIATURE CYMBIDIUM puts on a grand show for months.

A TYPICAL WHITE-FLOWERED moth orchid (phalaenopsis) towers over a rare pink variety.

STRIPED, FRAGRANT FLOWERS make zygopetalum deliciously exotic.

Cymbidium

The first cymbidiums to bloom are miniatures, which top out at 2 feet. They do well indoors in warm, sunny spots like south- or west-facing windows.

Standard cymbidiums have large, dramatic, long-lasting flowers (eight weeks or more is a typical bloom time) and graceful, strappy leaves. They're blissfully easy to care for too. But they need some chill during the fall to set flower buds. They're happier outdoors than indoors—as long as temperatures don't drop much below 32° or rise above 100° for more than a few hours.

In frost-free areas, all cymbidiums can grow outdoors through winter. Elsewhere, protect them from cold by placing containers in a greenhouse or under deep overhangs. In summer, they thrive on lath-covered patios.

Standard cymbidiums are sold in 8- to 10-inch pots, miniatures in 6-inch pots. BLOOM TIME: September–January (miniatures), February–early May (standards). LIGHT: As much as possible, without burning leaves. Plants with yellow-green leaves usually flower best. TEMPERATURE: Minis: 70° or higher (day), 60° (night). Standards: 60°–75° (day), 50°–55° (night) is ideal, but higher summertime temperatures (to 90° or so) and near-freezing winter temperatures are tolerated if plants are sheltered. POTTING MIX: Packaged cymbidium mix. Or fine-grade fir bark mixed with peat moss or perlite or both. WATERING: Keep soil moist during growing season, March–September. In winter, water just enough to keep bulbs from shriveling. FEEDING: January–July, feed with complete liquid fertilizer high in nitrogen every 10 days to 2 weeks; August–December, feed as frequently with low-nitrogen fertilizer.

Phalaenopsis

Familiarly known as moth orchid because its blooms resemble moth wings, phalaenopsis is among the easiest orchids to grow. If there's enough light for your hand to cast a faint shadow, that will do. Moth orchids do appreciate high humidity, so they are happiest in a bathroom or near the kitchen sink. Phalaenopsis flowers endure a long time, and the plants send up new blooming shoots frequently. If it's happy, a plant can bloom for several months. BLOOM TIME: Varies. LIGHT: Filtered light; no direct sun. TEMPERATURE: 75°–85° (day), 60°–65° (night). POTTING MIX: Orchid mix or medium- to coarse-grade fir bark. Some growers add perlite and charcoal to the mix. WATERING: Keep the potting mix continually moist but not soggy. Provide additional humidity as recommended for oncidium (page 21). FEEDING: Fertilize monthly year-round with a high-nitrogen fertilizer.

Zygopetalum

All orchids seem exotic, but zygopetalum looks downright otherworldly. The upper petals are usually tiger-striped green and maroon, and the lower lips patterned with violet lines on white: the Nicolas Cage of the orchid world—slightly menacing-looking, perhaps, but that's part of the appeal. Growing requirements are similar to those of standard cymbidiums, but plants are slightly more sensitive to cold. All are pleasantly fragrant. BLOOM TIME: Most varieties are fall and winter bloomers. LIGHT: Full morning sun or bright shade all day outdoors; while indoors, try a south- or west-facing window. TEMPERATURE: 60°–75° (day), 50°–55° (night) is ideal, but can take higher summer daytime temperatures if sheltered. POTTING MIX: Commercial orchid mix or medium-grade bark with perlite added. WATERING: Keep the potting mix moist most of the year, but let it dry out slightly for two to three weeks at the end of summer. FEEDING: Feed with high-nitrogen fertilizer monthly for the first six months after bloom; use low-nitrogen fertilizer for the next six months.

Orchid sources

Winter-flowering orchids are widely available at nurseries, florists, and supermarkets. You can also mail-order directly from **Rod McLellan Co.** (800/467-2443). ◆

Roses for the 21st century

These new landscaping roses are easy-care, blooming over a long season without fuss

BY LAUREN BONAR SWEZEY
PHOTOGRAPHS BY NORMAN A. PLATE

LIKE A QUICK-CHANGE artist, 'Kaleidoscope' (above) transforms from orangy tan with a yellow center to mauve pink as it ages. Top right is Flower Carpet 'Pink'. Bottom right is clear white 'Ice Meidiland'.

■ IMAGINE THE PERFECT ROSE BUSH—GORGEOUS FLOWERS, NONSTOP BLOOM, AND lush, disease-free foliage. Wishful thinking? Happily not. Now on sale at nurseries are carefree landscape roses that perform like the best flowering shrubs, pumping out colorful blooms all season long.

These spectacular roses are the culmination of decades of breeding by the Conard-Pyle Co., the House of Meilland, Weeks Roses, and other rose companies. Pink-flowered 'Bonica' was the first of the modern easy-care roses to storm the market; it won the 1987 All-America Rose Selections (AARS) award, and led to the establishment of a new "shrub rose" class.

Since 'Bonica' arrived on the scene, only six other shrub roses (listed on page 24) have garnered the prestigious AARS award. All are disease-resistant and fantastic bloomers. The latest AARS winner, 'Knock Out', made its debut this season. One of the best, it's nearly everblooming.

Ground cover types, which are also classed as shrub roses but are lower-growing, are best planted en masse. The earliest ground cover roses—such as 'Scarlet Meidiland', for instance—were sprawlers, introduced during the 1970s as no-care plants for commercial use. But the newest ground cover roses created the biggest stir. Flower Carpet roses, Meilland's latest Meidiland roses ('Ice Meidiland', 'Magic Meidiland'), and Poulsen Roser's Towne & Country roses ('Aspen') are more restrained in habit and more disease-free and easy-care than their forebears.

These new shrub roses don't require spraying to stay healthy, and they need little or no pruning to remain shapely. Because they bloom almost continuously, they make excellent partners for perennials and other shrubs in borders. They're perfectly suited to the demands of busy, no-nonsense gardeners of the 21st century.

ABOVE: 'Carefree Delight'. RIGHT: Bed of roses includes bright pink 'Carefree Wonder', pale pink 'Bonica', 'Carefree Delight', and 'Fuchsia Meidiland'. BELOW RIGHT: 'Knock Out'.

Seven winning shrub roses

'All That Jazz' (1992 AARS winner): Large (4½-inch-wide), single deep coral blooms on a 4- to 5-foot-tall shrub.

'Bonica' (1987 AARS winner): Clusters of 2½-inch-wide, double shell pink flowers on a 5-foot-tall shrub.

'Carefree Delight' (1996 AARS winner): Clusters of 2½- to 3-inch-wide, single pink flowers, each with a white eye, on a 3½-foot-tall shrub.

'Carefree Wonder' (1991 AARS winner): Large (3-inch-wide), semidouble hot pink and white flowers on a 5-foot-tall shrub.

'First Light' (1998 AARS winner): Clusters of 3½- to 4-inch-wide, single soft pink flowers on a 2- to 3-foot-tall shrub.

'Kaleidoscope' (1999 AARS winner): Small (2- to 2½-inch-wide), double flowers are orangy tan with yellow centers on a 2- to 4-foot-tall shrub.

'Knock Out' (2000 AARS winner): Medium (3- to 3½-inch-wide), single raspberry blooms on a 3-foot-tall plant.

Top ground cover roses

All spread wider than they grow tall and have very glossy foliage. Small to medium-size flowers develop in clusters.

Flower Carpet. A low grower 2 to 2½ feet tall; spreads 3 to 3½ feet wide. Flowers come in white and shades of pink and red.

Meidiland roses. Low grower 2 feet tall by 4½ to 5 feet wide. Colors: 'Fire Meidiland' (deep red), 'Fuchsia Meidiland' (mauve pink), 'Magic Meidiland' (medium pink). 'Ice Meidiland' (white) is a medium grower, to 3 feet tall by 6 feet wide.

Towne & Country. 'Aspen' grows to 1½ feet tall by 2½ feet wide with yellow flowers; 'Old Charleston' grows 1 foot tall by 4 to 5 feet wide with white flowers; 'Napa Valley' grows 2 feet tall by 2½ feet wide with red flowers.

Rose care

HOW TO PLANT

- Plant in a spot that receives at least six hours of full sun and has well-drained soil.
- Dig a planting hole 15 to 18 inches wide and 15 to 18 inches deep. For heavy soils, mix in one part organic matter, such as compost or peat moss, to two parts soil. Do not add fertilizer.
- In the bottom of the planting hole, form a cone-shaped mound to fit the conical shape of the roots.
- Remove the rose's packaging, then prune the canes back to 6 to 8 inches

long. Make each pruning cut above an outward-facing bud. Prune the roots to remove any broken or overly long ones that won't fit in the planting hole.
• Position the rose on the mound so the graft (bump at the base of the canes) sits just above the soil surface. Spread the roots over the cone.
• Fill in the hole to within 2 inches of the soil surface, firming the soil down around the roots.
• Fill the hole with water, then let it drain. If needed, adjust the rose so the graft is still at the right level. Finish filling in the hole and firming down the soil.
• To protect canes from drying out, completely cover the exposed canes with compost, peat moss, or soil. When new shoots appear in two to three weeks (or longer), carefully remove the mounded material (if it's sunny and hot, remove it in stages).
• Water regularly to keep the soil moist. Fertilize when blooms appear.

ONCE ROSES ARE ESTABLISHED

• **Water** often enough to keep the soil constantly moist, but not soggy, to a depth of 16 to 18 inches (check soil with an auger or trowel).
• **Fertilize** after dormant-season pruning and again after each flush of blooms (or according to package directions).
• **Prune** shrub roses only if they need shaping, or to remove dead or weak canes. To reduce their height or width, cut back growth by about a third. Prune back the remaining stems by about a third.

Where to buy roses

Shrub roses are sold at nurseries. Or mail-order from one of these sources.
Edmunds' Roses; (888) 481-7673 or www.edmundsroses.com.
Michael's Premier Roses; (916) 369-7673 or www.michaelsrose.com.
Petaluma Rose Company; (707) 769-8862 or www.petrose.com.
Ray Reddell's Garden Valley Ranch Nursery; (707) 795-0919 or www.gardenvalley.com. ◆

Other easy-care favorites

We asked four growers around the West to name their favorite easy-care roses, regardless of category.

'Playboy'. Floribunda; yellow, orange, and cerise flowers. "The flowers are nicely shaped, and the plant blooms continuously and consistently," says Michael Fischer of Michael's Premier Roses in Sacramento. "It's a beautiful plant even when not in bloom." Other favorites: 'Baby Grand' (miniature, medium-pink), 'Sally Holmes' (white climber).

'Gift of Life'. Hybrid tea; soft yellow with a touch of pink. "Lovely, well-formed flowers are ideal in bouquets and have light fragrance—all on a plant that's very disease-resistant," says Phil Edmunds of Edmunds' Roses in Oregon. Other favorites: 'Full Sail' (white hybrid tea), 'Moody Dream' (lavender shrub), 'New Zealand' (soft pink hybrid tea).

'Just Joey'. Hybrid tea; big (4-inch) apricot flowers. "Most disease-resistant roses don't have strong fragrance, but this one does," says Rick Weeks of Petaluma Rose Company in Petaluma, California. Other favorites: 'Ingrid Bergman' (red hybrid tea), 'Sally Holmes' (white climber).

'Baby Love'. Shrub; yellow flowers. "One of the few yellow easy-care roses," says Tom Carruth of Weeks Roses in Southern California; yellows are typically more disease-prone than other colors. This one has "superlative black-spot resistance and clean, glossy green foliage," says Carruth. "It's also a prolific bloomer, producing many small [1½- to 2-inch-wide] single flowers throughout the season." Carruth's other favorites: 'Easy Going' (deep gold floribunda), 'Livin' Easy' (apricot-orange floribunda).

NORMAN A. PLATE (3)

Succulents in the spotlight

These easy-care beauties fill tiny pockets between pavers in Sunset's Demonstration Garden at the L.A. arboretum

BY SHARON COHOON

Succulents have the stage presence of divas but the undemanding dispositions of chorus members. Take *Echeveria* 'Afterglow', the lavender-gray rosette in the photo below left, for example. No matter where you place this plant, it's going to be a star—its strong, sculptural shape and out-of-this-world color are virtual guarantees. But unlike a diva, 'Afterglow' performs with few demands. Its roots are shallow, so it gets by with little soil. It evolved to survive without a lot of rain or soil nutrients, so it doesn't require frequent watering or

Tips & tricks

•**Ensure good drainage.** Though many succulents will adjust to surprisingly heavy soils, correcting poor drainage before planting is always advisable. To test drainage, dig a hole about the size of a 1-gallon pot and fill it with water. If the hole takes more than four hours to drain, add compost and sharp sand or pumice to improve the soil's texture.

ABOVE: Succulents masquerading as a sculpture gallery include (from left): *Senecio mandraliscae;* purple 'Afterglow' echeveria; variegated 'Sunburst' aeonium; and fan-shaped *Aloe plicatilis.* A small-leafed sedum meanders between pavers.
TOP LEFT: The cool blue-green leaves of *Agave attenuata* complement the red-blushed foliage of 'Camp Fire' crassula. Since *A. attenuata* is a spineless agave, you can safely plant it close to walkways. BOTTOM LEFT: The lavender-gray leaves and pinkish flower stalks of 'Afterglow' echeveria play off 'Camp Fire' crassula.

fertilizing (but it won't object to the more pampered existence of a perennial bed). Aeoniums, agaves, aloes, senecios, and most other succulents behave the same way. Their appearances may be dramatic, but their natures are forgiving.

Nick Williams of Nick Williams & Associates in Tarzana, California, relied mostly on succulents to embellish the dining and entertainment patio he designed for the *Sunset* Demonstration Garden at the Arboretum of Los Angeles County. Succulents are natural choices for outdoor rooms that are primarily hardscape, says Williams. They fit into small planting pockets and are slow to outgrow them. Their architectural shapes look good against stone, stucco, and concrete, and the reflected heat that bounces off these surfaces doesn't bother them. They're inherently neat—leaf drop and other plant litter is slight, and you don't have to cope with a lot of irrigation runoff.

Succulents look good outside houses of nearly any architectural style, from mission revival to sleekly modern. They even give guests something to talk about. "Each of these plants has amazing details if you stop and look," says David Bernstein of California Nursery Specialties Cactus Ranch in Reseda (818/894-5694), which supplied the succulents. "Every one is a conversation piece."

•**Water regularly.** Just because succulents can survive on sporadic watering doesn't mean they'll look best if they stay too dry. Most will look better with weekly watering during their active growing season (spring and summer).

•**Keep thorny types well away from paths.** You don't have to eliminate succulents cloaked in thorns. These details have their own fierce beauty. But you do have to position these plants carefully so no one will accidentally bump into them.

•**Arrange them like artwork.** You can manipulate succulents the same way you would a group of paintings on a wall or objets d'art on a side table. Position the larger and most dramatic players first, then place the rest around them, playing colors and textures off one another until you're pleased with the arrangement. You don't have to provide large gaps between succulents when planting; an agave isn't going to double in size in a season like a buddleia or lavatera. ◆

PETER MALINOWSKI / INSITE

FREESTANDING greenhouse glazed with single-pane glass costs $7,500; from Smith & Hawken.

Ready for a greenhouse?

Knowing your options can help you decide

BY JIM McCAUSLAND

For avid gardeners a greenhouse is an essential outdoor room for plants. It's a cozy year-round home for orchids or other exotics, a winter shelter for tender perennials like geraniums, and a nursery for starting seeds weeks before the last spring frost.

If you're in the market for a greenhouse, consider these factors.

Space, style, costs

"Greenhouse space is like money; you never seem to have enough," one owner told us. As greenhouse size increases, the cost per square foot decreases. Unless you plan to use a greenhouse only for seed-starting and potting, get one that's at least 6 feet wide and 8 feet long. If finances dictate a smaller unit, buy a model that can be extended later.

Rectangular freestanding greenhouses are very stable and designed to stand up under a fair snow load (ask the manufacturer for details). Many good units are in the $2,000 to $3,000 range, with top-of-the-line models running $7,000 to $8,000.

Lean-to models fit well in tight spaces, such as on a patio facing an exterior wall. They tend not to do as well under heavy snow loads (again, ask before you buy). Prices start at about $900 for a unit with double-walled polyethylene glazing, $1,200 for polycarbonate, and $1,300 for glass.

Collapsible greenhouses ($270 to $370) are good where space is a problem.

Framing

Most greenhouses have frames of wood or aluminum. Wood will lose no significant heat through the frame. Over time the wood fades unless you keep it painted or finished, and it may rot or warp.

Aluminum frames retain shape well, won't corrode, and are often color-coated. Some heat is lost through the aluminum (some units minimize heat loss with neoprene gaskets that separate the metal from the glazing).

Foldout greenhouse

Designed by a company that makes ice-fishing shelters, the collapsible Germinette sells for $270. Measuring 4 feet wide, 6 feet long, and just over 6 feet high, it's covered with sturdy woven polyethylene sheeting. When not in use, the unit folds up.

You'll need to cut and install shelves (we spent about $85 for rough-sawn redwood) and provide a platform—a foundation of 2-by-4s, a paved patio, or a deck (put down indoor-outdoor carpet or ply-

One manufacturer uses rigid steel-core PVC pipe for framing and shelving.

Glazing

Although traditional glass greenhouses have single panes, double- or triple-walled panels trap more air and thus have greater insulation value—a crucial consideration in cold-winter climates.

Glass. Fireproof, but breaks more easily than other options.

Fiberglass. Diffuses light well; good shatter resistance, a plus where hailstorms are common. Flammable.

Polycarbonate plastics. Transparent, almost unbreakable. Flame-resistant. Usually double-walled.

Acrylics. Like polycarbonates, but less resistant to breakage or fire. Clarity and rigidity approach those of glass, with better shatter resistance.

Double-walled polyethylene. Milky white, flexible. Diffuses light well and resists ultraviolet light. Flammable.

Accessories

Some greenhouse sellers offer just the shells, others fully equipped units. When you compare prices, your bottom line should include at least the following accessories: benches or shelves for plants ($10 to $25 per linear foot); a small fan for air circulation ($25); automatic solar-powered vent openers ($40 to $100); a heater ($50 to $100 for electric, considerably more for gas) in any area where it freezes; a minimum-maximum thermometer (about $20); and shadecloth ($50 to $130) to filter summer sun and reduce heat buildup.

Make sure electrical wiring and heating systems meet safety codes, and follow the manufacturer's instructions for heater placement and setup.

Site

Ask your city or county building department if you need a permit to erect a greenhouse.

Select a site that's near water and electric outlets and gets at least six hours of sun per day. Unless you set the greenhouse on an existing paved surface or deck, you'll need to level the ground and install a foundation for the frame. Pressure-treated 4-by-4s or 4-by-6s provide sufficient support for most greenhouses. Finally, install a floor of loose-laid bricks, pavers, or pea gravel.

Manufacturers

Many of these firms sell direct; others refer you to dealers.

Aluminum-frame models

- B.C. Greenhouse Builders; (888) 391-4433 or www.bcgreenhouses.com.
- Garden Grower's Greenhouse; (888) 929-8383 or www.gardengrower.com.
- Sunglo Greenhouses; (800) 647-0606 or www.sunglogreenhouses.com.

Redwood-frame models

- Santa Barbara Greenhouses; (800) 544-5276 or www.sbgreenhouse.com.
- Sturdi-built; (800) 334-4115 or www.sturdi-built.com.
- Sunshine Gardenhouse; (888) 272-9333 or www.gardenhouse.com.

Steel-core PVC-frame models

- Farm Wholesale; (800) 825-1925 or www.farmwholesale.com.

DIAN MOORE DESIGN

LEAN-TO with double-walled polyethylene glazing costs $900; from Farm Wholesale.

Retail dealers

- Charley's Greenhouse Supply sells temporary and permanent aluminum-frame models and supplies; (800) 322-4707 or www.charleysgreenhouse.com.
- Rain or Shine sells aluminum- and redwood-frame models and supplies; (800) 248-1981.
- Smith & Hawken sells freestanding aluminum-frame models; (800) 776-3336 or www.smithandhawken.com.
- Yard Works sells aluminum- and redwood-frame models, collapsible units, and supplies; (800) 369-8333 or www.yardworks-greenhouses.com. ◆

NORMAN A. PLATE (3)

wood to keep cold air from circulating through the gaps). A larger Germinator I unit (6′ by 8′ by 7′2″) sells for $329. For more information, call Millennium Industries at (800) 925-4639.

CLAIRE CURRAN

WHEN GRAPES DROP THEIR LEAVES, evergreen trumpet vines take over to keep this arbor covered. For details on planting bare-root grapevines, available at most nurseries in February, see page 37.

February

gardenguide

NORMAN A. PLATE

LILIES, tulips, and Queen Anne's lace are held in place with strips of transparent tape that form a grid atop a water-filled vase.

Sweetheart bouquets

■ What's your valentine's pleasure? Long-stemmed red roses from the florist? Camellia blossoms or branches of sweetly scented Chinese witch hazel (*Hamamelis mollis*) from your garden? Or your own mix-and-match arrangement of flowers purchased at a grocery store?

Any bouquet can bring a smile to your valentine's face. And if you arrange the flowers yourself (a less expensive proposition than a florist's creation), you'll have a guaranteed heart-warmer. **Here are tips to make your bouquet a standout.**

• Match the flower colors to the vase. For the arrangement pictured above, we chose a square vase of red glass, then bought flowers to match. Red tulips echo the color of the vase; pink tulips and white Queen Anne's lace fill in around them. Pink Oriental lilies splashed with red add punch, and variegated 'Needlepoint' ivy softens vase edges.

• Mix flower sizes and shapes. Buy or cut the bulk of your flowers in smaller sizes for the supporting cast, and use as few as three or four stems of larger flowers (such as Oriental lilies) as the stars.

• To prolong the lives of the flowers, plunge their stems into a bowl of hot water, keeping them submerged as you cut off the stem ends with pruning shears (make diagonal cuts).

• Arrange the ivy fringe first, then the supporting cast of flowers, and finally the stars. — *Kathleen N. Brenzel*

A pair of big, tasty slicers

■ If you enjoy really big slicing tomatoes, two newly introduced varieties may well satisfy you. 'Caspian Pink' (on right in photo) and 'Jetsetter' (on left) bear fruit so large that a single slice amply covers a hamburger and a whole tomato yields enough wedges for a salad.

Sunset staffers grew both in their home gardens. Even in an exceptionally cool California summer, they produced good crops of fruit weighing as much as 14 to 17 ounces apiece. Both of these tomatoes require tall cages or stakes to keep plants in bounds.

'Caspian Pink'. This heirloom tomato from Russia yields sweet, mild, pink-fleshed fruit whose flavor was preferred to that of 'Brandywine' in some recent tastings. Averaging 10 to 12 ounces each, the fruit colors from the bottom up, turning deeper shades of pink as it ripens. Pick when the top "shoulders" are still yellow; let fruit sit on a counter until it is fully colored and ready to eat. Expect 80 days from transplanting to maturity.

'Jetsetter'. As its name implies, this hybrid matures quickly (about 64 days after transplanting), making it a good choice where summers are cool or short. Globe-shaped fruit averaging 8 ounces has firm, meaty flesh with rich flavor. The plants resist many of the diseases that affect other tomatoes.

You can order seeds of either variety from Tomato Growers Supply Company (888/478-7333) and Totally Tomatoes (803/663-0016).

— Dick Bushnell

Alaska-style coldframe

■ Teena Garay of Homer, Alaska, gets an early start on annuals, perennials, and vegetables by growing seedlings in a coldframe designed and built by her husband, Pete. He used pressure-treated 2-by-4s to build the frame, which measures 9 feet long and 4 feet wide. It's covered by three hinged lids (framed with 2-by-2s) that slope from 30 inches at the rear to 18 inches in front. Translucent fiberglass sheeting encloses the sides and lids. To make it easier to open the lids for ventilation, he rigged them with pulley-drawn cords that tie off to cleats in a 2-by-4 mounted above the frame. A fine mesh screen is fastened across the bottom to prevent voles and other critters from tunneling up to the seedlings. *— Steven R. Lorton*

NORMAN A. PLATE (2)

NEW SHRUB

TERRENCE MOORE

A living valentine for the low desert

■ Plant a valentine for your sweetheart this month—*Eremophila* 'Valentine'. This Australian shrub adds a bright burst of late-winter color in low-desert gardens. Flower buds start appearing in December, followed by a profusion of red tubular blossoms that open from February through March. 'Valentine' has proven hardy to 25° and may tolerate even lower temperatures. The rounded shrub reaches 4 feet tall with a 5-foot spread.

In the landscape, plant 'Valentine' with shrubs that bloom in different seasons, like Texas ranger and Mexican bird of paradise, to create a succession of color. The medium-green foliage also makes a handsome backdrop for bold-leafed plants such as agave.

Nurseries sell 'Valentine' in 5-gallon containers for $17 to $20 each. If you can't find it, ask your nursery to order from Mountain States Wholesale Nursery in Glendale, Arizona. Plant 'Valentine' in full sun. Water once or twice a week during the summer, less often in the cool months. Lightly prune the branches in early April to promote new woody growth that will bear next year's blooms.

—Judy Mielke

Grow your own pistachios

■ With wrinkled husks turning from green to red, the cluster of pistachios shown at right is almost ready for September harvest. To get nuts like these, you need to plant a pair of *Pistacia vera:* the fruiting female 'Kerman' and the pollinating male 'Peters'.

Commercial growers raise pistachios in Arizona and southern New Mexico. Home gardeners can grow them in *Sunset* climate zones 10–12 (zone 13 does not get enough chill).

These trees eventually reach 30 feet tall with a broad, bushy habit. Green, roundish leaves are deciduous or semievergreen, depending on how cold the winter gets. Once established, the trees can take some drought. Expect a few nuts three or four years after planting, with full harvest coming in seven or eight years.

Look for pistachio trees at well-stocked nurseries or order from Pacific Tree Farms in Chula Vista, California ($62 per tree, shipping included; 619/422-2400). Because the young trees have delicate, fibrous root systems, they're usually sold in 5-gallon containers (plants about 3 feet tall), with as much soil as possible around the roots. As soon as you get them, plant in a site with full sun and well-drained soil. — *Jim McCausland*

SHARON COHOON

TERRENCE MOORE

PUNCTUATED BY CACTUS, a narrow bed edges a patio shaded by a lath-topped pergola.

Desert classic in Palm Springs

■ Bud and Barbara Hoover's garden complements their 1920s house so gracefully you'd assume it was installed at the same time. Not so. Palm Springs homes of that era rarely had gardens: "They had sand," says Barbara. Water wasn't as plentiful then, plus people usually spent only a few weeks in residence.

When the Hoovers renovated this home in 1989, they planned to live there a good part of each year. So, without compromising the structure's character, they added a few comforts like the pergola over an outdoor dining area.

Then they asked landscape architect Michael Buccino of Palm Desert, California, to take a similarly restrained approach with the garden. To provide shade, he brought in mature trees such as mesquite and jacaranda. He covered much of the ground with handsome hardscape, including native stone and river rocks for texture and pattern. In the remaining spaces, he placed plants with bold, sculptural shapes like golden barrel and organpipe cactus and fan palms. Containers of flowers, such as the pelargoniums and petunias shown in the photo, add dashes of seasonal color. The resulting garden "reflects the tranquillity and strength of the desert," says Buccino.

— Sharon Cohoon

'Himrod'

MICHAEL S. THOMPSON (2)

Hardy grapes for your table

■ During late winter when my grapes are sleeping, it's hard to imagine that the leafless vines will spring forth with lush green foliage, followed by colorful, delicious fruit. But they do, faithfully, year after year. That's why I planted my garden fence with a variety of seedless table grapes. When the harvest starts, I can reach out and savor the fruit right off the vines.

Here are four hardy, self-pollinating varieties that have proved themselves in home gardens in the Pacific Northwest, including mine.

• **'Canadice'.** Tight clusters of medium-size red fruit have deliciously sweet, slightly spicy flavor. Fruit ripens early, from late August on. *Sunset* climate zones 1–7.

• **'Glenora'.** Large clusters of plump, midnight blue fruit have a unique flavor that smacks of 'Concord' grapes and blueberries. Ripens early to midseason, beginning in September. Hardy to -20°.

• **'Himrod'.** Clusters of small to medium-size grapes turn golden yellow when fully ripe; they're crisp and sweet with a hint of spiciness. Ripens very early, from mid-August on. Zones 1–3 and 5–7.

• **'Interlaken'.** Large clusters of small amber-colored fruit have crispy, sweet flesh. Ripens midseason, from September on. Zones 1–7.

Grapes prefer full sun and well-drained, slightly acidic soil. Before planting, install a trellis or other sturdy support for vines to climb. For pruning instructions, refer to the *Sunset Western Garden Book*. The first full harvest usually comes in the third year.

Order bare-root stock for planting in late winter or early spring, or shop nurseries for container-grown plants in spring, summer, or early fall. 'Canadice', 'Glenora', and 'Himrod' are available from One Green World in Molalla, OR (503/651-3005). 'Canadice', 'Glenora', and 'Interlaken' are sold by Raintree Nursery in Morton, WA (360/496-6400).

— Kris Wetherbee

BACK TO BASICS

NORMAN A. PLATE

How to fertilize a lawn

To apply a dry lawn fertilizer evenly when using a spreader:

1. Overlap the spreader's wheel marks, so that the swaths of fertilizer just touch as you pass back and forth.

2. Don't go over the same area twice. Double doses kill the grass.

— Lauren Bonar Swezey

Meet the new minis

■ Standard Transvaal daisies (*Gerbera jamesonii*) bear bold 4-inch flowers atop 1½-foot-tall stems.

Now there's a petite version—a true miniature with small leaves and 1½-inch-wide flowers. New from Bloom-Rite, these little beauties show off best at close range; they're perfect in pots and tight places.

NORMAN A. PLATE

Indoors, miniature Transvaal daisies need bright, indirect light. Water plants thoroughly when the soil feels almost dry to the touch (avoid getting water on the leaves). Apply a dilute solution of liquid fertilizer weekly.

After the last frost, move daisies outdoors. Grow them in full sun (acclimate the plants by slowly introducing them to part sun, then full sun, over a period of a week or so). Like all gerberas, miniatures demand good potting soil with excellent drainage: Plant them so their crowns (where the leaves meet the main stem) are about ½ inch above the soil surface. Miniature Transvaal daisies are available this month ($5.50–$6) at floral departments in grocery stores. — *L.B.S.*

Japanese Friendship Garden reopens

STEVEN GUNTHER

■ The Japanese Friendship Garden in San Diego's Balboa Park has a new look. New features, designed by renowned garden designer Takeo Uesugi, include a new entry gate, an open-air plaza, and a tea pavilion—"hopefully the central gathering point the park has long needed," says board president Tom Yanagihara. Beyond the entry are a large new koi pond, an activity center for classes, and a ceremonial plaza for weddings and other festive rites. The garden's old memorial gate was relocated here from the original entry; it now serves as a beautiful photographic backdrop for this area. Throughout the garden, new plants and stones—each carefully placed by Tokushirou Tamane, master gardener of the Golden Pavilion in Kyoto, Japan—add masterful touches.

10–4 Tue-Sun; $3, $7 family. Balboa Park between the House of Hospitality and the Organ Pavilion; (619) 232-2721. — S.C.

Tunnel of vines

■ Cheri Maggiano had always wanted a covered walkway. So when she began looking for a way to visually separate one part of the garden from the other at her new home in Santa Ana, she decided on a tunnel of vines (see photo on page 30).

The arbor, designed and built by Mike Parsons of Saddleback Valley Ornamental Iron (949/830-9513), consists of a series of bent tubular steel arches, 6 feet wide and spaced 5 feet apart, connected with crossbeams. The arches were sandblasted, coated in zinc, and painted with black urethane. "They'll last forever," Parsons predicts.

Maggiano took a landscaper's suggestion to plant two red trumpet vines for every 'Flame' grape. The evergreen trumpet vines keep the arbor covered when the grapevines drop their leaves in winter, and prevent Maggiano from being totally inundated with grapes.

"The vines are only a year old, but we've already had tons of fruit," she says. "It was an amazing harvest."

Bare-root grapevines are available at most nurseries in February. European varieties ('Flame', for instance) do best in warm inland locations. American grapes such as 'Concord' are more successful near the coast. Plant grapevines in full sun, deep enough so that only the two top buds are aboveground.

— *Sharon Cohoon*

NORMAN A. PLATE

MADE FROM FRUIT TREE PRUNINGS, this freestanding trellis supports a mandevilla. Design: Françoise Kirkman.

Make a rustic trellis

■ Bentwood trellises are pretty, but most of us don't have access to the green willow saplings you need to make them. Dry wood, on the other hand, is fairly easy to come by, since trees get thinned and excess bamboo gets harvested. You can make a simple trellis from such prunings, or substitute 1-by-1 stakes from the nursery or lumberyard. The finished structure is 7 feet 4½ inches tall and 3 feet wide.

TIME: about 2½ hours (plus pruning)

COST: $5, $30 if you buy stakes

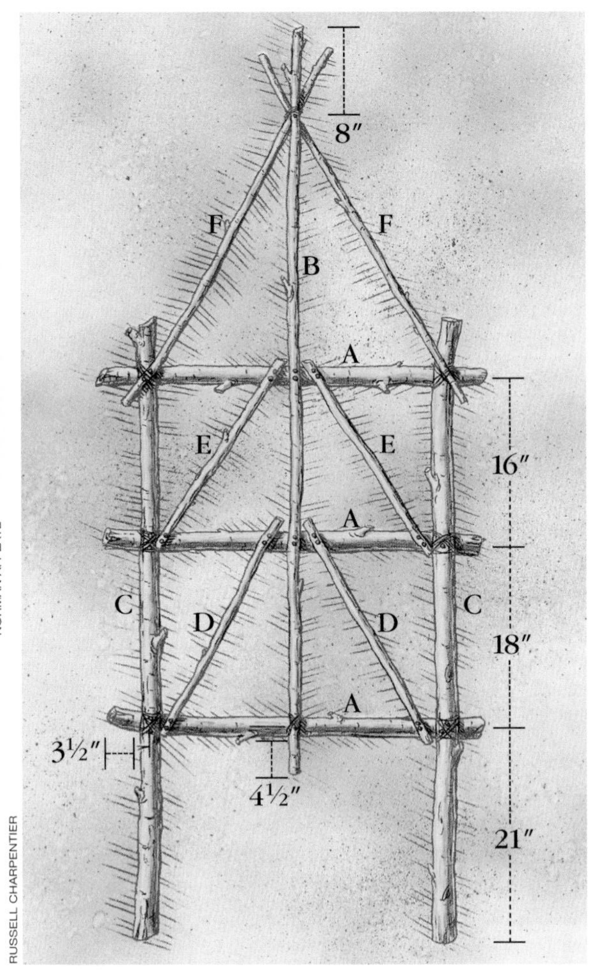

RUSSELL CHARPENTIER

TOOLS AND MATERIALS

12 straight branches, limbs or canes, each approximately 1" in diameter. These include (letters correspond with those on drawing above):

- Three pieces, each 3 feet long **(A)**
- One piece, 6 feet long **(B)**
- Two pieces, each 5 feet long **(C)**
- Two pieces, each 25 inches long **(D)**
- Two pieces, each 22½ inches long **(E)**
- Two pieces, each 39½ inches long **(F)**

One box 1¾-inch nails

Hammer

Spool of floral wire

DIRECTIONS

1. Trim from the prunings any side branches.

2. Lay the crosspieces **(A)** horizontally on a flat surface, with two of them 18 inches apart, and the third 16 inches above the center one.

3. Lay the centerpiece **(B)** vertically across the crosspieces. The bottom end of the centerpiece should overlap the lowest crosspiece by 4½ inches. Nail centerpiece to crosspieces at center joints.

4. Lay side pieces **(C)** vertically over crosspieces as shown, setting them about 3½ inches in from the ends of the crosspieces. Nail to crosspieces at the joints.

5. Place **D** and **E** pieces diagonally between crosspieces, slightly overlapping the horizontal crosspieces as shown. Nail them to the horizontals at the joints.

6. Place top pieces **(F)** so they cross behind the centerpiece **(B)** and on top of the side pieces **(C)**.

7. For additional stability, turn structure over and nail joints from the back side, then wrap wire several times around the main intersections.

— *S.C.*

QUICK TIP

Get sweet peas off to a quick start

■ Hard outer shells make sweet pea seeds slow to germinate, especially in cool soil. To get them off to a quick start, soak them in thick paper towels for three to four days right before planting.

Lay one towel on a waterproof surface. Scatter pea seeds evenly over it, allowing plenty of room between seeds. Cover the seeds with the second towel. Thoroughly moisten both towels, then roll them up carefully, so the seeds stay separated. Place the roll in a plastic bag, zip or twist it closed, and set the bag in a warm room. Check the seeds three to four days later to see if they have germinated. Plant them outdoors as soon as they have sprouted (if the seeds are left in the towels too long, they will mold). Poke holes in prepared soil and gently drop in each seed, handling it carefully to avoid damaging the root. — *L.B.S.*

Pacific Northwest Checklist

PLANNING AND PLANTING

✔ PLANT BARE-ROOT STOCK. Zones 4–7, 17: Plant berries, grapes, roses, vines, shrubs, and ornamental and fruit trees this month. In colder zones, plant as soon as bare-root plants are available and the ground is workable.

✔ SHOP FOR CONTAINER STOCK. The Pacific Northwest is a great place to plant winter-flowering trees and shrubs. Buy containers of Chinese witch hazel, Cornelian cherry, corylopsis, daphne, early-flowering rhododendrons, sarcococca, Sasanqua camellias, viburnums, and wintersweet.

✔ SET OUT PRIMROSES. Two kinds of English primroses are commonly sold this month: Acaulis types usually have one flower per stem; polyanthus types have multiple flowers growing from a strong single stem. Zones 1–3: Buy acaulis primroses for indoor display (they're perfect on windowsills). Zones 4–7, 17: Use acaulis primroses indoors or group them in outdoor containers. Plant taller polyanthus types in garden beds.

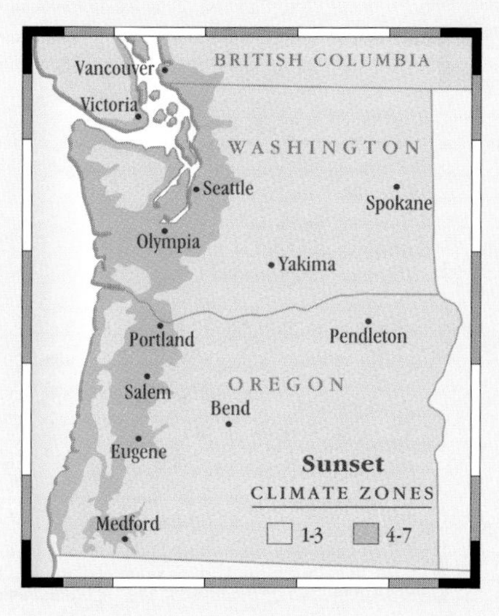

✔ SOW EARLY VEGETABLES. Zones 4–7, 17: Peas and spinach will both germinate in cool soil; sow seeds in mid- to late February.

✔ SOW HARDY ANNUALS. Direct-sow seeds of calendulas, clarkias, English daisies, California and Iceland poppies, and snapdragons.

✔ START SWEET PEAS. Sow seeds of flowering sweet peas indoors in 4-inch pots; transplant in March or April.

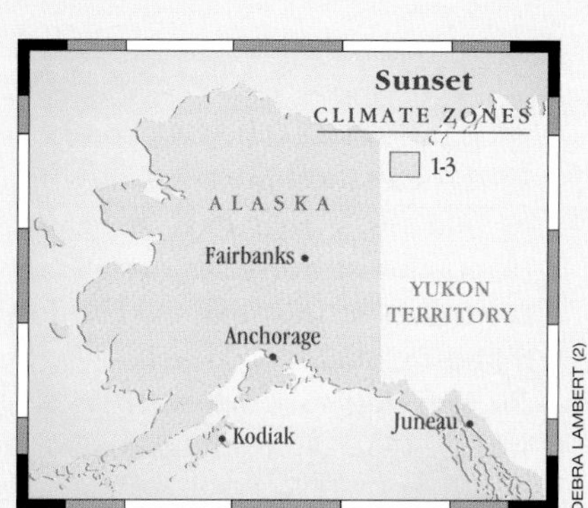

DEBRA LAMBERT (2)

MAINTENANCE

✔ CLEAN UP HOUSE PLANTS. Feed any that bear flowers or fruit at this time of year; wait to fertilize other kinds until spring growth begins. Give plants a shower of lukewarm water every month or two to wash dust off leaves and inhibit insect buildup. Then snip off yellowing leaves and cut back leggy plants to force new growth.

✔ PRUNE ROSES. Zones 4–7: Start by removing dead, injured, or diseased canes and suckers emerging from below the graft. Then prune hybrid teas for shape: Select the three to five strongest canes and cut them back by a third. Each cane should be left with one robust, outward-facing bud. Remaining canes should form a vase shape. In zones 1–3, wait to prune until just before new growth starts. ◆

WHAT TO DO IN YOUR GARDEN IN FEBRUARY

Northern California Checklist

PLANTING

✔ BARE-ROOT LILACS. Zones 7–9, 14–17: Call local nurseries this month to find those that deal in bare-root plants—most nurseries carry lilacs in containers at this time of year. In the mildest climates (zones 14–17), look for low-chill varieties, such as 'Angel White', 'Blue Skies', or 'Lavender Lady'.

✔ BULBS. Zones 7–9, 14–17: If you discovered a bag of unplanted bulbs in your garage or garden shed and the bulbs are still firm, don't toss them out; plant them. There's a good chance they'll bloom. Zones 1–2: Plant the bulbs in low 6- to 8-inch bowls to force in a cool place. Chill daffodils for 10 to 12 weeks, tulips for 12 to 14 weeks, and other bulbs for 8 to 10 weeks.

✔ EVERGREEN VINES. Zones 7–9, 14–17: Good choices for planting against fences and walls, or training over sturdy arbors, are fragrant, yellow-flowered Carolina jessamine (*Gelsemium sempervirens*), white-flowered evergreen clematis (*C. armandii*), pink or purple *Hardenbergia violacea* 'Happy Wanderer', pink *H.v.* 'Rosea', fragrant pinkish white *Jasminum polyanthum,* pink or white *Pandorea jasminoides,* and violet trumpet vine (*Clytostoma callistegioides*). All are very vigorous, growing 15 to 20 feet or longer.

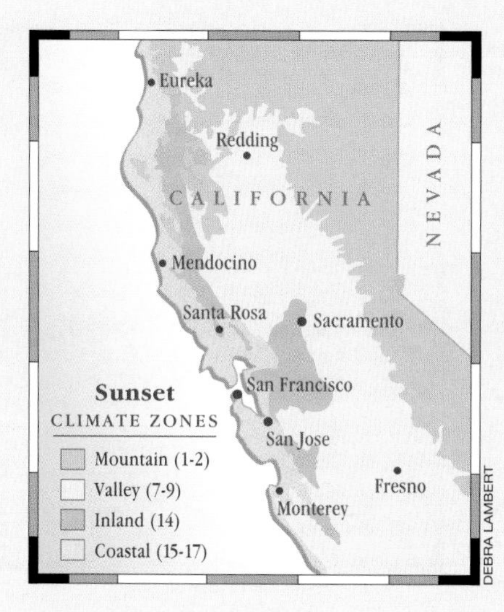

✔ TOMATOES FOR INLAND VALLEYS. Zones 7–9: 'Early Girl' is the best early-season tomato, but it stops producing when heat sets in. For later harvests, plant a midseason tomato such as 'Ace' or 'Celebrity' (all were flavor winners in valley tomato tastings). Seeds are available from Tomato Growers (888/478-7333).

✔ VEGETABLES. Zones 1–2: To get a jump on the season, start seeds of broccoli, cabbage, and cauliflower indoors or in a greenhouse at the end of the month. When seedlings are ready to plant (in six to eight weeks) and the ground can be worked, set them out, then drape them with floating row covers. Zones 7–9, 14–17: Set out artichokes and asparagus, and seedlings of broccoli, cabbage, cauliflower, celery (only in zones 15–17), green onions, kohlrabi, and lettuce. From seed, plant beets, carrots, chard, lettuce, peas, and spinach. Sow seeds of eggplant, pepper, and tomato indoors using bottom heat to speed germination (try a heating coil or set containers on a water heater until seeds germinate, then move them into bright light); allow them six to eight weeks to reach transplant size.

MAINTENANCE

✔ CUT BACK WOODY PLANTS. Zones 7–9, 14–17: To stimulate new, lush growth on artemisia, butterfly bush, fuchsia, and Mexican bush sage, cut back woody stems close to the ground. If left unpruned, plants get leggy and scraggly-looking.

✔ MAINTAIN HUMMINGBIRD FEEDERS. Change nectar and thoroughly wash feeders every three to four days. To make nectar, mix 4 parts water with 1 part sugar in a pan. Heat to dissolve the sugar, then cool. Store leftover mixture in the refrigerator. ◆

Southern California Checklist

PLANTING

✔ BARE-ROOT PLANTS. It's not too late to plant bare-root roses or fruit trees. But before planting, soak the roots overnight—the plants may have been in the nursery for several weeks.

✔ COOL-SEASON VEGETABLES. In coastal (zones 22–24), inland (zones 18–21), and high-desert (zone 11) gardens, continue to sow seeds of beets, carrots, chard, kale, lettuce, mustard, onions, peas, potatoes, radishes, spinach, and turnips. Plant nursery-starts or your own seedlings of broccoli, cauliflower, and other members of the cabbage family.

✔ STRAWBERRIES. February is the ideal time to plant strawberries. If you haven't been successful with strawberries in the past, try growing them in raised beds heavily amended with compost or other organic material. Mulch with hay or plastic to keep plants and fruit clean.

✔ SUMMER VEGETABLES. In the low desert (zone 13), plant tomatoes, peppers, and other warm-season vegetables late this month (making sure to protect them from late frost with cloches or hot caps). Elsewhere, start summer vegetables from seed in flats or pots indoors. Seedlings will be ready to move to the garden in six to eight weeks.

DEBRA LAMBERT

✔ WINTER COLOR. In coastal areas and inland, fill in the garden's bare spots with calendulas, cinerarias, Iceland poppies, nemesias, pansies, primroses, schizanthus, snapdragons, stock, and sweet peas. If the soil is too soggy, plant in containers.

✔ PERENNIAL WILDFLOWERS. In the low desert (zone 13), plant coreopsis, desert marigolds, evening primroses, penstemon, and salvia.

MAINTENANCE

✔ FINISH DORMANT-SEASON PRUNING. Prune deciduous fruit and ornamental trees, grape and wisteria vines, roses, and summer-blooming shrubs. Wait until after bloom to prune spring-flowering shrubs, and until the weather warms up before pruning tropicals.

✔ START SPRING FEEDING. Feed ground covers, shrubs, perennials, trees, and other permanent plants with a controlled-release fertilizer such as bonemeal, cottonseed meal, or well-rotted manure; this regimen will provide the plants with gradual nutrition throughout the season. Or scatter a granular complete fertilizer throughout garden beds and water in well. Feed cool-season lawns like tall fescue.

PEST AND WEED CONTROL

✔ SPRAY FRUIT TREES. Now, while trees are still leafless, is your last chance to smother overwintering insect pests such as scale, mites, and aphids with horticultural oil. Spray the trees when growth buds begin to swell but before they color and open. For fungal diseases such as peach leaf curl, add lime sulfur or fixed copper to the oil, following package directions. Spray the branches and crotches between them, as well as the trunk and the ground beneath the canopy. ◆

WHAT TO DO IN YOUR GARDEN IN FEBRUARY

Mountain Checklist

PLANNING AND PLANTING

✔ BARE-ROOT PLANTS. As soon as your garden soil can be worked, plant bare-root stock. Many nurseries carry small fruits such as grapes, strawberries, blackberries, and raspberries; all kinds of ornamental, fruit, and shade trees; and perennial vegetables such as asparagus and horseradish.

✔ STOCK UP ON SUMMER BULBS. Garden centers start carrying lilies and other summer bulbs this month. Plant lilies as soon as your soil has thawed. Store begonias, caladiums, cannas, dahlias, gladiolas, and other nonhardy bulbs in a cool, dry place until March, when they can be started indoors. Or wait to plant them directly in the garden in May.

✔ VEGETABLES. Indoors or in a greenhouse, start seeds of cool-season vegetables, including broccoli, cabbage, cauliflower, kale, and onions, for transplanting outdoors four weeks before the average date of the last frost in your area.

MAINTENANCE

✔ DEAL WITH ICE. Spread sand or unscented, nonclumping kitty litter on icy driveways and sidewalks. Icemelting salts can burn plants.

✔ FEED WILD BIRDS. When natural foods are scarce, birds seek out feeders. Seed-eating birds prefer sunflower seeds, millet, and mixed birdseed. Insect eaters go for peanut butter and suet (animal fat available from butchers).

✔ PREPARE BEDS. As soon as the ground can be worked, dig or till compost or other organic matter into the soil to prepare flower and vegetable beds for spring planting. If you live in an area where spring comes late, you can dig in manure that's not yet fully rotted. By planting time, it will have mellowed enough to feed plants without burning them.

✔ PREVENT CROCUS DAMAGE. Stop sparrows and finches from shredding crocus blossoms by placing foil pinwheels—the kind sold as children's toys—every few feet among the flowers. The flashing foil frightens away the birds.

✔ PRUNE SUCKERS. It's easier to remove suckering stems from the bases of trees and shrubs while the ground is still frozen and before new foliage emerges. Leave a few well-placed suckers to replace broken or old woody stems, if needed.

✔ PULL WEEDS. Freezing and thawing cycles create loose, friable soil that makes it easy to pull large-rooted weeds such as mallow and salsify with a firm tug, or to pop them out with a trowel.

✔ REMOVE SNOW. To prevent broken or permanently bent branches, remove heavy snow from trees and shrubs after each storm. Use a broom to gently lift and shake all branches within your reach.

✔ SPRAY DORMANT PLANTS. Spray horticultural oil on deciduous fruit and ornamental trees and shrubs to kill overwintering insect eggs and disease spores. — *Marcia Tatroe* ◆

WHAT TO DO IN YOUR GARDEN IN FEBRUARY

Southwest Checklist

PLANTING

✔ AGAVE, CACTUS. Zone 13 (Phoenix): Planted this month, they'll have time to get established before stressful summer weather arrives.

✔ BARE-ROOT PLANTS. Plant blackberries, grapes, raspberries, strawberries; ornamental, fruit, and shade trees; and perennial vegetables including asparagus and horseradish.

✔ GROUND COVERS. Zones 12–13: Plant perennial verbena, star jasmine, and trailing indigo bush (*Dalea greggii*).

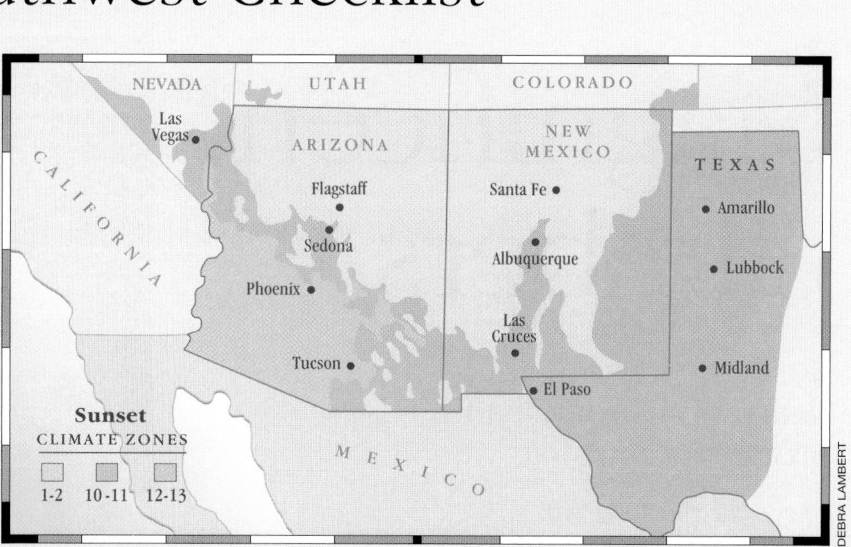

✔ NECTAR FOR HUMMINGBIRDS. Zones 12–13: Hummingbirds are frantically active this month, enticing mates, building nests, and brooding eggs—all of which makes them hungry. Plant nectar-bearing autumn sage (*Salvia greggii*), Mexican bush sage (*Salvia leucantha*), firecracker penstemon (*P. eatonii*), Parry's penstemon (*P. parryi*), or chuparosa (*Justicia californica*).

✔ SPRING COLOR. Zones 12–13: Plant desert marigolds, evening primroses, and paperflowers (*Psilostrophe cooperi*) for bloom this spring.

✔ VEGETABLES. Zones 1–2: Order seeds now for sowing when the weather warms up. Zones 10–11: Start seeds of cool-season crops (broccoli, cabbage, cauliflower, and lettuce) indoors after midmonth. Zones 12–13: Set out tomato seedlings, but prepare to protect them from frost. Direct-sow root crops (beets, carrots, radishes), peas, and spinach in prepared soil. Start seeds of warm-season crops—including cucumbers, eggplant, melons, peppers, and squash—indoors for transplanting after frost danger is past.

MAINTENANCE

✔ FEED BEARDED IRISES. Late in the month, scratch a complete fertilizer into the soil over rhizomes; water well.

✔ FEED ROSES. Late in the month when nighttime temperatures are forecast to remain above freezing, water established plants, apply a complete fertilizer, and water again.

✔ PREPARE SOIL. Zones 1–2, 10–11: Get flower and vegetable beds ready for spring planting by digging compost into the soil. Especially in zone 10 (Las Vegas), refresh soil in raised beds by adding plenty of organic matter.

✔ WEED, THIN WILDFLOWERS. Zones 12–13: As you weed beds of annual wildflowers, thin out crowded plantings by cutting off unwanted plants at the soil line with scissors. Plants should be spaced so they just touch. — *Mary Irish* ◆

Magnificent climbers

Roses with glorious canopies need solid support and proper training

BY STEVEN R. LORTON

ABOVE: White 'Lace Cascade' and bicolored 'Berries 'n' Cream'. RIGHT: Two plants of 'Cl. Cécile Brunner' form an arch over a porch roof.

NORMAN A. PLATE LEFT: STEVEN GUNTHER

■ IN THE SEEMINGLY DEMURE WORLD OF ROSES, THERE ARE TITANS: towering climbers that reach 20 to 35 feet, with an equal or wider spread, and form canopies big enough to hold a class reunion under. Just one of these plants may eventually bear hundreds, even thousands, of blossoms at the same time.

While it may look well mannered in a nursery container, one

of these young roses can soon produce enough growth to flatten a wimpy trellis. An established plant can generate vegetation—canes, foliage, and flowers—weighing several hundred pounds. That's why a sturdy arbor is the safest stage for the biggest show-offs. Smaller roses that reach 7 to 12 feet can be trained on a well-anchored trellis or fence. Whatever support you use, it must allow free air circulation around plants to reduce the risk of diseases. February is a good month to select roses and plan a structure. In mild-winter areas along the Pacific Coast, you can plant bare-root roses this month (in cold-winter areas, hold off until April). It's best to install the support structure before you plant so you won't disturb the roses later.

SAXON HOLT FAR LEFT: NORMAN A. PLATE BELOW: DEIDRA WALPOLE

Choice climbers for Western gardens

For mild-winter areas.

'Berries 'n' Cream': 10 to 12 feet; ruffled semidouble blossoms with swirls of rose pink and cream.

'Cl. Cécile Brunner': 20 feet or more; small, soft pink sweetheart buds.

'Cl. First Prize': 12 feet or more; deep pink double blossoms; light fragrance.

'Kiftsgate': To 35 feet; small, white single flowers; sweet fragrance.

'Gardenia': To 20 feet: buff yellow buds open to creamy white blooms; light fragrance.

'Lace Cascade': 7 feet; cream buds open to large white blossoms; pleasant fragrance.

Lady Banks' (*Rosa banksiae*): 20 feet or more; 1-inch double flowers in white ('Alba Plena') or yellow ('Lutea').

'Lawrence Johnston': 20 feet; large yellow flowers; strong fragrance.

'Mermaid': 15 feet; large, bright yellow single flowers with amber stamens.

'Paul's Himalayan Musk': 30 feet; shell pink double flowers; rich fragrance.

'Rambling Rector': 20 feet; creamy white semidouble flowers; pungent fragrance.

'Treasure Trove': 35 feet; soft apricot blossoms; strong fragrance.

'Wedding Day': 30 feet or more; creamy white single flowers tinged with pink.

For cold-winter areas. These roses are very hardy but don't reach titanic heights.

'Altissimo': 10 feet; blood red single blossoms with golden yellow stamens.

'Dream Weaver': 12 feet; deep coral buds open to ruffled, rich pink blossoms.

'Dublin Bay': 10 feet; deep red semidouble flowers.

'Madame Alfred Carrière': 15 to 20 feet; white double blossoms with pink blush at centers; musk fragrance.

'William Baffin': 12 feet; strawberry pink semidouble blooms with white centers and golden stamens.

TOP LEFT: Just one 'Gardenia' covers the entire arbor. TOP RIGHT: 'Altissimo' climbs a wall. ABOVE: 'Cl. First Prize' has spiral buds that unfold to double blossoms.

Growing tips

SITE. Most roses bloom best when they get at least six hours of full sun every day. They prefer loose, well-drained soil.

CARE. Water plants deeply and regularly for the first two years. During the roses' first year, feed them lightly with a balanced liquid plant food (such as 12-12-12) in late May and again in mid-July, advises John Clements, owner of Heirloom Old Garden Roses in St. Paul, Oregon. The second year, he suggests, feed with ½ cup of a complete granular fertilizer around the base of the plant in late February.

TRAINING. Rose canes don't climb like vines, so you'll need to train them. As they grow, tie the canes to supports with sturdy twine, heavy-gauge plastic ties, or plastic-coated wire.

PRUNING. Since it takes plants several years to develop strong climbing canes, prune only to remove dead stems, weak growth, and faded flowers for the first two to three years after planting. Prune during the dormant season (November to February) in mild-winter areas, early spring (April) in cold-winter areas. ◆

Clusters of tasty tomatoes

BY JIM McCAUSLAND

Bunches of ripe tomatoes still clinging to the vine have become a familiar sight at produce markets. These so-called cluster tomatoes are cultured in hothouses for sale during seasons when field-grown crops aren't available. But you can easily grow such tomatoes in your summer garden. Which are the most rewarding? To find out, *Sunset* grew several varieties last summer in Northern California and near Puget Sound, Washington. Then we conducted a tasting, rating each tomato for texture, flavor, and sweetness or acidity. Our seven favorites are shown and described in the chart at right.

Some varieties, like 'Juliet', are commonly sold as seedlings in nurseries; others you'll need to start from seed (sources are listed below). Sow seeds indoors about six weeks before the average date of the last spring frost in your area.

Plant seedlings in full sun and in soil amended with plenty of compost, leaf mold, or peat moss, plus some low-nitrogen fertilizer (5-10-10). You can grow plants in a tomato cage or train them up stakes.

Most kinds will start setting fruit in two months. Fruit ripens from the base of the cluster (closest to the main stem) outward to the tip. Pick ripe tomatoes one at a time to enjoy the best flavor.

***SEED SOURCES:** JS=Johnny's Selected Seeds; (207) 437-4301 or www.johnnyseeds.com. TG=Tomato Growers Supply; (888) 478-7333 or www.tomatogrowers.com. TS=Territorial Seed Company; (541) 942-9547 or www.territorial-seed.com. TT=Totally Tomatoes; (803) 663-0016 or www.totallytomato.com. WC=West Coast Seeds; (604) 482-8800 or www.westcoastseeds.com.

'Early Cascade'

FRUITS PER CLUSTER: 5–8
AVERAGE FRUIT LENGTH, WEIGHT: $2\frac{1}{2}$ in., $3\frac{1}{2}$ oz.
NOTES: Large fruit has meaty flesh with well-balanced flavor.
SEED SOURCES*: JS, TG, TS, WC

'Garden Peach'

FRUITS PER CLUSTER: 6–9
AVERAGE FRUIT LENGTH, WEIGHT: $1\frac{3}{8}$ in., $\frac{3}{4}$ oz.
NOTES: These tomatoes look like small peaches, complete with fuzzy skin. Full flavor.
SEED SOURCES*: TG, TS

'Juliet'

FRUITS PER CLUSTER: 6–9
AVERAGE FRUIT LENGTH, WEIGHT: $1\frac{1}{4}$ in., $\frac{3}{4}$ oz.
NOTES: First tomato to ripen in our trials, this 1999 All-America Selection produced large crops of firm, acidic fruit. Plant needs sturdy support.
SEED SOURCES*: JS, TT

'Principe Borghese'

FRUITS PER CLUSTER: 6–9
AVERAGE FRUIT LENGTH, WEIGHT: $1\frac{5}{8}$ in., $1\frac{1}{2}$ oz.
NOTES: Standard drying tomato in Italy; its meaty flesh has rich flavor. Plant has a vigorous habit.
SEED SOURCES*: JS, TG, TS, TT, WC

'Santa'

FRUITS PER CLUSTER: 6–13
AVERAGE FRUIT LENGTH, WEIGHT: 1 in., $\frac{1}{4}$ oz.
NOTES: Rated the most flavorful tomato in our tasting, it has a nice sweet-tart balance—and the fruit doesn't split. Vigorous vine resists late blight.
SEED SOURCES*: JS, TT

'Sausalito Cocktail'

FRUITS PER CLUSTER: 6–8
AVERAGE FRUIT LENGTH, WEIGHT: $1\frac{1}{4}$ in., $\frac{3}{4}$ oz.
NOTES: Small plant grows well in hanging baskets, since its vines grow to about 2 feet. Mild flavor. Fruit splits in rain.
SEED SOURCES*: TG, TS

'Sun Gold'

FRUITS PER CLUSTER: 8–14
AVERAGE FRUIT LENGTH, WEIGHT: $1\frac{1}{8}$ in., $\frac{1}{2}$ oz.
NOTES: Gold-fleshed cherry tomato is as sweet as candy. Fruit splits in rain.
SEED SOURCES*: JS, TG, TS, TT, WC ◆

NORMAN A. PLATE (3)

ROBIN CUSHMAN (4)

OAKLEAF LETTUCES, cress, and nasturtiums are tasty in salads, pretty as companions.

NORMAN A. PLATE

Salad in a pot

Perk up your salads with these easy-to-grow crops

BY SHARON COHOON

It doesn't take much to turn a head of romaine or a prepacked bag of greens into a gourmet first course. Toss in a few burgundy, bronze, or apple green leaves to make it pretty. Then, for zest, add a snippet or two of something peppery like arugula, mustard, or cress.

The same gourmet greens that make a restaurant salad pricey are, surprisingly, among the easiest to grow (they are expensive in markets because they need to be hand-harvested and have a short shelf life). Their seeds germinate quickly; leaves can be harvested when only a few inches high. In fact, young leaves taste best. If you use scissors to snip off only the leaves you need, the plant will quickly grow new ones for additional harvests. Keep cutting until the greens bolt (go to seed) or turn bitter.

To find the best salad enhancers, we asked greens specialists at three mail-order seed companies—Nichols Garden Nursery, Shepherd's Garden Seeds, and Territorial Seed Company—to name their favorites (listed on the facing page). Then we planted seeds of these varieties in containers as cut-and-come-again crops. With regular watering and periodic feeding with fish emulsion, the plants thrived.

There's no excuse for dull salads. If you have room for a half-barrel, a window box, or even a terra-cotta pot (at least 16 inches in diameter), you have room to grow your own designer salad greens.

Two ways to grow salad greens

As a mix. Combine seeds of all the greens you want to try, then broadcast them over the surface of potting soil for a blend similar to the salad mixes found in supermarkets. Sow mustard after other salad greens have sprouted; this vigorous grower can crowd out everything else.

In rows or blocks, by kind. To customize your salad to your meals—sometimes piquant, sometimes mellow—grow different greens separately. Sow seed in individual rows, blocks, or in concentric circles. This is a good method if you are trying greens you haven't tasted before. If there's one you don't like, it's easy to replace it.

Pretty leaves

OAKLEAFS. Though all looseleaf lettuces can be grown as cutting lettuces, oakleaf varieties are particularly popular because of their distinctive leaf shapes, buttery textures, and sweet flavor. Many are pretty, too, with leaf colors that spark up the greens: yellow-green varieties such as 'Salad Bowl' and 'Pom Pom', bronzy types like 'Red Sails' and 'Cocarde', and real reds like 'Red Oakleaf', 'Red Rebosa', and 'New Red Fire'.

ROMAINES. Choices include 'Deer Tongue', an heirloom variety with thick, succulent lime green leaves; 'Cimarron', a red-shaded romaine; and 'Freckles', a green romaine with dark red speckles and splotches.

'LOLLO ROSSO' TYPES. These are frilly-leafed lettuces, often used as a garnish in restaurants. Leaves of the regular variety are chartreuse with burgundy edges. 'Lovina', an improved selection, has mostly red leaves and is slower to bolt.

NORMAN A. PLATE (2)

ABOVE: A piquant mix of Italian dandelion, giant red mustard, and onion, with some oakleaf lettuce for sweetness. Shadecloth over bamboo hoops protects greens from afternoon sun and discourages bolting. LEFT: Red lettuces such as ruffly 'Lollo Rosso' add dash to greens.

Peppery partners

ARUGULA. The favorite gourmet green at restaurants. Extremely easy to grow. Plants bolt quickly, too, so sow seeds in small batches every few weeks.

MUSTARD. Many varieties; all usually taste pleasant in salads if harvested young. 'Red Giant' is particularly mild and has the additional advantage of burgundy-tinted leaves.

ITALIAN DANDELION. Tastes pleasantly bitter, like endive or chicory, but requires only a fraction of the space. Harvest when leaves are 3 to 4 inches tall; later, they're too tough for salad.

MOUNTAIN CRESS (also known as peppergrass or garden cress). Pleasantly piquant. A quick crop; you can harvest leaves in 10 to 14 days. Sow seeds frequently in small batches.

'WRINKLED, CRINKLED, CRUMPLED CRESS'. A cross between mountain cress and broadleaf cress, which is a mustard-family green. Adds interesting texture as well as flavor to salads.

LEEKS AND ONIONS. When harvested young, leaves are tender and mild-tasting.

NASTURTIUMS. Both flowers and leaves are edible and mildly peppery. 'Empress of India', a scarlet-flowered variety with slightly bluish green leaves, is especially handsome.

Where to buy seed

Plants of some greens mentioned at left, such as arugula, mustard, and 'Red Sails' lettuce, are available in cell-packs at garden centers. Seeds of other varieties are available by mail from the following sources.

Nichols Garden Nursery, 1190 N. Pacific Hwy., Albany, OR 97321; (541) 928-9280 or www.gardennursery.com. Sells 'Cimarron', 'Deer Tongue', 'Empress of India' nasturtiums, 'Lovina', 'Red Rebosa', 'Red Sails', 'Salad Bowl'.

Shepherd's Garden Seeds, 30 Irene St., Torrington, CT 06790; (860) 482-3638 or www.shepherdseeds.com. Sells 'Cocarde', 'Deer Tongue', 'Freckles', 'Red Oakleaf,' 'Wrinkled, Crinkled, Crumpled Cress'.

Territorial Seed Company, Box 157, Cottage Grove, OR 97424; (541) 942-9547 or www.territorial-seed.com. Sells seed of 'Catalogna Frastagli' Italian dandelion, 'New Red Fire', 'Pom Pom', 'Red Giant' mustard. ◆

Spring blooms aloft

Create clouds of color with flowering trees that thrive in the Northwest

BY STEVEN R. LORTON

PHOTOGRAPHS BY JANET LOUGHREY

ABOVE: 'Rubra' star magnolia. RIGHT: 'Tai Haku' flowering cherry. OPPOSITE PAGE: 'Orange Beauty' Chinese witch hazel.

■ WHEN IT COMES TO DECIDUOUS SPRING-FLOWERING TREES, FEW AREAS OF THE WORLD CAN MATCH THE RICH diversity of the Pacific Northwest. Take a walk through one of the older neighborhoods around Puget Sound or Portland and you're sure to see some in bloom. Their blossoms form golden veils on bare branches or hover like pastel clouds over sweeps of bulbs. They glow in the sunlight and glisten in the rain. And just when you think the show is over, a wind kicks up and the ground is covered with a blizzard of petals.

Our listings on page 52 describe many of the Northwest's proven performers. By choosing one or more plants from each group of flowering trees, you can enjoy a succession of bloom that will last from the first of the year until the end of spring.

Plant them now from nursery cans for instant bloom. Most will take partial shade, but they flower best in full sun. East of the Cascades, where summers can be blistering, give dogwoods light afternoon shade. All these trees like rich soil with good drainage. To encourage a robust flower crop, feed them in early spring and again in midsummer with a balanced fertilizer broadcast around the base of the tree.

Early spring

Chinese witch hazel (*Hamamelis mollis*) bears bright yellow, tassel-like flowers as early as January in the mildest winter climates. Flowers have a spicy fragrance. Reaches 10 feet (occasionally taller) with a 15-foot spread. For more exotic flower colors, try these varieties of *H. intermedia:* 'Diane' (bright burnt-red flowers), 'Orange Beauty' (coppery orange), and 'Ruby Glow' (medium red). *Sunset* climate zones 4–7, 17.

Cornelian cherry (*Cornus mas*) carries masses of small yellow flowers on bare twigs in early spring, followed by clusters of bright scarlet fruit (good for making jelly or attracting birds). Reaches 20 feet tall, 15 feet wide. Zones 2–6.

Thundercloud plum (*Prunus cerasifera* 'Thundercloud'). Its charcoal bark makes a handsome foil for rosy pink to white blossoms. Summer leaves are rich burgundy red. The tree grows to 20 feet tall with an equal spread. Zones 3–7, 17.

Midspring

Crabapple (*Malus* hybrids) bears pink, red, or white blossoms, followed by showy fruit in red or yellow, and some have autumn leaves in shades of red, orange, or yellow. Named varieties range in size from 12 to 25 feet tall and 12 to 20 feet across. Zones 1–7, 17.

Flowering cherry (*Prunus*). 'Daybreak' cherry (*P. yedoensis* 'Akebono') has rich pink, lightly fragrant flowers and grows to 25 feet tall in an open, graceful pattern. For a mass of white, consider *P. serrulata* 'Shirotae' (the 'Mt. Fuji' cherry), which grows to 20 feet tall in a handsome horizontal pattern. For the most spectacular white, look for *P.s.* 'Tai Haku', with 2½-inch-wide blooms. Zones 3–7, 17.

Magnolia (deciduous species and varieties). Early-flowering kinds that bear their blossoms on naked branches are breathtaking. Star magnolia (*M. stellata*) has glistening white blooms composed of star-shaped petals; *M.s.* 'Rubra' has rosy pink blossoms. The trees reach 10 feet or taller with an eventual 20-foot spread. Yulan magnolia (*M. denudata*), which carries fragrant, white, tulip-shaped flowers 6 to 7 inches across, reaches 35 feet tall with a nearly equal spread. Zones 2–7, 17.

ROSY PINK BLOSSOMS of 'Cherokee Chief' dogwood complement the plum-colored spring leaves of Japanese maples beneath.

Redbud (*Cercis canadensis*) sports bright pink flowers on black branches. The tree eventually reaches 25 feet with nearly horizontal branches. *C.c.* 'Forest Pansy' has heart-shaped, wine red flowers. Zones 2–7, 17. Chinese redbud (*C. chinensis* 'Avondale'), the most profuse bloomer, has deep purple flowers. Zones 4–7, 17.

Late spring

Dogwood (*Cornus*). Varieties of Eastern dogwood (*C. florida*) flower in shades of pink, deep rose, and near white. They top out at about 30 feet. Zones 2–7.

'Eddie's White Wonder', a hybrid of *C. florida* and the native *C. nuttallii,* bears big clusters of cream-colored flowers. This upright tree reaches 25 feet in time. Zones 2–7, 17. ◆

These pots are plastic?

The look of terra-cotta or stone with the durability of synthetics: These lightweight new pots have it all

BY JIM McCAUSLAND

Switching parents is a tricky business. But synthetic garden containers seem to have managed it. Originally, when they were just cheap plastic alternatives to terra-cotta, they looked like clay's poor relations and crumbled after a year or two in hot sun. But now manufacturers are marrying classic Italian design with modern materials to produce synthetic offspring that have all the advantages of terra-cotta or stone, and none of the liabilities. These new synthetic containers look so much like the real thing that—without hefting them—you might never know they're fakes.

These days, the most widely sold synthetic containers are made from polyurethane or polyethylene. You can usually tell the difference between the two just by feeling them.

Polyurethane is up to an inch thick, and extremely light—10 to 20 percent the weight of terra-cotta. It has the feel of hardened styrene foam.

This material is a very good insulator, keeping roots inside from overheating in summer, and inhibiting freezing in winter. Most pots are guaranteed for at least 36 months against chipping, cracking, fading, and freeze damage.

Polyethylene pots are more common. Planted, they can be indistinguishable from terra-cotta. Unplanted, they are identifiable by the way the rim is rolled over to the inside. Rolling makes the rim appear as thick as terra-cotta, though the wall of the rest of the pot measures only ¼ to ⅜ inch thick. The result is a great-looking pot, but one without the insulation that thicker polyurethane offers. Still, this material is very tough and resists damage from sun and frost.

Synthetic containers pictured here: garland window box ($44) and basic pot ($38) of polyethylene, and stone-colored urn of polyurethane ($75).

MARION BRENNER (3)

EVEN THE LARGEST plastic pot is easy to lift. ABOVE RIGHT: A 16¼-inch polyethylene pot with grape-garland motif ($20) has the look of granite.

Getting what you want

All these materials are available in a full palette of textures (some mimic granite or sandstone) and colors—from white and gray to pale rust and black. (Be wary of black polyethylene if you live in a hot climate: It can cause the soil inside to heat up substantially compared with soil inside light-colored containers, possibly damaging plant roots.)

While most synthetic containers work well right off the shelf, some come without drain holes, or with drain holes too small to make a difference. Fortunately, holes are easy to drill, so you can fix the problem yourself in minutes.

Sources

Plastic pots are widely available in garden centers and nurseries around the West. Or call manufacturers for catalogs and retail locations. For polyurethane, try American Designer Pottery (800/550-5761 or www.amdesignerpottery.com). For polyethylene, contact Campania International (215/538-1106 or www.campaniainternational.com); Riverside Plastics (606/849-3383 or www.riverside-plastics.com); Rotocast (800/423-8539 or www.rotocast.com/products); or Telcom USA (978/688-6130). ◆

CLAIRE CURRAN

ORANGE BLACK-EYED SUSAN VINE offers a refreshing contrast to white larkspur in the distant bed, and to white marguerites and Sally Holmes roses in the foreground. For details on this cheerful performer, see page 61.

March

gardenguide

CHARLES MANN

PINK-FLOWERED rock soapwort and golden tall bearded irises bloom along the stream.

A serene retreat

This Boulder backyard soothes the frazzled soul

■ When Larry and Sally Steinmetz built their dream home in Boulder, Colorado, they envisioned a garden where they could relax and unwind from their busy schedules. Landscape designer Mike Ransom of Robert Howard Associates in Boulder turned their 1-acre property into a personal sanctuary. Now, the Steinmetzes enjoy the serenity of a mountain retreat without ever leaving home. Ransom's design won a grand prize in a competition sponsored by the Associated Landscape Contractors of Colorado.

A natural-looking stream is the centerpiece of the backyard. Flowing 150 feet past a series of patios and pathways, the recirculating stream makes a dramatic backdrop for entertaining, and the soothing sound of splashing water helps mask traffic noise from a nearby highway. Poised along the stream are a pair of coyote sculptures cut from sheet metal and allowed to develop a rusty patina. The scene is illuminated by 12-volt lights for nighttime viewing.

The plantings surrounding the watercourse are kept simple for an uncluttered look and ease of maintenance. Perennials arranged in masses among boulders provide a succession of color from early spring to the first hard frost. The photo above shows the garden in June, when a pink froth of bloom covers low, spreading rock soapwort (*Saponaria ocymoides*) and golden yellow flowers rise from tall bearded irises and 'Moonshine' yarrow. Ornamental grasses (blue oat grass, feather reed grass, and *Miscanthus sinensis* 'Morning Light' and 'Yaku Jima') are planted singly as accents. The grasses sway softly in the slightest breeze, and their dry leaves and seed heads form buff silhouettes in the winter.

— Marcia Tatroe

Southwest style in Santa Monica

■ How do you convert a Santa Monica front yard into a desert dry wash? Susanne Jett, the landscape designer responsible for this transformation, makes it sound easy. Remove lawn. Reshape flat earth into gentle swells and swales. Add boulders. Plant aeonium, echeveria, and agave, along with other succulents and perennials that have compatible water requirements, such as *Athanasia*, Matilija poppy, and pride of Madeira. Cover remaining bare earth with rock mulch. Then create a walkway through the area that feels more like a path, so as not to spoil the effect.

A 2-inch layer of Del Rio (a relatively inexpensive, 3/8-inch-diameter stone) forms the base of the mulch. Arizona mix (slightly larger and with lavender tones) covers it. And Lodi (a 1½-inch ocher stone) is used as an accent around focal plants such as large agave. The mulch covers drip irrigation (½-inch tubing), conserves soil moisture, and provides reflected heat the plants appreciate. The different sizes and colors of stone make it all look natural. *—S.C.*

CLAIRE CURRAN ABOVE: STEVEN GUNTHER

WALL-MOUNTED BASKET mixes pink ivy geraniums, white 'Surfinia' petunias, 'Ann Folkard' true geraniums, dianthus, lobelia, and trailing pink 'Million Bells' (*Calibrachoa*). A gnarled piece of driftwood adds a sculptural element.

Cottage garden on high

■ Gregg Davila of Organic Art creates hanging baskets that look like cottage gardens in miniature—his blends of perennials, herbs, evergreens, and a sprinkling of annuals have the same casual, billowy style. Despite their carefree appearance, however, Davila's compositions are meticulously crafted. His method: Line the bottom two-thirds of a 12-inch wire basket with moistened sphagnum moss and fill it with potting soil. For the sides, slide the rootballs of small, cell-pack-size plants through the basket's wires, resting them on top of the soil, then cover the rootballs with strips of wet moss. Line the remainder of the basket with moss and fill it with soil. For polish, hide the top wire of the basket with a wrap of moss. Finally, plant the top, starting at the center and working toward the rim.

Davila sells examples of his living art at his kiosk at the Marketplace, 6577 E. Pacific Coast Hwy., Long Beach. He also conducts basketmaking classes occasionally. To get on his mailing list, call (562) 598-3838. — *Sharon Cohoon*

CLIPPINGS

•Unusual plants on-line. More and more nurseries are going high-tech by putting their entire catalogs on-line. Find an incredible array of plants at Forestfarm (www.forestfarm.com), the Great Plant Company (www.greatplants.com; includes photos of plants), Heronswood Nursery (www.heronswood.com), and Mountain Valley Growers (www.mountainvalleygrowers.com; includes photos).

•Growing veggies in Hawaii. Try finding a book that tells you how to grow breadfruit or taro. Or how to prepare daikon or pipinola once you figure out how to grow them. Kathy Oshiro couldn't. So she wrote her own book, *Growing Vegetables in Hawai'i: A How-to Guide for the Gardener.* Mainlanders with a soft spot for the Islands might want it just for the recipes: lomi salmon, sweet potato with coconut milk, and 68 more. *Bess Press, Honolulu, 1999; $14.95; (800) 910-2377 or www.besspress.com.*

•Rosy website. Visit www.helpmefind.com/sites/rrr/rosetest.html for details about rose varieties (hybridizer, parentage, size, color), as well as rose gardens, publications, suppliers, and more.

Clematis with blooms sweet as honey

MAGGIE MacLAREN

■ Later this month, when evergreen clematis (*C. armandii*) bursts into bloom, masses of fragrant white blossoms will glisten on fencetops and roof gables in many parts of the West.

In the photo at right, you see it spilling over a fence at the entry to Carolyn Temple's Seattle garden. Large clusters of 2½-inch-wide flowers with a honeylike scent stand out against the glossy dark green foliage.

Evergreen clematis grows well in *Sunset* climate zones 4–9, 12–24. A rampant grower, the vine reaches 20 feet in two to three years.

Like other clematis, this one should be planted so its roots are in shade and its leaves in sun. It does well in loose, acidic soil with good drainage. Train it so its clinging tendrils can wrap around fences or other supports.

Once the plant is established, feed it with a complete granular fertilizer in late winter, again after bloom, and in early summer as it sets next year's flower buds. After flowering, prune it hard to prevent tangling and the buildup of thatch. As soon as blooms fade, cut the plant back to the height you want; in a few weeks, new growth will emerge, and soon you'll hardly know the plant was pruned.

— Steven R. Lorton

TERRENCE MOORE

A grassy meadow in Paradise Valley

■ A desert wash runs through part of Sallye Schumacher's front yard near the slopes of Mummy Mountain in Paradise Valley, Arizona. To soften the austere look of the wash, she planted it with ornamental grasses and shrubs that require no supplemental irrigation.

Schumacher had the wash lined with granite boulders, then planted deer grass (*Muhlenbergia rigens*), fountain grass (*Pennisetum alopecuroides* 'Hameln'), and sacahuista (*Nolina microcarpa*), an evergreen shrub with narrow, grasslike leaves. She added brittlebush (*Encelia farinosa*) for its yellow spring flowers and Mexican honeysuckle (*Justicia spicigera*) for its deep orange blooms, which appear from late fall through spring.

Now fully established, the grasses form arching clumps among the boulders. In late October, Schumacher cuts them back to prevent reseeding and to encourage dense new growth in the spring. When occasional heavy rains run off the mountain and fill the wash, the water flows around the boulders and collects in a pond Schumacher formed in a low area.

— Nora Burba Trulsson

PROJECT

An easy azalea bonsai

■ This remarkable Kurume azalea bonsai, created by *Sunset* associate art director Dennis Leong, is just five years old. Leong started it by pruning the canopy of a small azalea to a miniature tree shape. Then he pruned the roots and secured the plant in a bonsai dish.

Kurume and Satsuki azalea hybrids make the best bonsais. They're easy to train; wherever you make a cut, they'll sprout new growth. Bonsai supplies are available at most retail nurseries.

TIME: About 2 hours

COST: $50–$65

TOOLS AND MATERIALS

- Wire cutters
- 6-inch-square piece of plastic mesh screen
- Bonsai dish (Leong's is 11 inches long by 6½ inches wide)
- 24-gauge copper wire
- Four sturdy wood matchsticks or 2-inch-long pieces of ⅛-inch-thick wood
- Potting soil
- An azalea
- Pruners and spray bottle
- Chopstick
- Moss spores

CLOUDS OF PINK BLOOMS cover this Kurume azalea bonsai—started from a 1-gallon-size plant—in spring.

NORMAN A. PLATE (7)

A

B

C

D

E

F

DIRECTIONS

1. Cut two 2-inch-square pieces of plastic mesh and lay one over each drainage hole on the inside of the bonsai dish. For each piece of mesh, make two loops in a 4-inch-long piece of wire (**A**) and slip ends through the mesh and drainage hole. Turn the pot over and bend the wire outward.

2. Cut heads off the matchsticks. Cut two 20-inch lengths of wire and wind each wire six times around a matchstick at the wire's center point.

3. Cut two 3-inch-long pieces of wire and bend in half. Attach a wired matchstick to the inside of each drainage hole (**B**) by placing another matchstick on the outside of the drainage hole and slipping the ends of the short wire over the wired matchstick, through the mesh and the hole, and around the outer matchstick; twist ends tightly (**C**). Fill the dish partway with potting soil.

4. Remove the azalea from the pot (**D**). Prune to thin out the top growth to make the plant's structure more open and to form a tree shape.

5. Carefully tease the soil away from the roots (**E**) and gently untangle them; mist the roots frequently with water while working.

6. Cut off two-thirds of the roots, flattening the bottom of the rootball and rounding the sides to decrease its diameter—the pruned roots should cover about two-thirds of the surface area of the bonsai dish. Position the base of the plant in the dish just off-center. Add soil to hold the rootball in place, working it in around the roots with the chopstick.

7. Cut two ¾-inch-wide by 4-inch-long strips from the remaining screen. Lay a strip across each side of the rootball. Run an anchoring wire through the ends of both screens, then tightly twist the wire ends across the mesh to firmly hold the rootball in place. Clip off the excess wire (**F**).

8. Finish filling the pot with soil. Water well. Sprinkle moss spores over the soil surface, and mist regularly with water.

— *Lauren Bonar Swezey*

Asian hybrid lilacs flaunt rich color, fragrance

■ American gardeners are familiar with the legendary scent of the common lilac (*Syringa vulgaris*). But other members of the lilac clan, including most of the Asian relations and their hybrids, have luscious fragrances and other attributes that make them worth seeking out.

When hybridizers noticed that broadleaf lilac (*S. oblata*) flowered a week or two earlier than common lilac, they crossed the two and came up with a series of beautiful, early-flowering hybrids called *S. hyacinthiflora*. All have classic lilac fragrance. The plants, which can be grown in *Sunset* climate zones 1–7, may reach 15 feet tall with equal width.

Many *S. hyacinthiflora* hybrids rank among the best lilacs in their color classes.

ROYAL BOTANICAL GARDENS

'GLORY' bears fluffy clusters of flowers on a 4- to 5-foot-tall shrub.

These include blue-white 'Blanche Sweet'; bluish pink 'Excel'; light lavender 'Assessippi'; pink 'Annabel', 'California Rose', and 'Esther Staley'; purple 'Glory'; violet purple 'Pocahontas'; and white 'Mount Baker'. Some of these, such as 'Annabel' and 'Excel', are very early bloomers that react to unseasonably cold temperatures by delaying flowers until the weather becomes milder.

Order bare-root plants to set out now or plant container-grown stock later. For a good selection by mail, check out Heard Gardens (5355 Merle Hay Rd., Johnston, IA 50131; 515/276-4533 or www.heardgardens.com; catalog $2) or Select Plus International Nursery (1510 Pine Rd., Mascouche, Quebec, Canada J7L 2M4; 450/477-3797 or www.spi.8m.com; catalog $1).

—Jim McCausland

JANET LOUGHREY

Artichokes from seed

■ Homegrown artichokes in the Northwest? You bet! On the west side of the Cascades, you can grow artichokes as perennials; on the east, grow them as annuals. Among the most reliable perennial varieties are 'Green Globe' (shown at left), which has proved the most hardy, and slightly later-maturing 'Violetto', with striking purple-tinged buds. In cold-winter climates (*Sunset* zones 1–3), the best bet is 'Imperial Star'. Seeds of all three are sold by Territorial Seed Co. (541/942-9547 or www.territorial-seed.com).

In February to mid-March, start seeds indoors in 4-inch pots. Grow seedlings under fluorescent lights or in a sunny window or greenhouse. Feed plants every 10 days with a liquid fertilizer diluted to quarter-strength.

Transplant 8- to 10-week-old plants outdoors in a sunny spot, spacing them 4 to 6 feet apart. Work a shovelful of well-aged manure or 1 cup of complete fertilizer into each planting hole. Spread 4 inches of organic mulch around plants. In colder areas, protect plants with cloches at night if frost threatens; buds can take light frost, but a hard frost will kill the plants. About 90 to 100 days after transplanting, the first artichokes should be ready to pick.

If you grow artichokes as perennials, cut plants back to 4 to 6 inches above the ground in late October, then generously mulch with compost or straw. *— Kris Wetherbee*

Two tasty slicing tomatoes

'Jetsetter' 'Caspian Pink'

■ If you enjoy really big slicing tomatoes, two newly introduced varieties may well satisfy you. 'Jetsetter' and 'Caspian Pink' bear fruits so large that a single slice covers a hamburger and a whole tomato yields enough wedges for a salad. *Sunset* staffers grew both in their home gardens; even in an exceptionally cool summer, the plants produced good crops of fruit weighing 14 to 17 ounces apiece. Both are indeterminate tomatoes that require tall cages or stakes to keep plants inbounds.

'Jetsetter'. As its name implies, this hybrid matures early (about 64 days after transplanting), making it a good choice where summers are cool or short. Globe-shaped fruits averaging 8 ounces have firm, meaty flesh with rich flavor. The plants resist many of the diseases that affect tomatoes.

'Caspian Pink'. An heirloom tomato from Russia, it yields sweet, mild, pink-fleshed fruits. Averaging 10 to 12 ounces each, tomatoes color from the bottom up, turning deeper shades of pink as they ripen; pick when the top "shoulders" are still yellow and bring them indoors until they're fully pink and ready to eat. Expect 80 days from transplanting to maturity.

Order seeds of either variety from Nichols Garden Nursery (541/928-9280), Tomato Growers Supply Company (888/478-7333), or Totally Tomatoes (803/663-0016). — *Dick Bushnell*

BACK TO BASICS

NORMAN A. PLATE (2)

How to pop a plant out of a nursery pot. Follow this time-tested method for easing plants out of nursery pots (you may need to cut the pot off seriously root-bound plants). Lay the pot on its side and roll it back and forth, placing pressure on the side of the pot. Turn the pot upside down while holding one hand across the top of the rootball; carefully slide the plant out. If it doesn't come out, repeat the process. — *L.B.S.*

Warm welcome, year-round

■ Black-eyed Susan vine (*Thunbergia alata*) is grown as a summer annual in most of the country. But in coastal Southern California (*Sunset* climate zones 23–24), this cheerful performer is rarely out of bloom. That's why Kathy Donovan Icaza chose it to cover the metal arbor that frames the entrance to her Tustin garden (see photo on page 54). She knew visitors would be welcomed with flowers year-round.

T. alata grows very fast—two 1-gallon-size plants covered the arbor in a single season. The vine resists pests and diseases and requires little or no feeding—Icaza saves the chicken manure from her four hens (two shown in photo) for more demanding plants like roses. Icaza has discovered that it's better to manicure *T. alata* regularly to keep it in line, just as you would a hedge, than to hard-prune—which results in woody plants and fewer flowers for a while.

Those orange blooms are too versatile to do without, says Icaza. They are a nice contrast to the cool purples and blues she favors in spring, a great complement to her zinnias in summer, and a cheerful sight in winter when little else is in bloom. — *S.C.*

TERRENCE MOORE

Is that a pony under the palo verde?

■ A creator and collector of ceramics, Lynn Myers knows how well sculpture in general—and clay in particular—fits into desert landscapes. She has placed many of her own pieces around her home in Borrego Springs in the California desert. But she wanted a sculpture larger than any of her own pieces to place beneath a native palo verde tree on the edge of her property. What she found was a nearly life-size pony sculpted in clay by Rodney Mott. "I knew that horse would look right at home under that tree," says Myers. "And the taller the tree grows, the more natural it looks." First-time visitors to her home often mistake it for a real pony grazing in the shade, she says. As for the sculpture's durability, clay fired at 2,000° can easily tolerate the worst desert heat. — *S.C.*

'Remembrance' columbine

■ This spring, a columbine called 'Remembrance' is being introduced to honor the victims of the shooting tragedy at Columbine High School in Jefferson County, Colorado. 'Remembrance' bears flowers with white rosettes poised on velvety purple stars with long spurs of the same color. Clusters of blossoms dance on 24-inch stems above delicate, fernlike foliage from late spring through early summer.

Like other columbines, 'Remembrance' is hardy in all *Sunset* climate zones and can be grown at elevations to 9,000 feet. Plant 'Remembrance' in well-drained soil in borders, woodland gardens, or containers. At lower elevations, the plant prefers morning sun and afternoon shade; at higher elevations, give it full sun. Water regularly during dry spells.

Look for plants bearing a distinctive blue label in garden centers and nurseries. Thanks to corporate and community sponsors, all proceeds from the sale of this plant will fund programs to teach tolerance and appreciation of diversity in schools across the nation. — *M.T.*

NEW PRODUCT

No more potting mess

NORMAN A. PLATE

■ Whether you pot your plants indoors or outdoors, cleaning up spilled soil is always part of the process. Well, say good-bye to your dustpan and brush. The Table-Top Gardener, a portable potting tray, turns any flat surface into a potting table. Its tall side walls keep the soil from spilling out, while its cutaway front allows you to work at a more comfortable angle as you fill pots with soil, seeds, or bulbs. (The tray can also be used for other messy tasks like root pruning and pumpkin carving, as well as craft projects.)

The lightweight plastic tray also features flared handle grips at the sides and a shallow shelf along the back to hold tools, gloves, seed packets, or other gardening paraphernalia.

Measuring 23½ inches wide, 21 inches deep, and 6 inches tall, the tray costs $13.95 (including shipping and handling). To order, phone the Argee Corporation at (800) 449-3030.

— *Peter O. Whiteley*

WHAT TO DO IN YOUR GARDEN IN MARCH

Pacific Northwest Checklist

PLANTING

✔ CAMELLIAS. Zones 4–7: Winter-flowering Sasanquas are at the end of their bloom cycle, while spring-flowering Japonicas are just coming into their own. Put them in the ground now or keep them in nursery containers and enjoy them up close until blooms are past, then plant them out.

✔ COOL-SEASON CROPS. Zones 4–7: Sow or set out seedlings of lettuce, peas, spinach, and Swiss chard; cabbage family members (broccoli, brussels sprouts, cabbage, cauliflower, kale, kohlrabi, mustard); root crops (beets, carrots, potatoes, radishes); and the onion clan (chives, elephant garlic, soft- and hard-neck garlic, leeks, onions, shallots). In zones 1–3, plant late this month or next.

✔ LAWNS. This is one of the best times to start new lawns and patch old ones. You can save time by laying sod, money by sowing seed. Either way, till the top 6 inches of soil, pick out roots and rocks, then till in a 2-inch layer of organic matter such as compost. Level the soil, then rake in seed or lay sod and roll. Water regularly until the grass is well established and growing strongly. To patch worn lawns, rough up the bare areas, rake in seed, cover lightly with compost, and water.

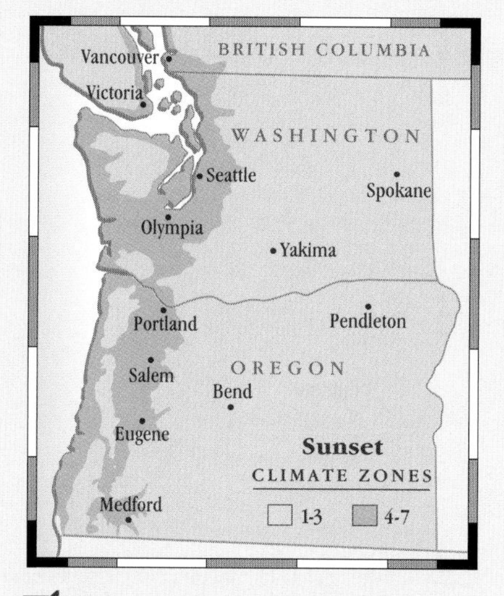

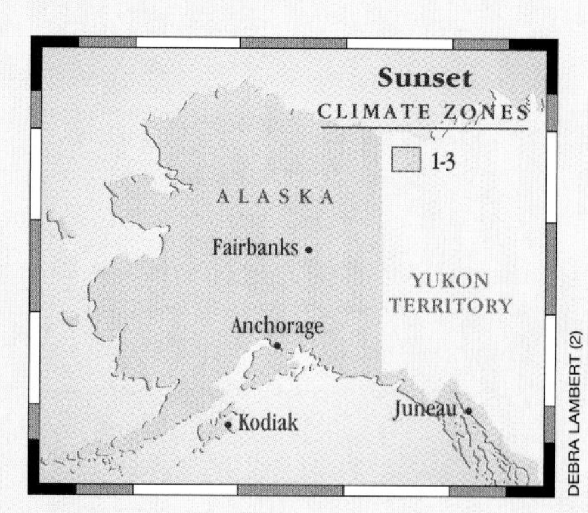

DEBRA LAMBERT (2)

✔ WARM-SEASON CROPS. Start seeds indoors for warm-season crops, including basil, cucumbers, eggplant, melons, peppers, and tomatoes. Transplant seedlings into the garden in mid-May.

MAINTENANCE

✔ CONTROL SLUGS. They show up at the first hint of mild, damp weather. Like weeds, they're easiest to control when they're small. A new alternative to poison bait is iron phosphate–based products (sold as Escar-Go! or Sluggo), which are nontoxic to humans and pets.

✔ DIVIDE PERENNIALS. Zones 4–7: This is the best time to divide summer- and fall-flowering perennials like asters, chrysanthemums, and Shasta daisies. In zones 1–3, divide these plants in April. In all zones, wait until autumn to divide spring-flowering perennials.

✔ FEED LAWNS. Zones 4–7: Grass starts growing rapidly this month. Support it by applying ½ pound nitrogen per 1,000 square feet. You can't go wrong with a fertilizer formulated in an N-P-K ratio of 3-1-2: 3 parts nitrogen, 1 part phosphorus, 2 parts potassium.

✔ PRUNE CLEMATIS. Zones 4–7: Cut back summer- and fall-flowering clematis to the strongest stems now, then scratch fertilizer in around the base of the plant. Prune back spring-flowering varieties immediately after bloom. In zones 1–3, wait to prune until after the danger of hard frost is past. ◆

WHAT TO DO IN YOUR GARDEN IN MARCH

Northern California Checklist

PLANTING

✔ ORIENTAL LILIES. Zones 7–9, 14–17: You can't beat lilies for drama. 'Casablanca' (white) and 'Stargazer' (dark pink with white edges) are two of the most stunning. Other great choices include 'Arena' (white with red and yellow), 'Aruba' (medium pink and white), and 'Kissproof' (dark pink-red). All are available from Dutch Gardens (800/818-3861 or www.dutchgardens.com).

✔ PERENNIALS. Shop for perennials such as 'David's Choice' or 'Powis Castle' artemisias, coreopsis, *Diascia* (coral, pink, or purple), gaillardia, *Gaura lindheimeri* 'Siskiyou Pink', purple-leafed heuchera, ornamental oreganos, penstemons, perennial foxglove (*Digitalis mertonensis*), salvias, Santa Barbara daisies, and wallflowers. Many perennials are available in six-packs, 4-inch pots, and 1-gallon cans.

✔ POTATO TUBERS. Zones 7–9, 14–17: Try potatoes in different colors and flavors, such as yellow 'Bintje' or 'Yukon Gold'; red 'All Red' or 'Red Dale'; blue 'All Blue' or 'Caribe'. Order these or any of 85 disease-free varieties from Irish Eyes with a Hint of Garlic, Box 307, Ellensberg, WA 98926; (509) 925-6025 or www.irish-eyes.com; catalog $2.

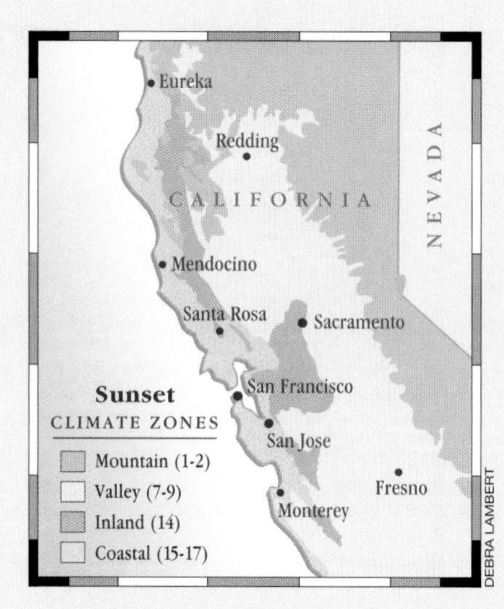

✔ TREES. Zones 7–9, 14–17: Celebrate California's Arbor Day by planting a tree between March 7 and 14. Choose a variety that's suitable to your climate and the site. Always learn the mature height of a tree before planting. For instance, California's state tree, the redwood—which grows 3 to 5 feet a year, has a branch spread of 14 to 30 feet, and grows 90 to several hundred feet tall—isn't suitable for small yards. But lower-growing Chinese tallow tree and crape myrtle make handsome patio trees.

✔ VEGETABLES. Zones 7–9, 14–17: To ensure a continuous crop of beets, bush peas, carrots, lettuce, radishes, spinach, Swiss chard, and turnips, make successive sowings two weeks apart. Set out broccoli, cabbage, and cauliflower seedlings. If the last frost has passed, you also can start planting the first warm-season crops when they appear in nurseries. Most need warm (at least 60°) soil to thrive. To give vegetables a boost, plant through black plastic and use floating row covers.

MAINTENANCE

✔ CHECK DRIP SYSTEMS. Zones 7–9, 14–17: Flush out sediment from filters and check screens for algae; clean with a toothbrush, if necessary. Turn on water and check to make sure all emitters are dripping water; clean or replace clogged ones (if you can't get an emitter out, install a new one next to it). Check for and repair leaks in lines. For supplies, visit a home center or irrigation supply store. Or order by mail from the Urban Farmer (415/661-2204).

✔ FEED LAWNS. Zones 7–9, 14–17: Bent, blue, fescue, and rye grasses begin their spring growth spurts now. Feed with a high-nitrogen lawn fertilizer (try one of the new organic ones available at many nurseries), according to label directions. ◆

Southern California Checklist

PLANTING & HARVEST

✔AZALEAS AND CAMELLIAS. Purchase plants while they are still in flower, and plant them as soon as possible thereafter. Amend the soil well with organic material and a soil acidifier such as oak leaf mold or peat moss. Plant both shrubs a bit high so that the tops of the rootballs are 1 inch or so aboveground after the soil settles.

✔CULINARY HERBS. Sow seeds of arugula, chervil, cilantro, cress, and dill. Plant chives, oregano, parsley, rosemary, sage, savory, tarragon, and thyme. Experiment with some new herbs, such as anise hyssop, French sorrel, or even Vietnamese coriander (*rau răm*).

✔CUTTING FLOWERS. Sow seeds of cleome, cosmos, nicotiana, and sunflowers—all make great cutting flowers and germinate easily. Also try annual scabiosa. 'Fire King', with burgundy and white flowers, is especially showy. Available from Seed Savers Exchange; (319) 382-5990.

✔PERENNIALS. Nurseries are well stocked with blooming perennials in early spring. Reliable choices include campanula, coral bells, coreopsis, dianthus, diascia, kangaroo paws, lavenders, limonium, geraniums, marguerites, nemesia, penstemon, salvia, scabiosa, and yarrow.

DEBRA LAMBERT

✔SUMMER BULBS. Plant acidanthera, cannas, dahlias, gladiolus, liatris, lilies, tigridia, tuberose, and tuberous begonias now for color this summer.

MAINTENANCE

✔CONTINUE SPRING-FEEDING. If you didn't do it last month, feed ground covers, shrubs, perennials, and trees with a controlled-release fertilizer such as bonemeal, cottonseed meal, or well-rotted manure—or, if preferred, a faster-acting complete fertilizer. Feed azaleas and camellias with cottonseed meal or an acid-type fertilizer after bloom. Both warm- and cool-season turf grasses will benefit from an application of high-nitrogen fertilizer now too.

✔JUMP-START ROSES. If you garden in heavy clay soil, try Marty Hammond's formula for getting your roses off on the right foot. Mix together ½ cup gypsum, ½ cup Epsom salts, 1 tablespoon soil sulfur, and 1 tablespoon chelated iron. Spread around base of the plant. Repeat for each rose. Water in well.

✔THIN FRUIT TREES. Begin thinning apples, pears, and stone fruit when they are about ½ inch in size. Space fruit 4 to 6 inches apart or leave one fruit per spur.

PEST CONTROL

✔CONTROL APHIDS. These sucking insects are attracted to tender new growth. Dislodge them with a strong blast of water from a hose. Or don disposable plastic gloves, and strip aphids off stems with your fingers.

✔MONITOR GIANT WHITEFLY. Look for white spirals on the undersides of target plants (avocado, banana, hibiscus, plumeria, xylosma, and many others)—whitefly eggs are often deposited here. Pick, bag, and dispose of leaves, or wash off the spirals with a strong stream of water. ◆

Mountain Checklist

PLANTING

✔ BARE-ROOT ROSES. Remove packaging material and soak the rose in a bucket of water for as long as 24 hours. Dig a hole 2 feet deep and 2 feet wide. Plant the roots so the bud union or graft is 2 inches below the ground level. Mix a shovelful of compost into the backfill, refill the hole, then water. Mound soil over the canes to protect them from freezing. Gradually remove the soil so the canes are completely uncovered by the last frost date in your area.

✔ EARLY SPRING COLOR. Brighten up the garden by setting out frost-hardy English primroses and pansies in beds or frost-proof containers. Before planting, harden off these greenhouse-grown flowers by placing them outdoors in a shady area for a few hours a day, gradually increasing their exposure to sunlight over a week; bring them indoors at night. After planting, cover the flowers with an old sheet or frost blanket (available at garden centers) if freezing temperatures threaten.

✔ SOW COOL-SEASON VEGETABLES. If you didn't prepare your vegetable beds in fall, dig in several inches of well-rotted manure or compost now. Sow seeds of beets, carrots, chard, endive, kohlrabi, lettuce, onions, parsnips, peas, radishes, spinach, Swiss chard, and turnips as soon as the soil is free of frost.

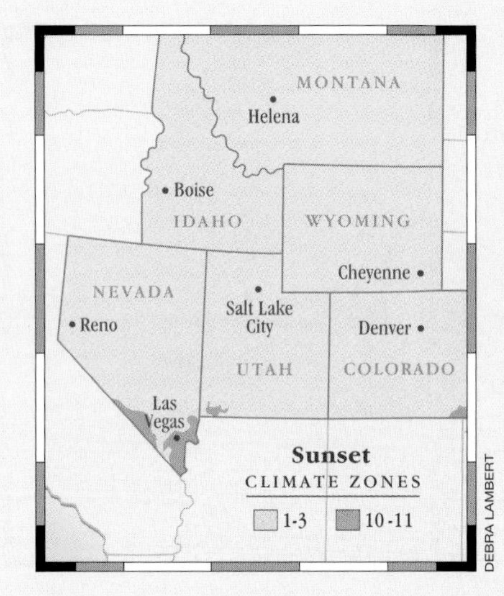

DEBRA LAMBERT

✔ SOW HARDY ANNUALS. Scatter seeds directly into the garden where you want them to grow. Among the flowers that germinate best in cold, moist soil are annual phlox (*P. drummondii*), bachelor's buttons, calendulas, California desert bluebells (*Phacelia campanularia*), California poppies, clarkias, Johnny-jump-ups, larkspurs, love-in-a-mist (*Nigella damascena*), moss roses, Shirley poppies, snapdragons, sweet alyssums, and wallflowers.

MAINTENANCE

✔ CARE FOR LAWNS. If your lawn is covered with gray snow mold, rake it off. Dehydrated turf grass attracts damaging winter mites; to control them, keep the grass well watered, especially on south-facing slopes and along sidewalks and foundations.

✔ FEED BULBS. When early-flowering bulbs like crocuses and species tulips finish blooming, drench the leaves with a foliar fertilizer or manure tea. The nutrients absorbed through the leaves will make their way to the bulbs and nurture next year's flowers.

✔ GROOM GRASSES, SHRUBS. Trim ornamental grasses close to the ground before new growth starts. It helps to wrap an elastic cord around the whole bunch and use a saw to cut the old stems below the cord. To keep shrubs compact, cut all stems of beautyberry, bluebeard, butterfly bush, dyer's greenweed (*Genista tinctoria*), rubber rabbitbrush, and snakeweed (*Gutierrezia sarothrae*) to within a few inches of the ground before they leaf out.

✔ TRANSPLANT SHRUBS. Move shrubs while they are dormant to reduce risk of transplant shock. Water thoroughly to keep the rootball moist until new growth appears. — *M.T.* ◆

WHAT TO DO IN YOUR GARDEN IN MARCH

Southwest Checklist

PLANTING

✔ ANNUALS. Zones 12–13: Set out warm-season flowers such as celosia, cosmos, gaillardia, globe amaranth (*Gomphrena*), lisianthus, Madagascar periwinkle, marigold, and portulaca.

✔ CITRUS TREES. Zone 12 (Tucson): Plant mandarins such as 'Fairchild', 'Fortune', and 'Fremont'. Zone 13 (Phoenix): Try grapefruits, lemons, pummelo hybrids 'Melogold' and 'Oroblanco', and sweet oranges such as 'Marrs', 'Trovita', and 'Valencia'.

✔ GROUND COVERS. Zones 12–13: Set out Mexican evening primrose, trailing indigo bush (*Dalea greggii*), verbena, and *Vinca major.*

✔ PERENNIALS. Zones 10–11: Plant asters, chrysanthemums, coreopsis, feverfews, hollyhocks, Maximilian sunflowers (*Helianthus maximilianii*), Shasta daisies, and statice. Zones 12–13: Plant blackfoot daisy (*Melampodium leucanthum*), lantana, penstemon, *Zauschneria,* and summer-flowering shrubs like yellow bells (*Tecoma stans*).

✔ SUMMER BULBS. Zones 10–13: Shop for caladium, canna, and crinum but wait until soil warms to 65° before planting. Set out dahlia tubers and gladiolus corms after danger of frost is past.

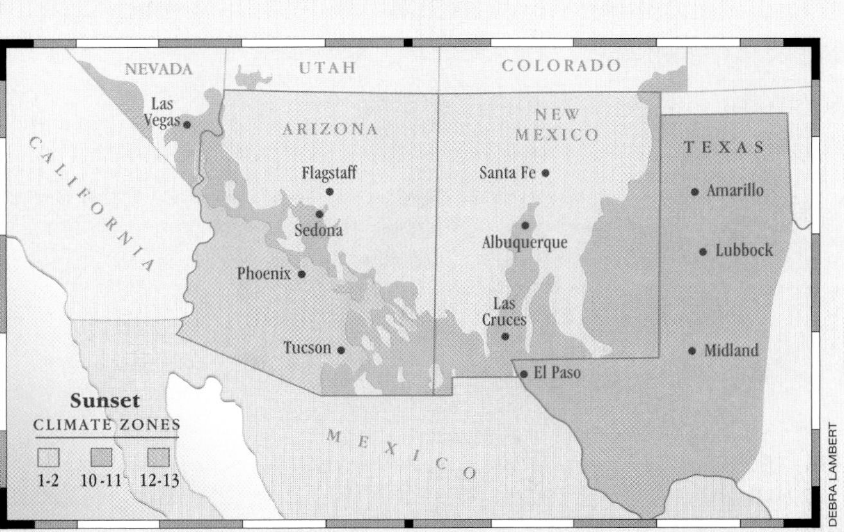

✔ VEGETABLES. Zones 1–2: Sow seeds of cool-season crops like broccoli, cabbage, carrots, cauliflower, lettuce, potatoes, radishes, and spinach right away; start tomatoes indoors from seed by midmonth. Zones 10–11: Set out seedlings of peppers and tomatoes now, but be ready to cover plants if frost threatens. Zones 12–13: Sow asparagus beans, black-eyed peas, bush beans and limas, corn, cucumbers, melons, and summer squash.

MAINTENANCE

✔ CARE FOR HERBS. Zones 10–13: Cut back ratty-looking perennial herbs like mint and sage, then fertilize and water. Mint often dies back from the center; to reinvigorate it, stab a sharp spade down through the roots several times in a crosshatch pattern.

✔ DIVIDE PERENNIALS. Zones 10–13: Dig and divide clumping perennials like chrysanthemum and daylily.

✔ MAINTAIN DRIP SYSTEMS. Clean out sediment and algae, replace clogged emitters you can't clear, and clean filters.

✔ WATERING. Zones 10–13: As days lengthen and get warmer, adjust watering schedules. Irrigate high-water-use plants once a week, less thirsty ones twice a month. — *Mary Irish* ◆

CANDY-COLORED BLOOMS include dahlias ranging from burgundy and rose to pink; pink Oriental lilies; and Asiatic lilies in yellow and apricot. DESIGN: Ann Leyhe.

GARDEN BED shows off gladiolus, pink cactus dahlias, and lilies. BELOW: Tuberose is cool complement to banksia.

Bulbs for bouquets

BY SHARON COHOON
PHOTOGRAPHS BY NORMAN A. PLATE

Grow voluptuous favorites in your summer garden

■ It's summer bulb time, and the lilies are easy. Dahlias, gladiolus, crocosmias, and tuberoses are a breeze too—they're as effortless as their spring-blooming cousins. Just bury, water, and watch them grow. Their bold rather than blushing style is dazzling under the bright summer sun.

Since the majority of them come from warm climates, summer bulbs are tender. But frost is about the only thing they can't handle. Sizzling heat rarely fazes them.

There's something else special about these bulbs: They look as good in vases as they do in the garden. Most sport large, bright, sturdy flowers on long, strong stems. Some are intensely fragrant. And many will last a week or longer once cut. So don't deprive yourself—plant the bulbs listed here now for bouquet flowers all summer.

■ Acidanthera bicolor (***Gladiolus callianthus***). Pure

white, 3-inch, star-shaped flowers with mahogany-blushed throats have a delightfully clean, sweet fragrance. Four to six blossoms bloom in succession on each 2- to 3-foot stem over a monthlong period. In cool climates, lift and store the corms over winter.

■ Calla (***Zantedeschia***). Colored callas grow 1½ to 2 feet tall, and they come in exotic colors, as their names—'Mango', 'Garnet Glow', 'Flame'—suggest. The big, white trumpet-shaped flowers of common callas look wonderful when displayed solo in vases. White callas (*Z. aethiopica*) are nearly evergreen in

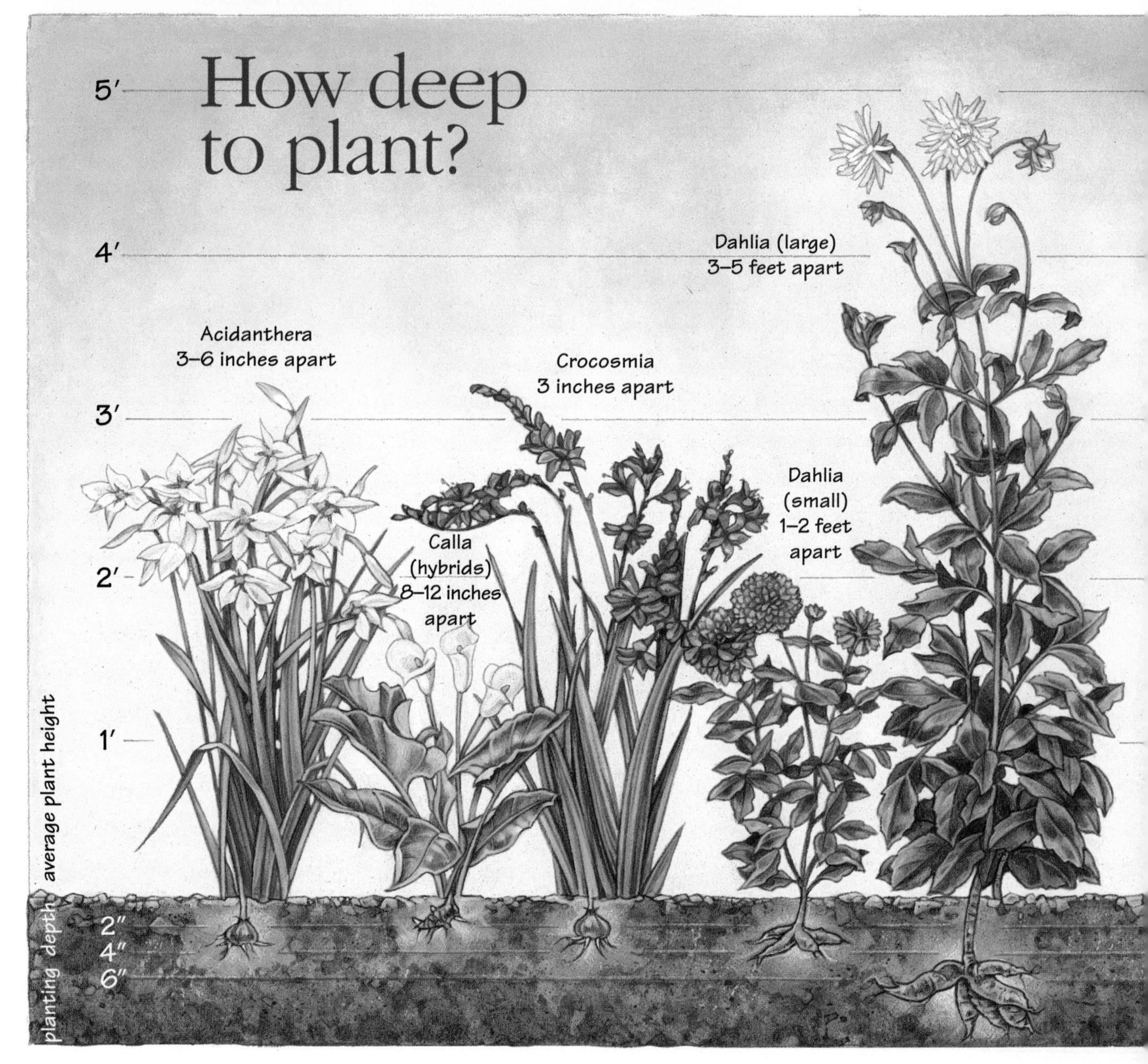

mild climates but deciduous in cold climates; they grow in *Sunset* zones 5–6, 8–9, 14–24.

■ Crocosmia **(Montbretia).** Traditional hybrid favorites like 'Lucifer' are big, bold plants—their sword-shaped leaves make upright fans to 4 feet tall with zigzagging flower spikes. Newer hybrids tend to be smaller—2-foot 'Emily MacKenzie', for instance. All flowers are fiery-hued—reds, oranges, yellows—and make long-lasting cutting flowers. Plants can naturalize in zones 5–24. Where winter temperatures dip below 10°, give them protective mulch.

Crocosmia

■ Dahlia. Tuberous-rooted plants come in an amazing variety of heights (from 1 foot to taller than 7 feet), flower sizes (from 2 to 12 inches in diameter), and shapes (from tight pompoms to loose cactus types), and every hue but blue. All but the shortest make good cutting flowers; small to medium-size flowers are the most versatile. Dahlias appreciate light afternoon shade in hot summer areas. They can be left in the ground if winter temperatures remain above 20°, but most gardeners lift them each year and replant after the danger of frost is past.

■ Gladiolus. These are mainstays of the

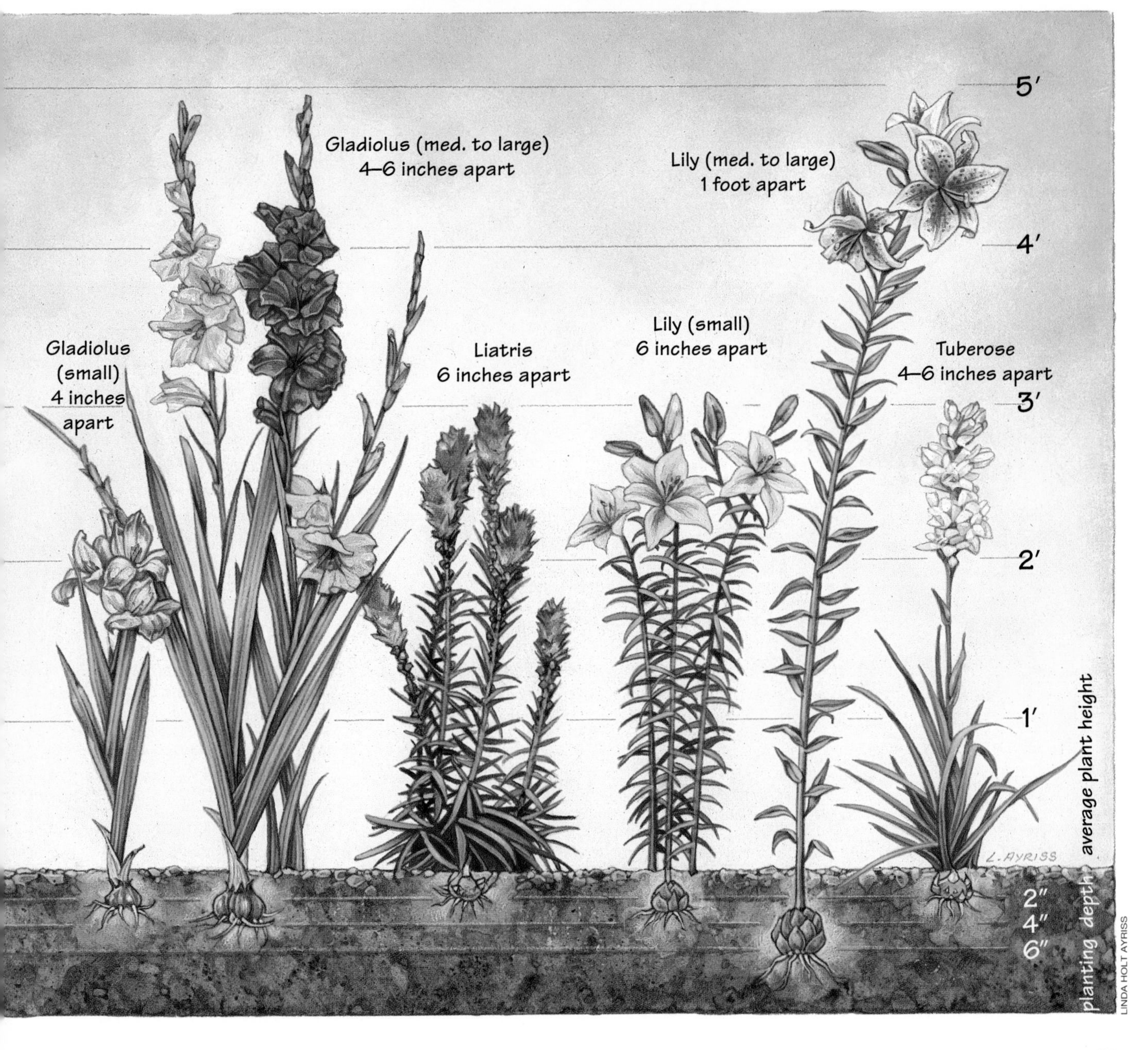

LINDA HOLT AYRISS

Dahlia

Gladiolus

RICHARD SHIELL

floral industry for good reason—all varieties create dramatic vertical accents in bouquets. Grandiflora hybrids, also called garden glads, are the largest; individual flowers grow as wide as 8 inches with stems 4 to 5 feet tall. Butterfly glads are shorter (2 to 3 feet) and usually have contrasting blotches of color across the throats (hence the name). Baby glads are shorter still (1½ feet); in zones 4–9 and 12–24, these can be left in the ground for the winter. Most other glads need to be lifted and stored at the end of the growing season. (If your soil is sandy, set tall gladiolus several inches deeper than shown on chart on pages 70–71.)

■ Liatris **(Gayfeather).** This tough, tuberous-rooted perennial, often sold as a bulb, endures cold, heat, drought,

How to plant and care for summer bulbs

PLANTING. Plant in groups of three or more for a clump effect. The rule of thumb for all bulbs is to plant at a depth three times the widest diameter of the bulb. Some summer bulbs, however, should be planted deeper (see chart on pages 70–71). For dahlias, for instance, dig a hole 1 foot deep and several feet wide for each tuberous root. Add several inches of loose soil to each hole, then plant tuber. Cover tuber with 3 inches of soil; water. As shoots emerge and grow, gradually fill hole with soil. Plant all bulbs pointed side up, root side down; when in doubt, plant sideways.

FERTILIZING. Bulbs contain most of their own food supply, but for best performance: 1) Add a high-phosphorus bulb food to the bottom of the hole when planting, to encourage root production. 2) Feed with an all-purpose fertilizer when the plants start to grow. 3) Feed again after flowering to help bulbs store up energy, if you are going to replant them next year.

STORING. After leaves have died back, bulbs can be prepared for winter storage, if necessary. (In frost-free areas, these bulbs can overwinter in the ground.) Dig up, or knock them out of their containers. Remove dried leaves and soil. Spread the bulbs on newspaper and let them dry in a shady spot for a few days. Bulbs that have their own protective tunics, such as glads and crocosmias, can be stored in baskets, boxes, or mesh bags. Store the rest between layers of vermiculite, sand, or peat moss. Store all summer bulbs where they will be protected from cold, heat, and moisture.

and poor soil. Foxtail-like spikes of rosy purple or pure white flowers emerge from grassy clumps of foliage. At 2 to 4 feet tall, they make good fillers for bouquets. They'll attract butterflies to the garden. Zones 1–10, 14–24.

■ **Lily.** There are many species and eight divisions of hybrids, but let's make it simple: Asiatic hybrids are the earliest to bloom. Oriental hybrids come later. Both types happen to be terrific cutting flowers. Lilies have large, trumpet-shaped blooms on strong, tall (up to 5-foot) stems. They grow in a wide variety of colors, often with contrasting throats, speckles, or "brushstrokes." They need ample moisture and prefer filtered sun or afternoon shade in most regions; the root zones like to stay cool. Hardy to -30°.

■ **Tuberose (*Polianthes tuberosa*).** Intensely fragrant, waxy white blossoms emerge on stems as tall as 3 feet above grassy basal foliage and tuberous roots. Both single- and double-flowered forms are very long-lasting. Tuberoses need a long (four-month or longer) warm period before flowering; if you have a short summer season, start them indoors in pots. The scent alone makes tuberoses worth the extra effort. Zones 15–17, 22–24 (in zones 8–9 and 14, plant in pots and move to a protected place for winter).

Liatris

Lily (Oriental)

Tuberose

Bulbs for bouquets

true bulb

corm

rhizome

tuberous root

Bulb basics

Though gardeners generally refer to them all as bulbs, of the flowers listed, only lilies qualify as true bulbs. Glads and crocosmia come from corms (swollen underground stems, each with a growth point on the top); dahlias grow from tuberous roots (small potato-like roots); and callas and tuberoses come from rhizomes (thickened stems that grow horizontally on or beneath the soil surface). Despite their differing underground structures, corms, tuberous roots, and rhizomes are all referred to as bulbs. They come with their own cafeterias attached—subterranean storage organs that hold reserves of food to keep the plants alive from one growing season to the next. It's this built-in food supply that makes these types of plants more forgiving of casual care and attention.

Sources

Most nursery centers carry the bulbs listed here. But if you are looking for additional sources, try the following mail-order catalogs. Buy early for the best selection.

Brent & Becky's Bulbs, 7463 Heath Trail, Gloucester, VA 23061; (877) 661-2852 or www.brentandbeckysbulbs.com.

McClure & Zimmerman, Box 368, Friesland, WI 53935; (800) 883-6998 or www.mzbulb.com.

Swan Island Dahlias, Box 700, Canby, OR 97013 (catalog $3); (800) 410-6540 or www.dahlias.com. ◆

Fabulous ferns

These Northwest favorites actually can grow just about anywhere

BY STEVEN R. LORTON

ALLAN MANDELL

WESTERN MAIDENHAIR FERN'S delicate fronds spill from spaces between wet, mossy rocks, mimicking a mountain waterfall.

The Pacific Northwest *is* fern country. Thanks to a cool, moist climate, magnificent stands of sword fern (*Polystichum munitum*) grow in great sweeps on forest floors and form delicate tufts of green lace on rocky cliffs. In cities, wind-driven fern spores land and take root on bits of debris caught along downspouts, making feathery little clumps that march up the sides of old brick buildings. Ferns fill gardens and bouquets. Their decorative leaves are sometimes pressed into concrete steppingstones, and, sometimes, into our memories.

Once, when my son was a toddler, we walked through an alder forest on the Olympic Peninsula. A thick carpet of sword ferns covered the ground. As the fronds bobbed gently in the wind, my son stretched out his arm, pointed to them, and shouted, "Butterflies!" The little guy was in good company. Renowned Northwest garden writer George Schenk once called ferns "the wings of the garden."

The fern family is as diverse as the plants are lush and beautiful. Many of them grow well throughout the West (except in the low desert) if you give them shady locations; rich, loose, acid soil; and plenty of water.

In the coldest regions of the West (*Sunset* climate zones 1–3), many ferns can survive if they're planted close to a house foundation, with some winter protection such as a thick mulch of leaves or straw over the crown. In hot, dry climates, ferns grow best in pots placed in shaded courtyards or patios. In coastal Southern California, tropical and subtropical ferns can easily duplicate the effects of a Northwest forest planting.

How can you use ferns in the landscape? Northwest gardens and woods offer great design lessons. Ferns are especially handsome as accents among swaths of lower-growing plants such as sweet woodruff or oxalis (*O. hirta* or *O. oregana*) or growing beside ponds. Mossy rocks, especially when wet, make beautiful foils for ferns. Mixtures of green can be as vivid in their own right as any bed of gladiolus or zinnias.

Where to buy ferns

These six Northwest nurseries sell a wide selection of ferns by mail.

Collector's Nursery, 16804 N.E. 102nd Ave., Battle Ground, WA 98604; (360) 574-3832. Catalog $2. Open by appointment only.

Fancy Fronds Nursery, Box 1090, Gold Bar, WA 98251; (360) 793-1472. Catalog $2. Open by appointment only.

Foliage Gardens, 2003 128th Ave. S.E., Bellevue, WA 98005; (425) 747-2998. Catalog $2. Open by appointment only.

Robyn's Nest Nursery, 7802 N.E. 63rd St., Vancouver, WA 98662; (360) 256-7399. Catalog $2.

Russell Graham, 4030 Eagle Crest Rd. N.W., Salem, OR 97304; (503) 362-1135. Catalog $2.

Siskiyou Rare Plant Nursery, 2825 Cummings Rd., Medford, OR 97501. Catalog $3.

Best bets: 10 ferns we can't resist

■ ***Adiantum aleuticum*** (five-finger fern, Western maidenhair fern). Zones 1–9, 14–21. Deciduous. Thin, papery, green fronds have large leaflets in a fan shape atop glistening black stems. Will take some early-morning or late-afternoon sun. To 2 feet tall.

■ ***Athyrium filix-femina*** (lady fern). Zones 1–9, 14–21. Deciduous. Feathery, lance-shaped fronds are soft yellow-green. Easy to grow. Prefers moist shade. To 3–5 feet tall.

■ ***Athyrium nipponicum* 'Pictum'** (Japanese painted fern). Zones 4–9, 14–24. Deciduous. Plant arches over, giving it a sprawling look. Glowing burgundy stems have fronds that are silvery at the center, gray-green around the edges. Needs moist soil, even in winter when dormant. To 1–2 feet tall.

■ ***Blechnum spicant*** (deer fern). Zones 1–9, 14–17. Evergreen sterile fronds are narrow, dark green, and leathery, with closely set leaflets. Deciduous fertile fronds are stiff and upright, with widely spaced leaflets. To 1–2 feet tall.

■ ***Dryopteris erythrosora*** (autumn fern). Zones 4–9, 14–24. Evergreen. Firm fronds open from coppery pink fiddleheads—golden green in youth, developing to rich, dark, glossy green. Prefers some high, filtered light or early-morning or late-afternoon sun to get intense coloration. To 2–3 feet tall.

■ ***Dryopteris* 'Robust'.** Zones 1–9, 14–24. Semi-evergreen; hangs onto its fronds well into winter in mild climates. Bold foliage is deeply divided and ruffly-looking. Fronds unfold apple green, getting darker with age in shade, yellowish green in sun. With good water this plant will take full sun. Stands up to a wide variety of soils. Fast-growing and easy. To 3–5 feet tall.

■ ***Osmunda regalis* 'Purpurascens'** (European royal fern). All zones. Deciduous. New growth emerges deep purple-red. Stems maintain red color, but fronds age to pea green. Leaflets are reminiscent of locust leaves. This tough plant withstands full sun and wind in soggy conditions. To 6 feet or taller.

■ ***Polystichum munitum*** (sword fern). Zones 4–9, 14–24. Evergreen. Tall, stiff, slightly arching, spear-shaped fronds are dark green in shade, lighter green in sun. Happiest in moist soil with some shade but will tolerate dry conditions and full sun. A Northwest signature plant, it is the most common fern in the region. To 3–4 feet tall.

■ ***Polystichum polyblepharum*** (tassel fern). Zones 4–9, 14–24. Evergreen. Dense and lacy dark green fronds have a varnished look. Likes evenly moist soil. Will not take full sun. To 2 feet tall.

■ ***Polystichum setiferum*** (soft-shield fern). Zones 4–9, 14–24. Evergreen. Slightly arching fronds have a soft, plumelike texture. The many cultivated varieties, each with its own characteristics, include dwarf *P.s.* 'Congestum cristatum' and lacy *P.s.* 'Divisilobum'—also called Alaska fern (a misnomer, since it is not native to Alaska). Soft-shield ferns are almost as sun- and drought-tolerant as sword ferns, but for best results, plant them where they won't get midday sun and give them even moisture. To 2 feet tall. ◆

TASSEL FERN has lacy, shiny foliage on coarse, dense fronds.

MICHAEL S. THOMPSON (2)

FIVE-FINGER FERN spreads its pea green fronds like fingers on a hand.

PAM SPALDING/POSITIVE IMAGES

WESTERN MAIDENHAIR FERN spreads like a parasol above white foamflowers.

DEREK FELL

JAPANESE PAINTED FERN'S silvery fronds fan out over sweet woodruff.

Grow a floral fantasy

Designers at Sherman Gardens share their planting secrets for a spectacular color show

BY SHARON COHOON • PHOTOGRAPHS BY STEVEN GUNTHER

■ AS PUBLIC GARDENS GO, SHERMAN LIBRARY & GARDENS IN CORONA DEL MAR, CALIFORNIA, IS small—just 2.2 acres. Lack of space, however, has forced it to be sharply focused; for highest impact, gardeners here devote most of their energy and acreage to a glorious celebration of seasonal flowers.

Massed bedding plants have always been this garden's specialty: Martha Washington geraniums in spring, marigolds in summer, chrysanthemums in fall, primroses in winter. Unfailingly gorgeous, but perhaps a tad too predictable?

That was Janelle Wiley's gentle suggestion upon joining the Sherman Gardens team as color specialist. Coming from a floral design background, Wiley longed to see more variation in stem height and a broader spectrum of flower colors. She wanted the beds—especially the spring ones—to have the giddy exuberance of bouquets. When Sherman Gardens removed a row of overgrown shrubs and offered Wiley the newly cleared bed to plant, she got a chance to demonstrate what she had in mind.

The lavender trumpets of *Clytostoma callistegioides,* a spring-blooming perennial vine growing on the fence behind the bed, inspired her color scheme. She repeated the pale red-violet hue and bell shape of the vine's flowers by planting the tall, stately spired Foxy strain of foxglove (*Digitalis purpurea*) in front. Then she mixed in foxgloves with flowers in closely related colors—pink, lilac, and lavender. Sticking to hues immediately next to each other on the color wheel, as Wiley did here, is a foolproof way to ensure a harmonious blend of blooms in a garden planting.

For sparkle, Wiley added a few spires of white foxglove, plus a ruffle of daisies (*Chrysanthemum paludosum*). "I rarely plant without including some white," she says. "It makes every color scheme look fresher."

In the central flower bed, Wiley continued the color scheme with two shades of Martha Washington geraniums. She edged this border with blue-violet petunias; adding another, but still related, color to the garden provided drama and kept the display from looking monochromatic. "That mysterious deep purple is a great final note, isn't it?" Wiley asks.

You can copy the scheme in a garden of any size; plants are available at nurseries around the West this month. See "Lessons in Color" on page 78.

Geraniums (pink and magenta) in front bed are edged with deep purple petunias. Lavender trumpet vine (on fence), foxgloves, and white *Chrysanthemum paludosum* in the back bed repeat this color scheme. Coral tree (*Erythrina*) adds a dash of red-orange.

Lessons in color

1

START WITH A FLOWERING BACKDROP. To re-create the color saturation of the scene at right, you need a cascade of blooms in the background. Evergreen foliage just won't provide the same level of energy. You may already have an existing climber to use as background—wisteria, downy clematis, a pink climbing rose like 'Cécile Brunner', or a pink trumpet vine (*Pandorea ricasoliana*), for example. Or you could plant a fast-growing annual vine such as a cup-and-saucer vine (*Cobaea scandens*) to get a similar effect this year. Whatever vine you choose, plan your color scheme around it.

2

CHOOSE FLOWERS IN SHADES OF A SINGLE COLOR, plus closely related hues, instead of a two-color scheme such as red with white or blue with yellow. If you don't like pinks, opt for yellows—lemon yellow, pineapple yellow, and golden yellow, for instance, with a dash of peach or lime for contrast and a ruffle of white for sparkle. Or try a blue palette—from cobalt to sky blue. Play off the blues of delphiniums with a dash of purple for definition.

Sherman Library & Gardens, 2647 E. Pacific Coast Hwy., Corona del Mar, CA; (949) 673-2261. Open 10:30–4 daily.

3

REPEAT COLORS IN ADJACENT BEDS. The foxglove border and the geranium bed in the photo above would each be pretty if used individually. But you need both beds, reflecting each other's colors, to create the illusion of a sea of flowers. You don't need a big space for two beds: A circle of potted pink geraniums and a second row of dark petunias or pansies around a courtyard fountain could create the same effect near a small garden bed.

4

ADD A VERTICAL ELEMENT. Few flowers create as striking a vertical display as foxgloves. Despite its flashy appearance, *Digitalis purpurea* is surprisingly easy to grow. Provide a stake for support at the time of transplanting, bait for snails and slugs, and water frequently, especially once flower spikes show. For maximum performance, amend soil before transplanting and fertilize regularly. (Wiley feeds foxgloves with a 10-10-5 formula every other week during their growing season.)

For the best chance of a big show this year, buy the largest foxgloves you can find now. If you like instant gratification and want maximum height this year, substitute Pacific Giant delphiniums for the foxgloves. They are available in the same range of colors. ◆

The cutting edge

Japanese steel blades make pruning easier

BY LAUREN BONAR SWEZEY

For many professional arborists, the current tools of choice are Japanese saws and shears made of high-carbon steel. Why? "It's their superior cutting blades," explains arborist Kevin Raftery of Palo Alto. The blades are thin and razor-sharp, which makes for easier pruning and more precise cuts.

What makes this metal so different? Japanese manufacturers press the steel. This process retains the steel's carbon content, so blades can be made much thinner and sharper than those of conventional drop-forge steel, explains Tish Nakayama of Shark Corporation in Wilmington, California.

Today, home gardeners, too, are discovering the value of Japanese pruning tools, and more firms are importing them.

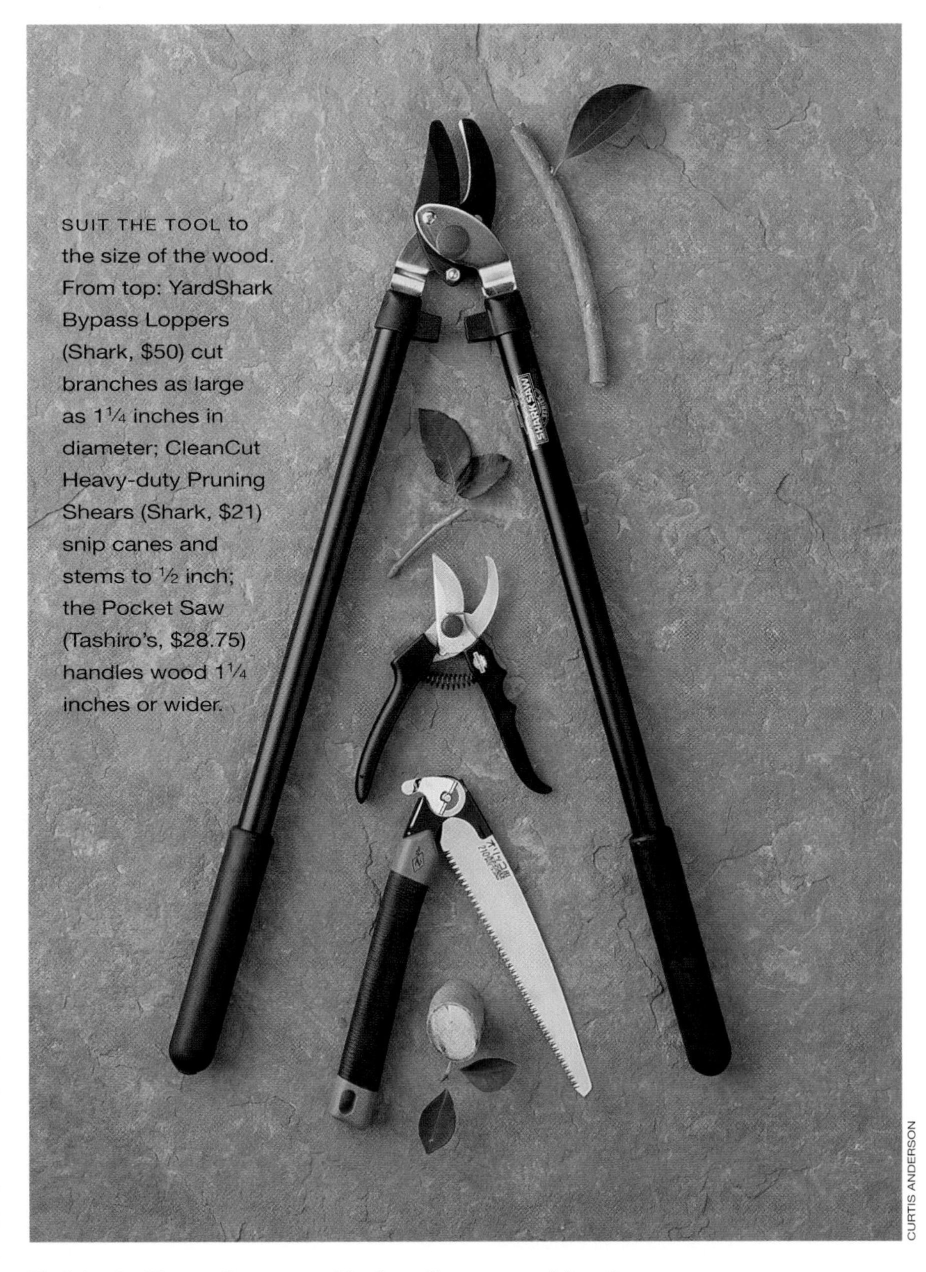

SUIT THE TOOL to the size of the wood. From top: YardShark Bypass Loppers (Shark, $50) cut branches as large as 1¼ inches in diameter; CleanCut Heavy-duty Pruning Shears (Shark, $21) snip canes and stems to ½ inch; the Pocket Saw (Tashiro's, $28.75) handles wood 1¼ inches or wider.

CURTIS ANDERSON

TOOLS AND SOURCES

Barnel Tiger Tooth folding saws, featuring an ergonomic design and nonslip grips, come in a range of blade sizes, from 6 inches ($20 to $25) to 14 inches ($25 to $30). The saws are available at some nurseries and hardware stores, or you can order the 9½-inch model by mail from the Urban Farmer (800/753-3747). For other suppliers, call (800) 877-9907.

Shark Corporation sells pruning shears, trimming shears, and loppers, as well as a folding saw and a pole pruning saw with both upper and lower teeth so you can undercut branches to avoid splitting the bark. Prices range from $21 (shears) to $50 (loppers). These tools are available at garden and some home supply centers. If you can't find them, call (800) 891-7855 for a supplier near you.

Tashiro's Sharp Japanese Tools sells the Pocket Saw ($28.75 plus shipping), a folding pruning saw with a nonslip grip and interchangeable blades that can be locked into position every 10° along a 270° arc. To order, call (206) 328-7641.

SPECIAL CARE

While Japanese steel is heat-treated and very strong, it's also brittle: never twist these blades when cutting or they might break. After each use, wipe the blades clean and rub them with vegetable oil to prevent rust.

Japanese saws cut on the back (pull) stroke; don't attempt to cut as you push. Because the blades are ground on three edges instead of the typical two, they can't be sharpened, but even a heavily used blade will last as long as five years. When one does wear out, pop it out and insert a replacement blade ($12 to $20). Shears and loppers must be sharpened with a 300- to 400-grit diamond file.

If shears get stuck during pruning, rotate them up and down. ◆

GOLDEN SAGE laps at the edge of the box at rear, while green- and purple-leafed basils and rosemary reach for the sun.

SAXON HOLT

Raised-box herb garden

Easy-to-build wood planters provide perfect conditions for growing herbs in tight spaces

BY KATHLEEN N. BRENZEL

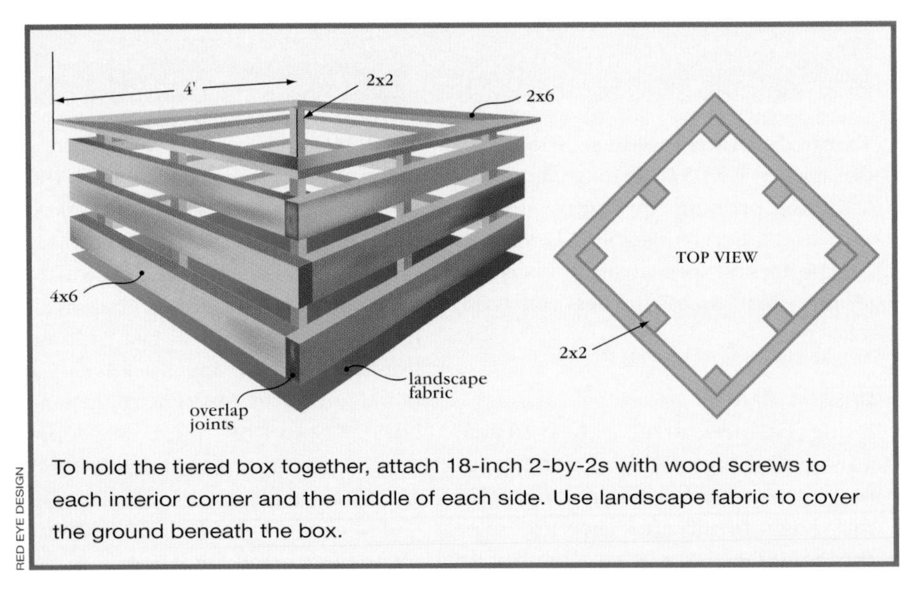

To hold the tiered box together, attach 18-inch 2-by-2s with wood screws to each interior corner and the middle of each side. Use landscape fabric to cover the ground beneath the box.

RED EYE DESIGN

A sliver of ground with heavy clay soil was the only site left for an herb garden on a hilltop lot in Cupertino, California. Yet landscape architect Jim Ripley found a way to shoehorn the garden into the space and overcome the poor soil at the same time. He designed five raised planter boxes and arranged them corner-to-corner in an inverted V formation. Filled with rich soil mix, the boxes provide the perfect drainage that herbs need.

The garden's sunny exposure and its proximity to an outdoor kitchen make it an ideal spot for growing culinary herbs, as well as compact summer vegetables and flowers for cutting.

The 4-foot-square boxes, made of redwood 4-by-6s capped with 2-by-6s, stand 20 inches tall, making it easy to harvest crops from them without stooping. Follow the construction details at left to build your boxes, then fill them with herbs drawn from the selection described on the facing page.

A cook's garden of culinary herbs

Basil. Bushy annuals, 1 to 2 feet tall, come in a variety of flavors. In addition to sweet Italian types, try spicy cinnamon basil, zesty lemon basil (*Ocimum basilicum citrodorum*), or pungent purple-leafed kinds like 'Dark Opal' and 'Purple Ruffles'. 'African Blue' basil (pictured at right) is a tender perennial. Use fresh leaves in pastas, pesto, salads, and soups.

Chives. Clumping perennial, 1 to 2 feet tall, with grasslike leaves bears edible rose-purple flowers in early summer. Grow onion-flavored chives (*Allium schoenoprasum*) or garlic chives (*A. tuberosum*). Use the leaves in salads and sauces, the flowers as garnishes or salad toppings.

French tarragon (*Artemisia dracunculus*). Upright perennial, 1 to 2 feet tall, has narrow green leaves with spicy anise flavor. Give plants sun and excellent drainage; too much fertilizer produces tender growth with little flavor. To harvest, snip out tips. Use in egg, chicken, and fish dishes, or in béarnaise sauce.

Lavender. Perennial English lavender (*Lavandula angustifolia*) forms mounds of gray-green foliage topped by flower spikes. Compact varieties such as *L.a.* 'Munstead' (1½ feet tall) and *L.a.* 'Hidcote' (1½ to 2 feet) fit best in raised beds. Toss the fragrant leaves on the grill to flavor meats, or steep the flowers for lemonade.

Mint. These hardy perennials, 1½ to 3 feet tall, have invasive roots that can choke out less vigorous herbs, so give them their own box. Set plants 12 to 18 inches apart. In addition to familiar spearmint (*Mentha spicata*) and peppermint (*M. piperita*), try apple mint (*M. suaveolens*), pineapple mint (*M.s.* 'Variegata'), and chocolate mint. Use spearmint for cooking, others to flavor tea.

Nasturtium. Annual flowers in vivid shades of yellow or red. Dwarf kinds (to 15 inches tall) work best in raised beds. Edible blossoms and leaves add a peppery, cresslike flavor to salads.

Planting and growing tips

- Don't waste space on herbs you won't use. Put in three or four plants each of tender-leafed herbs such as basil or parsley that you use frequently. For larger woody plants like rosemary, a single plant can supply enough sprigs for years.
- For added visual appeal, combine plants by color: purple-leafed basil with 'Tricolor' sage, for example.
- With basil, French tarragon, and parsley, remove flower heads regularly so the leaves retain their best flavor. Remove flower buds from chives to encourage new leaves; use the edible blooms in salads.
- If chives, mint, or sage grow leggy, cut back to promote new growth. Replace basil and parsley every year. ◆

Oregano. Bushy perennial grows 1 to 2 feet tall. Choose pungent Greek oregano (*Origanum vulgare hirtum*) or milder Italian oregano (*O. majoricum*). Use in pastas, pizza toppings, sauces, soups, and stews.

Parsley. A biennial grown as an annual, it forms 6- to 12-inch tufts. Dark green curly-leafed types make a handsome garnish; many cooks prefer the stronger flavor and smoother texture of flat-leafed Italian parsley.

Rosemary (*Rosmarinus officinalis*). Prized for its aromatic, evergreen leaves, this Mediterranean native comes in upright and trailing forms. Chefs prefer the resinous foliage of bushy, upright varieties like 'Tuscan Blue' (6 feet or taller), which bears edible bright blue flowers in winter and early spring. Use the leaves to flavor pork, lamb, and poultry.

Sage. Bushy perennial reaches 1 to 2 feet tall. For the classic flavor associated with turkey stuffing, try garden sage (*Salvia officinalis*) or dwarf sage (*S.o. minumus*). More decorative varieties are golden 'Icterina' and variegated 'Tricolor'. Use in soups, stews, and poultry stuffings.

Sweet marjoram (*Origanum majorana*). Usually grown as a summer annual, this plant reaches 1 to 2 feet tall. Its tiny leaves are sweet with a milder flavor than Greek oregano. Use to flavor eggs, soups, herb butters, and vinegars.

Thyme. Hardy perennial English thyme (*Thymus vulgaris*) grows about 1 foot tall; its tiny, pungent leaves add mild tang to fish, pork, poultry, and vegetables. Similar-tasting silver thyme (*T.v.* 'Argenteus') is more ornamental but less hardy. For zesty citrus flavor (and pretty yellow-green foliage), try lemon thyme (*T. citriodorus*) or lime thyme.

SAXON HOLT

A BASKET of freshly cut sweet basil, parsley, sage, and nasturtium blossoms is ready for the kitchen. 'African Blue' basil blooms behind.

NORMAN A. PLATE (2)

▲
Protea power

Bizarrely beautiful **proteas** feature blooms ranging from velvety pink rosettes to neon pincushions. Dramatic in bouquets, protea blooms are long-lived—they'll hold color for two weeks in water. Commercial proteas thrive around Kula on the Hawaiian island of Maui, where conditions—well-drained soil, warm days, cool nights—are right for them. The plants are tricky to grow; if you can't give them what they need, buy blooms at florists and markets, or order from Maui. *Sunrise Protea Farm; (800) 222-2797 or www.sunriseprotea.com. Maui Floral; (800) 543-2727 or www.mauifloral.com.*

Gift of gardening

Though gardening isn't usually numbered among the privileges of the wealthy, it does take land, tools, and some education to grow plants. That's where the **Kitchen Garden Project** of Olympia, Washington, comes in. "We build 200 gardens per year for low-income families," says director Richard Doss. Three raised-bed gardens are built for each participant, complete with soil, trellis, seeds, fertilizer, and instructions.

Volunteers check on the gardens during the growing season to aid success. "One of our biggest rewards," says Doss, "is seeing our gardeners take homegrown produce back to food banks that have helped them in the past." *(360) 943-9188 or www.olywa.net/kgp.*

Most bird-friendly town

It's no surprise butterflies and songbirds head south this spring to Alpine, California, just east of San Diego.

This foothills town has been designated the **first community wildlife habitat** by the National Wildlife Federation. The reason? Maureen Austin and her organization, Chirp for Garden Wildlife, inspired more than 120 residents and businesses to transform their gardens into certified backyard wildlife habitats. *Chirp; (619) 445-7675 or www.chirp.org. National Wildlife Federation; (703) 790-4100 or www.nwf.org/habitats.*

Wake-up call for containers

No plant receives more oohs and aahs from visitors to our test garden than **variegated Jacob's ladder** (*Polemonium caeruleum* 'Brise de Anjou'). This shade-loving perennial, with its white-edged leaves, is a perfect partner for container-grown begonias: Both thrive in partial or full shade and rich, moist, well-drained soil. *Woodside Gardens; (800) 473-1152 or www.woodsidegardens.com.*

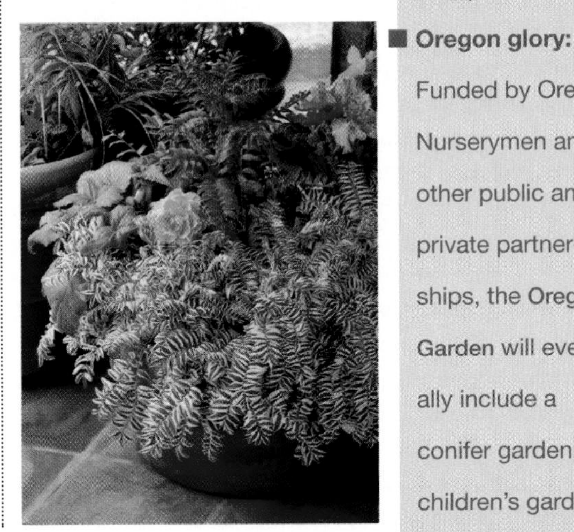

■ **Best book:** Daniel J. Hinkley has roamed the world in search of plants for his nursery, Heronswood, near Seattle. Now Hinkley narrates his peregrinations in *The Explorer's Garden: Rare and Unusual Perennials* (Timber Press, Portland, 1999; $39.95; 800/327-5680).

■ **Oregon glory:** Funded by Oregon Nurserymen and other public and private partnerships, the **Oregon Garden** will eventually include a conifer garden, a children's garden, and other plantings on 240 acres in Silverton, 10 miles east of Salem. A 60-acre Phase I opens informally in May with tours and a summer concert series. *(877) 674-2733 or www.oregongarden.org.*

JIM BROWN

No tool like an old tool

Denman & Company, the garden tool specialty store in Orange County, California, is *the* place to find eye, heart, and finger hoes; bulb, nurseryman's, and rockery trowels; post hole and trenching spades, sod lifters, trombone sprayers, and stone pickers; and 1,900 or so other tools you didn't know you needed. "After the Industrial Revolution, all kinds of specialized tools were developed," says owner Bob Denman, "but many disappeared. Our mission is to give gardeners all the tool choices Victorians had." Denman will also refurbish old tools, custom-build new ones, or modify handles or grips to suit your needs and preferences. *401 W. Chapman Ave., Orange, CA 92866; (714) 639-8106.*

Bright rockets of bloom

The new giant lupines from England are perfect for summer borders

BY JIM McCAUSLAND

COLORFUL SPIKES of New Generation lupines stand well above foliage. In gardens, these gorgeous perennials bloom better when well spaced (18 to 24 inches apart) than when crowded.

GREG LEE (2)

The classic perennial lupines, with flower spikes that tower above their foliage like colorful candles, just got better. New Generation lupines have all the merits of the older Russell hybrids, with a new vigor and a broader color range.

These new lupines—rebred, refined, and revitalized versions of the Russells—are husky plants that don't need staking. They come in a rainbow array of colors, including clear red, white, yellow, orange, pink, mauve, blue, and purple. Flower spikes reach about 4 feet tall, with foliage about half that tall. (Leaves are divided into many leaflets, like fingers of a hand).

If planted this month, these new lupines can splash your perennial border with color from June until the end of summer and, if you cut off the spent blooms, sometimes even rebloom in fall.

Both the Russells and the New Generations descended from plants native to Western America. But both were bred in England—the New Generations by Brian and Maurice Woodfield, English brothers who own a nursery in Stratford-on-Avon.

Seedlings of New Generation lupines are available at retail nurseries in the Pacific Northwest and parts of California, or you can order them by mail from Jackson & Perkins (800/292-4769).

Plant lupines 18 to 24 inches apart in full sun. Soil should drain well and doesn't have to be particularly fertile, but plants live longer if you feed them early in the season with a mild fertilizer like 5-10-10 or mulch them with composted manure. Water plants regularly.

Expect modest bloom the first summer, then heavy bloom for four or five years after that. Plants will need replacing every seven to eight years or so. Cut off spent flowers to prolong bloom, and to encourage a flush of fall color. Snip off spent flowers in fall, too, then allow plants to overwinter in the ground. In early spring, prune plants to remove any winter damage; new growth will soon overtake the old.

Flowers are excellent in big bouquets (stems are 2 feet long) and last in vases about a week if cut when most of the flowers on a spike are open.

Lupines are attractive to aphids. Control the pests by blasting them from the plants with a strong jet of water from the hose and, if necessary, following up with insecticidal soap. New Generation lupines resist powdery mildew. ◆

A quick guide to fertilizers

BY JIM McCAUSLAND

Native Americans once put a fish in a hole, covered it with earth, planted a corn seed, then harvested the crop a few months later. A biblical parable offers this advice for reviving a failing fig tree: "Dig about it and dung it." And indeed, fertilizing plants used to be as simple as applying fish and manure. Today, things aren't that simple: Take a look at the dizzying array of packaged fertilizers on nursery shelves. How do you decide which fertilizer to buy? First, read the label.

Check out the nutrients

Nitrogen (N), phosphorus (P), and potassium (K) are the primary plant nutrients. They are always listed on the labels of packaged fertilizers (look under Guaranteed Analysis) in the same order, known as the N-P-K ratio. For example, a fertilizer that's labeled 10-8-6 contains 10 percent nitrogen, 8 percent phosphorus, and 6 percent potassium. Any fertilizer that contains all three primary nutrients, such as a 10-8-6, is called a *complete* fertilizer.

Of the three primary nutrients, nitrogen is generally in shortest supply in Western soils and thus needs to be replenished most often. Fertilizers supply nitrogen in water-soluble (fast-release) or insoluble (slow-release) forms. Soluble nitrogen becomes available to plants quickly. Insoluble nitrogen must be broken down slowly by microorganisms in the soil for plants to use it. Most fertilizers contain both forms of nitrogen, although labels don't always specify the percentages.

Plants also need smaller amounts of secondary nutrients—calcium, magnesium, and sulfur—and trace amounts of micronutrients, including iron,

Charting the fertilizers

The charts below and on the facing page describe several commonly available natural and chemical fertilizers. The N-P-K ratios listed are typical, but they vary widely among manufacturers. In general, fertilizers formulated for lawns and other plants grown for their leaves have higher nitrogen levels; fertilizers that promote flowering and fruiting have higher phosphorus levels. When you shop, you'll also see specialty fertilizers formulated for citrus, lawns, roses, tomatoes, and other groups of widely grown plants. With any fertilizer, follow the directions on the package when you apply it.

NATURAL	Fertilizer type	N-P-K ratio	Benefits, uses
	Blood meal	13–0–0	Good source of nitrogen in both soluble and insoluble forms. Scratch it into the soil around plants. Store away from cats and dogs.
	Cottonseed meal	6–2–1	Acidifies soil as it fertilizes, making it useful for gardens with alkaline soil or for plants such as azaleas that like acidity.
	Fish emulsion	5–1–1	Acts fairly quickly and gently. Excellent for container plants and leafy vegetables. Fishy odor can attract cats and raccoons.
	Fish pellets	8–5–1	Blend the pellets into the soil of vegetable beds at planting time. Fishy odor can attract cats.

NORMAN A. PLATE (5)

CHEMICAL	Fertilizer type	N-P-K ratio	Benefits, uses
	Solid		
	Granules or pellets		
	•All-purpose	10–10–10	Abundant (often balanced) amounts of each major nutrient. Use to feed ground covers, perennials, trees, and shrubs.
	•Flower	6–10–4	Higher phosphorus content promotes flowering and fruiting.
	•Lawn	29–3–4	High nitrogen helps turf grass grow quickly between cuttings.
	•Vegetables	10–20–20	Boosts bloom and fruit for plants like beans, peppers, tomatoes, and squash.
	Spikes	16–8–8	Large spikes for feeding trees and shrubs last about three months. Small spikes for house plants (13-4-5) are also available.
	Liquid (water-soluble crystals)	20–20–20	Balanced formula works well for everything from vegetables to house plants.

NORMAN A. PLATE (3)

manganese, and zinc. These secondary and micronutrients are already present in most garden soils, so they're not always included in general-purpose fertilizers (check the label); they are commonly sold as separate supplements.

Natural or chemical?

You can buy fertilizers in either natural or chemical form. Plants can't distinguish nitrogen that came out of a chicken from nitrogen that came out of a chemical factory. People, however, seem to have their preferences. Some favor natural fertilizers, using them to complement organic gardening practices. Others prefer the convenience of chemical products in controlled-release form. Applied properly, both have their appropriate uses in the garden.

NATURAL FERTILIZERS are derived from dead organisms. These fertilizers include all kinds of animal manures, fish emulsion, and meals made from blood, bone, alfalfa, cottonseed, kelp, and soybeans. These products are usually more expensive, pound for pound, than chemical fertilizers.

Most natural fertilizers contain lower levels of nutrients than chemical products. Because they tend to release nutrients over a longer period of time, they're less likely to burn plants (although manures that aren't fully composted *can* burn plants). However, since they depend on soil organisms to break down the nutrients, they're not as effective in chilly weather, when such organisms are less active. On the other hand, the insoluble nitrogen they supply tends to stay put in the soil and not move into the water supply, where it could have harmful effects. Natural fertilizers also improve the texture of the soil and increase the amount of beneficial microorganisms. For best long-term results, dig them into the soil early in the season.

CHEMICAL FERTILIZERS are mass-produced by industrial means. They usually have higher levels of nutrients and a larger percentage of soluble nitrogen than natural fertilizers. The fast release of soluble nitrogen is a plus in chilly weather, when cool-season crops and spring-flowering shrubs and trees can use a boost. However, when fertilizer is applied too heavily and followed with excess irrigation or rainfall, the soluble nitrogen can run off the soil and pollute surface water as well as groundwater.

Liquid or solid?

You can buy natural and chemical fertilizers in liquid or solid form.

LIQUID FERTILIZERS, including fish emulsion and water-soluble crystals, get nutrients to the roots immediately. But, because the nutrients usually last only a couple of weeks in soil, liquid fertilizers need to be applied more often. Liquids are useful for feeding plants in containers and hanging baskets.

SOLID FERTILIZERS are usually sold as granules or pellets. They can be broadcast or spread over lawns and ground covers, or dug or raked into soil around the root zones of trees, shrubs, and perennials. To avoid burning plants, water soil thoroughly after application.

Other solids include controlled-release fertilizers. These are sold as spikes or beadlike granules that release nutrients over a period of time (usually three to nine months) with regular watering. Since they release nitrogen slowly and steadily, most of it is used by the plant and very little leaches out with irrigation water. Pound fertilizer spikes into the soil around trees and shrubs. Mix granules into the soil at planting time or scratch them into the soil. ◆

JAMES CARRIER

THESE "EGGCEPTIONAL" LITTLE VASES are just right for small spring bouquets. Easy directions appear on page 92.

April

How to make an azalea weep

Just prune it up, then let it drape

■ In spring when the azalea blooms on JoAnn Mazzoni's porch, it's the talk of her San Carlos, California, neighborhood. A cascade of magenta flowers drapes from the 8-foot-tall bush, giving it the look of a carefully groomed hothouse plant.

But this gorgeous azalea is not as labor-intensive as it looks, and its origins are humble. Mazzoni received it one Mother's Day as a demure 6-inch potted plant. As it grew, she began to train it into a tree shape. Each year after bloom, she trimmed the lower branches from the trunk but left the canopy. She transplanted the azalea into a 24-inch-wide wood pot. Since the plant received sunlight only from one side, its top growth began to weep. After six years, the azalea had developed its current shape.

Now Mazzoni trims only a little off the ends each year to maintain the plant's form. She feeds the bush once a month with an azalea food, except during bloom time, and waters it often enough to keep the soil moist, even during winter (the roof's overhang prevents rain from reaching it). A sturdy stake holds the plant upright.

— Lauren Bonar Swezey

NORMAN A. PLATE

HEAVY WITH BLOOMS, this 8-foot-tall azalea droops over its pot; a cymbidium grows at left.

Frequent flyer

■ John Schoustra, owner of Greenwood Irises + Daylilies, has been trying to find a bearded iris to match, bloom for bloom, the flower production of his best daylilies. The search may be over. 'Frequent Flyer', the tall bearded iris with the pure white flowers shown here, produces as many as 12 flowers per stalk and puts on this show at least four times a year. "It begins blooming in spring and doesn't quit until late fall," says Christine Mulligan, a Long Beach landscape designer.

Thanks to its unusually broad leaves, 'Frequent Flyer' is handsome even without flowers, says Mulligan. At the garden of Brent and Beth Harris in Rolling Hills, California, Mulligan paired 'Frequent Flyer' with creamy-plumed Oriental fountain grass. She also likes it with anything in the Mediterranean palette—especially artemisia, lavender, rosemary, or santolina.

'Frequent Flyer' is available in 1- and 2-gallon cans at many nurseries this spring. Or you can mail-order directly from Greenwood; (562) 494-8944 or www.greenwooddaylily.com.

— *Sharon Cohoon*

PURE WHITE BLOOMS of 'Frequent Flyer' iris mingle with ornamental grasses.

STEVEN GUNTHER (2)

Tool art

■ The spokelike arrangement of rakes, spades, and pickaxes attached to Julie Heinsheimer's barn in Rolling Hills, California, isn't there just to be pretty—these antique tools also recall pleasant memories. John Bauman, the owner of Palos Verdes Begonia Farm, collected the tools during antique-hunting trips in the Midwest and displayed them at the farm. When the popular nursery closed its doors a few years ago, Bauman offered his collection to Heinsheimer, and she accepted.

"I like having a little piece of local history in my garden," she says. The array of tools also reminds Heinsheimer of the hex signs that Pennsylvania Dutch farmers used to paint on their barns to promote good fortune—she likes that too.

Nails pounded into the barn siding (one at the head end of each tool and one at the handle), supplemented by wire, hold each tool in place.

Before hanging the tools, Heinsheimer arranged and rearranged them on the ground to come up with a pleasing design. — *S.C.*

NORMAN A. PLATE

YELLOW SNAPDRAGONS and blue salvias thrive in this raised bed's rich soil mix.

Homemade soil beats the odds in Las Vegas

■ If Las Vegans want to grow anything other than native plants, they have to make their own soil, says Clarita Huffman, master gardener at the University of Nevada Cooperative Extension. "Our native soil is so salty that it is actually toxic to many plants," she explains.

Since homemade soil is precious, it's best to corral it into raised beds. "They're efficient and effective," says Huffman, and her garden offers beautiful proof. Yellow snapdragons, violas, blue salvias, and chaste tree (*Vitex agnus-castus*) thrive in a raised front border (shown here), contained by interlocking concrete blocks. Beyond the border, perennials, roses, fruit trees, and vegetables all flourish in other raised beds.

For creating soil, Huffman swears by a recipe she found in *Super Nutrition Gardening,* by William S. Peavy and Warren Peary (Avery Press, New York, 1992; $14.95).

Spread a 3-inch layer of compost over the planting area. For each 100 square feet, apply 20 pounds of cottonseed meal and ½ cup of seaweed. Add soil sulfur according to manufacturer's directions. Till the amendments to a depth of 6 to 8 inches and water in thoroughly.

Allow the bed to rest for three to four weeks before planting. To refresh the soil in subsequent years, reduce the cottonseed meal by half and omit sulfur unless it's needed to adjust the pH.

— S.C.

Weaving a tapestry on a slope

■ Loose-laid stones and low-growing plants form a tapestry on a slope leading to Michael and Leslie Engl's home near Ketchum, Idaho. Instead of mortar, creeping perennials fill the cracks between the stones, knitting the composition together.

The 20° slope was excavated by hand to form inset shapes for steps and a bench facing a patio. The Engls chose Montana slate for the patio and local quartzite for the steps and the dry-stack bench.

Once the stonework was in place, the slope was planted with cold-hardy perennials and small shrubs—perfect for Ketchum's 5,750-foot elevation and short growing season—to control soil erosion and provide seasonal color. The photo at right shows the slope's fresh beauty in early summer. Bright bursts of chartreuse foliage come from *Spiraea bumalda* 'Limemound'. Along the steps are pink creeping phlox, orange geum, purple aubrieta, silvery snow-in-summer, and white candytuft (*Iberis sempervirens*). Red-flowered bitterroot (*Lewisia rediviva*) and *Sedum spurium* 'Dragon's Blood' spring from crannies between the bench stones. Creeping plants, including speedwell (*Veronica pectinata*), spring cinquefoil (*Potentilla tabernaemontanii*), woolly thyme, and common moss, form seams in the gaps between the steps and patio stones.

— Suzanne Touchette Kelso

SUZANNE KELSO BELOW: RICHARD D. RIFKIND

FRUIT TREE

'Centennial' crabapple

■ You might think of crabapples as puckery little critters good only for pickling or preserves. But not after you take a bite of 'Centennial'. Beneath its rosy apricot skin, the crisp flesh has a delicious sweet-tart taste. The 1½- to 2-inch oblong fruits can be eaten—core and all—in two or three bites. They also make good applesauce and pies.

'Centennial' is hardy in *Sunset* climate zones 1 to 3 and resists scab. The compact tree reaches about 8 feet tall. Showy white blossoms appear in spring, followed by brilliant green leaves that turn deep gold in fall. The fruits—which ripen in mid-August or September, depending on your climate—hold well on the tree and retain their crispness after they're picked.

You can set out young trees from nursery containers any time the soil is workable. If local nurseries don't carry 'Centennial', ask the staff to order from Bailey Nurseries (wholesale only; 800/829-8898) in Minnesota. Or order directly from Raintree Nursery in Morton, Washington (360/496-6400). Expect a dozen or so fruits the first year after planting. By the third year, you'll be harvesting by the bucketful. *— Dick Rifkind*

NEW FRUIT

LANCE WALHEIM

This orange is pink

■ 'Cara Cara', a new orange, is appearing in nurseries and some fruit markets these days. On the outside, it looks much like the familiar 'Washington' navel. But under its orange peel is deep salmon pink flesh that tastes sweet and fruity, with a slightly spicy finish. Fruit is medium-size and seedless.

Discovered as a limb sport (a natural mutation) on a tree in Venezuela, 'Cara Cara' grows anywhere 'Washington' navels do. Fruit develops the best flavor in warmer inland areas, but because it holds well on the tree for an extended period, it eventually sweetens up in cooler areas (except near the often foggy coast). Fruit is ready to harvest between late November and April.

Plants grafted onto standard rootstock reach 10 feet or taller with an equal spread; on dwarfing rootstock, they grow about 6 to 8 feet tall. 'Cara Cara' trees are often sold as patio trees in 5-gallon containers.

After the threat of hard frost is past, plant 'Cara Cara' trees in a sunny spot in well-drained, well-amended soil. Plants bear at a young age and should start producing fruit in two to three years.

— Lance Walheim

Eggceptional vases

■ The pretty little vases featured on page 86 are just right for small spring bouquets. Designed by Françoise Kirkman, they are simple to make: they're eggshells that have been emptied, cleaned, filled with water, and placed in egg cups. Filled with clusters of small flowers and grouped together on a dining table or sideboard, these bouquets make a festive centerpiece. Or display them individually with a name card propped against each one for seating at spring parties. *— L.B.S*

TIME: 20 to 30 minutes

COST: $2 to $30 for each egg cup (total cost dependent on quantity used)

DIRECTIONS

1. Gently knock one end of each egg on a counter so only the very top portion cracks.
2. Carefully peel off enough shell to create a hole ¾ to 1 inch wide.
3. Dump the yolks and whites into a bowl to save for your next breakfast or baking project.
4. Gently but thoroughly rinse the inside of each shell.
5. Fill eggs partway with water.
6. Poke small flowers into the "vases." Good choices are baby's breath, *Chrysanthemum paludosum,* English or fairy primroses, forget-me-nots, linarias, nemesias, pansies, succulents, sweet peas, and violas.

LAWN CARE

Tune-up for lawns

Follow these simple steps now to help your lawn look its best.

1. Mow the grass at least weekly, never cutting off more than the top third of the blades at one time. Use sharp mower blades so cuts are clean, not ragged.

2. Cut at the right height. Set your mower's cutting height to ½ inch for Bermuda, about ¾ inch for zoysia, about 1 inch for St. Augustine, and 2 to 2½ inches for tall fescue and bluegrass.

3. Let clippings stay on the lawn. Cut grass contains about 4 percent nitrogen. Cut your lawn with a mulching mower (it chops the grass blades into tinier pieces than a conventional mower) and let the clippings fall. They will dry up, decompose, and eventually recycle nitrogen into the lawn, so you spend less on fertilizer.

4. Attack weeds. If your lawn is full of crabgrass that has set seed, collect the clippings after mowing to prevent the weed from spreading. Or apply a low-toxicity, preemergence herbicide such as corn gluten (which also works on dandelions and other common weeds).

5. Water efficiently. To encourage deep rooting and avoid runoff, soak lawns deeply by repeating irrigation cycles. Water for 10 to 15 minutes, then turn off the water and repeat the cycle in an hour.

6. Feed the lawn with a high-nitrogen fertilizer, when needed (follow package directions).

— Jim McCausland

CABBAGELIKE AEONIUMS form the framework of this succulent bed brightened by sunny-hued dwarf gloriosa daisies. Bottomless pots planted with citrus provide focal points at the back of the bed.

Succulents: Bold and beautiful

■ Not having succulents in his new garden would have been unthinkable to Ernest Cohen. He grew up with them. His father, Robert, adored the strong personalities of these plants and developed a succulent fantasia. But including them was a little scary, Ernest says: "Like being Picasso's son and trying to paint."

Jeff Powers of Earthscaping in Laguna Beach created a succulent border that pleases both father and son. Powers laid out succulents in drifts: apple green aeonium rosettes, icy blue senecio fingers, and rose-tipped pads of kalanchoe. In between, he added herbaceous perennials with comparably modest water requirements: gloriosa daisies (*Rudbeckia*), coreopsis, dwarf alstroemerias, penstemons, foxgloves, *Salvia greggii,* and coneflowers. The style of Ernest's new garden is different from his father's (most of Robert's succulents are in containers), but both love its drama. "It's one of the boldest gardens I've seen," says Ernest. "But it's a soothing sort of bold."

GOOD IDEA

For accents, Powers set several potted 'Valencia' and navel orange trees behind the succulents. The bottom of each pot has been carefully sawed away, giving the citrus the best of both worlds: Thanks to its elevated position, the tree gets the good drainage that citrus requires, yet its longest roots are unrestricted. Each pot even has its own built-in drip irrigation system and an uplighting fixture.

— *S.C.*

CLAIRE CURRAN (2)

Trading lawn for flowers in Portland

■ The flowerful garden pictured here was a lawn not long ago. Covering more than an acre, the lawn was too large to strip off, so owner/landscape designer Margaret de Haas van Dorsser simply smothered it under several inches of horse manure. Over the next few months, worms tilled the manure into the soil, loosening it for planting. As de Haas van Dorsser set out shrubs and perennials, she placed the manure in the planting holes.

A Mexican orange (*Choisya ternata*) stands guard on the left side of the path. Roses grow on the opposite side; these include light pink 'Sharifa Asma' in the foreground, 'Mary Rose' in the center, and a big climber, 'Cl. Cécile Brunner', in the background.

Geranium himalayense (cranesbill) crowds the path to the left of 'Sharifa Asma', while *Euphorbia characias wulfenii* and coral bark maple (*Acer palmatum* 'Sango Kaku') line the way behind it.

To make the path, de Haas van Dorsser excavated the soil a few inches deep, added a layer of fist-size stones sifted from the vegetable garden, leveled it with sand, then surfaced it with a 2-inch layer of pea gravel. —*J.M.*

ROBUST PINK ROSES, underplanted with blue geraniums and chartreuse euphorbia, thrive in rich soil.

JANET LOUGHREY

Kiwis hardy enough for the Northwest

■ Unlike its fuzzy cousin, the fuzzless hardy kiwi (*Actinidia arguta*) is excellent in Northwest gardens. Not only does it take our winter cold in stride, but its tasty grape-size fruits can be enjoyed unpeeled, fresh off the vine or in preserves. The pest-free, deciduous vine grows well in *Sunset* climate zones 2–7 and 17.

Most hardy kiwis are not self-fruitful: To get a crop, you'll need to grow a male plant and at least one female plant in close proximity (one male will pollinate as many as three females). The most widely grown variety, 'Ananasnaya' or 'Anna' (shown at right), bears ½-ounce fruits with sweet-tart kiwi flavor. East of the Cascades, try earlier-ripening 'Geneva' or 'Jumbo', with mild-tasting 1-ounce fruits. For fruit with red skin and flesh, try 'Hardy Red' or 'Ken's Red'.

Planted in spring, most hardy kiwis will yield their first fruit in about three years. Plants grow about 16 feet in five years. If you have space for only one, grow 'Issai', a more challenging plant but a self-fruitful variety. Growing slowly to about 10 feet, it bears heavily, with the first crop coming just one year after planting.

Plant kiwis on opposite sides of an arbor and let the vines grow overhead; harvest the hanging fruits from below. Give the trunks shade to minimize cracking. Water weekly during warm weather and feed twice a year. To protect new growth from late frosts, water the vines with a sprinkler.

JANET LOUGHREY

Shop for container-grown plants at nurseries or order bare-root stock by mail from One Green World (877/353-4028) in Mollala, Oregon, or Raintree Nursery (360/496-6400) in Morton, Washington. Expect to pay $15 to $20 for each 2- to 4-foot-tall plant. —*J.M.*

CLIPPINGS

•**New iris catalog.** Maryott's Iris Gardens, a local iris supplier, recently moved from San Jose to Corralitos. Though you can no longer buy on-site, there's a showy new color catalog ($5; 831/722-1810 or www.irisgarden.com), so you can order tubers by mail or on-line.

•**Wildflower Hotline.** Scant rains this past winter mean that wildflowers will be spotty this year. For help in finding the best displays from San Diego to Ventura County, call the Theodore Payne Foundation 24-Hour Wildflower Hotline. Reports on more than 30 sites in Southern California are updated weekly through the end of May. *(818) 768-3533.*

BACK TO BASICS

NORMAN A. PLATE

Muscle up your potting mix. Whether you're starting seed, repotting house plants, or assembling big pots of flowers, it helps to use potting soil that already contains nutrients. You can buy ready-made, fortified mixes or make your own with the following controlled-release organic recipe.

Start by pouring a gallon of potting mix onto a potting bench. Add 1 tablespoon each of blood meal for nitrogen, kelp for trace elements, and greensand for potassium; then add 2 tablespoons of bone meal for phosphorus. Mix it all together and you're ready to plant. — *J.M.*

LEFT: Brilliant black-eyed Susans and lavender dianthus blanket this planting bed. BELOW: Snowy white petunias contrast with burgundy and purple verbenas.

Prizewinning beds in Colorado

■ Visitors to Greenwood Village, Colorado, enjoy eye-catching floral displays along city streets. The plantings (designed for maximum impact by John Probeck of Western Proscapes in Englewood) won a grand award for use of color from the Associated Landscape Contractors of Colorado. Pictured here are two of Probeck's planting beds.

The flower bed at right is planted exclusively with annual flowers. An edging of white petunias sets off a cool color scheme created by lavender, burgundy, and purple verbenas 'Sterling Star', 'Toronto Wine', and 'Imagination'. Spikes of 'Victoria Blue' salvia add deep blue accents. The plants are spaced close together to concentrate flower color and shade out weeds. This bed looks fresh from late May until the first hard frost.

The flower planting above is composed mostly of perennials and ornamental grasses. Sweeps of golden black-eyed Susans and lavender 'First Love' dianthus on the left contrast with fountains of zebra grass at the rear. "The grasses add texture and take over the starring role from the flowers during fall and winter," Probeck says.

— *Marcia Tatroe*

PAUL BOUSQUET (2)

Pacific Northwest Checklist

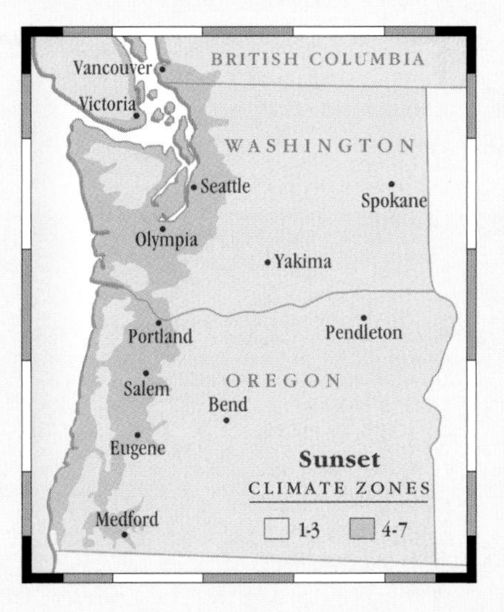

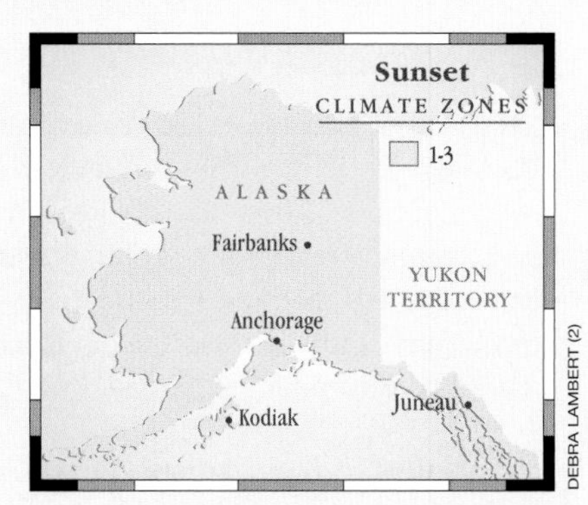

PLANTING

✔ANNUAL FLOWERS. Stick with cool-season annuals such as calendula, English daisies, pansies, snapdragons, stock, sweet alyssum, and violas until the danger of frost is past. Then start planting summer annuals such as marigolds, petunias, and zinnias.

✔COOL-SEASON VEGETABLES. Set out seedlings of broccoli, cabbage, cauliflower, chard, Chinese vegetables, kale, kohlrabi, lettuce, and spinach as soon as possible. Sow carrots, peas, and radishes, and plant seed potatoes now.

✔FRUITS. Zones 1–3: Plant bare-root cane berries, grapes, hardy kiwis, strawberries, and fruit trees while they're still available at nurseries and garden centers. Zones 4–7, 17: Plant all of these fruits from containers now.

✔HERBS. Set out seedlings of just about everything now, from chives and parsley to mint, rosemary, sage, and thyme. Wait until danger of frost is past to sow basil.

✔LAWNS. Zones 1–3: As soon as the soil thaws and warms, start lawns from seed or sod. Zones 4–7: Start lawns from sod or seed anytime; keep the grass well watered until it is growing at the rate of about 1 inch per week.

✔PERENNIALS. Nurseries are a sea of color now, featuring basket-of-gold, bleeding heart, columbine, Corsican hellebore, forget-me-not, primrose, rockcress, wallflower, and a host of others. Plant immediately.

✔TREES, SHRUBS, VINES. Zones 1–3: In cold-winter areas, you can still buy bare-root stock now; plant immediately. Zones 4–7: You can buy many container-grown flowering trees (especially crabapples, cherries, and dogwoods) in bloom now, as well as shrubs like azaleas, lilacs, and rhododendrons. Deciduous vines, from clematis to wisteria, are also available.

✔WARM-SEASON VEGETABLES. Start seeds of warm-season vegetables such as cucumbers, eggplants, melons, peppers, and tomatoes now for transplanting in six to eight weeks, after the danger of frost is past.

MAINTENANCE

✔CONTROL APHIDS. Blast them off tender new growth with a jet of water.

✔CONTROL SLUGS. Handpick slugs or spread bait around plants before their populations explode and start damaging new growth. Try one of the iron phosphate baits, which are safe for use around children and pets.

✔FERTILIZE. To give plants a boost while the soil is cool, apply liquid fertilizer on flower and vegetable beds or dig in an organic fertilizer with both fast- and slow-release forms of nitrogen, like blood meal. ◆

WHAT TO DO IN YOUR GARDEN IN APRIL

Northern California Checklist

PLANTING

✔ HARDY VEGETABLES. Zones 1–2: As soon as soil can be worked, sow seeds of beets, broccoli, cabbage, carrots, cauliflower, endive, kohlrabi, lettuce, onions, parsley, parsnips, peas, potatoes, radishes, spinach, Swiss chard, and turnips.

✔ HERBS. Zones 7–9, 14–17: Nurseries are stocked with many basic culinary herbs, including basil, chives, mint, oregano, parsley, and thyme. For greater variety, contact Mountain Valley Growers (559/338-2775 or www.mountainvalleygrowers.com) or Papa Geno's Herb Farm (402/423-5051 or www.papagenos.com).

✔ WATER GARDENING. Zones 7–9, 14–17: Choose a glazed ceramic container with no drainage hole. Fill it with water and add a pump, if desired (drill a hole under the lip of the pot for the cord to exit, or drape the cord over the pot edge and hide it among the plants). Add plants such as blue spike rush, dwarf umbrella palm, floating heart, Japanese iris, primrose creeper, water poppy, and white snowflake. A good source for plants is Lilypons Water Gardens (800/999-5459 or www.lilypons.com). Support the pots on bricks or upside-down pots. Add mosquito fish, if desired (see "Pest Control" at right).

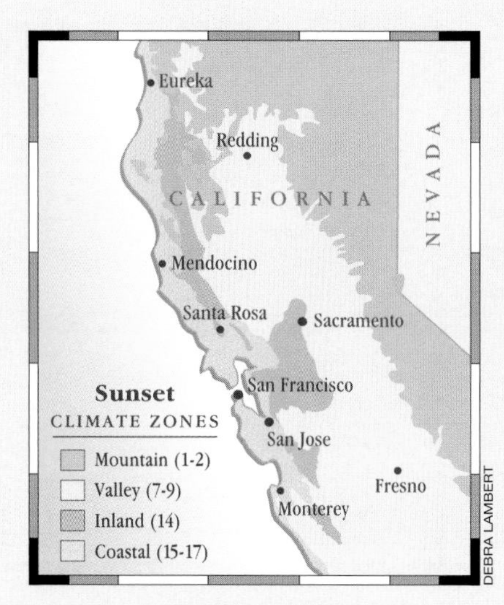

✔ XERISCAPE PLANTS. Zones 1–2, 7–9, 14–17: High Country Gardens specializes in water-wise perennials for the Western garden. The catalog includes shrubs, grasses, perennials, cactus, and ground covers suitable for a variety of zones. Contact the company at (800) 925-9387 or visit www.highcountrygardens.com.

MAINTENANCE

✔ FEED ACID LOVERS. Zones 7–9, 14–17: After azaleas, camellias, and rhododendrons finish blooming, feed them with an acid fertilizer (purchase bags or boxes of dry fertilizer for acid-loving plants). Also, pinch or snap off spent blooms, but be careful not to damage emerging growth.

✔ THIN VEGETABLE SEEDLINGS. Use scissors to snip out seedlings of basil, beets, carrots, green onions, mesclun, turnips, and other vegetables that have been sown too thickly; cut out at ground level (use beet and mesclun thinnings in salads).

PEST CONTROL

✔ CONTROL MOSQUITOES. Zones 7–9, 14–17: Eliminate breeding sites by draining away all excess water in drainage pipes, gutters, buckets, plant containers, saucers, and anywhere water may stand or collect. Stock ponds and fountains with mosquito fish (*Gambusia affinis*), available (often free) from nurseries that sell water plants. Many county mosquito and vector control departments also provide free mosquito fish.

✔ HOSE OFF APHIDS. These tiny soft-bodied insects feed on new growth by sucking out fluids. Many plants, particularly roses, are susceptible this time of year. In the morning, hose aphids off sturdy plants with a strong blast of water. Carefully wash more delicate plants, using your fingers to dislodge the insects. ◆

WHAT TO DO IN YOUR GARDEN IN APRIL

Southern California Checklist

PLANTING

✔ CONTAINER-GROWN ROSES. Buying roses in bloom is more expensive, but it allows you to judge flower color and form; this month, nurseries are well stocked with blooming plants. Choose roses with at least four strong canes and make sure the swollen bud joint at the base of the plant is at least 1 inch above soil level.

✔ SUMMER ANNUALS. Plant summer annuals such as ageratums, bedding dahlias, coleus, marigolds, nasturtiums, nicotianas, petunias, salvias, strawflowers (*Helichrysum bracteatum*), sunflowers, and Swan River daisies (*Brachycome*). Gardeners in the high desert (zone 11) still have the opportunity to plant pansies, snapdragons, stock, sweet alyssum, and violas this month.

✔ SUMMER VEGETABLES. Inland gardeners (zones 18–21) can start beans, corn, cucumbers, eggplant, lima beans, melons, okra, peppers, pumpkins, squash, tomatoes, and other warm-season crops now. Along the coast (zones 22–24), continue planting quick-maturing, cool-season crops such as chard, leaf lettuce, radish, and spinach; wait until late April to put in summer crops. Because of the possibility of frost, high-desert (zone 11) gardeners should delay summer planting two to four weeks as well.

DEBRA LAMBERT

MAINTENANCE

✔ ADJUST SOIL PH. In years without heavy winter rains, like this past one, salts don't leach out of the soil, causing pH levels to rise. That's why Steve Brigham of Buena Creek Gardens in San Marcos will be using an acid fertilizer, like azalea and camellia food, on *everything* in his garden this spring. Brigham suggests using half the recommended dosage and watering heavily after application to wash the fertilizer well into the soil.

✔ TREAT IRON DEFICIENCY. Gardenias, citrus, and other plants often exhibit signs of iron chlorosis in early spring. If leaves are yellow between green veins, treat with iron chelate (follow package directions).

PEST CONTROL

✔ MANAGE BUDWORM. Geranium budworm, also called tobacco budworm, attacks penstemons, nicotianas, and petunias, in addition to geraniums. Since the tiny worms burrow into the buds and feed from the inside, *Bacillus thuringiensis* (BT) and other insecticides are rarely effective. Instead release *Trichogramma pretiosum* (a tiny stingless wasp that parasitizes budworm eggs). Set out cards of these wasp eggs now and every few weeks through September. If you can't find them at your nursery, order from A-1 Unique Insect Control (916/961-7945) or Rincon-Vitova Insectaries (800/248-2847).

✔ ORDER BENEFICIAL INSECTS. Green lacewings eat aphids, thrips, mealybugs, and lots of other pests. *Encarsia formosa* parasitizes greenhouse whiteflies. Two predatory mites (*Galendromus annetens* and *G. helveolus*) prey on avocado persea mite. Order them from the sources listed above. ◆

WHAT TO DO IN YOUR GARDEN IN APRIL

Mountain Checklist

PLANTING

✔ ANNUALS. Four to six weeks before the average last frost date in your area, start seeds indoors for warm-season annual flowers (ageratums, lavateras, marigolds, petunias, statice) and vegetables (eggplant, melons, peppers, squash, tomatoes). In mountainous areas, start seeds of cool-season flowers and vegetables this month.

✔ HARDY VEGETABLES. Two to four weeks before your last frost date, it's safe to set out transplants of broccoli, brussels sprouts, cabbage, and cauliflower.

✔ SUMMER BULBS. Start begonias, caladiums, callas, cannas, and dahlias in pots indoors on a sunny windowsill. Wait to plant these outside until all risk of frost is past.

✔ SWEET CORN. Two weeks before last frost, sow seeds of sweet corn directly in the ground. In areas with short summers, try 'Yukon Chief', a dwarf variety that matures in only 55 days. It's available from Garden City Seeds (406/961-4837 or www.gardencityseeds.com).

MAINTENANCE

✔ CARE FOR LAWNS. Aerate lawns using a rental machine that removes plugs of soil; rake up the plugs and put them on the compost pile or leave them in place to decompose. To control crabgrass and dandelions before they sprout, apply a preemergence herbicide. If you prefer a more natural herbicide, try one of the corn gluten–based products such as WOW! (available from Gardens Alive!, Lawrenceburg, IN; 812/537-8650 or www.gardens-alive.com.).

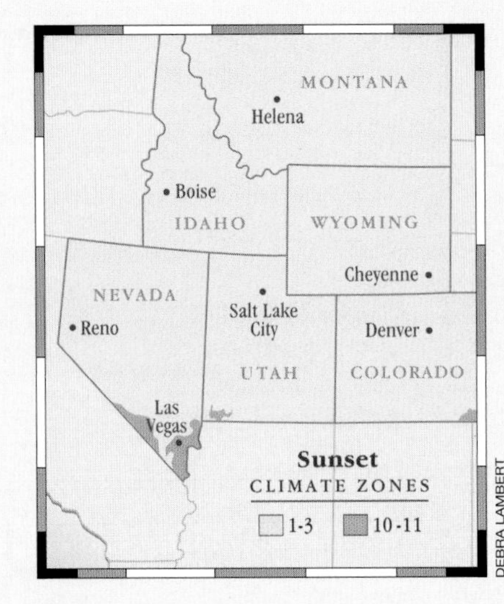

✔ CLEAN FLOWER BEDS. Gradually remove winter mulch and debris around perennials, then top-dress beds with 2 to 3 inches of compost.

✔ DIVIDE PERENNIALS. When new leaves appear, divide clumps of asters, bellflowers, chrysanthemums, daylilies, sedums, Shasta daisies, and yarrow. Dig a bucketful of compost into the soil before replanting divisions.

✔ ELIMINATE WEEDS. Hoe small weeds when the soil is dry; do it early in the day so the sun will dry them out. For larger weeds, water thoroughly, then use a hand weeder to pop them out of the ground.

✔ PRUNE ROSES. Toward month's end, after roses put out new foliage, cut off dead and blackened stems and canes. Seal each pruning cut with clear nail polish, white glue, or a commercial cane sealer to prevent borer damage. As the weather warms up, remove last year's mulch and leave the soil bare until hot weather arrives.

✔ REMOVE TREE WRAP. If you wrapped trunks for winter protection, take the wrap off now; otherwise it can harbor destructive insects during the growing season.

✔ SPRAY FRUIT TREES. After pruning but before flowers and leaves appear, spray fruit trees with a mixture of dormant oil and lime sulfur or oil and copper. If rain washes it off within 48 hours, reapply. ◆

Southwest Checklist

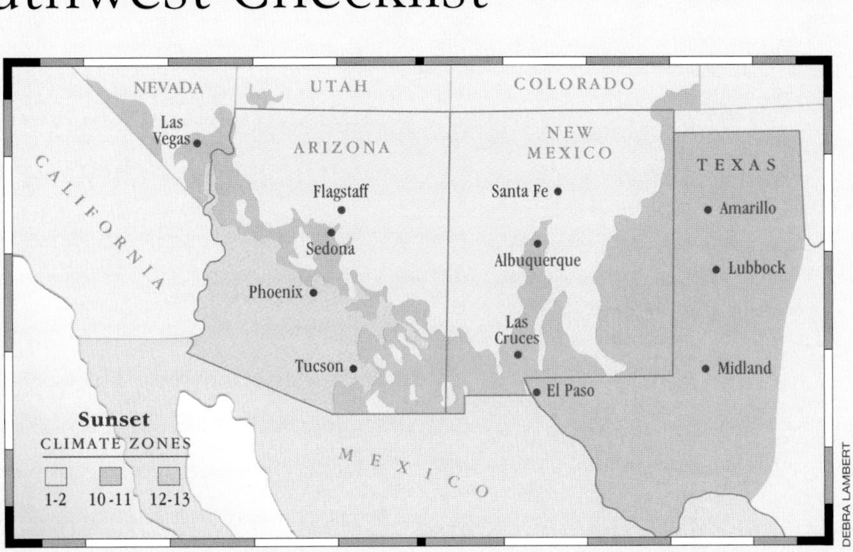

PLANTING

✔ ANNUALS. Zones 1–2: Set out pansies for early color. Zones 10–13: Plant ageratums, cosmos, globe amaranths, gloriosa daisies, lisianthus, Madagascar periwinkles, marigolds, Mexican sunflowers (*Tithonia*), portulacas, and zinnias.

✔ CITRUS. Zones 12–13: Set out container-grown citrus trees in full sun. Dig the planting hole as deep as the rootball and at least twice as wide. Wrap the exposed trunk in white cloth or paint it with white latex to prevent sunburn. Water two or three times per week for the first month, then every five to seven days through summer.

✔ LAWNS. Zones 1–2 and 10 (Albuquerque): Sow or reseed lawns with fine or tall fescue, perennial ryegrass, or a blend of these. In areas with long, warm summers, consider a blend of buffalo grass and blue grama. Zone 11 (Las Vegas): In addition to tall fescue or perennial ryegrass, you can grow common or hybrid Bermuda grass. Zones 12–13: When night temperatures are above 65°, sow common Bermuda grass or plant plugs or sprigs of hybrid Bermuda or zoysia.

✔ PERENNIALS. Zone 10–11: Plant chrysanthemums, columbines, gazanias, geraniums, gerberas, hollyhocks, Michaelmas daisies, and Shasta daisies. Zones 12–13: Plant coreopsis, gaillardias, and salvias.

✔ SUMMER BULBS. Zones 10–12: After the last frost, plant caladiums, cannas, crinus, gladiolus, irises, and montbretias (*Crocosmia crocosmiiflora*). Zone 13 (Phoenix): Plant cannas, crinus, and zephyranthes.

✔ VEGETABLES. Zones 10–11: Sow seeds of beans, corn, cucumbers, melons, okra, pumpkins, squash, and watermelons. Set out seedlings of eggplants, peppers, and tomatoes, plus tubers of Jerusalem artichokes. Zones 12–13: Sow seeds of beans, black-eyed peas, cucumbers, melons, okra, and squash by mid-April; set out eggplant seedlings, peanuts, and sweet potato tubers anytime this month.

✔ VINES. Zones 12–13: Plant tender vines, including bougainvillea, *Mandevilla* 'Alice Du Pont', pink trumpet vine, and queen's wreath (*Antigonon leptopus*) in a warm spot with good winter protection.

MAINTENANCE

✔ FERTILIZE PLANTS. Almost everything in the garden can use fertilizer now. To avoid burning plants, water thoroughly the day before you fertilize and again immediately afterward. ◆

quick-start

6 great gardens you can plant in a weekend, a day, or even an hour

GARDEN PHOTOGRAPHS BY NORMAN A. PLATE

The spring-planting clock is ticking, and your time is tight. Can you still enjoy a summer full of beautiful flowers, delicious vegetables, and savory herbs? Absolutely! On these pages, we present *Sunset*-tested plans to get your garden off to a fast start, easily. Just give yourself a day or weekend for planting (plus a few hours for planning), then let nature's spring growth surge fill in the garden in the days to come. Turn your work in spring—the season of possibilities—into your most fulfilling summer garden.

1 A garden in a day

SIZE: 12 by 18 feet

TIME: 1 week to plan, 1 day to install

COST: $750 (see cost breakdown, page 140)

Like a canvas awaiting a painter's brush, Linda and Rich Peters's barren courtyard fronting their home in San Mateo, California, cried out for color and life. Knowing that weeds would pop up if they didn't plant quickly, the Peterses were thrilled when friends from *Sunset's* garden staff offered to help design and plant a low-maintenance garden with flowers and a small lawn.

Sunset's test garden coordinator Bud Stuckey took measurements and designed the garden; then he calculated the number of plants and amount of turf grass sod it would require. The whole garden—lawn and all—was installed by two people in a single day. —*Jim McCausland*

PLANT LIST
(numerals indicate number of plants)

A. *Achillea* 'Coronation Gold', 3
B. *Artemisia schmidtiana* 'Silver Mound', 4
C. *Chrysanthemum frutescens* 'Summer Beauty', 1
D. Dahlberg daisy, 3
E. Delphinium (pink and purple), 4
F. 'Eureka' lemon, 1
G. Fountain grass, 2
H. Mexican bush sage, 1
I. *Nemesia* 'Blue Bird', 18
J. *Penstemon* 'Utah Mix', 1
K. *Petunia* 'Ultra Plum', 24 (grouped)
L. *Rudbeckia hirta* 'Goldilocks', 2
M. *Rudbeckia* 'Indian Summer', 2
N. *Salvia* 'Purple Majesty', 2
O. *Sedum spectabile* 'Autumn Joy', 2
P. *Sedum telephium* 'Carmen', 2
Q. Sweet alyssum (white and rosy purple), 12

ILLUSTRATIONS: MIMI OSBORNE

◀ Before: Small front-yard space enclosed on two sides by walls, on the other two sides by the house, is a blank slate with hard clay soil.
After: ▶ Closely spaced annuals, mature perennials (from 1-gallon cans), and shrubs (from 5-gallon cans) give the gently curving flower beds an established look.

gardens

gearing up for planting day ▼

Monday

Decide on the best turf grass for your site; order turf grass sod for delivery on the morning of planting day. (We used 16 rolls; order an extra roll or two more than you think you'll need, so you won't come up short.) Also call a rental yard to reserve a rear-tined rotary tiller and sod roller for pickup early on planting day.

Tuesday

Start shopping for plants, visiting different nurseries to obtain the best ones (buy a few extras). If your soil is hard, begin watering; you want it moistened several inches deep to make it easier to till.

Wednesday

Continue plant shopping. Pick up organic soil amendment and a 60-foot soaker hose to irrigate planting beds. A small lawn such as this one can be irrigated with a hose-end sprinkler.

Thursday

Gather garden tools, including spades, rakes, and trowels. Water nursery plants thoroughly, so they'll be ready for transplanting the next day.

Friday planting day ▶

Pick up the **rotary tiller** and **sod roller.** Receive delivery of the **sod.** Begin **installing the garden,** following the sequence shown in the photos at right.

costs*

Organic soil amendment	$20
Sod (16 rolls, 18 by 80 inches)	$60
Plants	$625
Soaker hose (60 feet)	$11
Total	$716

*Excluding rental of rotary tiller and sod roller, and optional flagstones and bench

Use a rotary tiller to work organic amendment deep into the soil (at least 8 inches). After tilling, level the ground, then rake it to remove any large rocks.

Push the sod roller (filled halfway with water) over the sod to press its root zone into firm contact with the soil.

Arrange the plants, still in their nursery containers, on the soil; move as needed to create the desired composition.

Spread powdered gypsum (flour or sand also works) on the ground to outline the lawn area.

Lay sod of dwarf tall fescue on top of the soil. Trim fescue edges with a sharp knife to fit the outline.

Remove the containers and set plants in the ground.

GARDEN BENCH COURTESY OF ALLIED ARTS GUILD, MENLO PARK, CA

When all planting is done, water the plants and lawn. As finishing touches, you can edge the beds with flagstones (cut out patches of sod to accommodate the stones, about $30) or add a bench (we chose a hand-carved wood bench, $600).

Perennials in a weekend

SIZE: 10 by 15 feet

TIME: 1 day for shopping and soil prep, 1 day to plant

COST: About $500 (chair and table not included)

This little garden, designed by Judy Wigand of Judy's Perennials in San Marcos, California, makes use of pillowy perennials that will produce a colorful show this season.

Wigand designed the garden around a willow chair and table, but a bench or a simple water feature, with a stone path leading to it, would also work.

In our plan, perennials with flowers in fiery oranges, reds, and yellows are outlined with cool whites and grays; the plants are mostly long-bloomers that provide all-season color. Those with shorter flowering cycles (santolina, for instance) were also selected for their attractive foliage color when not in bloom.

— Lauren Bonar Swezey

After planting: ▲The garden retreat looks neat, with a few flowers for interest. Two months later: ▶The garden is ablaze with colorful blooms, drawing visitors down its stone path.

PLANT LIST

(numerals indicate number of plants)

A. *Boltonia asteroides* 'Snowbank', 5

B. Cape fuchsia (*Phygelius capensis* 'Moonraker'), 4

C. *Chrysanthemum frutescens* 'Silver Leaf', 3

D. *Erodium corsicum* 'Album', 18

E. Lavender cotton (*Santolina chamaecyparissus* 'Compacta'), 3

F. *Nemesia* 'Innocence', 3

G. *Penstemon gloxinioides* 'Firebird', 5

H. 'Playboy' rose, 1

I. *Rudbeckia hirta* 'Irish Eyes', 5

J. Santa Barbara daisy (*Erigeron karvinskianus*), 4

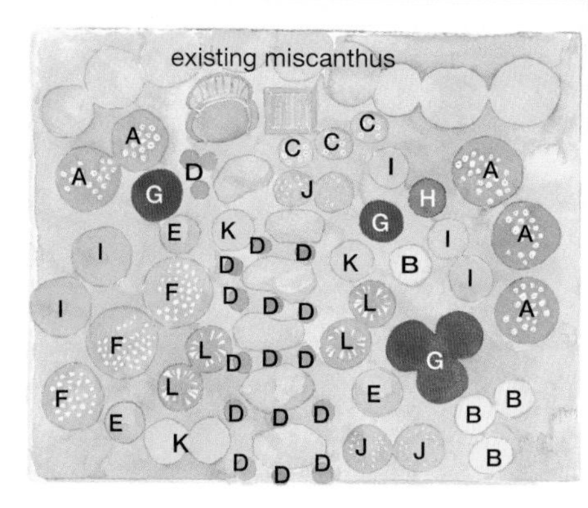

K. Silver thyme (*Thymus vulgaris* 'Argentus'), 4

L. *Veronica spicata* 'Icicle', 4

preparation, planting

DAY 1

1. **Prepare the soil.** Cover the planting bed with a 3-inch layer of compost and rotary-till it into the soil.

2. **Shop for plants.** Water thoroughly

when you bring them home.

3. Shop for stone pavers (at a building supply yard).

DAY 2

1. Position the plants, still in their nursery pots, on the bed; adjust as necessary.

2. Position stone pavers, firming them into the soil. Also position the chair or bench, offsetting it so the garden doesn't look too uniform.

3. Dig planting holes. As you dig, add controlled-release fertilizer to each planting hole.

4. Set out the plants.

5. Snake ooze-tubing around them for irrigation.

6. Mulch. To control weeds and keep evaporation down, spread ground fir bark around plants.

French-intensive bed is designed for tending from the perimeter. Low plants (basil, sage) grow in front, tall ones

Weekend vegetable beds

Two styles: The French-intensive garden shown above and a keyhole plan (page 110)

It's easy to have resounding success at vegetable gardening, even if you've never grown so much as a tomato before. All you need is a sunny site, good soil, and a simple plan (we offer two). If you prepare the soil well and start most crops from seedlings, you'll end up with enough fresh herbs and vegetables to fill your own table and give away too. The preparation and planting guidelines listed at right apply to both beds. —*J.M.*

(sunflowers, beans) in rear.

French-intensive garden

SIZE: 4 by 12 feet
TIME: 2 days to plant, plus prep
COST: $175

Shoulder-to-shoulder planting in double-dug soil delivers more food per square foot than any system we've ever used. Roots grow down instead of out, so you can space plants closer together and still get high production. In turn the close spacing shades out weeds, so they don't become major problems as they do in a more open garden.

The system demands extra-deep soil preparation, done by double-digging with a garden spade (with a squared-off blade). Dig out the top 10 to 11 inches of soil and pile it by the side of the bed. Then loosen the soil in the bottom of the bed another spade-length deep; simply dig and turn that bottom layer of soil in place with the spade, or (in traditional English garden fashion) loosen it with a spading fork.

When you're done, put the top layer of soil back into the garden bed, mixing ⅓ to ½ yard of compost into the whole bed. This process is very hard work but extremely rewarding.

PLANT LIST
(numerals indicate number of plants; spacing given in inches)

A. Pole beans, 24 seeds (2 tepees); 4″
B. Sunflowers, 6 (grouped); 18″
C. White cosmos, 12 (grouped); 6″
D. Tomatoes, 4; 21″
E. Parsley, 10; 6″
F. 'Tricolor' sage, 1; 15″
G. 'Golden' sage, 1; 15″
H. Chives, 2; 6″
I. Zucchini, 2; 15″
J. Sweet basil, 2; 6″

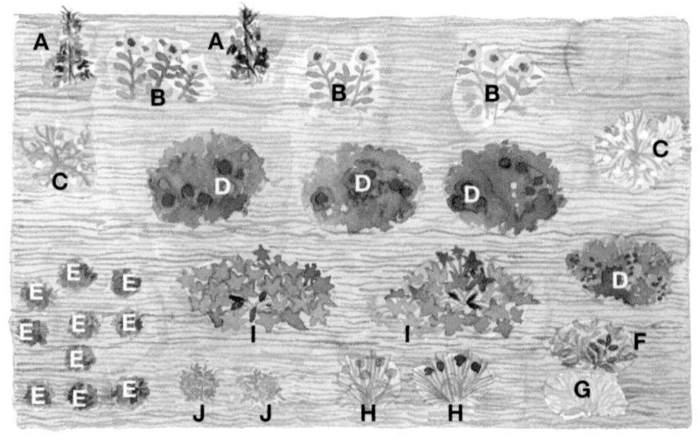

preparation, planting

A FEW DAYS AHEAD

1. Choose a sunny spot with access from all sides.

2. Order soil amendment, and if you're making the keyhole garden and don't want to hand-dig it, rent a rotary tiller.

3. Order seedlings. Choose varieties suited to your region (nurseries and garden centers usually have these). The varieties listed on page 111 are ones we used in our Menlo Park, California, test garden. Also buy bamboo poles and tomato cages.

4. Get rid of weeds.

WEEKEND, DAY 1

1. Prepare the soil. Follow directions above or on page 110.

2. Erect tepees to support pole beans: Tie four 8-foot bamboo poles together 6 inches from one end, then stand upright.

3. Water the bed thoroughly, then let it settle overnight before planting.

WEEKEND, DAY 2

1. Set out most plants in a diamond pattern, spacing as indicated on plant list.

2. Plant pole beans on tepees: three bean seeds at the base of each pole.

3. Support tomatoes with cages, putting one plant in the center of each (as it grows, it will fill the cage).

4. Snake soaker hoses through the beds as soon as seedlings are planted.

5. Apply mulch to keep down weeds and conserve water. We used Coco Grow mulch, but if you garden in the mountains or in a cool-summer climate, substitute black plastic mulch, which will make the soil warmer.

6. Fertilize at planting time with a spray of fish emulsion. Repeat about every two weeks. Stop feeding fruiting plants such as tomatoes, beans, and peppers as soon as they start flowering, but keep feeding leaf vegetables through the season. For an added boost, feed all plants with a dose of organic, complete vegetable fertilizer (a 5-5-5 formula) twice during the growing season.

4

Keyhole vegetable garden

SIZE: 11 by 12 feet
TIME: 2 days to plant, plus prep (see page 109)
COST: About $350

Veggies wrap around a central pathway in this garden, which makes working the beds a snap. Orient it so that the keyhole faces south; the larger plants (beans, tomatoes, and sunflowers) will be on the north side, where they won't shade smaller plants.

To prepare the soil, till it 8 to 12 inches deep, picking out roots and rocks as you go. Don't till the 3- by 7-foot center-access path (the keyhole); as long as the ground there is packed, weeds will have a hard time sprouting.

After the soil is well tilled, spread 2 yards of compost evenly over the beds and till again. Level the beds, which should form a 9-inch-tall, U-shaped plateau around the path. Rake the sides of the beds steep. Finally, spread 6 cubic feet of coarse ground bark or wood chips over the path to make an all-weather surface and to help keep down weeds.

PLANT LIST
(numerals indicate number of plants; spacing given in inches)

A. Sunflowers, 5; 18″
B. Pole beans, 60 seeds (5 tepees); 6″
C. White cosmos, 24 (grouped); 6″
D. Parsley, 18 (grouped); 9″
E. Tomatoes, 5; 24″
F. Peppers, 9; 10″
G. Zucchini, 4; 18″
H. Swiss chard, 9; 9″
I. Herb mix, 6; 15″
J. Chives, 3; 9″
K. Sweet basil, 4; 9″

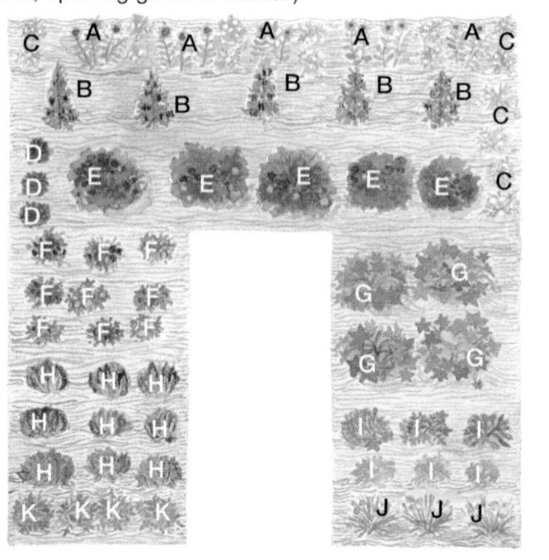

Right: Keyhole plan has a center path. Below: Varieties we grew include (from left) 'Golden Bell' pepper, 'Red Bell' pepper, 'Yellow Disk' sunflower, 'Blue Lake' pole bean, 'Ronde de Nice' zucchini.

which varieties to grow

Choose varieties of vegetables and flowers that are suited to your climate. For reference, here's what we chose (and the sizes they come in) for our test garden in Menlo Park, California.

Basil: 'Cinnamon', 'Dark Opal', and 'Sweet'; sixpacks

Chives: Common (blue flowers) and garlic (white flowers); sixpacks

Cosmos: White 'Sensation'; sixpacks

Garlic: 'California Giant White'; cloves

Oregano: 1-gallon cans

Parsley: Sixpacks

Peppers: 'Golden Bell', 'Long Italian', 'Red Bell', and 'Yellow Bell'; sixpacks

Pole bean: 'Blue Lake'; seed

Rosemary: 'Tuscan Blue'; 1-gallon can

Sage: 'Purple' for keyhole, plus 'Golden' and 'Tricolor' for French-intensive; 1-gallon cans

Sunflowers: 'Autumn Beauty', 'Double Sungold', and 'Lemon Gem'; 4-inch pots

Swiss chard: 'Rainbow' and 'Ruby'; sixpacks

Tarragon: 1-gallon cans

Thyme: English and lemon; 1-gallon cans

Tomatoes: 'Better Boy', 'Celebrity', 'Early Girl', and 'Sweet 100'; 4-inch pots

Zucchini: 'Eight Ball', 'Gold Rush', and 'Ronde de Nice'; 4-inch pots

FAR LEFT: SAXON HOLT (2)

Herbs in an hour

Plant culinary herbs in pots, in baskets

To perk up summer meals, try growing herbs in containers. Big terra-cotta pots filled with chives, parsley, and sage are perfect for patios; place them near a kitchen door or a backyard barbecue. Baskets make handsome portable herb gardens you can bring to the table to clip as you eat.

Start with plants from 2- to 4-inch nursery containers. Plant soft-stemmed herbs that you will harvest frequently—parsley and chives, for instance—or choose small plants of larger herbs such as sage to plant out in beds at the end of the season. Put low growers and draping plants (chives and nasturtiums) around sides. Build height in the center with tall, upward growers such as sweet basil and parsley.

Herbs in containers need more care than those in the ground; water frequently, feed regularly, and harvest liberally. Trim off yellow or dead leaves and replace plants as they outgrow their containers. Fresh herbs taste best when essential oils are at their peak—anytime before plants begin to flower.

— Kathleen N. Brenzel

5 Snip-and-serve herb baskets

TIME: 1 hour or less, plus shopping
COST: About $20

The basket should be sturdy and at least 9 inches wide, 12 inches long, and 6 inches deep. Line it with 3-mil plastic or a heavy-duty plastic trash bag, then use scissors to punch holes through the plastic. Fill partway with rich, fast-draining potting mix. Arrange herbs 3 to 4 inches apart on top of the soil. Gently loosen the rootballs, then plant. Put the basket outdoors where it gets at least four hours of sunlight every day (partial sun in hot inland areas). To counteract the leaching effect of watering, feed plants weekly with fish emulsion.

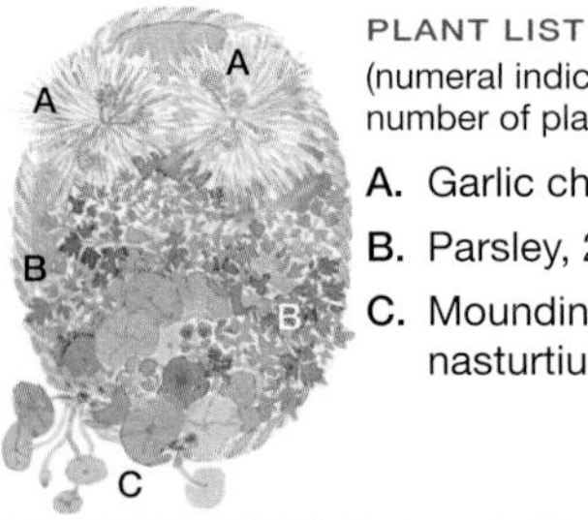

PLANT LIST
(numeral indicates number of plants)

A. Garlic chives,
B. Parsley, 2
C. Mounding nasturtium, 1

PLANT LIST

A. Parsley, 1
B. Thyme, 1
C. Oregano, 1
D. Sweet basil, 1
E. Sage, 1
F. 'Tricolor' sage, 1
G. Basil 'Red Rubin', 1

6 Kitchen garden in a pot

TIME: 1 hour or less
COST: About $65

You'll need a big pot; the one pictured at right is 14 inches in diameter (top) and 9 inches deep. Fill it slightly more than halfway with rich, fast-draining potting soil. Position the plants, still in their containers, about 4 inches apart on top of soil. When you're satisfied with their placement, knock each from its container and plant. Fill in around plants with potting soil. Feed every two weeks with fish emulsion.

PLANT LIST
(numeral indicates number of plants)

A. Oregano, 1
B. 'Golden' sage, 1
C. 'Tricolor' sage, 2
D. Chives, 2
E. Lemon thyme, 1

SILVERY leaves of 'Berggarten' sage (far left) and 'White Nancy' lamium (above) glow in the shade of an old apple tree.

ALLAN MANDELL

Shade gardens that shine

Beautiful ways to use shade plants in mountain or woodland settings

BY JIM McCAUSLAND

Like their counterparts in the sun, gardens made for the shade can take on formal or informal personalities. In Boulder, Colorado, for example, landscape designer Robert Howard created a shade border (shown above) with the formal look of an English garden. In Bellevue, Washington, Nita and Johnny Therrell planted a woodland garden (photo on facing page) that retains the informal look of the wild forest from which it sprang. Shade plants need little extra fertilizer if they're grown in good soil (nitrogen only makes them leggy), but competition for water can be intense when ground covers are planted over tree roots. Water whenever soil dries out.

BOULDER BORDER

Howard created this shady oasis beneath a pair of apple and pear trees. First he built a retaining wall of dry-stacked stone wall, then dug compost into the top foot of soil, avoiding the tree roots. He set the plants close together to keep weeds down.

Here, a mile above sea level, the light is so intense that it spurs strong growth, even in shade. This light made it possible to combine true shade-loving plants—including dead nettle, hosta, and meadow rue—with perennials that tolerate bright shade at higher elevations, such as catmint, 'Berggarten' sage, and veronica.

WASHINGTON WOODLAND

The Therrells filled their entry garden with azaleas, rhododendrons, Japanese maples, and other shade-tolerant exotics, but left most of the rest of their property as woodland.

The ground is carpeted with moss and a generous array of ferns. Spring-blooming woodland flowers, including bleeding hearts, trilliums, and violas, dot the forest floor from March through May; red-flowering currants and bunchberries pop out in April; and native azaleas and rhododendrons light up the woods in May. Ocean spray and twinflowers close out the season in June. After that, the exotics, including hostas and impatiens, carry on the floral show.

Shade plants in general and native plants in particular tend to have an open, informal look—a characteristic that leads many gardeners to think of them as plants suitable only for the wild garden. But Nita Therrell calls them rambunctious plants that simply want a little training. Therrell shears her huckleberry, ocean spray, Oregon boxwood, and salal plants close, and and she even maintains a perfectly sheared rhododendron hedge in the entry garden.

SHADES OF DIFFERENCE

Ironically, although shade plants usually cannot tolerate full sun during the hottest part of the day, most grow and flower best when they get plenty of light. They love the light shade cast by high-arching tree canopies, as well as the shade common in gardens that are shaded to the south but open to sky on the north. Generally, they don't perform as well in full shade.

Experiment to see what works for your garden: If your plants grow too leggy and fail to flower, they're probably getting too much shade. Transplant them in a brighter spot (or thin out any overhead branches that are casting shadows).

Because so many shade plants come from woodlands, they thrive in the

MAGGIE MACLAREN (2)

ABOVE: Big blue-leafed *Hosta sieboldiana* plays off smaller variegated hosta and astilbe.
LEFT: Variegated English ivy joins maidenhair and sword ferns in a half-barrel set atop a tree stump.

kind of porous, humusy soil typically found in the forest. If you have this kind of soil, maintain it by mulching with compost or leaf mold twice a year. If you don't, create your own by tilling a 3- to 4-inch layer of composted organic matter into your soil. Or combine 2 parts organic amendment (compost or peat moss) with 1 part sand and 1 part garden loam to form a layer of soil at least 8 inches deep to spread over the ground.

Plants made for shade

GROUND COVERS & PERENNIALS

■ Bunchberry (*Cornus canadensis*). Deciduous. White flowers appear in May, then red berries; 6-inch plant. *Sunset* climate zones 1–7.

■ Dead nettle (*Lamium maculatum*). Deciduous in hard winters. Silvery white leaves have green edges; usually pink or white flowers; 6 inches tall. All zones.

■ Hosta. Deciduous. Solid or variegated, blue to green leaves; sometimes-fragrant flowers. Zones 1–10, 12–21.

■ Japanese spurge (*Pachysandra terminalis*). Evergreen. Attractive, 6-inch leathery leaves. Zones 1–10, 14–21.

■ Meadow rue (*Thalictrum* species). Deciduous. Airy foliage grows 3 to 6 feet tall. All zones.

■ Redwood sorrel (*Oxalis oregana*). Deciduous. In spring, pink or white flowers rise over a cloverlike carpet. Resists slugs. Zones 4–9, 14–24.

■ Sweet woodruff (*Galium odoratum*). Deciduous. Delicate ground cover with white, mellow-smelling May flowers. Resists slugs. Zones 1–6, 15–17.

■ Vanilla leaf (*Achlys triphylla*). Deciduous. Butterfly-like leaves emerge in April; flowers are cream-colored; to 1 foot tall. Zones 2–7.

■ Wild ginger (*Asarum caudatum*). Evergreen; native to the woods of the Coast Range. Big, heart-shaped leaves have gingery scent when crushed; handsome, dark green carpet to 10 inches. Zones 4–6, 14–24.

FERNS & SHRUBS

■ Coast rhododendron (*R. macrophyllum*). Evergreen. Pink flowers in May or June. Tends to be leggy unless you prune hard after bloom; 10 to 20 feet tall. Zones 4–6, 15–17.

■ Maidenhair fern (*Adiantum aleuticum*). Deciduous in hard winters. Airy-looking, delicate fronds; 1 to 2 feet tall. Zones 1–9, 14–24.

■ Ocean spray (*Holodiscus discolor*). Deciduous. Western native with toothed leaves bears clusters of creamy white summer flowers; 3 to 20 feet (taller in very rich, moist soil). Zones 1–7, 14–17.

■ Oregon boxwood (*Paxistima myrsinites*). Evergreen. Looks like a dark, dense boxwood; 2 to 4 feet tall. Zones 1–10, 14–21.

■ Oregon grape (*Mahonia aquifolium*). Evergreen. Holly-shaped leaves; yellow spring flowers followed by sour, grapelike fruit; to 8 feet. Zones 1–21. Longleaf mahonia (*M. nervosa*) grows to 2 feet; zones 2–9, 14–17.

■ Red huckleberry (*Vaccinium parvifolium*). Deciduous. Airy branches with light green leaves are dotted with edible red berries in summer; 4 to 12 feet tall. Zones 2–7, 14–17.

■ Salal (*Gaultheria shallon*). Evergreen. Dense, unthirsty shrubs produce edible (if bland) purple summer fruit; 2 to 10 feet. Resists slugs. Zones 3–7, 14–17, 21–24.

■ Sword fern (*Polystichum munitum*). Evergreen. Takes some drought. Shiny, dark green fronds; 2 to 4 feet tall. Zones 4–9, 14–24.

■ Western azalea (*Rhododendron occidentale*). Deciduous. Fragrant white or pink flowers with yellow throats; to 8 feet tall. Zones 4–9, 14–17, 19–24. ◆

CENTURY PLANT points the way to an outdoor dining area.

TERRENCE MOORE

Making shade in the desert

Airy shelters and shade trees create cool oases in this Arizona garden

BY NORA BURBA TRULSSON

Hugging the slope of Camelback Mountain in Paradise Valley, Arizona, Elizabeth Alpert's house is surrounded by oases that provide respite from the blazing summer sun. Overhead shelters and leafy canopies cast pools of shade, making her 1-acre garden livable even during the hottest months.

When Alpert moved here in 1981, the garden consisted of native cactus, palo verde trees, and a small citrus grove. Working with Phoenix landscape contractor Ron Farone, Alpert began renovating. Trees were carefully placed to cast shade on the house, paved areas, and planter beds where annuals and roses enjoy a longer season of bloom in the filtered light.

An evergreen Indian laurel fig (*Ficus microcarpa nitida*), now more than 30 feet tall, shelters the house from intense sun in the morning; in the afternoon, it shades a courtyard planted with banana and jacaranda trees. A deciduous Brazilian butterfly tree (*Bauhinia forficata*) casts filtered shade over a large, south-facing window during the summer, but lets in winter light.

Alpert formed a leafy entry tunnel over the driveway by pruning a Brazilian pepper tree (*Schinus terebinthifolius*), fern-of-the-desert (*Lysiloma microphylla thornberi*), and a desert ironwood (*Olneya tesota*) to arch over the pavement. In the motor court, California and Mexican fan palms (*Washingtonia filifera* and *W. robusta*) and Canary Island date palm (*Phoenix canariensis*) provide cooling shade for parked vehicles and annual flowers tucked into beds.

Behind one seating area, Alpert planted a sweet acacia (*Acacia smallii*) to screen the late-afternoon sun. In the citrus grove, lemon, orange, and grapefruit trees surround an outdoor room paved with canterra stone tiles.

Two main structures serve as shady retreats. Near the house, a Spanish colonial–style gazebo serves as an outdoor dining room and kitchen complete with a barbecue, fireplace, and sink. The hexagonal gazebo's red-tiled

TERRENCE MOORE (2)

ABOVE: A sweet acacia tree casts filtered shade over a patio.
LEFT: Cactus and other desert plants flank the path to a palapa; its thatched roof shelters another seating area.

roof is supported by carved wood columns and corbels from Mexico. Vintage wrought-iron furniture complements the gazebo's formal style.

Tucked between boulders and cactus on the hillside, a Mexican-style palapa shelters an informal seating area. Unpeeled saplings were used for the posts and beams, and the roof was made from thatched palm fronds. Each summer when Alpert's palms are trimmed, she saves a few fronds to patch the palapa's roof.

Shade trees for desert patios

Spring and summer are good times to assess your needs for shade and decide which trees fit best into your home's landscape. The trees listed below are well suited for shading patio areas, according to Janet Rademacher of Mountain States Wholesale Nursery in Glendale, Arizona; the nursery specializes in native and drought-tolerant plants and trees.

■ **Arizona mesquite** (*Prosopis juliflora*); 25 feet tall and as wide. With a craggy, sculptural form and shaggy bark, this deciduous tree is a good choice for places where you want summer shade and winter sun. Keep thorny branches pruned and away from patio areas. *Sunset* climate zones 11–13.

■ **Blue palo verde** (*Cercidium floridum*); 30 feet tall and as wide. A desert classic, this deciduous tree provides filtered shade and an early-spring cloud of small yellow blossoms. Be sure to keep thorny branches pruned and away from patios. Zones 10–13.

■ **'Desert Museum' palo verde** (*Cercidium* hybrid); 20 feet tall and as wide. This thornless hybrid developed at Tucson's Arizona–Sonora Desert Museum grows rapidly and bears bigger, longer-lasting blossoms than other palo verdes. Small trees are hard to find. Zones 11–13.

■ **Escarpment live oak** (*Quercus fusiformis*); 35 to 50 feet tall and as wide. This West Texas native produces a dense, rounded canopy of small, leathery deep-green leaves. A slow-growing, long-lived tree, it is evergreen in lower desert areas, deciduous at higher elevations. Sheds blackish brown acorns in fall. Zones 10–13.

■ **Shoestring acacia** (*A. stenophylla*); 20 to 35 feet tall, 10 to 20 feet wide. Native to Australia, this fast-growing tree bears slim, weeping leaves that cast filtered shade. Plant in groves to provide denser shade. Seed pods are easy to clean up. Zones 12–13.

■ **Sissoo** (*Dalbergia sissoo*); 25 to 50 feet tall, 35 to 50 feet wide. Relatively new, this cottonwood look-alike from India is also known as a rosewood. Shiny green leaves give it a lush appearance. A frost-tender tree, it becomes more evergreen once established. Zone 13.

■ **Sonoran palo verde** (*Cercidium praecox*); 25 to 30 feet tall and as wide. Native to Mexico, this frost-sensitive tree has an umbrella form with lime green trunk and branches. Zone 13.

■ **South American hybrid mesquite** (*Prosopis* hybrids); 20 to 25 feet tall and as wide. Briefly deciduous in midspring, this fast-growing, thornless tree can be pruned into classic canopy shape. Seasonal bean debris is easy to clean up; trees occasionally ooze sap, so keep patio furniture elsewhere. Zones 10–13.

■ **Sweet acacia** (*A. smallii*); 25 to 35 feet tall, 15 to 25 feet wide. This deciduous tree bears lacy leaves and fragrant yellow puffball blossoms in spring. Prune the thorny branches to keep the tree from looking bushy. Fallen blooms are easily brushed away. Zones 11–13.

■ **Texas ebony** (*Pithecellobium flexicaule*); 20 to 25 feet tall, 15 feet wide. Slow-growing evergreen tree with dark green leaves and a zigzagging branch pattern. Keep its thorny branches pruned and away from patio areas. Big seed pods are easy to clean up. Zones 10–13. ◆

An English garden basket

Assemble this spring bouquet in an hour or less

BY SHARON COHOON

PHOTOGRAPHS BY NORMAN A. PLATE

■ "The easiest floral arrangements to make are the ones that look like you lifted them right out of the garden," says Janelle Wiley, color specialist and floral design instructor at Sherman Library & Gardens in Corona del Mar, California. To prove her point, Wiley demonstrates an "English border in a basket." To assemble it, you just stick the stems of large, showy flowers such as roses and Dutch irises into floral foam, then tuck smaller flowers around them. "If you've ever held a trowel, you can make a bouquet like this. Trust me—it's instinctive," Wiley says.

TIME: About 1 hour

COST: $12 for materials (not including flowers)

MATERIALS

- One brick of florist's foam, 3 inches high, 4 inches long, and 9 inches wide*
- One green papier-mâché floral basket, 6 inches in diameter*
- One small roll of florist's tape*
- One package of sphagnum moss, at least 8 ounces*
- 3 feet raffia or string*
- Two stems of curly willow, at least 36 inches long
- 12 or more sprigs of ivy, rosemary, or other greenery with pliable stems
- 16 to 20 tall cut flowers, at least three of each kind (Wiley used both blue and yellow-and-white Dutch irises and pink roses)
- 16 or more shorter flowers (Wiley used white freesias, yellow button pompom chrysanthemums, and pink Geraldton waxflowers)
- Florist's scissors or hand pruners to trim stems as needed

**Sold at floral supply shops*

DIRECTIONS

1. Immerse the brick of florist's foam in water until thoroughly soaked, about 30 minutes.

2. Drain the brick and cut approximately $2\frac{1}{2}$ inches from its width. Push the brick partway into the basket; it will fit snugly. At least 1 inch of foam should extend above the rim. Firmly secure foam to basket with tape (**A**).

A

3. To conceal the papier-mâché, wrap spaghnum moss around the basket, tying it in place with raffia (**B**). Make sure the moss doesn't touch the foam or it will absorb water and possibly dampen a tabletop.

B

C

D

4. To form the handle, insert stems of curly willow into the foam on both sides of the basket (**C**), then weave the stems together at the top (**D**). Insert ivy stems into the foam on both sides of the basket and twine them around and through the curly willow (**E**). Insert additional ivy stems at the front and back of the basket to form a skirt to conceal the foam.

5. Place taller flowers in the basket first, grouping them by kind. Repeat the process with the shorter flowers, using the daintiest blooms to fill in the last few spaces. ◆

E

Privacy, with plants

Well-mannered trees and shrubs can create sheltered garden spaces

BY LAUREN BONAR SWEZEY

Fences are fine between neighboring properties, as far as they go. But often—especially in communities where lots are small—standard 6-foot-tall fences don't block views of unsightly roof lines or a looming multistory building next door, or do enough to ensure your privacy. And building codes generally don't allow for constructing anything taller than 6 feet. The temptation may be to plant a hedge, such as *Pittosporum eugenioides,* which will grow too fast and need too much pruning for most suburban gardens. Fortunately, there's a better solution.

PHOTINIAS GROWING in 24-inch-wide clay pots block out the neighbor's roof line in this Berkeley Hills garden. Design: Abbey Kletz. Top: Just two years after planting, *Tristania laurina* gives Nancy and Michael Fogel's patio in Stanford, California, plenty of privacy from their neighbors' two-story home. Trees were planted 5 feet apart, then underplanted with *Liriope muscari* and species geraniums. Star jasmine grows on the fence. Design: Lisa Moulton.

The plants listed on the facing page (brush cherry, for example, which is back after nearly being wiped out by an insect pest) create screens that grow fast enough to block undesirable views within a few years but stay in bounds so you and your neighbor aren't constantly hacking away at them to keep them under control.

"Brush cherry is one of the best," says landscape architect Lisa Moulton of Redwood City, California. "The lower leaves hang on even as the plant ages, and growth stays fairly narrow." Dense, small-leafed evergreen plants are Moulton's favorite types for screens.

Landscape designer Abbey Kletz of

NORMAN A. PLATE (2)

Berkeley favors plants with a variety of textures, such as black bamboo and photinia. "I look for plants that have charm and that complement the garden," she says. That means creating intimate and private spaces using plant screens with interesting foliage.

To start your own screen, choose from the list a plant whose foliage colors, growth habit, and size suit your garden. Set smaller plants 4 feet apart, larger ones 5 to 6 feet apart. When planting next to a long fence, Moulton sometimes combines several types of plants to break up and disguise the fence's linearity. For instance, she might group five brush cherries with five strawberry trees (*Arbutus unedo*) trained as standards.

Water plants regularly the first year to get them established. After that, follow the watering requirements listed for each plant. If you want to slow growth, water less often. To speed growth, water and fertilize more frequently (but don't keep the soil soggy).

TOP 9 PLANTS FOR SCREENING

BLACK BAMBOO. New culms (stems) are green, turning black in the second year. Leaves are greenish yellow. To restrain its spread (black bamboo produces underground runners), sink an 18- to 24-inch-wide aluminum barrier around the planting area and limit water after the first year. Thin culms when they get crowded. Black bamboo can also grow in pots but needs regular watering. 10–15 feet tall. Full sun to part shade. Water during growth periods. *Sunset* climate zones 4–9, 14–24.

BRUSH CHERRY (*Syzygium paniculatum*). Young foliage is reddish bronze; mature leaves are 1½ to 3 inches long and glossy green. 30 feet or taller but can easily be trimmed to stay at 10 feet. Full sun to light shade. Water regularly. Zones 16–17, 19–24 (foliage or stems may freeze at 25° but usually resprout).

FLOWERING MAPLE (*Abutilon hybridum*). Flowering maple isn't a dense shrub and is even rangy if not pruned. Pinch back new growth to encourage branching and fullness. When the plant is full grown (about 10 feet tall), cut back by at least 3 feet every winter to keep lower foliage full. The pink-, red-, white-, and yellow-flowered varieties grow tallest (others may not screen). Full sun on the coast, partial shade inland. Water regularly. Zones 8–9, 12–24.

LUMA APICULATA. Reminiscent of brush cherry, it has dense, dark green leaves ½ to 1 inch long and cinnamon-colored bark. 8–20 feet tall. Full sun. Little to regular watering. Zones 14–24.

PHOTINIA FRASERI. In the ground it's a tall, wide shrub, but in pots it stays more compact. New leaves are bronzy red, turning glossy green as they age. About 8 feet tall in pots, 10 to 15 feet tall in the ground. Plant standards to save space and to allow room for underplanting with flowers. Full sun. Water regularly. Zones 4–24.

***RHAPHIOLEPIS* 'MAJESTIC BEAUTY'.** Glossy, leathery leaves to 4 inches long. Pink flowers in spring. Slow-growing to 15 feet tall. Plant standards for screening. Stake at planting time. Full sun or light shade. Little to regular watering. Zones 8–10, 12–24 (often survives in 4–7).

STRAWBERRY TREE (*Arbutus unedo*). Oblong, dark green leaves are 2 to 3 inches long with red stems. Clusters of urn-shaped white flowers and yellow-and-red strawberry-like fruits appear at the same time in fall and winter. 8–35 feet tall. Plant standards to save space. Full sun to light shade. Little to regular watering. Zones 4–24.

SWEET OLIVE (*Osmanthus fragrans*). Dense, compact plant 10 feet or taller with glossy green, oval leaves. Inconspicuous flowers that appear in spring and summer are very fragrant. Full sun to part shade. Little water once established (more in hot areas). Zones 8–9, 12–24.

***TRISTANIA LAURINA* 'ELEGANT'.** Narrow, 4-inch-long, glossy leaves open red and turn green with age. Bark is mahogany-colored. Yellow flowers appear in late spring or early summer. 10 feet or taller. Plant standards. Full sun. Little watering. Zones 15–17, 19–24. ◆

Gentle pest controls

Common garden pests and safe, effective remedies

BY LAUREN BONAR SWEZEY WITH BUD STUCKEY

Warming spring weather means one thing: Pests and diseases are coming out in force, ready to attack tender new foliage and flowers. Before you get mad and reach for a chemical arsenal to do away with the nuisances, consider this: A cautious approach makes sense for the overall health of your garden, not to mention the children and pets who play there. Check the plants' growing conditions—healthy, vigorous plants are better equipped to resist pests and diseases.

• *Is the affected plant growing in the conditions it requires?* Make sure it has plenty of room to grow, the correct amount of light (sun or shade), and sufficient air circulation around it.

• *Is the soil healthy?* Flowers and vegetables thrive in well-amended soil with plenty of compost. Trees and shrubs don't need soil amendments, but covering the soil around them with an organic mulch such as bark chips helps keep the roots cool and encourages beneficial organisms in the soil.

• *Does the plant receive the amount of water and nutrients it needs?* Water-stressed plants are weak and susceptible to attack. Water early in the morning when the temperature is rising.

If good care isn't enough to keep insects or diseases at bay, identify the problem (the most common are shown and described on these pages), then choose the correct control method from the chart on the facing page. Give the control a chance to work before trying something stronger.

GINO HASLER (4)

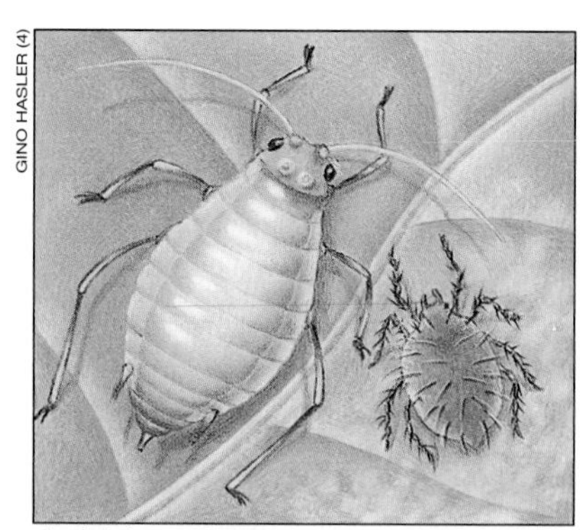

Aphids, mites

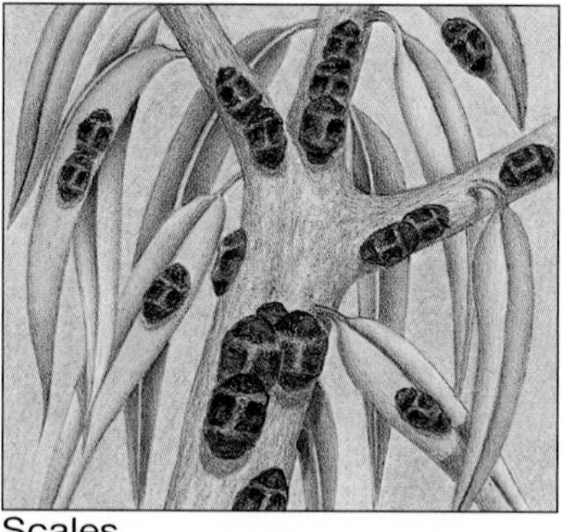

Scales

Whiteflies

Slugs, snails

APHIDS. Soft-bodied insects from 1/16 to 1/4 inch long, aphids can be found in a range of colors from black to pink to white and pale green. They usually cluster on the new growth of perennials, roses, and woody plants. Adults and nymphs damage plants by sucking out sap. In small numbers, aphids do little harm. But they can rapidly build up to destructive numbers.

MITES. These tiny, eight-legged pests of black, green, red, or yellow are nearly invisible. They destroy plants by sucking juices from the leaves, giving the leaves a stippled, bleached, or spotted appearance. Mites are most severe in hot, dry weather.

SCALES appear as clusters of crusty, waxy, or smooth bumps on leaves, branches, and the bark of trees and shrubs. There are numerous types varying in size, color, and shape. They spend most of their lives immobile, sucking nutrients out of their plant victims. Black sooty mold fungus may cover parts of the plant; heavily infested twigs and branches may die. Scales have protective coatings that help prevent sprays from affecting them; young crawlers are most susceptible to sprays.

WHITEFLIES. These tiny, winged insects appear in large numbers, typically on the undersides of leaves; vegetables and ornamental plants are favorites. Both the adults and wingless, transparent nymphs suck sap from plants. Affected leaves may be stippled yellow and covered by black sooty mold fungus. When the infested plants are disturbed (by humans, pets, or the elements), whiteflies scatter.

SLUGS AND SNAILS are mollusks, not insects. Snails have brown shells; slugs do not. Slugs come in many colors and sizes, but the 1-inch-long brown garden slugs are the most common pest of plants. Both snails and slugs rasp large, ragged holes in leaves and flowers.

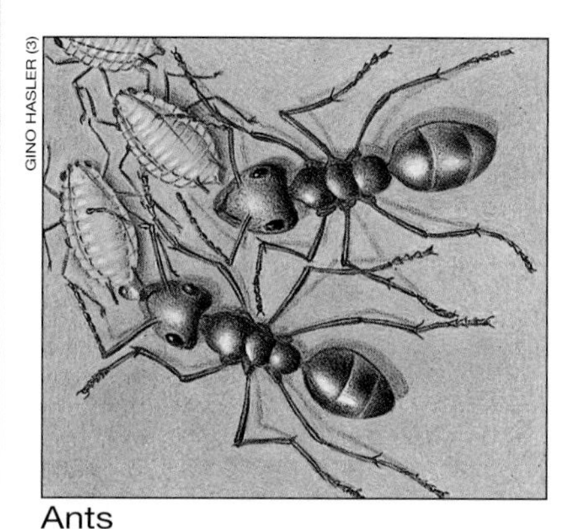
GINO HASLER (3)

Ants

Powdery mildews

Blackspot, rusts

ANTS. These small six-legged insects live in colonies in the soil, under rocks, or in crevices between paving stones. Newly hatched ants have wings; adults can be distinguished from termites by their narrow midsections. Ants encourage and protect sap-sucking insects such as aphids and scales.

POWDERY MILDEWS. These white or gray fungi attack the foliage and flowers of many kinds of plants, turning infected leaves yellowish green to brown, and stunting and distorting new growth. Mildews thrive when cool nights are followed by warm days—particularly in fall.

BLACKSPOT, fringed black spots on leaves, is a fungus disease that can defoliate a plant.

RUSTS are orange-yellow to rusty brown fungi that attack many plants. Powdery pustules appear on the undersides of leaves, but the first sign of infestation may be a yellow mottling on the upper leaf surfaces.

Have you seen beneficial insects in your garden?

Ladybugs, green lacewings, and other "good" bugs can keep aphids, scales, and other "bad" bugs in check. Encourage them to stay in the garden by setting out plants to feed and shelter them.

Mix annuals and perennials that bloom over a long season. Favorites of beneficial insects include coreopsis, corn cockle, cosmos, sweet alyssum, and yarrow. Avoid indiscriminate spraying, which kills good bugs too.

One way to be certain that beneficial insects inhabit your garden is to introduce them yourself. You can order them by mail or on-line from the following sources.

Harmony Farm Supply, Box 460, Graton, CA 95444; (707) 823-9125 or www.harmonyfarm.com.

Natural Pest Controls, 8864 Little Creek Dr., Orangevale, CA 95662; (916) 726-0855 or www.natpestco.com.

Peaceful Valley Farm Supply, Box 2209, Grass Valley, CA 95945; (888) 784-1722 or www.groworganic.com.

EARTH-FRIENDLY ALTERNATIVES

PROBLEM	SOLUTIONS Commercial product	 Home remedy
Aphids Mites Scales Whiteflies	Insecticidal soap spray (such as Safer), horticultural oil	Homemade soap spray (add ½ teaspoon mild dish soap and 1 teaspoon cooking oil to a 1-quart sprayer filled with water)
Slugs, snails	Iron phosphate (Sluggo, Escar-Go!, Worry Free Slug and Snail), copper barrier	Handpick at night Apply coarse sand
Ants	Citrus spray (Orange Guard, Bugs 'R' Gone), boric acid baits, sticky barrier (Tanglefoot)	Caulk entry cracks Wipe up trails with soap and water
Powdery mildews (PM) Blackspot (B) Rusts (R)	Lime sulfur (calcium polysulfide) PM, R	Baking soda spray (mix 1 teaspoon baking soda and 1 teaspoon horticultural oil in 1 gallon of water) B, PM

STEVEN GUNTHER ILLUSTRATIONS BY SUSAN CARLSON

HYACINTH BEAN VINE cloaks tepee at the Fullerton Arboretum's Children's Garden.

A vine-covered tepee

Create your own secret hideaway

BY SHARON COHOON WITH LAUREN BONAR SWEZEY

The leafy tepee shown here is the favorite hideout in the Children's Garden at the Fullerton Arboretum in Fullerton, California. "Kids want to get inside the minute they spot it," says Joyce Toy, an arboretum volunteer. Grown-ups need a bit of coaxing. "They hang back until their kids pull them in, but they always come out smiling," says Toy.

Be adult about it, we say. Admit you can picture yourself under these leaves—sitting cross-legged, palms up, practicing your mantra perhaps. Or in a beach chair with Puccini on the headset and a perfectly shaken martini in hand. Or curled up in an Indian blanket, sneaking a snooze. Pick your pleasure. Don't you deserve your own tepee?

Hyacinth bean vine (*Dolichos lablab*), a prolific bloomer, covers this tepee formed by bamboo poles. For other fast-growing annual vines to try, see the facing page.

Bean Tepee

TIME: About 1 hour
COST: About $20
MATERIALS

- Six bamboo poles, 8 feet long and 1 inch in diameter (thicker timber bamboo was used for the tepees shown)
- About 60 feet of sturdy hemp or jute twine
- About 80 feet of 1/8- or 7/32-inch-diameter clothesline rope
- Annual vine seeds (20–25)

TEPEE ASSEMBLY

1. Line up poles on the ground, alternating thick and thin ends. Pull the second, fourth, and sixth poles to the right, until only 2 feet of the six poles overlap in the center.

2. Fasten a 10-foot length of twine to the first pole by tying a sturdy hitch or knot. Loop the twine loosely around all six poles three or four times, allowing some space between poles (**A**).

3. Secure the loops by binding twine

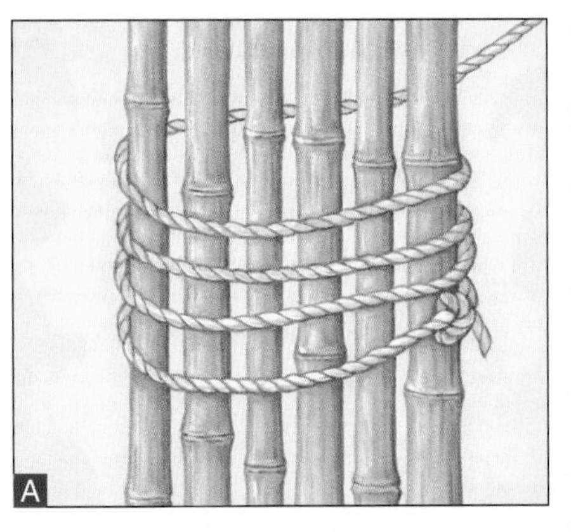

SUSAN CARLSON

around them at right angles, weaving it between the poles (**B**). At the final pole, fasten off the binding by tying a hitch or knot.

4. Pick up the poles and spread them in a circle—arranging poles so that the six thin ends cross at the top—to form a tepee with a diameter of about 8 feet. Allow extra space between the two poles that will frame the entrance.

SUPPORT GRID

1. String clothesline horizontally around the tepee at 1-foot intervals, except at the entrance (**C**). As you work, wrap the clothesline once around each pole and give it a tug to take up the slack.

2. To complete the grid, attach two or three lengths of twine vertically to the clothesline between pairs of poles.

PLANTING

Sow seeds directly in well-cultivated soil around the circumference of the tepee, except in front of the entrance. Train the vines up the poles and the twine. It takes about two months for the vines to cover the whole tepee.

DEIDRA WALPOLE

CLIMBING NASTURTIUMS ascend the 8-foot-tall poles that form this tepee at St. Paul's preschool in Tustin, California. Place logs or kid-size chairs inside the tepee for seating, or line the ground inside with a water-resistant mat.

Four pretty, fast vines to try

•**Climbing nasturtium** bears flowers in shades of orange to gold among broad green leaves.

•**Hyacinth bean vine** forms a dense green canopy; lots of violet, sweet pea–like flowers are followed by ornamental purple pods.

•**Morning glory** (*Ipomoea tricolor*) 'Heavenly Blue' bears 3- to 4-inch blue flowers; 'Pearly Gates' produces white ones of the same size. Note: Seeds are poisonous if ingested.

•**Scarlet runner bean** (*Phaseolus coccineus*) bears bright scarlet blossoms that develop into tasty shelling beans.

Seeds for these vines are available at nurseries, or you can order from Park Seed Co.; (800) 845-3369 or www.parkseed.com. ◆

VERBENA RIGIDA, 'Irene' trailing rosemary, 'Firebird' penstemon, and other intensely colored, heat-loving perennials tumble from a 3-foot-tall rock retaining wall at the base of a steep slope. Below it, a gravel path meanders past perennial beds.

Flower power

Maile Arnold transformed a dry slope in Sonoma County into a dazzling flower garden. Her secret? Choosing the right plants

BY LAUREN BONAR SWEZEY
PHOTOGRAPHS BY SAXON HOLT

"If you're given lemons, you make lemonade," says landscape designer Maile Arnold of the "lemon of a backyard" that she turned into the beautiful garden pictured here. Steep slopes and hard soil made this site in Glen Ellen, California, a gardening challenge. Construction cuts had left a hot, dry bank of white volcanic soil so desolate that it looked like a moonscape.

By choosing flowering plants that tolerate heat, aridity, and poor soil, Arnold was able to create a dazzling "lemonade" garden for owners Helen and Tom McCrea. She knew it would take a while for new plantings to cover the bare slope, so to draw attention away from it, she created drama at its base. First she formed a dry stone wall 6 feet out from the slope's base and filled it with fertile soil. Then she planted it with long-blooming perennials in vibrant purples and reds to echo the house's colorful Mexican interior.

On the upper slope, Arnold experimented with a range of plants to see which ones would tolerate the heat and poor soil. The proven winners? Lavender, Mexican bush sage, *Myoporum parvifolium* 'Putah Creek', red-leaf Japanese barberry, rosemary, and smoke tree. She planted figs and persimmon trees at the bottom of the slope so their

Color makers for hot, dry gardens

Blooming plants

CROWN-PINK (*Lychnis coronaria*). White-foliage perennial or annual to 2½ feet tall with magenta flowers. All *Sunset* zones.

DAYLILY (*Hemerocallis* hybrids). Deciduous or evergreen perennials with grassy leaves and flowers in many colors; grow 1–6 feet tall, depending on variety. All zones.

'FIREBIRD' PENSTEMON. Bushy, upright perennial 2 to 4 feet tall with red tubular flowers. All zones (annual in cold climates).

'IRENE' TRAILING ROSEMARY. Trailing evergreen bush 1 foot tall by 6 feet wide with violet blue flowers. Zones 4–24.

MEXICAN BUSH SAGE (*Salvia leucantha*). Shrubby perennial to 4 feet tall with velvety purple flower spikes.

MYOPORUM PARVIFOLIUM 'PUTAH CREEK'. Ground cover to 3 inches tall with bright green leaves and white flowers in summer. Zones 8–9, 12–16, 18–24.

'PROVENCE' LAVENDER. Upright, rounded evergreen shrub 2 to 3 feet tall with highly fragrant flowers. Zones 4–24.

ROSES. 'Altissimo', red climber; 'Joseph's Coat', multicolored (red, pink, orange, and yellow) climber. All zones.

SALVIA GREGGII. Evergreen shrub to 4 feet tall with small flowers from spring through fall. Comes in many colors. Zones 8–24.

SANTA BARBARA DAISY. Spreading evergreen perennial ground cover, 1 foot tall by 4 to 6 feet across. White or pinkish daisies appear all year in mild climates. Reseeds. Zones: 8, 9, 12–24.

'SISKIYOU PINK' GAURA. Long-blooming perennial to 3½ feet tall with rose pink flowers. All zones.

TEUCRIUM FRUTICANS 'AZUREUM'. Evergreen shrub 4 feet tall by 5 feet wide with dark blue flowers and gray leaves. Zones 4–24.

VERBENA BONARIENSIS. Airy, branching perennial with 3- to 6-foot-tall flowering stems topped with purple flowers. Reseeds. Zones 8–24.

V. RIGIDA. Spreading perennial 1 to 1½ feet tall by 3 to 4 feet wide with rough, dark green leaves. Lilac to purple-blue flowers appear on tall, stiff stems from summer through fall. All zones.

Foliage plants

RED-LEAF JAPANESE BARBERRY (*Berberis thunbergii* 'Atropurpurea'). Graceful, deciduous shrub 4 to 6 feet tall with bronzy red to purplish foliage all summer. All zones.

SMOKE TREE (*Cotinus coggygria*). Deciduous shrub or tree to 25 feet tall with green leaves that turn red in fall and smokelike flowers. 'Royal Purple' has purple leaves. All zones. ◆

RIGHT: Pink-flowered lychnis mingles with 'Siskiyou Pink' gaura and Santa Barbara daisy. BELOW: A flawless 'Cranberry Baby' daylily rises above a mound of Santa Barbara daisy.

canopies will eventually provide some shade and screening.

Throughout the rest of the backyard, Arnold planted informal, irregularly shaped beds with billowy perennials. Each bed contains an accent plant, such as a tree or rose, and is surrounded by grass and gravel paths made from decomposed granite.

Two years after planting, the garden is awash with colorful blooms from spring through fall. "The hot, bright, difficult place is now soft and beautiful," says Arnold.

DESIGN: Maile Arnold, Sebastopol, CA (707/823-1373).

Passionate about plants

A Bolinas plant lover keeps her enthusiasm for collecting in check with a few simple rules

BY LAUREN BONAR SWEZEY

Terry Camiccia is a plant collector. Her garden in Bolinas, California, overflows with an amazing assortment of plants gathered from friends, relatives, and nurseries throughout California. "I call it friendship through flowers," she says. But unlike most collectors' gardens, hers isn't a mishmash of exotic species. Terry understands how to combine textures and colors in borders and island beds, and she accents her garden carefully with trellises and garden art. The pictures on these pages show how plants and structures work together to tame her exuberance for collecting.

"When I first started gardening, I was so excited, I wanted one of everything," she says. "But I soon discovered it's hard to make all of those plants look like they're married." Visits to Italian Renaissance gardens and six years of studying ikebana flower arranging taught her a valuable lesson: Simplicity is key.

Terry's first adventure in gardening was with vegetables, thanks to her Italian grandfather's influence. Tiring of seeing bare ground in winter, she turned her

SAXON HOLT (2)

LIGHT PINK 'CÉCILE BRUNNER' rose climbs around a circle trellis made by Ralph Camiccia (top). The trellis was constructed by cutting out the center of an old fence and framing it with metal. Another metal trellis, covered with grapes, arches over the gravel path leading to the back deck, repeating the line formed by the rose trellis. Above: Terry Camiccia in her garden.

Terry's design tips

■ **Blend foliage color the way you do flower color.** Terry starts with the foliage of one plant—yellowish green *Scleranthus biflorus,* for instance—then selects additional plants with harmonizing colors. In one bed, she combined it with yellow and green leaves of 'Golden Rain' rosemary and bright yellow 'Limemound' spiraea.

■ **Repeat forms.** Err on the side of simplicity. Edge a path or patio with low-mounding plants of differing foliage colors. Use pyramidal dwarf conifers to duplicate shapes of garden art nearby, as shown in the photograph at top left.

■ **Naturalize rocks.** Create rock outcroppings. Partially bury the rocks to mimic the way they look in nature.

■ **Use trellises and arbors.** These sculptural elements give form to the garden and add whimsy. Put two arching trellises side by side as shown in the photograph on the facing page. Train grapevines over one, and roses, such as climbing 'Cécile Brunner', over the other.

■ **Have fun with pruning.** Allow some plants to grow naturally, but don't be afraid to experiment. Terry stripped the lower leaves off black bamboo so she could see through it and shaped other shrubs so she could see over them. But her most creative pruning has been her sculptured shrubs—boxwood clipped into doughnut shapes, for example.

SAXON HOLT (3)

LIMESTONE COLUMNS embedded with 225-million-year-old fossils (top) form the focal point of Terry Camiccia's "green room," where lumpy-looking *Scleranthus* and lime thyme creep over rocks (center). Ralph Camiccia's handmade copper bench is adorned with flowers, so it "looks like it's growing," explains Terry. A gazing ball sits on a metal foxglove plant. 'Helene von Stein' large-leafed lamb's ears grows around it.

vegetable beds into flower beds. That's when she started collecting cuttings, roots, and seeds from her friends' plants. Her first flowering plant was a valerian cutting from her great-grandfather. "Now it's happily reseeded everywhere," she says. Other "friendship" plants include a lacy-leafed bleeding heart from a 90-year-old gardener and a hydrangea from her adopted mom, Madeline. "I can look at the garden and tell you where every plant came from," she says.

Terry's husband, Ralph, a metal artist, played an important role in the garden's development; his sculptural trellises, arbors, and bench accent the plantings and help divide the garden into "rooms." "The structures give the garden oomph," Terry says.

Even though space is at a premium now, Terry continues to collect plants from friends and nurseries ("I can't help myself") and saves them in her "plant bank"—a lath house filled with container plants for future projects. ◆

JACK DYKINGA

YELLOW SIERRA SUNDROPS and magenta four o'clocks bloom in the new Moth Garden at the Arizona–Sonora Desert Museum in Tucson. For details, see page 140.

May

DEIDRA WALPOLE

Ivy geraniums, trumpet vines, and pink 'Bermuda's Kathleen' rose (center) echo the rosy hues of this used-brick terrace.

Mystery rose is the star of this patio

'Bermuda's Kathleen' pairs well with other shrubs and perennials

■ "I love growing roses that Charles Darwin could have sniffed, or Teddy Roosevelt might have worn in his lapel," says Sharon Milder. So in some ways, mysterious 'Bermuda's Kathleen', the big, pink shrub rose gracing her backyard patio (pictured above), is a surprisingly undocumented choice. Rosarians know that Bermuda roses were brought to the island by Europeans, but not much more about them has been proved.

Milder knows a few other things about 'Bermuda's Kathleen', though. It's easy to grow—"an ideal coastal rose," she says. "No mildew, no rust—about as carefree as roses get." It's also big. "I keep it at 5 or 6 feet tall with an annual winter pruning, but it would like to be bigger." And its small, plentiful flowers are pure delight. The single blooms open blush pink and gradually deepen to dark pink, creating a charming multicolored effect. This mutable habit, she says, makes the rose an interesting companion for *Brunfelsia pauciflora* 'Floribunda', a shrub that exhibits purple, lavender, and white flowers simultaneously.

Other good companions for Milder's star rose include (clockwise from bottom left) a pale pink zonal geranium in a pot, deep rose royal trumpet vine (*Distictis* 'Rivers'), pink ivy geraniums, and pink-flowered true geraniums (*G. oxonianum* 'Claridge Druce'). Foliage plants in pots—variegated ivy and wall rockcress (*Arabis caucasica*)—provide a cooling counterpoint beside the table.

'Bermuda's Kathleen' is available from the Antique Rose Emporium. For a free catalog, call (800) 441-0002.

— Sharon Cohoon

Grand gazebo

JANET LOUGHREY

■ As an architectural anchor to a grove of trees and shrubs or as a shady place to sit, there's nothing like a gazebo. But in the often rainy Pacific Northwest, these classic structures have another use: They can act as giant umbrellas, allowing people to sit outdoors any time when temperatures are mild.

James Britt and Jerry Heade of Milwaukie, Oregon, put a gazebo at the far corner of their brick patio. Based on an Asian design, it is 11 feet wide and made of cedar, which weathers handsomely. It comfortably seats four on teak benches. It's a spot to sit, or a place to set up a small table and serve dinner. Rhododendrons, hostas, and other lush greenery grow around it.

The gazebo was built from a kit (often sold at home and garden stores). If you're thinking about adding a gazebo to your garden, a good place to start is with *Sunset's* how-to book *Patio Roofs and Gazebos* (800/526-5111 or www.sunsetbooks.com). Filled with design ideas, plans, and construction techniques, it will help you select the style you want.

— *Steven R. Lorton*

CLIPPING

•**New book.** *The Tree and Shrub Finder: Choosing the Best Plants for Your Yard,* by Northern California resident Robert Kourik (Taunton Press, Newtown, CT, 2000; $27.95; 800/888-8286), helps you select the best plants for foliage, privacy, shade, windbreaks, and more. It also provides essential information on planting and care.

Now blooming in Federal Way

DAVID MCDONALD

■ Spring explodes this month at the Rhododendron Species Foundation gardens in Federal Way, Washington. Not only are the gardens blurs of blooms in every direction, but the lacy spring green of newly emerging leaves makes all that color look as though it's wrapped in green gauze.

The shrubs have never looked better. The foundation, started in 1964, moved to its present 22-acre site 10 years later. Its goals were to grow the largest collection of rhododendrons in the Western Hemisphere and to show visitors how handsome they can be in the landscape. RSF has accomplished both.

The breadth of the collection is amazing: 10,000 plants of 450 species come from Asia, North America, Europe, and Australia. The diminutive *R. radicans,* from Tibet, hugs the ground, its lavender, flat-faced flowers peering up like elves. The robust *R. hodgsonii,* from the Himalayas, has leaves that measure 12 to 18 inches long, purplish pink flowers, and startling silvery new growth.

Take time to linger in the gazebo at the top of the hill; this quiet, shady vantage point has a 360° view of the gardens.

In peak bloom months (March through May), RSF is open 10–4 daily, except Thursday. Admission costs $3.50, $2.50 students and seniors; children under 12 are admitted free but must be accompanied by an adult. To reach the gardens, take Interstate 5 to exit 143 and follow the signs less than 1 mile to the entrance. RSF also publishes a catalog of plants for sale. For details, contact (253) 927-6960, (253) 661-9377, or www.halcyon.com/rsf.

— *S.R.L.*

◀ A feast of flowers fills four buckets of varying sizes. A 5½-gallon bucket (on chair) contains white gauras, 'Cinnamon Red Hots' dianthus, yellow 'Goldmarie' bidens, 'Blue Bird' nemesias, annual phlox, and pink petunias. Three 4-gallon buckets each contain dianthus, brachycomes, helichrysum 'Baby Gold', marigolds, yellow pansies, and petunias.

Plant a country garden—in buckets

■ Change your planting containers, and your approach to planting may change. That's what happened recently at M&M Nursery in Orange, when designers planted seasonal color in galvanized tin buckets and tubs instead of the usual terra-cotta pots. The casual containers imposed their own style—clean, cheerful, carefree. Nursery staffers found themselves using annuals with stems longer than usual, combining colors with a freer hand, and producing more informal compositions. "The buckets look like you've just picked a bunch of flowers out of a country garden," says Ted Mayeda, the nursery's owner. "Customers love them." — *S.C.*

STEP-BY-STEP

1. Find a suitable bucket or tub, either new or used.
2. Drill drainage holes in the bottom, using a ½-inch metal drill bit; create at least three holes for a 12-quart bucket, six or more for a 5½-gallon tub.
3. Add potting soil to the bucket until it's about two-thirds full.
4. Move the bucket handle to the upright position; begin planting. For the breezy styles seen here, include some leggy plants like gauras, nemesias, and carnations, as well as middle-of-the-pot candidates such as annual phlox and marigolds. Then add edge-spillers like petunias.

DEIDRA WALPOLE (2)

▲ Galvanized tin bucket contains dianthus, at back, and scaevolas and annual phlox, in middle. Alyssums and rosy pink petunias edge the front.

Reno's arboretum comes of age

■ Like any good garden, Wilbur D. May Arboretum and Botanical Garden might have looked a bit raw at the beginning. But now, at age 15, this fast-maturing landscape is becoming the garden its designers had envisioned.

Visit this month and you'll see just how much can be accomplished in your garden in the space of a few years. At 20 to 25 feet, the oaks of the arboretum's Kleiner Grove are tall enough now to give the garden meaningful shade and depth. Forsythia and quince are working their spring magic in Burke Garden, with snowballs and lilacs not far behind. The wildflower garden is ablaze with flax, lupines, and early penstemons.

Beautiful as it is, this landscape has its challenges. Just a couple of blocks north of downtown, it sits on a 12-acre plot that gets only about 7 inches of precipitation per year. But Reno's climate is relatively mild for Nevada, and the gardens are nursed along by a dedicated horticulture staff that knows how to blend native and exotic plants for maximum impact using minimum water.

This time of year, you may find staff members tending the arboretum's MacDonald Rock Garden (shown at right), where evening primroses, globe mallows, lewisias, and pussy toes jostle for space with three colors of wild buckwheat. Or they might be working with the bearded irises, wisteria, crabapples, and flowering magnolias in Kristen's Garden.

CONNIE COLEMAN   LEFT: DAVID WINGER

May Arboretum, at 1502 Washington Street in Rancho San Rafael Regional Park, is open 8 to sundown daily. Admission is free; call (775) 785-4153 or visit www.maycenter.com for information.

— Jim McCausland

BOOKSHELF

Van Houtte spiraea

Unthirsty plants for Rocky Mountain gardens

A longtime advocate of waterwise gardening, Jim Knopf has just produced a companion guide to his widely popular *Xeriscape Flower Gardener* (Johnson Books, Boulder, CO, 1991; $19; 303/443-9766). *Waterwise Landscaping with Trees, Shrubs & Vines* (Chamisa Books, Boulder, 1999; $24.95; order from BookMasters, 800/247-6553) focuses on woody plants but also discusses ground covers and drought-tolerant lawn grasses. Here's a sampling of Knopf's proven performers.

■ PLUCKY SHRUBS

Fern bush (*Chamaebatiaria millefolium*). A native beauty with clusters of white flowers in midsummer. **Van Houtte spiraea** (*S. vanhouttei*). This shrub can stand up to chinook winds, shade, and high elevations. White flowers in spring, orange foliage in fall.

■ TERRIFIC TREES

Cockspur hawthorn (*Crataegus crus-galli* 'Inermis'). Versatile small tree that has it all: glossy green leaves, showy white flowers, autumn orange, and red berries in winter. **Bur oak** (*Quercus macrocarpa*). At maturity, bur oak is a stately, spreading shade tree.

■ EVERGREEN TREES

Piñon (*Pinus edulis*). With age, assumes irregular, picturesque forms. **Austrian black pine** (*P. nigra*). A large tree, adaptable to high altitudes, hot and cool summers.

■ ROBUST VINES

Sweet autumn clematis (*C. dioscoreifolia*). This large, vigorous vine bears masses of white flowers in fall. **Trumpet honeysuckle** (*Lonicera sempervirens*). This semievergreen vine produces tubular red flowers irresistible to hummingbirds. — *Marcia Tatroe*

Nurturing nature

■ It's hard to tell where nature leaves off and the plantings begin in this garden in Grand Junction, Colorado, next to Colorado National Monument.

Rugged terrain creates a dramatic backdrop, while indigenous plants such as evening primrose, Indian paintbrush, Indian rice grass, juniper, piñon, rabbitbrush, sage, and saltbush trail down the park's slope and into the garden beds.

Reintroduced native and locally adapted plants—which include desert four o'clock (*Mirabilis multiflora*), mountain mahogany (*Cercocarpus montanus*), perennial blue flax, Rocky Mountain white oak, yarrow, and yucca—mingle in the yard.

"When we designed and built the house and garden beds, we did our best to preserve as much of the natural terrain and vegetation as possible," says owner Virginia Beemer. Her botanist daughter, Jennifer Straus, helped select plants.

At the front of the house, blue cranesbill, chocolate flower, hummingbird flower, and clusters of penstemon (*P. eatonii, P. grandiflorus, P. palmeri,* and *P. strictus*), with underplantings of sedum, soapwort, and speedwell, flank a natural wash.

CHARLES MANN

Native and adapted plants merge on a garden berm. Clockwise from upper left, golden currant, sagebrush, apache plume, and goldenrain tree create the backbone. Perennial flowers (desert four o'clock, salvia, paperflower, blue flax, dwarf Shasta daisy, coreopsis) add splashes of color.

At the end of the wash, blooms of blanket flower, coreopsis, dwarf Shasta daisy, penstemon, perennial blue flax, salvia, and yarrow sparkle like gems against silvery green native shrubs. An arbor wrapped in table-grape vines connects the front garden to a side-yard patio.

— Pam Cornelison

Citrus in a bottomless pot

■ Many citrus varieties grow happily for years in containers. But they do appreciate plenty of room around their roots, and they demand good drainage. Here's a way to have both, while showing them off to best advantage: Grow them in big, bottomless pots.

The 'Valencia' orange pictured at right is one of several potted citrus trees used as accents behind a succulent border in a garden designed by Jeff Powers. The bottom of each pot has been carefully sawed away, giving the citrus the best of both worlds. Thanks to its elevated position, the tree gets the good drainage citrus requires, yet its longest roots are unrestricted. Each pot even has its own built-in drip-irrigation system and an uplighting fixture. Small succulents grow at the base of each tree. — *S.C.*

CLAIRE CURRAN

Desert rockery: Ideas from Las Vegas

■ Though salty desert soil and alpine plants are completely incompatible, a rock garden in the Southwest is not a far-fetched notion, says Peter Duncombe, administrator of the Las Vegas Valley Water District's Desert Demonstration Gardens. Substitute cliff rose (*Cowania mexicana stansburiana*), two kinds of desert zinnia (*Z. acerosa* and *Z. grandiflora*), angel's hair (*Artemisia schmidtiana*), and other Western natives for the alpines, he says, and rock gardening becomes an ideal landscaping style for the desert. The demonstration gardens' new rock garden, shown below, proves Duncombe's point.

Most desert plants thrive among rocks—in fact, wild, boulder-strewn washes and rocky slopes are their preferred habitat. The plants benefit from the root protection the stones provide and the extra water that collects beneath them.

Using boulders generously in the landscape also reduces the amount of ground that needs to be planted and watered. More traditional hardscape materials like flagstone and pavers do this, too, but boulders also support life. Lizards find shelter among them, and butterflies, insects, and birds sip the water that collects in the rocks' natural indentations.

Visit and see for yourself. The rock garden is in peak bloom now, as are the cottage, native wash, and terraced gardens.

Desert Demonstration Gardens is at 3701 W. Alta Drive, just east of Valley View Boulevard in Las Vegas. It's open 8–5 daily except major holidays; admission is free. For more details, call (702) 258-3205. — *S.C.*

NORMAN A. PLATE

Purple *Verbena rigida,* white Blackfoot daisies, and yellow 'Moonshine' yarrow thrive in the Rock Garden. Also in bloom are desert zinnia, *Dalea capitata* 'Sierra Gold', fountain grass, cliff rose, and foothills palo verde.

DAVID WINGER

The word on clematis

■ Clematis *does* grow in Southern California. That's the message Edith Malek has been preaching since at least 1996, when she formed the American Clematis Society. I've seen enough healthy, handsome "clemmies" in her converts' gardens that by now I'm convinced she's right.

Malek's book, *American Clematis Society's Guide to Growing Clematis in the United States* (American Clematis Society, Irvine, CA, 1999; $19.99), should swell the ranks of "clematized" gardeners. According to Malek, the reason Southern California gardeners failed with this plant before was lack of information. "'Feet in the shade, head in the sun' is fine, but that's not all there is to know about clematis," she says. Amending the soil, adjusting pH, planting deeply, watering amply, and fertilizing correctly are all equally important. Her book addresses each of these issues and more in deliciously precise detail, and provides descriptions and photos of the 48 varieties she believes are best suited to American gardens. Many, including 'Ville de Lyon' (pictured at left), deep violet 'Lady Betty Balfour', white 'Marie Boisselot', velvety purple 'Polish Spirit', mauve-pink 'Proteus', and soft rosy purple 'Victoria', are especially good in Southern California.

The book is available at several specialty nurseries. Send a check for $26.44 to American Clematis Society, Box 17085, Irvine, CA 92623. Or order on-line from www.clematis.org.

— S.C.

CLIPPINGS

•**Trusty reference, newly revised.** After the *Sunset Western Garden Book*, one of the best references for Southern California gardeners is *Pat Welsh's Southern California Gardening.* Welsh has a completely revised edition, which now includes information on true geraniums, ornamental grasses, and other plants that were not in general use when her book was first published. *Chronicle Books, San Francisco, 2000; $24.95 paperback; 800/722-6657. — S.C.*

BACK TO BASICS

THOMAS J. STORY

How to score a rootball. Ideally, plants grown in containers should have well-formed rootballs. But sometimes the roots are wrapped around the rootball. To encourage these circling roots to grow out into the surrounding soil after planting, knock the plant out of its can, score the sides of the rootball with a knife in four to six places, then make a cut across the bottom. Don't use this method for delicate-rooted plants such as bougainvilleas. — *L.B.S.*

MARK TURNER

In spring, azaleas in shades from crimson and pink to white splash this otherwise all-green woodland garden with vivid color.

The color of spring in the forest

■ Other than the Himalayas, the best place in the world to grow azaleas, rhododendrons, and woodland perennials must be the Pacific Northwest—a fact not lost on Darcie and Gary Cousins as they planned their Gig Harbor, Washington, garden 15 years ago. With garden space carved out between the house and the native firs and cedars, their site was exactly right for spring-flowering shrubs.

The evergreen rhododendrons and azaleas that grow along the garden's gently curving path shade out weeds below. Adjacent perennials and ground covers like blue ajugas, strawberries, and montbretias grow so densely that weeds have trouble competing.

The path is graveled to help keep weeds down and to keep guests and gardeners out of the mud when they stroll through the landscape during rainy months.

The Cousinses chose hardy evergreen azaleas, including the pink Kurume hybrid 'Sherwood Orchid', *Rhododendron mucronulatum* 'Delaware Valley White', pink 'Caroline Gable', and 'Hino Crimson' azaleas. All blend well with the taller, later-flowering rhododendrons behind them, and all are solid with color early every spring.

The Cousinses water with sprinklers on risers and feed plants with a complete fertilizer in early spring, before bloom begins.

—J.M.

SAXON HOLT (2)

Train a lacy, live umbrella

■ Virgil and Eady Wheatley of Santa Rosa, California wanted a shade maker, and they did not want to wait six to eight years for a tree to grow. So Virgil constructed an umbrella frame from poles, then planted a fast-growing potato vine (*Solanum jasminoides*) next to it. In just three years, the potato vine covered the frame to create a handsome live umbrella that fans out over a corner of the deck and blooms for at least eight months of the year.

Virgil, a retired engineer, was inspired by a rose arbor he saw at a nursery. First, he drilled a hole in the deck's wood planks to accommodate a pole 10 feet tall and 5 inches wide. He sank the pole through the hole in the deck, then bolted the pole to a beam on the deck's underside. To make the 12-foot-wide frame, he screwed together 3-inch-diameter tree stakes. The frame, bolted atop the pole, is supported by umbrella-like stays screwed into the center post.

Virgil planted the potato vine in the soil next to the deck, then trained it up the pole, which is about 2 feet from the railing.

The only maintenance the vine requires is an annual trim around the bottom of the canopy to keep it about 7 feet off the ground. — *L.B.S.*

A garden for moths

■ Sierra sundrops (*Calylophus hartwegii*), the plant with butter yellow flowers in the foreground of the photo on page 130, is symbiotic. So is the magenta four o'clock (*Mirabilis multiflora*) just behind it. Both plants need couriers to reproduce: Since neither plant can travel to find a mate, to set seed they depend on moths to carry pollen from the stamens of one flower to the stigma of another. In exchange for this service, the moths get to feast on the flowers' nectar.

These plants are part of the new Moth Garden, one of seven Pollination Gardens at the Arizona–Sonora Desert Museum in Tucson.

In the Butterfly Garden, a portion of which is visible in the background of the photo, are plants such as trailing lantana (*L. montevidensis*), Goodding's verbena (*V. gooddingii*), and Texas ebony tree (*Pithecellobium flexicaule*) that rely on butterflies for pollination assistance. In the other gardens, plants attract specific seasonal pollinators including bees, bats, hummingbirds, and yucca moths.

Demonstrating how dependent plants—and people—are on pollinators is the main mission of the Pollination Gardens. Planting flowers like these in home gardens can help keep pollinators around.

The museum, at 2021 N. Kinney Road, is open 7:30–5 daily March through September, 8:30–5 the rest of the year. June through September, it will stay open until 10 on Saturdays, when you might be able to see moths that work the night shift. For more information, call (520) 883-1380.

— *S.C.*

CLIPPINGS

•Ultimate rose reference. *Botanica's Roses: The Encyclopedia of Roses,* by Peter Beales et al. (Welcome Rain Publisher, New York, 1999; $59.95; 212/967-7961), contains color photos and descriptions of some 4,000 roses and more.

•Sneezeless gardening. Allergy sufferers will appreciate *Allergy-Free Gardening: The Revolutionary Approach to Healthy Landscaping,* by Thomas Leo Ogren (Ten Speed Press, Berkeley, 2000; $19.95; 800/841-2665), which describes plants' allergy-causing potential.

Pacific Northwest Checklist

PLANTING

✔ ANNUALS. As soon as danger of frost is past in your area, sow or plant annuals. If you start plants from nursery seedlings, harden them off first by placing the containers under a tree or on a sheltered patio for a few days, then plant out. Good choices for sun include cosmos, geraniums, marigolds, petunias, and zinnias; for light shade, try begonias, coleus, impatiens, and violets.

✔ FUCHSIAS. Among the best plants for large patio pots and hanging baskets, fuchsias also thrive in garden beds. Most like partial shade or (near the coast) full sun. Pinch them back as they grow to make them bushy, and feed and water regularly through the summer for optimum bloom.

✔ HERBS. Plant all kinds now from nursery containers. Basil is a perfect companion for tomatoes, both in the kitchen and in the garden bed, while thyme is the best candidate for a crack-filling ground cover. Plant mint where it gets plenty of water, and chives, oregano, and parsley as edgings.

✔ SUMMER BULBS. Callas and cannas (usually sold as pot plants by this time of year), dahlias, and gladiolus are among the summer bulbs that can be planted now. All like full sun; callas and cannas appreciate places that get plenty of water.

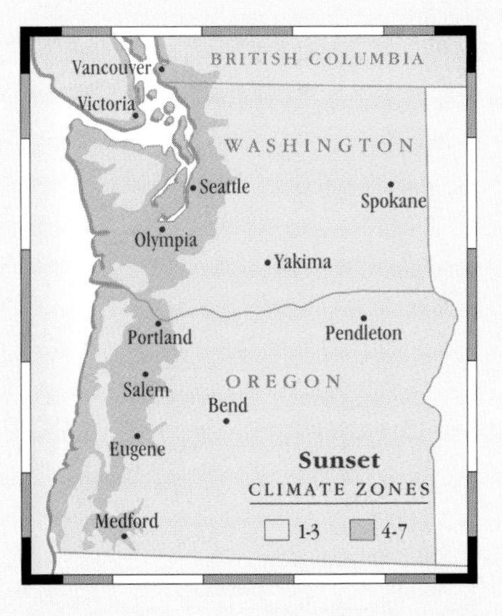

✔ VEGETABLES. All warm-season veggies can go into the ground as soon as danger of frost is past. Try beans and corn from seed; eggplant, peppers, and tomatoes from plants; and cucumbers, melons, and squash from seed (if your area has a long, warm growing season) or transplants (if it doesn't).

MAINTENANCE

✔ CONTROL APHIDS. Spray them off with a jet of water from the hose whenever you see them. In bad cases, control with insecticidal soap.

✔ DISPATCH SLUGS. Baby vegetables and flowers are their favorite munchies. Go on slug patrol at night with a flashlight and a machete, cutting them in half as you see them, or put out a pet-safe bait like iron phosphate. If you use a methaldehyde-based bait, put it where pets and birds can't get to it, since it can kill or sicken them.

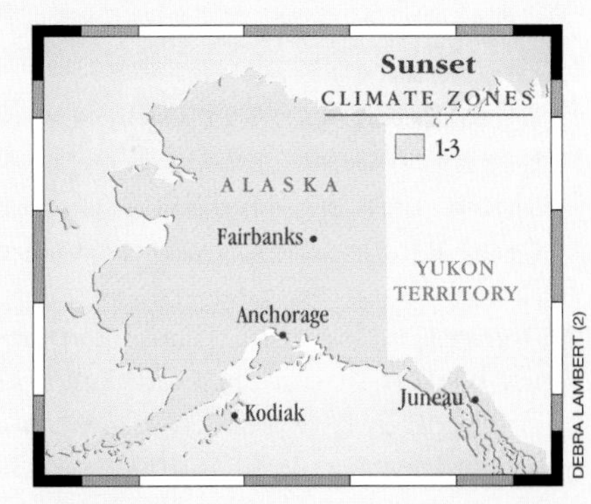

DEBRA LAMBERT (2)

✔ FERTILIZE LAWNS. Apply 1 pound of nitrogen per 1,000 square feet of lawn early this month and water it in well. This is the last major feeding your lawn should get until late summer.

✔ FERTILIZE PLANTS. You have three choices: Dig controlled-release organic fertilizer into the backfill for everything you plant this month, apply liquid fertilizer two weeks after planting, or scatter complete granular fertilizer over the root zones two weeks after planting and scratch it in with a rake. Then water well. ◆

WHAT TO DO IN YOUR GARDEN IN MAY

Northern California Checklist

PLANTING

✔ DAHLIAS AND BEGONIAS. Both flowers provide a long season of bloom that lasts into fall. Choose dwarf dahlias, dahlias with plate-size flowers that grow 6 feet tall, or tuberous begonias—either hanging types for baskets or upright kinds for pots and beds. Both flowers grow in vibrant or soft pastel colors. Antonelli Brothers Begonia Gardens sells them by mail (888/423-4664), on-line (www.infopoint.com/sc/market/antnelli), or at the nursery in Santa Cruz (2545 Capitola Rd.).

✔ DWARF LAVENDER. Good compact varieties for the front of a border include 'Baby Blue' (dark purple, 12–14 in. tall), 'Grosso' (violet, 18 in. tall), 'Hidcote Compact' (violet-blue, 12–15 in. tall), and 'Jean Davis' (soft pink, 16 in. tall). All are available from Woodside Gardens (call or fax 800/473-1152, or visit www.woodsidegardens.com).

✔ PLANT FOR PERMANENCE. Now is a good time to plant almost any perennial, shrub, tree, or vine. (Zones 1–2: Wait until last frost to set out tender plants.) When shopping at the nursery, look for plants that have good leaf color (green leaves should be a deep green, not pale yellow) and attractive form. Check container bottoms to make sure roots aren't growing out of them, which may mean plants are rootbound. Plants should also have been well watered.

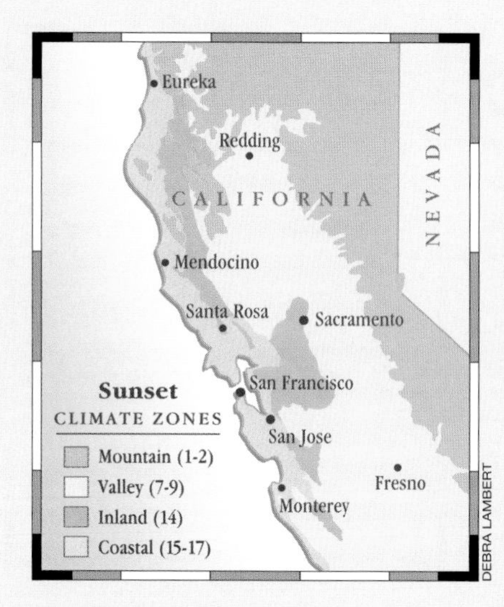

✔ PLANTS FOR MOM. Perfume and pajamas are nice, but chances are, Mom would rather have a beautiful blooming gift plant for Mother's Day. Good bets include azaleas, callas, hydrangeas, miniature roses, moth orchids, and Oriental lilies.

✔ SPECIALTY VEGETABLES AND HERBS. Gardeners now have a much wider selection of seedlings to choose from, thanks to several growers who offer European and specialty vegetables and herbs through local nurseries. You can also order organic seedlings by mail or on-line from the Natural Gardening Company (707/766-9303 or www.naturalgardening.com) or from Seeds of Change (888/762-7333 or www.seedsofchange.com).

MAINTENANCE

✔ AERATE COMPACTED LAWNS. To help improve air and water movement to the grass roots, aerate lawns that get a lot of use and have compacted soil. You can rent an aerator from an equipment supply store (look in the yellow pages under Rental Service Stores & Yards). Rake up the cores and top-dress with mulch. If you haven't fertilized recently, apply a lawn fertilizer and water in well.

✔ PREPARE FOR FROSTS. Zones 1–2: At highest elevations, frosts can occur in late spring and early summer, so have stakes and plastic sheeting handy to protect plants.

✔ PRUNE COLD-CLIMATE PLANTS. Zones 1–2: To promote compact growth, tip-prune evergreens. Remove winter-killed branches from euonymus, juniper, pyracantha, and yew. Finish pruning roses. Prune spring-flowering shrubs after they bloom. ◆

WHAT TO DO IN YOUR GARDEN IN MAY

Southern California Checklist

PLANTING

✔ SUBTROPICALS. This is the ideal time to plant avocados, bananas, cherimoyas, citrus, guavas, mangoes, and other tropical and subtropical fruits appropriate for your area. They'll have all summer to grow before hardening off for winter. For the same reason, late spring is also a good time to add subtropical ornamentals such as bougainvilleas, clerodendrums, ginger, hibiscus, justicias, and mandevillas. Subtropical flowering trees—like bauhinias, chorisias, crape myrtles, and tabebuias—can also be planted now.

✔ SUBTROPICAL LAWNS. Plant Bermuda grass from sod, plugs, or seed; plant St. Augustine from sod or plugs.

✔ SUMMER COLOR. Fill bare spots in the garden with summer-bedding plants. Heat lovers like ageratums, amaranths, dianthus, marigolds, petunias, portulacas, salvias, verbenas, vincas, and zinnias are the best choices for sunny spots. Or start cleomes, cosmos, sunflowers, or zinnias from seed. In the shade, plant bedding begonias, caladiums, coleus, and impatiens.

✔ VEGETABLES. Sow seeds of beans, corn, cucumbers, melons, pumpkins, and summer and winter squash. Set out basil, cucumber, eggplant, melon, pepper, and tomato plants. In the low desert (zone 13), plant Jerusalem artichokes, okra, peppers, and sweet potatoes.

MAINTENANCE

✔ FEED AZALEAS AND CAMELLIAS. After they finish blooming, fertilize azaleas and camellias to support strong growth and heavy set of flower buds for next year. Use an acid-type fertilizer formulated for these plants at half-strength. Feed camellias two or three times more at six- to eight-week intervals during their growth period.

✔ PINCH BACK CHRYSANTHEMUMS. For an ample supply of flowers and attractive, bushy plants, continue pinching back the growing tips of chrysanthemums through July.

✔ PRUNE SUBTROPICALS. Remove frost-damaged growth. Cut back leggy hibiscus, lantanas, princess flowers, and other overgrown subtropicals by as much as half.

✔ RENEW MULCH. To keep roots cool, preserve soil moisture, and discourage weeds, renew mulch around trees, shrubs, and established perennials. Use compost, shredded bark, or wood chips. To prevent diseases, leave several inches clear around the bases of plants.

✔ THIN FRUIT. Thin fruit on apple, nectarine, peach, and other deciduous fruit trees to allow 6 inches of branch space between fruit.

PEST AND WEED CONTROL

✔ MANAGE PESTS. Control aphids, mites, and whiteflies with a strong spray of water from the hose; concentrate on the backs of leaves, where the pests hide. Or try insecticidal soap or horticultural oil. Trap, handpick, or bait for snails and slugs. Apply copper strips to trunks of citrus trees to keep snails and slugs from climbing into branches. Copper strips also protect sturdy-stemmed shrubs like camellias. ◆

Mountain Checklist

PLANNING AND PLANTING

✔ ANNUALS. At high elevations, start annuals after May 1 for transplanting after June 1.

✔ FLOWERS. This month, nurseries are filled with annuals and perennials. Shop early to get the best selection. Cover annual seedlings with floating row covers for frost protection on cold nights. Remove covers when danger of frost is past.

✔ ORNAMENTALS. Trees, shrubs, roses, evergreens, vines, and perennials can go into the garden now. Use floating row covers for the first two weeks to shade plants imported from coastal nurseries. To help prevent transplant shock, apply liquid fertilizer diluted to half the recommended amount.

✔ SUMMER BULBS. When the soil starts to warm up, plant bulbs of calla lilies, cannas, dahlias, freesias, gladiolus, ixias, and lilies-of-the-valley.

MAINTENANCE

✔ CARE FOR LAWNS. Begin watering and mowing lawns as needed. Mow using the highest setting, ideally 2 to 3 inches. Never cut off more than a third of the grass blade at one time or the lawn may scorch. Leave grass clippings on the lawn to provide extra nutrients and organic matter. To keep the clippings short so they don't mat down on the lawn, use a mulching mower or mow more frequently.

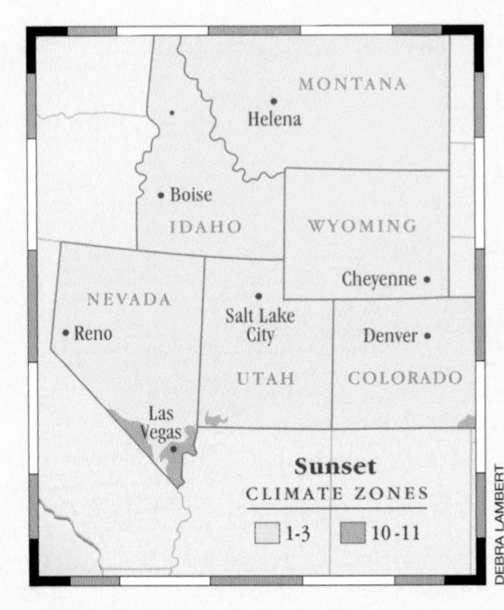

✔ CHECK IRRIGATION SYSTEMS. Clean and flush irrigation systems, checking emitters, sprinklers, and filters to make sure everything works.

✔ DIVIDE BULBS. After the leaves turn brown, dig up crowded clumps of tulips and daffodils and gently pull the bulbs apart. Before replanting, till 2 inches of compost and a handful of complete fertilizer into the soil.

✔ FERTILIZE. Feed spring-flowering shrubs after they bloom, and start a monthly fertilizing program for long-blooming perennials, annuals, and container plants. By midmonth, apply fertilizer to bluegrass lawns. Feed roses this month and then once a month through mid-August.

✔ HARVEST COOL-SEASON VEGETABLES. Pick before they go to seed. When the bed is empty, get ready for planting summer vegetables by tilling in 2 inches of compost.

✔ STAKE PERENNIALS. When plants are 6 to 8 inches tall, place peony hoops or other supporting devices over them.

PEST CONTROL

✔ BLAST APHIDS. Pay particular attention to tender new growth. If you notice an infestation of aphids starting to develop, blast them off with a strong spray of water, or spray with insecticidal soap.

✔ OYSTER SHELL SCALE. These pests are nearly impossible to kill except in their newly hatched crawler stage, which usually occurs around Memorial Day. Check infested plants weekly with a magnifying glass, and if you find pinhead-size hatchlings, spray with summer horticultural oil. — *M.T.* ◆

Southwest Checklist

PLANTING

✔ FLOWERS. Zones 1 (Taos) and 2 (Santa Fe): Set out ageratum, celosia, coreopsis, cosmos, four o'clock, gaillardia, globe amaranth, gloriosa daisy, lisianthus, nicotiana, portulaca, salvia, strawflower, vinca rosea (*Catharanthus roseus*), and zinnia after all danger of frost is past, or plant when available and protect with row covers. Zones 10–13: Early in the month, set out ageratum, coreopsis, cosmos, four o'clock, gaillardia, lantana, salvia, and zinnia.

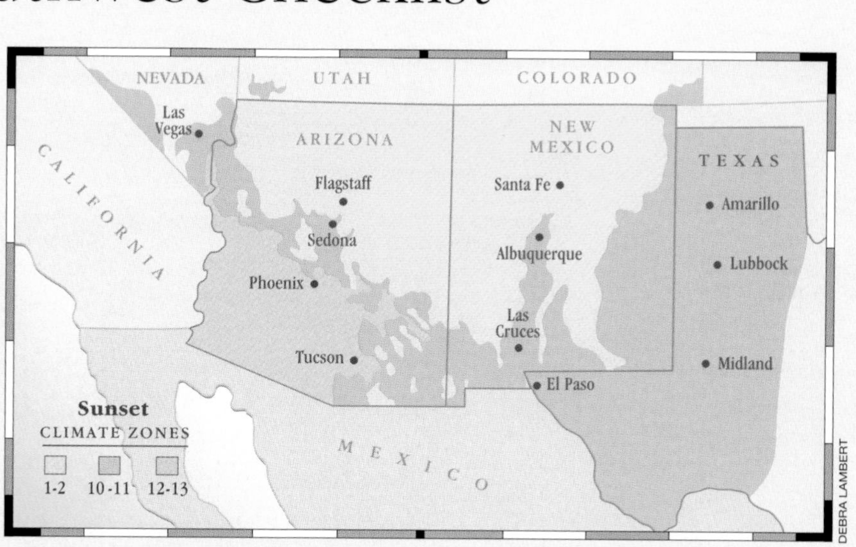

DEBRA LAMBERT

✔ LAWNS. Zones 1–2, 10 (Albuquerque): Early in the month, plant or overseed with bluegrass, fescue, rye, or a mixture of these. Zones 12 (Tucson), 13 (Phoenix): Plant or seed Bermuda or improved buffalo grass.

✔ PERENNIALS. Zones 1–2, 10, 11 (Las Vegas): Plant trees, shrubs, vines, and ground covers from containers this month. Divide mums and keep pinching back until July. Zones 12–13: Try two recent summer-flowering introductions: *Ageratum corymbosum,* a perennial that is attractive to butterflies, and scarlet bush (*Hamelia patens*), a shrub or small tree with orange to scarlet or crimson flowers.

✔ SUMMER BULBS. Zones 1–2: Plant caladium, dahlia, and elephant's ear (*Colocasia esculenta*). Zones 10–11: Plant acidanthera (*Gladiolus callianthus*), canna, dahlia, daylily, gladiolus, montbretia, and tiger flower (*Tigridia*), as well as those listed above. Zones 12–13: Plant crinum and zephyranthes.

✔ VEGETABLES. Zones 1–2: When soil temperature is above 60°, plant beans, corn, cucumber, okra, pumpkin, sweet potato, and watermelon. Sow seed of eggplant, melon, pepper, squash, and tomato to set out when danger of frost is past. Zone 10: Set out beans, corn, cucumber, melon, pumpkin, radish, Southern peas, and tomato. Zone 11: Plant the above vegetables early in May, okra and sweet potato through midmonth. Zones 12–13: Set out eggplant, okra, pepper, summer squash, sweet potato, and watermelon.

MAINTENANCE

✔ CARE FOR ROSES. Zones 11–13: As heat starts to take its toll, water plants deeply, then mulch and fertilize.

✔ INCREASE WATERING. When 100° days arrive, check plants (especially newly planted ones) at least twice a day for wilting. Increase watering for all plants, even cactus and succulents.

✔ MULCH PLANTS. Mulch everything in the garden to cool roots, keep weeds down, and hold in soil moisture.

— *Mary Irish* ◆

California

foothills fantasy

around the west in 21 pots

Each Western state inspires its own container plantings

BY KATHLEEN N. BRENZEL
PHOTOS BY NORMAN A. PLATE

From coastal chaparral to alpine meadows, the West is blessed with an awe-inspiring range of landscapes and vegetations. Taking our cue from nature, we set out to design container gardens that celebrate the diverse beauty of our 13 Western states. We turned to the West's magnificent landscapes—deserts, wildflower meadows, rain forests, prairies, and beaches—and to the plants that grow there. We visited nurseries to see which plants combined well for color and texture. We gathered pots. Then we planted.

Each design starts with an anchor plant—a small tree, shrub, or ornamental grass. Around the anchors, we arranged annuals and perennials, some of them native to the state. Whenever possible, we included state flowers (to learn which ones can grow in pots, see page 155). Most of the plants came from

4-inch pots, some from gallon cans.

The largest pots are really like small gardens; display them singly on a patio. The smaller pots are handsome in groups of two or three. With a few exceptions, most of these plantings can grow anywhere in the West. (Desert gardeners might find growing vine maples a bit of a stretch, and gardeners up north would find tender tropicals a challenge to keep growing beyond one season without a greenhouse.) For pot sources, see page 153.

California

FOOTHILLS FANTASY (PAGES 146–147)

Grasses, reminiscent of those that cover California's foothills in late summer, fill these large containers. Their billowy forms and earthy hues contrast pleasingly with the cool blue flowers and rich green foliage planted around them. Sun or light shade. Design: Tisa Watts.

Plants. Left: Fountain grass (*Pennisetum setaceum* 'Rubrum'), with *Salvia sinaloensis* (deep blue flowers). Center: Lavender (*Lavandula angustifolia* 'Goodwin Creek Grey'), with blue-flowered *Convolvulus mauritanicus*. Right: *Miscanthus sinensis* 'Yaku Jima', with *Scaevola aemula* 'New Wonder'.

Pots. Glascrete bowls; 24 inches wide, 22 inches deep.

HOLLYWOOD HEAT

Hot colors that stand up to bright sun keep this pot sizzling with blooms all season. A splash of blue-purple tempers the visual heat. Sun. Design: Bud Stuckey.

Plants. Left: Purple bougainvillea, with yellow *Lantana montevidensis* 'Spreading Sunshine', orange-and-yellow *L.m.* 'Radiation', and sea lavender (*Limonium perezii*). Right: 'Radiation' lantana.

Pots. Ocher-stained terra-cotta: tall pot 20 inches wide, 16 inches deep; small pot 14 inches wide, 10½ inches deep.

California
hollywood heat

Washington

PUGET SOUND'S PRIDE

Plants that thrive in woodland gardens west of the Cascades fill this large container. The rhododendron blooms in late May, followed by astilbe's feathery pink-coral blooms in June and July. Choose a dwarf rhododendron such as 'Bow Bells' or 'Ginny Gee'. Or buy a young, small rhododendron in a 1- or 2-gallon can and grow it in the pot for a season before transplanting to the garden. Filtered shade.

Plants. Vine maple (*Acer circinatum*), with *Astilbe japonica* 'Bonn', leatherleaf fern (*Rumohra adiantiformis*), and rhododendron.

Pot. Glazed ceramic; 20 inches wide, 20 inches deep.

Alaska

NORTHERN LIGHTS

The state flower of Alaska (forget-me-not) and the ferns and conifers that grow in southeastern Alaska's lower elevations inspired this arrangement. A flat gray stone, reminiscent of those found in glacial rivers, adds a finishing touch behind the forget-me-nots. Sun to partial shade.

Plants. Dwarf hinoki false cypress (*Chamaecyparis obtusa* 'Verdoni'), with deep blue *Anchusa capensis* 'Blue Angel', sky blue forget-me-not (*Myosotis sylvatica*), Johnny-jump-up (*Viola tricolor*), Scotch moss (*Sagina subulata*), and tassel fern (*Polystichum setosum*).

Pot. Glazed stoneware; 13 inches wide, 12½ inches deep.

Oregon

COLUMBIA GORGEOUS

Oregon grape, the state flower, determined the companion plants in this pot. The grape's young leaves are bronze, and scattered mature leaves are red. To echo this coloring, we chose plants with purplish bronze foliage, and New Guinea impatiens with red-orange blooms. For a softer, more natural look ("reminiscent of the plant life in Columbia Gorge," says Steve Lorton, *Sunset's* Northwest bureau chief), substitute rosy maidenhair fern (*Adiantum hispidulum* 'Rosy Maid') for the impa-

Washington
puget sound's pride

Alaska
northern lights

Oregon
columbia gorgeous

tiens. Part shade.

Plants. Oregon grape (*Mahonia aquifolium*), with dwarf Japanese barberry (*Berberis thunbergii* 'Crimson Pygmy'), *Heuchera* 'Palace Purple', New Guinea impatiens, and Scotch moss (*Sagina subulata*).

Pot. Glazed ceramic; 16 inches wide, 15 inches deep.

Hawaii

SOUTH PACIFIC SUNRISE

Big-leafed foliage and flamboyant flowers fill three huge pots that have a scorched, volcanic look. Most of the plants thrive in sun and heat (tuberous begonias do better in filtered shade). Cannas and tuberous begonias go dormant for winter. Sun. Design: Bud Stuckey.

Plants. Left: *Canna* 'Tropicanna', with 'Flame Orange' tuberous begonia, flowering maple (*Abutilon* 'Vesuvius'), and trailing *Lotus maculatus* 'Gold Flash'. Center: Shell ginger (*Alpinia zerumbet* 'Variegata'), with *Acorus gramineus*, bromeliads, and croton (*Codiaeum variegatum*). Right: *Cordyline stricta*, with *Canna* 'Tropicanna' and 'Pink Splendor' mirror plant (*Coprosma repens*).

Pots. Left: Nubby ceramic; about 24 inches wide, 22 inches deep. Center: Stained terra-cotta; 18 inches wide, 18 inches deep. Right: Stained terra-cotta; 19 inches wide, 20 inches deep.

Nevada

SAGEBRUSH AND SILVER

Rugged red earth backed by snow-capped mountains inspired this pot's color theme. The artemisia's lacy gray foliage stays beautiful for a season; after that, the plant quickly outgrows the confines of a pot. Dusty miller (*Senecio cineraria*) makes a handsome and slower-growing substitute. Sun.

Plants. *Artemisia* 'Powis Castle', with *Carex buchananii* (straw-colored sedge) and *Zinnia angustifolia* 'Crystal White'.

Pot. Chocolate-colored stoneware; 14 inches wide, 12 inches deep.

Arizona

DESERT IN BLOOM

The Southwest deserts are filled with plants both soft (wildflowers) and sculptural (yuccas and cactus). This pot combines the two, with the bloomers surrounding a single yucca.

Plants. *Yucca whipplei* (from a 1-gallon can), with red *Salvia greggii* and *purple Verbena peruviana* (from 4-inch pots).

Pot. Glazed terra-cotta with Southwest motif; 16 inches wide, 13 inches deep.

New Mexico

SANTA FE SALSA

Bright primary colors—the sassy shades of folk-art wood carvings and fiesta decorations—inspired these two pots filled to bursting with summer-blooming annuals and perennials. The pots' textured surfaces and rosy tones blend well with sandstone pavers. Most of the plants are from 4-inch nursery pots. Sun.

Plants. Center: *Gaura lindheimeri,* with blue *Salvia farinacea,* creeping zinnia (*Sanvitalia procumbens*), dwarf French marigold (*Tagetes patula*), light blue *Lobelia erinus,* 'Profusion Orange' zinnia, red *Geum chiloense* 'Mrs. Bradshaw', and red *Salvia greggii.* Right: Carmine *Cosmos bipinnatus* Sonata series, with blue *Lobelia erinus* and dwarf French marigold.

Pots. Center: Tapered jar; 13 inches wide, 18 inches deep. Right: Textured ceramic; 15 inches wide, 7½ inches deep.

New Mexico
santa fe salsa

How to plant a big pot

1. Fill the pot with just enough fast-draining potting soil that the top of the biggest plant's rootball will nest about 2 inches below the pot rim (**A**). Tamp the soil to firm it.
2. Mix a granular fertilizer into the potting soil, according to package directions (**B**).
3. Arrange nursery plants, still in their pots, inside the big container. Once the design is set, remove the plants from the big pot. Knock the anchor plant from its nursery container, rough up its rootball, and position it in the big pot, putting its best side forward (**C**).
4. Fill the pot with potting soil (up to the top of the biggest rootball).
5. Plant smaller flowering and foliage plants, packing soil firmly around rootballs (**D**). Put trailers (ferns and mosses) near pot edges.
6. Give the planting a thorough watering.

NORM PLATE (4)

Tips

- Choose plants to coordinate with the container and the setting.
- Choose a few permanent plants, such as low-growing shrubs, as anchors, then fill in around them with colorful annuals and perennials. Make sure the plants have the same needs for exposure, water, and fertilizer.
- Put the pot where you want it, then plant. Big containers are heavy, especially when filled with soil.
- Permanent plants such as woody shrubs can grow two to three years in pots.

Idaho

WILDERNESS RIVERS

Spilling conifers and earth-toned flowers capture the spirit of Idaho with its many lakes, rivers, and forests. The tall golden Hinoki false cypress echoes the yellow of the yarrow, while the bronze-red flowers of coreopsis and gaillardia add punch and contrast handsomely with the shore pine's cool blue needles. Sun. Design: Bud Stuckey.

Plants. Left: Hinoki false cypress (*Chamaecyparis obtusa* 'Aurea'), with *Coreopsis tinctoria,* gaillardia, gloriosa daisy (*Rudbeckia hirta*), shore pine (*Pinus contorta*), and yarrow (*Achillea*). Right: Shore pine, with baby's tears (*Soleirolia soleirolii*) and gloriosa daisy.

Pots. Left: Green-stained terra-cotta, 19½ inches wide (inside), 14 inches deep. Right: Stone bowl, 14½ inches wide (inside), 7 inches deep.

Utah

ALPINE SNOW

Snow-covered peaks, and the alpine plants that grow there, inspired this arrangement. Rosy-tipped *Sedum spurium* 'Dragon's Blood' rambles around a single firecracker penstemon (from a 4-inch pot), with a silvery lamb's ears shimmering in front. Sun.

Plants. Red firecracker penstemon, with lamb's ears (*Stachys byzantina*) and 'Dragon's Blood' sedum.

Pot. Stone bowl; 14¼ inches wide (inside), 7 inches deep.

Wyoming

PRAIRIE FLOWERS

Grassy prairies strewn with wildflowers are captured in this composition. Sun.

Plants. Mexican feather grass (*Stipa tenuissima*), with blanket flower (*Gaillardia grandiflora*), blue fescue (*Festuca ovina* 'Glauca'), gloriosa daisy (*Rudbeckia hirta*), and purple coneflower (*Echinacea purpurea*).

Pot. Stone bowl; 18 inches wide (inside), 9 inches deep.

Colorado

ROCKY MOUNTAIN HIGH (PAGE 154)

Wispy blooms in pale lavender, blue, and yellow recall shaded woodlands where columbines grow wild.

Plants. Chinese meadow rue (*Thalictrum dipterocarpum*), with blue-and-white Johnny-jump-up (*Viola tricolor*), perennial blue flax (*Linum perenne*). Dalmatian bellflower (*Campanula muralis*), and sweet woodruff (*Galium odoratum*).

Pot. Glazed stoneware; 14 inches wide (top), 14 inches deep.

Montana

BIG SKY MEADOW (PAGE 154)

Grasses and perennials with golden and purple blooms are combined with snowy white Shasta daisies to give this planting the look of a flower-strewn meadow in summer.

Plants. Blue oat grass (*Helictotrichon sempervirens*), with *Coreopsis verticillata* 'Moonbeam', dwarf Shasta daisy, *Verbascum bombyciferum* 'Arctic Summer', *Verbena bonariensis,* and yellow yarrow (*Achillea* 'Moonshine').

Pot. Deep green glazed stoneware; 18 inches wide (inside top), 17 inches deep.

All pots purchased at nurseries, except the following: "Aquarian" Glascrete planters (California; pages 146–147) from Dura Art Stone; (800) 821-1120. Brighton hypertufa bowls (Utah, Wyoming) from Stonesmith Garden Vessels, Cambria, CA; (805) 927-0827. Glazed and textured terra-cotta pot (Arizona), chocolate-colored nubby ceramic pot (Hawaii, left), ceramic pot (Nevada), tapered jar (New Mexico), and glazed ceramic pots (Oregon, Washington), all from AW Pottery, Oakland, CA; (510) 533-3900.

Colorado
rocky mountain high
Montana
big sky meadow

Can you grow your state flower in a pot?

1. Alaska: Forget-me-not (*Myosotis*). Beautiful in pots; use as an underplanting for Iceland poppies or a pink rose such as 'The Fairy'. Plants are easy from seed and 4-inch pots.

2. Arizona: Saguaro blossom. Plants don't start blooming until too old (about 60 years) and too big for pots. But they are slow-growing; young ones can live for years in pots.

3. California: California poppy (*Eschscholzia californica*). Can get rangy in pots and doesn't transplant well (sow seed directly). Nurseries sell potted garden varieties in colors other than orange. Bright yellow *E. caespitosa* is smaller (to 6 inches) and does well in pots.

4. Colorado: Rocky Mountain columbine (*Aquilegia caerulea*). Most beautiful in mixed plantings in woodland gardens, but fine in pots for short-lived display. Ferny foliage is susceptible to mildew and starts to look ratty after flowers fade. Many outstanding long-spurred strains in a variety of flower colors.

5. Hawaii: *Hibiscus brackenridgei.* A large, rugged-looking plant with bright yellow flowers. Hard to find. Compact forms of *H. rosa-sinensis* are better suited to pots; plant them singly and give them room (pots at least 18 inches wide and deep).

6. Idaho: Wild mock orange (*Philadelphus lewisii*). Deciduous shrubs with fragrant white flowers are too big for pots. Try a dwarf kind, such as *P. virginalis* 'Dwarf Snowflake'.

7. Montana: Bitterroot (*Lewisia rediviva*). Its short leaves usually die back before the appearance of rose or white flowers, which look like single water lilies. Other species (*L. cotyledon, L. tweedyi*) are especially showy. Handsome in stone troughs with gravel mulch. Needs excellent drainage; let roots dry out a little between waterings.

8. Nevada: Big sagebrush (*Artemisia tridentata*). This wild-looking plant with insignificant flowers, native to the Great Plains, is not suited to life in pots. Choose other members of the artemisia clan, such as *A.* 'Powis Castle', for instance. Give them big pots, and pinch tips regularly.

9. New Mexico: *Yucca glauca.* Young plants of this and some other species are fine in pots; buy them small—in gallon cans—and grow them in mixed plantings for a year or two.

10. Oregon: Oregon grape (*Mahonia aquifolium*). Most kinds grow too big; try 'Compacta' (to 2 ft. tall) and give it room to spread, or grow young plants (1-gallon size) of taller mahonias for a season before moving them out into the garden.

11. Utah: Sego lily (*Calochortus nuttallii*). These beautiful little white flowers with lilac or purple markings grow from bulbs that can be difficult to find and need more than ordinary care. Check mail-order suppliers of rare bulbs. Lift bulbs after spring bloom and allow them to dry out in summer.

12. Washington: Rhododendron. Try low-growers such as 'Bow Bells' (4 ft. tall) and 'Ginny Gee' (2 ft. tall). After several years in large containers, plant them out in the garden.

13. Wyoming: Indian paintbrush (*Castilleja linariaefolia*). Spectacular red to orange blooms on big, wild plants (2–5 ft. tall). Tricky and slow to grow from seed in pots. Try a red-flowered penstemon, such as *P. eatonii* or *P. gloxinoides* 'Firebird', instead. ◆

ILLUSTRATION BY LOIS LOVEJOY

The front garden's color scheme includes pink from a David Austin rose ('Mary Rose') and *Salvia greggii;* blue from delphiniums, statice, and English lavender; and yellow from African daisies (*Arctotis*) and bidens (baby snapdragons or nemesia could be substituted). White potato vine (*Solanum jasminoides*) along the roof line adds sparkle.

The ultimate spring garden

Sheri Workman's plantings are works of art. Here's how she combines roses, perennials, and annuals for spectacular beds and borders

BY SHARON COHOON
PHOTOGRAPHS BY STEVEN GUNTHER

■ How do you turn a typical suburban yard—mostly lawn with narrow flower beds around the edges—into the star of a popular spring garden tour? Sheri Workman of Fountain Valley, California, has the answers. And the results, shown here, are an encyclopedia of ideas for novice and experienced gardeners alike.

1. Give yourself room to create and run wild

By tripling the 3-foot depth of planting beds at the perimeter of the property, Workman gained room to replace a single row of shrubs and a small ruffle of bedding plants with climbing and shrub roses, lots of perennials, blocks of tall and short annuals, and a fringe of handsome foliage plants. The bigger canvas also gave her room to paint broader strokes and experiment with more complex color harmonies. "Visitors to the garden come around the corner and gasp," she says.

2. Give the garden structure

Shrub roses such as 'Graham Thomas' and 'Mutabilis' are the backbone of Workman's bigger, better border. "Nothing provides more flowers over a longer period than roses," Workman says. "That's why they were my starting point." Most of them are planted across the middle of the border, close enough to snip stems for bouquets but far enough back to leave space in front for lower-growing perennials and annuals.

Between the shrub roses and the property line grow tall flowering shrubs such as *Salvia guaranitica* and climbing roses such as 'Sombreuil'. For most of the year, flowers completely camouflage a block wall behind the border.

Workman deliberately leaves blocks of the border empty for showy

The backyard explodes with color. LEFT: A green-and-white *Helichrysum petiolare* 'Variegatum', deep pink 'International Herald Tribune' and 'Mutabilis' roses, multicolored linaria, and bright orange geum above purple verbena. In the background are red Jupiter's beards, dark purple clematis, and lavender Virginian stock. RIGHT: Orange geum picks up peach tones of 'Mutabilis' rose. Purple verbena and linaria and lavender-and-white 'Waverly' salvia grow in front.

annuals. Tall exclamation points such as delphiniums are planted near the back, with "fluffy stuff" like linaria and Virginian stock (*Malcolmia maritima*) placed closer toward the front. In late summer, dahlias and sunflowers replace the delphiniums.

3. Choose core colors, then play around

Though the beds and borders include every shade in the rainbow, the basic colors are pink and blue. Most of the pink comes from the roses, but perennials such as alstroemeria, Jupiter's beard (*Centranthus ruber,* also called red valerian), and rose campion (*Lychnis coronaria*) contribute. In late spring and early summer, delphiniums provide most of the blue. Summer through fall, salvias take over.

Workman also uses a lot of red-violet, a blend of her two major colors. Examples are 'Polish Spirit' clematis and purple verbena.

Yellow, white, and orange play roles in her borders as well, but she makes sure they remain accents. "As long as the pinks and blues predominate, you can get away with it," she says. Last year was the first time she was brave enough to include orange flowers, "but now I really like them."

Workman achieved perfect harmony as much by playing as by planning. "Most of life has to be organized," she says. "Gardening is the one place where it's safe to experiment."

4. Add focal points and final touches

Since the garden doesn't have much in the way of architectural details, ornaments are used to draw the eye to and through the garden. The frog in the picture above left, though small in comparison with the size of the border, is positioned to pull you into the scene visually and make you wonder what is

Plan shows how the gently curving border wraps the lawn. A gazebo sits at the upper left.

MIMI OSBORNE

beyond the curve of flowers.

At another point, a stone birdbath makes you stop and applaud the high-voltage combination of a rose-and-peach 'Mutabilis' rose, lavender-and-white 'Waverly' salvia, orange geum, purple verbena, and yellow-green Westringia 'Morning Light'.

How does she do it?

January and February, when East Coast gardeners are still daydreaming over their seed catalogs, are Workman's busiest months in the garden; she puts in about 18 hours a week during that period. Most of January is devoted to pruning back her 75 roses. In February she cuts back all of her perennials. (In climates that aren't as mild as Southern California's, cut back perennials when new basal growth appears.) Next Workman scratches a humus-based, all-purpose granular fertilizer into the soil around each of her plants. Finally she replenishes her mulch.

During March, when plants are growing slowly, she takes a well-deserved rest. Deadheading flowers, giving roses a little extra fertilizer, putting in summer annuals, and other light chores give her excuses to putter, but none of these tasks are hard labor. (Mulch and dense planting keep weeds at bay, and pest and disease problems are rare in her garden.) In late fall, Workman transplants her delphiniums and other cool-season annuals.

Careful soil preparation is the secret to her healthy plants. When Workman tripled the size of her beds, she spaded up the soil to a depth of 2 feet, then rotary-tilled a "truckload" of soil amendments—composted redwood, peat moss, perlite, bone meal, and gypsum—and a granular fertilizer into the soil to lighten and enrich it. "It was a ton of work," she says, "but the rewards made it all worthwhile." ◆

TOP: The 10-foot-deep border permits a richly detailed design: fuzzy lamb's ears in front; verbena, Shasta daisies, and linaria behind; pink shrub roses and towering delphiniums; and finally the white climbing rose 'Madame Alfred Carrière'. LEFT: Purple pansies in a wall-mounted terra-cotta pot stand out against a background of Boston ivy. RIGHT: Garden art is used to draw attention to particularly compatible plant combinations in the border. Here, a small concrete frog peeks out between yellow-green licorice plant (*Helichrysum petiolare* 'Variegatum') and darker green *Gaura lindheimeri* 'Siskiyou Pink'.

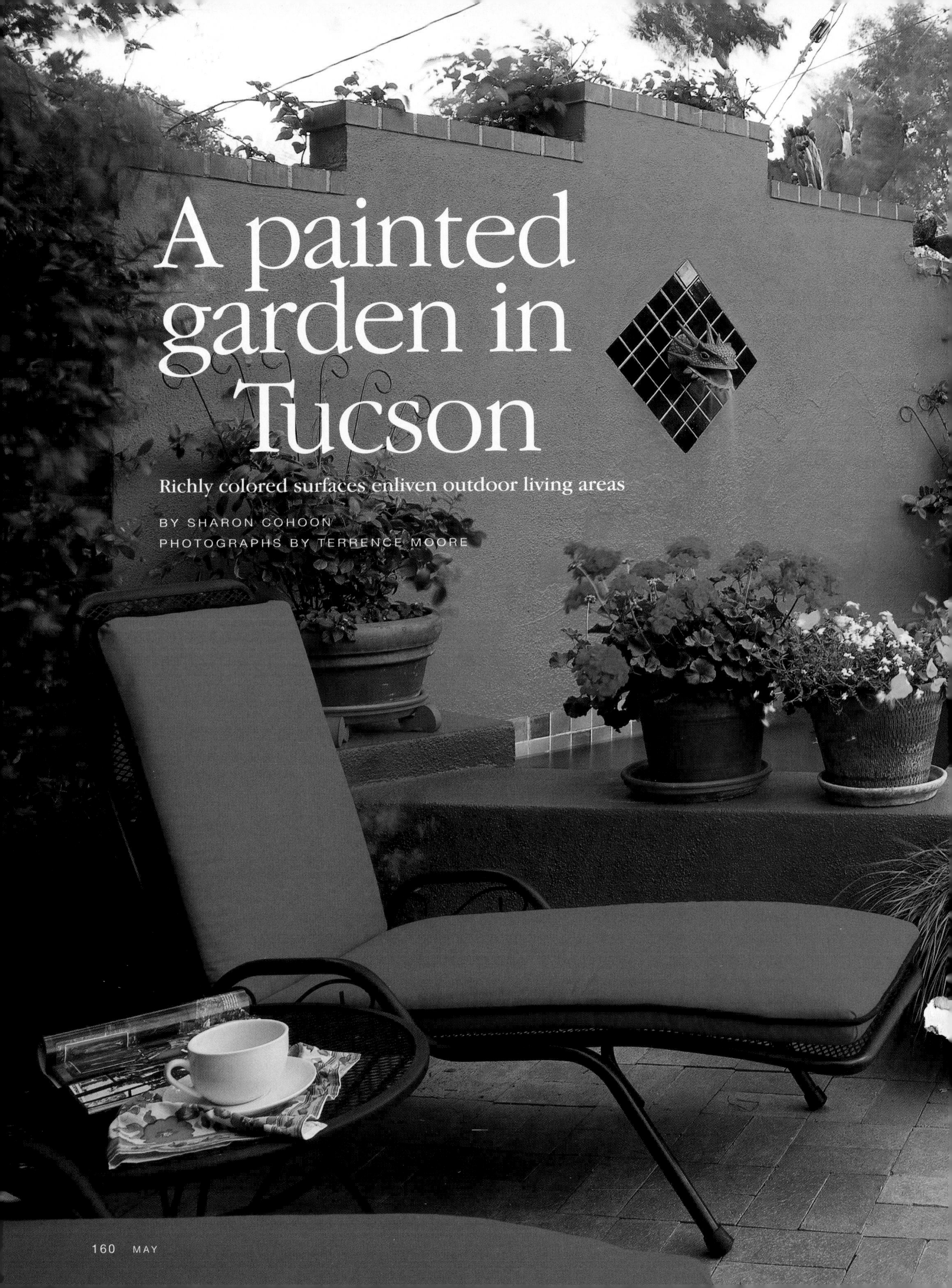

A painted garden in Tucson

Richly colored surfaces enliven outdoor living areas

BY SHARON COHOON
PHOTOGRAPHS BY TERRENCE MOORE

Richly colored walls, benches, and accessories stand up to blazing sunlight and act as a beautiful foil for potted plants.

An egg yolk–colored rocking chair, a red wicker basket, and a blue-and-white porcelain pot add dots of color to a shady corner. Pots hold petunias, nasturtiums, and other colorful annuals.

■ Bright pinks, dark reds, and deep purples: At first glance these colors may seem entirely too forceful to consider living with. But when Margaret West, a Tucson-based landscape designer, shows clients photographs of the colorful walls in John and Susan Harper's garden, the dazzling hues invite smiles. A visit to the garden turns those smiles into broad grins. Such fearless colors, chosen by Susan Harper, look friendly, playful, alive, and entirely at home under the Southwest sun.

Show some courage and use color boldly, Susan urges. "Pastels don't work in our hot climate—they just look exhausted." It takes deep, saturated colors like the ones shown here to stand up to the most blazing sunlight. Despite their intensity, these rich hues actually have a calming, cooling effect.

Susan's advice is not as risky as it sounds. "The great thing about paint is that no decision is ever final," she says. "If you don't like a color, you can always paint over it."

The Harpers weren't always so brave about color. It took a garden renovation to liberate them.

Renovation equals liberation

Originally a stucco wall cut across the garden, with an area behind the wall reserved for utilitarian items like a toolshed or clothesline or camper—a common practice when the tract house was built in the early 1950s. When the Harpers added a family room to the back of the house, however, the yard suddenly seemed cramped. So they decided to knock out the wall, build a new one farther back, and revamp the garden. They hired Margaret West to do the job.

West suggested leaving the existing lawn intact and creating several small patios around the perimeter of the property, where there were established shade trees. She also proposed raising sections of the new wall from 6 to 8 feet to screen out unwanted views of neighboring yards and adding built-in seating and a pool at these spots to make them focal points. The Harpers liked the plan, but Susan Harper worried that the garden would lack color, since the patios used up most of the plantable area. But when she and West came up with the idea of making the walls themselves bear the burden of color, she was sold.

Susan wanted to choose the paint herself. After ruling out midtones such as orchid ("horrible, glaring"), she settled on four shades: Drama Red from Behr Paints (Home Depot) and deep rose Monsignor, Purple Lake, and Woodlawn Green from Dunn-Edwards Paints. All are semigloss latex exterior paints. "Semigloss holds up better, and the gloss intensifies the colors," says Susan. The

MIMI OSBORNE

The new family room (at right in drawing) looks out on the area of the garden where the color is concentrated—the fountain and bench seating.

Pink, red, and purple walls meet harmoniously in this seating area. A large bronze sun sculpture adds further drama. Pots in front contain gold nasturtiums and purple pansies and petunias.

A wall-mounted ceramic pot, filled to overflowing with dazzling red-orange impatiens, is a brilliant complement to the purple wall.

block wall painted Woodlawn Green is mostly hidden by the foliage of podocarpus and other shrubs, but the dark paint almost makes the wall disappear.

Intense color shows off potted plants

The walls' saturated colors turned out to be a surprisingly good foil for potted plants. "I don't have to match plants to the wall colors, but everything seems to look good against them," Susan says. Pots are stuffed with bright flowers—scarlet geraniums, white and hot pink petunias, orange marigolds, blue lobelias. Her setting, in fact, was so conducive to container planting that she became quite skilled at combining plants. West noticed, and so did the clients she brought to visit. (At West's suggestion, Susan started a container plant business, called Flowerscapes.)

Colorful furnishings and beautiful details—including red-orange impatiens spilling from a yellow pot set into a purple wall and a purple horned toad lizard head protruding over a fountain—are like icing on the cake.

Playing with color in the garden seems to have intensified Susan's color cravings. Now she's tackling the indoors. "Maybe it's delayed rebellion," she says. "My mother had a white-on-white living room, and I always hated it." Now that she has started, Susan is fearless. "If I feel myself getting timid, I remind myself it's only paint and I can always change it." ◆

Happy Mother's Day bouquets

They're elegant and surprisingly easy to arrange

BY JILL SLATER AND LAUREN BONAR SWEZEY

A spring bouquet is sure to make a mother feel special, particularly one with a look as joyous as a flower garden. Two of ours start with handsome containers (stone, terra-cotta, or plastic; we used lightweight plastic urns that look like stone). The big bouquet at right is especially showy, but you need a lot of flowers to fill the 13-inch-diameter container; you can create a similar, smaller arrangement in a 6- to 8-inch vase. The third bouquet, a French twist, is shown on page 166.

Use the same technique to make the first two bouquets. Mentally divide the design into sections: middle, left, right, front, and back. Using flowers and foliage from your garden or the florist, add large clusters of a single flower to each section, starting in the middle with the tallest. We chose a palette of pink, cream, and rose with splashes of lime green; you can mix and match your own color favorites. On the facing page are directions for the big

Big-bouquet flowers

Anemones, white (30 stems)

French tulips, purple (7)

French tulips, cream (4)

Irises, white (5 stems)

Larkspurs, white (5 stems)

Larkspurs, pink (10 stems)

Heather, pink (20 stems)

Pussy willows (10 stems)

Roses, long-stemmed light pink (12)

Viburnums, green (5 stems)

Foliage: camellia, New Zealand flax, pittosporum, variegated ivy

NORMAN A. PLATE

1. Insert the tallest flowers, such as pussy willows and larkspurs, in the middle, varying their heights slightly.

2. Add shorter-stemmed flowers (such as roses and tulips) to the left and right sides of the arrangement, graduating their heights slightly.

3. Insert the shortest stems in front and back; then fill spaces between flowers with foliage. Finish by adding ivy around the pot's base.

bouquet. For a smaller version, set the moist florist's foam directly inside the vase and eliminate the chicken wire.

Big bouquet

TIME: About 1 hour
COST: $100 or more (depending on the number of flowers purchased or picked from the garden), plus container. Smaller bouquet is about $30, plus container.

MATERIALS AND TOOLS

- Three bricks of florist's foam
- Pruning shears or a florist's knife
- Waterproof papier-mâché liner to fit the container (12 inches wide by 5½ inches deep)
- Florist's tape
- 10-inch-square piece of chicken wire (for extra support)
- Wire clippers
- Pot or bricks (optional)
- Large container, 13 inches wide (inside)
- Flowers and foliage

DIRECTIONS

1. Saturate the florist's foam in a bucket of water. Cut one block of foam into 2-inch cubes and put the cubes into the waterproof liner. Place two bricks of soaked foam atop the cubes. The foam should rise about 1 inch above the top of the liner.
2. Secure the florist's foam to the liner with florist's tape.
3. For extra support, cut a strip of the chicken wire to fit the diameter of the liner, if necessary, and place it over the florist's foam. Secure the chicken wire to the liner by running florist's tape from one side of the chicken wire around the bottom of the liner to the other side of the chicken wire.
4. Set an upside-down pot or bricks in the bottom of the decorative container if necessary to make the edge of the liner even with the edge of the pot. Place the liner in the container.
5. Arrange flowers and foliage as shown above.

(Continued on page 166)

NORMAN A. PLATE (4)

The smaller version uses the same design principles and palette but fewer flowers—white anemones, pink tulips, heather, and foliage.

French twist

TIME: 20 minutes

COST: $20 to $35 (depending on the number of flowers purchased or picked from the garden), plus bowl

NOTE: Use flowers with long, strong stems, and mix blooms of different colors for a carefree, country-garden look. Add green foliage for accent and texture. Supplement garden flowers with florist's blooms as needed.

MATERIALS AND TOOLS

- Flowers, about 55 stems (we used yellow 'Peace' roses, peach spray roses, feverfew, orange-red bouvardias, blue brodiaeas, and others)
- Foliage or grasses (we used hypericum, oregano, zebra grass)
- Shears
- 2 yards of waxed floral string or raffia
- Scissors
- 2 yards of decorative ribbon
- Low, round bowl

DIRECTIONS

1. Separate flowers and foliage into piles by variety; lay each pile flat on a table.

2. Gather and twist the stems as shown in the photos below.

3. Using sharp shears, cut all the stems to the same length.

4. Recut the center stems about 1 inch shorter than the outer ones (this helps to ensure that the bouquet will stand up easily).

5. Tie all stems together with string or raffia, just below flower heads, then tie a decorative ribbon around the bouquet to cover string. Spread the stems with your fingers so the bouquet will stand up.

6. Place the spiral bouquet in a low, wide bowl filled with water. ◆

Hold the first flower stem vertically between thumb and fingers. Place another stem next to the first. Repeat this step with about five flowers. Add three more flower stems to the bunch, one at a time, placing them at a 45° angle, as shown (**A**). Fill with foliage stems as desired.

Twist the bouquet clockwise in your hand. Add three more stems, then twist the bouquet in the same direction; repeat this step until the bouquet looks full, as shown (**B**).

Wind string tightly around the stems several times; leave a 2-inch length dangling free. Pull the free end up through the middle of the stems, as shown (**C**), then tie it in a knot.

A

NORMAN A. PLATE (4)

B

C

Proven plants—from a pro

Rob Proctor of Denver Botanic Gardens shares his Rocky Mountain favorites

By Lauren Bonar Swezey

Rob Proctor knows Colorado well. He has traversed the state—from Grand Junction to Denver to Steamboat Springs, Pueblo, and Monte Vista—capturing its fleeting growing season on film.

"I'm not a good traveler," he confesses in the preface to his book *Colorado's Great Gardens* (Westcliffe Publishers, Englewood, CO, 1998; $15; 800/523-3692). "I sleep poorly in motels, forget to pack shaving cream or socks.... I'd much rather be at home in Denver working in my own garden."

But travel he does, for the love of plants and the people who grow them. That passion has led him to his current position as the new director of horticulture for Denver Botanic Gardens, where he has been charged with supervising the design, planting, and maintenance of display gardens and collections. What has he learned from his many adventures in the home gardens of Colorado's plains, mountains, and plateaus? That any way you look at it, "gardening in the climate extremes of this state is a challenge, but not an obstacle."

Sure, you can never be too certain of the weather here. Winter temperatures may hover at a balmy 65° one day, then—thanks to an arctic air mass—plunge to 0° a night or two later. Summer temperatures, on the other hand, can soar to blast-furnace highs. Such extremes are tough on plants.

Fortunately for mountain gardeners, this past decade has seen a large influx of plants that are adaptable to cold climates—from areas with similar climate extremes—and new varieties developed by nurseries. Native plants are also becoming more available, and Denver Botanic Gardens has developed its own plant introduction program, Plant Select, in conjunction with Colorado State University; its plants have been thoroughly tested and are proven winners (some are listed in "Proctor's top 10 plants," at right).

But finding adaptable plants isn't the only hurdle for Colorado gardeners. Soil and water are limiting factors too. "Most Western cities are located in an artificial urban forest," says Proctor. "We don't have eons' worth of leaf litter accumulated in our soils. On the Western plains, the soil is grass-based so there's little humus." As a result, many Coloradans add lots of soil amendments. But that's not necessary if you avoid introduced plants, like hostas and astilbes, that need rich soil. Plenty of plants can thrive in lean soil.

"Gardeners new to our region have a tendency to pamper plants," explains Proctor. "They kill them with kindness—too much water and too much compost." That sets them up for an early demise. "I always tell gardeners to grow their plants lean and mean."

Proctor should know: He has seen plenty of gardens during his travels. *Denver Botanic Gardens, 909 York St.; (303) 331-4000.*

DWAYN CAVENDISH

Proctor's top 10 plants

These sun-loving plants are proven winners in Colorado, standing up to poor soil and temperature extremes.

- Blanket flower (*Gaillardia grandiflora*). "A plains native that adapts to heat and clay soil."
- Blue fescue (*Festuca ovina* 'Glauca'). "The color and texture work beautifully in our mountain and plains gardens."
- *Gaura lindheimeri*. "This white-flowered perennial is super-tough."
- Globe thistle (*Echinops exaltatus*). "It balks at pampering."
- *Miscanthus sinensis* 'Morning Light'. "A grass with four seasons of interest."
- *Oenothera macrocarpa v. incana* 'Silver Blade'. "A ground cover that loves abuse."
- **Penstemon mexicali* 'Pikes Peak Purple'. "It blooms all summer."
- Rocky Mountain penstemon (*P. strictus*). "It's terrifically adaptable."
- *Salvia superba* 'May Night'. "A long-season bloomer."
- *Wine cups (*Callirhoe involucrata*). "A ground cover that thrives in heat."

**Indicates a Plant Select variety. For a complete list, visit www.botanicgardens.org.* ◆

How to attract good bugs to your garden

The right flowers will invite ladybird beetles, lacewings, and other beneficial insects to your backyard

BY SHARON COHOON

RICHARD SHIELL (2)

A hover fly (syrphid fly) controls houseflies by laying its eggs in housefly's pupae. Above, it draws nectar from a sweet alyssum blossom. At left, red clover (*Trifolium pratense*), which attracts ladybird beetles and parasitic wasps.

Successful organic growers don't wait for crop pests to invade before recruiting an opposing army. They build up reserves of beneficial insects, poised for counterattack, to kill insect pests. Their fields, orchards, and gardens teem with ladybird beetles (ladybugs), lacewings, big-eyed bugs, and other predators, with tachinid flies, parasitic wasps, and other parasitoids as backup. (Parasitoids destroy insect pests by laying their eggs on the eggs, larvae, pupae, or adults of the enemy; when the eggs hatch, the parasitoid larvae devour their hosts.)

Organic growers keep predators and parasitoids on hand by providing the adult forms with a steady supply of nectar and pollen. Some adult beneficials get all their food from flowers—protein from pollen, carbohydrates from nectar—while others use these resources to supplement their diets when prey is scarce. The flowering plants they rely on for food are called insectary plants.

Nutrient-rich flowers give adults the energy they need to thrive, mate, and lay eggs on or near the vegetable crops that attract pests. By the time the pests arrive, the eggs will have hatched into larvae—the hungry teenager stage of beneficials—ready for some serious chomping. These voracious adolescents provide most of the pest control.

The above scenario is, obviously, ideal. Arriving at an optimal balance between beneficials and pests doesn't happen overnight. It requires patience and could take several years to build up enough beneficials to neutralize pest invasions. It means using the least toxic pesticides applied only to the plants under attack or, better yet, using none at all; beneficials are also susceptible to pesticides. It requires close observation to determine who's living in your yard—a 10x or 15x hand lens and an insect guidebook are handy. A little tolerance for chewed leaves will also help.

This scenario can come true in your garden in the not-so-distant future. To manage pest problems, growing numbers of agricultural professionals are turning from pesticides to a combination of insectary plants and beneficials. Educational institutions such as the University of California at Davis and Oregon State University are supporting the efforts with research.

To compile our list of insectary plants most likely to lure beneficials (see the facing page), we've drawn from this research, as well as from the experience of seasoned organic growers like Frank and Karen Morton of Shoulder to Shoulder Farms in Philomath, Oregon. From these sources we also learned how to incorporate insectary plants into home gardens.

8 ways to use insectary plants

1. Intersperse vegetable beds with rows or islands of annuals. Corn cockle (*Agrostemma*), cosmos, marigold, sunflower, sweet alyssum, and tithonia add decorative elements while luring beneficials toward prey.

2. Plant an herb garden. Coriander (cilantro) in bloom is one of the top insectary plants throughout the West, so let it bolt with your blessings. Caraway, chervil, dill, fennel, lovage, and parsley flowers also score high as insectary plants. The blooms of many ornamental herbs, notably tansy and santolina, also attract beneficials.

3. Include perennials that are rich in nectar and pollen in permanent flower beds. Agastache, a showy, aromatic summer perennial in the mint family, also happens to be nectar-rich, making it irresistible to beneficials. Bees and hummingbirds like it too. Other beneficial plants that look good in a border include coneflower, coreopsis, golden marguerite, goldenrod, scabiosa, and yarrow.

4. Find room for native plants. The tiny flowers of wild buckwheat (*Eriogonum*) are irresistible to many beneficials, and there are buckwheats that are low and compact enough to tuck into even the smallest garden. If you have more space, consider ceanothus, coffeeberry, and toyon.

5. Fill empty corners with a border mix. Nichols Border Mix (Nichols Garden Nursery; 541/928-9280) contains many of the insectary plants listed at right, with some extras for bees and butterflies. Clyde Robin Seed Company's Border Patrol, available at many garden centers, also works well.

6. Experiment with hedgerows. Organic growers plant mixed hedges of tall insectary plants at the edges of their fields as both shelter and a food source for beneficials. A row of sunflowers or fennel along the fence or encircling the compost could have the same effect. Or let a silver lace vine (*Polygonum aubertii*) cover a chain-link fence or arbor.

7. Grow green manure. Clover and vetch, often sown as cover crops between vegetable crops and then turned under to enrich the soil, happen to be excellent insectary plants.

8. Allow some of your salad and cabbage crops to bloom. Beneficial insects love the flowers of arugula, chervil, chicory, and other greens. Brassica flowers (bok choy, for instance) are also appreciated.

RICHARD SHIELL

Rice-shaped yellow eggs of a ladybird beetle are clustered on the underside of a fennel leaf.

For additional reading

The Wild Garden seed catalog of Shoulder to Shoulder Farm is targeted to professional growers, so seeds are sold in large quantities—½ ounce or more ($50 minimum purchase required). The catalog, however, is a fascinating read and well worth its $5 price. Write to Box 1509, Philomath, OR 97370.

13 top insectary plants and the insects they attract

Letters indicate the insects that these plants attract (see key at bottom)

ANNUALS

Cosmos. Spring through fall. HF, LB, LW.

Sunflowers. Summer into fall. HF, LB, PW.

Sweet alyssum. Summer; year-round in mild areas. HF, LW, PW, TF.

HERBS

Coriander. Spring. HF, LW, PW, TF.

Dill. Spring and summer. HF, LB, PW.

Fennel. Spring through fall. HF, LB, PW, TF. (Reseeds readily; not for small gardens.)

PERENNIALS

Agastache. Summer. HF, PW.

Clovers. Spring and summer per type. LB, PW.

Coreopsis. Spring through fall. HF, LB, LW, PW.

Pincushion flower (*Scabiosa*). Spring to fall. HF, PW.

Tansy. Summer. HF, LB, LW, PW.

Wild buckwheat (*Eriogonum*). Spring through fall. HF, PW, TF.

Yarrow (*Achillea*). Spring through fall. HF, LB, PW.

ABBREVIATION KEY

HF: Hover flies (syrphid flies)
LB: Ladybird beetles
LW: Lacewings
PW: Parasitic wasps
TF: Tachinid (parasitic) flies ◆

Cottage garden know-how

A coastal California garden offers lessons in creating controlled exuberance

BY LAUREN BONAR SWEZEY

Bountiful cutting garden filled with long-blooming annuals and perennials provides a constant source of flowers from spring through fall. A V-shaped cobblestone path divides the garden into three sections, with annual color focused around a birdbath.

You can't help but feel elated when you enter this exuberant Northern California coastal garden filled with annuals, perennials, flowering shrubs, and whimsical artifacts. "It's a country garden with lots of colors, textures, and weathered wood," says owner Kerry Olson of Santa Cruz. "Nothing is too uniform. The style is light and loose."

Olson isn't a landscape professional, and she didn't start with a plan. But her methods offer good ideas for creating similar projects with minimal help.

The garden was developed over several years, with the aid of Olson's friend Dianne Olivieri. "I knew I wanted a path, a pond, and a cutting garden," says Olson. "When I started, the yard seemed really teeny. But now that it has many separate areas with many discoveries in each one, it seems huge. It's counterintuitive."

If Olson has learned one lesson over the years, it's that there's a fine line between abundance and chaos. The key is to simplify by repeating elements.

Since the path and initial beds went in, Olson has worked with landscape designer Lynn Robinson to develop the cutting garden—a breezy blend of perennials and long-lived annuals.

Everywhere you turn there's something to see: A giant birdhouse framed against a wall. Brilliant borders overflowing with roses. An antique garden swing at the end of a path. Old weathered doors as backdrops to beds. The cutting garden has an arbor, the pond has sculpture and an aviary, and each garden includes seating.

Olson is constantly on the lookout for objects—sculpture, old chairs, pottery—to place around the garden. She also works with Crawford's Antiques of Soquel, California (4401 Soquel Dr.; 831/462-1528), to develop new structures out of antique remnants. The garden swing is a composite of at least eight different antique structures.

Keeping up the abundance

To keep the garden looking its best, designer Robinson spends about three hours per week clipping spent blooms, watering, and feeding. (For a calendar of Robinson's seasonal chores, see box on facing page.)

Cottage garden plants

Flowers for cutting

Tall plants for backgrounds: delphiniums, Foxy strain foxgloves, *Nicotiana alata,* Rocket series snapdragons, variegated summer phlox.

Medium-size plants: 'Apple Blossom' and 'Firebird' penstemons, asters, Champagne Bubbles strain Iceland poppies (*Papaver nudicaule*), gloriosa daisies (*Rudbeckia hirta*), lamb's ears (*Stachys*

Lynn Robinson's maintenance schedule

Early spring. Mulch the soil with a 2- to 3-inch layer of high-quality compost (hers contains horse manure).

Spring. Pull out faded cool-season annuals, plant summer-fall annuals (such as cosmos and sweet alyssums), prune off frost-damaged growth, and shape plants where needed.

Spring through fall. Foliar-feed every month with a liquid fertilizer (Robinson's favorite is Peters 20-20-20).

Fall. Cut back faded perennials, pull out summer annuals, and plant cool-season annuals.

All year. Trim or shear overgrown plants; remove dead flowers.

OLSON'S COTTAGE GARDEN DESIGN TIPS

• AVOID STRAIGHT LINES. Keep the shape of the beds and the color patterns informal.

• DIVIDE THE GARDEN INTO ROOMS with trellises or walls of plants.

• REPEAT PLANTINGS to avoid visual chaos. Either scatter the same plants throughout a bed (Olson uses multiple plantings of delphiniums and foxgloves in her cutting garden) or plant in drifts (Santa Barbara daisies fill in under rose beds).

• VARY PLANT HEIGHTS AND TEXTURES. Plant in layers, and combine large- and small-leafed plants.

• ADD STRUCTURAL ELEMENTS. Sculptures, birdhouses, pots, and arbors anchor plantings and serve as points of interest.

• GROW PLANTS VERTICALLY. Break up the monotony of a fence by covering it with vines. Also train vines up poles and over arbors.

• TAKE ADVANTAGE OF LOCAL SOURCES. Ask lots of questions when you visit nurseries.

PAUL BOUSQUET (2)

ABOVE: Covered porch is furnished with antique rocking chairs and potted plants; baskets dangle flowers at eye level. TOP: A honeysuckle-covered arbor leads to the cutting garden. Swing is made of remnants. Yellow rose beside the path is 'Pilgrim'.

byzantina), 'Salmon Beauty' yarrow (*Achillea*), Sonata series cosmos.

Fillers for the front of borders: 'Butterfly Blue' scabiosas, *Chrysanthemum paludosum,* sweet alyssums (*Lobularia maritima*), pansies, violas.

Permanent plants for pots

Cape mallow (*Anisodontea hypomandarum*) topiaries, citrus, fern pines (*Podocarpus gracilior*), *Fuchsia thymifolia,* roses, wax-leaf privets (*Ligustrum japonicum*). Fill in around them with seasonal annuals.

Roses

'Bonica', 'First Light', 'Gertrude Jekyll', 'Graham Thomas', 'Just Joey', 'Sun Flare', 'The Fairy'.

Vines for fences and walls

Banana passion vine (*Passiflora mollissima*), clematis, climbing roses ('Kathleen', 'Madame Alfred Carrière'), honeysuckle (*Lonicera*), wisteria. ◆

CLAIRE CURRAN (3)

Freshly picked fruits are these gardeners' rewards. From left: Eunice Messner shows off her cherimoyas, Elva West samples his papayas, and Gary Matsuoka holds his mangoes.

A taste of the tropics

How to grow cherimoyas, mangoes, and papayas in Southern California gardens

BY SHARON COHOON

Your friends back East may envy you your winter days in shirtsleeves while they're bundled up in heavy layers. But to make their envy index really rise, tell them you're harvesting tropical fruit from trees you planted in your garden. If you plant trees now and are willing to wait a couple of years, you'll be able to have fruit to enjoy yourself—and to impress any visitors from colder climates.

Late spring into early summer is ideal for planting tropical and subtropical fruit trees; they'll have maximum time to put out new growth before winter comes. Choices abound—loquat, litchi, white sapote, Surinam cherry. But cherimoya, mango, and papaya have the edge. Not only are their fruits irresistible, but in the right climate, they require no more attention than more familiar fruit trees like plums and apples. Here are tips on growing these tropical trees from three experienced growers.

■ Cherimoya

"Cherimoya is one of the best-tasting fruits in the world," says Eunice Messner of Anaheim Hills. Mark Twain would agree. He described the fruit as "deliciousness itself." The flesh has a creamy, custardlike texture and a flavor that is a mixture of banana and pineapple. "If it didn't have seeds," says Messner, a contributing editor to *The Fruit Gardener*, the bimonthly magazine of the California Rare Fruit Growers, "it would be perfect."

Unpruned trees reach 20 feet, but pruning in March and August keeps trees at an easy-to-harvest 8 to 9 feet.

BEST VARIETY. Messner's choice is 'Pierce', which has "great flavor and doesn't turn dark in the refrigerator like some other varieties."

PREFERRED LOCATION. Cherimoya likes marine influence and does well in coastal and foothill Southern California.

FROST TOLERANCE. Mature trees can endure short periods of temperatures in the low 20s. Young trees need more protection.

POLLINATION. Self-pollinating, so only one tree required. For maximum production and perfectly formed fruit, you'll need to hand-pollinate, as commercial growers do. (There are no known natural cherimoya pollinators in California.) Gardeners such as Messner, however, don't find this necessary. "I get as much fruit as I want without it," she says, "especially if I mist the foliage regularly while they're in flower to help things along." To hand-pollinate, collect pollen from fully open (male) flowers in late afternoon with a slender paintbrush. The next morning, apply pollen to partially open (female) flowers. (Flowers are female in the morning, male by late afternoon.)

YEARS TO HARVEST. Two to three years for grafted trees; five to eight years for seedlings. (Named varieties are always grafted; unnamed ones are seedlings.)

HARVEST TIME. October through May.

CARE. In midwinter, feed trees with compost and well-aged chicken manure. Repeat when the trees leaf out again in May after a brief deciduous period. Messner also gives new leaves a single foliar feeding of kelp and fish emulsion during the growing season ("if I get around to it"). She waters twice a week with drip irrigation for most of the year, less when soil cools and winter rains begin.

■ Mango

"Rich, juicy, spicy, both sweet and tart"—every adjective used to describe a mango's taste is true, says Gary Matsuoka, president of Laguna Hills Nursery in Lake Forest. Mangoes' requirements are very similar to those of avocados: ample summer moisture and excellent winter drainage, which is not the easiest combination to pull off. But the fruit is so delicious, Matsuoka says, the trees are worth the effort. The small stature of the tree, which rarely exceeds 15 feet in our climate, also makes it suitable for home gardens.

BEST VARIETIES. Matsuoka's choices: 'Edward' ("stingy producer but superb flavor"), 'Carrie' ("small-size but rich, spicy fruit"), and 'Glenn' ("large fruit, little fiber, great taste").

PREFERRED LOCATIONS. Ideal are frost-free foothills, away from immediate marine influence: Fallbrook, Tustin, and San Joaquin, for example. But gardeners closer to the coast are reporting success. Matsuoka lives in Mission Viejo, and the fruit can also be grown in the Coachella Valley.

FROST TOLERANCE. Hardy to 26° at maturity. Until it has developed enough wood to give it some protection, it is more frost-sensitive.

POLLINATION. Self-fruiting, so only one tree required.

YEARS TO HARVEST. Two years for grafted tree; 7 to 10 for seedlings. Most people opt for grafted trees, which more quickly bear fruit that's reliable in quality.

HARVEST TIME. August through December.

CARE. Give mangoes your garden's sunniest, best-drained spot—a south-facing slope is ideal. If your soil is heavy, lighten it by digging in pumice or sponge rock. Mangoes like plenty of water, so keep soil consistently moist. Fertilize often with compost during summer and early fall, when trees are actively growing.

The chief problem with mangoes is winter rot, which is why drainage is so critical. Near the coast, powdery mildew can also be a problem. Dust or spray with wettable sulfur.

The first year or two, pinch off developing fruit on grafted plants, or you'll get mango vines instead of trees.

■ Papaya

Papaya is for risk-takers in most of Southern California. But if you live close enough to the coast not to get frost and far enough away not to get ocean breezes, you could succeed. The reward is a melon-textured fruit whose taste transports you to Hawaii. The 12-foot tree is also handsomely ornamental, particularly in subtropical gardens. Elva West lives in Anaheim Hills, which is one of those magic zones. For at least 25 years, he has been growing papayas with 90 to 95 percent success. He's also the papaya specialist for the California Rare Fruit Growers.

BEST VARIETY. 'Florida Jack'.

PREFERRED LOCATIONS. Frost-free foothills.

FROST TOLERANCE. Unknown, but West reports trees surviving 26°.

POLLINATION. Papaya trees have three sexes: male, female, and self-fertile hermaphroditic. Since papayas are grown from seed and you don't know what sex your tree is until it flowers, plant two or three to ensure fruit.

YEARS TO HARVEST. Two.

HARVEST TIME. April through September.

CARE. Keep the soil dry enough in winter to avoid root rot. (Hawaiian 'Solo' is especially vulnerable to this malady.) Plant on a slope, in a raised bed, or in a 15-gallon or larger container. Apply a 3- to 4-inch layer of mulch—leaves, grass clippings, or commercial products—in summer to keep soil moist, then remove mulch in winter so the sun can warm the soil.

Give the trees plenty of water and fertilizer during the growing season, May through September. West foliar-feeds seedlings with a 10-10-10 formula, then switches to a granular form when foliage has grown out of easy reach. He prefers using half the recommended dosage and fertilizing twice as often. Problems with pests and diseases have been minor, West reports.

Where to buy plants

Elva West, (714) 637-4084. West propagates and sells 'Florida Jack' and other papaya varieties.

Laguna Hills Nursery, 25290 Jeronimo Rd., Lake Forest; (949) 830-5653. Always well stocked with tropical fruit in season.

Pacific Tree Farms, 4301 Lynwood Dr., Chula Vista; (619) 422-2400. Walk-in or mail-order nursery; catalog $2.

Papaya Tree Nursery, 12422 El Oro Way, Granada Hills; (818) 363-3680; by appointment only. Specialty nursery for tropical and exotic fruit trees. Sells only fruit trees and other tropical edibles.

For more information on the California Rare Fruit Growers, check out the group's excellent website, www.crfg.org, or write to it in care of Fullerton Arboretum–CSUF, Box 6850, Fullerton, CA 92834.

■ From garden to kitchen

Here's a tasty, refreshing shake that starts with mango or papaya; it's easy to make too.

Mango-Yogurt Shakes

PREP TIME: About 10 minutes
SERVES: 2

- 1 cup chopped **firm-ripe mango** or papaya
- ¾ cup **orange juice**
- ½ cup cooked or canned **sweet potato**
- 1 cup **vanilla nonfat frozen yogurt**

In a blender, whirl mango, orange juice, and sweet potato until smooth. Add frozen yogurt; whirl until smooth. Pour into tall glasses.

Per serving: 282 cal., 1.6% (4.5 cal.) from fat; 4.4 g protein; 0.5 g fat (0.1 g sat.); 66 g carbo (3.5 g fiber); 58 mg sodium; 0 mg chol. ◆

How to make the most of a short season

The secret: Proven winners planted in the right place at the right time

By Dick Bushnell

Late springs, short summers with cool nights, and early frosts are among the constraints mountain-region gardeners face when growing flowers and vegetables. If you live in such areas—from Boise to Denver—you can meet these challenges and get the most out of your summer garden by following these tips.

Select a proper site

Most annual flowers thrive in borders and island beds that get full sun, or in containers. For flowering perennials, an east-facing site with morning sun is ideal. For a vegetable bed, choose a south-facing site that gets full sun all day. In windy areas, plant near boulders and walls to provide protection.

ROB PROCTOR (3)

Amend the soil

If you're growing introduced plants, including flowers and vegetables, add organic amendments to the soil to support healthy growth (mountain soils are typically shallow and rocky). Digging in plenty of compost, peat moss, or well-composted manure helps the soil retain moisture and air.

Choose the right plants

These plants have proved themselves in mountain gardens.

•ANNUAL FLOWERS. Calendula, cleome, cosmos, gazania, geranium, impatiens (for shade), marigold (*Tagetes*), nicotiana, petunia, snapdragon (*Antirrhinum majus*), sunflower (*Helianthus*), sweet alyssum (*Lobularia maritima*), 'Victoria' salvia, zinnia.

Hollyhocks are old-fashioned standouts in a sunny border. Mingled in mixed beds are marigolds and snapdragons (top right) and Shasta daisies and pansies (bottom right).

•FLOWERING PERENNIALS. Black-eyed Susan (*Rudbeckia hirta*), blanket flower (*Gaillardia grandiflora*), bleeding heart (*Dicentra*), catmint (*Nepeta faassenii*), columbine (*Aquilegia*), creeping phlox (*P. stolonifera*), daylily (*Hemerocallis*), delphinium, dianthus, hollyhock (biennial and perennial types), ice plant (many genera), Maltese cross (*Lychnis chalcedonica*), penstemon, Shasta daisy (*Chrysanthemum maximum*), snow-in-summer (*Cerastium tomentosum*), thrift (*Armeria maritima*), yarrow (*Achillea*).

•SHORT-SEASON VEGETABLES. Breeders have developed plants that mature in two months or less. Seed companies based in mountain states report success with the following early-bearing varieties.

Bush green beans: 'Earliserve', 'Provider', 'Venture'.

Corn: 'Candy Mountain', 'Earlivee', 'Early Sunglow', 'Kandy Kwik', 'Yukon Chief'.

Cucumbers: 'Northern Pickling', 'Sweet Success' (slicer).

Peppers: 'Ace' bell; 'Early Jalapeño', 'Olé' jalapeño; 'Hungarian Hot Wax'.

Summer squash: 'Early Prolific Straightneck' squash; 'Cocozelle', 'Dark Green', 'Grey', 'Seneca' zucchini.

Tomatoes: 'Gem State', 'Glacier', 'Gold Nugget' (cherry), 'Medina', 'Prairie Fire', 'Rocket', 'Siberia', 'Siletz', 'Stupice', 'Sub-Arctic Plenty'.

Because eggplant and melons take longer to mature, they often can't survive at higher elevations. In warmer intermountain areas, try 'Dusky' eggplant, 'Earlisweet' or 'Fast Break' cantaloupe, 'Earligold' or 'Minnesota Midget' muskmelon, and 'Cream of Saskatchewan' watermelon.

Look for seedlings in nurseries or order seed from these companies: *D.V. Burrell Seed Growers,* Rocky Ford, CO (719/254-3318); *Garden City Seeds,* Hamilton, MT (406/961-4837); *Seeds Trust/High Altitude Gardens,* Hailey, ID (208/788-4363).

Plant after the last frost

The date of the last frost varies with elevation. For example, in mile-high Denver the safe date is May 18, while at 8,200 feet in Vail, it's June 15. To find the date in your area, check with your local cooperative extension or Master Gardener program. Of course, at higher elevations frost can strike any night of the year.

Boost soil warmth around vegetables

There are several ways to do this. You can grow vegetables in raised beds, where soil drains better and warms up more quickly in spring than the surrounding soil does. Build raised beds by raking soil into flat-topped mounds or by framing the beds with lumber. You can also plant seedlings of warm-season crops through black plastic or fabric. Or place floating row covers over crops to warm the soil, to increase humidity around plants, and to provide protection from nighttime cold.

For tomato plants, surround with water-filled plastic collars such as Wall-O-Water, available from Garden City Seeds (see above).

Keep frost protection on hand

If frost is predicted, cover vegetable seedlings with one of these devices: cloches, plastic 1-gallon milk jugs with cutout bottoms, plastic sheeting rigged over lumber or schedule 40 PVC pipe, floating row covers. ◆

CLAIRE CURRAN

IN JUNE, roses, sea lavender, white gaura, light purple buddleia, and crimson bougainvillea are in peak bloom in the gardens at Mission San Juan Capistrano. For details, see page 181.

June

Crimson azaleas blaze in a mixed bed at the foot of a tree.

An Oregon garden gets new life

Impressive plantings restored in Lincoln City

■ An accomplished plantswoman, Connie Hansen worked tirelessly for 20 years on her 1-acre garden in Lincoln City on the Oregon coast. After she died in 1993, the property was in danger of falling into disrepair. To preserve the plants Hansen so lovingly cared for, local residents formed a nonprofit organization, the Connie Hansen Garden Conservancy, to buy the grounds and Hansen's home. Since then the conservancy has renovated the house (with an art gallery, library, offices, and gift shop), provided handicapped access, built a new parking lot, and redesigned areas of the garden. Other improvements include a new pond and pergola.

Visitors are welcome to stroll through the Connie Hansen Garden to see her impressive collection of rhododendrons (more than 100), as well as hostas, primulas, and most kinds of irises except bearded. Azaleas, dogwoods, Japanese maples, magnolias, and viburnums complete the wooded tapestry. A creek meanders through the garden, which offers sanctuary to birds, butterflies, and other wildlife.

The Connie Hansen Garden is always open but is staffed 10 to 2 on Tuesdays and Thursdays. One of the best times to visit is during the Festival of Gardens, late in June. Events include a plant sale, workshops, and tours of private gardens. Proceeds from the festival benefit the Connie Hansen Garden, which is privately funded and maintained entirely by volunteers. *Open daily; donations welcome. 1931 N.W. 33rd St., Lincoln City, OR; (541) 994-6338 or www.conniehansengarden.com.*

—Janet Loughrey

Scaling down in the desert

■ The popular hobby of garden railroading depends for much of its appeal on getting everything to scale. It's tough enough to find plants that will look like trees in miniature layouts; in the Southwest, there's the additional challenge of the climate, says Cathy Morgan, chief landscaper for the Morgan Creek Railroad, located in her Las Vegas yard. The dwarf conifers commonly used in other areas of the country usually fail in the desert, she says. "They don't like our summers or our soil."

Better choices for the desert are small-leafed shrubs such as dwarf myrtle, like the one Morgan is pruning above. This plant can take heat and alkalinity, yet its diminutive stature is perfectly scaled to the Morgans' G-gauge railroad (each boxcar is about the size of a loaf of bread). Rosemary is another good choice, says Morgan. "Prune it into a conical shape, and it looks just like a pine."

Morgan has incorporated a few true miniature trees that do stand up to desert conditions: dwarf Alberta spruce (*Picea glauca* 'Conica') and Hokkaido elm (*Ulmus parvifolia* 'Hokkaido'). Both were purchased from Miniature Plant Kingdom, Sebastopol, California (707/874-2233).

To find out more about the hobby, pick up *Garden Railways* magazine (sold at shops that sell model trains), check out the magazine's website, www.gardenrailways.com, or call (877) 547-2253 to get the free booklet "Beginning Garden Railroading." — *Sharon Cohoon*

Cathy Morgan prunes a dwarf myrtle near a church on her garden railroad layout.

Party lights for festive nights

■ Nothing brings romance into the garden faster than warm, subdued lighting. For a backyard party, there's a wonderful array of decorative indoor/outdoor string lights now available, ready to brighten up an arbor, a tree, or a patio umbrella.

Catalogs and on-line stores sell playful and sophisticated styles to please a range of tastes. Witness the sampling pictured here: Little white lights are covered with weatherproof shades made of (1) perforated metal, (2) a rice paper look-alike, (3) multicolored vellum, or (4) a natural Indonesian vetiver (a grass), which releases a woodsy scent when the lights warm up. The cone-shaped lights (5) are made of paper and should be used indoors or under protection outside.

Light strands, which range from 13 to 15 feet long, generally contain 10 lights each; number 5 has 20 lights. Strands can be plugged together. Prices range from $24 to $49, depending on the style.

NORMAN A. PLATE (2)

SOURCES **Discovery Store;** (800) 938-0333 or www.discoverystore.com (1, 4). **Garden.com;** (800) 466-8142 or www.garden.com (1, 2, 3). **Smith & Hawken;** (800) 776-3336 or www.smithandhawken.com (5). — *Lauren Bonar Swezey*

Garden caretakers Dana Ecelberger (right) and Melissa Attanasio show off their bountiful harvest. At right, colorful mixed salad greens grow in raised beds.

Dana's favorite tastes

- **Tomatoes for coastal climates:** 'Burbank Slicing', 'Early Cascade', 'Northern Delight', 'Red Currant', 'Stupice', 'Sweet Million', and 'Yellow Currant'.
- **Tasty greens:** 'Blue Solaise' leeks, 'Bright Lights' Swiss chard, 'Champion' collards, 'Ching Chiang' dwarf bok choy, 'MacGregor's Favorite' beet greens, 'Merlot' lettuce, 'Tah Tsai' mustard, and 'Valeria' lettuce.
- **Seed sources:** Territorial Seed Company (541/942-9547 or www.territorial-seed.com) and the Cook's Garden (800/457-9703 or store.yahoo.com/cooksgarden).

Gardening lessons

This Mendocino inn is not just a place to dine or spend a few nights—it's an education center for gardeners

■ The Stanford Inn by the Sea in Mendocino, California, isn't just *any* inn. Situated on a forested hilltop with panoramic views of the Pacific Ocean, it's surrounded by gorgeous gardens, including a certified organic garden that supplies produce for the inn's gourmet vegetarian restaurant. Owners Jeff and Joan Stanford describe it as a "garden with an inn."

Just downhill from the inn, raised beds are filled with seasonal produce that thrives near the coast. "We're primarily a salad and greens garden," says head gardener Dana Ecelberger. But heirloom leeks, gourmet crops such as edible podded peas and alpine strawberries, and a variety of flowers also grow here.

The inn also serves as an educational center, offering hands-on gardening workshops. Examples of topics that might be covered this month are propagation techniques, composting, and kitchen gardening. The inn is sometimes one of the stops on Mendocino coast garden tours. Weekend tours of the produce garden are also offered.

The innkeepers welcome kids and dogs too—they'll even supply blankets and dishes for your pet. For details, call (800) 331-8884. — *Lauren Bonar Swezey*

MARY-KATE MACKEY

■ When I was redesigning a bed in my Eugene, Oregon, garden, I knew that *Spiraea nipponica tosaensis* 'Snowmound' and lemon daylily (*Hemerocallis lilioasphodelus*) would make a harmonious pair. Sure enough, early the next summer, the spiraea's fluffy white flowers bloomed in concert with the daylily's clear yellow trumpets. Then serendipity came into play. I'd forgotten about the common chives already growing at the front of the bed. When the chives burst into bloom, their rosy lavender blossoms added another element to my composition, turning a nice duet into a merry trio.

All three plants have similar needs: They bloom best in full sun and well-drained soil. A light feeding in early spring and regular water during the dry summer months keep the show coming back year after year.

— *Mary-Kate Mackey*

Mission revival

Gardens have come back to Capistrano, beautifully. This month is a perfect time to visit

■ If it has been more than two years since you visited Mission San Juan Capistrano, drop by again. Thanks to the efforts of a volunteer group called the Gardening Angels, directed by president Jan Sorensen, the gardens have undergone such a remarkable transformation that the whole mission seems renewed.

When Sorensen and fellow angel Ann Thiel formed the group three years ago, the mission grounds needed help. There were struggling rose bushes and some dusty clumps of bird of paradise, but mostly there was bare earth. Now there are well-tended roses, perennials (such as buddleia, gaura, and statice), herbs, succulents, flowering shrubs, and old-fashioned annuals like hollyhocks in abundance, all complementing century-old pepper trees. The grounds (see photo on page 176) look more like the work of passionate, skilled home gardeners, offering visitors plenty of ideas for beautiful plant combinations.

CLAIRE CURRAN

This month offers the perfect opportunity for a visit. During the Mission San Juan Capistrano Flower & Garden Festival, most of the plants will be in peak bloom and there will be vendors, related lectures and displays, treasure hunts and other children's activities, and a living-history-pageant.

Mission San Juan Capistrano is off Interstate 5, at the Ortega exit. For other events during the summer, call (949) 443-2060 or check www. missionsjc.com. — *S.C.*

DAVID WINGER

These clippers aren't just for grass

■ Most scissorslike grass shears require a continual squeezing motion, which can eventually cause pain in hands and forearms, or even carpal tunnel syndrome. Now, a new battery-operated model—the Ryobi 12-volt Grass Shears—makes the job quick, easy, and pain-free.

With just the push of a safety button and press of a trigger, the dual blades clip the grass instantly. The clippers are also useful for deadheading flowers on herbaceous perennials such as coreopsis, lavender, and Santa Barbara daisy, but they should never be used to cut tough, woody growth. Maintaining the shears is simple. After each use, pull out the battery, wipe the blades with a clean cloth, and plug the battery into its 120-volt AC charger for at least eight hours.

Ryobi Grass Shears are available at many home improvement centers; the suggested retail price is $69.99. To find a retailer near you, contact Ryobi at (800) 345-8746.— *L.B.S.*

THOMAS J. STORY

A summer blizzard of bloom

■ From the end of May until the end of June, the front yard of Kiyoshi and Erika Agena's home in Lakewood, Colorado, is blanketed by drifts of snow-in-summer (*Cerastium tomentosum*). Even after the blizzard of flowers subsides, its silvery gray foliage shimmers in the sun.

The Agenas planted the rugged perennial six years ago as a water-saving lawn replacement. The snow-in-summer has turned out to be a nearly maintenance-free alternative to turf grass. Reaching 6 to 8 inches high, it shades out most weeds and doesn't require mowing or fertilizing. It needs only a couple of deep soakings in July after the bloom to keep it from going brown in the heat of summer.

Snow-in-summer is hardy in all *Sunset* climate zones. This sun-loving plant is not finicky about soil as long as it is well drained. Space plants 18 inches apart and water once or twice weekly until they grow together into a dense mat. Established plants can be mowed or sheared in late spring and again after bloom to remove shabby foliage. As a ground cover, snow-in-summer has two drawbacks: It does not tolerate foot traffic, and it does not stay green in winter. — *Marcia Tatroe*

BACK TO BASICS

Should you prune tomatoes? In cool-summer climates, where tomatoes often don't get enough heat for the fruit to ripen, you can prune plants to let the sun in. As shown, pinch out suckers that sprout from the crotches between the main stems and side branches. On plants trained to stakes, keep one vertical leader. For caged plants, train three or four vertical leaders along the sides of the cage and thin out congested growth to improve air circulation.

In warm-summer climates, tomatoes should be pruned only minimally to prevent sunburned fruit. Be sure to keep enough leaves to shade the fruit. — *Jim McCausland*

LINDA HOLT AYRISS

CLIPPINGS

•**Support local farmers.** Community Supported Agriculture (CSA) is a network of farms that offers fresh seasonal produce directly to consumers, bypassing grocery stores. To find a CSA farm near you, visit www.sare.org/san/csa/index.htm.

A fresh approach to desert gardening

RIZZOLI INTERNATIONAL PUBLICATIONS (2)

■ Some desert gardens mirror nature so closely that it's hard to tell where the wild desert ends and the cultivated landscape begins. Other gardens prefer to "borrow the plants but leave the desert behind," writes Gary Lyons, the former curator of the desert plant collection at San Marino, California's Huntington Botanical Gardens and author of the newly published book *Desert Gardens* (Rizzoli International Publications, New York, 2000; $50; 800/522-6657). Such gardens bring together cactus and succulents from Southwest deserts, Mexican thorn scrub, the African savanna, and other arid lands, then reassemble the plants in original ways. The garden at the top of this page is a prime example. Created by Boyd and Mary Ev Walker in Pacific Palisades, California, it employs succulents, rather than perennials, to achieve the effect of a traditional English herbaceous border. Or consider the living tapestry above, at the home of Gunther Schwartz in Santa Barbara. Altogether, 18 gardens are described by Lyons and photographed by Melba Levick. They are all in Southern California, but they may inspire gardeners throughout the Southwest to use some of nature's toughest plants in beautiful new ways. — *S.C.*

Flower beds for sun and shade

■ It's not too late to spark up your garden with colorful flowers and foliage—nurseries are filled with perennials in 4-inch pots and 1-gallon cans.

The two beds shown here measure just 8 to 9 feet in diameter; each is designed around a focal point—a birdbath or boulder.

Before planting, rotary-till the soil or turn it over with a shovel. Mix a 2- to 3-inch layer of organic mulch into the soil, then level the planting area with a rake. Set the boulder or birdbath in the center of the planting area (bury the boulder only halfway). Position plants, still in their containers, setting them far enough apart so they have room to spread. Dig the holes and plant. Water well and cover the area with mulch.

— L.B.S.

Sunny yellows and pastels

Pink and purple penstemons decorate the outer edges of this sunny bed, with coreopsis and yarrow filling the spaces in between. Low-growing clusters of diascia and blue-flowered catmint grow in the foreground.

DESIGN: Bud Stuckey
TIME: ½ day (including shopping)
COST: About $80 for plants
MATERIALS: Medium-size boulder (20 to 24 inches long); catmint, 2; coreopsis, 2; *Diascia vigilis,* 2; lavender blue delphinium, 2; penstemon, 1

A shady bird sanctuary

Burgundy foliage mingles with bright flowers in this handsome bed. Corydalis softens the edges of the birdbath, while, at front, heucheras mingle with orange-flowered geum. Low-growing ajuga grows between the corydalis and heucheras.

DESIGN: Maile Arnold, Sebastopol (707/823-1373)
TIME: ½ day (including shopping)
COST: About $130 for plants
MATERIALS: Small birdbath. The one pictured here is from Smith & Hawken (800/776-3336 or www.smithandhawken.com; $98). *Ajuga* 'Catlin's Giant', 1 sixpack; *Corydalis lutea,* 4; *Geum borisii,* 6; *Heuchera* 'Palace Purple', 3; *Heuchera* 'Pewter Veil', 3

NORMAN A. PLATE (2)

southern california· checklist

WHAT TO DO IN YOUR GARDEN IN JUNE

PLANTING

☐ CULINARY HERBS. This is a good season to plant most herbs. Try basil, chervil, chives, fennel, lemon grass, mint, oregano, parsley, rosemary, sage, savory, tarragon, and thyme from nursery pots. Cilantro and dill are best started from seed.

☐ SUMMER COLOR. It's not too late to plant summer annuals. Choices include ageratum, celosia, dahlia, gomphrena, marigold, nicotiana, petunia, portulaca, salvia, sanvitalia (creeping zinnia), sunflower, verbena, vinca (*Catharanthus*), and zinnia. In shade, take advantage of the gorgeous coleus varieties recently made available. Or plant the reliable standbys—impatiens and begonias. Also look for summer-to-fall-blooming perennials such as daylily, gaillardia, lion's tail, rudbeckia, scabiosa, Shasta daisy, and varieties of salvia.

☐ SUMMER VEGETABLES. Set out seedlings of cucumbers, eggplant, melons, peppers, squash, and tomatoes. Sow seeds of beans, corn, cucumbers, New Zealand spinach, okra, pumpkins, and summer and winter squash. (If you want pumpkins by Halloween, plant before June 15.) In the high desert (zone 11), sow seeds of corn, cucumber, melon, okra, squash, and watermelon.

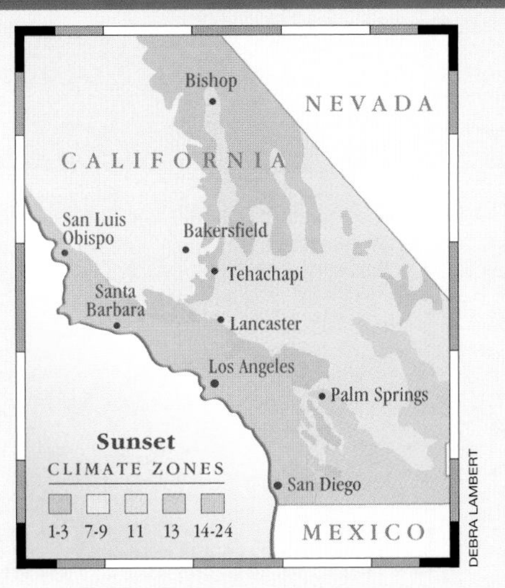

DEBRA LAMBERT

MAINTENANCE

☐ CUT BACK DELPHINIUMS. For a second bloom by summer's end, cut back delphiniums after flowers are spent. Leave only a pair or two of leaves at the bottom of each bloom spike.

☐ STAKE TOMATOES. To ease picking and to prevent fruit rot, provide support for tomato plants. Concrete-reinforcing wire cages are quick to make and very sturdy. Cut a 76-inch-long piece out of 6-inch concrete-reinforcing wire or galvanized mesh. Bend around plant, creating a 2-foot-diameter cage. Crimp ends. For a prettier option, build a wood framework: Secure 2-by-2 wood stakes, 8 feet long, on opposite sides of the plant, about 2 feet apart. Nail three or more 1-by-1 crosspieces between them. As plants grow, tie vines to the support with plastic ties.

☐ TREAT IRON DEFICIENCIES. Azaleas, citrus, gardenias, hibiscus, and other susceptible plants often exhibit green veins on upper leaves at this time of year—a signal they are not getting enough iron. To correct, apply chelated iron as a foliar spray or soil drench, following package directions.

PEST AND WEED CONTROL

☐ COMBAT ROSE PESTS. Along the coast, "June gloom" creates ideal conditions for powdery mildew. Combat by frequently hosing off foliage early in the morning to wash off spores. Or spray with 1 tablespoon each baking soda and fine-grade horticultural oil diluted in a gallon of water. Avoid spraying when temperatures exceed 85°. Inland, watch for spider mites. Keep mite populations in check by spraying foliage, particularly the undersides of leaves, often.

☐ MANAGE WHITEFLIES. Examine the undersides of leaves of target plants like banana, hibiscus, and plumeria for white waxy spirals, where eggs are often deposited. Remove leaves—bag them in plastic and dispose of them—or wash away the spirals with a strong stream of water. ◆

WHAT TO DO IN YOUR GARDEN IN JUNE

PLANTING

☐ SUMMER FLOWERS. When the weather warms up, sow seeds of cosmos, marigold, morning glory, portulaca, nasturtium, sunflower, and zinnia for splashes of color. For instant impact, set out nursery seedlings of ageratum, amaranth, celosia, China aster, coleus, gazania, geranium, heliotrope, impatiens, Madagascar periwinkle, nierembergia, ornamental pepper, petunia, and scarlet sage.

☐ VEGETABLES. After the late frost date for your area, set out transplants of warm-season vegetables, including cucumbers, eggplants, melons, peppers, pumpkins, squash, and tomatoes. Sow seeds of beans, corn, and tender herbs like basil directly in the ground.

☐ WATER GARDENS. Put tropical water lilies and other frost-tender aquatic plants into outdoor ponds when water temperature reaches 70°. Fertilize at planting time and monthly through September.

MAINTENANCE

☐ MULCH BEDS. Once the soil warms up, spread organic mulch over flower and vegetable beds to keep down weeds and hold in soil moisture.

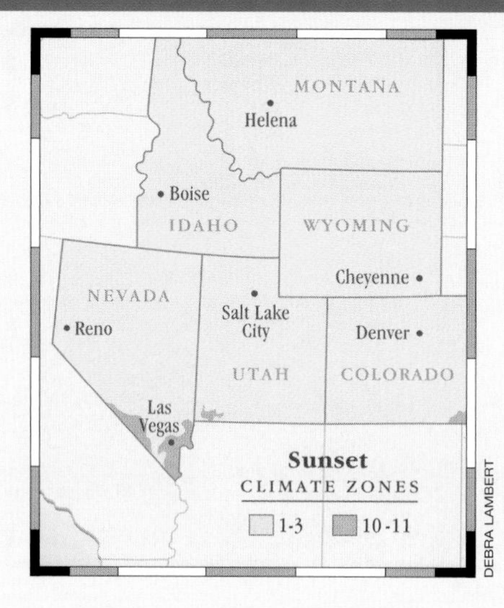

☐ PINCH ASTERS, MUMS. To encourage branching, compact growth, and extra flowers, pinch or shear fall-blooming asters and chrysanthemums until mid-July. Remove the top few inches of each stem whenever plants reach 1 foot tall.

☐ PRUNE SPRING-BLOOMING SHRUBS. If needed, prune bridal wreath spiraea, forsythia, lilac, mock orange, quince, and wiegela immediately after flowering.

☐ THIN FRUIT. For larger fruit and to prevent stress to the tree, thin apples, apricots, peaches, and plums when they reach ¾ inch in diameter. Apples should be spaced 6 inches apart, peaches 4 to 6 inches apart, apricots and plums 2 to 3 inches apart.

☐ TREAT CHLOROSIS. When leaves turn yellow while veins remain green, it's a sign of chlorosis, a condition caused by an iron deficiency in the soil. Correct chlorosis by applying a chelated iron product directly to the foliage and to the soil around the root zone, following the package instructions.

PEST CONTROL

☐ MELTING-OUT DISEASE OF TURF GRASS. If large, irregular patches of lawn turn yellow and die suddenly during warm weather, suspect melting-out fungus. Proper lawn care can prevent this fungal disease. Be careful not to overwater, overfertilize, or cut the lawn shorter than 2½ inches. Aerate lawns at least once a season to help prevent thatch buildup.

☐ WESTERN CABBAGE FLEA BEETLE. Numerous small holes in the leaves of both vegetable and ornamental members of the cabbage family are usually the work of this tiny black beetle. Damage can be severe enough to kill plants. Early in the season, use floating row covers to protect small seedlings of broccoli, cabbage, and kale. Fungicides containing sulfur will repel flea beetles on rockcress and sweet alyssum. The insecticide rotenone provides some control. Flea beetles are usually not a problem after midsummer. — *M.T.* ◆

WHAT TO DO IN YOUR GARDEN IN JUNE

PLANTING

☐ PALMS. Zones 11–13 (Las Vegas, Tucson, Phoenix): Plant or transplant them into a hole the same depth as the rootball and twice as wide. Tie the fronds up over the bud to protect it. After new growth begins, cut the twine.

☐ SUMMER COLOR. Zones 1–2 (Taos, Santa Fe): Plant calendula, marigold, and zinnia early in the month. Zones 10–12: Plant celosia, four o'clock, globe amaranth, kochia, Madagascar periwinkle, portulaca, and zinnia early in the month in a place that gets only filtered sun.

☐ VEGETABLES. Zones 1–2, 10 (Albuquerque): Sow Brussels sprouts, cabbage, and carrots anytime this month. Zones 10–11: Plant corn during the first days of the month and cucumbers, melons, and summer squash by midmonth. Wait until midmonth to sow broccoli and cauliflower. Zones 12–13: You can still sow seeds of Armenian cucumbers, black-eyed peas, corn, melon, okra, and yard-long beans. Set out transplants of sweet potatoes early in the month.

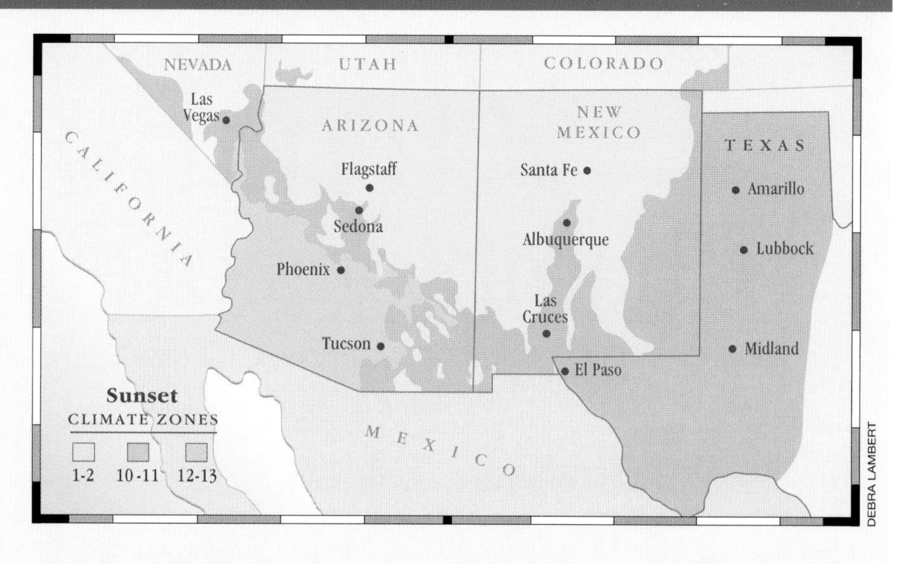

DEBRA LAMBERT

MAINTENANCE

☐ CARE FOR ROSES. Zones 11–13: Cut off faded flowers, then build a moat around each plant to concentrate water in the root zone. Mulch each plant well. Afternoon shade will help reduce heat stress. Zone 10: After first bloom, wet the soil, fertilize, and water again.

☐ MOW LAWNS. Cut Bermuda, St. Augustine, and zoysia grass to 1 to 1½ inches tall. Keep hybrid Bermuda at about 1 inch.

☐ MULCH PLANTS. Zones 10–13: Spread a 2- to 4-inch layer of organic or gravel mulch over the root zones of trees, shrubs, vines, flowers, and vegetables.

☐ TREAT CHLOROSIS. Zones 10–13: Iron deficiency (chlorosis) causes plants to develop yellow leaves with contrasting green veins. Apply a chelated iron product to the soil around the root zone, following package instructions.

☐ WATER. Zones 12–13: For fruit trees, adjust watering schedule to every 7 to 10 days. If you use a drip irrigation system, flood-irrigate monthly to wash accumulated salts out of the root zone.

PEST CONTROL

☐ BEET LEAFHOPPERS. These greenish yellow, inch-long insects spread curly top virus to cucumber, melon, and tomato plants. Protect crops by covering them with shade cloth. Remove and destroy infested plants.

☐ SQUASH VINE BORERS. Look for tiny eggs on squash vines. Rub them off before borers hatch out and drill into the vine, weakening the plant. — *Mary Irish* ◆

Zinnias: Champions of summer

Grow these favorites, old and new, for dazzling beds and bouquets

By Sharon Cohoon

■ If there were a summer Olympics for garden flowers, zinnias would surely emerge as gold medalists. These dazzling blooms have already won enough accolades to make fans everywhere sit up and take notice. In 1999, a dahlia-flowered zinnia series called Benary's Giants was selected as cut flower of the year by the Association of Specialty Cut Flower Growers. The All-America Selections (AAS) committee awarded another zinnia—the Profusion series—a gold medal for its faultless behavior as a bedding plant. And the National Garden Bureau is celebrating 2000 as the year of the zinnia.

It couldn't happen to nicer plants. *Sunset's* garden staff have always thought zinnias were tops, and we rarely let a year go by without planting a few varieties in our test gardens in Menlo Park, California. We adore zinnias' carnival-bright colors, starchy stems, and the way you can plop a bunch in a container for a great living bouquet. We admire their easy disposition—seeds germinate in a snap, and plants thrive on heat, don't require tons of water or fertilizer, and rarely need staking. The bedding varieties bloom their hearts out. Zinnias aren't plants you have to fuss with—you can just enjoy them. Isn't that what summer is all about?

Profusion Orange and Profusion Cherry score perfect 10s in the bedding plant category. At right, a bouquet of winning long-stemmed zinnias from our test garden. DESIGN: Jill Slater.

Last year, when we decided to plant many varieties at the test garden, everyone lobbied for a favorite. Garden editor Kathleen Brenzel pushed for 'Persian Carpet', an old-fashioned type with a sweet country-garden look that's becoming popular again. Senior editor Dick Bushnell made a pitch for Star White, a bedding plant with a rugged disposition and a dainty appearance that goes with everything. Senior writer Lauren Swezey made a strong case for *Zinnia peruviana,* a subtle flower that is almost as pretty dried as fresh—and can be dried right on the plant. *Sunset's* test garden coordinator, Bud Stuckey, is a fan of the Splendor series, whose large, beautifully formed flowers come in scarlet, pink, orange, and yellow. I love the range of colors and mix of singles and doubles in the Yoga series, and I have filled vases with these zinnias for several summers running.

We grew them all, plus a few others, with design help from Shirley Kerins, a Pasadena-based landscape architect with a well-honed sense of color. (Kerins's plan for our all-zinnia border appears on page 192.) Our experiment didn't change any opinions; we just added new loves to

NORMAN A. PLATE LEFT: SAXON HOLT

NORMAN A. PLATE BELOW: ALEXIS SEABROOK

All-zinnia border includes Star Gold (A), Star White (B), Profusion Orange (C), Profusion Cherry (D), 'Persian Carpet' (E), Splendor (F), Yoga (G), and Blue Point (H).

our lists. Following is our (semi-objective) report.

Zinnia elegans: A cut-flower favorite

When you think of zinnias, these are the flowers you picture. Though this group includes dwarf bedding plants, we concentrated on the star blooms for summer bouquets—long-stemmed, large-flowered types. These annuals love heat and aren't particularly demanding, but they *are* prone to powdery mildew, especially late in the season. Adequate spacing and no overhead watering or late-afternoon irrigations help gardeners get several months of good bloom before these plants become unsightly. Spraying with sulfur will delay the inevitable, as does stripping off affected leaves, which is much easier.

But the best preventive is planting disease-resistant varieties. Benary's Giants are probably the most disease-resistant *Z. elegans* on the market. These beauties have extra-long stems, very large (5-in.) flowers, jewel-bright colors, and long vase life. They are more costly than generic zinnias but are well worth the price.

Among the unresistant kinds, Splendor is a gorgeous series—fully double flowers with ruffly, slightly squared petals and a pretty crown of gold stars at the center. The Yoga series isn't as fancy, but it comes in singles and doubles, and in a wide color range that includes lilac, salmon, coral, and burgundy.

Other zinnia favorites include 'Envy', a chartreuse-flowered zinnia that has always been popular with floral designers (lime makes every other color sing), and 'Candy Cane' and 'Candy Stripe', which bear white flowers splashed with pink, rose, or red, or orange flowers with gold flecks; both varieties are good mixers in bouquets.

SAXON HOLT

A ribbon of hot pink Profusion Cherry meanders through the center of a Profusion Orange bed. This series blooms so liberally that it creates a carpet of pure color.

Other zinnias for cutting

Zinnia haageana is quite different from *Z. elegans.* The plant has narrower leaves, is more compact (1½ ft. tall), and has relatively small flowers (1 to 2 in. diameter). But it's a fantastic cut flower in its own casual, wildflower-looking way. 'Old Mexico' is a double-flowered type that bears mahogany blooms tipped with gold. (It won an AAS award in 1962.) 'Persian Carpet' (an AAS winner in '52) is similar, but its flowers also include orange and deep red shades with more variations in pattern. Mildew is not a problem for *Z. haageana* or any of the plants that follow.

Z. peruviana bears tiny flowers (1½ in. diameter) in subtle colors (brick red or soft gold), but it's surprisingly effective in the garden or in a vase. *Z. peruviana* (also called the Bonita series or *Z. pauciflora*) beautifully complements yarrow, coneflower, salvia, and other casual flowers in bouquets. At the same time, it looks great solo. No need to get out silica crystals or even hang the stems for drying the buttonlike blooms; the flowers dry in the vase or on the plant.

Spreading zinnias

Zinnia angustifolia (like the Star series) and interspecies crosses with *Z. angustifolia* in their parentage (such as the award-winning Profusion series) have stems that are too short for cutting; they range from 12 to 18 inches in length. But they're superb in beds and borders: They flower quickly, pump out blooms until frost, and are nearly maintenance-free. They're wonderful in beds and borders. They're also great edgers for a traditional mixed border or to give a cutting border a finished appearance, and they thrive in containers.

Planting

From nursery starts. Zinnias come in sixpacks, jumbo-packs, and 4-inch pots, depending on variety and local growers' practices. Tip pots on their sides to gently remove the tender transplants; with sixpacks, use your thumb to push rootballs up from the bottom. Dig a planting hole larger than the plant's rootball. Set the plant in the hole, making sure the top of the rootball is even with the surrounding soil surface. Firm soil around roots and water well.

From seed. Sow seeds directly in the ground in an area with full sun. Average soil is acceptable, but if you add compost and all-purpose fertilizer to the soil before sowing, you'll get lusher crops, especially from *Z. elegans.* Sow seeds 2 to 3 inches apart in rows 12 inches apart or as recommended on seed packets. Barely cover seeds with soil; they need light to germinate. Keep soil moist until seeds germinate, in 5 to 10 days. Then thin seedlings according to packet instructions, usually 10 to 12 inches apart.

Care

- Protect seedlings from slugs and snails until they're older and tougher.
- Water young plants frequently—always at ground level to avoid wetting foliage—until they reach several inches tall. Then water less often but more deeply, approximately 1 inch of water per week.
- To encourage strong growth and flowering, feed lightly with a general fertilizer once a month.

Where to find zinnias

You'll find many varieties of zinnias at your local nursery. You can also find a wide selection at these mail-order sources.

NORMAN A. PLATE

A splash of *Z. angustifolia* Star White makes a cool contrast to the hot colors of most other zinnias.

Burpee Seeds & Plants (BS), 300 Park Ave., Warminster, PA 18974; (800) 888-1447 or www.burpee.com.

Nichols Garden Nursery (NGN), 1190 Old Salem Rd. N.E., Albany, OR 97321; (541) 928-9280 or www.nicholsgardennursery.com.

Park Seed (PS), 1 Parkton Ave., Greenwood, SC 29647; (800) 845-3369 or www.parkseed.com.

Renee's Garden Seeds (RG), available at many nursery and garden centers; (888) 880-7228 or www.reneesgarden.com.

Select Seeds (SS), 180 Stickney Hill Rd., Union, CT 06076; (860) 684-9310 or www.selectseeds.com.

Shepherd's Garden Seeds (SGS), 30 Irene St., Torrington, CT 06790; (860) 482-3638 or www.shepherdseeds.com.

Territorial Seed Company (TS), Box 157, Cottage Grove, OR 97424; (541) 942-9547 or www.territorial-seed.com.

A dozen dazzlers for summer gardens

Variety/type	Color	Plant height	Flower size	Sources
ZINNIA ELEGANS				
Benary's Giants (Blue Point or Park's Picks)	Wide range	40–50″	4–5″	PS, RG, SGS, TS
Splendor	Scarlet, pink, orange, yellow	22″	4–5″	BS
Yoga	Wide range	30–36″	3–4″	SGS
'Envy'	Lime green	24–30″	2½–3″	NGN, SGS
'Candy Cane'	Striped	17″	4″	BS
'Candy Stripe'	Striped	24″	4″	PS
ZINNIA HAAGEANA				
'Old Mexico'	Copper and gold	18″	2″	SS, TS
'Persian Carpet'	Burnished colors	18–28″	2″	RG, SGS, SS
ZINNIA PERUVIANA (Bonita)	Brick red, soft gold	24″	1½″	SGS, SS, TS
ZINNIA ANGUSTIFOLIA				
Star	White, gold, orange	14–16″	1″	BS, SGS
Profusion	Orange, cherry pink	12–18″	2–2½″	BS, NGN, RG ◆

A dry stream meanders through plantings and boulders as a natural wash would. Gnarled wood "bridge" is the trunk of a tea tree (*Leptospermum*) that formerly grew on this spot. This area measures about 800 square feet.

It's Big Bear, in Arcadia

The Woodland Garden at *Sunset's* Demonstration Garden captures the spirit of the mountains, with Mediterranean plants

By Sharon Cohoon

If you inherit a property where mature pine trees grow, the natural impulse is to create a woodland garden beneath them. The problem is that most of us carry around a mental image of a woodland garden that is totally incompatible with Southern California's Mediterranean sunshine, alkaline soil, and sparse rainfall. The trick is to pull off the same effect with plants that grow best in an *arroyo seco* (dry stream). It can be done. The Woodland Garden in the *Sunset* Demonstration Garden at the Arboretum of Los Angeles County in Arcadia, shown above, offers proof.

To come up with the design, Anna Armstrong and Richard Walker, of Armstrong & Walker Landscape Architecture in Monrovia, turned for inspiration to California's coastal redwood forests and the riparian habitats of our canyons. They planted Western redbuds instead of dogwoods. In place of rhododendrons, they put in abutilons. And instead of columbines and trilliums, they brought together an assortment of grasslike plants, including Douglas iris, blue-eyed grass, *Festuca glauca,* kangaroo paw (with mustard and brick red blooms), and blue tall bearded iris

Without the riverbed running through them, these fine-textured plants probably wouldn't look as convincingly woodland. But the stream does more than set the scene. It solves a problem. The soil here was heavy and drained poorly. The streambed they created acts like a reservoir, allowing rainfall to percolate deeply into the soil, and feeding tree roots.

Woodland-style gardens, says Armstrong, are good choices for people who appreciate low-maintenance, natural-looking landscaping.

For a firsthand look, visit the arboretum at 301 N. Baldwin Avenue, Arcadia (9–4:30 daily). The *Sunset* Demonstration Garden is just beyond the arboretum entrance. ◆

The world's most popular annual celebrates 50 years

SUMMER PLEASURES

irresistible impatiens

of breeding, with more flower colors and patterns than ever

Move over, marigolds and petunias: Impatiens (*I. wallerana*)—the spectacular ever-blooming beauty queens of the summer shade border—are now the most popular bedding plants on the planet. And not by a small margin. Many garden centers report that today these jungle beauties, which were relatively obscure before World War II, account for 25 percent of sales.

In spite of impatiens' odd common names—like busy Lizzie, touch-me-not, and snapweed—their meteoric rise to fame isn't surprising. Impatiens are extraordinarily easy to grow: "Just dig a hole, put the green side up, water, and stand back," one specialist jokingly advised. Insects and diseases don't bother them, and the plants are incredibly adaptable to almost any climate. They're floriferous, blooming nonstop from spring until first frost—and even throughout winter in mild coastal areas. They're among a few colorful annuals that thrive and bloom in full shade. And they come in every color of the rainbow, except true blue and true yellow, and in a host of interesting flower patterns.

New Firefly Violet mini-impatiens edge a path of baby's tears, at left. DESIGN: Robert Clark, Oakland, CA (510/633-1391)

The impatiens clan wasn't always so impressive. Native to Africa and naturalized in Costa Rica, wild impatiens are gangly, 3-foot-tall plants with only scattered blooms. Thanks to breeding efforts over the past 40 years (see "Meet the father of modern impatiens," page 200), modern impatiens are much more refined, with an improved branching habit, a more compact form, and new flower colors and patterns.

SAXON HOLT (2)

By Lauren Bonar Swezey

From dainty minis to superstars

Gardeners can now choose from a wide assortment of impatiens to fit any garden style.

Tall to small. Elfin, the first series developed for the consumer market, was originally 2 feet tall. After years of breeding and a name change to Super Elfin, the series now includes some of the most compact plants—8 to 10 inches tall. Most other series (Dazzler, Infinity, and Starbright, for instance) range from 10 to 14 inches in height.

NEW FOR 2000: Firefly series, a charming mini-impatiens, tops out at 6 to 8 inches tall. Dainty ½-inch-wide flowers come in orange, red, salmon, lavender, violet, or white.

Colors and more colors. Impatiens come in an amazing array of colors from coral, orange, and salmon to burgundy, red, pink, purple, and white and every shade in between. Accent, a popular series with large (2- to 3-inch diameter) flowers, comes in 26 single colors and 8 mixes.

Super Elfin has 23 individual colors and 4 mixes. Super Elfin Sunrise is one of the most unusual colors of any series. It starts out iridescent salmon-orange with purple edges, then ages to purple. Another striking color in the series is Blue Pearl, which is the closest breeders have come to a true blue.

Although *I. wallerana* does not come in true yellow, a related impatiens series, Seashell, was introduced two years ago that includes yellow flowers. The blooms are shell-like, rather than flat and open.

Designer mixes. Some impatiens grow in mixed colors, which have come a long way in the past few years. Formerly random, with clashing colors like pinks and oranges, mixes nowadays are well matched and are sold in designer colors—Mystic Mixture (lavender), Cranberry Punch Mixture, Merlot Mix, and Sunrise Mixture—that nod to interior design and fashion trends.

NEW FOR 2000: Super Elfin Parfait Mix (pinks) and Paradise Mix (tropical colors) are now available. As part of Goldsmith Seeds' Plant for the Cure program, a portion of the proceeds from the sale of Accent Miracle Mix (three shades of pink) goes to the Susan G. Komen

Planting and care

Follow these planting and care guidelines for a glorious show all season.

- Choose a site with dappled shade, morning sun, or late-afternoon sun. On the coast, you can also plant in full sun as long as there's no reflected light or heat from pavement or a wall.
- For border plantings: Before planting, mix compost or an organic amendment into the soil.
- For container plantings: Mix soil polymers (such as Broadleaf P-4, available from the Urban Farmer Store; 800/753-3747) into the potting mix to help reduce watering frequency.

NEW LOOKS

swirl pink

fiesta pink ruffle

NORMAN A. PLATE (6)

Breast Cancer Foundation.

Swirls and stars. Novelty impatiens, such as Mosaic (white patterning scattered over a color) and Swirl (dark-edged, pastel-colored flowers), are relatively new. Breeders have taken the look of impatiens one step farther with these markings.

NEW FOR 2000: Stardust series is the latest addition to the star-patterned impatiens. Its stars, which appear in the center of bright petals, have blurred edges that look dusty.

Double delight. At first glance double impatiens look like miniroses. They're propagated from cuttings to achieve fully double blooms, and they include Fiesta, Tioga, and Victorian, the 1998 All-America Selections winner. These dainty flowers are best used in containers, where they can be appreciated up close.

Sunny-side up. The most popular shade plant isn't just for shade anymore. The Impact series, introduced two years ago, was bred to take more heat and sun. Though they don't do well in blazing heat or full sun reflected off of a white wall, in a mild to warm climate, Impact impatiens thrive in sunny borders if given plenty of water.

- Loosen the rootball before planting, especially if it looks rootbound.
- Fertilize monthly during the growing season or mix a controlled-release fertilizer into the planting hole.
- Water after planting, then keep the soil constantly moist (but not soggy) all season.

Annuals and perennials make perfect partners for impatiens in borders. LEFT: Lobelias, green heucheras, and maidenhair ferns are interplanted with Dazzler White and Super Elfin Blue Pearl, Pearl, Pink, and Rose. ABOVE: Accent Orange impatiens and lime and red coleus spice up a partly sunny border.

Designing with impatiens

Since impatiens come in such a wide array of colors, both soft-hued and bold, they pair beautifully with shade plants. Here are ways to use them.

Plant them en masse.

- Mix two or three complementary or contrasting colors and then add a few whites to spark up the palette.
- For a refined look, weave swaths of sophisticated single colors (coral or lilac, for instance) in and out of permanent shrubbery.
- Use pale impatiens to brighten up dark borders or add a spot of light below trees.

Mix them with other shade lovers.

- Mix one or several colors with ferns, corydalis, or other fine-textured shade plants in borders.
- Combine white impatiens with white-edged hostas.
- Interplant orange impatiens with lime coleus and ferns.

Cluster plants in containers.

- Impatiens thrive in any kind of container, including

super elfin sunrise

stardust rose

NORMAN A. PLATE

TUCKER AND HOSSLER

Impatiens add color to pot plantings. LEFT: Accent Coral pairs with sweet alyssum and *Helichrysum* 'Limelight' in a terra-cotta container. RIGHT: Intensely colored New Guinea impatiens enliven a two-tiered patio planter.

terra-cotta pots, glazed urns, moss-lined hanging baskets, and window boxes. Plant impatiens with begonias, coleus, ferns, fuchsias, hydrangeas, and lobelias.

The other impatiens

New Guinea impatiens—hybrids of several different impatiens species native to New Guinea—first stormed the market about 20 years ago. Generally more vigorous than *I. wallerana,* they have bigger leaves and flowers; some have striking variegated foliage. They were originally touted as impatiens for full sun, but time has shown that they perform much better in partial shade (or morning sun and afternoon shade), particularly in inland climates.

New Guinea impatiens put on a great bloom show, with large flowers (2–2½ inches wide) held high above foliage on plants 12 to 24 inches tall. But Celebration—a popular series that regularly wins top marks in university trials—grows 18 to 22 inches tall and bears flowers up to 3 inches wide. Once considered container plants, many of the newest series of New Guinea impatiens (Celebration, Paradise, and Pure Beauty, for instance) also perform well in the landscape. Baby Bonita, a miniature that grows to 8 inches tall, is best for window boxes and small containers.

Meet the father of modern impatiens

Claude Hope, 93, is a living legend in the seed business. For nearly 50 years, he's been hybridizing impatiens, petunias, salvias, and other annuals at his farm in Costa Rica. • Hope first arrived in Central America in 1943 to work on quinine research for the U.S. Army. While there, he became enchanted by the impatiens he saw growing throughout the countryside. "Charmed at first sight," Hope says. • After the war, Hope pursued his passion for plant breeding. In the early 1960s, he began tinkering with impatiens to increase the size and number of blooms and to improve growth habit. "I don't know of any other plant that shows as much variation in color and patterning," he notes. In 1967, Hope introduced Elfin to the world. • Almost every impatiens available today is a descendant of the first cross he made at his farm. ◆

ROB CARDILLO

Best of the West

By Steven R. Lorton • Illustration by Charlene Rendeiro

A regional romance

Westerners dote on their roses, and roses love the West

■ The West is rose country.

As far back as 35 or 40 million years ago, fossils testify, roses were growing in Colorado, Oregon, and Montana. When the first Europeans arrived in the West, they found wild roses all about, as far north as Alaska. Cultivated varieties such as the damask rose, introduced by a Frenchman in 1786, took to the region with enthusiasm.

Nowadays the West starts off the nation's year with Pasadena's Tournament of Roses. As the year progresses, roses emerge throughout the region: by April in the Southwest, by May in the San Francisco Bay Area. Come June, Portland's Rose Festival is in full swing, and the climbers and ramblers of Washington and British Columbia sprawl floriferously over garden walls. The mountain states are abloom by July.

Roses are also big business in the West. Ninety-five percent of the nation's roses are field-grown in Western states, over half in Wasco, California, which celebrates its agricultural prowess with a Festival of Roses in September (661/758-2616).

A changing and improving palette of blooms has resulted from Western hybridizing: 'Charlotte Armstrong', 'Chrysler Imperial', and 'Queen Elizabeth', all developed by Dr. Walter E. Lammerts; 'Brandy', 'Double Delight', and 'Sutter's Gold', created by Robert C. Swim. A modern master is Ralph Moore, a miniature-rose specialist who introduced 'Cal Poly' and the Halo series (Halo Fire, Halo Sunrise, and the new Halo Sunset).

The young wonders join cherished old plants, many of them heirlooms. When you visit a Western garden, it's not uncommon to be escorted to a venerable shrub rose and told, "My great-great-grandmother brought this out as a cutting on a covered wagon."

To savor the richness of roses, you need only visit one of the region's many gardens. Here are some of the West's best.

ARIZONA. Mesa: Rose Garden at Mesa Community College. Open 24 hours daily; free. 1833 W. Southern Ave.; (480) 895-7793.

CALIFORNIA. Berkeley: Berkeley Municipal Rose Garden. Dawn-dusk daily; free. Euclid Ave. and Bayview Place; (510) 644-6530.

La Cañada Flintridge: Descanso Gardens. 9–4:30 daily; $5, $3 seniors and students, $1 ages 5–12. 1418 Descanso Dr.; (818) 952-4401.

Pasadena: Wrigley Rose Gardens. 9–dusk daily; free. 391 S. Orange Grove Blvd.; (626) 449-4100.

San Diego: Inez Grant Parker Memorial Rose Garden in Balboa Park. Dawn-dusk daily; free. 1114 Park Blvd.; (619) 239-0512.

San Jose: Heritage Rose Garden. Dawn-dusk daily; free. 715 Spring St.; (408) 298-7657.

San Marino: Huntington Botanical Gardens. 10:30–4:30 Tue-Sun; $8.50. 1151 Oxford Rd.; (626) 405-2100.

Woodside: Filoli. 10–2 Tue-Sat; $10, $1 ages 1–12. 86 Cañada Rd.; (650) 364-8300.

COLORADO. Longmont: Longmont Memorial Rose Garden. Dawn–11:30 daily; free. 700 block of Bross St.; (303) 651-8446.

IDAHO. Boise: Julia Davis Municipal Rose Garden. Dawn-dusk daily; free. Julia Davis Dr.; (208) 384-4327.

MONTANA. Missoula: Missoula Memorial Rose Garden. 6–11 daily; free. Brooks and Mount streets; (406) 721-7275.

OREGON. Portland: International Rose Test Garden in Washington Park. 7–9 daily; free. 400 S.W. Kingston Ave.; (503) 823-3636.

WASHINGTON. Seattle: Woodland Park Rose Garden. Dawn-dusk daily; free. 700 N. 50th St.; (206) 684-4863.

Tacoma: Point Defiance Park Rose Garden. Dawn-dusk daily; free. 5400 N. Pearl St.; (253) 305-1000.

BRITISH COLUMBIA. Brentwood Bay (near Victoria), Vancouver Island: **Butchart Gardens.** 9–8 daily; $16.50. 800 Benvenuto Ave.; (250) 652-4422. ◆

Living lettuce bowl contains romaine, 'Red Oak Leaf', and butter lettuce. Smaller pots around it hold chives, parsley, rosemary, and basil.

MARION BRENNER

Snip-and-serve greenery

Dress your barbecued burgers with garden-fresh lettuce and herbs from tabletop pots

By Jill Slater
Recipes by Andrew Baker

When summer barbecues call for backyard buffets, why not put crops from your garden on the menu? A pot of salad greens, surrounded by smaller pots filled with herbs such as basil, chives, parsley, and rosemary, makes an attractive garden centerpiece for a patio table. As a bonus, guests can snip bits to garnish grilled burgers (provide cutting tools beside the pots—bonsai clippers work well).

Fragrant basil is always a crowd pleaser, and on a burger topped with chives and melted cheese, it's a taste treat. Maybe you prefer cilantro or Italian parsley. No matter which greens you grow, plant them about three weeks before the barbecue to give them time to fill out. (In hottest weather, grow the lettuce under a lath.) Or stagger planting times, a pot per week, so you always have plants ready for snipping.

To reinforce the garden theme, fill harvest baskets with fresh-picked tomatoes, peppers, corn, and cucumbers, and place them near the barbecue and buffet, with slicing knives and cutting boards at the ready. Many vegetables—such as pattypan squash, peppers, and tomatoes—are delicious when sizzled on the grill; they'll complement garden-fresh salads and barbecue fare (for a beef burger recipe, see the facing page).

Garden Projects

Lettuce Centerpiece

TIME: About 30 minutes
COST: About $45

MATERIALS

- Large terra-cotta bowl, at least 16 inches in diameter, with drain holes
- Small bag of potting soil
- Lettuces (about five sixpacks)—choose several varieties, such as butter lettuce, romaine, 'Red Oak Leaf', and Swiss chard
- Trowel

PLANTING AND CARE

1. Fill the container halfway with potting soil.

2. Push plants from their sixpacks, then plant them about 2 inches apart. For best effects, group them by kind, with the tallest plants (such as romaine) in the back. Fill in around them with more potting soil.

3. Set the lettuce centerpiece in filtered shade and water it well.

4. Continue to water regularly; fertilize once a week with dilute fish emulsion.

The day of the barbecue, thoroughly mist the leaves with water to clean them before placing the container on the patio table.

Herb Garnishes

TIME: About 15 minutes

COST: About $30 for eight pots

MATERIALS

- Eight 4-inch clay pots with saucers
- Potting soil
- Eight herbs, such as basil, chives, parsley, and rosemary, in small pots

PLANTING

1. Fill each container about one-quarter full with potting soil.

2. Remove plants from nursery pots, loosen the rootballs, then slip them into the 4-inch pots.

3. Fill in around plants with more potting soil.

4. Water thoroughly.

Recipes

Beef Burgers for a Garden Barbecue

PREP AND COOK TIME: About 40 minutes

NOTES: Snip herbs from the table garden to embellish these burgers. If desired, lay herbs on the grilling patties, then top them with cheese; the cheese will help anchor the herbs in place. Before serving, sprinkle additional herbs atop the melted cheese. Accompany the burgers with grilled vegetables, such as peppers, from the garden or market.

To grill bell peppers, rinse them and cut them in half lengthwise; then discard stems and seeds. Lay peppers skin side down beside beef burgers; cook until charred on the bottom, about 6 minutes. Let them cool slightly; if desired, pull off pepper skins and discard.

MAKES: 12 servings

TUCKER & HOSSLER

Thinly sliced cheese melts over tender basil laid on burger while it's on the grill. Chives garnish the top.

3 **large eggs**

About 1¼ teaspoons **salt**

¾ teaspoon **pepper**

3 pounds **ground lean beef**

¾ cup **fine dried bread crumbs**

12 thin slices **Swiss cheese** (about 5 oz. total; optional)

12 **round sandwich buns** (4 to 4½ in.), cut in half horizontally

Condiments (choices follow)

1. In a large bowl, beat eggs, 1¼ teaspoons salt, and pepper to blend. Add beef and bread crumbs; mix gently to avoid compacting meat. Form 12 equal patties, each ½ inch thick.

2. Lay patties on a barbecue grill over a solid bed of hot coals or high heat on a gas grill (you can hold your hand at grill level only 2 to 3 seconds); close lid on gas grill. Turning once to brown evenly, cook until a thermometer inserted in center of thickest part reads 160° (no pink in the center), 6 to 8 minutes total.

3. When patties are almost done, if desired, top each with a slice of cheese. Also lay buns, cut side down, on grill and toast about 30 seconds.

4. With a wide spatula, transfer patties to bun bottoms. Add condiments and salt to taste. Cover with bun tops.

Per serving: 432 cal., 46% (198 cal.) from fat; 29 g protein; 22 g fat (8.9 g sat.); 27 g carbo (1.1 g fiber); 649 mg sodium; 134 mg chol.

Condiments

BLUE CHEESE AIOLI. In a bowl mash to blend 1 teaspoon minced **garlic,** ¼ cup **crumbled blue cheese,** and 1 cup **mayonnaise.** Makes about 1 cup.

Per tablespoon: 106 cal., 93% (99 cal.) from fat; 0.6 g protein; 11 g fat (2 g sat.); 0.5 g carbo (0 g fiber); 108 mg sodium; 9.7 mg chol.

CHIPOTLE CATSUP. Discard seeds and veins from 1 or 2 **canned chipotle chilies.** In a blender, combine 2 tablespoons of the canned chipotles' sauce, 1 cup **catsup,** and 1 chipotle chili; whirl smooth. Taste, and if desired, add remaining chili and whirl smooth. Makes about 1 cup.

Per tablespoon: 18 cal., 5% (0.9 cal.) from fat; 0.2 g protein; 0.1 g fat (0 g sat.); 4.5 g carbo (0.3 g fiber); 201 mg sodium; 0 mg chol.

MARGARITA MUSTARD. In a bowl stir together 1 cup **Dijon mustard,** ¼ cup **tequila,** 2 teaspoons **lime juice,** and 1 teaspoon grated **orange** peel. Makes about 1¼ cups.

Per tablespoon: 20 cal., 0% (0 cal.) from fat; 0 g protein; 0 g fat; 0.1 g carbo (0 g fiber); 288 mg sodium; 0 mg chol. ◆

Fresh Flower Project

Singular sensations

Arrange a festive, 1-bunch bouquet in minutes to dress up a garden party table

By Kathleen N. Brenzel
Designs by Jill Slater
Photographs by Norman A. Plate

Fresh, casual, and as colorful as candy, lollipop-shaped arrangements are the perfect way to show off luscious summer blooms. They couldn't be simpler: You just gather a bunch of sunflowers, gerberas, Oriental lilies, roses, or other favorite flowers, then anchor them in moist florist's foam in a terra-cotta pot. A single type and color of flower is an eye-catcher. For extra punch, paint the pot to match the blooms; patio paints suitable for use on terracotta are available at well-stocked nurseries. Or for a country look, mix several types of flowers and leave the pot unpainted. Beautiful ribbons add festive finishing touches.

A single pot can center a small, round patio table; three to five pots—filled with the same flowers—can march in a line down a long, rectangular table.

Use flowers with long, sturdy stems from your own garden or from a florist. Kept moist, flowers can last a week or more (use a spray bottle to moisten the florist's foam every few days, if needed).

Nothing says summer like this arrangement of yellow sunflowers in a sky blue pot.

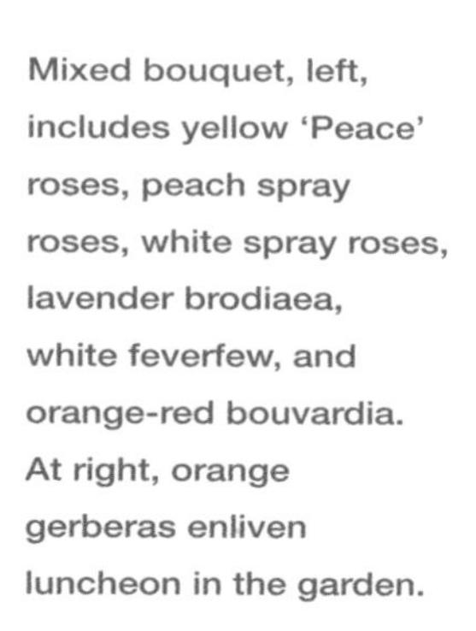

Mixed bouquet, left, includes yellow 'Peace' roses, peach spray roses, white spray roses, lavender brodiaea, white feverfew, and orange-red bouvardia. At right, orange gerberas enliven luncheon in the garden.

HOW TO MAKE IT

TIME: About 15 minutes, plus drying time for paint (optional)

COST: $25–$30 (less if you use your own flowers)

TOOLS AND MATERIALS FOR ONE POT

- 4-inch, tapered terra-cotta pot (leave natural or paint with patio paint, sold at nurseries)
- Plastic food bag (to line the pot)
- Scissors, knife to cut florist's foam, and clippers
- Block of florist's foam
- 7 to 10 stems of flowers such as China asters, dahlias, gerberas, lilies, roses, or sunflowers
- Rubber band
- Sphagnum moss
- 1 yard of French ribbon (with wired edges)

DIRECTIONS

1. Line the pot with the plastic food bag; trim excess with scissors.

2. Soak the florist's foam until thoroughly moistened.

3. Using the knife, cut the foam in half, then round the corners; push the foam into the pot.

4. Gather the flower stems in one hand, holding them just under the bloom while you arrange them in a lollipop shape (**A**). Turn the flower stems upside down and secure them with a rubber band, sliding it down the stems to just under the blooms (**B**). Cut the stems to the desired length. Holding the bundled stems toward the bottom, insert stem ends into the center of the foam (**C**). Cover the florist's foam with moistened sphagnum moss. Finish with ribbon, covering the rubber band, as shown (**D**). ◆

A mirror mounted on a garden wall looks like an opening to another landscape.

BEN WOOLSEY

Mirror magic

Through the looking glass: Three ways to use reflective illusions in your garden

By Steven R. Lorton

Imagine an opening in a garden wall. You move closer, attempt to peer through it to glimpse the leaves, flowers, and branches moving gently in the breeze on the other side. But then a person comes into view. It's you.

Startling? Perhaps. Magical? For certain. And therein lies the shimmering wonder of a garden mirror. It tricks, illuminates, and doubles the beauty.

Western gardeners are discovering the power of mirrors, using the reflective glass in creative ways in the garden; three examples are shown on these pages. On a wall, a mirror seems to expand a garden beyond its boundaries. Small mirrors can look like windows on the outside world. On the ground, a mirror is a surprisingly good substitute for a real pond, especially when you edge it with boulders and small weeping conifers or grasses.

Outdoor mirrors are installed differently than those indoors; for one thing, you need to protect the glass from moisture damage. Installation tips are on the facing page.

Reflected glory

Barbara and Jack Thomas put a mirror on the wall of their Seattle garden, behind a shallow pool (above).

The 4- by 8-foot mirror looks like an opening in the wall that frames a garden beyond, making the pool and patio appear twice as large as they really are. A stone lion's head, which seems to float above a potted plant, drips water into the pool. It was mounted through a hole in the mirror, drilled at a glass shop. Ivy obscures the mirror's edges, adding to the illusion.

THOMAS J. STORY

Stones of different sizes flank this small mirror, giving it the look of a mountain pool.

A glacial "pool"

Water can turn a tiny garden from ordinary to interesting. Here's a way to bring the look of a small pool to a bed or border without disturbing existing roots: Build an illusory pool.

In the alpine border pictured here, *Sunset* test garden coordinator Bud Stuckey used a mirror to create the look of a glacial lake. Among boulders and plants, he placed a 16-inch-square mirror. He masked the edges by adding a layer of smooth river rocks of varying sizes and colors to mimic a rocky beach. Low, mounding grasses such as blue fescue soften the look. The mirror reflects the sky and surrounding rocks and plants the way a mountain pool would, bouncing light throughout the space.

Installation tips

Working with mirrors

- Wear heavy leather gloves and protective glasses.
- If you will be placing the mirror where children play, use safety glass.
- To prevent moisture damage, seal mirror edges by painting "edge seal" (a lacquerlike substance available at glass shops) around all sides.

Vertically mounted mirrors

- Add a backing such as exterior-grade ¾-inch plywood. Use mirror mastic, a strong waterproof adhesive that's available at large hardware stores and glass shops, to mount the mirror to the plywood.
- Give the mirror proper support.
- Frame the mirror with wood, metal, plastic, or even tile.

Mirrors on the ground

- Choose a level spot among plants.
- Dig out 2 inches of soil and replace it with builder's sand, packed firm.

Windows in the wall: Easy to make from mirror tiles

They look like deep, framed portholes in the fence, inviting you to peek through them. But each "porthole" pictured below is really a foot-square mirror tile set into the back of a box frame made with 2-by-4s. The garden they reflect is your own.

PETER O. WHITELEY (2)

COST: About $5 each

TIME: Less than 2 hours

MATERIALS (for one mirror)

- 6-foot length of rough-sawn 2-by-4
- Eight 2-inch galvanized finish nails or deck screws
- Wood stain (we used gray semitransparent)
- 1-foot-square mirror tile
- 1-foot-square piece of ⅛-inch hardboard or plywood (optional)
- Staples
- Two 1-inch eye screws
- Picture-hanging wire

TOOLS

To make a mirror frame, you'll need a table saw, circular saw, or router to cut a rabbet (notch) in the edge of the 2-by-4. Use a hammer and nail set or an electric drill with countersink bit to join the frame pieces.

DIRECTIONS

1. Cut a ⅝- by ⅝-inch rabbet along one edge of the 2-by-4.

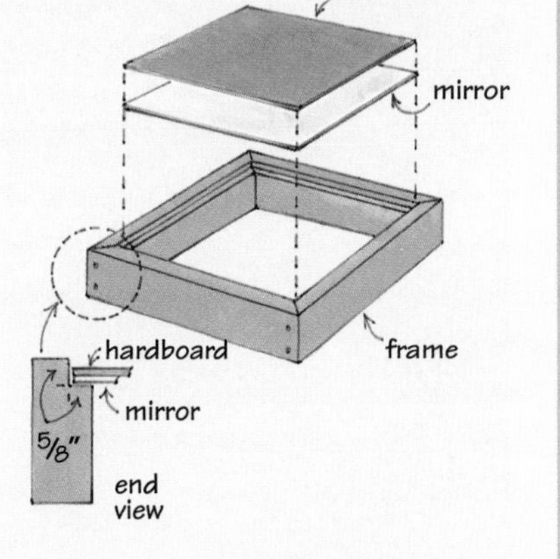

2. Cut the 2-by-4 into four 14-inch-long pieces with mitered ends. Position the rabbets on the inside edge of the rear of the frame.

3. Assemble frame with nails or countersunk screws.

4. Stain wood.

5. Insert mirror (and optional backing). Hold in place with staples.

6. Add eye screws and wire. Hang on fence. — *Peter O. Whiteley* ◆

Splendor in the grass

The perfect summer lawn starts now

By Jim McCausland

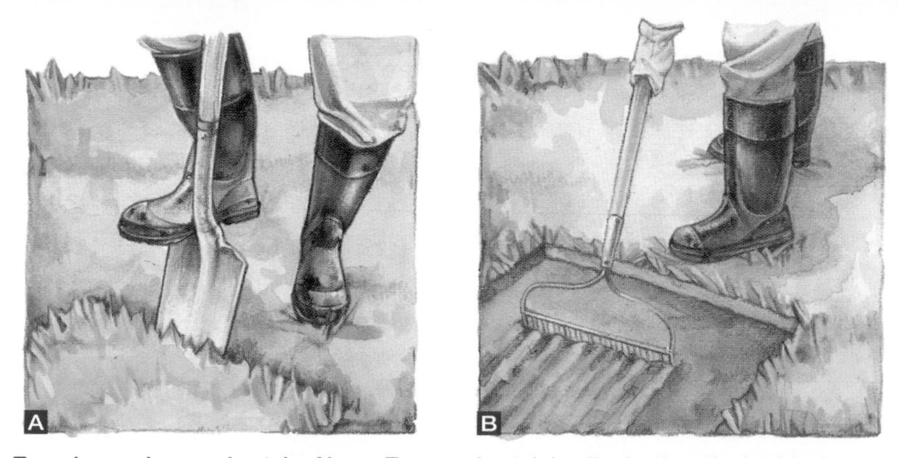

To replace a damaged patch of lawn: Trace sod patch by digging into the healthy lawn around it with a spade (A). Remove patch; cut away lawn at trace marks. Remove 3 to 4 inches of soil and level the surface with a rake (B); sprinkle soil with granular fertilizer. Lay sod patch in place, stretching and pressing it to fit (C). Tamp to firm, then water well.

In summer, lawns get hammered. There's extra wear and tear from weekend play, stress from summer heat, and corresponding pressure from utilities in some areas to cut back on watering. But if you start a sensible lawn-care program now, you can strengthen your turf going into summer, help it stay greener, and give it a better chance against the ravages of insects and disease.

Fertilize. If you haven't fertilized yet this year—or if you're growing heavy feeders such as perennial ryegrass, tall fescue, Kentucky bluegrass, hybrid Bermuda, or St. Augustine—apply 2 pounds actual nitrogen per 1,000 square feet. If you've fertilized during the past four months and aren't growing a heavy feeder, give the grass 1 pound actual nitrogen per 1,000 square feet. (The first number in a fertilizer bag's large, three-number label gives the percentage of nitrogen in the bag. A 100-pound bag of 29-3-4 fertilizer, for example, contains 29 percent actual nitrogen, or 29 pounds.)

Mow. Cut often, so you never have to shorten the grass by more than a third at one mowing. Use a mulching mower with a sharp blade. Since

LINDA HOLT AYRISS (3)

grass clippings contain 3 to 5 percent nitrogen, they feed the lawn if you let them drop (don't bag them). This allows you to reduce your annual lawn-feeding program by half. Mow warm-season grasses at 1 inch ($^3/_4$ inch for hybrid Bermuda) and cut cool-season grasses at 2 inches ($^1/_2$ inch for bent grass).

Dethatch. Most warm-season grasses develop thatch, a spongelike layer of roots, runners, and grass blades just above the soil surface. Thatch interferes with the downward flow of fertilizer and water, depriving plant roots; thin it now, if you haven't already done so (use a dethatcher from a rental yard). The lawn will recover quickly and will perform better through summer. Dethatch cool-season grasses like Kentucky bluegrass and fine fescue in fall.

Water. Most lawns need about 1 inch of water per week. Apply it deeply and infrequently rather than often and shallowly—and early in the morning when there's less wind and evaporation than during the heat of the day.

Control pests and diseases. To keep the lawn looking its best, watch for signs of critter damage or disease, and deal with either immediately.

DOGS. If a dog urinates on your lawn, flood the area with hose water. Don't try to repair doggy spots (dead spots among healthy green grass) by fertilizing; the excess nitrogen in dog urine kills the grass, so adding more nitrogen won't help. Remove dead patches along with 3 to 4 inches of soil underneath; fill the hole with a fresh piece of sod, as shown above, or overseed.

INSECTS. Insect problems vary regionally and seasonally. In Idaho's Snake River basin, billbug is a summer problem. In California and the Southwest, chinch bugs can suck the life out of zoysia and St. Augustine in summer. Treat both chinch bug and billbug with Dursban.

DISEASES. Highly maintained lawns (mowed low, heavily fertilized, liberally watered) are the most subject to disease. Fight disease by backing off on fertilizer and water, and by raising the mowing height by 25 percent.

WEEDS. On cool-season lawns, weeds really take hold when the grass starts to go dormant in July. Hand-weed small infestations as soon as they appear. For larger infestations, try a preemergence herbicide made from corn gluten meal (available at nurseries).

Tall fescue, a cool-season grass, grows into a lush emerald carpet .

NORMAN A. PLATE (5)

What's my lawn?

Lawn care depends on whether your turf is made up of warm- or cool-season grasses. Here's how to tell which kind you have.

Cool-season grasses include bent grass, fescue, Kentucky bluegrass, and ryegrass. If you live in the Pacific Northwest or any cool-summer or high-altitude area of the West (the Rockies, for example), your lawn is probably a blend of cool-season grasses. These grasses grow best in mild weather—that's winter in the southern parts of the West, spring and fall most other places, and summer in cold-winter areas.

Warm-season grasses include Bermuda grass, blue grama, buffalo, St. Augustine, and zoysia. These grow best in warm-summer parts of California and the Southwest, and they peak in summer. ◆

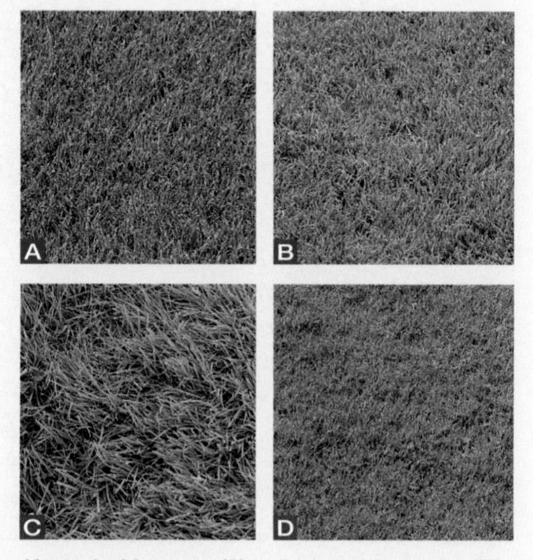

Kentucky bluegrass (A) and perennial ryegrass (B) make good cool-season lawns. Warm-season choices include buffalo (C) and hybrid Bermuda (D).

Tufts of ornamental grasses sweep around boulders and a small pond.

A grassy meadow for mountain gardens

Mix billowy grasses, boulders, and a pond for a natural look

By Nora Burba Trulsson

A wash runs through part of Sallye Schumacher's front yard. To soften its austere look, she planted it with ornamental grasses that require no supplemental irrigation. She had the wash lined with granite boulders, then planted fountain grass (*Pennisetum alopecuroides* 'Hameln') and other grasses that billow softly. Schumacher's garden is near the slopes of Mummy Mountain in Arizona. Rocky Mountain gardeners can duplicate her meadow effect using ornamental grasses suitable for mountain climates (see box at right).

Now fully established, the grasses form arching clumps among the boulders. In late October, Schumacher cuts them back to prevent reseeding and to encourage dense new growth in spring. When occasional heavy rains run off the mountain and fill the wash, the water flows around the boulders and collects in a pond Schumacher formed in a low area.

One good mail-order source for ornamental grasses is High Country Gardens of Santa Fe (800/925-9387 or www.highcountrygardens.com).

4 great plants for a mountain meadow

Delicate leaves and fountainlike forms make these ornamental grasses especially showy among boulders and beside ponds.

BLUE OAT GRASS (*Helictotrichon sempervirens*). Perennial. Fountains of bright blue-gray, narrow leaves, 2 to 3 feet tall, are wonderfully graceful. Combines well with other grasses and broadleafed plants, or with boulders in rock gardens. Full sun. Needs good drainage and regular water.

BULBOUS OAT GRASS (*Arrhenatherum elatius bulbosum* 'Variegatum'). Perennial. Narrow leaves, 6 to 12 inches long, are boldly edged and striped in white. Erect, oatlike flower spikes appear in summer. Makes a handsome accent in perennial borders and large rock gardens, and can brighten a dark place under trees or big shrubs. Sun or part shade. Needs moderate water.

EULALIA GRASS (*Miscanthus sinensis*). Perennial. This graceful clumping grass, 5 to 6 feet tall, is a standout in borders or as a focal point. 'Yaku Jima' is smaller (to 4 ft.). Can take sun or shade, and needs lots of water; perfect beside ponds.

FOERSTER'S FEATHER REED GRASS (*Calamagrostis arundinacea* 'Karl Foerster'). Perennial. Clumping grass with upright form, 4 to 5 feet tall. Feathery flower spikes, which emerge in early summer, ripen to wheat-colored seedheads in fall. Full sun. Tolerates some drought. ◆

LEFT: Brilliant black-eyed Susans and lavender dianthus blanket this planting bed.

BELOW: Snowy white petunias contrast with burgundy and purple verbenas.

Beautiful beds

The secret to these prizewinning beds: dazzling color contrasts

By Marcia Tatroe

The eye-catching floral displays pictured here—designed for maximum impact by John Probeck of Western Proscapes in Englewood, Colorado—won a grand award for use of color from the Associated Landscape Contractors of Colorado. And though the plantings line city streets in Greenwood Village, Colorado, they can be easily duplicated by gardeners from Seattle to San Francisco to Phoenix.

The planting above is composed mostly of perennials and ornamental grasses. Sweeps of golden black-eyed Susans and lavender 'First Love' dianthus contrast with fountains of zebra grass at the rear. Here and there, annual flowers add splashes of color. "The grasses add texture and take over the starring role from the flowers during fall and winter," Probeck says.

The flower bed at right is planted exclusively with annual flowers. An edging of white petunias sets off a cool color scheme created by lavender, burgundy, and purple verbenas 'Sterling Star', 'Toronto Wine', and 'Imagination'. Spikes of 'Victoria Blue' salvia add deep blue accents. At planting time, the flowers are spaced close together to concentrate color and shade out most weeds. ◆

PAUL BOUSQUET (2)

A RECIRCULATING POND covered with lily pads makes a cool centerpiece for an enclosed patio in Tucson. For details on this backyard oasis, see page 220.

July

Cottage garden combines tropical colors with Mediterranean soul.

PETER MALINOWSKI / INSITE

Fashioning a garden

A Santa Barbara clothier shows how to use fiery and icy plant colors with panache

■ Wendy Foster, the owner of four clothing stores in Santa Barbara, puts together a garden in much the same way she lays out her stores every season. At her shops, Foster begins the season by choosing two or three colors for her major collections. Then, when she has her basic inventory lined up, she adds accessories in complementary colors.

The exuberant border in front of her rosy pink stucco cottage came together in similar fashion. Since the spot was very sunny, Foster chose to build her color scheme around the most sizzling hues in the spectrum—yellow and reddish orange. First, she put in the foundation plants: shrubs and vines with yellow to red flowers (see "Fire," at right). Then, as she does at the store, she stepped back and asked herself, "Now, what do I need?" A little blue to temper the flames, she decided. So she added plants such as blue-flowered echium, blue-leafed senecio, and a generous splash of chartreuse supplied by *Euphorbia characias wulfenii* to bridge the gap between fire and ice. It's a color combination that works especially well in Mediterranean-style gardens.

Despite its lush look, the garden is reasonably drought-tolerant. Weekly watering suffices for everything except the hibiscus, which get water about twice a week.

— Sharon Coboon

FIRE
- Butter yellow hibiscus
- Blood red trumpet vine
- Orange marmalade bush (*Streptosolen jamesonii*)
- Golden coulter bush (*Athanasia parviflora*)

ICE
- Silver-leafed agave
- Blue-flowered *Echium pininana*
- Blue-gray foliage of *Senecio mandraliscae*
- Frosty purple 'Midnight' penstemon

Inspiring nursery gardens in Eugene

■ If you're looking for horticultural inspiration, take time to stop by the Northwest Garden Nursery in Eugene. Landscapers–turned–nursery owners Ernie and Marietta O'Byrne love hard-to-find perennials. They have especially good collections of Himalayan poppies, hardy geraniums, and hellebores.

The couple has built a business around display gardens filled with great plant combinations like the one pictured at right. In the foreground is *Carex siderosticha* 'Variegata', a broad-leafed sedge. Try it in a woodland garden with other shade-loving plants like the Japanese lace fern (*Polystichum polyblepharum*) behind it. The gold-leafed plant in the back is *Berberis thunbergii* 'Aurea'.

The Northwest Garden Nursery is about 3 miles south of Fern Ridge Reservoir. *10–6 Thu-Fri, 10–5 Sat. (To visit other days, the owners suggest you call for an appointment about a day or two in advance; they'll accommodate you if they can.) 86813 Central Rd.; (541) 935-3915.*

—Jim McCausland

ROBIN CUSHMAN

WATER GARDENING

NORMAN A. PLATE

Natural pond filters

■ Keeping even the smallest ponds clear and free of algae can be challenging. Biological filters, which combine mechanical and bacterial filtration, help. But introducing water plants and scavengers such as water snails and tadpoles into a pond is an easier and less expensive solution.

Water plants keep ponds shaded, protecting them from heat buildup that stimulates algae growth. They also provide oxygen for fish and consume carbon dioxide, which helps keep water clear. Snails and tadpoles are nature's garbage disposals, feeding on decaying plant material and fish waste.

Plants. Water plants should consist of oxygenating grasses and other types of aquatic plants. The small pot shown at left contains water lettuce (*Pistia*), dwarf papyrus, a water lily, and anacharis (*Egeria densa*), an oxygenating grass.

Scavengers. A variety of snails are sold for ponds. You can buy tadpoles (when they become frogs, they may even hang around). Add mosquito fish (often free at nurseries) to keep mosquitoes at bay.

Sources. Try a local nursery or order by mail from ***Lilypons Water Gardens*** (800/999-5459 or www.lilypons.com) or ***Van Ness Water Gardens*** (800/205-2425 or www.vnwg.com).

— Lauren Bonar Swezey

CHARLES MANN

Celebrate lavender in New Mexico

■ In the summer, graceful wands bloom in clean-scented profusion in Jody Apple's lavender field. Guests at Rancho Manzana, Apple's bed-and-breakfast inn in Chimayo, find themselves wanting to plunge into that fragrant purple sea. That's fine with Apple. Come harvest time, she's likely to hand a guest a pair of scissors with an invitation to start clipping.

Apple, who transformed a historic, 200-year-old building on the property into the Rancho Manzana, once grew chilies in the field. But after a class with landscape designer Randy Murray, she decided instead on a mass planting of lavender—*Lavandula intermedia* 'Provence', to be precise. Grown for its tall stem and strong fragrance, 'Provence' is also prized for its subtle flavor as a culinary herb.

Every year, in late July, the guest rooms close for the annual Lavender Festival, hosted by Apple and Murray. From 11 to 4, visitors can buy lavender plants as well as potpourri and tea. There are also classes in aromatherapy, cooking, and propagation.

Chimayo is about 25 miles northeast of Santa Fe. From Santa Fe, go north on U.S. 84/285 to State 503, then east to Chimayo. Just beyond Rancho de Chimayo restaurant, turn left on County Road 98 and go ¼ mile to Rancho Manzana. For reservations or tours, call (888) 505-2227.

— *Linda Thornton*

BOOKSHELF

GARY IRISH (3)

Fresh landscaping ideas for agaves and yuccas

■ With their bold structures and textures, agaves and yuccas look right at home in cactus gardens, but how do you use them in other landscape situations such as a perennial border, a Mediterranean-style courtyard, or a lush, subtropical garden? Coauthors Mary and Gary Irish address that question in *Agaves, Yuccas, and Related Plants: A Gardener's Guide* (Timber Press, Portland, 2000; $34.95; 800/327-5680). Nearly every plant listed in this illustrated guide comes with suggestions for landscape use. For example, among the agaves, the authors say, the big, silver *Agave franzonsinii* (shown in the photograph at far left) is a wonderful choice for brightening a dark corner; *A. parryi truncata* (left) is especially striking planted en masse; and *A. victoriae-reginae* (top) looks great when viewed from above, as from a deck.

This encyclopedic book supplies all the information you need to succeed with these plants, including detailed guidance on care and cultivation. Both authors know their subjects extremely well: Mary, a regular contributor to *Sunset,* was the former director of public horticulture at the Desert Botanical Garden in Phoenix, and Gary, who took most of the photographs, is an avid grower and collector of agaves and yuccas. — *S.C.*

JERRY PAVIA

Long-spurred columbines nod on 2-foot-tall stems in the filtered shade under a tree.

Columbines forever in Ketchum

■ Every year columbines in shades of red, pink, purple, yellow, and white put on a summer-long show in Betty Taylor's garden in Ketchum, Idaho. The fairylike flowers are the result of plants Taylor started a dozen years ago. Although columbines are considered short-lived perennials, the plants in Taylor's garden replenish themselves by self-sowing so freely that she has never had to replant. "I've found that columbines seem to go on forever," says Taylor.

She started by sowing an outdoor seedbed with a mixture of McKana Giants, a tall hybrid strain, then transplanted the seedlings into garden beds where they would get filtered sun. Now the carefree flowers require little maintenance. Taylor fertilizes the beds in early and late spring. Since columbines like damp soil, she waters them for 30 minutes a day during the growing season. Once the plants finish blooming, she lets the flowers go to seed. Then in autumn, after the seeds have dropped, she cuts the plants back to the ground and covers the beds with a 3-inch blanket of mulch made from compost, manure, and peat moss. When new seedlings emerge in spring, Taylor transplants them to other parts of the garden.

A good seed source for columbines is Nichols Garden Nursery (541/928-9280).

— Suzanne Touchette Kelso

JANET LOUGHREY

A rich tapestry—from chartreuse lady's-mantle to burgundy Japanese maple—nearly envelops this shallow pond.

Landscaping a woodland pond

Thanks to a skillful combination of plants and rocks, this little pool looks like a natural part of the landscape

■ Imagine hiking through a forest on a hot day. You're looking for a place to stop and rest when you come across a cool, spring-fed pool lit from above by shafts of sunlight poking through tall conifers. Sounds like a place you'd like to linger awhile, right? The pool in the picture above could be that oasis in a deep forest, but it's in a backyard garden. And those "shafts of sunlight" come from yellowish foliage and flowers, not from the summer sky.

The pond is scarcely bigger than a puddle—less than 4 feet long and about 2 feet at its widest. Owner Sandra Adams built it by digging a shallow impression in the soil, then lining the hollow with a PVC liner. She covered the liner with small stones, edged it with river rock, and set a slab of basalt upright in the water's center to make the pool look deeper.

Behind the slab, she planted bright yellow *Carex elata* 'Bowles Golden'. In the foreground, a haze of chartreuse flowers covers lady's-mantle (*Alchemilla mollis*). At the left of the pond, the red-tipped blades of Japanese blood grass (*Imperata cylindrica* 'Rubra') echo the red-leafed Japanese maple that forms a lacy canopy overhead. At bottom right, coral bells (*Heuchera sanguinea*) send up hot pink flower spikes that play off the maple leaves and blood grass. — *Steven R. Lorton*

A plant lover's paradise

■ You won't find any highway signs leading to Hortus Botanicus nursery in Fort Bragg: It's located off the beaten path down a gravel road. But word of mouth has put this nursery on the road maps of many passionate gardeners since it opened five years ago. "People seem to find us," says owner Robert Goleman, a Fort Bragg native.

This "collector's nursery" is a jewel; it's well worth a detour off State 1. Situated on 14 acres with 2 acres of plants, display gardens, and greenhouses, it's home to more than 800 heirloom and modern roses planted in the ground, 50 clematis (Goleman sells 40 kinds), thousands of orchids (a passion of his since he was 12 years old), and a rare succulent collection inherited from the previous nursery owner—not to mention a healthy collection of container trees, shrubs, and perennials for sale.

TED BETZ

Owner Robert Goleman chats in front of his begonia lath house.

Stop by this month and see an entire lath house dedicated to begonias in full bloom. 10–5 Thu-Mon. 20103 Hanson Rd.; (707) 964-4786 or www.hortusb.com.

— L.B.S.

In Vista, a forest of ideas

STEVEN GUNTHER

■ Mardy Darian dreams big. On the 15-acre site that the city of Vista (east of Carlsbad) has set aside for a botanical garden in Brengle Terrace Park, he pictures a subtropical rain forest containing thousands of palms, ferns, orchids, and other exotic species. At the very crown of this hilltop site, he envisions a transparent conservatory, housing a true tropical forest.

An impossible fantasy? The city of Vista doesn't think so. They've already given the proposed project a name (Vista Botanical Forest) and appointed Dr. Darian as its executive director.

If you visit Dr. Darian's home garden, you'll understand the city's confidence. Darian has spent the last 35 years turning a rocky, exposed hillside into a subtropical fantasy. His rain forest has a lacy canopy, a shady understory, and plenty of orchids and tree ferns in between. In essence, it's the prototype for the new botanical garden. Now Darian just has to think a little bigger—obviously something that comes naturally.

To encourage interest in the Vista Botanical Forest, Darian is opening his home garden for tours. Call (760) 945-3954 for an appointment and details. *— S.C.*

CLIPPINGS

• **Website for herb lovers.** To find exotic herbs, visit the Lingle's Herbs website at www.linglesherbs.com. The Long Beach–based, family-owned company carries 175 different herbs. Basil mint, Cuban oregano, Vietnamese coriander, Egyptian walking onion, and Moujean tea (leaves smell like Earl Grey) are a few of the most unusual offerings. For a catalog, send $2 (refundable with purchase) to 2055 N. Lomina Ave., Long Beach, CA 90815, or call (800) 708-0633.

• **Perfuming the garden.** If you would like to have more fragrant plants in your garden but don't know where to start, pick up a copy of *A Garden of Fragrance,* by Suzy Bales (ReganBooks, New York, 2000; $29.95; 800/242-7737). This 192-page book is filled with suggestions for bringing fragrant plants into a garden. Edge a vegetable bed with scented annuals, Bales tells us, or plant herbs such as thyme between pavers.

• **Kids' gardening online.** Find gardening ideas for families and classrooms, a gardening store for youngsters, and a discussion forum on kids gardening at National Gardening Association's new website, www.kidsgardening.com.

CHARLES MANN

See plants on trial in Fort Collins

■ For a chance to observe many new flower introductions, visit the trial garden for annuals at Colorado State University in Fort Collins. Twenty-five seed and plant companies provide nearly 950 varieties of annuals for evaluation in this High Plains environment. Flowers must withstand intense sunlight, large daily temperature fluctuations, drying winds, hailstorms, and heavy clay soils.

Peak viewing runs from mid-July through mid-August. The photo above shows a sampling of the 125-plus zonal geraniums displayed in the 2-acre trial garden. Magenta 'Brazil 99' was chosen as the best zonal geranium last season. Among the ivy geraniums, 'Picasso', with bicolored burgundy and white flowers, was judged the favorite, while the overall best of show was a mildew-free giant zinnia, Benary's Giant Formula Mix. Ninety percent of the varieties tested are commercially available; others should become available within a year or two.

The trial garden is located on the southwest corner of the CSU campus. You can also view the adjoining test plots for vegetables and turf grasses. There is a 1-acre perennial display garden, an ornamental grass garden, and an arboretum that showcases more than 1,000 different varieties of trees and shrubs. The grounds are open during daylight hours year-round. *Free. 630 W. Lake St.; (970) 491-7019. — Marcia Tatroe*

BACK TO BASICS

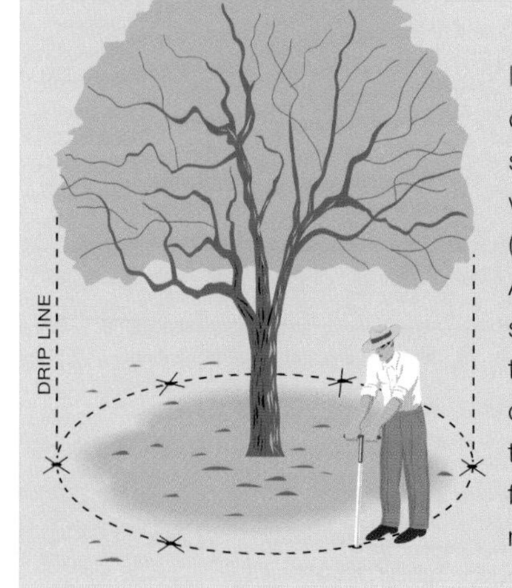

How to water trees. Trees need periodic deep watering to get them through the dry season. If they're not being watered deeply with drip irrigation, use a deep-root irrigator (about $30) to get water down to the roots. Attach the irrigator to a hose, insert the stem 6 to 12 inches into the soil beneath the drip line of the tree, and turn the water on gently for 5 to 10 minutes, depending on tree size. Repeat the process at three spots for younger trees, five to seven for large, mature trees. — *L.B.S.*

MAX SEABAUGH

A pond turns a patio into a desert oasis

A recirculating pond is the cool centerpiece of a Tucson retreat

■ With its soothing dark walls and shady mesquite trees, the enclosed patio featured on page 212 would be a pleasant spot even without water. But the addition of a water lily–filled pond turns the space into a genuine oasis.

Landscape designer Michelle Hearon and architect Diana Osborne designed the patio as a restful retreat at Osborne's home in Tucson. The pond is an irregularly shaped cement basin, roughly 9 feet in diameter, set into flagstone paving and generously embellished with hefty boulders from the nearby Catalina Mountains.

One particularly dramatic stone with a crevice was turned into a water feature. Osborne drilled a hole through the top of the stone, inserted flexible tubing, and attached the tubing to a recirculating pump. The pump releases a slow, steady trickle down the crevice, creating the illusion of water seeping from a natural spring.

The pond is planted with cattails, dwarf papyrus, water irises, and water lilies and is stocked with goldfish and koi. Except for needing the vegetation thinned occasionally, the pond takes care of itself. "I don't feed the fish or the plants," says Osborne. "The fish eat the algae, and they provide the fertilizer for the plants."

— S.C.

DIXI CARRILLO (2)

An arched arbor frames a view of the herb garden. Below, a path of Navajo sandstone laces the fragrance garden.

Treat yourself to the Terrace Gardens in Salt Lake City

They're a delightful blend of plants and landscaping ideas

■ There are many ways to judge the quality of a public garden: how it fits into the landscape, how it blends foliage and flowers, and how well it tells the stories of the plants themselves. On all these counts, the Terrace Gardens at Red Butte Garden in Salt Lake City are a magnificent piece of work. Indeed, they recently earned an award in a nationwide competition sponsored by the Utah chapter of the American Society of Landscape Architects.

Occupying a 1.5-acre site, the gardens put herbs at your feet and the Wasatch Range at your back. You can sun yourself on one of the sandstone walls, breathing in the scents from the fragrance garden. If the day is hot, you'll probably be tempted to sit on a bench beneath the wisteria arbor or splash your arms with water from one of the basins or fountains that decorate the gardens.

The herb garden shows off plants used in cooking, including several varieties of oregano, sage, and thyme to garlics and horehounds.

The fragrance garden features plants whose scents come from their flowers (like nicotiana) or leaves (mint), while the medicinal garden includes healing types such as coltsfoot, purple coneflower, potentilla, and willow.

The Terrace Gardens are a part of the University of Utah's Red Butte Garden, located at the mouth of Red Butte Canyon. *9–8 Mon-Sat, 9–5 Sun; $5, $3 seniors and ages 4–17. 300 Wakara Way; (801) 581-4747. —J.M.*

Leafy coolers for a garden party

■ Inexpensive galvanized tubs make handy drink coolers to place around the garden within easy reach of thirsty party guests. With a few snippets of foliage and some green moss, you can cloak these tubs in appropriate party dress.

The 10-inch-diameter bucket pictured at right, which can hold several bottles of wine, is attired in green moss. It is elegant enough to hold its own on an outdoor buffet table. The 22-inch-diameter tub shown below, for cooling bottles of sodas or beer, is perfect for a casual picnic; it was spray-painted seafoam green, then accented with strands of ivy.
DESIGN: Françoise Kirkman

THOMAS J. STORY (5)

TIME: 20 to 30 minutes each
COST: $30 to $45, depending on the size of the bucket

MATERIALS

For moss-covered bucket:
- 3-inch-wide paintbrush
- Tacky glue
- Galvanized bucket
- 1½–2 pounds sheet moss

For ivy-covered tub:
- Spray paint
- Galvanized tub
- Long strands of ivy or other vine
- Florist's wire
- All-weather polyethylene repair tape

DIRECTIONS

▶ **Moss-covered bucket.** With the paintbrush, spread a layer of glue over the outside of half the bucket, including the rim and the top 2 inches of the inside. Apply sheet moss to the glued area, wrapping it over the rim and pressing it down inside. Repeat the process until the whole bucket is covered. Let glue dry for a few hours.

▶ **Ivy-covered tub.** Spray-paint the entire tub, inside and out. Attach pieces of ivy end to end with wire until they encircle the rim of the bucket twice. For small-leafed vines, wrap them around several times. Secure the ivy on the bucket in four or five places with the clear repair tape. — *L.B.S.*

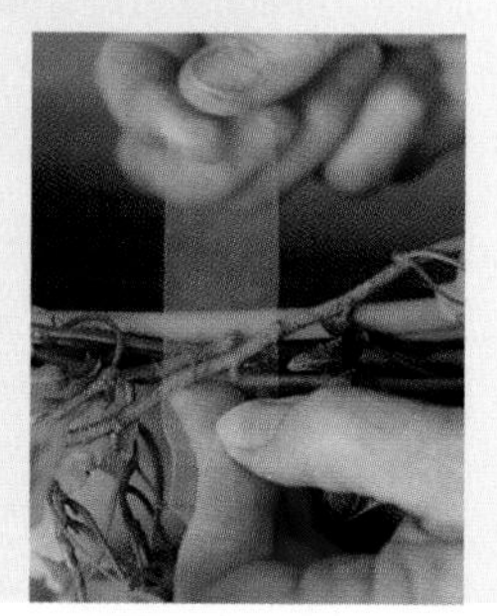

pacific northwest • checklist

WHAT TO DO IN YOUR GARDEN IN JULY

PLANTING

☐ SUMMER ANNUALS. There's still time to plant annuals that will bloom until frost, often putting on a better late-summer show than ones that were planted in May. But act fast—by the end of the first week in July, if possible.

☐ VEGETABLES. Sow seeds or plant seedlings of beets, broccoli, bush beans, carrots, cauliflower, Chinese cabbage, kohlrabi, lettuce, peas, radishes, scallions, spinach, Swiss chard, and turnips. If you plant a second crop of potatoes right away, you'll be able to harvest them this fall.

MAINTENANCE

☐ COMPOST. Keep adding organic matter. Turn the pile at least weekly, spraying it down with a hose to keep it as moist as a wrung-out sponge.

☐ CONTROL SLUGS. Put bait in cool spots (such as around the base of a woodpile or in ground covers). If you have pets, put the bait in pet-proof slug traps or under boards held up by bricks.

☐ FEED MUMS. For best bloom this autumn, feed plants with a low-nitrogen, high-phosphorus liquid fertilizer (often called a bloom formula) every three weeks until buds start to show color. When the first blooms open, feed weekly.

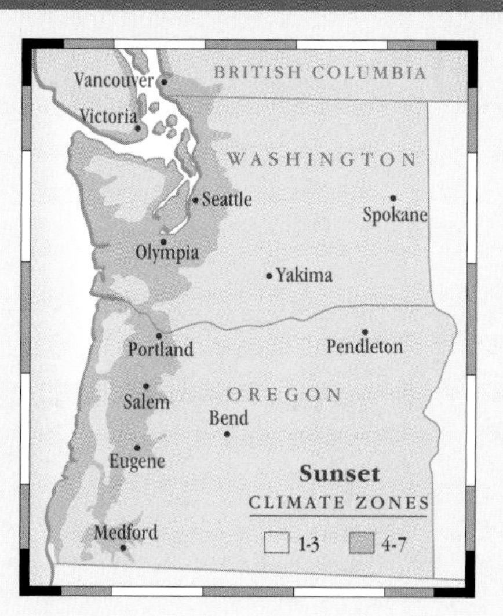

☐ IRRIGATE. Water annuals, perennials, and shrubs early in the morning to minimize evaporation and to allow plants time to dry off to discourage mildew. Remember that plants growing in containers and under eaves need extra water all summer long.

☐ MAINTAIN FUCHSIAS. Pick off faded flowers to stimulate bloom, but expect it to decrease during hot weather. Apply a complete liquid fertilizer monthly (every two weeks if plants are in containers).

☐ MONITOR HOUSE PLANTS. Watch for a buildup of aphids, mealybugs, mites, and scale insects; their populations can explode this time of year. Rinse off dusty leaves in a lukewarm shower.

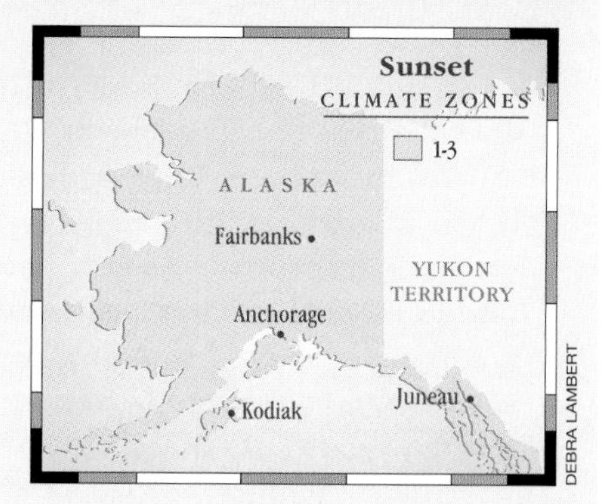

DEBRA LAMBERT

☐ MULCH TREES, SHRUBS. To conserve moisture, spread 3 to 4 inches of organic mulch under moisture-loving trees and shrubs, especially azaleas, camellias, kalmias, maples, and rhododendrons.

☐ TEND ROSES. When you harvest hybrid tea roses, cut stems ¼ inch above a set of five leaflets (*not* three) to stimulate new bloom.

☐ TEND STRAWBERRIES. Keep berries picked on everbearing kinds so they'll keep producing fruit. After the harvest of June-bearing varieties, feed with 2 pounds of 10-10-10 fertilizer per 100 square feet.

☐ WEED. Hoe off young weeds on a warm, dry morning, and the sun will kill them by evening. Water before you pull mature weeds, so taproots come out more easily. ◆

WHAT TO DO IN YOUR GARDEN IN JULY

PLANTING

☐ FALL VEGETABLES. Zones 1–2: For fall harvest (except at highest elevations), plant beets, broccoli, bush beans, cabbage, carrots, cauliflower, green onions, peas, spinach, and turnips. Below 5,000 feet, plant winter squash among spinach; the spinach will be ready to harvest before the squash takes over.

☐ PERENNIALS. To get ready for fall planting, take cuttings of dianthus, geraniums, salvias, Shasta daisies, verbena, and other herbaceous perennials. Dip them in rooting hormone, then plant them in a mixture of one part perlite and one part peat moss. Keep cuttings out of direct sun and cover them with plastic to keep the humidity high. Lift the plastic for air circulation every few days. Check for rooting in about two weeks.

☐ SUMMER FLOWERS. Nurseries still have a wide variety of summer flowers that will bloom into fall. Choices include ageratum, celosia, dahlia, marigold, petunia, portulaca, salvia, sweet alyssum, and zinnia. Look for healthy plants that aren't rootbound.

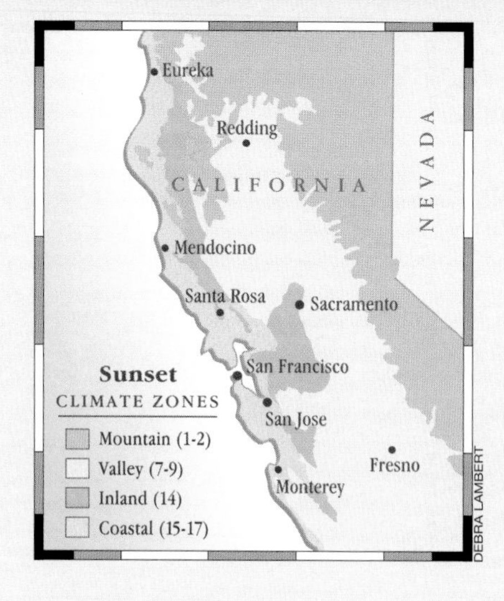

MAINTENANCE

☐ ADJUST AUTOMATIC CONTROLLERS. Depending on where you live, the weather this month can be hot, or it can be cool and foggy. If an automatic controller manages your irrigation, make sure it runs the system often enough so plants get the water they need, but not so often that the soil stays overly wet. As a test, check soil moisture just before the system is due to come on by digging down with a trowel or using a soil probe. If the soil seems too dry or too moist, adjust the controller. (For information on new types of controllers, see "Is your watering under control?" on page 237.)

☐ BUILD A POND. Dig a hole and fill it with a flexible plastic liner or a plastic pond. Obscure pond edges with flat rocks, then plant around it. Or use a large glazed urn that has no drainage hole. Add water, aquatic plants, and scavengers (see "Natural pond filters" on page 215).

☐ CUT BACK CANE BERRIES. After harvesting June-bearing blackberries, boysenberries, and raspberries, cut spent canes back to the ground and tie up new canes.

☐ WATER AND FEED CONTAINER PLANTS. Flowers and shrubs growing in containers dry out quickly in summer, and constant watering drains away nutrients. Drip irrigation is the easiest way to keep pots watered. Or use a watering wand attached to a hose that delivers water in gentle streams. Water pots often enough to keep the soil moist. Fertilize every time you water with a half-strength solution of fertilizer or every couple of weeks with the recommended dosage. If the soil dries out and water rolls off the top, use a wetting agent (available at nurseries) diluted in water to re-wet the soil thoroughly.

PEST CONTROL

☐ CONTROL BUDWORMS. Zones 7–9, 14–17: If your geraniums, nicotianas, penstemons, and petunias appear healthy but have no flowers, budworms are probably eating the flowers before they have a chance to open. Look for holes in the buds and black droppings. If you find such evidence of budworms, spray every 7 to 10 days with *Bacillus thuringiensis* (BT), available at most local nurseries or by mail from Harmony Farm Supply and Nursery (707/823-9125). ◆

southern california • checklist

WHAT TO DO IN YOUR GARDEN IN JULY

PLANTING

☐ BIENNIALS. For blooms next spring, sow seeds of Canterbury bell, foxglove, hollyhock, sweet William, and verbascum now, in flats or pots. Transplant seedlings to the garden in fall when they are 4 to 6 inches tall.

☐ SUBTROPICALS. Set out palms, philodendrons, tree ferns, and other evergreens; flowering shrubs like angel's trumpet (*Brugmansia*), cestrum, hibiscus, and princess flower (*Tibouchina*); avocado, cherimoya, citrus, mango, and other exotic fruits; and bougainvillea, passion flower, thunbergia, and trumpet vines.

☐ SUMMER VEGETABLES. Gardeners in coastal and inland zones (22–24 and 18–21, respectively) can continue to plant summer vegetables. Set out cucumber, eggplant, pepper, squash, and tomato plants. Sow snap beans and corn. Or plant the crops that can go in year-round—beets, carrots, Swiss chard, and turnips, In the low desert (zone 13), start pumpkins and winter squash.

MAINTENANCE

☐ FERTILIZE SELECTIVELY. Feed annual flowers and vegetables, cymbidium orchids, ferns, fuchsias, roses, tropicals, and warm-season lawns. If you didn't do it last month, fertilize avocado and citrus trees. Feed bromeliads with an acidic fertilizer diluted to half strength or less. Fertilize evergreen shrubs if you didn't do so in spring.

☐ HARVEST CROPS. To encourage further production, pick beans, cucumbers, peppers, and tomatoes frequently. Fast growers like squash should be checked almost daily. Cut off seedheads of cosmos, dahlias, rudbeckias, and zinnias to encourage more flowers.

☐ MOVE HOUSE PLANTS OUTDOORS. House plants grow faster and look healthier if they can spend all or part of the summer outside. Give them a shady spot protected from strong winds and harsh sunlight. Spray foliage occasionally to wash off dust.

☐ MOW LAWNS. To keep their roots shaded and conserve soil moisture, allow tall fescues to grow 2 to 3 inches tall. Warm-season grasses like Bermuda and St. Augustine, on the other hand, should be kept shorter than 1 inch tall to lessen thatch buildup.

☐ WATER. Shade trees will appreciate a slow, deep soak about now (see "Back to basics" on page 220). Repeat monthly while weather is warm. Also water established shrubs and perennials deeply. Shallow-rooted avocado and citrus need more frequent irrigation. In inland areas, water once a week; along the coast water every other week. Container plants dry out quickly during the summer and may need daily soakings.

PEST CONTROL

☐ MANAGE WHITEFLY. Examine the undersides of leaves of target plants such as banana, hibiscus, and plumeria for white waxy spirals where eggs are often deposited. Remove leaves, bag them in plastic, and dispose, or wash away the spirals with a strong stream of water.

☐ WASH AWAY PESTS. Keep spider mites and thrips in check by spraying plant foliage often, particularly the undersides of leaves. Clean foliage also encourages beneficial insects to move in—they don't like dust. If water alone doesn't work, treat with insecticidal soap or summer horticultural oil. ◆

mountain • checklist

WHAT TO DO IN YOUR GARDEN IN JULY

PLANTING

☐ DRESS UP PERENNIAL BEDS. When spring-blooming perennials such as bleeding heart, fernleaf peony, and Oriental poppy go dormant in summer, cut off their yellowed foliage and fill the gaps with container-grown annuals. Dig the planting holes for the annuals off to the side of the perennials, being careful not to disturb their roots.

☐ REPLACE COOL-SEASON ANNUALS. Clarkias, Iceland poppies, pansies, and stock can't stand intense summer heat. When they start looking ragged, pull them out and replant beds and containers with heat-tolerant annuals such as gazania, globe amaranth, gloriosa daisy, Madagascar periwinkle, marigold, moss rose, petunia, sunflower, and zinnia.

MAINTENANCE

☐ BE KIND TO BLUEGRASS LAWNS. When temperatures regularly exceed 90°, bluegrass goes dormant and turns brown if it does not receive adequate moisture. During heat waves, water every other day to prevent stress to the grass.

☐ CARE FOR CONTAINER PLANTS. In really hot weather, check containers daily and water when they start to dry out. Foliar-feed container plantings with a liquid fertilizer weekly. If annuals become leggy, cut their stems back by half to renew their vigor and restore their shape.

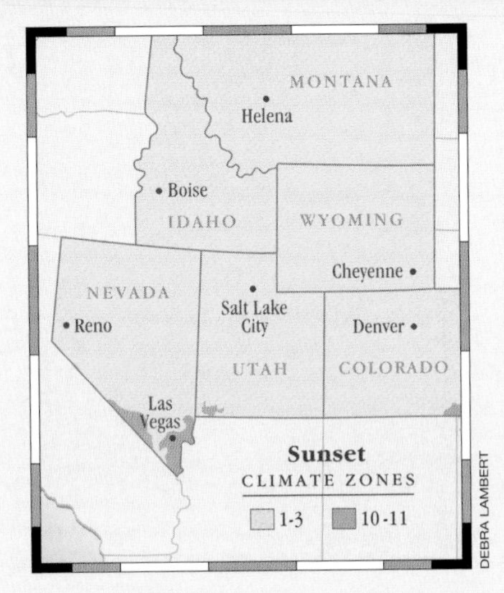

☐ DIVIDE TALL BEARDED IRIS. The best time to divide overcrowded clumps of tall bearded iris is six weeks after they finish blooming. Toss out all old rhizomes and replant only healthy new fans. Irises are heavy feeders, so before replanting dig in a bucketful of compost or well-rotted manure and a handful of balanced fertilizer.

PEST CONTROL

☐ APPLE MAGGOTS. These pests damage apples by tunneling into the ripening fruit. Instead of spraying insecticide, hang one or two traps—red balls coated with a sticky product formulated to trap insects—in each apple tree.

☐ POWDERY MILDEW. One warm, humid summer day is all it takes to trigger an outbreak of powdery mildew, a fungal disease that causes leaves to look as if they have been sprinkled with talcum powder. To prevent infection, spray plants that have succumbed to this disease in previous years with liquid sulfur or a fungicidal soap product every 7 to 10 days from midsummer through autumn.

☐ SPIDER MITES. Leaves that become coppery or yellow and curled in midsummer may indicate an infestation of spider mites. Close examination with a hand lens will reveal these tiny, tick-shaped pests and their webs. Blast spider mites off plants with a strong jet of water from the hose or spray with summer horticultural oil. To help prevent future infestations, rinse foliage with water once a week from midsummer until the first hard frost.

☐ TOMATO HORNWORMS. These chubby 3-inch-long caterpillars can decimate a tomato plant within a few days. They are easier to spot early in the morning, when they can be found feeding at the tips of stems. Handpick the caterpillars or spray plants with *Bacillus thuringiensis*. — *M.T.* ◆

southwest • checklist

WHAT TO DO IN YOUR GARDEN IN JULY

PLANTING

☐ CROPS. Zones 1–2 (Taos, Santa Fe): Plant pumpkins early in the month to ensure maturity before frost; plant second crops of beans, cabbage, lettuce, and spinach. Zone 10 (Albuquerque): Plant cantaloupes, eggplant, okra, peppers, pumpkins, tomatoes, watermelons, and winter squash. Potatoes go in at month's end. Zone 11 (Las Vegas): Plant bush beans, corn, cucumbers, and squash. Zones 12–13 (Tucson, Phoenix): Plant black-eyed peas, corn, pumpkins, and winter squash.

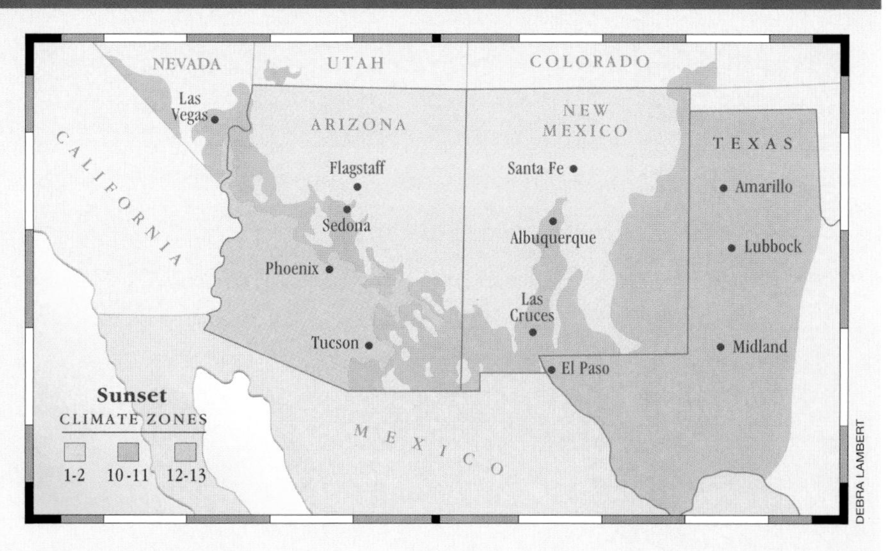

☐ PERENNIALS. Zones 1–2: Plant perennials through the end of the month so plants can get established before winter.

☐ SUBTROPICALS, SUCCULENTS. Zones 11–13: Plant hibiscus, lantanas, and palms. If you plant succulents, including agaves, aloes, and cactus, provide shade to reduce transplant stress.

MAINTENANCE

☐ CARE FOR CONTAINER PLANTS. Fertilize at least monthly with liquid fertilizer and pick off spent flowers.

☐ CARE FOR ROSES. Zones 1–2, 10: After each bloom cycle, remove faded flowers, cutting them off just above a leaf node with five leaflets (nodes closest to the flower have three leaflets). Then fertilize and water plants deeply to stimulate the next round of bloom. Zone 11: Apply fertilizer at half strength monthly. Zones 12–13: Do not fertilize this month since plants are not actively growing at this time, but keep them well watered.

☐ COMPOST. Water the compost pile weekly and turn it frequently to keep it working. Zones 11–13: Compost piles need afternoon shade to prevent drying out. Build the pile under a large tree, in the shelter of an east-facing wall, or provide a cover such as shadecloth.

☐ FERTILIZE. Feed annuals and vegetables with high-nitrogen fertilizer, and water it in well. Zones 11–13: Fertilize lawns monthly. Feed established palms with a balanced fertilizer and an iron chelate formulation.

☐ MULCH. Apply a 3-inch layer of organic mulch to reduce soil evaporation, keep down weeds, and give plants a cool root zone.

☐ PRUNE SPRING-BLOOMING SHRUBS. Zones 1–2: Prune to thin out lilacs, forsythias, and other spring-flowering shrubs by removing old, thick stems.

☐ PRUNE PALMS. Zones 11–13: This is a good month to prune palms because blooming stalks can be removed before fruit is set. Prune only dead leaves and blooming stalks, leaving at least half the crown in place after pruning.

— *Mary Irish* ◆

CLAIRE CURRAN RIGHT: STEVEN GUNTHER

Gorgeous grasses

Ornamental grasses bring beauty, motion, and a soft, romantic look to beds and borders

By Sharon Cohoon

■ Born mixers, ornamental grasses belong *in* the garden, not banished to the outskirts with only each other for company, says Rick Darke, an internationally recognized authority on grasses and author of *The Color Encyclopedia of Ornamental Grasses.* He points out that these fluid, subtle plants are at their best playing off of perennials, shrubs, annuals, and trees.

"A border composed solely of flowering perennials can be colorfully bland," Darke says. Adding grasses brings texture, motion, light, and even sound to the garden. More important, grasses are graceful threads that weave all other plants in the garden together, making them look more like family members than a convention of strangers.

As the photos on these pages show, Western designers have found beautiful new ways to integrate grasses into the garden. Lew Whitney, vice chairman of Roger's Gardens in Corona del Mar, California, combines grasses with shrubs in low-maintenance but high-interest foundation plantings, where flowers are clearly secondary to foliage. The nursery's demonstration garden (shown at left) is a good example. Grasses with vertical thrust, such as blue oat grass (*Helictotrichon sempervirens*) and pheasant's tail (*Stipa arundinacea*), look like "fireworks erupting between the hills," he says, when combined with dense, round shrubs like apple green *Pittosporum crassifolium* 'Compactum'. Billowing white cascades of ribbon grass (*Phalaris arundinacea*) and a green carpet of autumn moor grass (*Sesleria autumnalis*) contribute additional textures, shapes, and colors.

Flowing grasses play off stiffer flaxes and broad-leafed shrubs. ABOVE: Feathery flowers of maiden grass.

A walkway lined by maiden grass blends a tiny suburban garden with its surroundings.

Burgundy-colored fountain grasses, bronze carexes, ultrablue fescues, and bold variegated grasses capture the most attention in nurseries, but some designers prefer more ordinary greens. "Not every plant in the garden should call attention to itself," says Laguna Beach, California, landscape architect Jana Ruzicka. "You need some respite." That's why Ruzicka's favorites include unvariegated greens such as maiden grass and sheep fescue (*Festuca ovina*).

Simple grasses are particularly appealing when used in gardens close to wilderness, as is the case with Kelley and Stanton Perry's home in Laguna Niguel, California, overlooking coastal chaparral (pictured above). "In this situation, a variegated grass would have been too fussy," says Carole McElwee, the garden's designer. "I wanted everything to be very soft and subtle—mostly grays, greens, and blues—just like the view." Despite the formal columns and the bench, this garden feels a bit wild. And grasses are primarily responsible for that mood.

Design tips

Containers. Ornamental grasses make great companions to potted annuals, perennials, herbs, succulents, and broad-leafed plants. If the container is particularly striking, let the grass go solo—so it complements its setting rather than competes. Blue lyme grass (*Elymus arenarius* 'Glaucus'), for instance, looks dyed to match when paired with a weathered copper pot. The arching shape of eulalia grass (*Miscanthus sinensis*) mimics the shape of an urn. Bronze carex or blonde feather grass pairs beautifully with rusty iron.

Ground covers. Neat little tuft grasses—such as carex and festuca—look good with practically anything. Ruzicka uses green *Carex texensis* with coral bells and other woodland plants under trees.

Santa Monica landscape designer Susanne Jett creates meadows of blue fescue, rosy pink yarrow, and snow-in-summer, and she mixes fescue with aloes and other succulents for a Mediterranean look. (Slightly taller, looser grasses like blue oat grass and autumn moor grass also work.) To make any of these simple grasses look natural, use them in clusters—they rarely occur in widely isolated clumps in the wild.

Where to buy

Most nurseries sell a variety of grasses that thrive in your area. The following mail-order sources also carry good selections.

Forestfarm, 990 Tetherow Rd., Williams, OR 97544; (541) 846-7269; catalog $4.

Digging Dog Nursery, Box 471, Albion, CA 95410; (707) 937-1130; catalog free.

Heronswood Nursery, 7530 N.E. 288th St., Kingston, WA 98346; (360) 297-4172 or www.heronswood.com; catalog $8.

Plants of the Southwest, Agua Fria, Rte. 6 Box 11A, Santa Fe, NM 87501; (800) 788-7333 or www.plantsofthesouthwest.com; catalog $3.50.

Further reading

The Color Encyclopedia of Ornamental Grasses, by Rick Darke (Timber Press, Portland, OR, 1999; $49.95; 800/327-5680 or www.timberpress.com). Darke, the author and primary photographer for the book, has spent decades researching, growing, photographing, and designing with grasses.

The Encyclopedia of Ornamental Grasses, by John Greenlee (Rodale Press, Emmaus, PA, 1993; $29.95; 800/848-4735 or www.organicgardening.com). The author is the owner of Greenlee Nursery, a wholesale ornamental grass nursery in Pomona, California. His passion for grasses has earned him the honorary title "the guru of grass."

Hedges and screens. Grasses 6 feet or taller, like many eulalia grasses, can form barriers, boundaries, and screens that catch the light and move gracefully. Eulalia grass is an outstanding screener, but also try *Calamagrostis acutifolia* 'Stricta' and *Molinia caerulea.*

Perennial companions. Grasses of medium stature—3 to 6 feet—or low clumping grasses with tall flower spikes all look good with perennials and flowering shrubs. Here are a few combinations that work well.

• Blue oat grass (*Helictotrichon sempervirens*), a metallic blue grass bearing wheat-colored flowers, combined with yellow Mexican tulip poppy (*Hunnemannia fumariifolia*), euphorbia with chartreuse bracts, orange monkey flower (*Mimulus*), or true blue *Salvia patens.*

• Feather reed grass (*Calamagrostis acutifolia*), a deep green, very vertical grass waving feathery plumes of blond flowers, paired with Russian sage (*Perovskia*), rudbeckia, or tall yarrows like 'Coronation Gold.'

• Mexican feather grass (*Stipa tenuissima*), a very fine-textured green grass sporting a bleached-blond mane of flowers in late summer, with Santa Barbara daisy, lavender, *Salvia greggii,* or small agaves.

• Oriental fountain grass, a dense blue-green mound of grass carrying fluffy pink, caterpillar-like flower heads, with 'Autumn Joy' sedum, bearded iris, and pink shrub roses.

• Pink muhly (*Muhlenbergia capillaris*), a dark green grass bearing a cloud of pink flower panicles, partnered with asters and smoke tree (*Cotinus coggygria*) or *Dalea capitata* and bush morning glory (*Convolvulus cneorum*).

SAXON HOLT

Ornamental grasses all look wonderful in pots, solo or with a partner. Here *Stipa arundinacea* shares space with coral impatiens.

How to care for ornamental grasses

Weekly irrigation is sufficient for most established grasses, and many get by with considerably less water. Don't bother with fertilizing—they look better without it. Leave your chemicals in the garage; pests and diseases rarely affect grasses. To keep plants from looking ratty, cut them back once a year in late winter or early spring when new growth appears at the base. Cut the clumps back to just a few inches above the base. Grasses also need dividing when they outgrow their area or develop bare centers.

Beware of invasive grasses

Though undeniably beautiful, many grasses need to be used with caution. They produce large amounts of seed, easily dispersed by wind, and have the potential to be invasive. If you live close to fragile wilderness, be especially careful. Choose grasses native to your region, or, before planting, check with county extension offices to see if any ornamental grasses are potentially invasive in your area. Don't plant giant reed (*Arundo donax*) in California or the Southwest, jubata grass (*Cortaderia jubata*) or pampas grass (*C. selloana*) in coastal California, or green fountain grass (*Pennisetum setaceum*) in Southern California or the Southwest. ◆

meet the new *Hibiscu*

Bigger flowers, smaller stature make these tender shrubs great for containers—indoors or out

By Sharon Cohoon
Photographs by Claire Curran

■ To call the flowers pictured on these pages "showy" would be an understatement. Many of them rival Gianni Versace's clothing designs in flamboyance and circus-bright color blends, with up to four or more colors in a single bloom. 'Rainbow Christie', for example, has a dark red eye encircled by a ring of rose pink, a ring of ivory, and finally, an edging of butter yellow. "Deliciously gaudy," says John Bagnasco, plant buyer for Armstrong Garden Centers, appreciatively. (The Southern California chain was the first major retailer to carry these plants, which they market under the label Hotbiscus.) Other blooms exhibit strange, subtle colors more likely to be found in an understated Giorgio Armani suit than in flower petals—like café au lait, pewter gray, and gunmetal.

LEFT: The sheer size of 'Fantasy Charm' brings a smile. BELOW: 'Georgia's Pearl'. RIGHT: 'Jami Lou'.

Where have these exotic hibiscus been before now? In the backyards of amateur hybridizers in Florida and Texas. Until recently, growers of Chinese hibiscus (*Hibiscus rosa-sinensis*) fell into two camps: those who propagate the large, loose shrubs with big, single flowers that are landscaping staples in Hawaii, the Gulf states, and Southern California; and the members of the American Hibiscus Society, mostly Floridians and Texans, who nurture the flashy hybrids you see here. The latter group grow hibiscus primarily to compete in shows or trade with each other. Until a few years ago, no one sold them commercially on a large scale.

No one, that is, until Charles Black—a California grower of ornamental plants—entered the picture in 1995. When he walked into his greenhouse one morning and saw the first huge bloom of lavender, yellow, and red 'Donna Lynn', an exotic hibiscus he'd purchased from a rare plant nursery, he knew he'd found his specialty. Black began sorting through the thousands of hybrids created by hibiscus society breeders, searching for the most garden-worthy candidates to produce on a mass scale. Today his company, Hidden Valley Hibiscus, supplies 300 varieties of connoisseur hybrids to nurseries in Alabama, Arizona, California, Florida, Georgia, Pennsylvania, and Texas, as well as Canada and Tahiti. (For a list of retailers or to order plants for delivery anywhere in the West, visit the company's website, www.hiddenvalleyhibiscus.com.)

Unlike most hibiscus now on the market, Hidden Valley's are not grown on their own roots. They are grafted to rootstock known to be vigorous and disease-resistant—a practice recently adopted for commercial propagation.

These plants differ in other ways from standard hibiscus, which can reach 10 to 15 feet tall. They're shorter—4 to 8 feet in the ground, 3 to 4 feet in containers—perfect for today's smaller gardens. Their suitability as container plants makes it possible for gardeners in colder climates to move them indoors during winter or to grow them as house plants. These hibiscus also tolerate more shade, which is useful for gardens with only filtered light.

But, let's face it, what makes these connoisseur hybrids so special is their flowers. They're huge—8 inches wide is standard, and 10 inches across is not rare. "They're so big, you think they're illusions," says François Paré, who imports the hibiscus as house plants for Scardera Floriste et Centre de Jardin, a nursery near Montreal. They come not only in single forms, but in crested singles,

'Bonnie B'

16 glorious new hibiscus

HYBRID	COLORS
'Amber Suzanne'	Pink and white
'Audrey'	Red-and-yellow marbling
'Bonnie B'	Maroon eye, bronzy orange body, gold edge
'Candy Manners'	Red and pink with white splashes
'Dragon's Breath'	Deep red with pure white rays emanating from center
'Fantasy Charm'	Pink and white with ruffled edge
'Fifth Dimension'	Gunmetal with yellow and orange edge
'Georgia's Pearl'	Yellow and peach with pink center
'High Voltage'	Bright red eye bleeds out into white body
'Jami Lou'	Maroon eye, red halo, pink body, tan edge
'Midnight Blue'	Vibrant contrast of medium red and dark blue
'Mystic Pink'	Pink and white
'Rainbow Christie'	Dark red eye, pink body, white and cream or yellow border
'Red Snapper'	Cherry red and white
'Silver Memories'	Subtle silver or cream with yellow or orange border
'The Path'	Fuchsia and yellow with large magenta eye

'Midnight Blue'

'The Path'

'Silver Memories'

'Candy Manners'

USES	COMMENTS
Container, landscape, house plant	Double flowers tolerate temperature extremes
Container	Prolific bloomer
Container, house plant	Slow-growing at first
Container, house plant	One of the prettiest doubles
Container, house plant	Unusual color
Container, house plant	Best variety for large blooms
Container, landscape, house plant	Can be grown in full sun; blooms profusely
Container, landscape	Likes sun; steady bloomer
Container, landscape	Tolerates sun and heat
Container, house plant	Blooms profusely
Container	Needs filtered light or shade
Container, landscape, house plant	Steady bloomer
Container, house plant	Heavy bloomer
Container, landscape	Vigorous plant with double flowers
Container, landscape	Well-shaped bush
Container, house plant	Grows in sun or shade

cup-and-saucer doubles, loose doubles, and full doubles. The chart at left lists Black's favorite performers.

Like other hibiscus, these new hybrids are tender; their ideal temperature range is 60° to 90°, but they will endure warmer temperatures—up to 115°—if they're given plenty of water. They will also withstand some cold, but growth and bloom stop when temperatures drop below 50°, and plants will not survive anything below 30°.

Flowers can be picked and used in bouquets. Immersing their stems in water won't prolong life of the blooms. Because their petals are thicker than regular hibiscus, most blooms last longer than a day, some up to four days. They're fun to toss into casual arrangements—a quintet on the coffee table, a trio on the bathroom counter, or solo on each plate at a dinner party. Wherever you display them, they're guaranteed conversation starters.

So how did hibiscus get so colorful?

"*Hibiscus rosa-sinensis* has the unusual distinction of being a manmade plant," says Black. It is not really a species at all, but a collection of hybrids developed over several centuries in disparate geographical areas.

Despite its botanical name (*sinensis* means *Chinese*) and common name (Chinese hibiscus), researchers now believe the plant originated in India, then was carried by traders to the South Pacific and ultimately to China, where it was first cultivated extensively.

During the early 20th century, the plant's already broad genetic heritage became even more complex when Hawaiians began crossing *H. rosa-sinensis* with native Hawaiian species and other hibiscus species. When grafting techniques became common practice, the flowers became bigger, better, and even more spectacular.

(Continued on page 236)

How to grow hibiscus

OUTDOORS. While standard hibiscus plants prefer full sun, these hybrids will take a little shade—filtered light with at least one hour of direct sun is optimal.

Water plants generously while the weather is warm and the plant is growing. In winter, water more sparingly. "It's better to let the soil get a little dry than to overwater," Black says.

All hibiscus need excellent drainage, and these hybrids are no exception. Add organic amendments to heavy clay soils before planting or plant in raised beds. When using pots, mix some pumice or sand into your potting soil.

Feed actively growing plants frequently. Ideally, apply a little diluted low-phosphorous fertilizer (such as 20-10-20) with every watering. If you find that regime difficult to maintain, try adding controlled-release granular fertilizer to the soil at planting time; if the foliage begins to lose its lush, dark green look, begin feeding with liquid fertilizer.

Aphids, spider mites, and whiteflies are the most likely pests. A blast of water will dislodge them: Attach a water wand or spray nozzle to a hose and spray the plant thoroughly, being sure to wet the undersides of leaves. For heavy infestations, use horticultural oil or insecticidal soap mixed with water, following instructions on the package. In areas where it is present, giant whitefly can also be a problem, though these plants don't seem to be as attractive a host as regular hibiscus.

INDOORS. Hibiscus thrive at room temperatures in the 60° to 70° range or higher. Plants bloom best when they receive one or two hours of direct sunlight per day. Good locations are south- or west-facing windows or under a skylight away from cold drafts. If you can't provide these, use grow lights. Water once or twice weekly, as needed. Feed twice a month with a low-phosphorous fertilizer, as recommended above.

The main pest problem indoors is spider mites. Place the plants in the shower and rinse the insects off with a strong spray of lukewarm water. ◆

Red-and-yellow marbled 'Audrey' (throughout center of bouquet) and cheerful companions make up this arrangement by Cindy McNatt.

Is your watering under control?

The new breed of automatic controllers offers worry-free irrigation

By Lauren Bonar Swezey
Illustration by Annie Gusman

Sprinkler and drip-irrigation systems can be turned on and off manually, but most gardeners appreciate an automatic timer or controller to manage the watering.

In recent years, automatic controllers have become more technologically sophisticated, with built-in features that can deliver the amount of water various plants need at precisely the time they need it. The best units allow you to take full advantage of hydrozoning—grouping plants with similar water requirements.

If you're planning to install an irrigation system or replace an old controller, check out your options.

Features

1. Multiple programs. A program runs one or more valves (called stations in irrigation jargon). If you have just a lawn and a sunny shrub border, an inexpensive two-program unit will handle the job. Most gardens have more complex watering needs and benefit from a controller that runs at least three programs.

2. 365-day calendar clock. A full-year clock lets you set the year, month, and day, giving the utmost flexibility in scheduling. Among the advantages: You can water only on odd or even days—a requirement in some water-rationed areas.

3. Water budgeting. This feature lets you adjust the run times of all stations with a push of a button, so if there's a sudden heat wave or prolonged cool spell, you can increase or decrease run times (usually in 10 percent increments) without tinkering with each program.

4. Longer run times. Run times of up to 10 hours allow you to deeply soak trees.

5. Self-diagnostic circuit breaker. It identifies a valve with an electrical malfunction while continuing to operate functioning valves. Controllers that don't have this feature can't operate any valves when just one malfunctions.

Accessories

6. Remote control device (about $150). This can turn stations or programs off and on from hundreds of feet away.

7. Programmer (about $100). You can program schedules on a personal computer, then download them into the controller.

Sources

Controllers are sold at home improvement centers, but to find the most versatile models, you'll probably need to visit an irrigation supply store. The units listed at left are also available by mail order from the Urban Farmer Store (415/661-2204 or www.urbanfarmerstore.com). ◆

Recommended makes and models

For the greatest watering flexibility, irrigation specialists most often recommend the controllers listed below. Boldface numbers listed after the model names correspond to the features and accessories described on these pages. Prices given are for six-station units without accessories (adding more stations increases the cost).

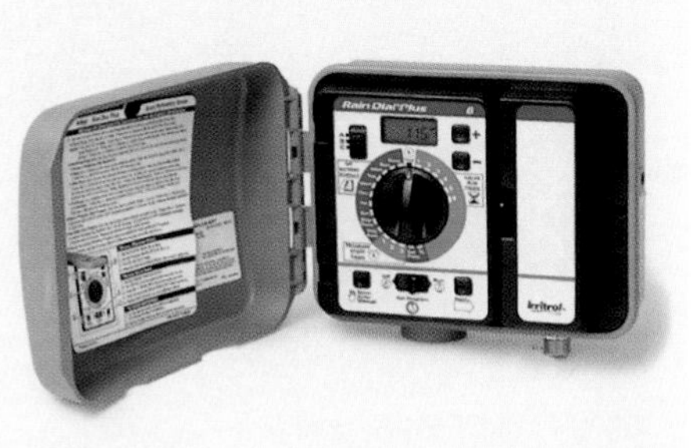

THOMAS J. STORY

■ HUNTER. *SRC* (about $110): **1** (three programs; up to nine stations), **2, 6, 7.**

■ IRRITROL. *Rain Dial Series* ($145): **1** (three programs; up to 12 stations), **4, 5.** *Rain Dial Plus Series* ($155): **1** (three programs; up to 12 stations), **2, 3, 4, 5.** *Total Control Series* ($200): **1** (four programs; up to 24 stations), **2, 3, 4, 5.**

■ RAIN BIRD. *E Class* ($100): **1** (three programs; up to 12 stations), **2, 3, 4, 5.** *ESP Series* ($145): **1** (four programs; up to 24 stations), **2, 3, 4, 5.**

practically perfect maples

JIM McCAUSLAND FAR LEFT: ALLAN MANDELL

Japanese maples add grace to small gardens. Here's a buyer's guide to the best varieties for northern climes

By Jim McCausland

■ IN ANCIENT JAPAN people would walk from their villages into the hills to view the delicate leaves and brilliant colors of their native maples. Over the centuries they brought the wild trees they liked best to their own gardens. By 1710, a writer named Ibei Ito had found 36 cultivated Japanese maples to include in his horticultural encyclopedia *Zoho Chikinsho.* • Today there are more than 1,000 named varieties of Japanese maple (*Acer palmatum*), which are distinctive for their leaf shape, foliage color, or growth habit.

Deeply cut leaves of green ('Filigree', left) or purplish red (above) characterize laceleaf maples.

Japanese maples grow in all Western climates except the coldest (*Sunset* climate zone 1). The trees reach near perfection along the Pacific Coast in places that are free from excessive heat, dry wind, and salty ocean breezes.

Characteristics to consider

The maples you see at the nursery will change as the season progresses. The following pointers and "A guide to Japanese maples," at right, will acquaint you with the characteristics of different trees.

Leaves often start out infused with red or purple, fade to green in summer, then color up again in fall. However, some leaves hold their spring color (be it green, purple, or red) until autumn, when they flush burgundy, scarlet, orange, or yellow before dropping.

- Laceleaf types, with deeply divided leaves, suffer more than most maples in hot, dry, and/or windy locations.
- Red-leafed varieties and the full-moon maples can handle more cold than other Japanese maples.

Bark can change color with the seasons. Coral-bark varieties develop the most color in winter on the sunny side of the tree. Green-bark varieties have good color year-round, showing deepest green on new twigs in summer.

Forms can be upright, spreading, or weeping; the weeping form often takes a distinctive mushroom shape.

- If you want a tree, buy an upright variety with a single trunk. If you prefer a shrubby look, choose one of the spreading varieties, which tend to have multiple trunks.
- Weeping varieties usually grow slowly, topping out in the 6- to 10-foot range.
- Laceleaf types are almost all grafted (the rootstock will be a plain maple species, while the top—the part that produces leaves and branches—will be a named variety from a different tree). The trunk will be straight below the graft, then start meandering and spreading above it, giving the tree a mushroom shape.

Planting tips

In your garden, Japanese maples will want a spot that gets about three

A guide to Japanese maples

'Garnet'
JIM MCCAUSLAND

The laceleafs

These are the maples with deeply dissected leaves. Usually much wider than they are tall, and characterized by their mushroom shape, most trees have a weeping form that does a nice job cascading over rocks and walls. The delicacy of the leaves makes them vulnerable to heat, wind, and hard water, all of which can burn leaf tips and edges.

- ***Acer palmatum*** **'Filigree'** (shown on page 238). Weeping; 7 feet. A classic green laceleaf, with very finely cut leaves. Yellow fall color.
- **'Garnet'** (shown at left). Weeping; 10 feet. With fairly intense, nonfading leaf color, this is one of many good laceleafs in the red-to-purple range.
- **'Seiryu'.** Upright; 25 to 30 feet. The only upright laceleaf, this has a distinctly feathery green look.

'Butterfly'
ALLAN MANDELL

Variegated leaves

Whether their foliage is stippled, marbled, edged, splashed, or striped with white or cream, variegated types can illuminate a lightly shaded corner of the garden. But you have to be careful, since they can scorch in sun or hot winds and turn all green if you give them too much shade or fertilizer.

- ***A. p.*** **'Butterfly'** (shown above). Upright; 7 feet. Scorch-resistant and nearly foolproof, this is the one to grow in borderline situations.
- **'Orido nishiki'.** Upright; 10 to 15 feet. This fast-growing variety has green leaves variegated with both pink and white.

'Osakazuki'

NANCY FIERS

Vibrant autumn color

Most vigorous and largest of the Japanese maples, this group bears thick, star-shaped leaves that develop the most intense fall color.

- *A. p.* **'Hogyoku'.** Upright; 20 feet. Green summer leaves, fiery yellow foliage in fall.
- **'Ichigyoji'.** Upright; 20 feet. Green leaves change to crimson in autumn.
- **'Osakazuki'** (shown above). Upright; 30 feet. Summer leaves are green, autumn leaves a glowing, deep red.
- **'Shishi gashira'** (lion's head maple). Spreading; 10 feet. Densely cloaked with crinkled green leaves. Fall color is yellow to golden brown.

Intense spring color

Many Japanese maples splash the garden with color in the spring, when leaves are fresh and almost waxy looking. A few weeks into the season, the colors fade to green or reddish green, then may (or may not) come back in fall.

- *A. p.* **'Shin deshojo'.** Spreading; 10 feet. The most spectacular: Brilliant coral-red leaves fade to greenish pink in summer and develop only a little color in fall.

Colored bark

Japanese maples can have wonderfully colored bark, in hues ranging from pea green to orange and pink. Colors tend to intensify in the winter sun (especially on the most exposed side of the tree), and in the coral-barked kinds, colors become more muted when summer leaves shade the bark.

- *A. p.* **'Ao yagi'.** Upright; 20 to 25 feet. Green bark and small, bright green leaves that turn yellow in fall.
- **'Sango Kaku'** (coral bark maple; shown above right). Upright; 25 feet. Its bark is yellow-red in summer, coral-red in winter. Green leaves turn gold in fall.

Reliable red-leafed uprights

Not all red-leafed Japanese maples are laceleaf types with weeping habits. Here are two vigorous upright varieties.

'Sango Kaku'

MICHAEL S. THOMPSON

- *A. p.* **'Bloodgood'.** Upright; 25 feet. One of the toughest Japanese maples, this one holds its red color well even during hot summers.
- **'Trompenburg'** (shown below). Upright; 30 feet. This one's small, narrow leaves look as though they've been pressed from burgundy patent leather. Fades to reddish green in summer; also comes in an all-green form.

'Trompenburg'

JIM MCCAUSLAND

Small-scale trees for containers, bonsai

These dwarf trees take naturally to containers. For serious bonsai, look for one of the small-leafed varieties in the Yatsubusa group.

- *A. p.* **'Beni maiko'.** Upright; 4 to 5 feet. A favorite in containers, it has leaves that open brilliant scarlet, then fade to reddish green.
- **'Kashima'.** Spreading; 15 feet. This has a natural multiple-trunk bonsai look. Leaves are green.

Hardy fullmoon maples

Fullmoon maple

Native to the mountain forests of Japan, the fullmoon maple (*A. japonicum*) can take 10° more cold than *A. palmatum* varieties, but not as much heat (they burn out in California's Central Valley and in southern Oregon). They're usually upright, strong growers with green summer leaves and red, orange, and gold fall color.

- ***A. japonicum* 'Aconitifolium'** (fernleaf fullmoon maple). Upright; 25 to 30 feet. Large, ferny, deeply dissected leaves make this a favorite.
- **'Green Cascade'.** Spreading; 4 feet. A diminutive version of 'Aconitifolium'.

ALLAN MANDELL

'Aureum'

Golden fullmoon maple

These trees are also extrahardy, and they like cool climates. They display exquisite golden green leaf color in summer. Fall color is usually soft gold, but hot fall weather can crisp the foliage. 'Aureum' variety is difficult to propagate, making it harder to find. New 'Autumn Moon' is easy and vigorous.

- ***A. shirasawanum* 'Aureum'** (shown above). Upright; 15 feet. This tree's large, undivided leaves are the color of pale moonlight.
- **'Autumn Moon'.** Upright; 20 feet. Much like 'Aureum', but its leaves develop a peach blush where the morning sun hits them.

MARK TURNER

A laceleaf Japanese maple displays its mushroom shape.

hours of morning sun, then filtered shade during the warmest hours of the day. The hotter your summers are, the more crucial this balance of sun and shade becomes. When maples get too much sun and heat, laceleaf and variegated types scorch, while red-leafed varieties take on a burned bronzy sheen. At the other extreme, dense shade causes variegated, red- and golden-leafed varieties to turn green, and it mutes the color of winter bark.

Plant Japanese maples in the ground in loose, porous soil that affords good air and water penetration. To improve native soil, amend the backfill from the planting hole with an equal amount of organic matter (use peat moss if your soil is alkaline) and cover the root zone with an organic mulch to keep the soil cool and moist.

Since maples have abundant surface roots, they do well in relatively shallow and broad containers. Plant them in a high-quality potting mix.

You can spur growth of all kinds of maples with an application of 5-10-10 fertilizer as leaves emerge in spring and in early summer. Potted plants need only one dose of controlled-release fertilizer in spring.

Water when the soil beneath the mulch dries out. Hard water is trouble, since it is usually accompanied by high pH and salts: Some gardeners use rainwater.

Plant sources

Nurseries commonly carry Japanese maples in 1-, 2-, and 5-gallon containers. If you have trouble finding a good selection of varieties in your area, try one of these mail-order growers.

Del's Japanese Maples stocks 150 to 200 varieties. *Ships year-round; free catalog. (541) 688-5587.*

Foliage Gardens lists more than 50, most in the dwarf to semidwarf range. *Ships May and September; catalog $2. (425) 747-2998 or www.foliagegardens.com.*

Greer Gardens offers about 130 varieties of Japanese maples. *Ships year-round; catalog $3. (800) 548-0111 or www.greergardens.com.*

Mountain Maples carries 200 varieties of *A. palmatum* alone. *Ships February-May, October-November; free catalog. (707) 984-6522 or www.mountainmaples.com.*

Whitney Gardens & Nursery lists about 100 varieties of Japanese and fullmoon maples. *Ships fall-spring; catalog $4. (800) 952-2404.*

Wildwood Farm Nursery & Sculpture Gardens lists 200 to 300 varieties. *Ships September-April; catalog $2. (888) 833-4181 or www.wildwoodmaples.com.* ◆

Centerpiece in a hurry

Mix low-growing plants to make these tabletop gardens

By Kathleen N. Brenzel

Consider the pizza: It's topped with goodies in interesting colors, textures, and shapes. It comes together fast. And it inspired these patio-table centerpieces, assembled in minutes using small-leafed plants.

The centerpieces start with a terra-cotta bowl at least 12 inches wide. Choose a bowl first, then buy plants to fit. Playing plant colors and textures off one another is what makes these living centerpieces interesting.

Perfect plants for this project include tiny sedums, succulents, and thymes like the ones shown in these two bowls as well as baby's tears, blue star creeper, dichondra, and Irish and Scotch mosses.

After planting, water the bowls regularly and feed weekly with half-strength fish emulsion. With good care, most centerpieces should last all summer.

SAXON HOLT (2)

▲ SWIRL OF SUCCULENTS

Bowl size: 14 inches wide, 5 inches deep (about $25).

Small sedums and succulents from sixpacks contrast beautifully in this textured terra-cotta bowl. The blue-gray palette includes wedges of white *Sedum spathulifolium* 'Cape Blanco' and blue-gray *S. anglicum,* a spray of pork and beans, and clusters of blue-green echeveria for accents.

◀ DEEP-DISH LIME THYME

Bowl size: 13 inches wide, 4½ inches deep (about $13).

Lemon and lime thyme—two plants of each, from 4-inch pots (about $3 apiece)—make up most of this fragrant centerpiece. Common thyme, from sixpacks, fills the spaces between them. Before planting, we placed a terra-cotta candleholder with a detachable hurricane glass (not shown) in the bowl's center, then added soil and plants. (You could substitute an upended narrow clay pot for the candleholder.) The finishing touch is a citrus-scented candle. ◆

PAUL BOUSQUET

ORANGE ASIATIC LILIES burst in one corner of Dodie Bingham's garden in Breckenridge, Colorado. For more information about this colorful display, see page 249.

August

STEVEN GUNTHER

A water-thrifty landscape in Las Vegas

■ This attractive landscape in Rex Bell's Las Vegas front yard is also a water saver: Landscaper Hal Love has installed drought-tolerant plants in place of much of the lawn.

After removing the turf grass in front of the house, Love planted a Chilean mesquite (*Prosopis chilensis*) to shade a west-facing window. A curvilinear raised planter of interlocking concrete blocks, filled with a mixture of topsoil and amendments, holds colorful perennials like lantana plus annuals such as the orange and yellow marigolds and blue salvia shown here.

Elsewhere Love made extensive use of unthirsty desert plants, including barrel and prickly pear cactus, century plant with variegated foliage, green desert spoon (*Dasylirion acrotriche*), Joshua tree (*Yucca brevifolia*), red bird of paradise (*Caesalpinia pulcherrima*), red hesperaloe (*Hesperaloe parviflora*), and Texas ranger (*Leucophyllum frutescens* 'Green Cloud'). He installed a drip-watering system to irrigate the plants until they established themselves; now they get by on rainfall alone. A 2½- to 3-inch-deep layer of crushed coral pink granite helps conserve soil moisture.

— Gail Mueller

Theme gardens of Seaside, Oregon

■ Stroll through the business district of the Oregon coast town of Seaside and you'll find a dozen small gardens composed of plants representing various themes appropriate to their locations. For example, at Pig 'n Pancake and Dooger's Seafood & Grill, there are kitchen gardens devoted to culinary herbs such as oregano, rosemary, and sage. Outside Holladay Drug Store, an apothecary garden contains plants said to have medicinal properties, like purple coneflower (*Echinacea purpurea*).

The community garden at the Downing Mall Pocket Park on Broadway has a diversity of plants intended to delight the senses of residents. There are fuzzy-leafed plants like lamb's ears to touch and fragrant plants like heliotrope to sniff. In the bed shown at right, red-flowered geraniums and red-leafed coleus (front) mix with deep burgundy hebe. Behind and to the left, *Spiraea bumalda* 'Goldflame' explodes in pink, while a rosy-flowered dahlia towers above. A native vine maple anchors the bed.

Sponsored by the Seaside Downtown Development Association, the plantings were laid out by designer Tina Miller of Garden Song Landscape Design (877/697-9555). — *Steven R. Lorton*

JANET LOUGHREY

FLORAL ART

SANDRA LEE REHA

Create an everlasting summer flower basket

■ Strolling among your flower beds on a summer morning and admiring the collage of colors is one of gardening's greatest pleasures. Savor that moment throughout the year by preserving a basketful of your favorite summer blooms.

Simply gather small bunches of flowers over the summer, loosely bind a few stems together with plastic twist ties, and hang them upside down to dry somewhere out of the way. (I often have several bunches hanging from the cord of my blinds.) Thorough drying takes from one to three weeks, depending on the size of the flowers. When the stems feel dry and brittle, take down the bunches and carefully place them in a paper bag. Put the bag in a dark, cool place until you've collected enough material for an arrangement.

Many flowers dry well. I've had success with baby's breath, bachelor's button, calendula, carnation, catananche, coreopsis, crocosmia, delphinium, foxglove, hydrangea, lavender (blooms and stems), love-in-a-mist, purple coneflower, roses, scabiosa, statice, sunflower, and yarrow. The foliage of dusty miller, ivy, and lamb's ears also dries nicely and contrasts well with the blooms.

Once you collect enough dried bunches, cut a piece of florist's foam to fit the base of a basket, then gently poke the dried and stiffened stems into the foam. Place the flowers close together to give the arrangement a rich, full look. — *Kaaren Graciano*

ONE-HOUR WONDER

THOMAS J. STORY (3)

Quick and easy garden markers

■ Have you forgotten the name of the beautiful dahlia blooming in your garden? Did the seed packet identifying your yummy corn disintegrate before harvest? Easy-to-make laminated garden markers will last for seasons with a little care. They also function as a quick chronicle of planting times, fertilizer schedules, and harvest dates when you write on the back with a grease pencil.

To make them, all you need are seed packets or representative photographs from garden magazines or plant catalogs. Glue a picture onto a sheet of paper; write in the plant name if the picture isn't identified, and get it laminated at a copy shop. Attach your artwork to a bamboo stake to mark your favorite bulbs and flowers; use sturdy wood stakes to mark vegetables. Hanging labels work well for trees, shrubs, and roses.

TIME: 1 hour for 3 to 5 garden labels

COST: About $1 per label

MATERIALS
- Seed packets, or plant drawings or photographs
- Colored or white construction paper
- Marking pen or computer with printer
- Glue stick
- Scissors
- 12-inch-tall wood or bamboo stake
- Pruning shears
- 4-inch strip of hook-and-loop (Velcro) fastener for wood stake
- Hole punch
- Leather shoelace, 6 to 8 inches
- Grease pencil

DIRECTIONS

1. Cut out a photograph of the plant or use the art on a seed packet. Glue the picture or packet on a piece of construction paper **(A)**; if necessary, write in the plant name. (For a more finished look, plan the placement of the photo but don't glue it; use the computer to print the plant name, then glue the photo.)

2. Cut out the label, leaving 1 inch of space below the plant name and 1/8 to 1/2 inch elsewhere.

3. Laminate at a copy store with the heaviest laminate available. You can usually get four labels on one sheet, which you can then cut apart.

4. ***For bamboo stakes,*** cut a 1-inch-deep slit into the top of the stake with pruning shears and insert plant tag into slit **(B)**.
For wood stakes, cut pieces of fastener to fit the width of the stake. Attach one piece to the top of the stake and the other piece to the top center of the label. Attach the label to the stake.
For banging labels, punch a hole in the top left corner of the label and thread a leather shoelace through hole. Tie the label to a branch.

—Jill Slater

A

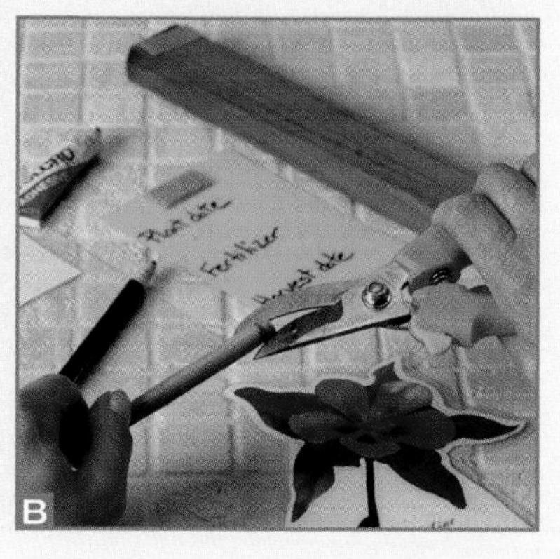
B

PAUL BOUSQUET

A crescendo of color, high in Colorado

■ Breckenridge may be best known as a winter skiing resort, but in summer this Victorian-era mining town puts on one of the grandest flower shows in the Rockies. Residents and shopkeepers fill gardens, hanging baskets, and window boxes with a profusion of hardy annuals and perennials. This colorful display is all the more amazing when you consider that Breckenridge sits at 9,600 feet and gardeners here can count on only 27 to 33 frost-free days each growing season.

The jewel of Breckenridge is the 20-year-old garden in front of Dodie Bingham's gift shop, the Bay Street Company. Flowers command the entire front yard of the charming 100-year-old cottage-style house in the town's historic district. Due to the short growing season, spring and summer flowers bloom together in a crescendo of color in July and August. To jump-start the season, Bingham plants 1,000 tulips each fall for late spring color. When the tulips are finished, she pulls them out and fills the gaps with cosmos and foxgloves.

The trick to creating a successful garden at such a high elevation is choosing flowers hardy enough to thrive in these conditions. The bright days and cool nights are exactly what many perennials enjoy—delphiniums have survived in Bingham's garden for 20 years. Her favorites are listed in the box at left.

— Marcia Tatroe

Dodie Bingham's favorites

• **Annuals:** Cosmos, godetia, lobelia, pansy, petunia, rose campion (*Lychnis coronaria*), salpiglossis, Shirley poppy.
• **Biennials:** Foxglove. • **Bulbs:** Asiatic lily, Darwin tulip.
• **Perennials:** Alpine aster, catmint, columbine, coreopsis, delphinium, gaillardia, Jacob's ladder, 'Johnson's Blue' geranium, lamb's ears, lupine, Maltese cross, meadow rue, mountain bluet, painted daisy, peach-leafed bellflower, Oriental poppy, Shasta daisy, Siberian iris, yarrow.

STEVEN GUNTHER

Room for a view

This deck is a stage for succulents by day, seating for a light show after dark

■ The low-profile deck shown above looks like a wood raft that drifted in with the fog, got hung up on some boulders, settled into the ground, and eventually came to look as if it had always been there. Exactly the effect Brent and Beth Harris had hoped for.

The garden sits on a hill with a beautiful city view below. The owners wanted a seating area where they could linger to enjoy the night skyline, as well as a place to display their plant collections, which include succulents. Since this viewing spot sits far from the house and close to the street, they also wanted the platform to disappear into its surroundings during the day. With the help of Marmol & Radziner Architects, the couple designed a sleek platform with built-in ledges that display plants and double as seating. The low stage hugs the ground yet appears to float slightly above it, thanks to short wood posts.

Landscape designer Christine Mulligan cloaked the structure in a cozy wrap of fine-textured shrubs such as *Anisodontea, Ceanothus,* and *Westringia.* She chose more delicate plants for the foreground—artemisia, lamb's ears, lavenders, and ornamental grasses—and plants with white or pale blue flowers (such as 'Iceberg' roses and 'Waverly' salvia) that would stand out at night and echo the city lights. What looks like meadow grass is actually 'Sultan', a hybrid Bermuda—"fine enough that you can let it reach 4 or 5 inches long to become nice and billowy," Mulligan says. Sunk into the grass are pavers of indigenous Palo Verde rock. "It glows in the moonlight like a lighted pathway leading to the view," Mulligan notes. — *Sharon Cohoon*

NORMAN A. PLATE

MATERIALS
- One pot, 22 inches in diameter and 8 inches tall
- $1\frac{1}{2}$ bags of potting soil

PLANTS
- Three 6-inch bromeliads
- Two 6-inch crotons
- Four 4-inch lady's slipper orchids (*Paphiopedilum*)
- One 6-inch *Spathiphyllum*
- 12 4-inch hot pink crown of thorns (*Euphorbia milii*)
- Six 4-inch variegated ivies

Plant a pot with tropical sizzle

■ Nothing brings the steamy jungle look to a patio faster than colorful tropicals in pots. Typically sold as house plants, they thrive outdoors during August's warm days. On a lath-covered patio or under a high canopy of lacy-leafed trees, bromeliads glow like torches, croton leaves fan the flames with broad, golden-veined leaves, and crown of thorns scatters tiny flowers like embers around the pot fringes. Ivy softens pot edges with a cool cascade of green leaves.

You can plant a tropical pot easily for a backyard party; see list above. Place your pot where it will be displayed, then fill it a little more than halfway with potting soil. Place the larger plants in the center, then fill in around the edges with the lower growers. Add potting soil around the plants. Water thoroughly. —*J.S.*

CLIPPINGS

New reference for old roses. Maybe you've admired Bourbons, hybrid perpetuals, polyanthas, or rugosas in friends' gardens or in glossy-paged books but have yet to plant your own. A new guide can help you decide: *100 English Roses for the American Garden* (Workman Publishing, New York, 2000; $17.95; 800/722-7202), by Clair Martin, curator of the rose collections at Huntington Botanical Gardens in San Marino. It includes some intriguing chapters about the history of cultivation, a solid section on care, and 100 scrumptious photos with lengthy descriptions.

BEVERLY HILLS

A classic Italian garden gets a new look

■ The Italian Terrace Garden at the Virginia Robinson Gardens in Beverly Hills is not new. Robinson, who was chair of the board for Robinson's department stores, added this section to her estate more than 65 years ago. But if you've ever visited this public garden, you may not recognize the scene pictured at right. This area had become so overgrown that the Italian Renaissance–style garden was hidden. Now dozens of trees and other extraneous plants have been removed, revealing once again the ageless features of a classic Italian garden: brick terraces carved into a hillside and an enviable view of the distant Pacific, all handsomely framed by cypress tree spires. Tim Lindsay, the gardens' new director, has restored the terrace's playful water feature, which begins at a pond encircled by three sculptural frogs and ends at a triple-tiered fountain in the middle of a persimmon grove. En route, the water courses down runnels in the stairs and trickles down grotto walls. It's as close to Florence's Boboli Gardens as you'll get in Los Angeles. The Virginia Robinson Gardens are open for guided walking tours; reservations are required. *10 and 1 Tue–Thu, 10 Fri; $8, $4 seniors and children. (310) 276-5367.* — S.C.

STEVEN GUNTHER

Rock garden art in Wyoming

CHARLES MANN

■ Jeanie and Roger Schlump live in a brick cottage in Laramie, Wyoming, next door to a large warehouse that used to be an eyesore.

The couple purchased the warehouse in 1994, and Jeanie, who is a professional artist and amateur gardener, set about transforming the east-facing side of the structure into one of Laramie's most distinctive landscapes. She covered the half-block-long wall with a distinctive trompe l'oeil mural and installed a rock garden in front of it.

For the mural, Jeanie painted a scene inspired by the Vedauwoo Rocks in Medicine Bow–Routt National Forest, near Laramie. Next she hauled in new soil and prepared a 10-foot planting strip. Collecting rocks from the surrounding countryside, she arranged them so that the garden would appear to be a three-dimensional extension of the mural.

With Laramie's hot, dry summers and bitterly cold winters in mind, Jeanie chose hardy plants for the rock garden.

A selection of tough perennials, including blue flax, delphinium, dianthus, fleabane, gaillardia, golden marguerite (*Anthemis tinctoria*), hens and chickens, rudbeckia, sage, sedum, Shasta daisy, snow-in-summer, and tall bearded iris, provide reliable color.

Annuals such as bachelor's button, begonia, coleus, and ornamental kale fill in the gaps. Rugged shrubs like barberry and potentilla give the garden permanent structure, while the rocks help protect the plants from searing winds and keep the soil from drying out. The mural garden is in the 1100 block of South Fifth Street, Laramie. — *M.T.*

BACK TO BASICS

MAX SEABAUGH

How to prune a hedge. Shrubs grow faster at the top. To counteract top-heavy growth, clip a hedge slightly wider at the base, slanting it in at the top. Use electric or hand-operated hedge shears for fine- to medium-leafed shrubs. Use pruning shears on large-leafed shrubs, cutting off growth branch by branch. Trim at least three times a year, when new growth is about 6 inches long.
— Lauren Bonar Swezey

CLIPPINGS

•**Shopping guide.** The fourth edition of *Where on Earth: A Guide to Specialty Nurseries and Other Resources for California Gardeners,* by Barbara Stevens and Nancy Conner (Heyday Books, Berkeley, 1999; $14.95; 510/549-3564) is updated and expanded. It describes more than 300 specialty nurseries and other gardening sources.

WHAT TO DO IN YOUR GARDEN IN AUGUST

PLANTING AND HARVEST

☐ FALL AND WINTER CROPS. Zones 4–7: See "Your Cool-season Kitchen Garden," on page 258, for information on what and when to plant. Also included are plans for laying out a keyhole garden and a French-intensive bed.

☐ LATE SUMMER COLOR. Zones 4–7: There's still enough time to plant seedlings of annual flowers for a show that will run clear to frost. Impatiens, marigolds, pelargoniums, and petunias are all good candidates.

MAINTENANCE

☐ HARVEST HERBS FOR DRYING. Pick herbs in the morning, just after dew has dried. To air-dry herbs such as basil, dill, lemon balm, rosemary, sage, tarragon, and thyme, secure stems with rubber bands and hang bunches upside down in a cool, dry spot out of direct sunlight and where dust won't blow on them. Once the leaves are completely dry, store them in airtight jars.

☐ PROPAGATE SHRUBS. This is a good time to start new plants from cuttings of all kinds of shrubs. Evergreen candidates include azaleas, camellias, daphnes, euonymus, hollies, and rhododendrons. Deciduous plants like hydrangeas and magnolias can also

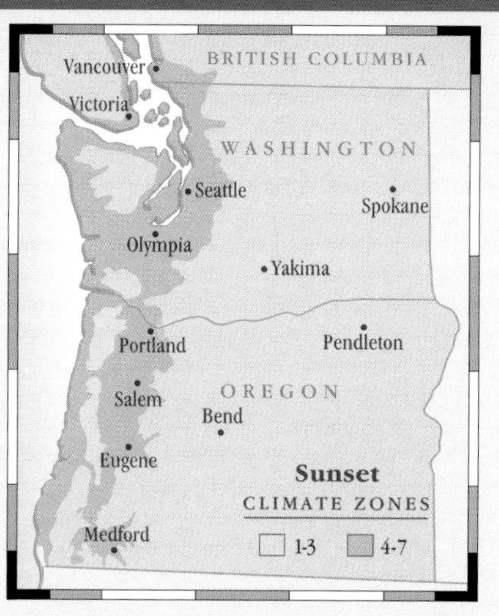

be propagated this way. Take 4- to 6-inch cuttings in the morning. Strip off all but the top three or four leaves. Dip the cut ends into rooting hormone, then insert them into 4-inch pots filled with sterile soil; water well. Place the cuttings in a spot out of direct sunlight and keep them thoroughly moist. Before frost hits, move them into a greenhouse or sunroom. Next spring, you'll have rooted plants to bed out or transplant into 1-gallon cans.

☐ PRUNE CANE BERRIES. On June-bearing plants, remove all canes that produced fruit this season. On everbearing varieties, cut back by half any canes that have already borne fruit.

☐ TEND LAWNS. Cool-season grasses tend to go dormant in late summer. Many gardeners let them turn straw brown and hold off on water; others keep them green by applying 1 inch of water per week. If weeds take hold in dormant lawns, pull or spot-spray them before they can go to seed and spread.

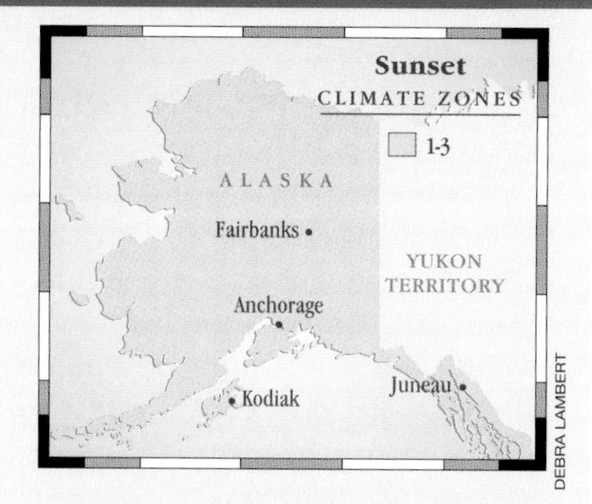

DEBRA LAMBERT

☐ WATCH FOR CARPENTER ANTS. You can recycle stumps and logs as garden sculptures, but if you do, keep an eye out for carpenter ants. They tend to march along well-defined trails: If those trails lead to your house, you're likely to develop an infestation. Hire a professional exterminating service to deal with it.

☐ WATER. Deeply irrigate moisture-loving plants like rhododendrons twice a week. Also spray the foliage; it washes dust off leaves and helps stressed plants absorb water quickly. ◆

WHAT TO DO IN YOUR GARDEN IN AUGUST

PLANTING

☐ LATE SUMMER, FALL COLOR. Many perennial borders reach their peak bloom in spring and summer, but that doesn't mean you can't incorporate color in late summer and fall. Choices for late-season color include aster, chrysanthemum, coreopsis, daylily, gaillardia, gaura, Japanese anemone, lavatera, *Nemesia fruticans,* rudbeckia, Russian sage, and summer phlox. (Before shopping, check to see which plants are adapted to your climate.)

☐ TREES FOR SHADE. For optimum cooling effect this summer and for many summers to come, plant a tree on the southwest side of your house in a place where it will shade windows. Use a deciduous tree to provide shade in summer and sun in winter. Zones 7–9, 14–17: Try camphor tree, Chinese hackberry, Chinese pistache, flowering pear, Japanese pagoda tree, 'Raywood' ash, or red oak. Zones 1–2: Try American hornbeam, Eastern redbud, honey locust, Japanese pagoda tree, little-leaf linden, or Marshall seedless green ash.

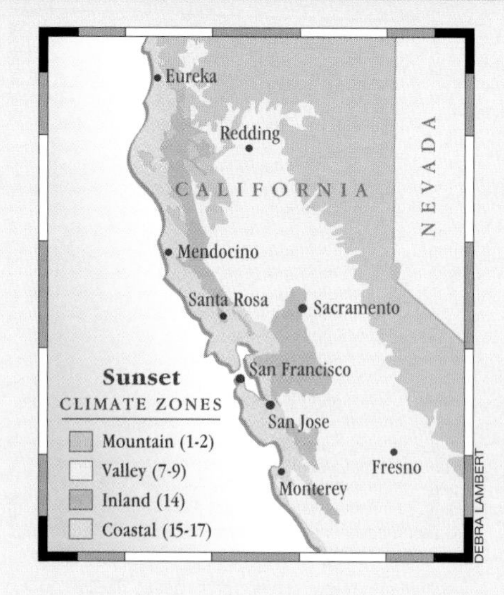

☐ SOW COOL-SEASON CROPS. Zones 7–9, 14–17: Start broccoli, cabbage, cauliflower, lettuce, spinach, and Swiss chard seeds in containers. Choose a well-draining potting mix, fill flats or pots, and moisten the mix thoroughly. Direct-sow carrots, onions, peas, and radishes. Till the soil, mix in compost, soak thoroughly, and plant. Sow fine seeds about ¼ to ½ inch deep, larger (pea) seeds about 1 inch deep. Zones 1–2: Where frosts aren't expected until late October, sow seeds of beets, carrots, spinach, and radishes; they should be ready to harvest by fall.

MAINTENANCE

☐ BUY A WATERING HOSE. Try the Gates Flexogen Garden Hose, reinforced with tough polyester cords. Various sizes available at building supply stores or from Peaceful Valley Farm Supply (888/784-1722 or www.groworganic.com); a ⅝-inch by 50-foot hose costs $23.50, plus tax and shipping.

☐ CHECK SOIL MOISTURE. Before watering, check soil moisture to see if plants need it. Dig down with a trowel (1 to 2 inches for shallow-rooted plants and 6 to 18 inches for deep-rooted shrubs and trees) or use a soil probe.

☐ HARVEST FLOWERS FOR DRYING. For dried arrangements, harvest plants that keep well, such as celosia, English lavender, globe amaranth, hydrangea, roses, statice, strawflower, and yarrow. Cut as long a stem as possible, stripping off any leaves you don't want. Fasten stems in small bunches (use rubber bands; as stems shrink, they won't fall out of the bunch), and hang upside down in a dark, dry, well-ventilated area. A clothes-drying rack works well for drying flowers.

PEST CONTROL

☐ CONTROL SPIDER MITES. These pests thrive during hot weather. Though to the naked eye they look like tiny specks of red, yellow, or green, they are spider relatives (each has eight legs). Signs of infestation may include stippling on leaves or fine webbing. Spray the undersides of leaves with insecticidal soap. To reduce the chance of infestation, rinse dust and grime off leaves periodically with water. ◆

WHAT TO DO IN YOUR GARDEN IN AUGUST

PLANTING

☐ ANNUALS AND BIENNIALS. Start annuals such as Iceland poppies, nemesias, phlox, snapdragons, stock, and sweet peas in flats; also start biennials such as Canterbury bells, foxgloves, hollyhocks, and verbascum in small pots or flats. Seedlings will be ready to transplant in the garden by October.

☐ SOUTH AFRICAN BULBS. Freesias, ixias, sparaxis, and other South African bulbs—the best picks for naturalizing here—arrive at nurseries this month. Shop early for best selection. Plant immediately.

☐ SUMMER CROPS. In coastal areas (*Sunset* climate zones 22–24), inland (zones 18–21), and the low desert (zone 13), gardeners can sow a final crop of beans and corn. Coastal gardeners can also set out transplants of peppers, squash, and tomatoes for fall harvest.

☐ WINTER CROPS. In coastal areas, inland, and the high desert (zone 11), start germinating cool-season vegetable seeds in flats. Candidates include broccoli, Brussels sprouts, cabbages, cauliflower, chard, collards, kale, Asian greens, peas, and spinach. Seedlings will be ready to transplant in the garden in 6 to 8 weeks. Sow seeds of beets, carrots, and turnips directly in the ground, or start them in peat pots and transplant seedlings, pot and all, into the garden.

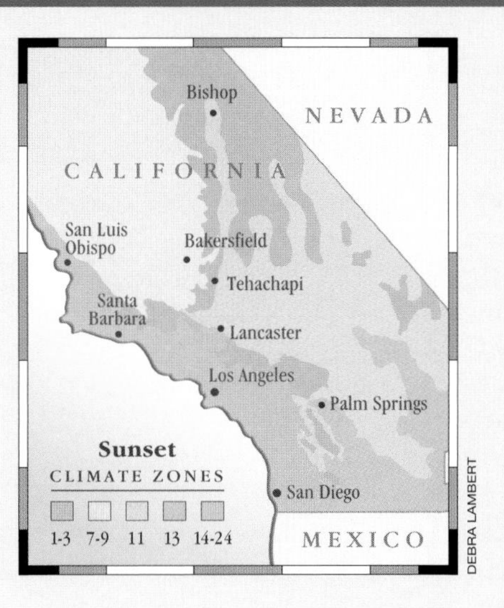

DEBRA LAMBERT

MAINTENANCE

☐ FERTILIZE. Continue feeding warm-season annuals and vegetables every two to four weeks, especially if they are growing in containers. Feed warm-season lawns such as Bermuda, St. Augustine, and zoysia every four to six weeks.

☐ GROOM PLANTS. Lightly trim plants that have grown rangy or leggy so they'll have time to put out new growth before winter. Watch for new basal growth on perennials; cut back spent stalks to just above this growth to shape plants and encourage rebloom. Prune roses lightly to stimulate fall bloom.

☐ RENEW MULCH. Mulch (such as bark chips) insulates plant roots, helps retain soil moisture, discourages weeds, and enriches soil when it decomposes. Apply a 3- to 4-inch-thick layer throughout the garden.

☐ WATER. Shade trees appreciate a slow, deep soak about now. Repeat monthly while weather is warm. Water established shrubs and perennials deeply too. Shallow-rooted avocado and citrus trees need more frequent irrigation. Water once a week inland and every other week along the coast. Container plants may need a daily soak.

PEST CONTROL

☐ FIREBLIGHT. This bacterial disease makes the foliage of susceptible plants (cotoneaster, pyracantha) look as if it has been scorched. To control it, prune out diseased twigs and branches. Cut to 4 to 6 inches below any visible damage on small branches—12 inches or more on large branches.

☐ LAWN PROBLEMS. Brown patches in cool-season lawns could indicate a fungal disease. Treat affected areas with fungicide, following label directions carefully. If grass is chewed off at ground level, the problem could be sod webworms. If grass is loose and rolls up like a carpet, the problem is white grubs. Your nursery can suggest controls. ◆

WHAT TO DO IN YOUR GARDEN IN AUGUST

PLANTING

☐ LAWNS. Lawns of cool-season grasses (bluegrass, creeping bent grass, crested wheatgrass, and fescues) should be seeded in mid- to late August (July at higher elevations). Prepare the site by tilling 1 to 3 cubic yards of compost into the soil per 1,000 square feet and raking the surface smooth. After seeding, water frequently until the seeds germinate.

MAINTENANCE

☐ CUT BACK PERENNIALS. When summer-flowering perennials such as bellflowers, geraniums, lychnis, Shasta daisies, and spiderworts finish blooming and start to look tattered, cut back their stems to the rosette of new foliage at the base of the plants.

☐ HARVEST POTATOES. Dig new potatoes when the plants flower. Harvest main crop after the foliage turns brown, or leave the potatoes underground until fall.

☐ START HARDENING OFF PLANTS. New growth this late in the season is highly susceptible to early frost damage. By midmonth stop fertilizing perennials, roses, shrubs, and trees and gradually cut back on irrigation to harden off plants for winter.

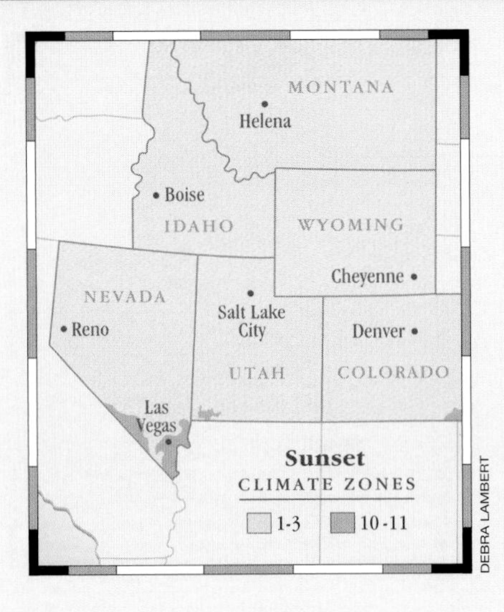

☐ TRANSPLANT PEONIES. This is the best time to divide peonies and to move plants to other parts of the garden. Cut the clump into large sections and replant the divisions in amended soil at the depth at which the mother plant grew. Planting too deeply can halt blooming.

PEST CONTROL

☐ ASTER YELLOWS. Stunted, twisted growth and oddly distorted flowers are the symptoms of aster yellows, a disease which often shows up in midsummer. Sucking insects, primarily leafhoppers, transmit this incurable disease. Affected flowers should be pulled up and discarded immediately to stop the spread of this organism.

☐ GERANIUM BUDWORM. Chewed or missing flowers on geraniums and petunias are usually the work of this small caterpillar. Handpick these pests early in the morning or spray *Bacillus thuringiensis* (BT) to kill them. Ivy geraniums are seldom bothered by geranium budworms.

☐ POTATO/TOMATO PSYLLIDS. Plants damaged by these tiny insects exhibit stunted growth and twisted, discolored foliage. The leaves also appear to have been sprinkled with granulated sugar. Spray affected plants with sulfur or lime sulfur to control these pests.

☐ POWDERY MILDEW ON PERENNIALS. By late summer, tall asters, monarda, and summer phlox inevitably become affected by unsightly powdery mildew. Monarda and phlox are usually finished blooming when the disease strikes; cut them down to the ground and new, healthy foliage will grow back. Mildew-resistant varieties of monarda and phlox are available. Plant late-blooming asters behind shorter perennials to hide the damage until they finish blooming.

☐ WEEDS. Continue to hoe or pull annual weeds as they come up. Spray perennial weeds such as bindweed and Canadian thistle with a glyphosate-based herbicide.

— *M.T.* ◆

southwest • checklist

WHAT TO DO IN YOUR GARDEN IN AUGUST

PLANTING

☐ PLANT VEGETABLES. Zones 1–2 (Taos, Santa Fe): Sow seeds of lettuce, peas, short-season beans, and spinach. Set out seedlings of broccoli and cauliflower for fall harvest. Zone 10 (Albuquerque): Early in the month, sow seeds of beans, cabbage family members, corn, cucumbers, potatoes, spinach, squash, and Swiss chard; or at month's end, set out seedlings of those crops. Zone 11 (Las Vegas): Sow beets, broccoli, cabbage, carrots, cauliflower, radishes, and spinach for fall harvest. Zones 12–13 (Tucson, Phoenix): Late in the month, sow beans, carrots, corn, and squash.

☐ SOW WILDFLOWERS. Zones 1–2, 10: Sow annual and perennial wildflower seeds now for bloom next spring. Try bachelor's buttons, blue flax, coreopsis, Mexican hat, poppies, prairie asters, and Rocky Mountain penstemons. Cultivate soil lightly, broadcast seeds, then cover with ¼ to ½ inch of ground bark or other organic mulch.

MAINTENANCE

☐ CARE FOR ROSES. Zones 1–2, 10: Discontinue feeding and pruning plants to avoid stimulating tender new growth that might be damaged by early frost. Zones 11–13: To prepare plants for strong fall bloom, feed now with a complete fertilizer. If leaves show signs of chlorosis (yellow leaves and green veins), apply iron chelate.

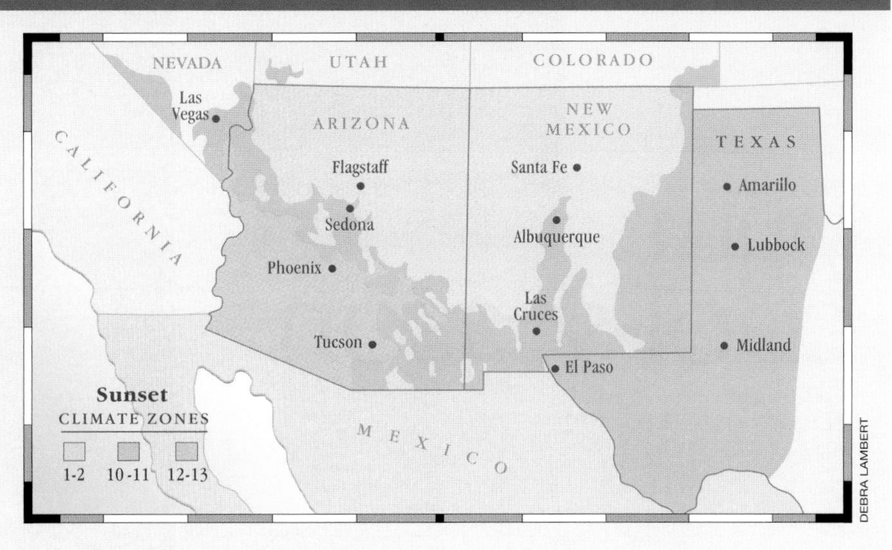

☐ FEED CITRUS. Apply a complete fertilizer to all citrus this month, following instructions on package. Thoroughly soak the soil before you apply the fertilizer and water immediately after. This late-summer feeding is particularly essential for navel oranges and tangerines.

☐ FERTILIZE SHRUBS. Zones 11–13: Apply a half-strength dose of a complete fertilizer to summer- and fall-blooming shrubs; water it in thoroughly. Do not feed desert shrubs such as black dalea and Texas ranger.

☐ WATER. Take care not to overwater desert shrubs—many are susceptible to root rot if given too much water in hot weather. For other shrubs and herbaceous plants, continue to water weekly, using a soaker hose, drip-watering system, or a hose slowly running into a basin built around the plant.

CONTROL PESTS

☐ OLEANDER GALL. Cut out affected parts and throw them away. Between cuts, disinfect pruning shears in a bleach solution (10 parts water to 1 part bleach).

☐ SOUTHWESTERN CORN BORERS. Translucent, skeletonized patches appearing on corn leaves are usually the work of corn borer larvae. Spray plants, especially where leaves join the stalk, with *Bacillus thuringiensis* (BT).

— *Mary Irish*

your cool-season Kitchen garden

In much of the West, it's time to start winter vegetables

By Jim McCausland • Photographs by Norman A. Plate

One of the blessings of gardening in mild-winter areas of the West is the opportunity to grow many vegetables during the fall and winter months. It's no wonder gardeners are fond of the cool season: Insects are fewer, rainfall is more abundant, and weeds aren't much of a problem. What's more, the list of crops you can grow during the cool months is surprisingly long if you live west of the Cascades or Sierra Nevada or at lower elevations in the Southwest. • To demonstrate what you can grow, we planted two vegetable plots in *Sunset's* test garden in Menlo Park, California. On the following pages, you'll find the plans for our keyhole garden (shown at right) and our French-intensive bed (page 261).

Snap peas climb poles at the rear of our keyhole garden. At top, 'Giant Red' and 'Green Wave' mustards.

Keyhole garden plan

A. **Snap peas,** pole-type 'Sugar Snap', 1 seed packet

B. **Edible flowers** (calendulas, pansies, violas)

C. **Cabbage,** 'Ruby Perfection', 6 plants

D. **Cauliflower,** 'Amazing', 9 plants

E. **Spinach,** 'Tyee', 6 plants

F. **Garlic,** 'Chesnok Red' and 'Spanish Roja'

G. **Broccoli,** 'Premium Crop', 8 plants, and Romanesco, 12 plants

H. **Mustard,** 'Giant Red', 6 plants, and 'Green Wave', 3 plants

I. **Carrots,** 'Babette' and 'Bolero', 1 seed packet *each*

J. **Onions,** 'Walla Walla Sweet'

K. **Radishes,** 'Cherry Belle' and 'Crimson Giant', 1 seed packet *each*

L. **Swiss chard,** 'Rainbow', 9 plants, and 'Ruby', 2 plants

M. **Kale,** 'Winterbor', 6 plants

N. **Lettuce,** curly endive, 'Dark Lollo Rossa', 'Lollo Rossa', 'Sierra', and 'Tom Thumb', 6 plants *each*

O. **Ornamental kale,** 26 plants

P. **Herbs** (assorted)

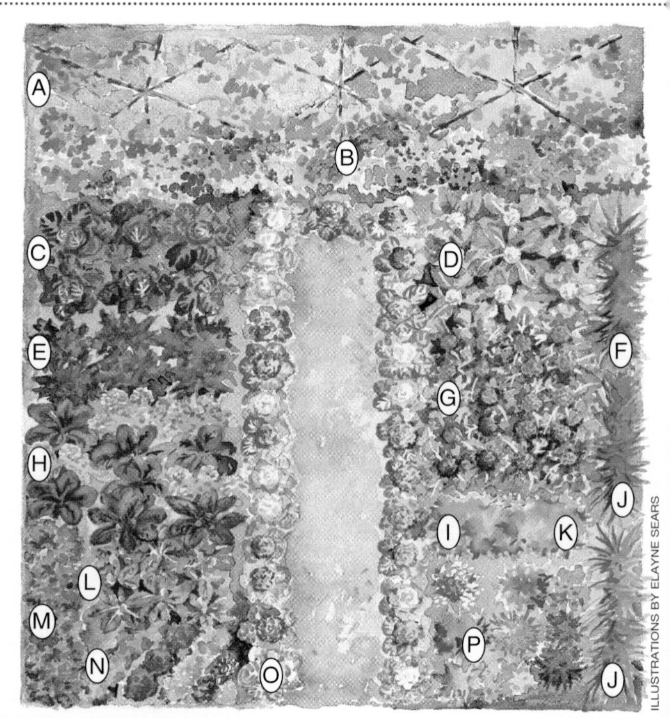

ILLUSTRATIONS BY ELAYNE SEARS

Keyhole garden is 12 feet long and 11 feet wide, with a 2-foot-wide path between beds. 'Cherry Belle' radishes are shown below.

Timing is everything

One of *Sunset's* editors once observed: "Starting a garden is like catching a train. If you're late, you miss it." The chart on page 262 shows when to plant so you'll be on track for fall and winter harvest. You can start cool-season vegetables from seeds if you sow early enough, or set out transplants later in the season.

The advantage of seeds is their low cost and great diversity. You can order from a seed supplier by computer, fax, or phone and obtain almost any variety of vegetable you want within a few days. Nurseries carry seedlings of many winter vegetables, but their selections may be limited.

Get your garden ready

Dig plenty of compost into your garden soil before planting. Loose, light well-amended soil is easier for roots to penetrate, retains nutrients better, and drains well after winter rains.

Since you're starting tender seedlings during the heat of summer, you'll need to shade them with floating row covers after planting. The row covers not only shield the young plants from the scorching sun but also help keep insects at bay and provide frost protection during the cold months.

Fertilize at planting time, then once every two months. You can use any complete fertilizer, but in our test garden, we used fish emulsion exclusively.

Raised beds give you an edge

By far the fastest and most effective way to start a vegetable garden—especially if you have poor soil—is to use raised beds. Filled with light commercial topsoil, raised beds afford excellent drainage and warm up quickly in mild, sunny weather. The loose soil is easily penetrated by roots, making it possible for carrots and radishes to develop perfectly.

You can frame raised beds with lumber or form unframed beds like ours by shaping soil into level, flat-sided mounds about 8 inches high.

French-intensive bed plan

A. **Ornamental kale,** 6 plants

B. **Cauliflower,** 'Amazing', 3 plants

C. **Broccoli,** 'Premium Crop', Romanesco, and 'Violet Queen', 6 plants *each*

D. **Snap peas,** bush-type 'Oregon Sugar Pod II', 1 seed packet

E. **Garlic chives** (*Allium tuberosum*), 6 plants

F. **Leeks,** 6 plants

G. **Mustard,** 'Giant Red' and 'Green Wave', 3 plants *each*

H. **Edible flowers,** calendulas, pansies, and violas, 12 plants *each*

I. **Lettuce,** curly endive, 'Dark Lollo Rossa', and 'Lollo Rossa', 6 plants *each*

French-intensive bed is 10 feet long and 7 feet wide. 'Violet Queen' broccoli is shown below.

Extra crop insurance

If there's room in your garden, try succession planting. Consider the salad crops you use up fastest—lettuce and radishes, for example—then plant a dozen seeds of each every two weeks until frost. That way you'll be sure to have enough plants at all stages of maturity to ensure against any losses caused by unseasonable heat or early frost.

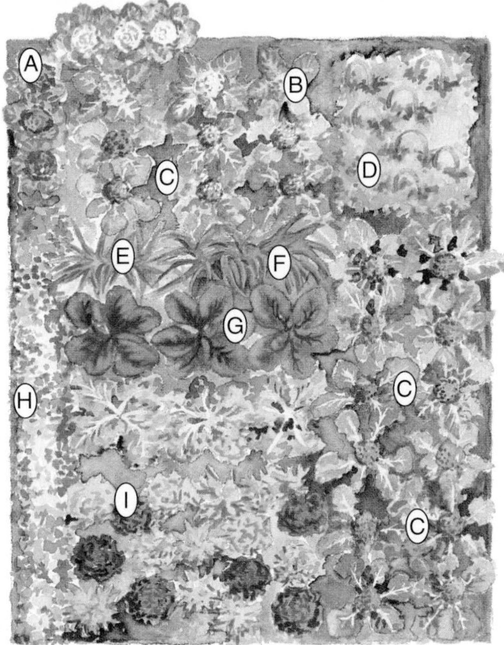

Manage your harvest

Leaf crops give you a bigger, longer yield per plant if you harvest a few outer leaves at a time instead of removing the whole plant. However, if you see flower buds start to emerge from any leafy vegetable except Swiss chard, harvest the whole plant right away; the flowering process (called bolting) makes leaves bitter on everything except chard.

Among the root crops, beets and carrots can stay in the ground until you're ready to use them. Radishes should be harvested as soon as they're big enough for salads. If you're growing onions for the green tops, pull them as soon as they're ready; if you're growing onions for bulbs, leave them in the ground until next summer.

Seed sources

You can buy seedlings of many winter vegetables at nurseries and garden centers. But for the widest selection, check out nursery seed racks or order from seed companies. Some good companies include Johnny's Selected Seeds (207/437-4301 or www.johnnyseeds.com), Nichols Garden Nursery (541/928-9280 or www.nicholsgardennursery.com), Shepherd's Garden Seeds (860/482-3638 or www.shepherdseeds.com), Territorial Seed Company (541/942-9547 or www.territorial-seed.com), and West Coast Seeds (604/482-8800 or www.westcoastseeds.com).

WHEN TO START COOL-SEASON CROPS

This chart gives rough planting times for most mild-weather parts of the West. In the following areas, you'll need to make adjustments.

- **In warm-winter areas** such as Palm Springs and Phoenix (*Sunset* climate zone 13) and in the hot interior valleys of Southern California, plant three or four weeks later than the times listed.
- **In high-desert areas** such as Albuquerque and Sedona (zone 10), start planting about two weeks earlier than the times listed.
- **In snowy-winter climates** (zones 1–3), wait to plant most crops except arugula, garlic, kale, and radishes until about a month before the average date of the last killing frost in spring.

	Crop type	Start seeds	Transplants	Dependable varieties
GREEN VEGETABLES	Arugula	Aug.-Oct.	Sept.-Oct.	
	Broccoli	Aug.	Aug.-Oct.	'Premium Crop', Romanesco, 'Violet Queen'
	Cabbage	Aug.	Aug.-Sept.	'Ruby Perfection'
	Cauliflower	Aug.-Sept.	Aug.-Oct.	'Amazing'
	Endive	Aug.–early Sept.	Sept.-Nov.	Curly and broad-leafed (escarole)
	Kale	Aug.	Aug.-Oct.	'Winterbor'
	Lettuce	Aug.	Aug.-Sept.	'Dark Lollo Rossa', 'Lollo Rossa', 'Sierra', 'Tom Thumb'
	Mustard	Aug.-Sept.	Sept.-Nov.	'Giant Red', 'Green Wave'
	Peas	Aug.-Sept.	Sept.-Oct.	'Oregon Giant', 'Oregon Sugar Pod II', 'Sugar Snap'
	Spinach	Aug.	Sept.-Oct.	'Tyee'
	Swiss chard	Aug.	Aug.-Sept.	'Perpetual Spinach', 'Rainbow', 'Ruby'
ROOTS AND BULBS	Beets	late July–Aug.	Not advised	'Early Wonder Tall Top', 'Red Ace', 'Winter Keeper'
	Carrots	late July–Aug.	Not advised	'Babette', 'Bolero'
	Garlic		Oct.-Dec. (cloves)	'Chesnok Red', 'Spanish Roja'
	Onions	Aug.-Sept.	Sept.-Oct.	'Walla Walla Sweet' north of Bakersfield, CA, 'Buffalo' anywhere
	Radishes	Aug.-Sept.	Not advised	'Cherry Belle', 'Crimson Giant'
HERBS	Parsley	Aug.-Oct.		'Forest Green' for garnishes, Italian flat-leaf type for cooking
	Rosemary	Any time		'Arp' or 'Sawyer's Selection' for cold climates, 'Tuscan Blue' elsewhere

A chef's cool garden

JIM McCAUSLAND (2)

A chef harvests purple kale (above). He lets artichoke bud go to bloom.

When the chefs at Café Pinceau want fresh herbs and garnishes, all they have to do is step out of the kitchen and into the garden behind the restaurant in Edmonds, Washington. In the photo above, curly 'Redbor' kale is gathered for dinner.

Restaurant owner Henry Arce, who developed the cafe's Cajun-influenced recipes, also grows edible flowers, including calendulas, pansies, and violas. He describes them as "the confetti that colors the salads."

You can visit the garden any time. Café Pinceau serves lunch and dinner. One wing of the restaurant is devoted to live blues bands 9 to midnight Thursday through Saturday and 6 to 9 Sunday. As Arce says, "Food, blues, and gardens—that's what we're about." *11:30–9 Tue-Thu, until 10 Fri-Sat. 610 Fifth Ave. S.; (425) 775-0199.* ◆

In praise of fences

For privacy, security, and aesthetic delight, fences serve well

BY PETER O. WHITELEY

Don't just stand there—do something! This familiar command seems to be the activating impulse behind every good fence. Participating in the landscape it inhabits, a fence can contribute qualities such as color, texture, scale, and levels of privacy.

The wood fences here and on pages 264 and 265 have personality—some restrained, others exuberant—that complements the architecture of a house and the design of a garden. But the role of a fence can vary with location or need. Some serve as unobtrusive backdrops for plants along property lines, while others step more prominently on stage by dividing gardens into zones or by editing views.

Functionally, these fences range from solid, unbroken surfaces that provide privacy to structures that are almost transparent. All help transform yards into intriguing outdoor rooms.

PETER O. WHITELEY (3)

▲ A LONG, TALL SIDE-YARD FENCE, made of Western red cedar, is composed of orderly grids of 1-by-2s between massive turned logs. Custom-fabricated rusting steel caps cover the log ends, which act as a base for a sturdy arbor; eventually vines will cover the grids and sprawl across the arbor. DESIGN: Todd Soli Architects, Langley, WA; (360) 221-6557.

▲ HORIZONTAL SIDING becomes a giant canvas for a painted morning glory vine. DESIGN: Turner/Alvet Fine Art Studio, Los Angeles; (800) 995-8533.

▲ VERTICAL AND HORIZONTAL BANDING establishes a graceful rhythm in this stately gray-stained arbor fence. Set across a rear corner of a garden, it screens a work area in addition to serving as a gracious backdrop for plants and a pond. DESIGN: Landscape architects John Herbst Jr. & Associates, Portland; (503) 246-8228.

PETER O. WHITELEY (2)

▲ PRESSURE-TREATED POLES of soft yellow-green unite this combination of fence, screen, and shallow trellis that divides a slender yard into zones. The top band of the fence echoes the proportions of the square openings in the taller screen. DESIGN: Landscape architect Richard William Wogisch, San Francisco; (415) 522-1335.

▲ A WHITE-PAINTED FORMAL FENCE separating a driveway from a brick patio has an inset panel of band saw–cut curves that establish fluid rhythm. The posts support a slender arbor; solid panels below ensure privacy for patio seating. DESIGN: Landscape architect Bill Derringer, Derringer & Associates, Atherton, CA; (650) 854-5111.

CHARLES CALLISTER

▲ ART DECO METAL RATTLESNAKE—framed in the top band of a 6-foot-tall redwood fence—adds a distinctive, unexpected accent. The verdigris color of the snake contrasts with the warm tones of the wood, which blends smooth-surfaced lumber and the craggier texture of split grapestakes. DESIGN: Martin Reutinger, Reutinger Design, Albany, CA; (510) 528-2000.

ALLAN MANDELL

▲ STEPPING IN AND OUT, rather than running arrow-straight along the property line, this fence forms little alcoves. The side-wall grids allow angled views to the street, but when seen straight on, the fence presents a solid surface broken only by an open horizontal grid on the upper section. DESIGN: Kevin Lane, Portland; (503) 233-1818.

▲ LIKE A CLOTH SUSPENDED between posts, the top of this fence forms a graceful arcing line below an orderly grid of 2-by-2s. The fence shields a front-yard deck on a sloping San Francisco site. DESIGN: Josephine Zeitlin Landscapes, Kentfield, CA; (415) 461-2429.

JAY GRAHAM (2)

▲ DESIGN AND SAFETY are combined in this fence. It steps down, becomes more transparent, and jogs inward the closer it gets to the corner, all of which allows drivers to see cars approaching on the intersecting street. The fence framework is filled with green-gray-stained board-and-batten and grids of overlapping 1-by-2s (stained a contrasting light gray). DESIGN: Chris Jacobson and Beverly Sarjeant, Gardenart, Los Gatos, CA; (415) 664-5913.

ANDREW DRAKE

◀ PREFABRICATED CEDAR PANELS called Ventwood boast clean architectural lines that blend with the heavier framework of the surrounding arbor to form the light and airy "walls" of this garden. The panels provide a sense of enclosure and screen angled vistas from passersby, without blocking all views. DESIGN: Architect David Hall, Henry Klein Partnership, Mt. Vernon, WA; (360) 336-2155. VENTWOOD: Howard Manufacturing Company, Kent, WA; (253) 395-7161.

PETER O. WHITELEY

◀ BUILT FOR PRIVACY, this brightly painted houselike fence boasts a board-and-batten façade with unglazed window-shaped openings extending above the fence line for visual surprise. The fence angles away from the living room window of a ranch-style house in order to block views of a cumbersome neighboring structure. The fence creates a backdrop for luxuriant plantings. DESIGN: Landscape architect Richard William Wogisch, San Francisco; (415) 522-1335. ◆

SCOTT ATKINSON

A deep-root irrigator (left) attaches to a hose to inject water 18 inches down into tree root zones (this one is pictured spraying water above ground to illustrate how it works). A rotating sprinkler (above) sends water through rotating arms.

Strategies for summer watering

Six easy steps you can take now to give your garden the amount of water it needs, without waste

By Lance Walheim

■ All over the mostly arid West, garden watering is a summer ritual—usually the first chore we tackle in the early morning or after work. On hot days in neighborhood after neighborhood, sprinklers whoosh, hoses gurgle, soaker hoses hiss, and drip systems silently plop their precious cargo into the soil to keep plants lush and green. Gardeners leaving for vacation set automatic controllers or pay a neighbor's kid to handle irrigation.

However diligent we may be about dispensing water, if we don't pay attention to *how* we're dispensing it, we waste it. Irrigate plants on windy days, and water can blow away from the intended area before it reaches the ground. Pour the water on faster than soil can absorb it, and rivulets and streams run down driveways and into streets. It's no secret that, in the West, water is liquid gold; in some pay-by-use districts, waste means higher water bills. Here's how to water your garden easily and efficiently.

CRAIG D. WOOD (2) ABOVE: NORMAN A. PLATE

The ideal hose (above) is made of a durable reinforced material, with brass couplings. Attachments include an oscillating sprinkler (left), which waters in an arc; a soaker hose (bottom right), held in place by U-shaped pins, that oozes water; and a long-armed nozzle (below left). A pop-up sprinkler (bottom left) sprays a fan of water.

GEORGE OLSON DIRECTLY ABOVE: A. M. LEONARD

DARROW M. WATT

1. Know your soil

The type of soil you have—sand, clay, or loam—influences how fast water penetrates before running off, how often plants will need to be watered, and how much water you'll need to apply with each irrigation. Observe what happens to your soil when you wet it.

Sandy soils absorb water quickly without puddling. Compared with plants growing in clay soils, those in sandy soils need water more often, but since water penetrates sandy soils faster, you don't need to apply as much. In sandy soils, irrigate more frequently, but don't apply so much water that it will flow through the root zone without stopping.

Clay soils absorb water more slowly than sandy ones do; when water is applied too quickly, it puddles or runs off before being absorbed. Clay soils are slow to dry out; plants that grow in them are particularly at risk of diseases and other problems that result from overwatering. Stretch the time between waterings so plants have a chance to partially dry out. Apply water slowly so it doesn't run off before it can be absorbed.

Loam soils absorb water at an even pace without heavy puddling or runoff. You can recognize loam by picking up a moist handful; when you let go, it holds together but falls apart easily with some gentle prodding.

Most soils are a mixture of clay, sand, and loam. Identify what predominates in your soil and adjust your watering accordingly.

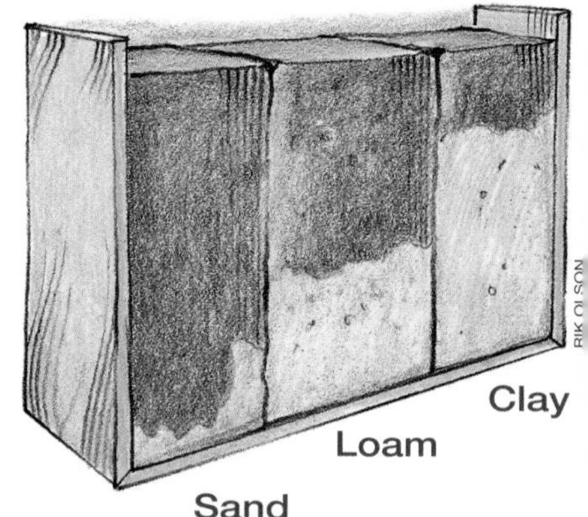

Soil texture and water penetration

Applied to sand, 1 inch of water penetrates about 12 inches. Applied to loam, 1 inch of water reaches about 7 inches down. Applied to clay, 1 inch of water soaks only 4 to 5 inches.

2. Match your irrigation system to your plants

Watering your garden need not be complicated or time-consuming; in fact, easy-to-use hoses or soaker hoses (perforated on one side, or porous overall) may be your best choice for some plants. The list that follows pairs plant groups with the watering methods that work best for each. In-ground sprinklers are certainly best for lawns. Drip-irrigation systems (made of PVC pipe and slender tubing with emitters that deliver water directly to individual plants), managed by automatic controllers, can be the most convenient method for irrigating flower beds, rows of vegetables, and even shrubs and trees, especially when you're on vacation. However, both systems must be mapped out and, in most cases, installed before you plant, so the list that follows focuses mainly on manual devices and techniques (building basins and furrows of soil around plants, for instance, to direct water to the roots and help avoid runoff). If you plan to install a larger automated system, it is best to do so before a seasonal planting.

■ Lawn

- For a small lawn, hose-end sprinklers can work well.

■ Vegetables

- Plant in rows with furrows; build basins around large individual plants. Hand-water.
- Use soaker hoses on flat ground.
- Seedlings and vegetables that are flowering or setting fruit need more water than mature ones.

Planning ahead? A drip-irrigation system is the best method. Group plants with similar watering needs.

■ Annuals and perennials

- Use soaker hoses or hoses slowly dripping over root zone. Overhead watering may cause flowers to tip or fade; some species are more subject to disease if showered from above.

Planning ahead? For closely spaced beds, choose drip-emitter lines; for widely spaced plants, use individual drip-emitters.

For lawns (A), use hose-end sprinklers. For vegetables (B), hand-water or use soaker hoses. Annuals and perennials (C) thrive when watered by soaker hoses or drip-emitter lines.

Ground covers

- Build basins of soil around large, shrubby plants.

Planning ahead? Use in-ground sprinklers; install stationary risers (pop-up types) for plantings more than 1 foot tall, and low-output sprinklers on a slope. Or install a drip-irrigation system for shrubby ground covers.

Trees and shrubs

- Build basins of soil around shrubs.
- Attach a deep-root irrigator to the end of a hose and inject water into the soil near a tree's roots.
- Soaker hoses work well for occasional deep watering of established trees. Lay them on flat ground; wrap them around the tree several times—starting a few feet out from the trunk and ending just beyond the drip line.

Planning ahead? Low-volume systems with drip-emitters or micro-sprinklers (miniature sprayers) are most efficient, especially on slopes.

Roses

- Build basins of soil around the plants to direct hose water to roots.
- On level ground, snake soaker hoses around plants.

Planning ahead? Install in-ground sprinklers with flat-head sprayers (on short risers, these send the spray out straight, rather than up, where it can wet the foliage); run them early so leaves will dry by midday. Or, for closely spaced bushes, install a drip-irrigation system with a drip-emitter line and individual drip-emitters.

Natives and unestablished drought-adapted plants

Warm, moist soils can be lethal to many native plants and to those of Mediterranean origins, especially in poorly drained soil.

- If plantings are less than a year old, use ooze-type soaker hoses at low pressure, very early or late in the day when soil is cool.

Planning ahead? Use low-flow drip-irrigation with a manual shutoff valve for the first year or so, until plants are established. After that, natives and drought-adapted plants need little to no water beyond rainfall.

Container plants

- Hand-water gently, using a hose fitted with a wide nozzle.
- Submerse hanging baskets and small pots for half an hour in tubs of water to saturate soil.
- Install drip tubing to water pots for two to five minutes, several times a day. Simple drip-irrigation kits for container plantings are sold at garden centers and nurseries.

(Continued on page 270)

Use soaker hoses or in-ground sprinklers for ground covers (D), soil basins for azaleas (E) and roses (F).

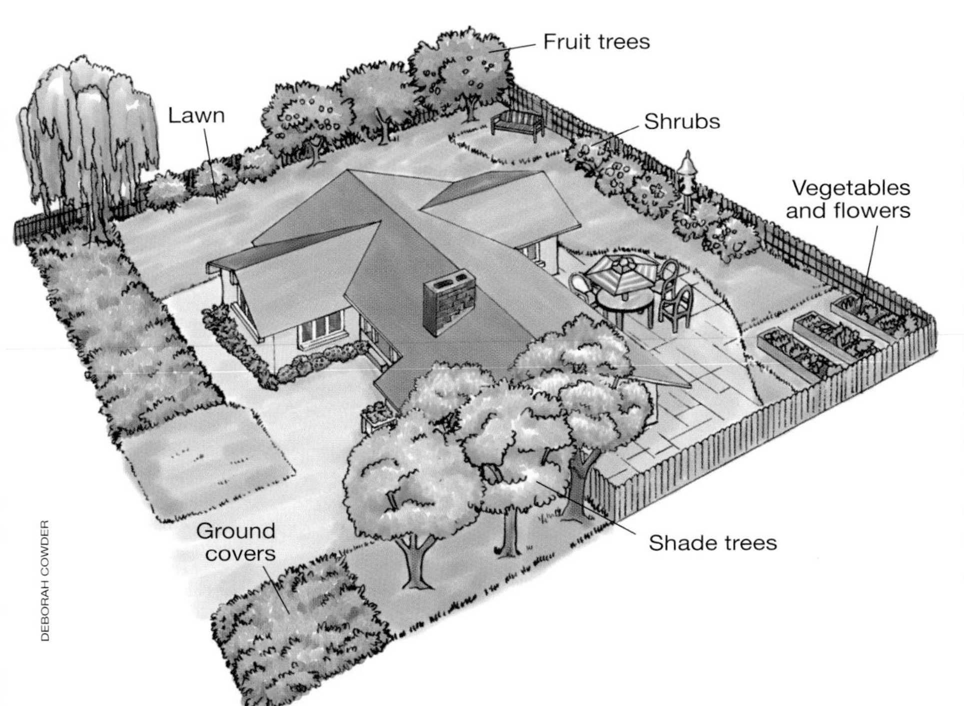

Irrigating by zone

By grouping plants with similar water needs, savvy Western gardeners can apply water efficiently, make the best use of low-volume irrigation systems, and be sure that no plants are being over- or underwatered. This illustration shows one way to group various plantings; the lawn can be watered by in-ground sprinklers, fruit trees by a drip-emitter line, vegetable and flower beds by a drip-emitter line, shrubs by individual drip-emitters, ground covers by pop-up sprinklers, and shade trees by a deep-root irrigator, as needed.

Hose sense

A hose is enough to handle your watering if you have just a few outdoor plants or even a small lawn.

Hoses vary in quality. Depending on the manufacturer, they may be made of rubber, vinyl, or a combination. The best hoses incorporate multiple layers of reinforcing fabrics such as nylon or rayon, and they have strong couplings made of brass (the thicker the better) and quality swivels (hexagonal-shaped for easy gripping). Also look for a protective collar just below the coupling, which prevents the hose from kinking at the faucet.

Garden hoses vary in length (25, 50, 75, and 100 feet) and inside diameter (½, ⅝, and ¾ inch). The larger the hose, the greater the volume it delivers. To tailor your hose to various water situations, you can choose from these attachments.

HOSE-END NOZZLES turn hose-flow into a variety of sprays, from strong jet to gentle mist. Some have long handles, making them especially helpful for watering hanging baskets. Many have built-in shut-off valves.

PORTABLE SPRINKLERS (impulse, oscillating, rotating, stationary, or traveling) help you water small lawns. Choose a sprinkler with a pattern that matches the shape of the lawn you need to irrigate.

DEEP-ROOT IRRIGATORS attached to hoses can inject water 18 inches down into tree root zones. (See photo on page 266.)

Extras:

ON-OFF TIMERS, at their simplest, are designed to fit between a faucet and a hose. You set a dial and the timer turns off the water at the designated time. You can also use an egg timer to remind you to turn off the water.

HOSE YS turn one faucet into two or more. On some models, each branch of the Y has a shutoff valve, so you can use them separately; this is handy if you are running several drip-irrigation lines or soaker hoses from one faucet.

3. Irrigate plants to the correct depth

Apply enough water to wet the entire root zone and to encourage deep rooting. Deeper roots are better able to withstand periods of drought; shallow watering, on the other hand, leads to shallow roots and plants that are susceptible to drought and strongly affected by fluctuating temperatures. (Properly irrigated, roots of lawn grasses grow about 6 inches deep, shrub roots about 12 to 18 inches deep. Most tree feeder roots, even of large trees, are within the top 2 feet of soil; they extend well beyond the tree's drip line.) How can you tell how deep water is penetrating? Push a stiff metal rod into the soil after watering. It will move easily through wet soil and will stop or become harder to push when it hits dry soil.

In heavy clay soils, you may have to pulse-irrigate—watering until puddling occurs, stopping until the water is absorbed into the soil, then repeating—to avoid wasteful runoff. Automatic controllers make this easy.

4. Apply water with care

Irrigate early in the morning, when winds are calm and evaporation is at a minimum, so that water goes into the soil and to plant roots.

Water only the target area. There's no need to sprinkle sidewalks, driveways, or the side of the house.

Apply a layer of mulch (such as ground bark or gravel) to the soil to reduce evaporation. Use a 1- to 2-inch-thick layer around annuals, perennials, and vegetables and a 3-inch-thick layer around trees and shrubs.

5. Maintain your irrigation system

To make sure your system operates efficiently, examine it frequently, checking for leaks, clogs, or misdirected sprinklers or drip-emitters.

Sprinklers. Look for signs of trouble. If sprinklers are spraying more water on paving or other unintended areas than on lawns, adjust them. Unclog heads, using a knife or a piece of wire. Water-filled valve boxes or leaking sprinklers may be a sign that valves need to be repaired or replaced.

Drip-irrigation system. Check for leaks—geysers, puddles, eroded soil. Secure tubing that has come loose. Replace or clean clogged drip-emitters and mini-sprinklers. Clean the filter as needed.

6. Adjust watering schedules with weather

Since plants use more water during hot, dry weather, you need to water more often in summer (and on windy days) than in spring or fall. In many regions, plants don't need any supplemental water in winter. ◆

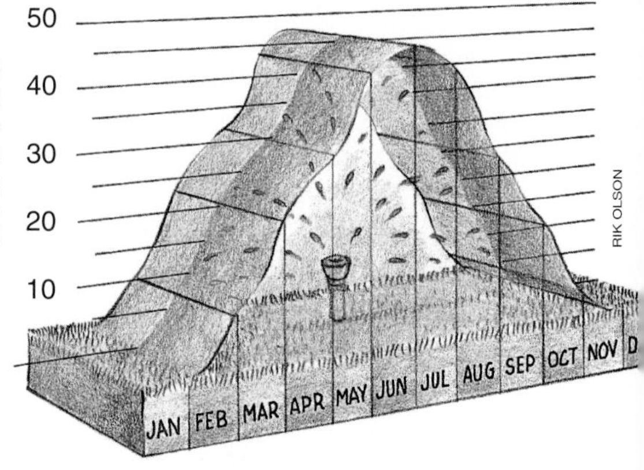

This irrigation schedule illustrates the maximum weekly water needs of lawns in a Northern California water district. The weekly sprinkler run time (the minutes column) is based on an application rate of 2 inches per hour spread out over a week.

JANET LOUGHREY

Nectar-bearing blossoms of delphinium attract a hummingbird.

Creating a bird-friendly garden

The keys are shelter, proper food, and water

By Jim McCausland

Abby and Ken Crouch adore wild birds, so when they bought a ⅓-acre lot in Portland a few years ago, they resolved to make it a bird sanctuary par excellence. They accomplished this by designing a landscape with bird-friendly plants, well-stocked feeders, and a constant water source. The garden now draws dozens of species of birds, from hummingbirds to flickers.

Plants for the birds

Trees, shrubs, perennials, and vines provide nesting space, seasonal food, and safe haven from predators. In the Crouches' garden, large evergreens, English boxwoods, and deciduous plants conceal many nests and provide cover from enemies.

Mountain ashes, crabapple trees, and a pear tree provide fruit in season, while trumpet vines and such flowering perennials as penstemon and sage supply nectar that sustains hummingbirds.

When trees die, the Crouches leave them standing so that birds such as flickers and chickadees can feed on the insects that invade the dead wood. Dead branches also make perfect perches for resting birds and are good places to hang feeders.

Food and feeders

Because different birds eat different foods, the Crouches put out several types of feed.

BLACK OIL SUNFLOWER and niger thistle seeds bring in seed-eaters such as evening grosbeaks, goldfinches, house finches, pine siskins, purple finches, scrub jays, and Steller's jays. The Crouches fill hanging tubular feeders with these seeds.

MILLET, favored by rufous-sided towhees and white- and golden-crowned sparrows, is scattered on an elevated platform feeder.

SUET draws insect-eaters such as chickadees, flickers, jays, and nuthatches.

SUGAR WATER is the beverage of choice for hummingbirds. Mix a solution of 1 part white granulated sugar (sucrose) with 4 parts water. Bring the solution to a boil, then let it cool before filling the feeder. Change the solution every two to three days in summer, washing the feeder out with hot water between fillings.

Water

The Crouches installed a ready-made bubbling pool. It's used by most of the birds, which bathe in the water all year long. However, the main job of the pool is to slake birds' thirst, not only on hot summer days but also in winter when natural sources of water may freeze solid. The water in the Crouches' pool circulates constantly so it freezes only around the edges. Avian Aquatics (800/788-6478 or www.avianaquatics.com) sells a variety of recirculating pools and heated birdbaths.

Warding off cats

Birds will fly down to the ground to eat seeds spilled from feeders; cats can exploit this situation with disastrous results for the birds. The Crouches cut thorny blackberry canes and place them in the spill zones under their feeders to prevent cats from pouncing.

No pesticides

Birds are vulnerable to many chemical pesticides. The Crouches simply don't use them. ◆

A secret garden

Create your own small, enchanted space with plants, pavers, and a water feature

By Steven R. Lorton • Photographs by Thomas J. Story

Ever dream of a secret place where only you can go—filled with flowers and fragrance, and sheltered from the rest of the world by hedges or trellises? A place where a softly dripping fountain soothes away the jangle outside, and time goes by so slowly that tomorrow seems like a distant dream?

Ancient Korean royals knew the value of privacy and a change of scenery. They built *beewons* (secret gardens) within their palace walls. Off-limits to everyone but the emperor or empress and their invited guests, these secluded retreats provided escapes from the rigors of court life.

You may not wear a crown of gold and jade or need daily escapes to a beewon, but don't leave the dream of a secret garden locked away in your imagination. Just find a spot away from your garden's center of activity—a forgotten corner under trees or alongside a fence, for example—and make it your own (see our plan, at right).

A small backyard beewon can be created in a weekend, often with inexpensive materials or items you may already have. You can lay pavers and a path this month, then plant next month after temperatures cool.

Rose-covered trellis marks the entrance to this secret garden in the back corner of a lot. It's sheltered on one side by a fence and on the other two sides by trees, shrubs, and vines.

Some things to consider

• **The site.** Locate your secret garden where it faces a great view or captures the magic of sunrise or sunset. If the northwest corner of the garden gets the first rays of morning sun in summer, this may be where you want to read the paper in your bathrobe and sip a mug of coffee long before the rest of the family stirs. Or you may look forward to disappearing after dinner to the top of a knoll, looking west to the sunset while enjoying a glass of wine and writing in a journal or curling up with a good book.

• **The size.** Smaller is better. The space should be private but allow you room to breathe. A circular patio of brick, stone, or concrete with a 6-foot diameter is more than enough for you and—on occasion—another person. It should feel intimate.

Elements of a secret garden

•**Art.** A favorite sculpture, piece of driftwood, gazing ball, or treasured stone can contribute to the feeling of personal ownership and give the garden a finished look.

•**Flower color.** A pot filled with blooming plants, a flowery vine (such as a lacy potato vine, *Solanum jasminoides,* scrambling along the fence), or a sweep of cottage pinks at your feet add seasonal cheer.

•**Fragrance.** In the ground or in a container, include at least one plant for scent. The perfume can be subtle—a lemon-scented geranium that needs a pinch to release its aroma—or sweetly pungent, as from jasmine or rose. We used stock and dianthus (plant both in fall), as well as purple heliotrope, with flowers that smell like baby powder (heliotrope is frost-tender; plant in spring).

•**Furniture.** All you need is one chair (two at most) and a little table or wide, low shelf on which to rest a glass of lemonade or a book; a bench can meet both needs. If this is a snooze garden, use a lounge chair or hammock.

•**Screening.** A garden wall, fence, hedge, high shrub, or a combination of these lend a sense of enclosure.

•**Sound.** A softly spilling fountain like the one shown below does a lot to mask the cacophony of the world outside. Two or three stalks of bamboo make a soothing rustle when a breeze blows (plant the clumping kind or grow small varieties in a big pot).

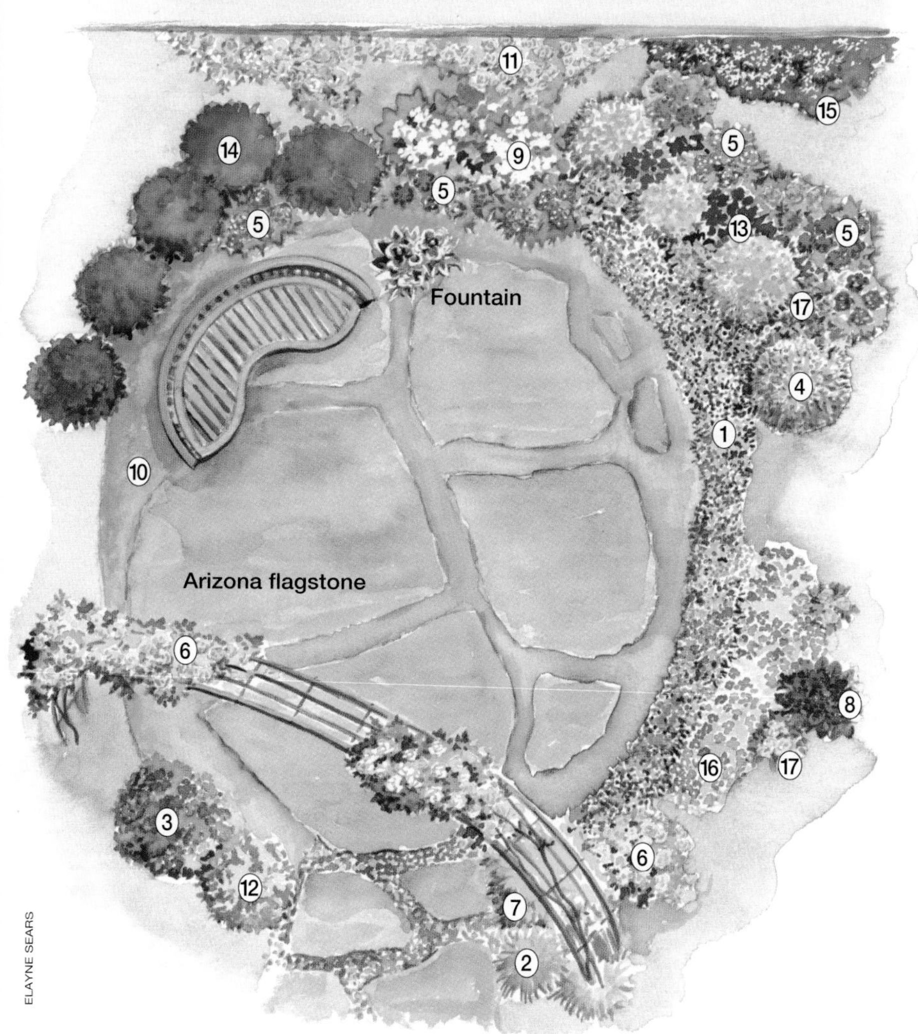

Plant list

1. Alyssum (2 jumbo flats)
2. Blue fescue (2)
3. Cape fuchsia (1)
4. *Coleonema pulchrum* (5)
5. Delphinium (17)
6. 'First Light' rose (1)
7. Golden juniper (1)
8. Heliotrope (4)
9. Hydrangea (2)
10. Irish moss (3 flats)
11. 'Mary Rose' rose (2)
12. *Oxalis crassipes* (1)
13. *Salvia superba* 'May Night' (3)
14. 'Skyrocket' juniper (6)
15. *Solanum jasminoides* (1)
16. 'Spotti' dianthus (4)
17. Stock (32 4-in. pots) ◆

Showstopping perennials

Star-power plants that command the spotlight in containers

By Steven R. Lorton

Container gardening is like opera. Fill a pot with many kinds of plants and you get a colorful chorus, but plant a star performer such as bear's breech or mullein singly in a unique pot and you have the leafy equivalent of a great tenor—Domingo or Carreras. True, you won't get the continuous floral show that a chorus of annuals puts on, but this is horticultural opera. High drama is the name of the game, and showing off plants with shapely leaves, soaring flower spikes, and magnificent presence calls for theatrical flourish.

When Steve Volpin needed a bold statement for the entry of his new Los Angeles home, he planted a hefty lily-of-the-Nile (*Agapanthus orientalis*) in a bright blue glazed pot. He liked the plant's strappy clumps of glossy evergreen leaves. And when the flower stems shot up with big spherical clusters of blue blossoms to match the container, he knew he'd struck pay dirt. Best of all, he says, the plant is easy to care for—"a little attention from the hose, a little liquid plant food, a little grooming, and that's it."

In Portland, Doreen Strong grows *Ligularia stenocephala* 'The Rocket' in a large pot. Early in March the deep burgundy buds show up, then the large, arrow-shaped leaves unfold on black stems that grow to 18 inches, sometimes taller. Finally 5-foot spires shoot up, holding yellow flowers that turn into handsome seed pods.

Honey bush (*Melianthus major*) has ferny leaves and flamboyant flower spikes that make it the star attraction in this Northwest patio.

BEN WOOLSEY

14 choices for center stage

ACANTHUS MOLLIS (bear's breech). Shiny, dark green, deeply cut leaves to 2 feet long. Flower spikes of tubular blooms 2 to 5 feet tall. Light shade; sun at coast. *Sunset* climate zones 4–24.

ACHILLEA FILIPENDULINA (fernleaf yarrow). Delicate silvery foliage in lacy mounds. Yellow flowers on stems 3 to 5 feet tall are flat-topped, like plates. Two good varieties are 'Gold Plate' and 'Coronation Gold'. Full sun. All zones.

AGAPANTHUS (lily-of-the-Nile). Clumping plant with broad, arching straplike leaves. In summer, it bears globes of tubular flowers. *A. orientalis* is the most commonly planted kind; in summer, stems up to 5 feet tall bear as many as 100 blue flowers. 'Albus' has white flowers. *A.* 'Peter Pan' has smaller clumps (8 to 12 in. tall) and shorter bloom stems (1 to 1½ ft. tall). Sun or part shade. Zones 7–9, 12–24. (In cold-winter areas, lift and store during winter.)

ANIGOZANTHOS (kangaroo paw). Clumps of dark green swordlike leaves 3 feet or taller. Bears striking woolly flowers of red, purple, green, or yellow atop 3- to 6-foot stems. Attractive to hummingbirds. Blooms from late spring to fall if spent flowering spikes are cut off at the base. Full sun. Zones 12–13, 15–24.

BERGENIA CORDIFOLIA and **B. CRASSIFOLIA.** Roundish, thick waxy green leaves in clumps to 1½ feet tall, turning burgundy in cool weather. Pink to rose flower clusters in late winter and early spring. Part shade; full sun on coast. Zones 1–9, 12–24.

EUPHORBIA CHARACIAS WULFENII. Upright stems to 4 feet filled with narrow blue-green leaves. Chartreuse flowers in big clusters in spring. Full sun. Zones 4–24.

HELIOTROPIUM ARBORESCENS (heliotrope). Heavily veined leaves with a dark purplish cast on a shrubby 4-foot plant. Flowers are dark violet to white, sweetly fragrant. Sun; part shade in hot-summer climates. Zones 8–24.

HEUCHERA 'Palace Purple'. Deep purple leaves form clumps 18 inches tall. Lacy white flowers grow on spikes in airy clusters. Sun; light shade in the hottest areas. All zones.

LIGULARIA STENOCEPHALA 'The Rocket'. Stately perennial with big (1-ft.-wide) leaves and yellow daisy-like flowers along spires to 5 feet tall. Sun near the coast; shade inland. Zones 3–9, 15–17.

MELIANTHUS MAJOR (honey bush). A robust plant to 14 feet that seldom exceeds 5 feet in a container. Gray-green foliage is topped by spikes of reddish brown flowers. Very theatrical. Sun; part shade in desert. Zones 8–9, 12–24.

THALICTRUM (meadow rue). Five species and several varieties of similar plants commonly sold. Their erect, ferny leaves stretch from 2 to 6 feet in height. Flowers are fine cloudlike puffs in white, pink, lilac, or yellow. Light shade. All zones.

VERBASCUM OLYMPICUM and **V. PHOENICEUM** (purple mullein). Most verbascums are biennial; these two are perennial and have the same downy leaves. Flowers are grand spikes 2 to 5 feet tall, most commonly yellow but also white, cream, and pink. Sun. All zones.

ALLAN MANDELL

Heliotrope, trained as a standard, fills center pot. Its dramatic clouds of small purple flowers are fragrant and contrast beautifully with bright red geraniums, fuchsias, and impatiens, plus yellow yarrow in pots beside it. DESIGN: Tina Dixon. Below, *Heuchera* 'Palace Purple' fills large urn.

What potted perennials need

Perennials do best in pots when given the following:

- Roomy containers (at least 16-in. diameter).
- Rich, fresh potting mix.
- The right sun exposure.
- Regular water.
- Fertilizer. Use a liquid plant food mixed to manufacturer's specifications when plants emerge in spring, then again in midsummer, if not monthly from April to October.
- Repotting. Plants may need dividing about every three years. Knock them out of their containers, divide, and repot. ◆

BEN WOOLSEY

AIRY, COOL-HUED FLOWER CLUSTERS and downy-textured leaves create soft clouds of color in this drought-tolerant Northern California garden. For details, see page 282.

September

COURTESY OF FULCRUM PUBLISHING

Passionate Colorado gardeners

■ Perched on the slope of a valley in northern Colorado, Lauren Springer's garden is a lovely blend of dwarf conifers and low-growing perennials that echo the wildflower fields of the surrounding Rocky Mountains. Some of the plants Springer chose, including red firecracker penstemon (foreground) and many of the sages and other penstemons in the background, look at home here because they're Western natives. Non-indigenous plants such as apricot-colored *Papaver triniifolium* (left), blue *Nepeta racemosa* 'Walker's Low' (center), and bright yellow *Alyssum markgrafii* (center right) were selected because they blend nicely into this setting.

Springer's experiences in creating her garden provide much of the pith of *Passionate Gardening: Good Advice for Challenging Climates* (Fulcrum, Golden, CO, 2000; $34.95; 800/992-2908). This book is a wonderful collection of garden essays written and photographed by Springer and Rob Proctor, horticulture director at Denver Botanic Gardens. The essays are by turns inspirational, instructive, and humorous. Here's Proctor on borders: "There are many books on making borders. I can boil their contents down to several sentences in plain English: plant the short things in the front and the tall things in the back... pairing large-leaved plants with small-leaved ones, and pairing contrasting shapes—round plants next to spiky ones. That's about it."

Springer says of her garden: "Someone asked me what I might name the garden. I am loath to do that, but the name that came to mind was Piles. Piles of manure, of rock mulch, of compost, pots, and labels. ... And I must say, from all those piles, a lovely garden has been born."

—*Jim McCausland*

These clippers aren't just for grass

THOMAS J. STORY

■ Most scissorslike grass shears require a continual squeezing motion, which can eventually cause pain in hands and forearms, or even carpal tunnel syndrome. Now, a new battery-operated model—the Ryobi 12-volt Grass Shears—makes the job quick, easy, and pain-free.

With just the push of a safety button and press of a trigger, the dual blades clip the grass instantly. The clippers are also useful for deadheading flowers on herbaceous perennials such as coreopsis, lavender, and Santa Barbara daisy, but they should never be used to cut tough, woody growth.

Maintaining the shears is simple. After each use, pull out the battery, wipe the blades with a clean cloth, and plug the battery into its 120-volt AC charger for at least eight hours.

Ryobi Grass Shears are available at many home improvement centers; the suggested retail price is $69.99. To find a retailer near you, call Ryobi at (800) 345-8746. — *Lauren Bonar Swezey*

JUDY DYER NORMAN A. PLATE (ABOVE)

Prickly pear wreath puts on a surprise show

■ In *Sunset's* December 1999 issue, we featured the Southwestern wreath made from prickly pear pads that's pictured at left ("Deck the Halls in Desert Style,"). Inspired by our story, Judy Dyer of Tucson made the wreath and recently sent us the following update.

"I made the wreath last December from a cactus in my yard. I hung it on the front of our house, where it has been ever since. Much to my surprise, it bloomed this April, as if the pads had never been cut. I have attached a photo of it [below, left]. Shows you how tough these cactus really are. It even has a new shoot off one lobe."

Judy Dyer's wreath was still bearing yellow flowers in early June.

BOOKSHELF

•Earth-friendly rose care. University of California Agricultural & Natural Resources has published another winner for gardeners eager to avoid using toxic chemicals. Hot off the press, *Healthy Roses: Environmentally Friendly Ways to Manage Pests and Disorders in Your Garden and Landscape,* by Mary Louise Flint and John F. Karlik (publication 21589, 2000; $10; 800/994-8849 or anrcatalog.ucdavis.edu), offers tips on rose care, pest and disease identification, and beneficial insects that attack rose pests. Photographs of the insects and diseases accompany the text. Don't miss Flint's other valuable books, *Pests of the Garden and Small Farm* (publication 3332; $35) and *Pests of Landscape Trees and Shrubs* (publication 3359; $35).

•Perfuming the garden. If you would like to have more fragrant plants in your garden but don't know where to start, pick up a copy of *A Garden of Fragrance,* by Suzy Bales (ReganBooks, New York, 2000; $29.95; 800/242-7737). This 192-page book is filled with suggestions for bringing fragrant plants into the garden. Edge a vegetable bed with scented annuals, Bales tells us, or plant herbs such as thyme between pavers.

CLIPPINGS

A fun read. *Orchid Fever: A Horticultural Tale of Love, Lust, and Lunacy,* by Eric Hansen (Pantheon Books, New York, 2000; $23). There's a serious message in this book. So-called orchid smugglers are actually conservationists, the author argues. And the laws they skirt prohibit collectors from rescuing plants that are doomed, while doing nothing to protect habitat. Yet Hansen introduces us to "perfectly eccentric" oddballs—illicit basement growers, visionary teenage breeders—who make the book a real page-turner.

A fountain without water

STEVEN GUNTHER (2)

■ Water used to spill from the conch shell on this cherub's shoulders, splashing into the giant clamshell beneath his feet. Or at least it did when Bill Anderson was a cherub-size visitor at his grandmother Glenna Anderson's home in Hollywood Hills. After Bill inherited the fountain and moved it to his home in Newport Beach, the Andersons decided against the expense of added plumbing. Instead, Bill's wife, Dana, planted a cascade.

The main spiller is white-flowered bacopa. The froth under the cherub's toes is campanula and Alpine strawberries. Planted nearly two years ago, this trio is thriving; species tulips and muscari have naturalized among them.

The surprise behind the success is that the basin has no drainage holes ("so we can keep the option of making it a fountain again")—a violation of the first principle of container planting. The width and shallowness of the shell are the saving grace. "The soil dries out quite quickly," Dana says. "That's what makes this work." — *Sharon Cohoon.*

Blooms on tap

■ There are dozens of reasons Laguna Beach landscape designer Jeff Powers of Earthscaping likes fairy lily (*Zephyranthes candida*). For one thing, though it's a bulb, its grassy leaves are evergreen and somewhat succulent. "That makes it a handsome, extremely low-maintenance ground cover—useful in many situations," he says. The bulb spreads quickly, choking out weeds, but it tolerates crowding so you don't have to divide it to keep it blooming. The white carpet of fairy lily under European white birch pictured at left is a prime example: It has flourished in this Corona del Mar garden for nine years without tampering.

Another plus: *Z. candida* puts on its best bloom show from late summer through mid-fall, when most gardens have little in flower. You can trick it into blooming again by letting it dry out, then giving it a good drenching. *Z. candida* is available in containers at nurseries now or in bulb form come January and February. — *S.C.*

MICHAEL S. THOMPSON

A dramatic entry to a Wright house

■ Six years ago, Rob Steiner bought a Frank Lloyd Wright house in the hills of Eugene, Oregon. Built in 1958, it was a Usonian-style house, Wright's term for his designs that were affordable for the average American. Steiner thought that the existing entry looked too average, so he enlisted Eugene landscape architect Brad Stangeland to revamp it. "The problem was how to introduce guests to this dramatic house—it is Frank Lloyd Wright, for goodness sake—while still keeping a sense of the natural Oregon environment," Stangeland says.

Stangeland's solution was to position the visitor parking area as far from the front door as possible. A curving driveway leads family cars down to the garage, but guests leave their cars outside the Craftsman-style gate pictured in the far right corner. Once inside the gate, the journey begins: A path of basalt steppingstones is laced with jewel mint of Corsica (*Mentha requienii*), a creeping ground cover whose leaves release a spicy fragrance when crushed underfoot. Next to the path, a stream appears, surrounded by low-growing plants such as 'Gumpo White' azaleas, Japanese blood grass (*Imperata cylindrica* 'Rubra'), and wild strawberries. The water splashes through a series of basins and disappears under the stone walkway, only to surface on the other side, flowing into several small pools where ferns, miniature cattail (*Typha minima*), and yellow flag (*Iris pseudacorus*) grow around moss-covered rocks.

Night lighting glows along the pathway, accentuating the branch patterns of Douglas firs and Japanese maples. As guests approach the front door, wide brick steps and a retaining wall signal a change from the natural to the formal, as the drama of the garden gives way to the drama of the house. — *Mary-Kate Mackey*

WILLIAM B. DEWEY

Gauzy textures, gutsy plants

The softer side of dry-climate landscaping

■ Throughout much of the West, a drought-tolerant garden is good insurance. Summers are dry, and prolonged periods of drought do occur. In many locations, landscape irrigation restrictions kick in when the water supply runs low. Knowing that, Bobby and Susan Shand planned accordingly. They asked landscape designer Pat Brodie to use unthirsty plants. But since their house is traditional in style rather than modern or Mediterranean, they didn't want cactus, agaves, or anything too austere.

To keep the look soft, Brodie chose plants with fine, downy-textured leaves and airy, cool-colored flower clusters. *Trachelium caeruleum,* the violet-blue cloud spilling over the rocks in the foreground of the photo above, is a prime example. It is backed by a complementary drift of Mexican bush sage (*Salvia leucantha*). To the left is a lavender-gray pillow of catmint (*Nepeta faassenii*). To the right are the creamy plumes of yarrow (*Achillea* 'Anthea'). "Except for the red flax, which lends contrast, everything has a soft and delicate appearance," Brodie says. "But they're actually all very tough."

Lavender-blue flowers of *Trachelium caeruleum* mix with catmint (left), yarrow (right), red flax, and Mexican bush sage (background).

Fall is an excellent time to plant a drought-tolerant border. Mexican bush sage and catmint, which are still in bloom, will be easy to find at nurseries. *T. caeruleum* flowers a bit earlier, so it might be harder to find; a service-oriented nursery can order it for you. — *S.C.*

A deerproof garden in Montana

■ Situated in a mixed conifer forest near Missoula, Montana, Mike and Joyce Nave's property includes the prolific raised-bed garden shown at right. Two features set this garden apart: a garden shed with a design that echoes that of the Naves' house, and a fence that shuts out ravenous local deer.

Designed by the Naves' son Jim, the 8- by 10-foot shed with a corrugated tin roof provides a place for potting and tool storage.

DAVID WAKELY

An 8-foot-tall wire fence surrounds the garden surrounded by forest.

The 8-foot-tall fence makes gardening possible: Without it, the deer would eat everything. Because the garden plot is so large (1,600 square feet), solid fencing would have been quite expensive and would have blocked views of the surrounding forest.

To avoid both problems, the Naves chose a wire-mesh fence. The 2- by 4-inch mesh of 11-gauge wire (called horse fencing) is supported every 10 feet by pressure-treated 4-by-4 posts anchored in concrete; 10-foot-long 2-by-4s provide horizontal reinforcement 4 feet above the ground and also cap the fence. The total cost to fence the 40- by 40-foot plot was about $1,000.

The Naves grow annual flowers and salad crops in the raised beds, feeding them with liquid fertilizer every two weeks during the growing season and adding chicken manure once a year when they turn the soil. —*J.M.*

Lawn grass of the future—today

SANDRA IVANY

■ Imagine a feathery emerald green lawn that needs watering only once a week and requires just two mowings a year. It may sound futuristic, but 'Rana Creek' fescue (*Festuca*)—a variety of a California native perennial bunchgrass—is available now.

Landscape designer Michelle Comeau discovered its charms on a field trip to Rana Creek Habitat Restoration, a Monterey-area nursery specializing in native grasses. "I wanted a grass that was soft enough to walk on barefoot," Comeau explains. She tried it in gardens around the Monterey Peninsula and found it the perfect solution for a cool coastal region plagued by droughts and water restrictions.

In the wild, this grass grows and turns green when fall rains come, and stays green until late spring when dry weather drives it into dormancy. But with supplemental water once a week during the dry season, it remains green all year long. Comeau irrigates this fescue only a few months a year (April or May through July). Then, to save water, she allows it to go dormant between August and the arrival of winter rains.

Mowing this grass is easy too. Comeau cuts it once in February or March and again when it's dormant—just before rains start. Between mowings, it can grow 1 foot tall.

To plant 'Rana Creek' fescue, prepare the soil as you would for a traditional lawn. After the first year, fertilize in fall using an organic (urea-based) nitrogen fertilizer that releases in cool temperatures.

Seed and plants (sold as plugs in 1-gallon cans) of 'Rana Creek' fescue are available from Rana Creek Habitat Restoration, 35351 E. Laurel Valley Rd., Carmel Valley; (831) 659-3820. — *L.B.S.*

JEFF GNASS (2)

Flowers spill from recycled trees in Juneau

■ A few years ago, Steve and Cindy Bowhay of Juneau bought 49 acres of land on the side of Thunder Mountain, planning to turn the property into a scenic attraction. Inspired by trees uprooted by a mudslide, Steve decided to try recycling some felled Sitka spruces and Western hemlocks elsewhere on his property to use as planters. So he buried the trunks of 30 trees into the ground and trimmed their roots to form giant bowls 10 to 14 feet in the air. Then he lined the bowls with fishnet and moss, filled them with potting soil, and planted them with trailing ground ivy (*Glechoma hederacea*) and flowering plants like begonias, bleeding hearts, fuchsias, lobelias, and petunias. The planters make a grand stand at the entry to the Bowhays' Glacier Gardens Rainforest Adventure.

Equally impressive are the dozens of hanging baskets spilling with begonias, fuchsias, and Surfina petunias (some cascading to 6 feet) in the indoor conservatory (shown at left), where there's a garden gift shop and cafe serving beverages and snacks.

Eight-person covered shuttles take visitors from the entry area up through the rain forest and to overlooks of downtown Juneau and the Chilkat Range. *Tours 9–6 daily, May-September; $14.95, $8.95 ages 6–12. 7600 Glacier Hwy.; (907) 790-3377.*

— Steven R. Lorton

How to harvest and store tomato seeds

■ Why save tomato seeds from year to year when buying packaged ones each year is so convenient? Because it's easy and satisfying, especially when the seeds you save are heirloom varieties. With tomato production winding down this month in Western gardens, now is a good time to harvest seeds. Before you start, here are a few guidelines.

•Preserve seed only from nonhybrid (open-pollinated) tomatoes. They produce offspring just like themselves, with only slight variations. On the other hand, hybrid tomatoes, which include most modern varieties, produce offspring that won't necessarily look or taste the same as the parents.

•Preserve seed that hasn't been cross-pollinated. All tomatoes are self-pollinating, but a few kinds (currant or potato-leaf types like 'Brandywine') can be cross-pollinated by some insects. If you're not growing currant or potato-leaf types, or you're growing just one of these in addition to other types of tomatoes, you can save seed from this year's harvest. To prevent cross-pollination in the future, cover flowers with a bag made from cheesecloth or spun-polyester fiber (available at nurseries) before blossoms open. Tag the covered flower stem with brightly colored yarn. Remove the cover when fruits are developing.

•Harvest fruits when they're thoroughly ripe and soft. Tomato seeds are enclosed in a gel sac; to remove the sac and to help destroy seed-borne diseases, put them through a fermentation process:

1

2

3

4

THOMAS J. STORY (4) UPPER LEFT: JAMES CARRIER

5

1. Wash the fruit, then cut it in half across the middle (not the stem end). Gently squeeze seeds and juice into a labeled glass or plastic container. Fill containers about half full, then set them out of direct sun in an area where you won't be bothered by the ripening odor or fruit flies.

2. Allow the seed mixture to sit until the surface is partially covered with whitish mold (in three to five days). In warm climates, you may need to add a little water midway through the process to keep the seeds afloat. Scrape off the white mold with a spoon, being careful not to remove seeds.

3. Fill the container with water, then stir; the good seeds will sink to the bottom.

4. Pour off and discard floating seeds and pulp. Repeat until the good seeds are clean. Pour the cleaned seeds into a fine strainer; rinse and drain.

5. Sprinkle seeds onto a plate and allow them to dry for one to three days, depending on the weather. Keep them out of direct sun. To make sure they dry thoroughly and don't stick together, stir twice a day. Store dried seeds in a cool, dry, dark place in individually labeled airtight containers such as glass canning or baby food jars until planting time next spring.

—L.B.S.

TERRENCE MOORE (2)

New desert garden respects Tucson tradition

■ Landscape designer Debra Huffman wanted the garden for her new home to blend into its older Tucson neighborhood, so she used traditional plants and hardscape materials that evoke the area's roots.

To create privacy from the street, for example, Huffman installed an old-fashioned ocotillo fence. Stems of 6-foot-tall ocotillo (*Fouquieria splendens*) were woven together with wire to make fence sections, sunk about 6 inches into soil mixed with sand, and lashed to steel crossbars on posts to provide extra stability. Huffman sprays the fence with water once a week; most of the ocotillo has taken root, sprouting leaves and red-orange blossoms. She also commissioned forged steel gates and trellises by Tucson sculptors Dan Lehman and Daniel Ptasnik.

To serve as the focal points of her front yard, Huffman relocated an existing date palm and planted a sculptural gray-green *Agave weberi,* both of which typify the region's flora. She also wove in some recent introductions to the Southwest, including *Acacia berlandieri,* a lacy shrub with fernlike foliage and creamy white puffball flowers in spring, and *Bulbine frutescens,* a low, shrubby South African native with succulent green leaves and yellow flowers from fall through spring. Pink penstemon and red-and-blue-flowered bat-faced cuphea dot the garden as well. By using unthirsty, desert-adapted plants and installing an efficient drip-irrigation system, Huffman's monthly water bill is $30 to $40—far less than the neighborhood average. — *Nora Burba Trulsson*

WHAT TO DO IN YOUR GARDEN IN SEPTEMBER

PLANTING

☐ COOL-SEASON CROPS. Up until Labor Day weekend, you can still sow seeds of arugula, kale, leaf lettuce, mustard greens, radishes, and spinach, or set out transplants of most winter crops. Set out onion transplants this month for harvest next summer. Order garlic now to plant in October and November.

☐ LANDSCAPE PLANTS. As the weather cools, plant all kinds of perennials, trees, shrubs, vines, and ground covers.

☐ LAWNS. This is also a good time to sow new lawns or to reseed bare spots in existing lawns (see "Tune up Your Turf," page 304).

☐ SPRING-BLOOMING BULBS. Shop for bulbs of crocus, daffodils, hyacinths, and tulips in nurseries just after Labor Day.

☐ WINTER COVER CROPS. As summer crops are removed from beds, sow seeds of crimson clover, Austrian field peas, and vetch. These cover crops minimize erosion caused by harsh winter weather, and they enrich the soil with organic matter when you till them under in spring.

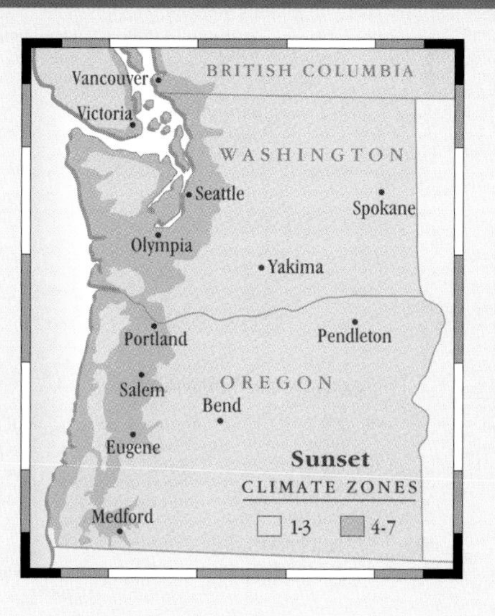

MAINTENANCE

☐ CARE FOR ROSES. After the fall flush of bloom, let the flowers form hips, which helps the plants wind down for winter.

☐ CLEAN GREENHOUSES. Before first fall frost, empty the greenhouse, wash it down (a combination of bleach and water makes short work of algae and moss), replace weather-stripping, check out heating and venting systems, and clean out flats, pots, and seedbeds.

☐ DIG AND DIVIDE PERENNIALS. Lift and divide spring- and summer-flowering perennials now, including astilbe, daylilies, Oriental poppies, peonies, Shasta daisies, Siberian irises, and violets. Divide fall bloomers like asters after they flower or wait until early next spring.

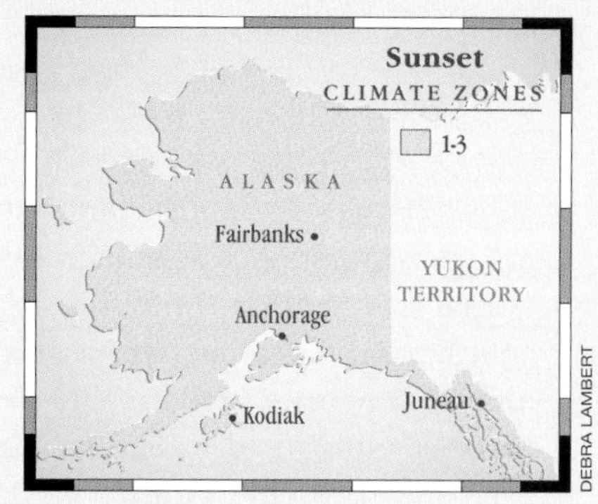

DEBRA LAMBERT

☐ MAKE COMPOST. Use grass clippings, fallen leaves, weeds, and vegetable waste to build a compost pile. Keep it damp and turned—you'll have compost to dig into the soil before winter.

☐ MULCH. Zones 1–3: Apply a 4-inch layer of organic mulch around perennials to minimize freeze damage and erosion. You can use shredded autumn leaves or coarse compost as mulch.

☐ TEND FLOWERS. Fertilize, water, and deadhead fuchsias, annuals, and long-flowering perennials to keep blooms coming until near frost.

☐ WEED. Fall weeds can be the most pernicious. Weeds that establish themselves now have the winter to send down roots, and they become very tough to remove in spring. Keep the garden hoed and mulched to prevent weeds from rooting. ◆

WHAT TO DO IN YOUR GARDEN IN SEPTEMBER

PLANTING

☐ BULBS. Shop soon for the best selection. Choose firm bulbs without soft or moldy spots. Good choices for mild-winter climates: anemone, crocus, daffodil, Dutch iris, freesia, homeria, hyacinth, ixia, leucojum, lycoris, oxalis, ranunculus, scilla, sparaxis, tritonia, tulip, and watsonia. It's not critical to chill bulbs such as crocus, hyacinths, and tulips in the refrigerator, but performance will be superior and tulip stems will grow 1/6 to 1/3 taller if you do (chill for about six weeks). In cold-winter areas (zones 1 and 2), tender bulbs such as freesias, homerias, and watsonias are not hardy; choose from what's available in local nurseries.

☐ EDIBLE-POD PEAS. Zones 1–9, 14–17: If you can't get your kids to eat green vegetables, plant some snap peas, which are tasty right off the plant. The best? Try 2½-foot-tall 'Super Sugar Mel' (from Renee's Garden at www.reneesgarden.com or in nurseries) or 2-foot tall 'Sugar Sprint' (new for 2000 from Nichols Garden Nursery; 541/928-9280 or www.nicholsgardennursery.com).

☐ MUMS. Chrysanthemums come in an amazing number of colors and forms. Brush, pompom, quill, spider, and spoon are a few of the forms designated by chrysanthemum hobbyists. To learn more about them, join the Northern California Chrysanthemum Society: Contact Jim Hackett at (916) 988-6081 or hackmum@aol.com.

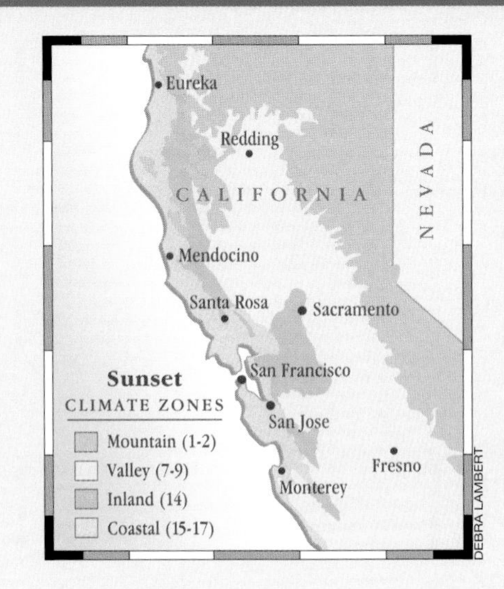

☐ NATIVE PLANTS. Zones 7–9, 14–17: You don't need a big garden to accommodate native plants. Any small bed set apart from heavily irrigated plants can become an attractive native border. Try *Arctostaphylos,* blue-eyed grass, bush anemone, fremontodendron, heuchera, lyme grass, mahonia, monkey flower, Pacific Coast iris, *Penstemon heterophyllus purdyi, Salvia clevelandii,* and Western columbine. For sources of these and other native plants, visit Baylands Nursery in East Palo Alto (650/323-1645), Intermountain Nursery in Prather (559/855-3113), Larner Seeds in Bolinas (415/868-9407), Mostly Natives in Tomales (707/878-2009), or Yerba Buena Nursery in Woodside (650/851-1668).

☐ VEGETABLES. Zones 7–9, 14–17: Early autumn is a great time to introduce kids to vegetable gardening. Select a small, sunny border, or plant in large containers. Choose carrots (try small, round 'Thumbelina' from Park Seed, 800/845-3369), onion sets (which are easy to handle), snap peas (kids love to pick and even eat them fresh), and radishes (try red, purple, and white 'Easter Egg Blend II', also from Park; they're fun to harvest).

MAINTENANCE

☐ RENOVATE LAWNS. Zones 7–9, 14–17: Late September is a good time for a complete lawn overhaul. Aerate compacted areas (equipment can be rented) and fertilize with a complete lawn fertilizer; water well. If you need to reseed bare patches, prepare the area by digging in organic matter, then firm down the soil, water well, scatter seed, and cover lightly with mulch. Water several times a day to keep seed moist; mow when new grass is well rooted in several weeks. For details, see "Tune up your turf" on page 304. ◆

southern california • checklist

WHAT TO DO IN YOUR GARDEN IN SEPTEMBER

PLANTING

☐ BULBS. Nurseries are well-stocked with spring-flowering bulbs. For a good selection, shop early. You can plant South African bulbs like babiana, freesia, ixia, sparaxis, and watsonia immediately. You can also plant oxalis, species tulips, star flower (*Ipheion uniflorum*), and Tazetta-type narcissus such as paperwhites. Buy anemones, daffodils, Dutch irises, and ranunculus now while supply is ample, but wait until October to plant. Dutch crocus, hyacinths, and tulips must chill at least six weeks before planting. Put them in a paper bag in the vegetable crisper of your refrigerator. In the high desert (zone 11), chilling is unnecessary.

☐ COOL-CLIMATE CROPS. Mid-month on the coast (zones 22–24) and inland (zones 18–21), begin planting winter crops. Sow seeds or transplant seedlings of beets, bok choy, broccoli, Brussels sprouts, cabbage, carrots, cauliflower, celery, collards, fava beans, garlic, lettuce, kale, kohlrabi, leeks, onions, parsnips, peas, radishes, spinach, Swiss chard, and turnips. In the high desert, plant lettuce, radishes, and spinach.

☐ COOL-SEASON ANNUALS. For flowers by Thanksgiving, plant spring bedding plants now. Good choices include calendulas, English and fairy primroses, Iceland poppies, nemesias, pansies, snapdragons, and stock.

DEBRA LAMBERT

☐ START HERBS. Plant mint, parsley, rosemary, tarragon, thyme, and other perennial herbs. Sow seeds of dill and cilantro.

MAINTENANCE

☐ FEED PERMANENT PLANTS. Fertilize established trees, shrubs, ground covers, and warm-season grasses like Bermuda. Coastal gardeners can feed tropical plants one last time. Stop feeding cymbidium orchids with high-nitrogen fertilizer; switch to a bloom formula such as 15-30-15. Don't feed Mediterranean or native plants.

☐ PROTECT AGAINST BRUSH-FIRES. Before the onset of Santa Ana winds, gardeners in fire-prone areas should cut and remove all dead branches and leaves from trees and shrubs, especially those near the house. Clear leaves from gutters and remove woody vegetation growing against structures.

☐ WATER CAREFULLY. Shade trees will appreciate a slow, deep soaking since winter rain is still a long way off. Give established shrubs and perennials the same treatment. Shallow-rooted citrus and avocado trees need more frequent irrigation—water once a week inland, every other week along the coast.

☐ DIVIDE PERENNIALS. After they've finished blooming, dig, divide, and replant overcrowded perennials such as agapanthus, daylilies, penstemons, and yarrow. Use a spading fork to loosen and lift clumps. Wash or gently shake off excess soil. Then divide into sections with a spade or sharp knife. Plant divisions immediately in freshly amended soil.

PEST CONTROL

☐ PROTECT CABBAGE CROPS. Squadrons of white butterflies (cabbage whites) seem to descend on broccoli and cabbage as soon as you plant them. To keep butterflies from laying eggs on crops, cover seedlings with floating row covers as soon as you plant. ◆

WHAT TO DO IN YOUR GARDEN IN SEPTEMBER

PLANTING

☐ HARDY PERENNIALS. Set out transplants of campanula, candytuft, catmint, coreopsis, delphinium, dianthus, foxglove, penstemon, phlox, salvia, and yarrow. In areas where soil freezes deep every winter, spread a thick layer of mulch around plants to keep them from being heaved out of the ground.

☐ INSTANT FALL COLOR. As tender perennials are damaged by frost, remove them and pop in fall-blooming asters, chrysanthemums, and pansies.

☐ TREES, SHRUBS. Cool fall temperatures are perfect for planting trees and shrubs. Apply several inches of organic mulch around the plants and don't let their rootballs dry out as they become established.

☐ VEGETABLES. Sow seeds of lettuce and other salad greens, radishes, and spinach for late-fall harvest. Keep the bed evenly moist and use a floating row cover to protect plants from early frosts. Spinach can be left in the ground over the winter for harvest in late winter or early spring.

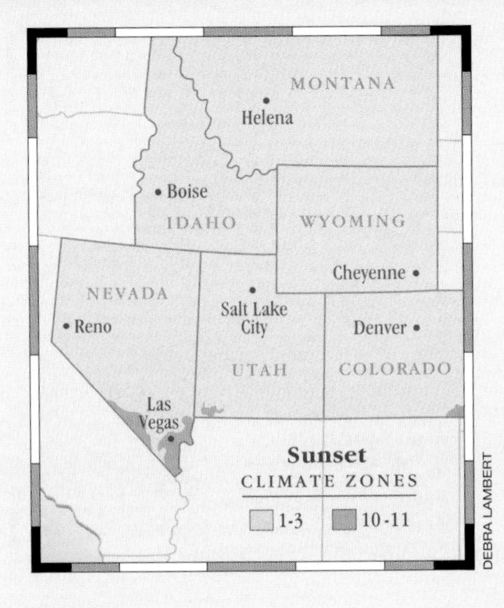

MAINTENANCE

☐ CARE FOR HOUSE PLANTS. Bring house plants back indoors before the first frost. Inspect them carefully for insects; if you find them, spray the foliage with insecticidal soap or a pyrethrum-based insecticide labeled safe for house plants. Be sure to spray tops and undersides of the leaves thoroughly.

☐ CONTROL PERSISTENT WEEDS. Spray perennial weeds such as bindweed and Canadian thistle with a glyphosate-based herbicide before first frost. Cut and discard any seed heads before spraying.

☐ DIVIDE PERENNIALS. Lift and divide overcrowded clumps of perennials, including campanulas, daylilies, hostas, peonies, sedums, and Shasta daisies. Pull the roots apart and replant the healthiest divisions in soil amended with compost. Cover with shredded bark mulch, straw, hay, or evergreen boughs to protect them over the winter.

☐ HARVEST VEGETABLES. Harvest tomatoes and peppers before first frost. Beets, carrots, parsnips, and turnips can be left in the ground for winter harvest if mulched with 6 to 12 inches of hay or straw.

☐ LIFT AND STORE SUMMER BULBS. After frost kills their foliage, dig up callas, cannas, dahlias, gladiolus, tuberous begonias, and other tender bulbs. Dry off the bulbs and pack them in vermiculite or sterile potting soil. Store in a cool place and keep the medium slightly moist all winter.

☐ OVERWINTER ANNUALS INDOORS. Take cuttings from coleus and geraniums to overwinter indoors. Root the cuttings in moist vermiculite or sterile potting soil. Bedding or wax begonias, heliotrope, impatiens, and Madagascar periwinkle can be moved indoors and grown as house plants over the winter. Clean up the plants, cut them back by one-third, place them in containers in a sunny window, and fertilize.

☐ TEND RASPBERRIES. Mow raspberry canes down to the ground with a power lawn mower when they have finished fruiting. After mowing, top-dress the bed with several inches of manure.

— *Marcia Tatroe* ◆

southwest • checklist

WHAT TO DO IN YOUR GARDEN IN SEPTEMBER

PLANTING

☐ ANNUALS. Zones 1–2 (Flagstaff, Santa Fe): Sow seeds of calendula, cornflower, larkspur, and poppies for spring bloom. Zones 11–13 (Las Vegas, Tucson, Phoenix): Set out transplants of delphinium, larkspur, lobelia, pansy, snapdragon, stock, and sweet alyssum late in the month.

☐ INDOOR PLANTS. All zones: Begin forcing bulbs of amaryllis and paperwhite narcissus by month's end to ensure indoor bloom for Christmas. Kalanchoe need 12 hours of darkness for 4 to 6 weeks beginning this month to promote flowering by Christmas.

☐ PERENNIALS. Zones 10–13: Moderate temperatures and, in most places, the approach of winter rains makes this a good time to plant many perennials, including campanula, catmint, coreopsis, dianthus, gaillardia, geum, penstemon, phlox, salvia, and yarrow. Set them out in well-prepared garden soil; water well. Start seeds of aster, carnation, columbine, feverfew, hollyhock, lupine, Shasta daisy, statice, and phlox. Transplant seedlings in about eight weeks.

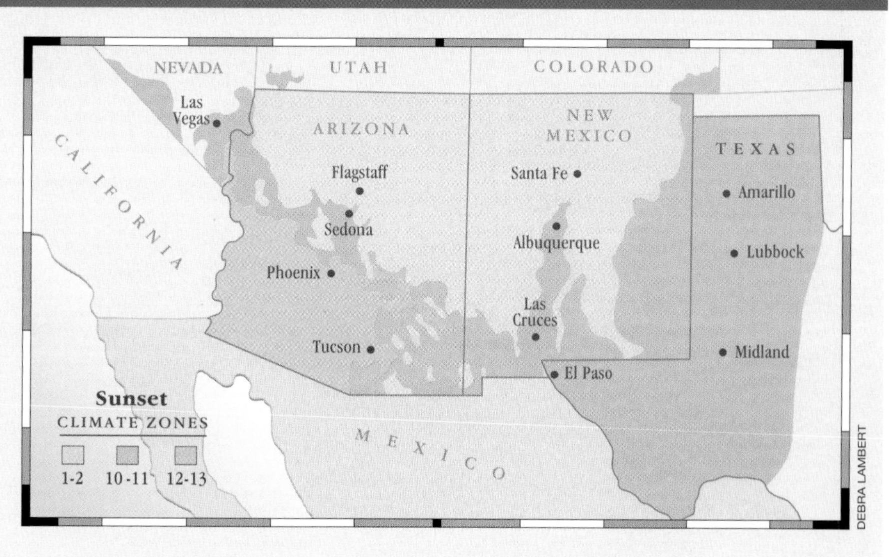

☐ VEGETABLES. Zones 1–2: Sow seeds of carrots, radishes, and spinach; set out garlic cloves. Zones 10–13: As soon as temperatures drop below 100°, sow seeds of short-season beets, broccoli, cabbage, carrots, cauliflower, celery, cucumber, fava beans, kale, kohlrabi, leeks, radishes, snap beans, Swiss chard, and turnips. Set out transplants of green onions, peppers, and tomatoes.

☐ SPRING-BLOOMING BULBS. Zones 1–2, 10 (Albuquerque): Plant spring-flowering bulbs, including crocus, daffodils, grape hyacinth, hyacinth, and tulips. Zones 11–13: Buy these bulbs now, place them in paper bags, and chill in the refrigerator until the soil cools enough to plant next month.

☐ TREES AND SHRUBS. Zones 10–13: Set out container-grown trees or shrubs that are not frost-tender. Most native desert plants establish best when planted in fall.

MAINTENANCE

☐ CARE FOR ROSES. Zones 1–2, 10: Leave blossoms on plants to slow growth before winter. Zones 11–13: Prune dead canes and clean up around the plant, then fertilize and water well to stimulate fall growth.

☐ DIVIDE PERENNIALS. Zones 1–2, 10: Lift and divide crowded clumps of daylilies, hostas, peonies, and Shasta daisies. Zones 11–13: Lift and divide the rhizomes of irises that have become crowded.

☐ PRUNE. Zones 11-13: Lightly prune evergreen shrubs such as Arizona rosewood, oleander, and Texas ranger to maintain their natural forms.— *Mary Irish* ◆

Garden make

overs

To edge a patio, the owner created beds of seasonal color, planted ground covers between pavers, and built a pond (far left, surrounded by ornamental grasses).
RIGHT: The second step in the garden remodel was covering an ugly chain-link fence with bougainvillea. (See "Scruffy to sensational," page 294.)

STEVEN GUNTHER (2)

RENOVATING YOUR GARDEN?

Here's how to give the whole yard, or just parts of it, a new look. Plus tips and advice from other weekend warriors

By Kathleen N. Brenzel

You've bought a fixer-upper with a neglected yard, and you want to make it pretty. Or you've lived for years with the same garden—allowing plants to scramble helter-skelter and trees to grow unchecked—and now you're ready to freshen its look. Either way, a landscape makeover can seem like a daunting task. It's a long journey, after all, from a wish to a dream garden.

Or is it? Last year we asked readers to tell us about gardens they've renovated, mostly by themselves. Hundreds responded, sending snapshots, plans, tips, and advice. On the following pages we share some of their stories.

Fall is the perfect time to start a landscaping project, to plant trees, shrubs, vines, and many perennials. The best way to start? Take it one step at a time (the guidelines on page 296 can help). That's what the owners of the gardens on these pages did, and they succeeded—brilliantly.

Scruffy to sensational: A garden retreat

TIME: Less than two years
COST: About $5,000

■ You might call this small (35- by 19-foot) outdoor room the yard that gave birth to a gardener.

When Alix Olson bought the Encinitas, California, property in 1986, tending plants was not on her to-do list. "I had neither the money nor the inclination to landscape," she explains. "So I kept the weeds, mowed when it rained, and ignored the ugly green chain-link fence."

But Olson knew she wanted greenery around her. Memories of her two-year stay in barren Saudi Arabia were still too fresh, and the idea of lush trees, flowers, and grass too appealing. Little by little, she began improving her land.

"I built a patio off the kitchen with French doors leading to it. I started watering the grass. Then I planted bougainvillea to hide the chain-link fence."

After a few months, Olson decided that a garden along the fence would be nice. She visited nurseries with her friend Sara Lynch to learn about plants. "I began to enjoy digging in the dirt," she recalls. Flowers lived and died, trees were planted, transplanted, lived, and died.

"I finally decided the soil—rather hard, packed clay with no drainage—was a problem. So last fall, inspired by magazine articles on small gardens, I ripped up the whole thing except the bougainvillea and the only tree that was happy with my haphazard care—an Australian willow.

An old lap pool was replaced by a sunny terrace (below).

BEFORE

AFTER

Fresh look for an overgrown slope

TIME: Two years
COST: About $6,000

■ "When we bought this house, the yard was overgrown with honeysuckle, ivy, and blackberries," writes Scott Terry of Oakland, California. "It had obviously been beautiful at one time but had been neglected for 10 years." Paths and retaining walls were crumbling; shrubs and trees were overgrown.

The biggest problem was an enormous lap pool at the bottom of the slope: Installed by the previous owner, the pool occupied the only spot on the property sunny enough for a vegetable garden. "We wanted it out," Terry says.

The first year, Terry and his partner, Todd Brower, hired an arborist to identify the trees on the property. Then they cleared out the ones that were ill or misplaced. They also repaired the retaining walls, paths, and sprinkler systems.

Since the budget to take out the pool and completely revamp the bottom terrace was a mere $5,000—not much considering the amount of work that needed to be done—Terry and Brower decided to do the work themselves, rather than hire landscapers to do it for them. "We wanted to integrate the pool area with the rest of the garden. But we also wanted a seating area where we could relax and look upslope to the rest of the garden, as well as a space for a vegetable garden, a small pond with goldfish, and additional fruit trees."

They asked landscape architect David Mandel to put their ideas on paper; for $800 (part of the $5,000), he measured the space, fine-tuned

TERRY'S ADVICE

Make a plan or hire someone to do it for you. Following a good plan is the best way to get exactly what you want—without making mistakes.

"I attacked the crabgrass, rototilled the soil, added every amendment the garden books recommended, put in a watering system, a pond with a solar-powered waterfall, and a flagstone path. I planted chamomile and thyme ground covers between the pavers, and waited for results while daily plucking tiny crabgrass sprouts with a paring knife."

Now, Olson says: "I have become a gardener. I can't stop. I go out in the morning and find myself still dead-heading at noon. I have even started landscaping around the mailbox."

A 2-foot-deep hole was dug to create a pond. Finished pond (right) is complete with liner, flat edging stones, and water plants. Flagstone pavers are set on a bed of gravel and sand.

the ideas, and provided a blueprint.

Then it was time to dig in. Terry and Brower tore up the pool themselves ("a bear of a job"). After six months of searching, they found aged pavers, similar to ones on the upper terraces, at a CalTrans disposal yard near the freeway.

Then they built raised beds for spring tulips and summer vegetables, edging the beds with recycled broken concrete and installing trellises for peas. They brought in ½ yard of planting mix, hauling it downslope in 5-gallon buckets—backbreaking work, but it paid off.

"We did all the work ourselves. Right on budget," Terry says proudly.

Downslope view from house shows paths and planting terraces. Benches and chairs provide seating on the lowest terrace.

MAKEOVER TIPS

Cost-savers

- Do the work yourself. Divide it up into small jobs spread out over weeks or months.

- Cover an ugly fence with vines rather than replacing it. Olson planted 10 bougainvilleas (*B. brasiliensis* 'Crimson Red') along the 54-foot-long fence. Other good choices are Lady Banks' rose (*Rosa banksiae*) and Japanese honeysuckle.

- Use recycled materials. "We were able to obtain free pavers from the disposal yard and from the neighbors' house," Terry says. "They were dismantling an enormous backyard barbecue. We used about 100 of those weathered concrete blocks."

Best ideas

- Use drought-tolerant plants. Even unthirsty plants can look lush and beautiful, and they're easy to care for.

- Plant tough but attractive ground covers between pavers. Chamomile and creeping thyme don't need mowing, and unlike lawn grass, they bloom in summer.

MARION BRENNER (2) TOP RIGHT: STEVEN GUNTHER

Outdoor room for an active family

TIME: Eight months, plus several months for planning

■ Unless you're a skilled outdoor builder, installing large retaining walls, waterfalls, pools, and gazebos is best left to professionals. That's what Bob and Debi Kahn, of Thousand Oaks, California, decided before tackling their dream garden—a "Victorian country" outdoor living room with a pool, spa, waterfall, gazebo, built-in barbecue, patio, pocket planters, and raised vegetable beds.

"The backyard is only 72 feet wide, and the distance from the back of the house to the base of the hill is only about 38 feet," Bob Kahn says. "But our landscape architect [Marsh Sanders of Design Concepts] drew up a plan that met all of our objectives." Landscape professionals cleared the land, leaving as many mature trees as possible, and Ken Palmer of K.C. Palmer Construction installed all the hardscaping. Then Bob took over, planting colorful flowers in poolside pockets and on the terraced hillside.

Work on the garden began October 2 and was completed May 2 (the photographs here show the garden's progression). Then the Kahns threw a party as a way to say to the neighbors, "Sorry for the inconvenience, trucks, and noise—we're done."

TOP LEFT: Backyard had lots of mature trees and a lawn. BOTTOM LEFT: The backyard is shown cleared of grass and unwanted plants. Some mature trees remain on the slope; others will be added. Stakes outline where the pool, spa, and planting beds will go. RIGHT: Water tumbles through a boulder-lined course into the pool, then recirculates. Timers turn it on and off. In pockets between the retaining walls, flowering plants are changed each season.

STEVEN GUNTHER (2)

Eight steps to a garden makeover

1. TAKE INVENTORY. Notice which plants are thriving, which ones aren't, and which ones have grown too big for the space allotted them. Notice how the sun moves across your property and which areas are mostly in shade or in sun. Check out the soil. Dig some up with a trowel and do the squeeze test: If it's heavy clay or very sandy, you'll need to add organic amendments such as fir bark or compost. Notice which materials, if any, can be reused in some way. A solid concrete path can be broken up into chunks to make a retaining wall, for instance.

2. CLEAN UP AND PRUNE. Identify plants that need pulling out or pruning. Remove or replant those with the wrong exposure (a shade-loving hydrangea growing in full sun with telltale bleached-out leaves, for example). Cut back overgrown, shapeless shrubs. Thin plantings that are crowding one another. If large trees are leaning toward your neighbor's yard or causing fences to buckle, consider cutting them down and replacing them with smaller ones planted farther from the fence. Pull weeds such as spurge from in between pavers, dandelions from lawns. Start a compost pile. Chop up and compost all garden prunings except weeds with seedheads or diseased plants. Use the compost later to enrich soil.

3. MAKE A WISH LIST. Jot down features you'd like your garden to have. A patio for entertaining? A small pond? Raised beds for vegetables? A gazebo? Beds for colorful annuals? A lawn for kids to play on? An English flower border, edged with winding stone paths? As you compile your list, keep in mind the following.

Your climate. Is it arid? Buffeted by afternoon winds? Gray and rainy much of the year? Climate and weather are key factors that determine the best plants to grow.

The land around you. Do you live in the foothills or near the beach? Desert or urban canyon? Is there a view you can borrow as a backdrop to frame with some of the same plants that grow wild beyond your fence? Or a view you'd like to block out (a neighbor's garage, for example) with hedges or trees?

The style of your house. A Spanish-style house lends itself to a Mediterranean garden with lavender, citrus, and a fountain, while a cedar-shingled house in a North-

MAKEOVER TIP

Best idea

- Install pipes to deep-water the trees. "Trees on hills are often unhealthy because they don't get the water they need," Kahn says. In the planting hole around each new tree, workers installed three perforated PVC drainage pipes for easy watering and fertilizing—setting them vertical and parallel to the tree trunks, then filling them with gravel. Each pipe measures 3¼ inches in diameter and 3 to 5 feet long, with ½-inch perforations. The pipes are really paying off, with healthy, robust trees.

KAHN'S ADVICE

Look at what you have, then decide what you can do with it. "We don't have a view; we have a hill. We made that our focal point."

Bob Kahn's finishing touch: A hammock.

west forest might be most at home among rhododendrons, vine maples, and conifers. A Southwest adobe might pair best with desert-adapted Palo Verde trees, cactus, and wildflowers.

4. DEVISE A PLAN OF ACTION. Determine how much work will be involved, from laying paths and patio pavers to installing sprinklers, edging strips, or a new lawn. Ask yourself whether you have the time, desire, and know-how to do the work yourself, or line up help where you need it. You might consider hiring a landscape architect to draw up a plan for you to follow. Ask friends or neighbors for recommendations. Local nurseries sometimes offer limited design services. Measure your garden and be ready to plan.

5. INSTALL HARDSCAPING, IRRIGATION, OUTDOOR LIGHTING. Paths, patios, decks, and gazebos are the bones of a garden, and in the West, irrigation systems are its lifeblood. Some gardeners, after scraping the ground bare, outline structures and plantings in the soil. You can use gypsum for this or lay down small stakes (as shown above, far left).

6. SHOP AT NURSERIES. Keep in mind your favorite colors, whether soft, romantic tones like pink, lavender, and pale apricot, or strong hues like purple and orange, then work your palette around those. As you draw up your shopping list, consider plants for fragrance (roses, jasmine), motion (ornamental grasses), and seasonal interest (spring bloom and fall color).

7. PREPARE THE SOIL, THEN PLANT. For all but native plants, most of which like their soil "lean," work generous amounts of compost or other organic amendment into the soil, about 2 to 3 feet deep. If possible, rent a rotary tiller to make the job easier. Plant most trees, shrubs, ground covers, vines, and perennials in fall. Tender tropicals and citrus should be planted in frost-free months.

8. ADD FINISHING TOUCHES. Containers, a great bench, outdoor sculpture, water features, and birdhouses make a garden look lived in and loved. ◆

A gardener's guide to the onion clan

Grow your own garlic, onions, leeks, and chives

By Jim McCausland • Photographs by Thomas J. Story

■ Capable both of bringing tears to your eyes and making your mouth water, members of the onion clan (the genus *Allium*) are among the most sensuous ingredients in the kitchen. Happily, it's also easy to grow onions, garlic, and their cousins such as chives, leeks, and shallots in home gardens. In most areas, you can plant from now through the end of autumn; they'll yield savory greens next spring and thick stems or mature bulbs next summer.

See the guide starting on page 300 for planting, harvest, and use tips for various allium family members.

The language of alliums

Members of the onion clan have their own vocabulary.

BULBING. The process by which onion bases swell into bulbs. The best bulbing conditions for onions are at temperatures between 60° and 104°.

CLOVE. One of many small bulbs that makes up each of garlic's larger bulbs.

LODGING. This is the process of bending the tops of bulbing onion and garlic plants to the ground after the leaves wither. During lodging the bulbs harden and cure for about three weeks before harvest.

PEARL ONIONS. These bulbing onions have been bred to produce bulbs that are walnut size or smaller.

SCALLIONS. Any bulbing onion harvested at the green stage before the bulbs mature; usually pencil width or slightly thicker.

SETS. Marble-size onion bulbs you plant instead of seeds or transplants. Sets are a dependable way to grow scallions (see above).

SHORT-, INTERMEDIATE-, AND LONG-DAY ONIONS. Most onions form bulbs in response to day length; growers and catalogs classify them accordingly. Choose bulbing onions from classes that correspond as closely as possible with your

'Evergreen Hardy White Bunching' onion

'Catawissa' topset onion

'Silverskin' garlic

White leek

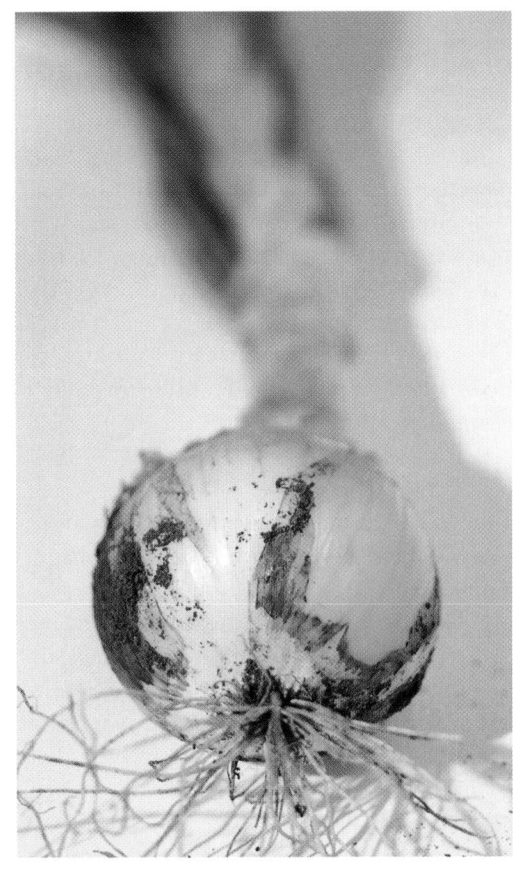

'Walla Walla Sweet' onion

'Dutch' shallots

Red, white, and yellow bulbing onions

'Korean Red' garlic

garden's latitude. For example, *short-day onions* grow in southernmost climes (from Brownsville, TX, north to San Juan Capistrano, CA, and Phoenix). *Long-day onions* do well in northerly climes from Bakersfield, CA, and Albuquerque all the way north to Fairbanks. You'll also find *intermediate-day onions* (they grow from El Paso, TX, north to Red Bluff, CA, Provo, UT, and Boulder, CO) and *day-neutral onions* (like 'Buffalo') that form bulbs anywhere.

SPRING ONIONS. Immature bulbing onions with green tops and slightly swollen bulbs; usually harvested at this stage in spring.

Growing tips

Because most alliums have shallow roots, they need rich, well-drained soil and steady irrigation to keep leaves growing and bulbs forming.

To nurture rapid growth in spring, give all alliums a dose of complete fertilizer and follow-up feedings of liquid fertilizer (fish emulsion is good) at least monthly through the season. Keep beds as weed-free as possible.

When flower buds appear on bulbing onions, pinch or snip them off since blooms divert energy away from bulb formation.

Don't plant different varieties of onions or garlic close together: As harvest approaches, you'll need to stop watering each kind at a different time.

Harvest hints

You can harvest green leaves from all kinds of chives, garlic, and onions at any time. Harvest garlic bulbs, bulbing onions, and shallots after the bulbs have swollen next summer. When onion and garlic leaves start to turn yellow at the tips, stop watering, then bend them to the ground as described previously, under "Lodging." Leave the dried tops on garlic so you can braid groups of the bulbs together. You can store bunching onions, most multipliers, and leeks in the ground, pulling them as needed.

You can grow any onion clan member in a raised bed. Clip bud stalks off onions and garlic to increase bulb size.

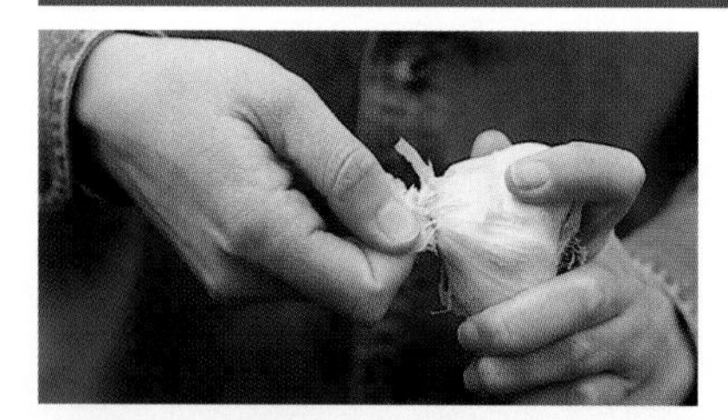

Pop goes the garlic

Before planting, break the "mother" bulb into individual cloves. Plant each clove with pointed end up, about 4 inches apart, and cover with 1 to 2 inches of soil in mild-winter climates. Cover with 3 to 4 inches in areas where the ground freezes.

CHIVES

■ CHOICE KINDS. Common chives (*Allium schoenoprasum*) have onion-flavored leaves and edible purple flowers that make pretty garnishes in salads. Chinese chives (*A. tuberosum*) have mild garlic flavor and edible white flowers.

■ PLANTING TIPS. Sow seeds ¼ inch deep in late summer, fall, or spring, or plant seedlings or divisions in early spring. These perennial plants are evergreen in mild climates but go deciduous where winters are cold.

■ HARVEST AND USE. Snip and chop fresh leaves for garnish (as on baked potatoes) or cooking (as in omelets).

GARLIC

■ CHOICE KINDS. ***Softneck*** (*A. sativum*) varieties include 'California Early' (also called 'Italian Early') and 'California Late' ('Italian Late')—the kinds you buy in the supermarket. They usually store well and grow in almost any climate. However, many are hard to peel and can taste rather sharp and hot when they're raw (cooking tempers their flavor). The silverskins ('Silver Rose' and 'Silverskin') make beautiful garlic braids and are especially well adapted to hot climates.

Hardneck varieties (*A. s. ophioscorodon*) have fewer, larger, easy-to-peel cloves and the most refined flavor of all garlics, with full rather than sharp taste. These garlics grow best where the ground freezes. They include the Asiatics ('Korean Red'), the rocamboles ('German Red' and 'Spanish Roja'), and purple-striped garlic ('Chesnok Red').

Garlic chives

Elephant garlic (*A. ampeloprasum*) is actually a leek that produces extremely large bulbs with mild garlic flavor. Use it as you would true garlic.

■ PLANTING TIPS. Plant cloves of softneck and hardneck kinds 1 to 2 inches deep from October through December (see photos on facing page); in cold-winter climates, wait until early spring to plant softneck or elephant garlic. Plant cloves of elephant garlic about 4 inches deep. True garlics sprout best at soil temperatures under 50°; if you live in a warm-winter climate, refrigerate cloves in a plastic bag full of potting mix until they sprout, then plant them. Keep soil evenly moist during the growing season for best results. If buds appear atop stalks, cut them off to boost bulb size.

■ HARVEST AND USE. You can eat any part of any garlic plant. Chop the fresh, young tops for stir-fry dishes. Harvest just-swelling bulbs in early spring. Wait until bulbs swell to full size and the tops die back, then use bulbs in cooking, or roast and eat them whole. For full-size bulbs of all kinds, withhold water after tops begin to yellow, then harvest and braid for storage in a cool, dry place.

LEEKS

■ CHOICE KINDS. White leeks (*A. porrum*) grow 1-inch-thick stems, used in soups and stews, while 'Varna' leeks grow to scallion size. Varieties with bluish or purplish leaves are hardier than those with greener leaves. Flavor is reminiscent of a very fine, mild onion, though hardy leeks have a stronger flavor than more frost-tender varieties.

■ PLANTING TIPS. Sow seeds ½ inch deep in late summer or early spring. In mild climates, set out transplants in fall and winter. When seedlings are 10 to 12 inches tall, hill up the soil around the plant bases to blanch the stems.

■ HARVEST AND USE. Harvest leeks at any stage after they reach pencil width. It's best to leave leeks in the ground until you're ready to use them, even if that means harvesting them from beneath the snow.

ONIONS

■ CHOICE KINDS. ***Bulbing onions*** (*A. cepa*) come in two classes. For fresh eating (but poor storage), try supersweet varieties like short-day 'California Red', 'Super Sweet', and 'Yellow Granex' (includes 'Maui' and 'Vidalia' onions), or long-day 'Walla Walla Sweet' onions. For longer storage life, try a day-neutral variety like 'Buffalo', an intermediate-day variety like 'Red Torpedo', or long-day onions like 'Early Yellow Globe', 'Ebenezer', 'Ruby', and 'Sweet Spanish'. For pearl onions, try one of the cipollini types, such as 'Gold Coin' or 'Purplette'.

Bunching onions (*A. fistulosum*) grow in clumps; instead of bulbs, they form thick stems. Use them like scallions. They include mild, refined Japanese varieties ('Evergreen Hardy White Bunching', 'Red Beard', and 'Santa Clause') and a more earthy-flavored Welsh variety ('White Welsh').

Multipliers (*A. c. aggregatum*) are quite hardy, perennial onions that grow by dividing into clusters of bulbs. They include shallots, which produce mild, sweet bulbs with a hint of garlic flavor. Shallots come in many varieties, from white-cloved 'Dutch' to purple-tinged 'Holland Red'. Harvest them in the cool months, since hot summers can give them a burning pungency. All multipliers taste best when cooked.

Topset onions (*A. c. viviparum*) form small bulblets aboveground on leafy green stalks; when the stalks hit the ground, the bulblets root in the soil, which explains why they're also called "walking" onions. Use these perennials like scallions. 'Catawissa' onions have robust flavor; 'Egyptian Walking' onions are milder and more tender (bulblets are good for pickling).

■ PLANTING TIPS. For bulbing onions, sow seeds ¼ inch deep or set out transplants in late summer or fall; where winters are consistently cold (below 20°), wait until spring. Plant sets 1 to 2 inches deep all winter long in mild climates north of Bakersfield, CA; most sets are long-day varieties that won't form bulbs south of there. In early spring, plant only small- to medium-size sets, since larger ones tend to bolt.

For bunching, multipliers, and topset types, plant divisions or small bulbs 1 inch deep in fall or spring. For shallots, plant bulbs 1 to 2 inches deep in fall or spring.

■ HARVEST AND USE. Harvest bulbing onions in summer after the tops have died down; store in a cool, dry place. For bunching onions, harvest up to half of each clump starting in spring; they'll quickly grow in again for summer harvest.

Sources

Many nurseries sell garlic cloves and onion seeds, seedlings, and sets. These mail-order companies offer a wide selection of alliums.

For garlic only. Try Filaree Farm (509/422-6940 or www.filareefarm.com) or Garlicsmiths (509/738-4470).

For many kinds of alliums. Try Irish Eyes with a Hint of Garlic (509/964-7000 or www.hintofgarlic.com), Nichols Garden Nursery (541/928-9280 or www.gardennursery.com), Territorial Seed Company (541/942-9547 or www.territorial-seed.com), and West Coast Seeds (604/482-8800 or www.westcoastseeds.com). ◆

Scent-sational sweet peas

Here are 16 of the most fragrant varieties you can grow from seed

By Lauren Bonar Swezey

THOMAS J. STORY (3)

'Cupani' (left), 'Butterfly' (center), and 'Painted Lady' (right) are old-fashioned sweet peas.

Few garden plants stir the senses like sweet peas. Sniff a billowy bunch, and you expect a delightful, spicy-sweet scent to greet you.

Which are the most fragrant sweet peas you can grow? To find out, we grew dozens of varieties in *Sunset*'s test garden in Menlo Park, California, and interviewed growers such as Patricia Sherman, whose Fragrant Garden Nursery in Oregon specializes in old-fashioned and Spencer sweet peas. The best varieties are listed on these pages. Plant one or several in your garden this fall or early next spring, and your nose won't be disappointed.

Sweet pea history

At the end of the 19th century, a Scot named Henry Eckford developed dozens of fragrant varieties with sturdier stems and larger flowers. But out of the approximately 300 varieties available in 1911, only about eight survived into the 1980s. Fortunately, 10 to 15 years ago, several seedsmen from England and New Zealand revived interest in the old varieties and have been reintroducing the aromatic ones. For example, purple-and-blue 'Cupani', the original cultivated sweet pea (discovered by a Sicilian monk in the 17th century) is powerfully fragrant. Rose-and-white 'Painted Lady', first introduced in the 18th century, is just as remarkable.

In England in 1900, the Spencer family's gardener, Silas Cole, discovered a large-flowered sweet pea with wavy petals, which he named 'Countess Spencer'. It caused a sensation and set in motion the hybridizers' quest for more large, wavy-edged flowers (known as Spencer sweet peas). In the process, much of the scent became diluted. Now breeders are getting scent back into Spencer hybrids.

Making sense of scent

Everyone perceives scent differently. What's strongly perfumed to one person might only be mildly so to another. Climate and the age of the flower also affect the pungency of a fragrance. Flower scents are stronger on warm, humid days than on cool, dry days. Older blooms are also subtler in fragrance than young, fresh blooms. Some flowers are inherently less fragrant: Red sweet peas, for instance, tend to have the least fragrance of any color.

PAT SHERMAN (3)

'Nora Holman' (left), 'Jilly' (center), and 'Annabelle' (right) are modern Spencer hybrids.

Old-fashioned favorites

These sweet peas have shorter stems and fewer, smaller flowers (three to four per stem) than Spencer hybrids; most are fragrant. The following varieties are standouts.

'Black Knight'. Hybridized by Eckford, 1898. Large, very dark maroon flowers.

'Butterfly'. Sutton Co., 1878. Mauve and white, tinged with lavender.

'Cupani' (also sold as 'Cupani's Original'). 1696. Purple standard (upper petals) and deep blue wings (lower petals).

'Dorothy Eckford'. Eckford, 1903. Large pure white flowers.

'Lady Grisel Hamilton'. Eckford, 1899. Light mauve standard, lavender wings.

'Painted Lady'. 1737. Rose standard, white wings tinged with pink.

'Perfume Delight'. A mixture of up to 26 old-fashioned varieties.

Spencer hybrids

All these have large wavy flowers on long stems, with four or five flowers per stem.

'Angela Ann'. Rose pink on white. A prizewinner in England.

'Annabelle'. Very frilly lavender flowers.

'Frolic'. Pink edge on cream.

'Jilly'. Large cream blooms.

'King Size Navy'. One of the darkest blue sweet peas available.

'Mollie Rilstone'. Rose pink edge on cream. A prizewinner in shows.

'Nora Holman'. Pink on cream. The most popular show sweet pea in England.

'Percy Thrower'. Pale lavender flush.

'White Supreme'. Large pure white flowers. Considered the best white sweet pea.

How to plant

In mild-winter climates from Arizona to Northern California, sow sweet peas directly in the ground, 1 inch deep and 2 inches apart, between late August and November. In the hottest areas, wait until September to plant; in colder areas of California and the Southwest, finish planting by October. In the Pacific Northwest and mountain areas, plant in February or March in 2-inch plastic pots, then transplant seedlings into the ground in March or April.

To speed germination, soak seeds overnight before planting.

Seed sources

FRAGRANT GARDEN NURSERY. Sells 23 old-fashioned varieties and 57 Spencer varieties. *Box 627, Canby, OR 97013; www.fragrantgarden.com.*

RENEE'S GARDEN. Sells Perfume Delight and 10 other mixes. *(888) 880-7228 or www.reneesgarden.com.*

SELECT SEEDS. Sells 25 old-fashioned varieties. *180 Stickney Hill Rd., Union, CT 06076; (860) 684-9310 or www.selectseeds.com.*

THOMPSON & MORGAN. Sells 'King Size Navy' and 29 other varieties and mixes. *Box 1308, Jackson, NJ 08527; (800) 274-7333 or www.thompson-morgan.com.* ◆

Tune up your turf

Fall is the ideal season for lawn maintenance

By Sharon Cohoon

If you'd like your lawn to look as well groomed as a PGA golf course, fall is the time to take corrective measures. Before you do, though, walk across the street, turn around, and view your lawn from your neighbors' perspective. It probably looks better than you expected. A little distance disguises a lawn's minor flaws, says Oregon State University extension turf specialist Tom Cook. "A good lawn is one that looks good from across the street," he says, "because that's how most of the world sees it." If yours looks healthy, your only chore right now is fertilizing it to keep it strong. On the other hand, if your lawn is the scourge of the neighborhood, get moving.

FERTILIZE ALL LAWNS. Both cool- and warm-season grasses benefit from feeding in early fall. Combination lawn fertilizers are a good choice, since they contain a small amount of fast-release nitrogen, which provides a quick green-up, and a larger portion of slow-release nitrogen, which continues feeding the lawn slowly and gently. Apply fertilizer as recommended on the label.

Another way to fertilize is by leaving your grass clippings on the lawn. As the clippings decompose, they release nitrogen into the turf. Cutting grass with a mulching mower, which chops the blades into finer pieces

If you can't easily push a screwdriver up to its handle into the turf (left), the soil is compacted and needs aeration. A power aerator (below) removes cylindrical plugs of grass and soil, leaving small holes in the lawn, as shown in cross section (bottom). You can leave the plugs on the lawn, where they will decompose rapidly.

ILLUSTRATIONS: LINDA HOLT AYRISS; PHOTO: MARION BRENNER

than a conventional mower, speeds up the process. By doing this regularly, you can eliminate one lawn feeding or more.

PATCH DEAD OR DAMAGED SPOTS. Always patch with the same type of grass as the existing lawn. Remove and discard the old turf, then loosen the top 3 to 6 inches of soil in the bare section, work in compost to improve the soil, and level the surface. Then either seed, plant new plugs, or insert a fresh piece of sod cut to fit the damaged area.

OVERSEED IF DESIRED. In mild areas of Arizona and Southern California, it is common practice in mid-fall to overseed winter-dormant grasses such as Bermuda and St. Augustine with ryegrass. Overseeding should take place when daytime highs range from 78° to 83° and nighttime lows are 55° or colder, typically between mid-October and mid-November.

Before overseeding, mow the grass very short. Mow in stages, taking off ¼ inch or so with each of three or four passes, until you've removed 60 to 70 percent of the blades' original height.

Apply seed generously: 14 to 18 pounds per 1,000 square feet. Top-dress with composted steer manure or other weed-free mulch and keep soil moist until seeds germinate. Don't mow until the ryegrass is 2 inches tall.

AERATE IF NEEDED. When your lawn gets heavy foot traffic, the soil underneath can become compacted, making it difficult for water, fertilizer, and especially oxygen to reach grass roots (to test for compaction, try the screwdriver test shown on the facing page). The remedy is to punch cylindrical holes into the soil so that the grass can breathe again and moisture and nutrients can penetrate more easily. Though manual aerating devices are available, for anything but a very small lawn you'll probably want to rent a power core aerator or hire a professional lawn care firm to do the job. Aeration works best on a moist lawn on a cool day.

CONTROL WEEDS. If you have lots of chickweed, dock, dandelion, plantain, or other broad-leafed perennial weeds in your lawn, apply a post-emergence systemic herbicide to control them (systemic herbicides circulate throughout the plant, killing all parts, including the roots). To identify weeds, take samples of your problem weeds to a nursery, where an experienced staff member can suggest appropriate chemical controls. Read labels carefully and follow directions.

For prevention of winter weeds like annual bluegrass, apply a pre-emergence herbicide to stop their seeds from sprouting.

Nonchemical weed controls are described at right.

WAIT TO DETHATCH. Turf experts no longer recommend dethatching lawns in early fall. Thatch is the tough fibrous layer of dead stems, rhizomes, and debris that builds up between the soil surface and the grass blades above it. When this layer gets thicker than about ½ inch, some of the thatch should be removed, preferably in early spring.

For cool-season grasses, like Kentucky bluegrass, do this in early spring; for warm-season grasses such as Bermuda, wait until summer. Grasses recover from dethatching trauma more quickly in warmer weather.

Nonchemical weed control methods

Chemical herbicides can help you reestablish control over a lawn where weeds have gained the upper hand. But if you prefer not to use these chemicals, here are some alternative measures.

- **Fill bare spots as soon as they appear.** If there's an empty space in your lawn, weeds will find and fill it. Don't give them the opportunity. Keep grass seed on hand and sow as thin spots appear.
- **Mow high and often.** The simple step of mowing high can eliminate a lot of weeds. To begin with, tall lawns are healthier. They have more leaf surface to collect sunlight and promote growth, and their roots tend to be deeper, with more access to water and nutrients. Over time, taller grass will crowd out and shade out many weeds.

Cut tall fescue such as Marathon to 2½ inches tall; annual ryegrass, buffalo grass, fine fescue, and Kentucky bluegrass to 2 inches; St. Augustine 1 to 2 inches; Bermuda and zoysia ½ to 1 inch. In summer, allow even more height. When you mow, never take off more than a third of the grass height at any one time; instead, mow often. Mowing frequently also helps reduce weeds by cutting off flowers before they can spread seeds.

- **Off with their heads.** You can kill many weeds by repeatedly cutting off their stems and leaves as close to the ground as you can. It may take a half-dozen decapitations, but eventually the weed will use up its reserves and die.
- **Hand-weed.** There are many weeding devices on the market, including some designed to pry out the monstrous taproots of dandelions. ◆

JAMIE HADLEY

FILL PUMPKIN “POTS” with flower and foliage to brighten a party table. See page 313 for easy-to-follow directions.

October

CHARLES MANN

A cozy courtyard in Albuquerque

Behind a wall, they created an intimate garden

■ A few years ago, Judy Propper and her husband, Tom Cartledge, bought a home in the Sandia Heights neighborhood of Albuquerque. At that time, Propper recalls, the backyard was a "wasteland" of brush and scraggly fruit trees. Looking for guidance, the couple enrolled in a course offered by the University of New Mexico titled "Master Planning for the Residential Landscape." Coincidentally, they wound up hiring the instructor, landscape architect Alana Markle, now with the Albuquerque BioPark. "We wanted an enclosed garden," Propper says. "We had the concept, and Alana did the design."

First, they removed an old wood fence and built a stucco-on-cinderblock wall around the yard. Inside the wall, which steps up in height from 5 to 6 feet, they planted aspens, desert willows, honey locusts, and piñons, installed tiered flower beds, and created inviting spaces for outdoor living. For example, in the northeast corner of the garden pictured here, they erected an arbor with a swing beneath. To cover the arbor, Propper and Cartledge planted climbing Lady Banks' rose (*Rosa banksiae* 'Alba Plena'). This frost-tender rose doesn't bloom every spring in the high-desert climate, but Propper likes the lush canopy of glossy leaves. "When it does bloom, it's really beautiful," she says.

A path of Colorado Red flagstones laced with woolly thyme leads to the arbor. Yellow-flowered coreopsis and purple Spanish lavender flank the path. Hall's honeysuckle climbs the wall to the left. Hardy perennials such as black-eyed Susan, catmint, delphinium, dianthus, purple coneflower, Russian sage, Shasta daisy, and yarrow provide seasonal color, with red, pink, and purple penstemons stealing the show in May and June. A drip-irrigation system waters the perennials and trees. *—Jeanne Hayden*

Sidewalk tapestry in Seattle

■ In this Seattle garden, ground covers, shrubs, and perennial flowers and grasses compose an elaborate living tapestry in a parking strip and along a stairway leading up a slope to the front entry.

Designed by Glenn Withey and Charles Price, the landscape combines plants with contrasting foliage forms, colors, and textures, as well as plants that add seasonal flowers. In this view from the curb along the parking strip, the left foreground is dominated by a clump of eulalia grass (*Miscanthus sinensis*), with its weeping leaves and feathery clusters of tan flowers. At lower right, Japanese barberry (*Berberis thunbergii* 'Crimson Pygmy') flaunts bronzy blood-red leaves on arching stems. Across the way, splashes of color come from the rosy flower spikes of an evergreen ground cover—*Polygonum affine* 'Darjeeling Red'—and the coral-pink blossoms of cape fuchsia (*Phygelius capensis*), a perennial.

The beds are groomed regularly to remove faded foliage and spent flowers. The owners do a major cleanup in fall and again in early spring, after which they apply a generous layer of compost to all beds. — *Steven R. Lorton*

JAMES FREDERICK HOUSEL

SHOPPING TIPS

Bulb buying

Nurseries and garden centers around the West carry spring-flowering bulbs for fall planting. You can increase your chances for success by being a smart bulb shopper. Follow these tips.

• Shop early for best selection. As more and more shoppers pick through bins, they inevitably mix unlike bulbs together—your bed of solid red tulips could wind up polka-dotted with other colors.

• Buy the largest bulbs you can find. Larger hyacinth and tulip bulbs give you larger flowers; top-size daffodils and ranunculus produce more flowers.

• Squeeze each bulb gently as you make your selections. Reject any soft or decayed bulbs and ones that have broken buds. Bulbs should not be shriveled, except anemones and ranunculus, which look that way naturally.

• Plant as soon as you can. Bulbs spend the first couple of months in the ground sending out roots to support the tops that emerge after the first of the year. If late planting curtails rooting, the tops won't be as vigorous. — *J.M.*

BEN WOOLSEY

JIM McCAUSLAND

A bountiful spring flowerpot

■ Designer Tina Dixon, owner of Plants à la Cart in Bothell, Washington, really likes to crowd her pots. The one shown here in April offers proof that her method works beautifully. Dixon planted the combination last October for Howard and Lynn Behar's garden on Mercer Island.

The 23-inch-diameter container holds 10 tulips (*Tulipa kaufmanniana* 'Stresa'), 10 daffodils (almost out of bloom in this photo), 7 pansies, a pair of sedges, 2 *Euphorbia purpurea*, and gallon-size plants of *Hypericum* 'Albury Purple' and *Leucothoe fontanesiana* 'Rainbow'. Dixon sets in the largest plants first, buries daffodil and tulip bulbs 6 inches deep, then overplants them with pansies.

—Jim McCausland

Pest tree alert

■ Until recently, Chinese tallow tree (*Sapium sebiferum*), an attractive small tree with outstanding fall color, was considered suitable for all residential landscapes. Recently, the California Exotic Pest Plant Council (www.caleppc.org) placed it on their "Red Alert" list of species with potential to spread explosively. Chinese tallow, already on the Nature Conservancy's "Dirty Dozen" list due to infestations in Southeastern states, is now naturalized along the American River near Sacramento and in Yolo County. Since a mature tree can produce 100,000 seeds annually, it can quickly crowd out native plants. If you garden near wetlands, rivers, or native plant habitats, it's best not to plant Chinese tallow tree. *— Lauren Bonar Swezey*

A larkspur meadow

■ You don't need wildflowers to create a backyard meadow—just flowers with an old-fashioned, country garden look, like larkspurs. In the planting bed pictured here, these candles of bloom in shades of pink and blue combine with linaria, tall-stemmed snapdragons, and sweet Williams. Pansies fringe the bed.

DEIDRA WALPOLE

Plant larkspur in fall for bloom in cool spring months. You can buy it in cell-packs at nurseries. For a mass planting, grow plants from seed—it's much less expensive. Sow seed in a sunny location in soil well amended with organic matter like compost. Heavy, slow-draining soils are not good for larkspurs. Cover seed with ⅛ inch of soil. For the biggest flowers, thin seedlings to avoid crowding.

— S.C.

Mock orange bears fragrant flowers.

CHARLES MANN

Preview select plants for the Rockies

New perennials and shrubs will debut in nurseries next spring

■ Since 1997, the Plant Select program has spotlighted some of the best plant introductions for gardens in the Rocky Mountains and the High Plains. Administered by Colorado State University and Denver Botanic Gardens, the program has designated seven selections for release in 2001. As you plan next year's garden, consider adding these plants. For more information, visit the Plant Select website, www.colostate.edu/Depts/CoopExt/PSEL.

'Cheyenne' mock orange (*Philadelphus lewisii*) is cloaked with sweetly fragrant 2-inch white blossoms in June. This plant's beauty belies its toughness: Its parent has thrived for decades at the U.S. Department of Agriculture field station in Cheyenne, surviving drought, hail, and howling winds. A deciduous shrub, it reaches 7 feet tall and 6 feet wide.

'Comanche' gooseberry (*Ribes uva-crispa*) bears sweet, $\frac{1}{2}$- to 1-inch oval red berries in midsummer. A very hardy deciduous shrub with bright green leaves and long thorns, it makes a good low hedge to $2\frac{1}{2}$ feet tall.

'Coronado' hyssop (*Agastache aurantiaca*), a Southwest native perennial wildflower, bears spikes of tubular orange-yellow flowers on 15-inch-tall plants from midsummer to frost. It takes drought in stride and can survive to -25°.

'Denver Gold' columbine is a 30-inch-tall plant that bears golden yellow flowers 3 inches wide with longer spurs. This perennial flowers in late spring and then reblooms later.

'First Love' dianthus blooms all summer long, bearing fragrant flowers that open white then age to deep rose. A clump-forming perennial, it grows about 18 inches tall.

'Orange Carpet' California fuchsia (*Zauschneria garrettii*), a perennial ground cover with a spreading habit, grows just 4 inches tall. Tubular orange-scarlet flowers appear in summer and fall.

'Remembrance' columbine bears dainty flowers with violet-blue petals and spurs, and white rosettes in late spring or early summer. Plants reach 14 to 24 inches tall.

—J.M.

ROBIN CUSHMAN (2)

Brick paths lead through lush plantings under tall evergreens.

Woodland paradise

Weaving a dreamy shade garden in Eugene

■ Shaded by mature Douglas fir and Oregon myrtle trees, the lawn fronting Sarah and Lance Robertson's home in Eugene, Oregon, grew so sparsely that it seemed to be "crying to be put out of its misery," Sarah recalls. So in the fall of 1996, with planting suggestions from landscape architect Brad Stangeland, they began a major renovation. They replaced the lawn with lush shade plantings and constructed a series of cobbled paths, transforming their front yard into an inviting woodland retreat.

In raised beds between the curving paths, rhododendrons provide structure and seasonal color. In contrast to the rhodies' darker evergreen foliage, plants with creamy white-edged leaves stand out like bright threads, knitting the composition together. Among the variegated plants are *Hebe elliptica* 'Variegata' with mauve flowers, hostas, and Solomon's seal (*Polygonatum odoratum* 'Variegatum'). The chartreuse flowers of lady's-mantle (*Alchemilla mollis*) and soft blue tufts of 'Elijah Blue' fescue contribute their color and texture.

At the base of the Douglas fir, the couple installed a teak bench. Sitting there in the midst of a tranquil shade garden sure beats mowing the grass, Sarah says. Maintenance is minimal. The plants are fed with organic fertilizer in March and June, and a thick layer of mulch keeps weeds at bay.

— Mary-Kate Mackey

Pumpkin pots

A medium-size pumpkin contains pansies and variegated ivy from sixpacks; a ghost white pumpkin holds a small ornamental pepper. Largest pumpkin shows off dusty miller and croton.

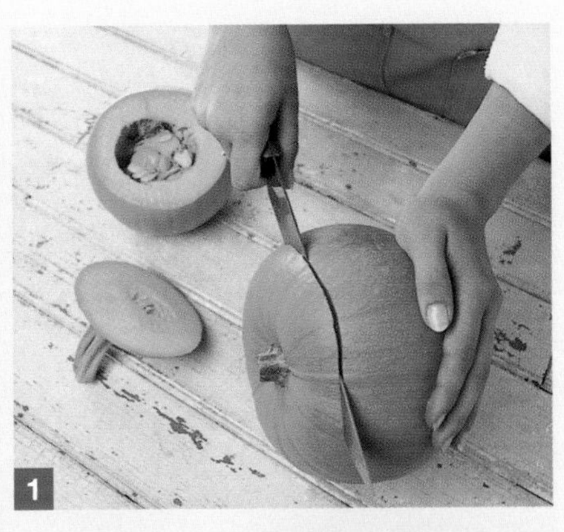

JAMIE HADLEY (4)

■ In "Theme in Yellow," Carl Sandburg wrote of "orange and tawny gold clusters" that "light the prairie cornfields." This month, orange globes carved with spooky faces will light up front porches. For a striking centerpiece to accompany the decor, fill a large pumpkin with flowers and foliage to brighten a party table. Since you start with moistened potting soil, you may not need to add water. If the top of the soil begins to dry out, moisten it gently—don't drench it.

Pumpkin vases will last 10 to 14 days in a cool area before they begin to soften and need to be discarded. Move the plants into the garden or a permanent container. For small and medium pumpkins, use sixpacks or 2-inch pots. For bigger pumpkins, use 4-inch or larger pots.

— S.C.

DIRECTIONS

1. Slice off the top third of the pumpkin.
2. Scoop out the pulp and seeds.
3. Fill the pumpkin cavity about two-thirds full with moistened potting soil. Give nursery seedlings a thorough soak, then pop them out of their containers and arrange them in a pleasing composition in the pumpkin. Fill empty spaces between plants with more moistened potting soil, tamping the rootballs firmly to stabilize the plantings.

TERRENCE MOORE

Desert spoon adds a native accent

■ Landscape architect Stephen Grede chose a native plant with powerful symmetrical shape—desert spoon, or sotol (*Dasylirion wheeleri*)—to accentuate the gently curving path in Carol Gordon's Tucson garden. This evergreen shrub reaches 3 feet tall with an equal spread, forming clumps of spiky blue-green foliage with tiny curved teeth along the margins of the leaves and spoon-shaped bases where they meet the trunk.

Native to southern Arizona and New Mexico, desert spoon grows best in *Sunset* climate zones 10–13. The plant demands excellent drainage, displaying its best form in full sun or light shade. Fall is a good time to set out nursery plants from 1- or 5-gallon containers.

In Gordon's garden, Grede used decomposed granite for the path and edged it with Salt River rock. The stones also serve as a mulch around the plants, holding moisture in the ground and preventing soil erosion in windy weather. The plantings and path were installed by Oasis Gardens Landscape, of Tucson. — *Mary Irish*

BACK TO BASICS

LINDA HOLT AYRISS

Whip weeds, not trees

Nothing knocks down weeds around saplings as well as a string trimmer, but nothing is more likely to girdle the tree and eventually kill it. Young, thin-barked trees just can't take such abuse.

To protect the trunk of a young tree, cut a short length of flexible black plastic pipe (it should be wide enough in diameter to fit around the tree), and split one side. Open up the pipe, then slip it around the trunk. As the trunk expands with age, so will the sleeve. With time, the tree will fill out and start casting enough shade to reduce the weeds around it. Then you can remove the sleeve.

— *Jim McCausland*

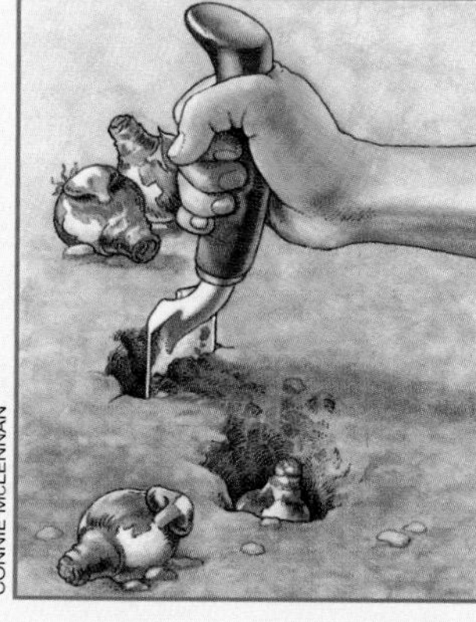
CONNIE McLENNAN

To plant bulbs quickly

in an established flower bed, plunge a stainless-steel trowel into the soil to a depth 4 times the height of the bulbs. (For large bulbs, use a 4-inch-wide tool, and for smaller ones, a 2-inch tool.) While the trowel is in the soil, pull it toward you to open a small hole. Remove the tool, then drop a bulb in the hole.

Plunge the tool into the soil directly behind the first hole, and again, pull it toward you (you're closing the first hole while creating another one). Repeat until all bulbs are planted. — *S.C.*

Great for shade

Fall is the time to plant this pretty perennial

Plectranthus ciliatus, a low-growing evergreen perennial, bears flower stems 8 inches long.

CLAIRE CURRAN (2)

■ Garden-worthy plants show up at public gardens long before they reach the nurseries. *Plectranthus ciliatus,* shown above, the star of the shade border at the University of California at Irvine Arboretum for the last several years, is a prime example. Its most obvious asset is its flowers—in a gorgeous goes-with-everything shade—which appear over an 8- to 10-week period in fall.

But *P. ciliatus* has many other virtues, says the arboretum's nursery manager, Laura Lyons. It tolerates most soils, has no disease or pest problems, and has no requirements other than regular watering and light feeding. Its foliage, with "lots of substance and attractive purple undersides," is exceptional, she says. Staffers at the arboretum prune the plant annually to keep it at about 3½ feet wide and 18 inches high.

If you want it, though, you'll have to come to the Arboretum's Fall Perennial Sale to get it. Despite its sterling character, *P. ciliatus* is still rare in the nursery trade. The Huntington Botanical Gardens will also sell the plant at its big four-day fall plant sale, October 12 to 15; see page 74 for details. *10–3, October 21–22; $2. UC Irvine Arboretum (on Campus St., south of Jamboree Rd.), Irvine; (949) 824-5833.*

— Sharon Cohoon

NORM PLATE (2)

Bulbs and friends

Brilliant beds call for great bulb-annual pairings

ABOVE: 'Queen of Sheba' tulips nod above nemesias. LEFT: 'Big Smile' tulips with purple pansies.

■ Tulips are beautiful enough when massed in beds and borders. But give them a support cast of annuals and perennials in complementary flower colors, and they're positively dazzling. In the Lafayette, California. garden pictured here, lily-flowered 'Queen of Sheba' tulips poke through a border of lush orange nemesias. The nemesias' deep green foliage provides a handsome contrast to the mix of orange flowers and the playful orange-checked sculpture in the background.

"Everyone hates orange," says Bob Clark, the garden's designer. "But here it's used in the best way." 'Queen of Sheba' is in the right company. In another part of the same garden, Clark planted drifts of yellow 'Big Smile' tulips under white birches; purple pansies, white Iceland poppies, and white ranunculus accent the sunny tulips. Clark also mixed in plenty of foliage, such as black mondo grass, feverfew, and Scotch moss to tone down the overall brightness.

Plant bulbs in fall in rich soil with lots of compost; water regularly between rains. After the blooms fade in spring, the annuals carry on the show. — *L.B.S.*

WHAT TO DO IN YOUR GARDEN IN OCTOBER

PLANTING

☐ BULBS. Nurseries and garden shops are awash with bulbs this month. See the buying tips for bulbs on page 309.

☐ COVER CROPS. Zones 4–7: As late as the first week of October, you can still sow cover crops such as Austrian field peas, crimson clover, hairy vetch, and tyfon greens. They'll grow slowly through winter and will add organic matter to the earth when you plow them under in spring.

☐ GROUND COVERS. If you want them to cover ground fast in spring, you should plant now. They'll become established over winter and will put on a strong burst of new growth when the weather warms up.

☐ LAWNS. Zones 4–7: There's still time to start a new lawn if you act early in the month. The easiest and best way to do it is to install sod, but you can also start from seed. Just prepare the soil by tilling a 2-inch layer of compost into the seedbed and leveling the site. Then put down sod or rake in seed; keep the site evenly moist until rains take over.

☐ PERENNIALS. Planted now, perennials will have the entire winter to put out roots in order to grow and flower next spring.

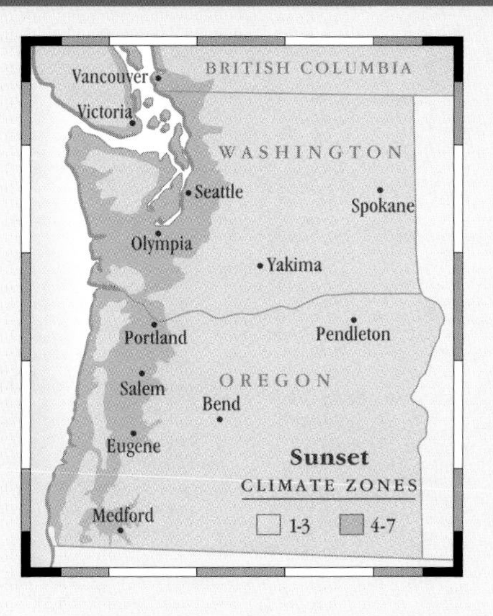

☐ TREES, SHRUBS. This is the best month for planting shrubs and trees—especially those that have great fall color. Shop now and you'll see just what you're getting.

MAINTENANCE

☐ ANNUALS. Zones 1–3: When frost hits, pull plants, shake soil off the roots, and toss them onto the compost pile. Zones 4–7: Continue to deadhead, and fertilize one last time early in the month.

☐ CARE FOR ROSES. Continue to remove faded blooms. As you cut flowers to take indoors, shape plants. Allow a few hips to form, since that process completes the flowering cycle and ushers plants into dormancy.

☐ MAKE COMPOST. As you clean out the summer garden, pile everything but diseased or thorny material onto the compost pile. Turn the pile and keep it moist. By next spring, compost should be ready to use.

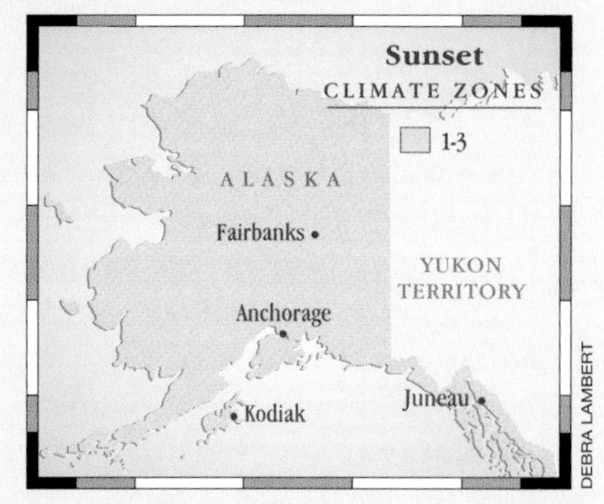

☐ MANAGE FUCHSIAS. Zones 1–3: Bring fuchsias into a protected, dark place for the winter (a cool basement or frost-free garage is fine). Zones 4–7: Give plants their last feeding on the first of October. Then let them wind down until just before frost, when you bring them inside or mulch them for the winter.

☐ WATER. Until rains begin, water established plants deeply. Drought-stressed plants are far more likely to be damaged in hard winters than healthy ones. ◆

WHAT TO DO IN YOUR GARDEN IN OCTOBER

PLANTING

☐ BERRIES FOR BIRDS. Zones 1–2, 7–9, 14–17: Set out plants that produce berries in winter, and invite birds to your garden. Many birds love berries of barberry, beautyberry, cotoneaster, currant, elderberry, gooseberry, holly, mahonia, mountain ash, nandina, pyracantha, and strawberry tree (not all plants grow in every zone).

☐ BULBS IN POTS. Zones 7–9, 14–17: For a big show in spring, plant bulbs of a single variety in big (16-inch diameter) flared pots. Follow this recipe from *Sunset* gardener Rick La Frentz: Fill pots with potting soil so the tops of bulbs will sit about 4 to 5 inches below the pot rim. Firm the soil, then set the bulbs (such as tulip or daffodil) close together. Cover with soil, leaving about 2 inches at the top for watering space. Set the pots in a cool, shady area, wet the soil, and cover with wood shavings or other mulch; water to make damp. Make sure the soil never dries out. Move pots into full sun when leaves develop. Flowers appear about four months after planting. A 16-inch pot will hold 40 to 50 tulips, daffodils, or hyacinths.

☐ COOL-SEASON FLOWERS. In zones 7–9, 14–17, plant forget-me-nots, pansies, primroses, and violas for a colorful show during winter. All are available at nurseries this month in sixpacks and in 4-inch containers.

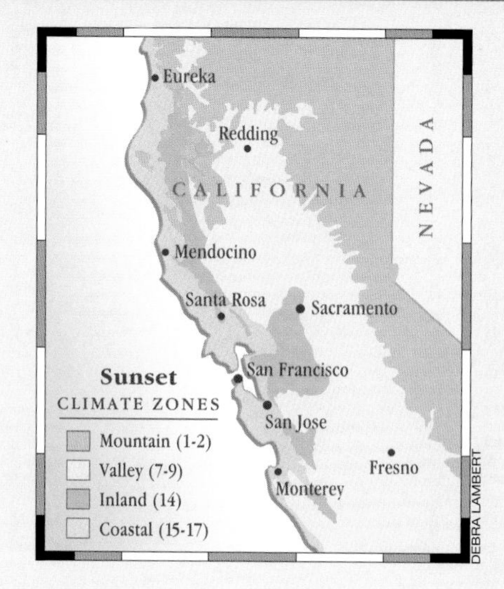

☐ GRAPES, FRUIT TREES, AND BERRIES. If you plan to purchase special fruit varieties by mail, get your orders in soon so that you get the types you want in time for dormant-season planting. For a taste treat, try 'Arctic Supreme' white-fleshed peach, 'Dapple Dandy' pluot (both from Bay Laurel Nursery; 805/466-3406), or 'Spitzenberg' apple (from Sonoma Antique Apple Nursery; 707/433-6420). Some nurseries will take a onetime special order this month; try Yamagami's Nursery in Cupertino (408/252-3347) and Orchard Nursery & Florist in Lafayette (925/284-4474).

☐ WINTER CROPS. Gardeners in frost-free areas can continue to sow beets, cabbage, carrots, lettuce, peas, radishes, and Swiss chard. Set out transplants of broccoli and brussels sprouts.

MAINTENANCE

☐ CLEAN UP DEBRIS. To reduce the number of sites that harbor insects and diseases over winter, pull weeds, spent annuals, and vegetables. Clean up all fruit and fallen leaves. Compost only pest-free plant debris. Add tainted material to your city's compost collection; commercially made compost normally gets hot enough to kill pests.

PEST CONTROL

☐ BAIT FOR SNAILS. Cool, damp fall weather brings out snails. To control them without risking the health of children and pets, use a bait containing iron phosphate, such as Sluggo (available at many nurseries or from Peaceful Valley Farm Supply; 888/784-1722 or www.groworganic.com). It's safe to use on all edible crops.

☐ CHECK COLE CROPS FOR CATERPILLARS. Zones 7–9, 14–17: If you see small holes in leaves or the new growth chewed on cabbage, cauliflower or other cole crops, the plants are probably being attacked by caterpillars. Search leaves for insects, pick off, and destroy, or spray with *Bacillus thuringiensis*. ◆

WHAT TO DO IN YOUR GARDEN IN OCTOBER

PLANTING

☐ BULBS. Continue to plant anemones, babiana, daffodils, Dutch irises, freesia, homeria, ixia, sparaxis, and watsonia. For a longer bloom period, plant groups of bulbs at two-week intervals. Give hyacinth and tulip bulbs a four- to six-week chill in the refrigerator before planting.

☐ COOL-SEASON ANNUALS. Low-desert, inland, and coastal gardeners (zones 13, 18–21, and 22–24, respectively) can set out transplants of African daisy, calendula, dianthus, English daisy, Iceland poppy, lobelia, nemesia, ornamental kale, pansy, phlox, schizanthus, stock, and viola. For even more variety—plus some longer stems for cut flowers—sow seeds (in raked, weed-free soil) of agrostemma, baby blue eyes, clarkia, flax, forget-me-not, larkspur, linaria, Shirley poppy, and sweet peas directly into the garden.

☐ MEDITERRANEAN AND NATIVE PLANTS. Mediterranean plants, such as rosemary and santolina, and California natives like toyon and ceanothus are accustomed to wet winter–dry summer climates. Fall is the easiest time to get them established in the garden—they'll take advantage of winter rains and develop deep roots before summer.

☐ RANUNCULUS. Ranunculus have a longer bloom period than most spring bulbs, and they're also great cut flowers. But because they're prone to rot, they can be tricky to grow. The most failproof method is to plant and thoroughly water them, then restrain from watering again until you see sprouts poking through the ground. Plant tubers

DEBRA LAMBERT

prong-side down about 6 inches apart. Plant 2 inches deep in sandy soil, 1½ inches deep in clay.

☐ WINTER CROPS. Gardeners in frost-free areas can continue to sow beets, carrots, fava beans, onions, peas, radishes, Swiss chard, and turnips, and set out transplants of broccoli, cabbage, and other cole crops. Those in coastal areas can start lettuces as well. This is also the month to start perennial crops such as artichokes, asparagus, horseradish, rhubarb, and sorrel.

MAINTENANCE

☐ FEED ROSES. If you deadhead and fertilize roses after their fall bloom, you can enjoy a final flush of blossoms around the winter holidays. On the other hand, you can give these hardworking shrubs a little extra rest this year by letting them form hips, which also happen to look wonderful in bouquets.

☐ PREPARE FOR SANTA ANA WINDS. Prevent branch breakage by thinning top-heavy trees like jacarandas. Check stakes supporting young trees to be sure they're strong enough. Also check to see that ties are strong but not cutting into bark. When winds are predicted, give trees, shrubs, and ground covers a deep soaking beforehand. Mist vulnerable container plants and hanging baskets frequently during the winds.

PEST CONTROL

☐ MANAGE INSECT PESTS. When the temperatures drop, aphids and whiteflies seem to multiply. Dislodge them from plants with blasts of water from a hose or use insecticidal soap. Repeat every three or four days. ◆

WHAT TO DO IN YOUR GARDEN IN OCTOBER

PLANTING

☐ **AMARYLLIS INDOORS.** Plant amaryllis bulbs in containers early this month for Thanksgiving bloom. For Christmas bloom, plant in late October.

☐ **GARLIC.** Choose hardneck types like 'Chesnok Red' or 'Korean Red'. Break bulbs into cloves and plant each clove 3 to 4 inches deep.

☐ **LANDSCAPE PLANTS.** Set out hardy ground covers and container-grown trees, shrubs, and perennials no later than six weeks before the ground generally freezes in your area. From fall through winter, water the transplants often enough to keep their rootballs from drying out.

☐ **SPRING BULBS.** Before the ground freezes, set out bulbs of crocus, daffodil, hyacinth, *Iris reticulata,* scilla, and tulip. Plant daffodils and tulips 6 to 8 inches deep, small bulbs 3 to 4 inches deep. Water the soil deeply and mulch the bed after planting.

☐ **WILDFLOWERS.** Sow seeds of bachelor's buttons, calendula, California poppy, desert bluebells (*Phacelia campanularia*), larkspur, love-in-a-mist, rose campion, Shirley poppy, skyrocket (*Ipomopsis aggregata*), sweet alyssum, and sweet William catchfly (*Silene armeria*). Broadcast seeds over soil, lightly rake them in, and cover with a thin layer of compost or soil. Fall rains and winter snows will provide moisture to germinate the seeds.

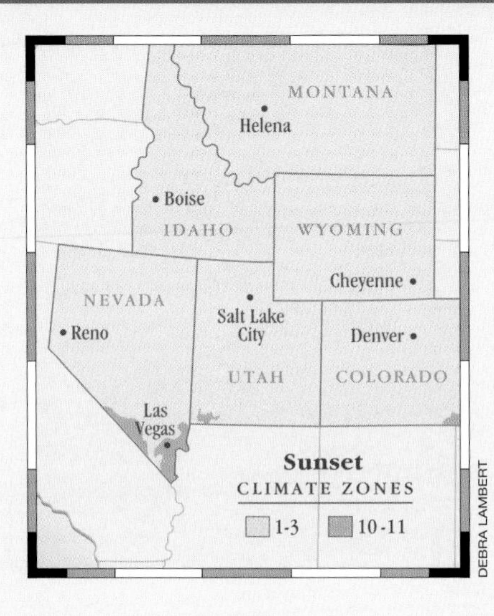

MAINTENANCE

☐ **CARE FOR LAWNS.** Give lawns their last feeding of the season. Use a power lawn mower to remove leaves from lawns. Add the ground-up leaves to the compost bin or spread them over perennial or bulb beds as mulch.

☐ **CUT BACK PERENNIALS.** After the first hard freeze, cut back perennials such as aster, campanula, daylily, phlox, and veronica, leaving 6-inch stubs above the ground. Leave those with attractive seedheads for winter interest.

☐ **DIVIDE RHUBARB.** For improved production next season, divide and transplant overcrowded roots after the first killing frost.

☐ **DRAIN DRIP SYSTEMS.** To prevent cracked tubing, drain drip-irrigation systems before the soil freezes. Remove end caps from the main lines, turn the water on for a few minutes to flush the lines, then shut it off. Drain all the water, then replace the end caps.

☐ **HARVEST, STORE CROPS.** Pick broccoli and brussels sprouts before a killing frost hits. Cut pumpkins and winter squash with 2-inch stems; store at 50° to 60°. Beets, carrots, potatoes, and turnips keep best at 35° to 45° in barely damp sand. Onions and shallots need cool, dry storage in mesh bags or slotted crates. Store apples and pears indoors in separate containers at 33° to 40°.

☐ **MULCH FOR WINTER.** After a hard freeze, spread 2 to 3 inches of compost, weed-free straw, or other organic mulch to protect bulbs, perennial flowers, vegetables, and strawberry beds. Mulch conserves soil moisture and helps minimize freezing and thawing of soil, which can heave plants out of the ground.

— *Marcia Tatroe* ◆

WHAT TO DO IN YOUR GARDEN IN OCTOBER

PLANTING

☐ COOL-SEASON FLOWERS. Zones 1–2 (Flagstaff, Santa Fe) and 10 (Albuquerque): Sow seeds of larkspur, snapdragon, and sweet alyssum for early spring bloom. Zones 11–13 (Las Vegas, Tucson, Phoenix): Set out calendula, dianthus, Iceland poppy, lobelia, ornamental cabbage and kale, pansy, snapdragon, and stock.

☐ COOL-SEASON VEGETABLES. Zones 12–13: Sow seeds of beets, carrots, kohlrabi, lettuce, peas, radishes, Swiss chard, and turnips. Fast-growing crops such as lettuce and radishes can be sown every two weeks to extend harvest. Set out transplants of broccoli, cabbage, and cauliflower. Plant garlic cloves and onion sets.

☐ GROUND COVERS. Zone 10: Plant low-growing cotoneaster, juniper, and trailing indigo bush (*Dalea greggii*). Zones 12–13: For fast cover try Baja and Mexican evening primroses, but beware of their tendency to spread quickly. Less-aggressive choices include ice plant, low-growing rosemary, and Goodding's and moss verbena.

☐ HERBS. Zones 10–13: Most herbs do best with fall planting. Set out transplants of chamomile, chives, lavender, Mexican tarragon, oregano, rosemary, salad burnet, thyme, and winter savory. Sow seeds of cilantro, dill, and parsley every two weeks for continuous harvest.

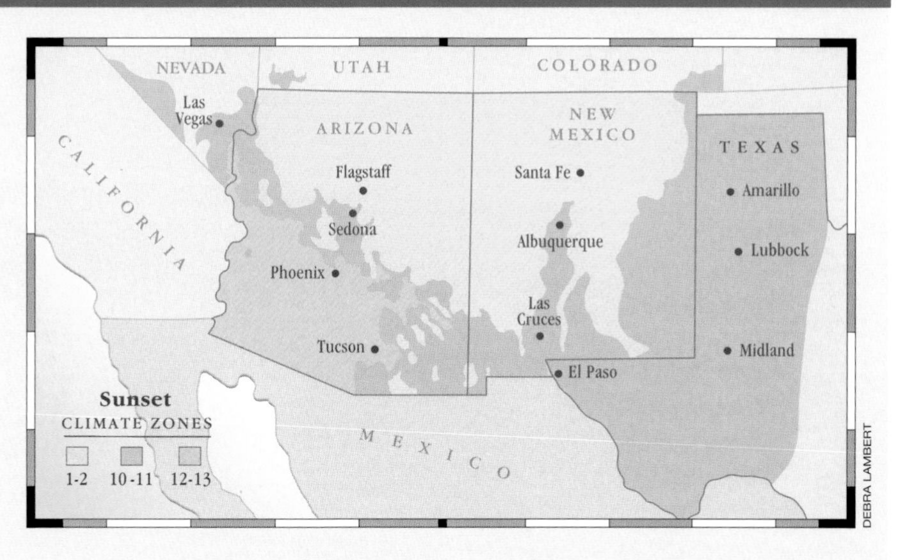

☐ SPRING-BLOOMING PERENNIALS. Zones 11–13: It's prime time to plant perennials, particularly natives, for spring bloom. Try blackfoot daisy (*Melampodium leucanthum*), chuparosa (*Justicia californica*), desert marigold, gaura, Parry's penstemon, and salvias.

☐ SPRING-FLOWERING ANNUALS. Zones 11–13: Sow seeds of African daisy, scarlet flax (*Linum grandiflorum* 'Rubrum'), Shirley poppy, and toadflax, plus wildflowers such as California poppy, desert bluebells, farewell-to-spring, Mexican tulip poppy, owl-clover, and tidytips. Prepare soil by running a rake over the surface, spread a 1- to 2-inch layer of organic mulch, broadcast seed over the mulch, then rake it in. Water daily until the seeds germinate.

☐ SPRING BULBS. Zones 1–2: Plant crocus, daffodil, hyacinth, and tulip. Zones 10–11: Plant all of these plus anemone, freesia, iris, and ranunculus. Zones 12–13: Plant these plus amaryllis, calla, homeria, oxalis, sparaxis, and watsonia. Bulbs of crocus, hyacinth, and tulip must chill in the refrigerator for at least six weeks before planting.

MAINTENANCE

☐ DIVIDE PERENNIALS. Zones 10–13: Dig and divide crowded clumps of bee balm, catmint, daylily, and Shasta daisy to reinvigorate plants and increase blooms next season. — *M.I.* ◆

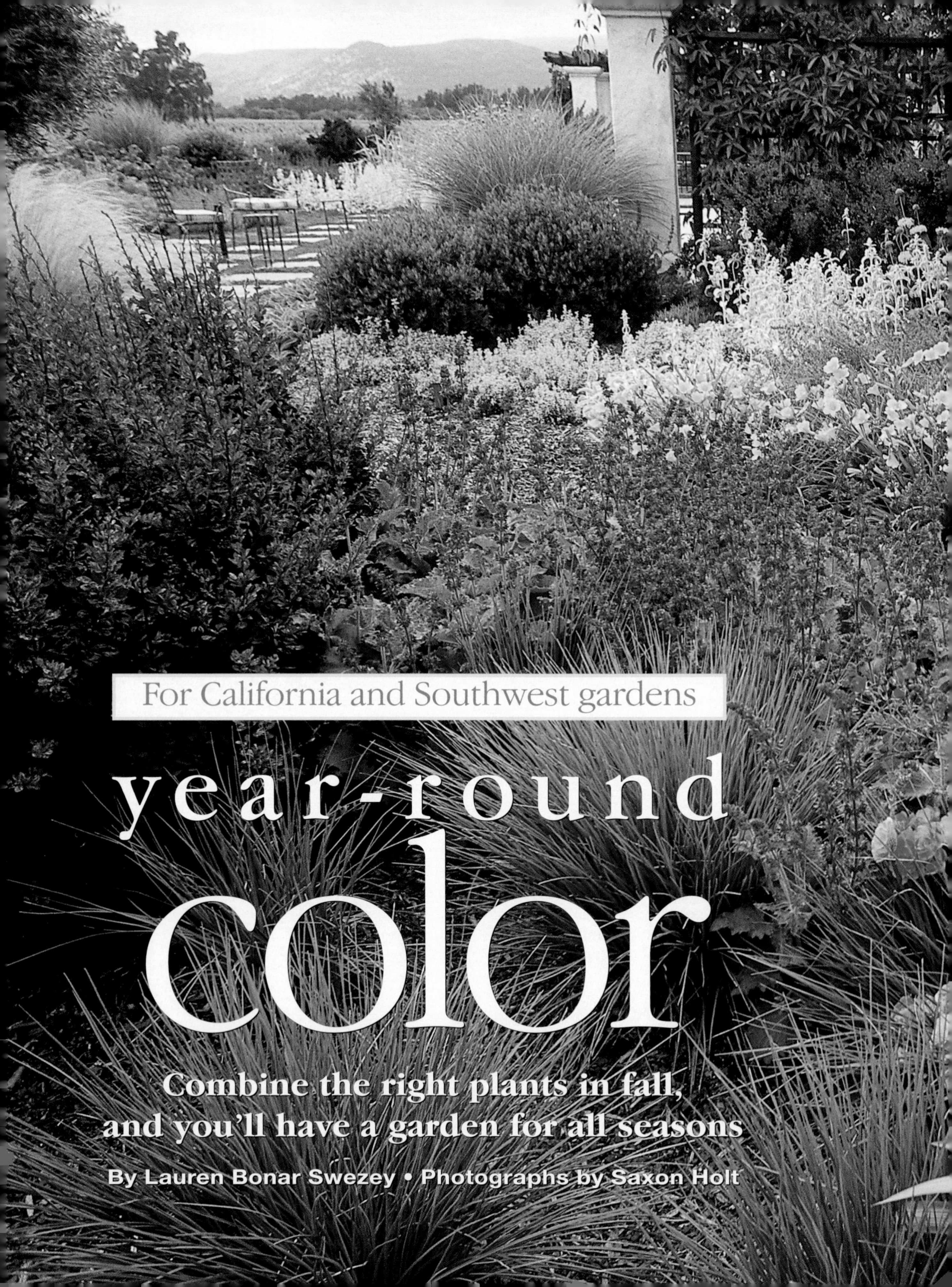
For California and Southwest gardens
year-round
color
Combine the right plants in fall, and you'll have a garden for all seasons
By Lauren Bonar Swezey • Photographs by Saxon Holt

Like a mysterious beauty, a great garden never reveals its charms all at once. Instead, it shows its different sides a little at a time, season by season. An ever-changing color palette—perhaps soft pastels in spring, followed by a cheerful summer mix of yellows and whites, then fiery foliage in fall—heightens its allure.

A garden of such enduring beauty takes careful planning. Freeland Tanner of Napa, California, who designed the St. Helena, California, garden pictured on these pages, compares its creation to staging a play. "Certain actors are always onstage as the drama unfolds, but the bit players shine as they come and go."

Tanner began this all-seasons garden by building good "bones"—arbors and patios define the spaces, and an undulating stone wall provides a handsome backdrop. Beds and borders are precisely orchestrated to shine in all seasons. Each is composed of a series of vignettes—groups of plants with compatible textures, shapes, and colors. To link these vignettes, Tanner used "blending plants" in neutral colors such as silver and gray.

Foliage is as important as flowers in this garden. "Flowers play their part, but they don't last," Tanner explains. "Colored foliage can be just as eye-catching, and it usually spans the seasons. I use it to stimulate and create color combinations. The flowers are icing on the cake." By producing waves of color that require no deadheading, foliage also makes a garden easier to maintain. These plants are particularly important for autumn color. When plants such as barberry, grapevine, ornamental grasses, and smoke bush are in their full glory, they create a garden's final drama of the year.

Fall is the best time to plan and plant a garden for all-season interest—it's the best time to choose trees and shrubs for fall color as well as to plant hardy trees, shrubs, and perennials. Use the design tips and plant selections here to stage your own year-round play.

fall and winter

Left: At the height of fall color, the garden glows with fiery red 'Rose Glow' Japanese barberry (*Berberis thunbergii*), deep purple grape (*Vitis vinifera* 'Purpurea'), and yellow and orange crape myrtle. **Above:** 'Yellow Wave' New Zealand flax mingles with 'Rose Glow' Japanese barberry. **Below left:** The tawny foliage and seed heads of *Miscanthus sinensis* 'Adagio' create a significant presence in the garden even though the plant is dormant. **Below right:** Purple grape leaves are highlighted against a soft-toned stucco post.

spring and summer

Left: 'Stella de Oro' daylily blooms on and off through summer. **Below left:** 'Yellow wave' New Zealand flax echoes the yellow of Jerusalem sage (*Phlomis fruticosa*). Behind the flax are *Salvia verticillata* 'Purple Rain' and 'Big Ears' lamb's ears. **Right:** *Campanula poscharskyana* mingles with 'Plum Delight' loropetalum in front of a terra-cotta urn. Yellow cape fuchsia grows at the back, and evergreen clematis climbs the fence. Small pot holds New Zealand flax and Santa Barbara daisy.

Tanner's design tips for an all-seasons garden

CREATE A SERIES OF VIGNETTES. Use groups of two, three, or four different kinds of plants with compatible textures, shapes, and colors.

TAKE INSPIRATION FROM NATURE. Study natural plant communities for ideas. Plant low growers in drifts of three, five, or more, set close enough together so they rub shoulders when mature. Interrupt the drifts with exclamation points—'Yellow Wave' New Zealand flax amid drifts of 'Primrose Heron' golden lamb's ears and catmint (*Nepeta faassenii*), for instance.

BORROW COLOR PALETTES. When choosing foliage and flower colors, take cues from indoor fabric colors, wall colors, and paintings.

MIX AND MATCH COLORS. Treat foliage and flower colors like paint swatches. Take a leaf or flower from one plant and hold it next to other plants to determine if they combine well.
DESIGN COLOR ECHOES. Repeat the same color two or three times within a vignette, in flowers, stems, or foliage. A yellow color echo might include zebra grass (*Miscanthus sinensis* 'Zebrinus'), 'Pretoria' canna, ground-hugging golden oregano, and spots of golden thyme. Other color echoes: *Phlomis fruticosa* with 'Yellow Wave' New Zealand flax, 'Stella de Oro' daylily, and golden oregano, or *Geranium cantabrigiense* with 'Rose Glow' Japanese barberry.
USE TRANSITIONAL COLORS. Plant silver or gray foliage to link two or more vignettes that feature different color themes. For example, Tanner might use silver artemisia to link a yellow bed of 'Stella de Oro' daylilies and 'Primrose Heron' golden lamb's ears with a purple bed of 'Dark Delight' New Zealand flax and catmint. Other blending plants: silver-leafed lamb's ears, 'Dutch Mill' lavender, silver thyme, or silver-leafed sunrose.
PLAY WITH BACKGROUND PLANTS. When planted behind catmint, dark-foliaged 'Palace Purple' heuchera makes the catmint's lavender-blue flowers stand out. On the other hand, brightly colored variegated ribbon grass planted behind catmint backlights the catmint and makes its flowers recede.
BRIGHTEN DARK CORNERS. To bring light to dark corners of the garden, use white and yellow flowers, and plants with gray, white, yellow, or variegated foliage.
CHOOSE LONG-SEASON BLOOMERS. Shrubs and perennials that bloom repeatedly—cape plumbago, Jerusalem sage, Flower Carpet roses, and repeat-blooming daylilies like 'Stella de Oro'—give you the biggest bang for your buck.
INTEGRATE TRANSLUCENT FOLIAGE. Choose some plants whose petals or leaves let light through. Grapevines, Japanese maples, ornamental grasses, and smoke trees are examples.

The best color-makers for California gardens

■ FOR FALL COLOR (foliage color, unless noted)

TREES: Chinese pistache, crape myrtle, Eastern redbud, floss silk tree (flowers), flowering dogwood, ginkgo, Japanese maple, liquidambar, ornamental pear, Persian parrotia, persimmon, scarlet oak, sour gum.

SHRUBS: Japanese barberry, oakleaf hydrangea, smoke tree, winged euonymus.

VINES: Grape, *Parthenocissus.*

■ FOR WINTER OR SPRING FLOWERS

TREES: *Acacia baileyana* 'Purpurea', crabapple, dogwood, locust (*Robinia ambigua* 'Idahoensis' or *R. a.* 'Purple Robe'), magnolia, orchid tree, *Prunus* (flowering cherry, flowering peach, flowering plum), redbud, *Tabebuia chrysotricha.*

SHRUBS: Azalea, blue hibiscus, cassia, ceanothus, *Coleonema pulchrum* 'Sunset Gold' (foliage and flowers), datura, heath, jasmine, lavender, princess flower, rockrose, rhododendron, rosemary, salvia, santolina (foliage and flowers), tea tree, viburnum, weigela.

GROUND COVERS: Ajuga (foliage and flowers), ceanothus 'Carmel Creeper'.

VINES, CLIMBERS: Clematis, *Hardenbergia,* rose (especially 'Cl. Cécile Brunner' or Lady Banks'), wisteria.

■ FOR SUMMER FLOWERS

TREES: Chinese fringe tree, jacaranda.

SHRUBS: Butterfly bush, *Caesalpinia,* fuchsia, gardenia, glorybower, hebe, hydrangea, *Justicia,* spiraea.

GROUND COVERS: Catmint, ceanothus, gazania, lantana, scaevola, verbena.

VINES: Bougainvillea, bower vine, cup-of-gold vine, *Distictis,* Guinea gold vine, honeysuckle, passion vine.

■ FOR A LONG SEASON OF BLOOM

TREES: *Chitalpa tashkentensis,* coral tree.

SHRUBS: Cape plumbago, escallonia, flowering maple, germander, hibiscus, oleander, salvia, shrub roses, tree mallow.

VINES: Mandevilla, potato vine, violet trumpet vine.

PERENNIALS: Alstroemeria, aster, begonia, blanket flower, brachycome, campanula, coreopsis, cranesbill, daylily, dianthus, diascia, gaura, Jerusalem sage, *Nemesia fruticans, Origanum,* penstemon, purple coneflower, *Rudbeckia,* Russian sage, Santa Barbara daisy, scabiosa, silene, statice, summer phlox, *Tagetes lemmonii.*

■ FOR BEAUTIFUL FOLIAGE ANYTIME

TREES: Bronze loquat, *Cercis canadensis* 'Forest Pansy', purple-leafed plum, 'Royal Purple' smoke tree, variegated dogwood, variegated Japanese maples.

SHRUBS: Juniper, mirror plant, silverberry, *Spiraea bumalda* 'Goldflame', *S. b.* 'Limemound'.

GROUND COVERS AND VINES: *Actinidia kolomikta, Euonymus fortunei.*

PERENNIALS. GRAY, GRAY-GREEN, WHITE: Artemisia, crown pink, dead nettle, ground morning glory, hosta, *Helichrysum petiolare,* lamb's ears, lungwort, Russian sage, silver spear, snow-in-summer, thyme, verbascum, yarrow. **BRONZE, RED, PURPLE:** Ajuga, canna, *Euphorbia amygdaloides* 'Purpurea', *Heuchera,* sedum. **YELLOW, GOLD:** *Bacopa* 'Olympic Gold', golden oregano, golden thyme, *Helichrysum petiolare* 'Limelight', hosta.

GRASSES AND GRASSLIKE PLANTS: Blue oat grass, Bowles' golden grass, eulalia grass, fairy wand, feather grass, feather reed grass, fescue, New Zealand flax, fountain grass, *Hesperaloe parviflora,* Japanese blood grass, *Muhlenbergia,* red-hot poker, ribbon grass, society garlic, sotol, tufted hair grass.

The best color-makers for Southwest gardens

Trees

Blue palo verde (*Cercidium floridum*). Yellow flowers, spring. *Sunset* climate zones 10–14, 18–20. **Cascalote** (*Caesalpinia cacalaco*). Yellow-gold flowers, winter. Zones 12–13. **Chaste tree** (*Vitex agnus-castus*). Purple flowers, spring and fall. Zones 10–13, 18–24. **Desert willow** (*Chilopsis linearis*). Pink-purple flowers, summer. Zones 10–13, 18–21. **Sweet acacia** (*Acacia smallii*). Yellow flowers, late winter to spring. Zones 12–13, 18–24. **Texas mountain laurel** (*Sophora secundiflora*). Purple flowers, spring. Zones 10–13, 18–24. **Texas red oak** (*Quercus buckleyi*). Orange-red fall foliage. Zones 10–13. **Western redbud** (*Cercis occidentalis*). Magenta flowers, spring. Yellow to red fall foliage. Zones 1–3, 10–13, 18–24.

Shrubs

Apache plume (*Fallugia paradoxa*). White flowers, spring. Feathery pink fruits. Zones 2–3, 10–13, 18–24. **Autumn sage** (*Salvia greggii*). Red, pink, or purple flowers; late fall through spring. Zones 10–13, 18–24. **Black dalea** (*Dalea frutescens*). Purple flowers, late summer through fall. Zones 12–13. **Brittlebush** (*Encelia farinosa*). Yellow flowers, spring. Zones 10, 18–24. **Chuparosa** (*Justicia californica*). Red flowers, spring and fall. Zones 10–13. **Fairy duster** (*Calliandra eriophylla*). Pink to red flowers, spring. Zones 10–13, 18–24. **Three-leaf sumac** (*Rhus* *trilobata*). Yellow, orange, or red fall foliage. Zones 1–3, 10. **Yellow bells** (*Tecoma stans*). Yellow flowers, late spring through early fall. Zones 10, 12–13, 21–24.

Vines

Cat's claw (*Macfadyena unguis-cati*). Yellow flowers, spring. Zones 10–13, 18–24. **Common trumpet creeper** (*Campsis radicans*). Orange flowers, spring through summer. Zones 1–3, 10–13, 18–21. **Queen's wreath** (*Antigonon leptopus*). Pink flowers, summer and fall. Zones 12–13, 18–21, 22–24 if sheltered from wind. **Yellow orchid vine** (*Mascagnia macroptera*). Yellow flowers, summer. Zones 12–13, 18–24.

Perennials

Angelita daisy (*Hymenoxys acaulis*). Yellow flowers, spring through fall. Zones 10–13. **Blanket flower** (*Gaillardia grandiflora*). Orange flowers, spring through fall. Zones 1–3, 10–13, 18–24. **Desert marigold** (*Baileya multiradiata*). Yellow flowers, spring through fall. Zones 1–3, 10–13, 18–24. **Firecracker penstemon** (*P. eatonii*). Red flowers, spring. Zones 1–3, 10–13, 18–24. **Gaura** (*G. lindheimeri*). White or pink flowers, spring. Zones 1–3, 10–13, 18–24. **Golden dyssodia** (*D. pentachaeta*). Gold flowers, spring and fall. Zones 10–13. **Goodding-verbena** (*V. gooddingii*). Lavender flowers, spring. Zones 1–3, 10–13, 18–24. **Hummingbird flower/California fuchsia** (*Zauschneria californica*). Orange-red flowers, summer through fall. Zones 2–3, 10, 12–13, 18–24. **Maximilian sunflower** (*Helianthus maximilianii*). Yellow flowers, summer through fall. Zones 1–3, 10–13, 18–24.

Mealy-cup sage (*Salvia farinacea*). Lavender-blue flowers, summer. Zones 1–3, 10–13, 18–24. **Paperflower** (*Psilostrophe cooperi*). Yellow flowers, spring. Zones 10–13. **Parry's penstemon** (*P. parryi*). Pink flowers, spring. Zones 12–13.

Ornamental grasses

Muhly grass (*Muhlenbergia capillaris* 'Regal Mist'). Rose-violet flowers, fall. Soft green foliage. Zones 10–13. **Purple fountain grass** (*Pennisetum setaceum* 'Cupreum' or 'Rubrum'). Fuzzy pink flowers, summer. Purplish brown foliage. Zones 10–13, 18–24.

— *Nora Burba Trulsson*

Elements of an all-seasons garden

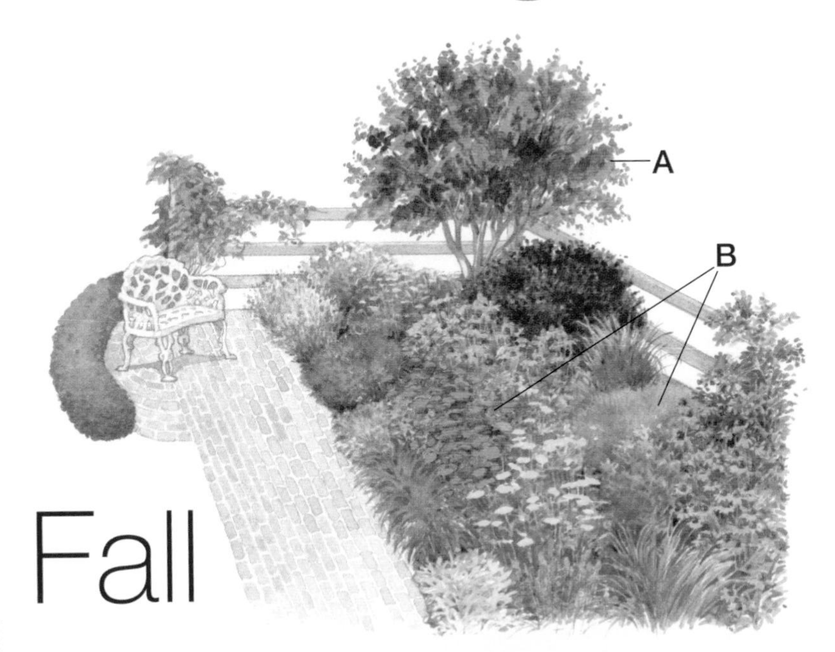

LOIS LOVEJOY (2)

A. TREES AND SHRUBS FOR FALL COLOR
Even a single tree and a few shrubs with foliage that turns autumnal hues can brighten a garden in October and November.

B. VINES, SHRUBS, AND PERENNIALS THAT COME AND GO WITH THE SEASONS
Mix plants that peak in each of the growing seasons—spring, summer, and fall—so there's always something flowering. Choose compatible flower colors.

C. EVERGREENS FOR YEAR-ROUND INTEREST
Choose trees, shrubs, and ornamental grasses that maintain beautiful foliage texture and color all year. Mix low-growing evergreens among flowering perennials. ◆

For Northwest and Mountain gardens

year-round color

Combine the right plants in fall, and you'll have a garden for all seasons

By Steven R. Lorton • Photographs by Allan Mandell

When does your garden peak? Is it with the explosion of bulbs, the first flush of roses, the blaze of autumn color on Japanese maples?

Thomas Vetter of Portland has a rather radical idea: His garden is always peaking. He's designed it to take your breath away from one day to the next, all year long. Every inch of his small city lot is carefully mapped and filled with plants chosen for color and texture.

Amble down his front path and you pass tall shrubs and small trees that screen the garden from the street. Wander under arbors where vines, meticulously trained, appear to scramble with abandon. The stuffed-with-plants look continues in the backyard, in beds that are horticultural treasure troves of shrubs, grasses, bulbs, and more. Foliage in golds and silvers, purples and greens, nudges the flowers of bulbs and perennials.

The plant show changes with the seasons. In spring, daffodils, tulips, scillas, hellebores, and pulmonarias herald the beginning of the new growing season. The white flowers of candytuft, the bells of styrax, and the emerging foliage of barberries and spiraeas like *S. bumalda* 'Goldflame' and 'Limemound' quickly follow.

As summer emerges, roses and perennials unfurl their flowers—among them, catmint, phlomis, yarrow, the spiny spikes of acanthus, and the foamy mounds of goat's beard. Autumn witnesses the appearance of seedheads on many grasses, and flowers on Japanese anemones, rudbeckias, and sedums. In winter, the garden takes on a sculptural look. Deciduous plants are placed so that their trunks and branches, sparkling with frost, cast long shadows under a low winter sun.

Evergreens anchor the garden year-round. Vetter likes to pit intense yellows against the gray Northwest skies. He uses golden conifers, gleaming gold *Elaeagnus pungens* 'Maculata', and glossy yellow *Choisya ternata* 'Sundance', among others. Golden evergreen sedges creep along the ground. And in winter, yellow flowers from Chinese witch hazel and winter-blooming mahonias and the

fall and winter

Left: Flowers splash the front garden in fall. They include brick red *Sedum* 'Autumn Joy', pink cleome, and golden rudbeckia. Shapely evergreens such as golden arborvitae (far left), weeping *Pinus strobus* 'Pendula', and mounding blue-gray *Genista lydia* will carry the show into winter. **Above (front to back):** Lime green *Choisya ternata* 'Sundance', white coneflowers, giant alliums, rose asters, and variegated *Pulmonaria* 'David Ward' are stars in the back garden. **Below:** Vetter pauses beneath a trellis.

white flowers of *Arbutus unedo* keep the landscape lively.

To create this colorful garden, Vetter combed nurseries, visited other gardens, read catalogs and gardening books, and mulled over his ideas with his friend Lucinda Packard. Then he laid out beds, dug organic matter into the soil, pruned up existing trees, and began to plant.

The "bones" of the garden—choice trees and shrubs for all-year interest—went in first. Vetter distributed these around the garden. Then he added the perennials and grasses, chosen for flower color, leaf form, leaf color, and texture. Vetter believes that leaves are as important as blossoms, if not more so, because they tie the beds together visually. But it's the continuous palette of bloom that keeps the garden's character changing through the year, a garden for all seasons.

Fall is for planting, spring is for tending

Vetter takes care of refurbishing in October, replacing tired plants and filling empty spots. Plants are going dormant now, and periods of active growth have passed. Temperatures are cooling, days are shortening, and the season of perpetual rain is on its way. New transplants will have the whole winter and early spring to develop sturdy root systems that will

spring and summer

support lush new growth in spring.

In March, Vetter top-dresses all planting beds with a 2- to 4-inch layer of mushroom compost, then covers the beds with an equally thick layer of mulch (his own, in addition to a commercial product). Throughout the summer, he waters the garden as needed and clips back spent blooms. Once chores are completed, he enjoys his garden, along with the insects and birds that have moved in and made it home.

Above left: Tulips are set off in front by *Viburnum davidii* and behind by lime green Corsican hellebore (*Helleborus argutifolius*). **Left:** Golden arborvitae combines with bronze-foliaged Japanese barberry, feather reed grass, and 'Frosty Morn' variegated sedum. **Top right:** Glorious spring bloomers include (left to right) *Pieris japonica,* 'Mt. Fuji' cherry, *Magnolia stellata,* and yellow forsythia. **Below right:** 'White Nancy' lamium blooms beneath white feverfew, variegated scrophularia, and blue hydrangeas.

Design tips for an all-seasons garden

CREATE A SERIES OF VIGNETTES. Use groups of two, three, or four different kinds of plants with compatible textures, shapes, and colors.

TAKE INSPIRATION FROM NATURE. Plant low growers in drifts of three, five, or more plants set close enough together so they rub shoulders when mature. Interrupt the drifts with exclamation points—sculptural golden conifers, for instance, or billowy groups of ornamental grasses.

BORROW COLOR PALETTES. When choosing foliage and flower colors, take cues from indoor fabric colors, wall colors, and paintings.

MIX AND MATCH COLORS. Treat foliage and flower colors like paint swatches. Take a leaf or flower from one plant and hold it next to other plants to determine if they combine well.

DESIGN COLOR ECHOES. Repeat the same color two or three times within a vignette. The color may appear in flowers, stems, or foliage. A yellow color echo might include *Phlomis fruticosa,* 'Stella de Oro' daylily, and golden oregano. A red echo could mix *Geranium cantabrigiense* with 'Rose Glow' Japanese barberry.

USE TRANSITIONAL COLORS. Plant silver or gray foliage to link two or more vignettes that feature different color themes. For example, silver lamb's ears (*Stachys byzantina*) might link the brick-colored flowers of *Sedum* 'Autumn Joy' with the yellow flowers of goldenrod.

PLAY WITH BACKGROUND PLANTS. Dark-foliaged 'Palace Purple' heuchera, when planted behind catmint (*Nepeta faassenii*), makes the catmint's lavender-blue flowers stand out. On the other hand, brightly colored variegated ribbon grass planted behind catmint backlights the catmint and makes its purple flowers recede.

BRIGHTEN DARK CORNERS. To bring light to dark corners of the garden, use white and yellow flowers, and plants with gray, white, yellow, or variegated foliage.

CHOOSE PLANTS WITH A LONG SEASON OF INTEREST. Shrubs and perennials that bloom in spring—such as *Pieris japonica,* with bronzy pink new leaves, drooping clusters of flower buds in fall, and flowers in early to midspring—give you the biggest bang for your buck.

INTEGRATE TRANSLUCENT FOLIAGE. Choose some plants whose petals or leaves let light pass through. Grapevines, Japanese maples, ornamental grasses, and smoke trees are examples.

Color-makers for Northwest and Mountain gardens

FOR FALL COLOR

TREES: *Acer palmatum* 'Bloodgood', *Betula jacquemontii* (Himalayan birch).

SHRUB: Japanese barberry 'Rose Glow'.

FOR SPRING BLOOM

TREE: *Prunus serrulata* 'Shirotae' ('Mt. Fuji' cherry).

SHRUBS: *Ceanothus* 'Victoria', *Choisya ternata* 'Sundance' (golden Mexican orange), *Cornus alba* 'Elegantissima' (variegated tatarian dogwood), *C. kousa* (kousa dogwood), *Genista lydia* (broom).

PERENNIALS: *Acanthus spinosus* (spiny bears breech), *Euphorbia amygdaloides* 'Purpurea' (purple wood spurge), *Phlomis russeliana* (sticky Jerusalem sage), *Pulmonaria rubra* 'David Ward' (red lungwort).

VINES: *Clematis macropetala* (downy clematis), *Solanum jasminoides* 'Album' (potato vine).

FOR SUMMER TO FALL BLOOM

TREES: *Stewartia pseudocamellia, Styrax obassia* (fragrant snowbell).

SHRUBS: *Hydrangea paniculata* 'Kyushu', *Hypericum androsaemum* 'Albury Purple', *Rosa rubrifolia* (formerly *Rosa glauca*).

PERENNIALS: Japanese anemone 'Honorine Jobert', *Artemisia lactiflora* 'Guizhou' (white mugwort), purple coneflower.

VINE: *Lonicera periclymenum* 'Belgica' (early Dutch honeysuckle).

FOR ALL-SEASON INTEREST

TREES: *Cryptomeria japonica* 'Elegans' (plume cedar), *Eucalyptus pauciflora niphophila* (snow gum), *Picea pungens* 'Bakeri' (Baker's blue spruce).

SHRUBS: *Mahonia* 'Arthur Menzies', *Pieris japonica* 'Mountain Fire'.

VINES: *Hedera canariensis* 'Gloire de Marengo', *Parthenocissus henryana* (silvervein creeper), *Vitis vinifera* 'Purpurea' (purple-leafed grape).

GRASSES: *Calamagrostis arundinacea* 'Karl Foerster', *Helictotrichon sempervirens* (blue oat grass), *Miscanthus sinensis* 'Cosmopolitan'.

Elements of an all-seasons garden

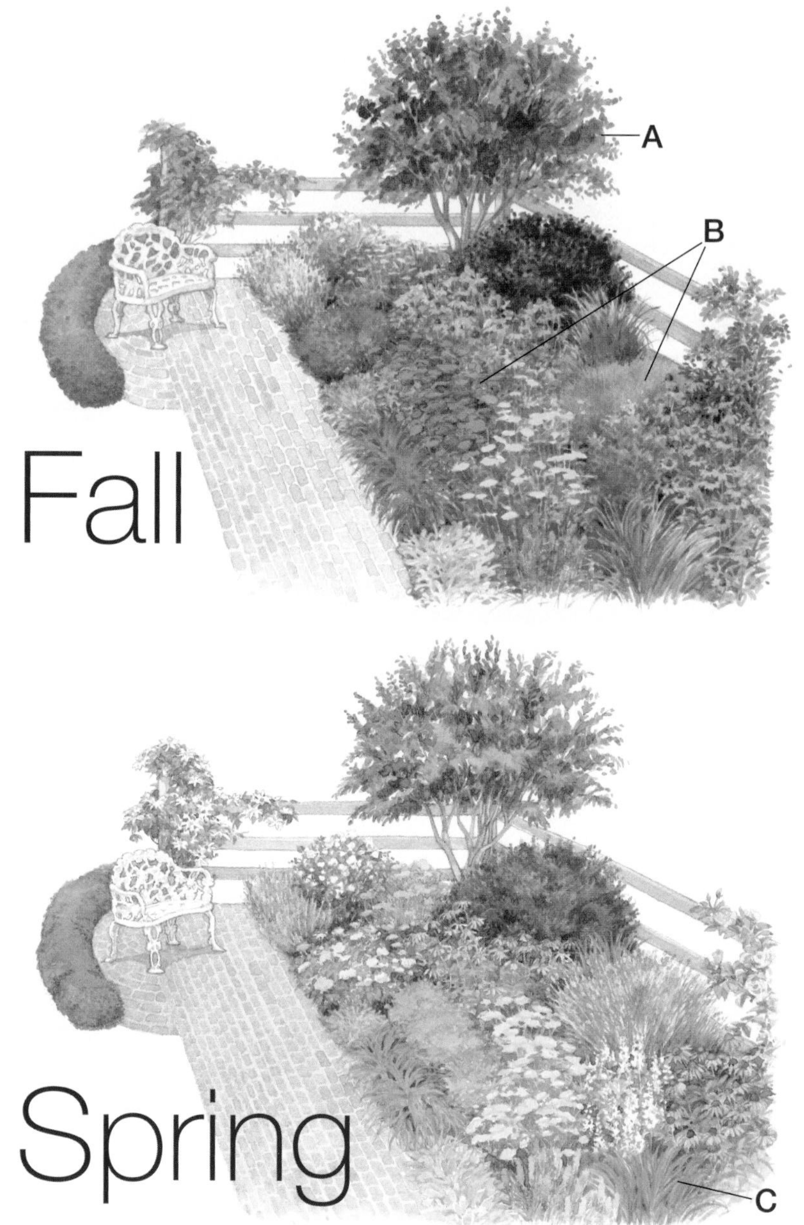

LOIS LOVEJOY (2)

A. TREES AND SHRUBS FOR FALL COLOR. Even a single tree and a few shrubs with foliage that turns autumnal hues can brighten a garden in October and November.

B. VINES, SHRUBS, AND PERENNIALS THAT COME AND GO WITH THE SEASONS. Mix plants that peak in each of the growing seasons—spring, summer, and fall—so there's always something flowering. Choose compatible flower colors.

C. EVERGREENS FOR YEAR-ROUND INTEREST. Choose trees, shrubs, and ornamental grasses that maintain beautiful foliage texture and color for most of the year. Mix some low ones among flowering perennials. ◆

A compost bin with a college degree

Five stackable sections make composting easy

By Jim McCausland

Finished compost (above) has the appearance and fine texture of coffee grounds.

ANDREW DRAKE (2)

When horticulturists at the University of California Cooperative Extension set out to design the perfect compost bin, they wanted one that was simple to build, easy to use, and efficient at making compost. The bin shown here meets those criteria.

This 3-foot-square unit consists of five sections. You start the compost pile by filling one or two sections with organic matter, then stack on the other sections as you add more material. By following the recipe (at right), you can have a load of finished compost in about six weeks.

TIME: Two to three hours

COST: $50 to $75, depending on the grade of wood (we used untreated pine)

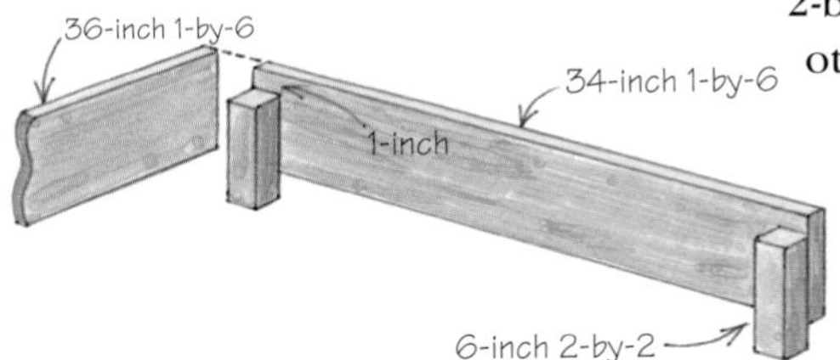

MATERIALS

60 feet 1-by-6 utility wood
10 feet 2-by-2 utility wood
80 2-inch woodscrews
1 quart of wood sealer

DIRECTIONS

1. Saw the 1-by-6s into 10 36-inch lengths and 10 34-inch lengths; saw the 2-by-2s into 6-inch lengths.

2. Lay each of 34-inch boards over two 2-by-2s, with one 2-by-2 flush with each end but offset from the top edge by 1 inch. Drive two screws through the 1-by-6s into each 2-by-2.

3. Place one 34-inch board upside down with 2-by-2s extending upward. Place a 36-inch board against one end, flush with the top, bottom, and outside edge. Attach with two woodscrews through the 1-by-6 into the 2-by-2. Add second 34-inch board at other end of 36-inch board. Complete section with other 36-inch board, making a 36-inch square. Repeat the process for each of the remaining four sections.

4. Apply two coats of wood sealer.

Recipe for homemade compost

Compost improves soil texture, fertility, and ability to hold water and air. Here's how to make it.

INGREDIENTS. Include grass clippings, dead leaves, and vegetable kitchen waste. Don't add diseased plants, plant parts that contain thorns, weed seedheads, or meat, fat, or bones from the kitchen. Chop or shred everything to speed decomposition. I run my lawn mower over fallen leaves.

ALTERNATE LAYERS OF BROWN AND GREEN MATTER. Put down a 3-inch layer of brown matter, such as shredded dead leaves, which contain plenty of carbon. Cover it with an equal layer of green matter, like grass clippings, which contain a lot of nitrogen.

If you're short on green matter, sprinkle the brown matter with high-nitrogen fertilizer (such as lawn fertilizer). To speed up decomposition in a new pile, add a few shovelfuls of old compost, which already contains bacteria and fungi.

KEEP THE PILE MOIST AND AERATED. Sprinkle the pile with water to keep it about as damp as a wrung-out sponge. Use a spading fork or pitchfork to thoroughly mix the ingredients and aerate the pile. When the compost is ready, its texture will be like that of fine soil. ◆

PETER O. WHITELEY

Softer steps

A garden designer shares ideas for pairing pavers with ground covers

By Sharon Cohoon
Photographs by Marion Brenner

■ A few bumps in the road can be a good thing. At least that's the premise of Oakland, California–based garden designer Bob Clark, who created the pathway plantings pictured on these pages. A smooth, swift course is a virtue on a speedway, he says, but not in a garden: "You're there to wander, not to race." If the surface underfoot alternates between stiff flagstone and springy Scotch moss, and that unevenness slows your steps, great. If there are clumps of grass or other vegetative obstacles to navigate around on the path, even better.

Bumpy walkways have other benefits too. Mosses and thymes between pavers make a garden appear more lush. "That's especially valuable in small gardens, where the proportion of hardscape to planting areas is always greater," Clark says. "These interplanted paths are great softeners."

Scotch moss and sweet grass make this pathway nearly disappear. ABOVE: For this much-used walk, lime thyme, sweet alyssum, and Mexican feather grass were used sparingly.

Gardens viewed mostly from above also profit from hardscape broken up with planting. From a second story, it's much nicer to look down on a tapestry of color and texture than on a solid expanse of flagstone or brick. In fact, in Clark's opinion, alternating between paving and plants is almost always a good idea. "Hardscape, for me, is just another opportunity to plant," he says.

ABOVE: Broad bands of red alyssum, lime thyme, and chamomile connect twin borders filled with pink petunias, pink geraniums, and chartreuse feverfew. BELOW: In a more-traveled section of the same garden, Irish moss adds a cool touch between sunny borders of petunias, salvia, and lavender.

three or more stones meet are a little more spacious and accommodating; these are good places to drop in carex, festuca, or other taller accent plants.

Plant as densely as you can. Purchase ground covers in flats, cut them apart into small squares, and plant the plugs as close as 6 inches apart. The quicker the gaps fill in, the less time you'll spend weeding.

Once the plants have filled in, an hour a month is about all you need to maintain a 30- by 5-foot path. Taller ground covers such as chamomile and sweet alyssum require more maintenance because they need occasional haircuts as well. About every three months should do it.

Fertilizer is rarely necessary for these tough plants, says Clark, but regular watering is. "Overhead sprinklers that water the pathways along with everything else are the simplest solution," he says.

Starting off on the right foot

To get ground covers between pavers off to a great start, you need good soil. Clark usually lays down at least 6 inches of high-quality planting mix before nestling the pavers among plants on top—the mix is not just in the areas where he anticipates planting, but under the whole path. "That's so I have the freedom to keep altering the pattern until I'm satisfied," he says, "but it's also to encourage plant roots to spread quickly."

Next, you should consider pedestrian impact. Where there's heavy foot traffic, create narrow gaps between pavers; where it is more occasional, leave up to 4 inches between stones for planting.

Choose lower-growing ground covers such as Scotch moss and dymondia for well-used areas; save the taller, more sprawling plants, such as thyme and chamomile, for side paths. The intersections where

Dymondia, the ground cover between pavers in the garden at left, is drought-tolerant, like its companions Santa Barbara daisy and upright rosemary. Its carpetlike habit makes it a witty companion to the stone sofa at the end of the path. (Seating by artist Donna Billick.)

Clark's favorite creepers

- BABY'S TEARS (*Soleirolia soleirolii*). Creeping plant, 1–4 inches tall, with tiny, round green leaves. Prefers shade; tolerates some sun near coast. *Sunset* climate zones 4–24.
- BLUE STAR CREEPER (*Pratia pedunculata,* also sold as *Laurentia fluviatilis* or *Isotoma fluviatilis*). Ground-hugging, as name implies—only 2 to 3 inches tall. Tiny green leaves much like baby's tears; blue flowers, spring through summer. Full sun to partial shade. Zones 4–9, 14–24.
- CHAMOMILE (*Chamaemelum nobile*). Soft-textured spreading plant with light green, finely cut aromatic leaves. Look for 'Treneague', a nonflowering variety. Full sun to partial shade. All zones.
- CORSICAN MINT. Very low (only ½ inch tall) mat with bright green leaves that release a delightful scent when walked on. Sun or partial shade. Zones 5–9, 12–24.
- CREEPING THYME. Lemon, lime, and variegated forms. Flat mat about 6 inches tall with small, round, pleasantly aromatic leaves. Prefers full sun but tolerates light shade. Best in areas with light foot traffic. All zones.
- DYMONDIA MARGARETAE. Low-growing (2 to 3 inches) ground cover with gray-green leaves with rolled white edges. Very drought-tolerant. Grows slowly—faster with regular watering. Full sun to partial shade. Zones 15–24.
- SCOTCH MOSS AND IRISH MOSS (*Sagina subulata*). Very dense, compact ground cover that looks like—but isn't—moss. Irish form, bright green; Scotch, more golden. Full sun to partial shade. Zones 1–11, 14–24.
- SWEET ALYSSUM (*Lobularia maritima*). Low, branching, trailing plant to 1 foot tall with generous clusters of tiny, four-petaled flowers. An annual but reseeds so profusely in zones 10–24 that the garden is rarely without blooms. Full sun or light shade. All zones. ◆

NORMAN A. PLATE

Fragrant hyacinth bulbs bloom in water-filled forcing vases.

The gentle art of forcing bulbs

Coax spring bulbs to flower indoors during winter

By Jim McCausland

In the dead of winter, spring-blooming bulbs are especially welcome in the house. They can easily fill a room with a delightful perfume and remind you that spring really is just around the corner.

The process of getting flower bulbs to bloom ahead of schedule is called forcing. Depending on the kind of bulbs you choose, you could enjoy your first blooms in less than 10 weeks.

We list several popular bulbs, which you can find at most nurseries and garden centers this month or buy through mail-order catalogs. Note that many bulbs require a certain amount of chilling; some need to be refrigerated, others can be planted then chilled outdoors (see "Forcing tips" on the facing page). Chilling periods given here are based on the recommendations of the Netherlands Flower Bulb Information Center.

CROCUS AND HYACINTHS must be chilled. They can be forced, one bulb per jar or vase, in water alone without any soil; there are special forcing jars and vases for crocus and hyacinths.

Crocus corms need to be refrigerated for 15 weeks. After chilling, place each corm in its own water-filled crocus forcing jar or vase at around 60°; flowers will emerge in about two weeks. Choose *Crocus vernus* in shades of purple, lavender, yellow, or white.

Hyacinth bulbs need to be refrigerated for 12 weeks. Then place each bulb in a water-filled hyacinth forcing jar or vase at around 70°; flowers follow in two or three weeks. Try fragrant Dutch hyacinths in shades of blue, purple, pink, or white.

FREESIAS AND TAZETTA NARCISSUS (PAPER WHITES) technically do not need chilling, but they do need cool night temperatures and plenty of time to root before they flower. They're powerfully fragrant.

Freesia corms take about 14 weeks from planting to bloom. Plant corms in a container filled with potting soil or sand, growing them in a spot that has daytime sun and nighttime temperatures in the 40s. Look for Dutch and Tecolote hybrids in shades of purple, blue, lavender, red, pink, orange, yellow, or white.

Tazetta narcissus bulbs take five to seven weeks from planting to bloom. Use any type of container that's twice as wide as it is high. Bulbs can be completely buried in potting soil or partially sunk in horticultural sand or decorative rocks or pebbles. Whatever medium you use, water well and put the container in a cool place (40° to 50° at night is perfect) until buds show color, then bring them indoors to bloom.

Many of these narcissus fall under the generic heading of "paper white," and all produce lots of flowers from each bud. Among the best for forcing are *Narcissus tazetta* 'Orientalis' (light yellow segments, deep yellow cup), 'Paper White' (all white), 'Grand Soleil d'Or' (golden yellow), and an Israeli-bred series that includes 'Galilee' (white), 'Nazareth' (also sold as 'Yael'; pale yellow segments, deep yellow cups), and 'Ziva' (white).

OTHER DAFFODILS AND TULIPS require a bit more effort to force. Because these bulbs need plenty of time to develop roots in order to support their tall, heavy tops, you must first plant them in potting soil, then chill at 45° or below for an extended period. Then bring the bulbs indoors to bloom at room temperature. Be sure to use a container that has a drain hole.

Daffodil bulbs need chilling for 16 weeks; bloom follows two or three weeks later. Try the strong-growing 'Salome' (pale yellow segments, apricot pink cup), the diminutive 'Tête à Tête' (all yellow), or 'Mount Hood' (all white).

THOMAS J. STORY

NORM PLATE

Freesia corms (upper right) were planted in sand, then covered with pebbles. Daffodil bulbs (above) sprouted in sand.

Tulip bulbs need chilling for 14 to 20 weeks; bloom follows about three weeks later. Choices range from low-growing species tulips to tall hybrids. Two of our favorites for forcing are red *T. greigii* (try 'Orange Toronto') and *T. kaufmanniana,* whose water lily–shaped flowers come in yellow or red ('Showwinner' is a superior red). Each holds its flowers about a foot high.

Forcing tips

CHILLING. To chill bulbs in the refrigerator, just store them in a mesh or paper bag in the crisper section until they're ready to be forced. Throughout much of the West (except mild-winter parts of Arizona and Southern California), you can chill bulbs after planting simply by putting the pots outdoors. In very cold regions, place them in your garage, greenhouse, or coldframe; in milder places, you can put them in a cool, bright part of the garden. Bulbs will root and sprout during chilling.

CONTAINERS. Shop for containers and special forcing jars and vases at garden centers and through mail-order catalogs. Tall glass vessels, like the hurricane-lamp chimney holding the freesias pictured above, do a good job of supporting spindly or extratall flower stems; you can also buy wire supports that keep stalks from leaning.

PLANTING. Most bulbs and corms can be put into containers almost shoulder-to-shoulder—certainly not more than 1 inch apart. Plant so that most of the bulb is buried, with just the tip poking above the potting medium. The level of the soil or sand should start out an inch below the container rim. As the bulbs start to grow, they'll push the soil or sand up and you'll be glad you allowed for that expansion. If you grow bulbs in soil, fertilize once with half-strength liquid fertilizer as soon as you bring them indoors. ◆

STEVEN GUNTHER

ROSES AND PERENNIALS create a riot of color in Deborah Landis's Beverly Hills garden. For details on this bright and beautiful garden, see page 351.

November

LINDA ENGER (2)

Playing plants off painted walls

■ Phoenix-based landscape designer Debra Burnette loves color and sculptural plants. Clients Rachel and George Klink found they shared these passions after Burnette created a walled garden at their home near the Phoenix Mountains Preserve.

Burnette positioned 7-foot-tall stucco-on-block walls to shield the house front from a crowded neighborhood and a two-story home next door. She covered the walls with rich shades of flat exterior latex paint. Then, in beds at the bases of the walls, she arranged plants chosen for their color and form.

TOP: Tall *Kalanchoe orgyalis* complements a yellow backdrop. ABOVE: Deer grass brushes a red wall.

She painted one wall yellow (Sunbury from Frazee Paint & Wallcovering) and used the shadier portion as a backdrop for two succulents, bronze-leafed *Kalanchoe orgyalis* and bright green *Crassula* 'Campfire'. Along the sunnier part of this wall, Burnette planted heat-tolerant agaves, bat-faced cuphea, and a Sonoran palo verde (*Cercidium praecox*) with chartreuse bark.

A patio wall on the side of the house is painted deep purple (Nocturne from Frazee), a tone accented by the white blossoms of *Gaura lindheimeri* and the yellow flowers of *Caesalpinia platyloba,* a small tree native to Mexico.

On the opposite side of the house, Burnette heightened a low wall that runs across the end of a swimming pool. She painted the wall red (Chinese Pagoda from Frazee) and used it to show off clumps of deer grass (*Muhlenbergia rigens*), a perennial that minds its manners in poolside plantings. *— Nora Burba Trulsson*

Window dressing

STEVEN GUNTHER

■ Dana Anderson decorated herself right out of a toolshed. When she bought the structure shown at right for her Newport Beach garden, it was a simple redwood playhouse. Then she made the mistake of dressing it up with white paint and, just to be playful, adding a working clock tower. She decked it out with family memorabilia—shutters from her parents' home, a brass letter *A* from their old retail store on the Dutch door, and a toy-size lantern that acts as a porch light, a remnant of her mother's childhood playhouse. As if the building weren't cute enough, Anderson also added a window box, planted it with pink geraniums and white gauras, and placed three boxwood topiaries underneath to create a "gardeny" scene. As a final graceful note, she trained an ivy garland to weave its way along the roofline.

No wonder her teenage daughters, Madeline (14) and Clementine (13), insist the building is too neat to be used for tools but is perfect for birthday parties and other gala events. "I think it's going to be a long time before that shed sees tools again," says Anderson with a resigned smile. — *Sharon Cohoon*

CRANDALL & CRANDALL

Canvas for a tool collector

■ Veteran gardener Barbara Baker has never been without some Peg-Board somewhere readily accessible from her backyard. "It's still the most convenient way to store garden tools I know," she says. "Everything is visible and easy to grab and put back." So when she moved and finally built the toolshed she'd been fantasizing about for decades, there was no question what the interior wallcovering would be—Peg-Board all around. "Practical, inexpensive, good-looking," Baker says. There's just one drawback. Friends, especially those in her gardening circle, see the walls as a canvas, and they keep showing up with antique tools, adding to what was already an ample collection. Baker isn't really complaining. "Peg-Board lets you rearrange at will, so it's no problem." Hooks keep the tools in place.

— *S.C.*

CLIPPINGS

•**Lake Tahoe landscaping.** If you garden in or near the Sierra or know someone who does, *Home Landscaping Guide for Lake Tahoe and Vicinity* (University of Nevada Cooperative Extension, Reno, 2000; $4) may prove useful. The new 150-page softcover book helps the region's homeowners develop environmentally appropriate landscapes to improve the lake's water quality. It's available from the University of Nevada Cooperative Extension in Incline Village (775/832-4150).

Great reference book. If you love out-of-the-ordinary plants but get frustrated because you can't find information about them, *Selected Plants for Southern California Gardens,* a new release from the Southern California Horticultural Society, should be in your library. The book describes 2,700 plants brought to the society's monthly plant forums over the last 65 years. No frills, no photos—just collective expertise of the best gardeners in the region. To order, send a check to the society, Box 41080, Los Angeles, CA 90041-0080. Cost is $34.95, plus $2.88 sales tax and $6 shipping.

Cool-season veggies in raised beds

■ In mild-winter areas of the West, it's still not too late to plant cool-season crops like lettuce if you set out nursery transplants immediately. Raised beds filled with rich soil provide ideal growing conditions. In the wood-framed beds pictured here, a Seattle family of six harvests vegetables, herbs, fruits, and cut flowers year-round. Altogether, the family maintains four 4- by 8-foot beds and one 4- by 4-foot bed. They've found a number of ways to get the most crops and color out of their beds.

• Grow ornamental edibles. Red- and green-leafed lettuces are clustered by color for a showy look. You can achieve a similar effect with red and green varieties of kale or mustard.

• Grow crops vertically to save space. Along the back of a bed (above), edible pole peas will twine up a framework of 5-foot bamboo stakes inserted into the soil in a crisscross pattern. Sweet peas planted at the base of a wood obelisk (left) will climb the sides, leaving plenty of room for strawberries to fill the rest of the bed.

More tips

• Plant cut-and-come-again vegetables that can be harvested a few leaves, sprigs, or stems at a time. Leaf lettuce, for example, will keep forming new leaves if you harvest mature leaves one at a time from the outside of the plant. Swiss chard can keep producing leaves for a couple of years. Grow curly parsley as a garnish and Italian flat-leaf parsley for cooking or salads. Japanese bunching onions yield a steady supply of stems you can use like scallions.

• Choose long-bearing or multi-purpose vegetable varieties when possible. Everbearing strawberries yield fruit from spring through fall. If you plant bulbing onions at 2-inch intervals, you can thin them in the green stage for scallions, then pick mature bulbs next summer.

• Interplant herbs with vegetables. Set oregano, thyme, and prostrate rosemary along the edges of raised beds and let them spill over the sides. Tuck a few pansies into the beds; use their edible flowers to garnish salads.

— *Jim McCausland*

JIM McCAUSLAND (3)

BEN WOOLSEY

'Robert Chapman' blazes like a campfire surrounded by stones.

Heathers that glow in frosty weather

After flowering, they display fiery winter foliage

■ In the Pacific Northwest, Scotch heather (*Calluna vulgaris*) is widely appreciated for delicate flowers that appear from midsummer to early autumn. Then, with the onset of frosty weather, many varieties of heather put on a second show as their foliage turns glowing shades of red, orange, or golden yellow.

Scotch heather grows well in cool, moist Western climates (*Sunset* zones 2–7 and 15–17), but is not suited for dry-summer, cold-winter conditions.

These varieties display especially vivid winter foliage; most bloom in August and September. Shop nurseries now for plants in 4-inch pots or 1-gallon cans. All plants listed below are available by mail from Heaths & Heathers in Shelton, Washington (catalog free; 360/427-5318 or www.heathsandheathers.com). Plant immediately in a site that gets full sun. Heathers need well-drained soil, enriched leaf mold, or peat moss.

'Beoley Gold'. Foliage turns rich gold in winter; white flowers.

'Firefly'. Terra-cotta-colored summer foliage turns vivid red; deep mauve flowers.

'Glenlivet'. Orange summer foliage becomes bright red; pink flowers.

'Gold Haze'. Gold hue deepens in winter; white flowers.

'Gold Knight'. Downy gold summer foliage develops a hint of red; lavender flowers.

'Hoyerhagen'. Bright gold summer foliage turns deep red in winter; pale crimson flowers.

'Robert Chapman'. Gold summer foliage becomes brick red in winter; lavender flowers.

'Sesam'. Gold foliage turns rich red-orange; lilac-pink flowers.

'Silver Knight'. Silver gray summer foliage develops purplish cast in winter; lavender flowers. — *Steven R. Lorton*

NORMAN A. PLATE

Poppies and perennials

Wildflowers don't need a meadow in which to shine—they thrive in garden beds

■ Some of the most appealing plants native to Mediterranean climates bloom in colors that many gardeners would never think of combining—vibrant orange and lime green, for instance. As the photograph above shows, these snappy hues translate well into garden beds.

This eye-catching, unthirsty planting, designed by *Sunset's* head gardener, Rick La Frentz, pairs chartreuse *Euphorbia characias wulfenii* with dazzling orange California poppies. Dark green feather reed grass and gray-leafed *Phlomis fruticosa* form a 3- to 4-foot-tall backdrop for the flowers. Perennial blue flax and red 'Mrs. Bradshaw' geum mingle behind the poppies.

La Frentz planted the border in fall in soil well amended with compost. He started the flax and poppies from seed, the others from 1-gallon containers. Planting in fall allows winter rains to help get the seeds and plants off to a good start. After the first year, the bed needs only infrequent summer irrigation in mild-summer areas (more frequent watering in hot inland climates). The California poppies will reseed themselves from year to year. — *Lauren Bonar Swezey*

Orange and cream California poppies, blue flax, red geum, and lime green euphorbia are style-setters in this unthirsty planting.

A showy winter garden

JIM McCAUSLAND

■ Winter visitors to Sooke Harbour House, a well-known country inn in Sooke, British Columbia, are surprised by the lush looks of its cool-season garden, pictured here in mid-November. The garden's success stems partly from its mild, waterside location on Vancouver Island and partly from plant selection, soil preparation, and maintenance. The portion of the garden shown in the photo also benefits from its southern exposure, which supplies extra light and warmth during the short, dark days of winter.

The garden relies heavily on ornamental cabbage and kale for color. The edible flowers of calendulas and pansies add colorful accents here and there.

Like any good winter garden, this one begins with well-amended soil that affords good drainage. The compost used to amend the soil at planting time supplies enough nutrients to carry the crops through winter. To insulate plant roots and hold down mud, head gardener Byron Cook uses aged Douglas fir sawdust to mulch beds and paths.

Sooke Harbour House is located about 23 miles west of Victoria via Provincial Highway 14. The gardens are open to visitors anytime. If you would like to spend the night or have a meal, which usually includes some crop from the garden, call (250) 642-3421 well ahead. —*J.M.*

Bright and beautiful

■ Controlled color schemes have their place in garden beds—lavenders and artemisia, for instance, all grays and blues, perfectly coordinated—but so do joyous mixes of bright colors.

That's what Deborah Landis, costume designer and wife of film director John Landis, discovered when she planted her garden in Beverly Hills (shown on page 344). The flower beds, which billow around her back patio, contain every color in the rainbow. When the Landises moved in, only a few scraggly foundation plants grew there—"very dreary," Landis says. Since the property was a rental, major landscaping renovations were not an option. "So, instead of long-term planning, I went for immediate gratification," she says. If a color was "just a shade shy of garish," she picked it.

Today, perennial blue morning glory races with 'Handel' roses up the walls of the house. Orange lion's tail and yellow Jerusalem sage vie for attention with pink lavatera and blue Cleveland sage in flower-filled beds.

Hoping to create a garden she could live with, Landis ended up with one she loved.

— *S.C.*

PLANT PROFILE

Weeping katsura

■ Every fall the weeping katsura (*Cercidiphyllum japonicum* 'Pendulum') in my Eugene, Oregon, garden becomes a cascade of golden leaves. Growing slowly to a height of 15 feet and a width of 12 feet, this graceful tree can be the centerpiece of even the smallest garden. In spring the heart-shaped leaves emerge with a pinkish hue. By summer they turn a soft blue-green. The glory days come in October or early November, when the tree is draped in a bright gold curtain that lasts for several weeks. Then all of the leaves drop at once into a pool of fallen gold.

The weeping katsura does best in zones 2b to 6. Give it full sun or partial shade, well-drained soil, and regular water.

— Mary-Kate Mackey

MARY-KATE MACKEY

TERRENCE MOORE

A terraced garden with year-round interest

Hardy plants and native stone blend beautifully on a Colorado hillside

■ When Charlotte Jorgensen and her husband, Rich, decided to revamp their garden on a steep hillside west of Boulder, they enlisted help from landscape designer Jack Geer of Azure Canyon Landscaping. The three worked closely together to ensure that the new landscape would harmonize with a surrounding woodland of aspens, Douglas firs, ponderosa pines, and river birches.

To give the garden a more natural look, existing straight-edged terraces of local red sandstone were reworked into multiple levels accented by large boulders moved from other locations on the property. Retaining walls of dry-stacked stone were rebuilt, and perennials, shrubs, and trees dug up from the old garden were transplanted into new soil-filled pockets. As a counterpoint to the hot, dry look of the sandstone, Charlotte chose cottage-garden flowers including campanulas, catmint, dianthus, peonies, and roses in shades of lavender, pink, blue, and wine red. She selected landscape plants that would provide interest during the prolonged winter here at 7,800-foot elevation: evergreen conifers, including 'Blue Star' juniper and dwarf Colorado blue spruce, and deciduous 'Miss Kim' lilac with its handsome bare-branched form.

Pyramidal forms of dwarf Colorado blue spruce punctuate some of the terraced beds.

Several flights of stone stairs lead down from a patio outside the dining room, through the garden to a lower patio. Woolly thyme and mother-of-thyme were planted in the seams between stone steps; their silvery gray leaves release a subtle fragrance underfoot. — *Marcia Tatroe*

WHAT TO DO IN YOUR GARDEN IN NOVEMBER

PLANTING

☐ AMARYLLIS. Garden shops and nurseries offer amaryllis as bulbs and as started plants. Buy budded plants to get exactly the color and size you want, or buy the bulbs and grow them yourself. Some will flower within a few weeks, while others may take three months or more to bloom. Give them plenty of light and regular water.

☐ CAMELLIAS. Winter-flowering camellias (mostly Sasanqua and Hiemalis types) start blooming later this month. Plant and mulch right away to protect roots from freezing, or be prepared to bring potted plants into shelter when hard freezes are predicted.

☐ FALL COLOR. This is the best time to scout nurseries for shrubs and trees with good autumn foliage color. Good choices, if you can find them, are burning bush (winged euonymus), fothergilla, maples, Persian parrotia, and weeping katsura (see page 351).

☐ SPRING-FLOWERING BULBS. Nurseries still have a good selection of flower bulbs on hand. Plant anemones, bluebells, crocus, daffodils, grape hyacinths, hyacinths, ranunculus, and tulips in drifts outdoors.

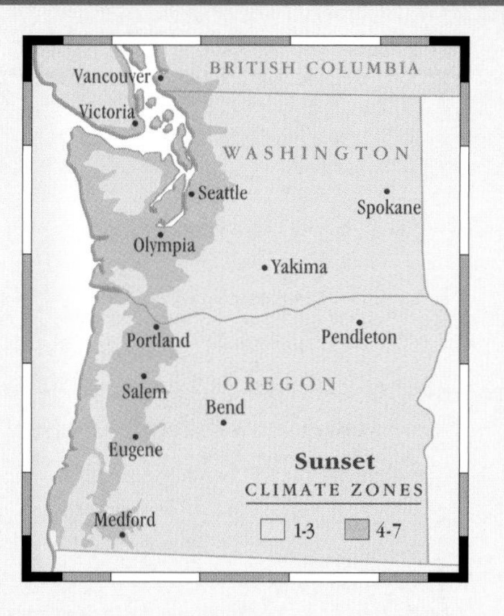

☐ WILDFLOWERS. Seedlings of fall-sown wildflowers will come up earlier than those sown in spring. Scatter seeds in amended, weeded beds.

MAINTENANCE

☐ COMPOST. As you gather fallen leaves and remove played-out annuals and weeds, run the lawn mower over them before you throw them onto the compost pile. Chopped garden debris breaks down faster.

☐ CLEAN UP GARDEN BEDS. If you weed, till, and amend beds now, they'll be ready for planting early next spring.

☐ LIFT AND STORE DAHLIAS. If you haven't already done so, dig up dahlia tubers, shake off the dirt, and let them dry before you put them in winter storage.

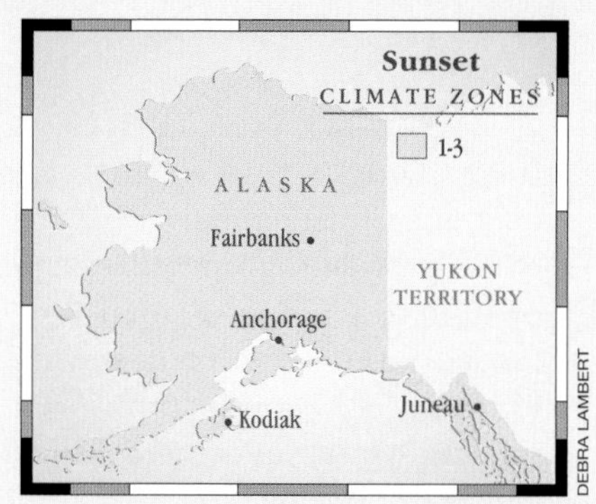

DEBRA LAMBERT

☐ MAINTAIN TOOLS. Service your tools before you put them away for the winter. Sharpen shovels, hoes, and pruners; rub down wood handles with linseed oil; and wipe tool blades with an oily cloth to protect them against rust. It's a bad idea to leave tools in an outdoor shed all winter, since high humidity causes rust. It's much better to bring them into a warmer, drier space (like your attic) until spring.

☐ MOW. Lawn growth slows to a snail's pace in winter. Mow one last time on a dry weekend in midmonth, and you shouldn't have to mow again until spring.

☐ PROTECT GERANIUMS, FUCHSIAS. Bring plants into a cool, dark, frost-free place for the winter. An unheated garage is usually adequate. ◆

WHAT TO DO IN YOUR GARDEN IN NOVEMBER

PLANTING

☐ AMARYLLIS FOR THE HOLIDAYS. Only 4 to 6 weeks after planting, Christmas-flowering amaryllis produce gorgeous single or double trumpet-shaped flowers as large as 9 inches wide. Flowers are coral, pink, red, salmon, white, yellow, and striped and feathered bicolors. Shop for bulbs at your nursery or order them from garden.com (800/466-8142 or www.garden.com), John Scheepers (860/567-0838 or www.johnscheepers.com), or Wayside Gardens (800/845-1124 or www.waysidegardens.com).

☐ TREES FOR FALL COLOR. Because the foliage of maples, Chinese pistaches, and other deciduous trees varies in color, now—while leaves are still on—is the best time to shop for these trees at nurseries. Other trees that crown themselves with beautiful autumn foliage in Northern California are crape myrtle, ginkgo, liquidambar, persimmon, Raywood ash, redbud, and sour gum. Keep in mind that plant health can also affect leaf color.

☐ WILDFLOWERS. For colorful spring bloom, choose a mix that's suited to your climate or create your own color combinations. You can also buy mixes for specific purposes, like attracting butterflies or

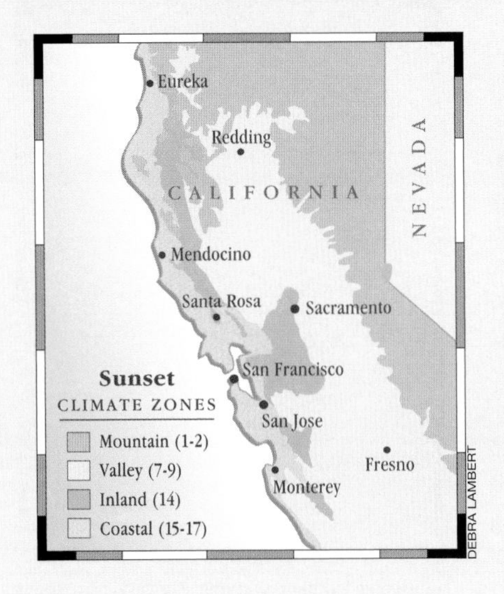

beneficial insects. Seed sources include Clyde Robin Seed Company in Castro Valley (510/785-0425 or www.clyderobin.com), Larner Seeds in Bolinas (415/868-9407 or www.larnerseeds.com), or Wildflower Seed Company in St. Helena (800/456-3359 or www.wildflower-seed.com).

MAINTENANCE

☐ DIG DAHLIA TUBERS. Withhold water to allow plants to go dormant. When foliage dies down, cut off stems to within 4 inches of the ground, carefully dig a 2-foot-wide circle around each plant, pry up the clump of tubers with a spading fork, and shake off loose soil (wait to divide until planting in late winter or early spring). Label each clump by tying a plant tag around the stem, and dry the tubers in the sun for a few hours before storing. Dust with sulfur to prevent rot; store in a cool, dry place in boxes or bags filled with peat moss, vermiculite, or sand.

☐ FIGHT EROSION. If you garden on a slope, make sure you have enough plant material growing there to curb erosion if rains are heavy this winter. If the slope is bare or covered with young plants whose roots haven't yet knitted the soil together, sow seeds of wildflowers and a perennial California native grass such as blue wild rye (*Elymus glaucus*). Seeds are available by the pound from Peaceful Valley Farm Supply (888/784-1722 or www.groworganic.com).

PEST CONTROL

☐ SPRAY FRUIT TREES. After leaves fall, spray peach and nectarine trees with lime sulfur to control peach leaf curl. For brown rot on apricots, mark your calendar to spray with a fixed copper spray at bud swell in spring. (Both sprays are available at local nurseries and home improvement stores.) Apply controls on dry days when no rain is predicted for at least 36 hours. Cover the branches, stems, and trunk thoroughly. ◆

WHAT TO DO IN YOUR GARDEN IN NOVEMBER

PLANTING

☐ COOL-SEASON ANNUALS. Except in the mountains, there's still time to set out early-blooming annuals such as African daisy, calendula, Iceland poppy, ornamental cabbage, pansies, snapdragon, and stock. For shady areas, try cineraria, cyclamen, and English and fairy primroses.

☐ WILDFLOWERS. Before sowing flower seed, water planting areas well to encourage weeds to sprout, then hoe out emerging weeds. Broadcast seeds of baby blue eyes, California poppies, clarkias, flax, godetias, and other wildflowers in weed-free soil. Rake the area lightly to cover seeds with soil. Keep soil consistently moist until seed germinates.

☐ WINTER VEGETABLES. Early November is a great time to start cool-season crops in many areas. Zones 13 (low desert) and 14–24: Sow seeds of beets, carrots, onions, parsley, peas, radishes, Swiss chard, and turnips and set out transplants of broccoli, cabbage, and other cole crops. Coastal gardeners can also continue to plant lettuces and other leafy crops. In the foothills and Central Valley (zones 7–9 and 14), sow peas and spinach; plant garlic and onions.

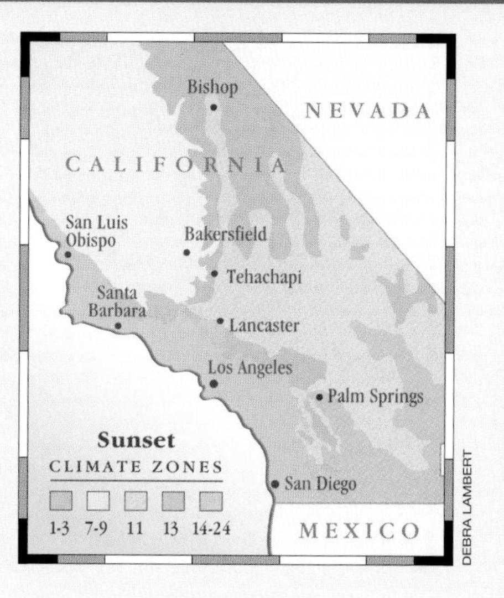

DEBRA LAMBERT

MAINTENANCE

☐ AMEND VEGETABLE BEDS. To ensure healthy, productive crops, condition your soil well before planting. Ralph Crane, who has taught home vegetable growing at the Arboretum of Los Angeles County for five years, recommends the following formula for new vegetable beds: For every 100 square feet of cultivated soil, spade in 10 pounds gypsum, ½ cubic yard compost, 6 pounds cottonseed meal, 2 pounds bonemeal, and ½ pound sulfate of potash. In subsequent years, reduce everything in the formula by half (except the compost) and add once a year.

☐ FIGHT EROSION. If you garden on a slope, make sure you have enough plant material in place to keep the hillside from eroding when winter rains are heavy. If your slope is bare or sparsely planted, consider sowing a mixture of fine fescues and wildflowers.

☐ OVERSEED BERMUDA. If you don't like the tawny look of dormant grass, overseed with annual rye. Mow the lawn short, scatter rye seed (1 pound per 100 square feet), cover it with top dressing, and water regularly until seed germinates.

☐ PRUNE BERRY PLANTS. On blackberry, boysenberry, and loganberry plants, cut old canes back to the ground. Keep the smooth-barked canes that grew this year; they'll bear fruit next year. Wait until December or January to cut back the canes of low-chill raspberries.

DISEASE CONTROL

☐ SPRAY FRUIT TREES. After the leaves have fallen, around Thanksgiving, spray peach and nectarine trees with lime sulfur or 50 percent fixed copper to control peach leaf curl, an airborne fungal disease. Rake up debris under trees before applying. Spray entire tree—trunk, branches, and twigs—as well as the ground underneath. Mark your calendar for two more treatments—around New Year's Day (the height of dormancy) and around Valentine's Day (just before bud break). ◆

WHAT TO DO IN YOUR GARDEN IN NOVEMBER

PLANTING

☐ COVER CROPS. After crops are harvested, spade several inches of manure into vegetable beds and sow a cover crop of white Dutch clover. Clover seeds will germinate when temperatures are cold. The plants will prevent soil erosion during the winter and add beneficial nutrients to the soil when they're tilled into beds next spring.

☐ PAPER WHITE NARCISSUS. Plant bulbs in a pot filled with horticultural sand or pebbles and store in a cool room (50° to 60°) until shoots emerge, then move the pot into a bright, cool window. Bulbs started by midmonth should bloom during the holidays.

☐ SPRING-BLOOMING BULBS. If you haven't set out hardy bulbs yet, get them into the ground immediately so they'll have a chance to develop roots before the soil freezes.

MAINTENANCE

☐ KEEP ON WATERING. Continue watering the landscape whenever soil is dry several inches beneath the surface. Don't forget to drain hoses and sprinklers after each use and store them indoors to avoid damage caused by freezing.

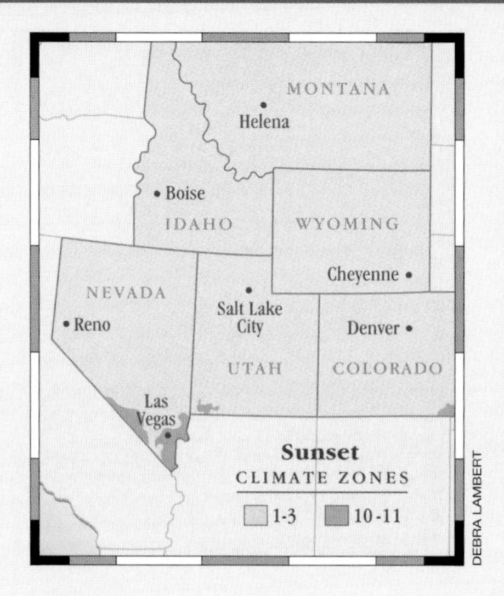

☐ MAINTAIN TOOLS. Sharpen blades of hoes, spades, and pruning shears, then wipe them with oil (machine oil for metal parts, linseed oil for handles) and store in a dry place for winter.

☐ PREPARE PLANTING BEDS. Before the ground freezes, till a 2- to 3-inch layer of composted steer manure or mushroom compost into planting beds. Leave the soil in large clumps; freezing and thawing will break them down, and the bed will be ready to plant as soon as the soil warms in spring.

☐ PREVENT WATER FEATURES FROM FREEZING. To prevent damage to fish and hardy water plants in ponds, use a stock tank heater (available from farm supply and feed stores) to prevent the water from freezing solid. Leaving a fountain or waterfall running prevents the water from freezing in all but the coldest weather.

☐ PROTECT YOUNG TREES. Trees with trunks less than 4 inches in diameter are vulnerable to sunscald, a damaging form of sunburn caused when the low winter sun shines on the tender bark. Paint the trunks with white latex, shield them with commercial tree wrap, or make a protective collar using corrugated plastic drainpipe (split it lengthwise and fit it around the trunk).

☐ SPREAD MULCH. If you haven't done so already, spread a 3- to 4-inch layer of organic mulch around half-hardy plants, on bulb beds, and under trees and shrubs. Shredded leaves, conifer boughs, or straw all work well as winter mulch.

☐ START A COMPOST PILE. Speed the composting process by grinding up plant waste before you toss it on the compost pile.

PEST CONTROL

☐ CONTROL INSECTS ON HOUSE PLANTS. If aphids, mites, or scale insects bother any of your house plants, slip a plastic clothing cover (the kind you get from a dry cleaner) over it, and then spray insecticidal soap on the leaves inside. The plastic tent will contain the spray. — *M.T.* ◆

WHAT TO DO IN YOUR GARDEN IN NOVEMBER

PLANTING

☐ ANNUALS. Zones 11–13 (Las Vegas, Tucson, Phoenix): Many colorful annuals thrive during the winter growing season. Set out plants of ageratum, aster, bells-of-Ireland, calendula, candytuft, coreopsis, dianthus, English daisy, foxglove, hollyhock, larkspur, lobelia, painted daisy, pansy, petunia, phlox, scabiosa, snapdragon, stock, and sweet alyssum. Sow seeds of clarkia, nasturtium, and sweet peas.

☐ PERENNIALS. Zones 10 (Albuquerque)–13: Through midmonth continue to plant perennials such as autumn sage (*Salvia greggii*), bush morning glory, globemallow (*Sphaeralcea* species), Mexican evening primrose (*Oenothera berlandieri*), Mexican honeysuckle (*Justicia spicigera*), penstemons, red justicia (*J. candicans*), and verbena.

☐ SHRUBS, TREES. Zones 10–13: Continue to plant frost-hardy and native woody shrubs and trees, including acacia, Apache plume, jojoba, mesquite, ocotillo, palo verde, Texas mountain laurel, and Texas ranger.

☐ SUCCULENTS. Zones 11–13: It's still a good time to set out cold-hardy or native succulents such as agave, desert spoon, and yucca. Water new plants once a week for the first month, gradually cutting back to once a month while weather is cool.

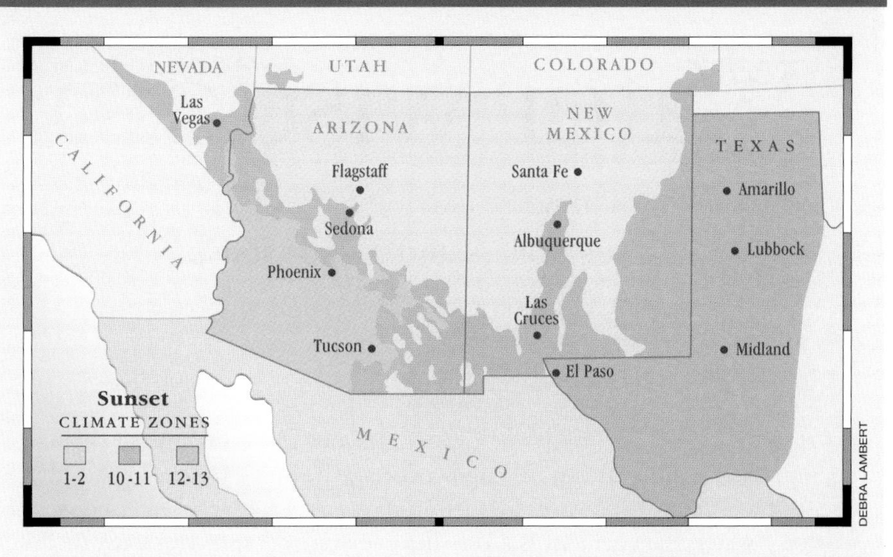

DEBRA LAMBERT

☐ VEGETABLES. Zones 11–13: Set out transplants of asparagus, broccoli, brussels sprouts, cabbage, and cauliflower. Continue to sow seeds of beets, carrots, lettuce, peas, radishes, spinach, Swiss chard, and turnips.

MAINTENANCE

☐ ADJUST IRRIGATION SCHEDULE. As temperatures fall, adjust irrigation controls to reduce watering frequency. For lawns, roses, and most ornamentals, water during daylight hours to avoid wet leaves at night (they provide ideal conditions for powdery mildew).

☐ CARE FOR ROSES. Zones 11–13: Continue to remove faded flowers, pruning lightly as you go. Give plants the last feeding of the year.

☐ CONTROL HOLLYHOCK WEEVILS. Zones 10–13: This weevil spends winter inside hollyhock seed heads, then lays eggs in emerging flower buds in spring. To reduce overwintering weevils, remove and discard all spent seed heads.

☐ PRUNE HERBS. Zones 11–13: This is a good time to do hard pruning on Mediterranean herbs (such as rosemary, sage, and thyme) that have become overgrown. Prune to the lowest new growth and remove all dead stems. Keep the plants well watered as they recover from pruning.

— *Mary Irish* ◆

Water wisdom

Managing garden irrigation saves dollars and makes sense

By Sharon Cohoon • Photographs by Bob Wigand

■ Contrary to common opinion, a water-efficient garden is not all cactus and decomposed granite. It can be English cottage, formal French, Italian Riviera, or Southwest chic. Even roses and tropicals are possible in a water-conserving garden. "Water management is a very flexible system," says Tim Barr, technical services coordinator for the Western Municipal Water District in Riverside, California. "You don't have to forgo thirsty plants. You just have to budget for them."

Getting the most out of your water allowance is a matter of following a few basic principles, says Barr. The garden of Nan and Bob Simonsen in Riverside is one of his favorite examples of these principles at work. Though the garden has been a stop on public garden tours regularly since 1997 and won first place in the individual category in the 1999 Water Efficiency Awards Contest, the Simonsens are relative newcomers to gardening, proving water-wise gardening is a learnable skill. "We visited the district's demonstration garden [Landscapes Southern California Style; see page 361] so frequently and took so many of their classes, I think we learned by osmosis," says Nan.

Nan's big indulgence is her rose garden. Though the roses need regular water, many plants here are moderate water users, including blue catmint (*Nepeta faassenii*) and Shasta daisies. Pea gravel walkways cover a large part of the space.

The Simonsens' property is quite large—2¼ acres. The thirstiest plants, including a lawn and rose garden, are confined to small areas close to the house, while plantings farther away thrive on much less water. A large slope drops down into a natural riparian area where Mediterranean plants grow. The slope on the other side of the riparian basin is planted entirely with California natives that, once established, will need little water beyond what nature provides.

Scrimping on the outlying areas saves irrigation money that can be spent on water for plantings near the house. *(Continued on page 360)*

Water management

LIMIT TURF. Turf grass is one of the thirstiest plants in our landscape. But that doesn't mean we have to eliminate it entirely. "There's really no satisfactory substitute," Barr says. Just limit turf to places where it serves a function, he says. On the Simonsens' property, only a tiny wedge near the front entrance has been planted with grass. "We put it in primarily for our dogs," Nan says, "but it also provides a cool welcome."

GROUP PLANTS WITH SIMILAR WATER NEEDS. From an irrigation standpoint, this approach makes perfect sense. If plants that need to be watered at the same frequency and for the same length of time are in the same place, you can dedicate a separate line or valve to them, delivering exactly the amount of water the plants need and no more. Plants such as rosemary, lavender, and pride of Madeira, which have adapted to rain-sparse Mediterranean climates, do best when they receive slow, deep, and not-too-frequent soaks. Forcing these plants to share the same irrigation valve with turf grass, which needs shallow and frequent watering, is not just wasteful, it shortens the lives of Mediterranean plants and can even kill them. Overwatering causes the demise of more plants than anything else.

Here's how the strategy plays out in the Simonsens' garden. Nan's biggest watering indulgence is her English flower garden near the house. The roses in this area are on a drip-irrigation system. However, the rest of this area, planted primarily with perennials and annuals, is watered with rotary-head sprinklers because this part of the garden changes significantly from season to season and year to year. "The flower garden is my area to experiment," says Nan. The English flower garden is watered twice a week during the hottest months.

The sunny hillside leading to the riparian habitat, which is planted with Mediterranean and other less-thirsty shrubs, trees, and perennials, is irrigated by impact-type sprinklers that put out water very slowly, minimizing runoff. Nan gives the plants about 1½ inches of water per irrigation period. During the hottest months, the area is watered once a week. When temperatures drop below 90°, the Simonsens stretch out the intervals between waterings.

The slope on the other side of the riparian area is only watered once a month—even in the worst summer heat. When the oaks and sycamores planted here mature, creating more shade, the slope will be self-sustaining and an irrigation system won't be necessary.

Mediterranean and native California plants create a sea of textures around the garden's perimeter. These include fountain grass, Mexican sage, New Zealand flax, and potted yucca (top) and variegated agave (above). In the small area devoted to thirsty flowers, 'Gertrude Jeykll' rose showers pink petals onto the ground (above right). In the larger area devoted to unthirsty plants, fountain grass arches over lavender and other gray-foliaged plants (below right).

"Though every garden is a little different, putting your thirstiest plants close to the house and using less and less water as you move away from it is a very sound approach," says Barr.

IRRIGATE EFFICIENTLY. Though drip-irrigation systems get all the press, they're not the best solution in every instance, says Barr. "You need to match the system to the situation, the soil, and the plants, as the Simonsens have done," he says. There are many factors to consider: drip-irrigation or underground systems, rotary or spray heads, output rates, and emitter sizes. Make your decisions based on research. Take advantage of the watering classes offered by your area water district. Talk to irrigation specialists, neighbors, and gardeners. Two booklets by *Sunset* can help. *Water-Wise Gardening for California* (16 pages) includes planting plans and plant lists. *How to Water Your Garden* (16 pages) explains options in watering systems and devices. To order, send $3.50 per copy to Sunset Water Booklets, 80 Willow Road, Menlo Park, CA 94025.

PLANT TREES. Plants under trees need less water because the shade lowers air and soil temperatures, reducing moisture loss. (People are also cooler under these leafy canopies.) Properly placed trees can reduce air-conditioning costs up to 40 percent, according to Southern California Edison. Yet, surprisingly, shade-tree planting is one of the most neglected water-conservation techniques. Not at the Simonsens': They surrounded their back patio with trees. (Western and southern exposures, like those here, particularly benefit.) The Simonsens added trees to their native and Mediterranean slopes. As the trees mature and shade more of the property, the Simonsens' irrigation usage will continue to decline.

IMPROVE SOIL; ADD MULCH. The Simonsens do both. Adding organic amendments to the soil improves its texture, enabling it to make better use of water. Giving soil a 3- to 5-inch layer of mulch helps conserve water by reducing water evaporation.

Though these principles were all new concepts to the Simonsens just a few years ago, now they're second nature. Practicing water-efficient gardening has taught them to be more successful gardeners, Nan says. Both Simonsens are now trained master gardeners with the University of California Cooperative Extension, and Nan teaches classes in gardening basics with an emphasis on wise water use through Riverside Community College.

Landscapes Southern California Style is a 1-acre site that demonstrates water-wise gardening. *10–4 daily; free. 450 Alessandro Blvd., Riverside, CA; (909) 780-4177.* ◆

More water wisdom

Unthirsty plants helped this Central Valley gardener save irrigation dollars

By Lance Walheim • Photographs by Norm Plate

■ Style and practicality determined the design of this water-conserving garden in Clovis, California. For owner Claudia Kus, the distinctively Southwestern house style suggested a less thirsty garden to match. But the real issues—a costly water supply, serious soil problems, and the hot, dry summers of the San Joaquin Valley—were the clinchers. As in many areas of Northern California, water is precious—a limited commodity. Kus needed to manage carefully the available water.

When she began to landscape her 3-acre property in the 1990s, she opted for good-looking plants that don't need a lot of water once established. In the front yard, she planted drought-tolerant shrubs and

In the front garden (right), fountain grass is accompanied by Santa Barbara daisy, blanket flower, and penstemon. White gaura, rosemary, and yellow santolina grow behind. The backyard fountain (above) is surrounded by olive trees, redbuds, spice bush, and grasses.

10528

flowering perennials. Throughout the property, Kus planted trees to create cooling shade—Australian melaleucas, chitalpa, cork oak, desert willow, hackberry, and shoestring acacia among them. Near a fountain in the back garden, she planted acacia, chitalpa, and redbud. Grapevines ramble over an arbor around the back patio.

These practical solutions to a hot, sunny site turned out beautifully, as the photos on these pages show.

Beautiful blooms start with good soil

Before the landscaping began, a cementlike hardpan (an impervious layer of compacted soil) underlay much of the property. To make matters worse, a natural creek that ran through the property in winter was blocked so that it no longer drained. Instead of trying to break through the hardpan, Kus brought in 80 tons of topsoil, which she amended with homemade compost. In the backyard, she sculpted this new soil into curving mounds. Gravel paths between the mounds cover perforated pipes that carry away the excess water to a partially manmade pond in front of the house. (Pipes are buried 2 feet deep in trenches.)

Choice plants from California and Australia

Three local nurseries helped Kus create an eclectic but stunningly beautiful mix of mostly drought-resistant plants. She worked with Planet Earth Growers in Fresno, which specializes in California and Australian natives, Intermountain Nursery in Prather, which specializes in native California plants, and Mountain Valley Growers in Squaw Valley, supplier of herbs. Kus kept plants that need more water, such as Japanese anemone and iris, closer to the house for an oasis effect.

More than 600 different species and varieties of plants now grow in this garden. Among the showiest are acacia, grevillea, melaleuca, olive tree, rosemary, and California natives such as ceanothus, manzanita, Matilija poppy, redbud, toyon, and four species of oak. There are native wildflowers, which reseed each year, a multitude of flowering perennials (including a diverse selection of salvias), and roses, ornamental grasses, and fruit trees.

Water-saving strategies

To manage the little water available, Kus has an elaborate drip-irrigation system that includes more than 1,000 emitters and microsprinklers, operated by 21 valves and 2 automatic controllers. Among the many features of these

LEFT: Purple spikes of *Salvia leucantha* rise between mounds of yellow-flowered marguerites.
ABOVE: Blanket flowers edge this island bed in front of the house; a big-leafed verbascum and other unthirsty plants grow behind.

state-of-the-art controllers is one that allows watering times to be easily adjusted to weather or water supply.

As automated as the irrigation system is, it still needs regular maintenance to deliver water efficiently. Cleaning emitters and repairing damage caused by rabbits and coyotes is a constant chore, but to Kus, it's well worth the effort. All beds are mulched with chunks of redwood bark.

Water management

LIMIT TURF. Turf grass needs more water than just about any other plant in our gardens. But none grows here—just flowering ground covers such as Santa Barbara daisies.

GROUP PLANTS WITH SIMILAR WATER NEEDS. From an irrigation standpoint, this approach makes perfect sense. If plants that need to be watered at the same frequency and for the same length of time are all in one place, you can dedicate a separate line or valve to them, delivering exactly the amount of water the plants need and no more. Plants like gaillardia, *Pennisetum setaceum* 'Rubrum', and penstemons, which have adapted to rain-sparse Mediterranean climates, do best when they receive slow, deep, and not-too-frequent soaks.

IRRIGATE EFFICIENTLY. Drip-irrigation systems get all the press, but they're not the best solution in every instance. Match the system to the situation, the soil, and the plants. There are many factors to consider: drip-irrigation or underground systems, rotary or spray heads, output rates, and emitter sizes. Make your decisions based on research. Take advantage of the watering classes offered by your area water district. Talk to irrigation specialists, neighbors, and gardeners. Two booklets by *Sunset* can help. *Water-Wise Gardening for California* (16 pages) includes planting plans and plant lists. *How to Water Your Garden* (16 pages) explains options in watering systems and devices. To order, send $3.50 per copy to Sunset Water Booklets, 80 Willow Road, Menlo Park, CA 94025.

PLANT TREES. Plants under trees need less water because the shade lowers air and soil temperatures, reducing moisture loss. People are also cooler under those leafy canopies. Properly placed trees can reduce air-conditioning costs up to 40 percent, according to Southern California Edison. Yet, surprisingly, shade-tree planting is one of the most neglected water-conservation techniques. Not at Kus's: Shade trees grow everywhere.

IMPROVE SOIL AND ADD MULCH. Adding organic amendments to the soil improves its texture, enabling it to make better use of water: Sandy soils hold more water, and clay soils drain better. Giving soil a 3- to 5-inch layer of mulch helps conserve water by reducing water evaporation.

— Sharon Cohoon ◆

Rock gardening

Grow gemlike plants in jewel-box gardens

By Jim McCausland • Photographs by Janet Loughrey

■ A classic rock garden has the visual quality of a jewel box, with tier upon tier of delicate plants sparkling like gems among the rocks.

Historically, rock gardening was the province of serious plant collectors (particularly English gardeners) who gathered rare plants from the world's alpine zones and grew them in greenhouses or rockeries. More recently, however, the definition of rock gardening as it is practiced by American gardeners has expanded to embrace not only the decorative use of natural stone in the garden but also "the cultivation of rock plants in any garden setting, with or without rocks," according to garden writer and landscape designer George Schenk.

LEFT: In Ernie and Marietta O'Byrne's garden, spring-blooming plants include rose pink *Armeria maritima* (front right).
TOP: A lupine native to Oregon, *Lupinus albifrons collinus,* blooms in Phyllis Gustafson's garden.

The definition of rock plants has also evolved. Once the term referred to wild plants, usually less than a foot in height, which most often grow in rock crevices. Now it may refer to virtually any plant a gardener wants to grow in a rock garden. The size range of rock plants has changed, encompassing taller species as they have been discovered, notes Baldassare Mineo in *Rock Garden Plants* (Timber Press, Portland, 1999; $59.95; 800/327-5680).

On these pages, we present a gallery of contemporary Western rock gardens and a sampler of rock plants. *(Continued on page 368)*

Elements of a rock garden

Site. In their natural habitats, many rock plants grow in exposed locations, so they will thrive in a site that gets full sun, especially near the coast. Most also grow well in a spot that gets filtered afternoon shade from high-branching trees.

Rock gardens don't need to be large to be effective. In fact, you can enjoy growing rock plants in a few square feet of ground or in containers as small as sinks, like the one shown on the facing page.

Rock. Rock itself is the main element, tying everything together visually and contrasting perfectly with the living detail of plants. Some of the best rock gardens mimic natural outcroppings. In most rock gardens, stone makes up 10 to 40 percent of the visible landscape. Rocks should be of different sizes of just one type of stone.

When Kathy Allen of Central Point, Oregon, created the rock garden shown above right, she first prepared a 2½-foot mound of soil, then dug rocks into place before planting. She buried about two-thirds of each rock and left the top showing. Her garden looks natural, and plants love it.

In so-called crevice gardens, where plants are tucked into crevices between adjacent rocks, stone makes up an even larger proportion of the landscape. When rocks or boulders are very large, as in Mineo's crevice garden in Medford, Oregon (top),

TOP: Dwarf mugho pines form the dark evergreen spine of Baldassare Mineo's crevice rock garden, designed by Josef Halda. ABOVE: Abloom in Kathy Allen's garden are violet *Campanula saxifraga* (left) and drifts of pink *Dianthus freynii* and *Aethionema pulchellum* (right).

soil is filled in as the rocks are placed, then plants are arranged.

When you set rocks in place, arrange their exposed surfaces so they form patterns. The faces of flat-sided rocks should lie in parallel planes; major crevices should be parallel so they resemble natural faults.

Plants. Evergreen plants, including dwarf conifers such as hemlocks, junipers, pines, and spruces, can form a backbone to anchor the design of a rock garden. For example, when Czech designer Josef Halda created Mineo's crevice garden, he planted several dwarf mugho pines (*Pinus mugo mugo*). Over time, as the pines encroached on rock plants, Mineo has removed about half of the trees.

As for rock plants themselves, there are thousands of perennials and small shrubs to choose from, including a host of dianthus, saxifrages, sedums, and sempervivums. Most of these hardy plants bloom in spring.

Soil. Horticulturists who hike above the timberline have noticed a remarkable phenomenon: Some of the most delicate and beautiful wildflowers grow in exposed scree. Such gems would quickly die if transplanted into normal garden soil, but they can flourish in a fast-draining mix formulated for rock gardens.

In Kathy Allen's garden, for example, the native soil is very heavy, so she covered it with an 8-inch layer of topsoil first, then topped that with a 2- to 3-foot layer of rock garden mix consisting of equal parts topsoil, crushed rock, sand, and compost. Many plants, especially alpines and Western natives like penstemons, need an even lighter mix (for these, Allen uses 1 part each sand, ½-inch bits of rock, and compost).

Such fast-draining mixes allow you to water rock plants during the hot summer months without causing constantly wet soil conditions, which lead to root rot and death. Drainage is further enhanced by mounded plantings.

Water. Water adds a natural complement to stone. That's why many rock gardeners include water features such as streams, waterfalls, ponds, or dish rocks—boulders with bowl-like depressions that collect rainwater. Keep in mind, though, that most rock plants can't stand too much water—make sure the water is well contained and doesn't soak the soil.

A container rock garden

Faux-stone containers formed from a mixture called *hypertufa* resemble sinks and water troughs popularized by English gardeners. Filled with a fast-draining soil mix, hypertufa containers make it possible to grow rock plants anywhere, even if you lack the space for a garden. Ernie and Marietta O'Byrne of Eugene, Oregon, make hypertufa troughs like the one above by mixing 3 parts peat moss, 3 parts perlite, 2 parts portland cement, and enough water to hold the ingredients together when molded by hand. They form this mixture into a trough with 2-inch-thick walls and drainage holes in the bottom. When the mixture dries, they rough up the hypertufa with a wire brush to mimic the look of natural stone.

Resources

For more information, check out the North American Rock Garden Society website, www.nargs.org. For a $25 annual fee, members receive *Rock Garden Quarterly,* access to the society's seed exchange and the Pennsylvania Horticultural Society's lending library, and connections to fellow enthusiasts. To join, send your check to Box 67, Millwood, NY 10546.

Well-stocked retail nurseries usually carry a standard selection of basic rock garden plants. Specialists, including the following mail-order sources, offer a much larger selection.

Mt. Tahoma Nursery. Classic alpine plants and new ones imported mostly from England. Catalog $2. *28111 112th Ave. E, Graham, WA 98338; (253) 847-9827 or www.backyardgardener.com/mttahoma.*

Porterhowse Farms. Extensive selection of dwarf conifers, plus some companion plants like saxifrages, sedums, and sempervivums. Free list. *41370 S.E. Thomas Rd., Sandy, OR 97055; (503) 668-5834 or www.porterhowse.com.*

Siskiyou Rare Plant Nursery. At any one time, offers about 1,000 plant species for the rock garden, including dwarf conifers. Catalog $3. *2825 Cummings Rd., Medford, OR 97501; (541) 772-6846 or www.wave.net/upg/srpn.*

Squaw Mountain Gardens. A comprehensive list of sedums and sempervivums. Catalog $2. *Box 946, Estacada, OR 97023; (503) 630-5458 or www.squawmountaingardens.com.*

Sunscapes Rare Plant Nursery. Heat- and drought-tolerant rock plants. Catalog $2. *330 Carlile Ave., Pueblo, CO 81004; (719) 546-0047 or www.sunscapes.net.* ◆

Magnificent minis

Miniature roses are beautiful, versatile, and once again, prizewinners

By Ruth Bird

Strolling along the aisles of my favorite nurseries or lost in the pages of a plant catalog, I know there are hidden forces at work—reasons why I gravitate toward certain plants out of all the ones available.

Scent, for one thing. The perfume of a damask rose instantly transports me across the years to my grandmother's garden. I love the way a vase of fragrant roses can transform a room. Roses lead the parade, the standard-bearers of scent. And close behind are the diminutive members of their court—the miniatures.

I am as fascinated by miniature roses as I am by a magician's sleight of hand. They're perfect scale models of their full-size counterparts, with small flowers, small leaves, and small stature (ranging from 6 inches to 2 feet tall). The only real difference between miniatures and regular roses is that miniatures are not divided into groups such as hybrid tea, floribunda, or rugosa. A world of varieties, with different flower colors and forms, falls under one simple classification: miniature.

Now, for the first time since 1993, a miniature has won the prestigious All-America Rose Selections for 2001. 'Sun Sprinkles' (see the facing page) has elegant buds that open to lovely 2-inch fully double, bright buttery yellow blooms that give off a spicy, slightly musky fragrance. Foliage is glossy green. Hybridized by John Walden and introduced by Bear Creek Gardens/Jackson & Perkins, the plant grows to 24 inches tall and blooms repeatedly throughout the season.

Miniatures are often given in lieu of cut flowers, not necessarily with the expectation that they will be planted in the garden. (Because they're so charming and easy, though, most gardeners opt to plant them out.) With the holidays fast upon us, you might consider giving these little charmers as gifts for your hosts. Or you could arrange them among some poinsettias.

Planting and care

Miniature roses have exactly the same needs as standard roses—fast-draining and slightly acid soil, full sun, and regular watering and feeding. Once established, they should be pruned once a year in early spring after the last hard frost; cut strong, healthy canes to about one-third their original length.

Where to plant

While young miniature roses are sometimes displayed indoors in sunny windows, these plants are at their best outdoors. They do well in border fronts and nestled in small beds. I have planted them with sweet peas in a bed surrounding a birdbath. Miniature roses also thrive in containers and window boxes; pair them with herbs or nasturtiums.

Right now, 'Sweet Chariot' perfumes my room, its delicious scent drifting in through the window from a planter box on my balcony. I can see its long sprays of polyantha-type magenta roses cascading nicely over the railing.

Today there are many varieties, one for every spot in your garden. Some favorites are listed on the next page. Don't settle for what is most readily available; dig a little deeper, and you'll find varieties that will have real presence in your garden. But be careful—minis are seductive. I'll bet you won't want to plant just one.

Choice miniature roses

Letters following each listing refer to sources listed below.

APRICOT, CINNAMON

'Cinnamon Delight'. A charming pink-brown with a strong fragrance; a similar one is 'Julia's Rose'. I plant these beautiful brownish roses with my lavenders. PT

'Loving Touch'. Lovely long apricot buds and flowers. PT, SN

'Savannah Miss'. A very fragrant apricot with double blooms on long stems. PT

LAVENDER, PURPLE

'Angel Darling'. Pointed buds that open to 10 wavy lavender petals. Unscented. JMR, PT

'Lavender Crystal'. Chinese peony–like petals and unfading clear lilac color. SN

'Sweet Chariot'. Clusters of fragrant purple blooms on trailing plant. JMR, PT, RN, SN

'Sun Sprinkles'

RED, PINK

'Baby Cécile Brunner'. An older miniature. Pink buds open to pale pink blooms. SN

'Cherry Hi'. Red double blooms hold well in hot weather. SN

'Chick A Dee'. Pure pink blooms with an occasional white stripe or two; blooms almost constantly. PT, SN

'Dresden Doll'. Scentless, very mossy buds open to perfect little cup-shaped shell pink blooms. PT, SN

'Renny'. Unique, old-fashioned flowers in a dark, dusty pink. Fragrant. PT, SN

WHITE, CREAM, YELLOW

'Cal Poly'. Blazing yellow blooms. RN, SN

'Popcorn'. A dainty, honey-scented white rose with yellow stamens and delicate foliage. PT, SN

'Rise 'n' shine'. Bright clear yellow flowers. SN

BICOLORS

'Magic Carrousel'. Well-formed buds open to white blooms with red edges. SN

'Rose Gilardi'. Mossy buds open to apple-scented flowers striped with pink and red. SN, UR

'Splish Splash'. Fragrant, porcelain pink petals blended with yellow. SN

Where to buy miniatures

Miniature roses are available year-round at florists and garden centers, and in floral departments of grocery stores. For the best selection of named varieties, order starts from specialists such as these listed below. 'Sun Sprinkles' is available from catalog sources, retailers, and through the All-America Rose Selections website, www.rose.org.

Justice Miniature Roses (JMR), Wilsonville, OR; (503) 682-2370.

Pixie Treasures Miniature Rose Nursery (PT), Yorba Linda, CA; (714) 993-6780.

Regan Nursery (RN), Fremont, CA; (510) 797-3222 or www.regannursery.com.

Sequoia Nursery (SN), Visalia, CA; (559) 732-0309 or www.miniatureroses.com.

Uncommon Rose (UR), Corvallis, OR; (541) 753-8871 or www.uncommonrose.com.

FAR LEFT: ALL-AMERICA ROSE SELECTIONS LEFT: CAROLYN SUPINGER

Meet Ralph S. Moore, miniature-rose hybridizer

California nurseryman Ralph Moore, 93, is often called the father of modern miniature roses. "He's the most innovative of American breeders," says Tom Carruth of Weeks Roses in Upland, California. Moore's miniatures have received 20 American Rose Society Awards of Excellence and have earned him the famous Dean Hole Medal of Great Britain's Royal National Rose Society.

For 65 years, Moore has devoted much of his time to creating miniature roses at his Sequoia Nursery in Visalia, California. "When I started," he says, "you could count the number of miniature roses on one hand." Since then, he's introduced more than 300 miniature varieties; 75 percent of all miniature roses have a Moore rose in their breeding background.

The first striped miniature rose and the introduction of moss characteristics (mosslike growth on the stems and buds) into repeat-blooming miniatures are among his most important achievements.

What's his favorite? "One I haven't developed yet, because it will be perfect and have no flaws," he modestly explains. Others might point to 'Rise 'n' Shine', considered the best yellow miniature, and award-winning 'Magic Carrousel'. — *Lauren Bonar Swezey* ◆

Prime time for native desert shrubs

They're perfectly suited to Southwest gardens, and this is planting season

By Mary Irish

CHARLES MANN FAR LEFT: RICHARD SHIELL

Baja fairy duster (left) bears puffy flowers 1½ inches across. Texas ranger (above) has rose pink flowers that stand out against silvery leaves.

Shrubs native to the Chihuahuan, Mojave, and Sonoran deserts are naturally adapted to the Southwest's aridity, summer heat, and soil conditions. Many such indigenous shrubs are valuable in home gardens and unrivaled at attracting birds and other wildlife. Several of the most worthy shrubs are listed below; they are evergreen plants except as noted. Shop for them at nurseries with good native plant selections.

Late fall is the ideal time to plant these shrubs in the Southwest deserts (*Sunset* climate zones 10–13). Cool fall and winter temperatures encourage newly set-out plants to develop roots and get established before hot weather arrives.

■ BAJA FAIRY DUSTER (*Calliandra californica*) grows to 4 feet tall and 4 feet wide, with an open habit. Brilliant red flowers occur year-round and attract hummingbirds. The leaves are composed of small dark green leaflets. Baja fairy duster is useful in very hot locations, even in the low desert (zone 13), as an accent, or in mixed plantings. Hardy to at least 25°.

■ BERBERIS: **Red barberry** (*B. haematocarpa*) reaches 5 feet tall with an equal width, bearing dark green hollylike leaves on stiff branches. Fragrant, bright yellow flowers in spring are followed by abundant red fruits that birds find irresistible. It's an excellent choice for a hedge or screen. Cold-hardy. **Agarita** (*B. trifoliata*) is a larger shrub, up to 6 feet tall and 4 to 6 feet wide, that also bears yellow flowers and red fruit. Hardy to 15°.

■ CORDIA: These are hardy to about 15°. **Texas olive** (*C. boissieri*) is a large shrub, 12 to 15 feet tall and 15 to 20 feet wide. Its oval leaves are gray-green on top and nearly silver on the bottom. Clusters of 1- to 2-inch papery white flowers appear in spring and continue over a long season. This plant can be trained as a small tree or pruned as a low shrub. It does best when watered deeply every two to three weeks during summer in low-desert elevations. **Littleleaf cordia** (*C. parvifolia*), a smaller species native to Baja California, reaches 6 to 8 feet tall and 8 feet wide. It bears tiny gray-green leaves and small white flowers from winter to late fall, and it blooms even during the hottest summer months.

■ CREOSOTE BUSH (*Larrea tridentata*), native throughout the Southwest, grows in an open form, reaching 4 to 8 feet tall and 6 to 8 feet wide. In spring, the plant is covered by yellow flowers, followed by small hairy fruit that birds relish. Its tiny dark green leaves are sticky. The foliage turns bright yellow when soil moisture is reduced, and the plant may lose up to 75 percent of its leaves during a drought. Creosote bush is effective in mass plantings, as a privacy screen, and in mixed plantings of native perennials and wildflowers. Hardy to at least 10°.

■ DALEA: All daleas have tiny leaflets that range from dark green to gray-green, often with a hint of silver. They work well as accent plants, as informal hedges, and in mixed plantings. They are hardy to 0°. **Black dalea** (*D. frutescens*), found from western Texas to deep into Mexico, reaches 3 feet tall and 4 feet wide, bearing round clusters of tiny purple flowers in spring and fall. **Indigo bush** (*D. pulchra*), a larger relative, grows up to 5 feet tall and 5 feet wide, bearing rose-magenta flowers in spring. **Wislizenus dalea** (*D. versicolor*) grows to 4 feet tall and 4 feet wide and bears elongated rose-purple flower spikes in winter.

■ HOP BUSH (*Dodonaea viscosa*) reaches 10 feet tall and 6 feet wide, with dense, willowlike leaves. The form native to Arizona has deep green foliage; two purple-leafed varieties are 'Purpurea' and 'Saratoga'. Small, barely noticeable flowers precede attractive, pinkish orange papery seeds. This fast-growing shrub makes a fine hedge or privacy screen. Hardy to 15°.

■ JOJOBA (*Simmondsia chinensis*) has a spreading habit, growing 6 feet tall and 6 to 10 feet wide, with leathery gray-green leaves on rigid branches. The female plants' inconspicuous flowers develop into edible acornlike fruit. Early settlers ground them as a coffee substitute, and jojoba oil is still used in cosmetics. Jojoba works well as a hedge or screen that can be formally pruned. Hardy to 15° when established.

■ LEUCOPHYLLUM: These plants are hardy to 5° to 10°. Poorly drained soils or overwatering in summer could result in root rot. **Chihuahuan sage** (*L. laevigatum*), native to northern Mexico, grows 4 feet tall and 5 feet wide, with an open branching pattern, medium green leaves, and blue-purple flowers in summer. It is useful in hedges and informal mixed plantings. **Texas ranger** (*L. frutescens*), a Chihuahuan Desert native, grows 6 to 8 feet tall and up to 8 feet wide, bearing light green to silvery green foliage and fragrant, pale lavender to rose pink flowers in summer. The variety 'Compactum' is smaller (3 to 4 feet tall) and more dense; 'Green Cloud' has dark green foliage and deep magenta flowers; 'White Cloud' has silvery foliage and white flowers. **Violet silverleaf** (*L. candidum*), as the name suggests, bears silvery to white leaves and, in late summer, bell-shaped violet flowers. Plants grow to 4 feet tall and 4 feet wide. 'Silver Cloud' has very white foliage; 'Thundercloud' is smaller (3 to 4 feet tall) with tightly packed flowers. All selections work well in mass plantings, as hedges, and in mixed plantings.

RICHARD SHIELL

Texas mountain laurel dangles flowers in 4- to 8-inch-long clusters.

■ MEXICAN BUCKEYE (*Ungnadia speciosa*) is a deciduous shrub or small tree that can reach 15 feet tall and nearly as wide, but rarely grows that large in the low desert. Its deep green compound leaves are more than 3 inches long. Small pink flowers in spring precede woody, light brown fruits resembling those of the buckeye tree. The shrub can be used as a background planting, as an informal hedge, or trained as a tree to provide a shady accent to a small patio. Hardy to about 5°.

■ TEXAS MOUNTAIN LAUREL (*Sophora secundiflora*), also known as mescal bean, grows slowly to 15 feet tall and 10 feet wide. Glossy dark green leaves are composed of rounded leaflets (a gray-leafed form is called 'Silver Peso'). In early spring, large clusters of purple flowers exude a grape soda aroma. The flowers are followed by silvery gray pods filled with poisonous seeds; gardeners with children or pets should clip off pods before seeds mature. It can be trained as a small tree for a patio; untrained it makes a good screen. Hardy to about 10°.

■ WOOLLY BUTTERFLY BUSH (*Buddleia marrubiifolia*) grows to 5 feet tall and 5 feet wide, bearing velvety silver-green foliage and rounded orange flower heads through the summer. This species is most useful in mixed plantings or informal hedges. Plant it near a patio or pool so you can watch butterflies flit among the flowers. Hardy to 15°. ◆

Planting tips

Dig the planting hole at least three times as wide as and equal to the depth of the plant's rootball. If caliche is present, break through the layer with a digging bar or pickax. Generally, native shrubs do not need organic soil amendments. Slide the plant out of its nursery container and brush away enough soil from the rootball to gently loosen roots. Set the plant in the ground so that its soil line is level with the top of the hole. Use backfill soil to refill the hole halfway, then lightly press the soil around the roots, and continue filling to the top. Firm the soil around the plant, and water thoroughly to soak the rootball. If mulching the soil surface to help conserve moisture, don't let the mulch touch the trunk or stems.

One stage, two stars

The flower bed stays the same, but the bulbs change

By Lauren Bonar Swezey

For sheer drama, few plants can compete with spring-blooming bulbs. Starting early in the season, straight green stems of daffodils and tulips shoot up like magic from the ground. Then the flowers unfurl.

As sweet as the show is, it's all too fleeting. Within a week or two, the flowers fade and shrivel, then the green, strappy leaves carry on for a few more weeks to help nourish the bulbs for next year's encore.

But there's an easy way to keep the beds pretty: "drop-in" bulb shows. Instead of planting bulbs directly in the ground this fall, plant early, midseason, and late bloomers in 1-gallon nursery cans or 8-inch plastic pots, then slip them into the ground when they bloom.

ABOVE: In early spring, pots of King Alfred daffodils enhance this little bed of blue violas, fringed with white sweet alyssum. RIGHT: After daffodils fade, they're replaced with pots of deep pink tulips, giving the bed a whole new look.

Getting started

■ Paper white narcissus bloom first. Then come daffodils and tulips. Pick bulb colors that complement a border's color scheme. For instance, in a bed of blue and white violas, you might try a succession of bloom from paper whites to white and apricot-pink 'Salome' daffodils, then pink 'Esther' and double white 'Mount Tacoma' tulips. If the bulb pots are going into an annual bed, plant the flowers first, leaving room between them to randomly space the pots. Hold the holes open with empty containers. Before bulb season, you can drop in other seasonal color, such as potted chrysanthemums.

TIPS

- Plant one bulb variety per pot or mix colors.
- For daffodils and other large bulbs, put three bulbs in some containers and five in others, so the final planting arrangement doesn't look too uniform.
- Plant a half-dozen or more pots of each variety, depending on the size of your bed.
- Cover large bulbs with 4 to 5 inches of soil, small bulbs with 3 inches. Add mulch; keep moist but not soggy.

NORMAN A. PLATE (2)

NORMAN A. PLATE

NOTHING SAYS "WELCOME" like an elegant wreath you've made yourself. Step-by-step instructions for the beauty shown here and four others begin on page 390.

December

Baubles and boughs

A nonelectric way to light up the garden

■ Outdoor Christmas decorating usually begins and ends with colored lights. Garden designer Laurie Connable decorates her garden to shine in daylight. She begins by securing shiny globes to her deciduous trees. "A bare-limbed tree hung with big, bright balls is a festive surprise," she says. "It looks great from indoors and is so unusual it draws guests out into the garden." To duplicate the look, buy plastic globes that won't break in windy weather and select a size considerably larger than you'd use indoors—"they'll disappear otherwise." According to Connable, red and gold are the most effective colors. Plastic globes are available at florists' suppliers and retailers such as Target.

JEFF LANCASTER RIGHT: STEVEN GUNTHER

Laurie Connable and friends attach red ribbon to pinecones. At right, a sycamore comes alive with glittering gold balls.

Connable doesn't stop there, though. She gilds the whole garden and makes a party out of the process. She invites her creative friends like floral designer Sissy MacAllister. Providing them with plenty of ribbons, greens, and other materials, Connable gives her guests free rein. Last year, they dressed up bare tulip magnolias with strings of beads, suspended a necklace of red cookie cutters above her garden swing, hung gilded pinecones from her pine tree, and trimmed the garden's entry arch with evergreens, clusters of pyracantha berries, and seeded eucalyptus. Everyone thought the garden-trimming party was so much fun, says Connable, she's making it a holiday tradition.

— *Sharon Cohoon*

NORMAN A. PLATE

A blooming dilemma

■ 'Winter Rose', a poinsettia with downward-curving petals, looks so much like a rose, you might be tempted to cut it and use it in holiday bouquets. Feel free. The flowers (actually colored leaves, or bracts) have a very long vase life. "They'll last up to four weeks," says Laurie Scullin of Paul Ecke Ranch, the company that introduced the cultivar. There's only one problem. 'Winter Rose' lasts even longer as a flowering container plant—it's been reported to look great for six months. So how to use the plant is a dilemma, but a rather nice one.

If you do use 'Winter Rose' as a cut flower, dip the stems in water after cutting to wash off any residue of milky sap. "That will keep the vase water from turning cloudy," says Scullin. (There's no need to burn the stems first, as you must with other cut flowers in the euphorbia family.) Some people find the sap irritating, so wash off any that comes in contact with your skin.

In addition to 'Winter Rose' red, there are now two other cultivars on the market: 'Winter Rose' white (not shown) and 'Winter Rose' pink. The original red cultivar is now widely distributed and should be easy to find; supply of the white and pink cultivars is more limited. — *S.C.*

Foxy garden gloves

■ They may look like something you'd wear with a string of pearls and a vintage gown, but Foxgloves are made for serious gardening. They're an especially good choice for gardeners who start the day gloved but always end up bare-handed. You won't peel off Foxgloves to perform a delicate operation like transplanting annuals, as you're used to, because you'll forget you're wearing them. The Supplex/Lycra fabric is extremely supple, nicely snug, and comfortingly supportive.

The gloves are available in two sizes (medium and large) and in four colors (compost, iris, moss, and periwinkle). The large gloves are designed especially for men. *$25. (888) 322-4450 or www.foxglovesinc.com. — S.C.*

THOMAS J. STORY

BOOKSHELF

■ *Landscape Plants for Dry Regions* (Fisher Books, Tucson, 2000; $39.95; 520/744-6110 or www.fisherbooks.com) is an excellent new reference book for desert gardeners. Authors Warren Jones and Charles Sacamano, both former professors at the University of Arizona and experts in Southwest horticulture, chose 600 of the best landscaping plants for the desert. Their detailed text covers all the criteria—hardiness, ultimate size, landscaping uses, cultural requirements, potential problems—you need to consider when deciding whether a particular plant is the right choice for your garden. A plant atlas fills most of the book, but many of the photos look fuzzy and washed out, as if they were shot at high noon on a summer day. — *S.C.*

Quick guide to gift plants

Many can live happily after the holidays

■ 'Tis the season when indoor display tables at garden centers and nurseries are decked with gift plants bearing colorful flowers, fruits, or foliage. Here's a rundown on the most common gift plants and how to maintain them indoors after the holidays.

Bulbs. Amaryllis, florists' cyclamen, and paper white narcissus are forced into bloom for the holidays. You can grow these bulbs indoors indefinitely, although they may not bloom at Christmastime again like they did this year.

For amaryllis, allow the bulbs to dry out from mid-August through mid-November, then water and feed to promote bloom.

For cyclamen, which grow from tuberous roots, cut back on watering after they finish flowering. When leaves die, stop watering completely and put the plant in a cool (65°) place for about three months, then water and feed.

For paper white narcissus, let the bulbs dry out from the time the leaves die back in spring through early fall, then start watering and feeding.

Cactus. Christmas cactus will grow for decades with only moderate light. To get bloom at Christmas again, keep the plant in an indoor area where it will be cool (50° to 55°) and will get 12 to 14 hours of darkness during November.

Flowering plants. Azaleas and kalanchoes can live and bloom indoors for years if given bright light and normal care.

After florists' chrysanthemums finish blooming, keep them in a frost-free place to transplant into the garden when the ground warms up.

Ornamental fruits. Jerusalem cherries and ornamental peppers are tender tropical plants. When they start looking shabby, consign them to the trash.

Poinsettias. After they start shedding flowerlike bracts and leaves, discard them. —*Jim McCausland*

BEN WOOLSEY

Azaleas (front) and other gift plants fill Watson's Greenhouses in Puyallup, Washington.

Manchurian ash is a hardy beauty

■ Mention an ash and most people think of a large, spreading tree. However, the Manchurian or mancana ash (*Fraxinus mandshurica* 'Mancana') is an ideal candidate for smaller yards, parking strips, or any area where a tree with a lush crown is desired but there isn't room for a big canopy.

Native to northeast Asia, the tree eventually grows to about 45 feet tall and about 25 feet wide. Its upward-arching branches are so strong and stout that they shrug off the heaviest snows and most ice storms. In summer, bright green, almost chartreuse leaves give the tree a cool, refreshing look. The real show comes in fall when the leaves turn intense chrome yellow; then almost as if on cue, they drop in unison—you only have to rake leaves once. After the leaves have fallen, the new wood displays its yellow color all winter.

Manchurian ash has proven hardy to -40°. The tree has no pest problems and tolerates poor, dry, or wet soils. With good soil and ample water, it grows about 2 to 3 feet a year. Many nurseries sell this tree in containers or as balled-and-burlapped stock. If your local nursery doesn't carry 'Mancana', ask to order it from a wholesale grower such as Apple Creek Propagators or Trees R Us in Bonners Ferry, Idaho. — *Dick Rifkind*

BACK TO BASICS

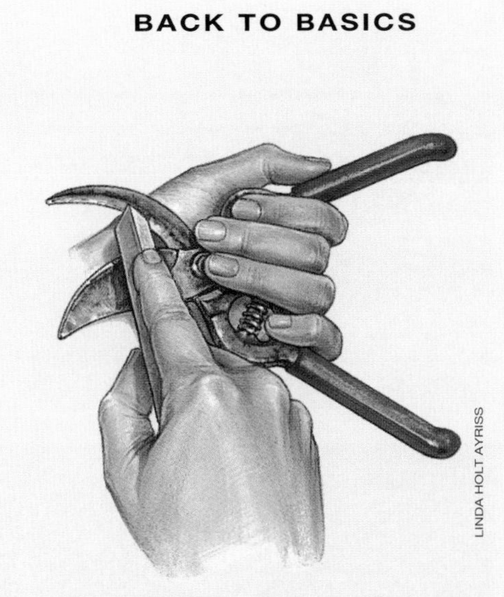
LINDA HOLT AYRISS

Fall tune-up for pruning shears. It's smart to clean and sharpen your tools before the pruning season. Sticky sap and grime cause dull blade edges, which make poor cuts. Use a rag dipped in kerosene or other solvent to wipe edges off (do this after each pruning). Use fine steel wool to remove any encrusted material. Sharpen blades with a sharpening stone. On anvil-type pruners, sharpen only the one blade (keep the sharpened edge perfectly straight). On bypass shears, sharpen both blades. Apply a thin coat of mineral or machine oil to the blades to prevent rust. — *L.B.S.*

MAX SEABAUGH

Finding your garden's cold pockets. Walk through your garden at dawn on a clear morning when the temperature is just below freezing. You'll notice that some areas are heavy with frost, while others are frost-free. The frost pockets (usually the garden's low spots and flat areas exposed to open sky) are cold microclimates, while the frost-free areas (slopes and areas that get protection from trees) are milder. The difference can mean life or death for semihardy plants. Keep this in mind when you plant.

— *J.M.*

NORMAN A. PLATE

Gifts that grow on you

■ Holiday gift giving becomes much more meaningful when the gift keeps on growing. Each of the pots pictured here contains a surprise garden—whether salad mix, paper white narcissus, or wildflowers. Choose an attractive container from the nursery, plant it with ground covers or flowering plants, then add the seeds or bulbs. Give the pot before seeds or bulbs germinate; with regular water, the plants emerge in a few weeks. Attach a gift card to the pot or basket, explaining how to care for the plants.

TIME: 15 to 20 minutes
COST: $25 to $30
MATERIALS: •Container (we used a 12-inch-long basket and 16-inch-wide bowls) •Sheet plastic •Potting soil •Plants, one sixpack (or use 2- or 4-inch plants) •Bulbs (three large) or seeds (one package)

DIRECTIONS

1. Fill the container with soil. Or line the bulb basket with plastic, then fill it halfway with potting soil.

2. *Salad mix pot:* Mix a controlled-release fertilizer into the soil. Plant three or four violas toward the perimeter of the pot. Sprinkle seeds of salad mix onto the soil surface between the plants. Scratch seeds into the soil and water well. CARE: Move pots outdoors to a sunny spot (protect from freezing) or to a cool, bright area indoors; keep the soil moist. Thin seedlings when they're an inch or so tall (use the trimmings in salads). Harvest individual leaves when they've reached 3 to 4 inches tall.

THOMAS J. STORY (3)

Harvesting a salad pot.

Wildflower pot: Plant four blue fescue plants around the outside of the pot and one in the center. Sprinkle seeds of low-growing wildflowers between the plants (we used dwarf toadflax and baby blue eyes, but tidytips also work). Water well. CARE: Grow outdoors in full sun; water regularly to keep soil moist.

Paper white narcissus basket: Plant bulbs several inches apart, so there's room to plant chamomile (*Chamaemelum nobile*) in between. Cover with soil up to the base of the bulb neck. Plant the chamomile. Water just to wet the soil. CARE: Grow outdoors in bright light. Protect the basket from rain, since the liner provides no drainage, and water only lightly. When flower buds start to open, bring the basket indoors; display in bright light. *—L.B.S.*

Wildflower pot

Paper white narcissus basket

WHAT TO DO IN YOUR GARDEN IN DECEMBER

PLANTING

☐ **AMARYLLIS.** Buy amaryllis bulbs or budded plants at most nurseries this month. Most produce large multiple flowers in shades of red, orange, peach, and white. Give plants plenty of light and regular water during bloom.

☐ **BULBS.** It's late to plant spring-flowering bulbs, but you can still get them into the ground during the first week of December.

☐ **CAMELLIAS.** Zones 4–7: Sasanqua camellias and other winter-flowering types are blooming at nurseries now. Plant right away and spread mulch around plants to protect roots from freezing, or be prepared to provide frost-free shelter for potted plants if freezing weather is predicted.

☐ **TREES, SHRUBS.** Zones 4–7: Plant hardy varieties anytime, watering them well. This is also a good time to transplant trees and shrubs.

MAINTENANCE

☐ **CARE FOR HOUSE PLANTS.** Fertilize winter-flowering plants lightly at bloom time, but wait until spring growth before feeding other kinds. Check for aphids, mealy bugs, and mites. If you see infestations, rinse the plant in a lukewarm shower and treat with a systemic insecticide, or take it outside on a mild day, spray with insecticidal soap, and bring back inside before evening.

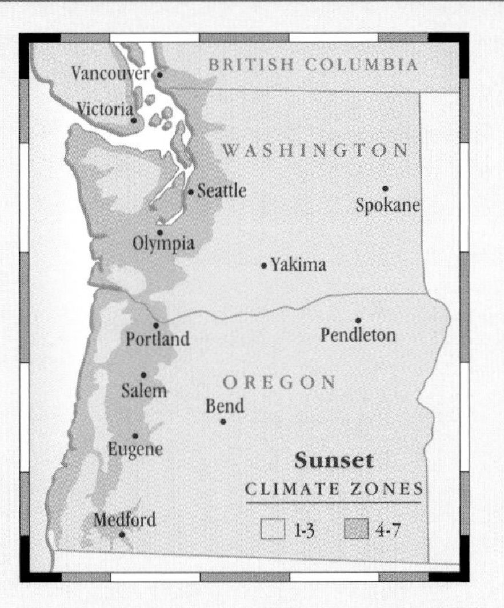

☐ **CARE FOR LIVING CHRISTMAS TREES.** If you select a living Christmas tree, leave it in its nursery container and try to limit its indoor stay to 10 days. Keep the tree away from heater vents and fireplaces. Water regularly; one easy way is to dump two trays of ice cubes on top of the soil daily. After its indoor stay, move the tree to a cool, bright porch or other protected place where the rootball won't freeze. You can transplant the tree into the garden or grow it in the container until next Christmas.

☐ **PROPAGATE EVERGREENS.** Use this technique to propagate new plants from broadleaf evergreens (azalea, camellia, daphne, mahonia, or rhododendron): Scrape a fingernail-size patch of bark off the bottom of a low-hanging branch of an existing plant, then dust the wound with rooting hormone and press it into the soil below. Firm

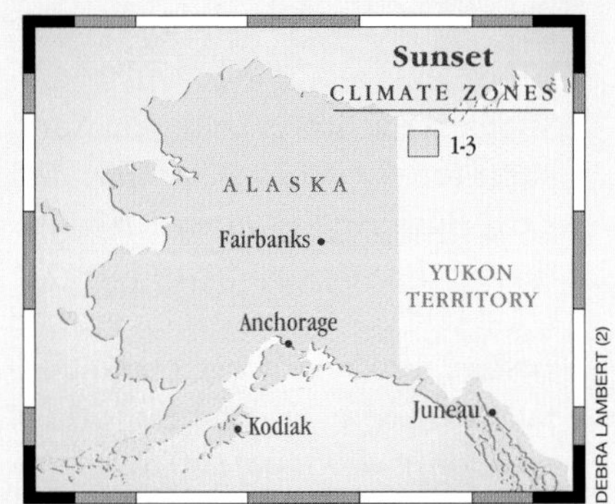

DEBRA LAMBERT (2)

more soil over the branch, leaving the tip and leaves exposed; lay a stone or brick on top of the branch to hold it firmly to the ground. Keep soil moist. Roots will form. By next fall, you can sever the branch from the mother plant and replant it wherever you want.

☐ **PRUNE CONIFERS, HOLLY FOR SWAGS.** Use sharp shears to cut boughs and sprigs for swags and wreaths. Make each cut just beyond a side branch (don't leave stubs). Work from the bottom of the plant to the top and from the inside out, keeping the plant's finished form in mind. ◆

WHAT TO DO IN YOUR GARDEN IN DECEMBER

PLANTING

☐ CAMELLIAS. Zones 7–9, 14–17: To select the flower color you want, shop for *Camellia sasanqua* and early-flowering *C. japonica* while they're blooming. Sasanquas are good choices for espaliers, ground covers, informal hedges, and containers. Some are upright, others spreading or vinelike. The plants tolerate a fair amount of sun. Some choices include 'Egao', 'Rainbow', 'Shibori-Egao', and 'Yuletide'. Japonicas are handsome as specimen plants and espaliers. Look for 'Alba Plena', 'Daikagura', 'Debutante', 'Elegans' ('Chandleri Elegans'), 'Nuccio's Carousel', 'Nuccio's Gem', and 'Wildfire'.

☐ CYCLAMEN. Zones 8–9, 14–17: Cyclamen come in a wonderful array of colors and flower sizes. You'll even find some flowers with ruffled petals. The best way to protect the flowers from rain spots is to plant cyclamen in a container and set the pot under an overhang or on a covered porch. Choose a spot that gets partial shade, morning sun, or late-afternoon sun. Place crowns (plant bases) slightly higher than the surrounding soil. Zones 1–2: Grow cyclamen in a cool, bright location indoors.

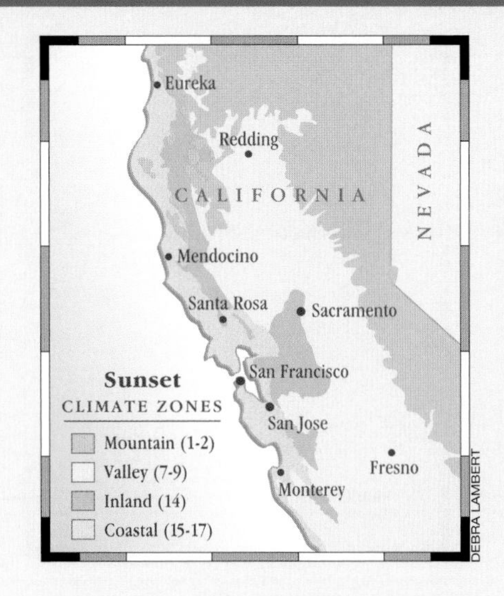

☐ FRUITS AND VEGETABLES. Zones 7–9, 14–17: Late this month, nurseries begin selling bare-root artichokes, asparagus, cane fruits (berries), grapes, rhubarb, and strawberries. Buy and plant early in the month while roots are still fresh. If the soil is too wet to plant, temporarily cover roots with moistened mulch to keep them from drying out.

☐ LIVING CHRISTMAS TREES. Most nurseries carry the following: Alberta spruce, aleppo pine, Colorado blue spruce, giant sequoia, and Monterey pine. Before bringing the tree indoors, water the pot thoroughly and spray the foliage with water. Indoors, set the pot in a cool location in a plastic waterproof saucer. If you are using a clay saucer, place the pot on plastic or a waterproof cork mat. Check soil moisture daily.

MAINTENANCE

☐ ADJUST IRRIGATION. Zones 7–9, 14–17: Rains in late fall and winter can be unpredictable. If they're light, continue to run your irrigation systems when the soil dries out. Also water containers when necessary and plants growing under eaves. If rains are adequate, make sure to shut off your automatic controller (or install a shutoff valve to do it automatically).

☐ APPLY DORMANT SPRAY. Zones 7–9, 14–17: To smother overwintering insect eggs and pests (such as aphids, mites, and scale), spray deciduous flowering trees, fruit trees, and roses with dormant oil after leaves have fallen. For complete coverage, spray the branches, branch crotches, trunk, and ground beneath the drip line. Also, rake up and destroy any fallen fruit and leaves.

☐ PRUNE FOR HOLIDAY GREENS. Long-lasting choices include evergreen magnolia, juniper, pine, and redwood. Conifers that drop needles sooner include deodar cedar, spruce, and Western hemlock.

☐ SPRAY GREENS. To keep greens and wreaths fresher longer, spray with an antitranspirant (available at nurseries) before bringing them indoors. ◆

WHAT TO DO IN YOUR GARDEN IN DECEMBER

PLANTING

☐ BARE-ROOT PLANTS. For the best selection in bare-root roses, visit nurseries soon—current favorites disappear quickly. Deciduous fruit trees, cane berries, grapes, and perennial vegetables will arrive later this month and next. Plant anything bare-root as soon after purchase as possible.

☐ BULBS. If you still have unplanted bulbs, get them in the ground by the end of this month. Bulbs that need chilling, like tulips, are the exception. Keep them in the refrigerator awhile longer, and plant them in early January.

☐ CYCLAMEN. Cyclamen come in an array of colors and flower sizes. You'll even find some flowers with ruffled petals. The best way to protect the flowers from rain spots is to plant cyclamen in a container and place the pot under an overhang or on a covered porch. Choose a location that gets partial shade, morning sun, or late-afternoon sun. Set crowns (plant bases) slightly higher than the surrounding soil. Zones 2–3 (Idyllwild, Julian): Grow cyclamen in a cool, bright location indoors.

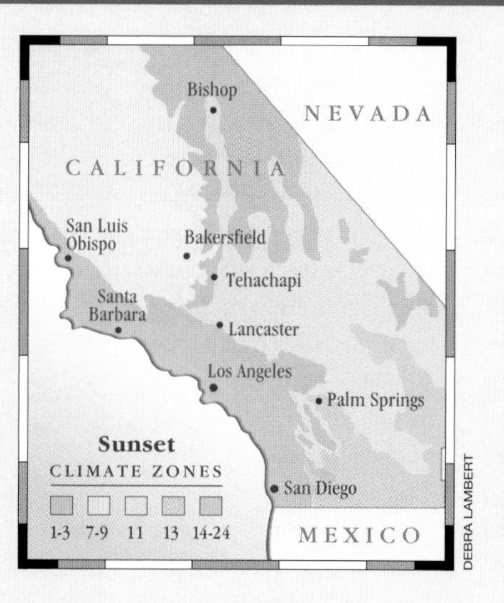

DEBRA LAMBERT

☐ WINTER VEGETABLES. As spaces open in the garden, add more winter vegetables. Leaf lettuces and salad mixes are particularly satisfying to start now. You can harvest their leaves as baby greens when they are only a few inches tall. Baby Mesclun Salad Paris Market Mix, a blend of sweet French lettuces and chervil, from Renee's Garden (888/880-7228 or www.reneesgarden.com), is a tempting new mix. Arugula, broccoli, cabbage, cauliflower, kale, kohlrabi, onion, peas, potatoes, radish, spinach, and Swiss chard are other options.

MAINTENANCE

☐ APPLY DORMANT SPRAY. To smother overwintering insect eggs and pests (aphids, mites, and scale), spray deciduous flowering trees, fruit trees, and roses with dormant oil after leaves have fallen. For complete coverage, spray the branches, branch crotches, trunk, and ground beneath the drip line.

☐ FERTILIZE CYMBIDIUMS. Continue feeding cymbidium orchids with a bloom-promoting fertilizer, such as 15-30-15, until buds open.

☐ HARVEST HOLIDAY GREENS. Prune cedars, cypresses, firs, pines, and other conifers, and use the boughs for making swags and wreaths. Cotoneaster, holly, juniper, pittosporum, podocarpus, pyracantha, and toyon also make good holiday decorations, and winter grooming is good for the plants. Cut to side branches or to about ¼ inch above buds.

☐ PRUNE LOW-CHILL RASPBERRIES. Low-chill raspberries bear fruit on new wood. Cut all canes to within a few inches of the ground this month or next, and let new growth emerge.

☐ REFURBISH TOOLS. Clean shovels, spades, forks, hoes, and other digging tools by filling a 16-gallon bucket with sand mixed with 1 quart vegetable oil. Dip tool heads into mixture several times until clean. *(Don't use this method for pruners or other crisscrossing blades.)* With sandpaper, gently remove rust spots on pruners, saws, and other tools (see also page 381). Sharpen blades with a bastard mill file, spray with machine or mineral oil, and wipe clean. Rub down wood handles with linseed oil. ◆

WHAT TO DO IN YOUR GARDEN IN DECEMBER

SHOPPING

☐ BUY LIVING CHRISTMAS TREES. Choose a tree you can plant in your garden later. Good choices include alpine fir (*Abies lasiocarpa*), Colorado blue spruce (*Picea pungens* 'Glauca'), Douglas fir (*Pseudotsuga menziesii*), and white fir (*A. concolor*). Keep the tree in its nursery container and try to limit its indoor stay to 10 days. Keep it away from heating vents and fireplaces. Water regularly; one easy way is to dump two trays of ice cubes on top of the soil daily.

☐ ORDER SEEDS, PLANTS. Place orders early for best selection. Most companies will hold plants for shipping at the proper planting time in your area. Check out catalog offerings of these regional sources. ***High Country Gardens*** (2902 Rufina St., Santa Fe, NM 87505; 800/925-9387 or www.highcountrygardens.com) specializes in drought-tolerant flowers and shrubs for xeriscape gardens. ***Plants of the Southwest*** (Agua Fria Rd., Rt. 6, Box 11A, Santa Fe, NM 87501; 800/788-7333 or www.plantsofthesouthwest.com) offers seeds and plants of native wildflowers, grasses, vegetables, and shrubs. ***Prairie Nursery*** (Box 306, Westfield, WI 53964; 800/476-9453 or www.prairienursery.com) features seed and plants for starting a prairie planting.

MAINTENANCE

☐ HARVEST HOLIDAY GREENS. Prune evergreen conifers and use the boughs for holiday wreaths or swags. Don't leave stubs; cut just above side branches that you want to grow. While you're at it, remove dead, diseased, and injured branches. Then prune for shape, working from the bottom of the tree to the top and from the inside out.

Find your garden's climate zone
The updated edition of *Sunset Western Garden Book* will be released in mid-February. Meanwhile, to learn your garden's *Sunset* climate zone, preview the book's newly revised climate maps of the mountain states starting on page 388.

☐ INSULATE ROSES. Don't prune roses this time of year except to remove broken or dead canes. After temperatures drop below freezing for a few nights, mound soil over the plant base; if it's a grafted rose, be sure the soil covers the bud union (the enlarged knob from which canes emerge). Once soil surface freezes, set a cylinder of chicken wire or a tomato cage around each plant and fill with a mulch of leaves, pine boughs, or straw. In spring, remove mulch and add it to compost pile.

☐ MULCH. Spread a 3- to- 4-inch layer of organic mulch over beds of bulbs, perennials, and shrubs.

☐ PREPARE CACTUS FOR BLOOM. Hold off watering spring-flowering indoor cactus from mid-December through February. Then resume watering, applying a dilute solution of fertilizer every second watering. If the cactus is in a bright spot, buds and blooms should follow.

☐ PROPAGATE HOUSE PLANTS. Chinese evergreen, philodendron, pothos, and other plants can become leggy in winter. To start new plants, snip off elongated stems and immerse the cut ends in water until roots form, then transplant rooted cuttings into fresh potting soil.

☐ SPRAY ANTIDESICCANT. Dwarf conifers and broadleaf evergreens such as holly and rhododendrons are susceptible to dehydration and windburn in winter. To protect them, spray the foliage with an antidesiccant product, following instructions on the label. One application lasts for several months.

☐ WATER. When temperatures stay above freezing, water dry spots in the garden, especially plants in containers and under house eaves.

— *Marcia Tatroe* ◆

WHAT TO DO IN YOUR GARDEN IN DECEMBER

SHOPPING AND PLANTING

☐ BUY LIVING CHRISTMAS TREES. Choose a tree you can transplant in the garden after the holidays. Zones 1–2 (Flagstaff, Santa Fe): Consider Colorado spruce (*Picea pungens*) and Douglas fir (*Pseudotsuga menziesii*). Zone 10 (Albuquerque): Try Arizona cypress (*Cupressus arizonica*), Colorado spruce, deodar cedar (*Cedrus deodora*), Douglas fir, and piñon (*Pinus edulis*). Zones 11–13 (Las Vegas, Tucson, Phoenix): Good choices include Afghan pine (*P. eldarica*), aleppo pine (*P. halepensis*), and Italian stone pine (*P. pinea*). Keep trees in their nursery containers, water them regularly, and try to limit their indoor stay to 10 days.

☐ PLANT BARE-ROOT ROSES. Zones 12–13: Buy bare-root plants at nurseries; ask the staff to pack the roots in damp burlap or sawdust and wrap them in a plastic bag to prevent them from drying out until you can get home. You should soak the plants in water for a day before planting.

☐ PLANT BULBS. Zones 11–13: You can still plant anemones, callas, crocuses, daffodils, freesias, hyacinths, ranunculus, and chilled tulips early in the month.

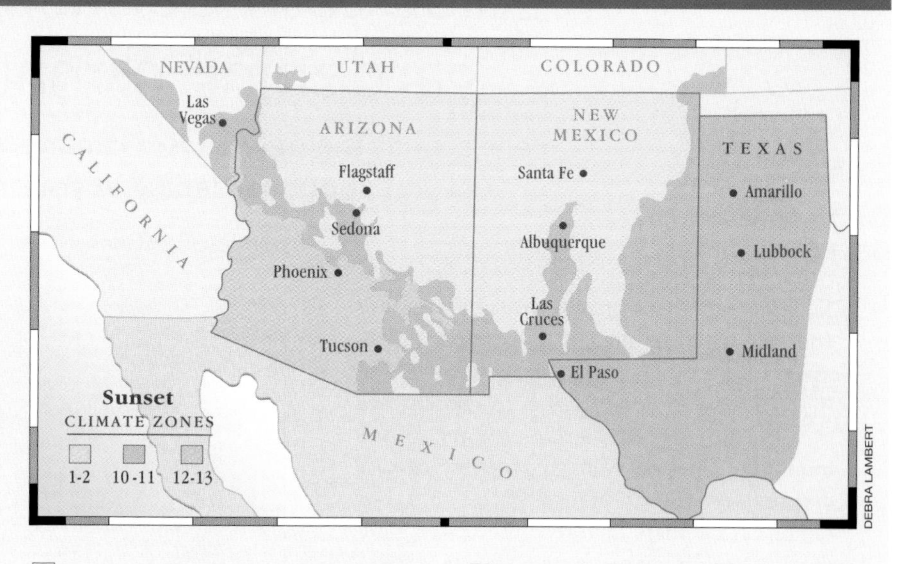

☐ START PEPPERS, TOMATOES. Zones 11–13: Start pepper and tomato seeds in containers filled with sterile potting soil in a warm, bright spot indoors. Seedlings will be ready to transplant outdoors eight weeks after sowing.

MAINTENANCE

☐ APPLY WINTER MULCH. Zones 1–2: Spread a 3- to 4-inch layer of organic mulch over beds of bulbs and perennials to protect roots from being heaved out of the ground during freezing and thawing cycles.

☐ CARE FOR GIFT PLANTS. To keep drainage free-flowing, remove decorative wrapping from potted plants. Place them away from heater vents and fireplaces. Check plants daily and keep soil moist.

☐ PREVENT GIRDLER DAMAGE. Mesquite twig girdlers are beetles that eat the bark off limbs in a circular pattern, which will kill the tree. To reduce girdler infestations, clean up fallen twigs and remove hanging deadwood.

☐ PROTECT CITRUS TREES. Zones 12–13: When temperatures are forecast to drop below 28°, cover tree canopies with burlap, blankets, or old sheets. Wrap the trunks of young trees with a blanket or cloth to protect their thin bark from splitting.

☐ WATER. Zones 1–2, 10: Water when the temperature is above freezing. Zones 11–13: Water established trees and shrubs deeply once this month if there has been no rain. — *Mary Irish* ◆

A guide to mountain states' gardening climates

Here's what the new *Sunset* climate zone maps tell you about gardening in your region

By Jim McCausland

Taking advantage of newly available weather and climate data, *Sunset* has refined the climate zone maps for our next edition of the *Western Garden Book,* available in bookstores in mid-February 2001. Maps for the West's mountain states, as well as gardening climate descriptions, appear on these pages. Find your region on the map, then read the corresponding description of your garden climate zone.

Gardening in the mountainous West is always a challenge, but understanding your climate zone will help you grow plants successfully. In fact, climate determines what plants you can and cannot grow in your garden. Once you know the characteristics of your zone, you can use the newly revised *Western Garden Book* to choose plants suited to that climate zone.

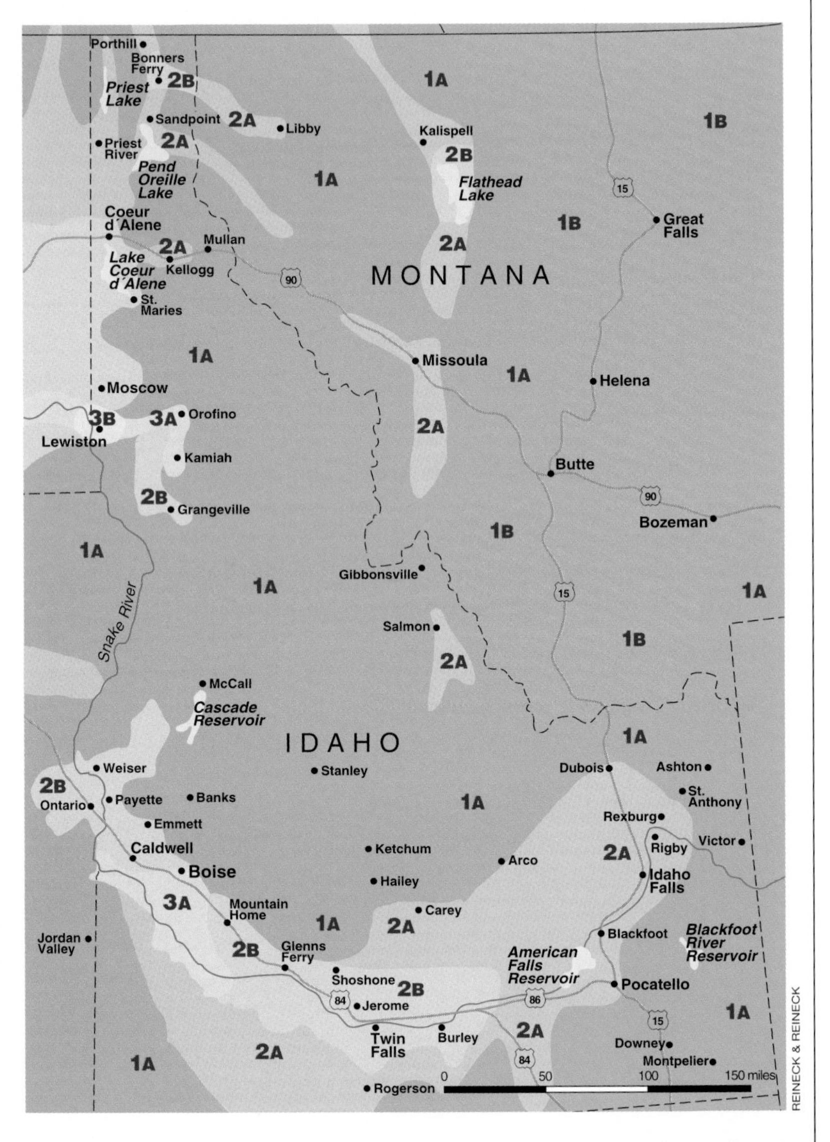

Zone 1A: Coldest mountain and intermountain areas

Marked by a short growing season and relatively mild summer temperatures, zone 1A includes the coldest regions west of the Rockies, and a few patches of cold country east of the Great Divide. The mild days and chilly nights extend bloom of summer perennials like columbines and Shasta daisies. If your garden gets reliable snow cover (which insulates plants), you can grow perennials listed for some of the milder zones. Along with hardy evergreen conifers, tough deciduous trees and shrubs form the garden's backbone here. Gardeners can grow warm-season vegetables as long as they're short-season varieties.

Winter lows average in the 0° to 11°F (-18° to -12°C) range; extremes range from -25° to -40°F (-32° to -40°C). The growing season averages 50 to 100 days.

Zone 1B: Coldest plains climate

Centered over the plains of Wyoming and Montana, this zone sees January temperatures from 0° to 12°F (-18° to -11°C), with extremes between -30° and -50°F (-34° and -46°C). Zone 1B lies east of the Great Divide, where the continental climate reigns supreme. Arctic cold fronts sweep through 6 to 12 times a year, sometimes dropping temperatures by 30° or 40°F in 24 hours. The summer growing season tends to be warm and generous at 110 to 140 days long, but constant winds—12 mph average, year-round, in many places—call for windbreaks and shade trees, such as hackberries and cottonwoods. Few shrubs are better loved here than lilacs or better adapted than smoke tree. With protection, annual vegetables and flowers thrive, as do wind-tolerant perennials like buckwheats, grasses, and penstemons. Where winters are dry and snow cover light, gardeners compensate with mulch and extra water.

Zone 2A: Cold mountain and intermountain areas

Another snowy winter climate, zone 2A covers several regions that are considered mild compared to their neighbors. This zone stretches over Colorado's northeastern plains, a bit of it along the Western Slope and Front Range of the Rockies, and in mild parts of river drainages such as the Snake, Okanogan, and Columbia. It also shows up in western Montana, Nevada, and in mountainous areas of the Southwest. This is the coldest zone in which sweet cherries and many apples grow.

Winter temperatures usually hover between 10° and 20°F (-12° and -7°C) at night, with drops between -20° and -30°F (-29° and -34°C) once every few years. When temperatures drop even lower, orchardists can lose their trees. The growing season is 100 to 150 days.

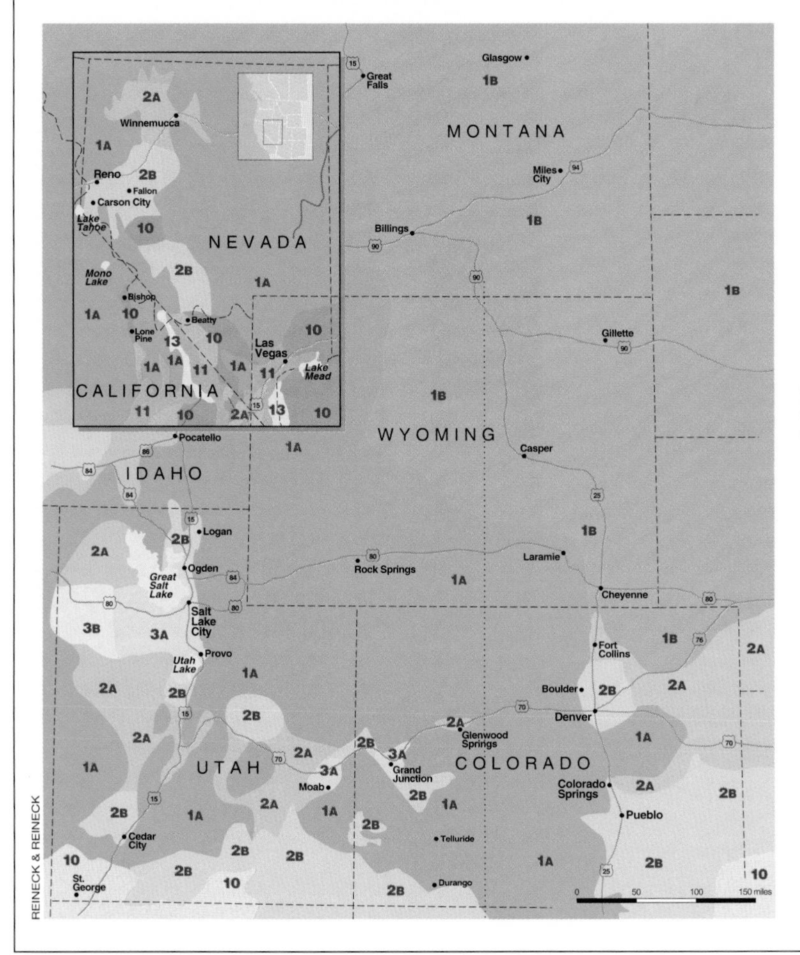

Zone 2B: Warmer summer intermountain climate

A good balance of long, warm summers and chilly winters makes this a perfect zone for commercial fruit growing, which is why you'll find orchards in this zone in almost every state in the West. You'll also notice this snowy-winter climate along Colorado's Western Slope and mild parts of the Front Range, in Nevada from Reno to Fallon and north to Lovelock, in large parts of northern Arizona and New Mexico, and in mild parts of the basins of the Columbia and Snake Rivers.

Winter minimum temperatures are milder than in neighboring zone 2A, averaging from 12° to 22°F (-11° to -6°C), with extremes in the -10° to -20°F (-23° to -30°C) range. The growing season ranges from 115 days in higher elevations and more northerly areas to more than 160 days in southeastern Colorado.

Zone 3A: Mild intermountain areas

East of the Sierra Nevada and Cascade Range, you can hardly find a better gardening climate than zone 3A. Winter minimum temperatures average from 15° to 25°F (-9° to -4°C), with extremes between -8° and -18°F (-22° and -28°C). Its frost-free growing season is 150 to 186 days in a normal year. The zone tends to occur at lower elevations in the northern states (Idaho, eastern Oregon, and Washington) and at higher elevations as you move south to Utah's Great Salt Lake and into northern New Mexico and Arizona. Fruits and vegetables that love long, warm summers—melons, gourds, and corn—typically do well here. This is another great zone for all kinds of deciduous fruit trees and ornamental trees and shrubs, as long as you water them well in summer.

Zone 3B: Mildest intermountain climate

Zone 3B is much like zone 3A, but with slightly milder winter averages (19° to 29°F; -7° to -2°C) and extremes that usually bottom out between -2° and -15°F (-19° and -26°C). Summer temperatures here are a bit higher than in zone 3A: They hover mostly in the high 80s and low to mid-90s. Zone 3B offers the longest growing season of all the intermountain climates. Gardeners here count on a growing season of about 180 to 210 frost-free days, with plenty of heat. However, it's one of the smallest zones, found mostly in the warmest parts of eastern Washington's Columbia Basin, in Lewiston, Idaho, and parts of southern Utah, New Mexico, and Arizona. ◆

easy & elegant wreaths

Bold and beautiful, these wreaths of flowers, foliage, and cones are easy to make

By Kathleen N. Brenzel
Designs by Bud Stuckey with Jill Slater
Photographs by Thomas J. Story

Flanked by fragrant carnation wreaths, Joanne Johnson (and Spanky) welcome visitors to their home in Los Gatos, California.

Few decorations say "welcome" like beautiful wreaths

California pepper berries decorate the wreath at right, finished with gold rope. A variation on our chapter-opening wreath, below, is embellished with pinecones and a golden green ribbon.

NORMAN A. PLATE

Whether bursting with crimson flowers, thick with red berries, or simply elegant in contrasting greens, a wreath you've made yourself offers the warmest of greetings. Florists or supermarkets supply festive flowers by the bunch, such as carnations in Christmas red or white with red stripes. In Western gardens, trees and shrubs offer up ripe-for-picking rose hips, California pepper berries, nandina berries, and pyracantha berries. Many shapes of cones are available; if trees in your own garden don't supply them, you can buy them at craft stores and florists' suppliers. Nontraditional greens such as golden junipers and arborvitae can add sparkle to an underpinning of more traditional pine, redwood, or spruce. A gorgeous ribbon or a cluster of flowers adds panache as a finishing touch.

Five wreaths are pictured on these pages—follow our directions to copy them exactly or let them inspire your own creations.

First, some tips. Each wreath starts with a base of wire, wood, plastic-backed floral foam, woven grapevine prunings, or twigs—most are sold ready-made at craft stores or specialty florists' supply stores. It's easiest to cover the inside edge of the base with plant material first, then the outside edge, and finally the front. To add flowers, foliage, pods, or cones, glue or wire them over the base.

Christmas carnations

Wreaths of puffy red carnations bring fragrance and color to Joanne Johnson's inviting entryway. Nearly invisible fishing line is looped around the tops of the wreaths and attached to the doorjamb with finishing nails to hold in place. For added support and color, ribbons run through the centers of the wreaths and fasten to the top of the door frame with tacks. The wreaths last for a week or more outdoors. (Johnson spritzes the floral foam ring with water from a spray bottle as needed.)

TIME: About 45 minutes

COST: About $25 (plus $60–$90 for carnations)

TOOLS AND MATERIALS

- 3½ feet fishing line (available at hardware stores)
- Clippers and scissors
- 15-inch plastic-backed floral foam ring
- One packet flower preservative
- 75 carnations
- 2 yards ribbon

DIRECTIONS

1. Tie fishing line around the top of the floral foam ring, knotting it and leaving the ends long for hanging.

2. Pour flower preservative into a water-filled tub, stir, then drop in the foam ring. Soak foam for 1 hour. Remove and let drain briefly.

3. Keep carnation stems in water while you work, removing several at a time to add to the wreath. While holding stem tips under water, cut several stems to about 2 inches long. Starting on the inside of the foam ring, poke these shortened stems into the foam so the flower heads sit flat and petals touch. Continue around the inside, then cover the outside; do the front of the wreath last.

4. Hang wreath by fishing line. Add ribbon.

Golden highlights

Many Christmas memories are associated with the smell and look of evergreens. This festive wreath uses fresh-cut golden conifer foliage to perk up the greenery. A lime-gold satin ribbon accents the golden highlights; pinecones can be added (see far left).

TIME: About 90 minutes

COST: $15 (plus about $20 for evergreens if your garden doesn't supply them)

TOOLS AND MATERIALS

- Clippers and wire cutters
- 10 branches green conifers
- 20 branches golden conifers
- Spool of coated 22- or 24-gauge florist's wire
- 16-inch heavy-gauge wire wreath base from a craft or florists' supply store
- 8 feet of wired, greenish gold ribbon
- About six pinecones (optional)

DIRECTIONS

1. Cut branches into pieces about 6 inches long. Separate by variety. Make bouquets of five to six stems that mix both kinds of greens; wrap wire several times around bouquet stems. Lash a bouquet to the wire base with florist's wire; do not cut wire.

2. Position another bouquet so the tips overlap stems of first bouquet; attach with the continuous strand of wire. Repeat, adding bouquets around the base. Tie off the florist's wire and cut off excess.

3. Make a decorative bow from the ribbon and attach it to the wreath with wire. Attach a sturdy loop of wire to the back of the wreath for hanging.

4. To attach pinecones (optional), wrap a length of florist's wire around the large end of a pinecone and twist the ends together. Nestle the cone in the foliage, wrap ends of wire around to the back of the wreath base, then twist ends together.

Berries by the bunch

Here's a great way to show off the beautiful red berries of the California pepper tree (*Schinus molle*). If you don't have a tree, you may be able to find the berries at a florist's or on-line at www.floralconcepts.com. A less pricey substitute is rose hips, eucalyptus pods, or pyracantha or holly berries.

TIME: Three hours

COST: $40 (plus about $100 to $150 for berries)

TOOLS AND MATERIALS

- One roll medium-gauge fishing line
- 21-inch plastic-backed floral foam ring
- 10 bunches California pepper berries (approximately 20 berry clusters per bunch)
- Spool of coated 22- or 24-gauge florist's wire
- 100 floral pins
- 3 yards gold cord
- One cluster gold faux berries

DIRECTIONS

1. Knot one end of fishing line onto the foam ring. Make small bouquets of California pepper berries, securing them with wire. Using floral pins, attach a bouquet to the front of the ring near the top, then pin down the stems. Next to this bouquet, attach additional bouquets to inside and outside edges of foam ring. Wrap the fishing line around foam and berry stems, pulling it tightly.

2. With one continuous strand of fishing line, repeat until the base is covered. Knot the fishing line several times at the top; cut off excess.

3. Tie gold cord around wreath, making a bow. Attach gold faux berry cluster to the center of the bow with wire or fishing line. Slip a piece of wire between the plastic back and foam ring to make a hanger.

Ring of roses

Magnolia leaves and rose-toned flowers give this wreath the look of a summer flower garden. (Camellia or citrus leaves are good long-lasting substitutes.) Small bouquets, each with a cluster of leaves and a few sprigs of dried flowers, are wired to a moss-covered grapevine wreath base; dried seed pods of poppies add accents.

NORMAN A. PLATE

TIME: About 90 minutes

COST: About $30

TOOLS AND MATERIALS

- Sphagnum moss
- 24-inch grapevine, twig, or wire wreath base
- Spool of coated 22- or 24- gauge florist's wire
- Wire cutters
- Clusters of magnolia leaves (enough to cover the wreath) and flowering branches of tea tree (*Leptospermum*), or greenery of your choice
- 12 dried rosebuds
- One bunch German statice, dried seed pods of poppies, or other dried flowers (from a craft store)

DIRECTIONS

1. Moisten the sphagnum moss to the consistency of a damp sponge, then pack it around the front and sides of the wreath base. Wrap the free end of the wire once around the top of the wreath base; tie it off, leaving about 6 inches on the end free.

2. Make a bouquet using a single cluster of magnolia leaves, plus a couple of roses and several sprigs of tea tree and statice, or substitutes. Pack a bit of sphagnum moss around the stems. Wind wire several times around the bouquet stems, then lash the bouquet to the base with a continuous strand of wire, pulling tightly.

3. Repeat, adding bouquets around the base. Tie off the florist's wire and cut off excess.

Forest jewels

From the Monterey pine belt to bristlecone country, conifers yield cones whose tawny beauty is worth celebrating. In this wreath, several kinds of cones are glued to a twig base. Gather cones in your yard or buy them from florists' suppliers like Columbia Pine Cones & Botanicals (888/470-6989 or www.pinecones.com).

TIME: 90 minutes

COST: About $15 (plus $40 for a box of assorted pinecones if your garden doesn't supply them)

TOOLS AND MATERIALS

- Spool of coated 22- or 24-gauge florist's wire
- Wire cutters
- 18-inch twig wreath base (from a craft store)
- About 120 pinecones (ours measure 2 to 3½ inches long)
- Glue gun

DIRECTIONS

1. To make a hanger, wrap a 9-inch length of wire around the top of the wreath base; twist ends together. Loop a 3-inch length of wire through the 9-inch length; twist ends together.

2. Using the glue gun, affix pinecones, one at a time, around the inside of the wreath base. Alternate big cones with small ones, gluing some right side up, some upside down, and some on their sides. Repeat to cover the outside of the frame, then the front of the wreath. ◆

The other conifers

Decorating is easy when you display juniper, cypress, and other handsome evergreens in containers

By Steven R. Lorton
Photographs by Thomas J. Story

ABOVE: Dwarf mugho pine is decorated with silver balls and tiny white lights. RIGHT: Japanese cryptomeria and 'Rheingold' arborvitae fill a rustic bowl. FAR RIGHT: Choice conifers include *Juniperus scopulorum* 'Gray Gleam' (A), limber pine (B), Colorado blue spruce (C), Verdoni dwarf hinoki cypress (D), dwarf Alberta spruce (E), *Chamaecyparis pisifera* 'Cyano-Viridis' (F), Japanese cryptomeria (G), and *Thuja occidentalis* 'Rheingold' (H).

■ Thanks to adventurous growers who are providing a continuous supply of new and exciting evergreens and to daring gardeners who are using the plants in creative ways, potted conifers have become nearly indispensable for holiday decorating. Buy one or more of these shapely plants to spruce up your porch, patio, or even a spot indoors. Or slip a conifer into a decorative container and embellish with ribbon or gleaming glass balls for a wonderful gift.

Set aside an afternoon to visit nurseries, where you'll find dozens of good plants that can add a natural accent to holiday decorations. Some of our favorites for containers are listed on page 398.

Keeping a contained conifer happy

If you display a living conifer indoors during the holidays, limit its time inside to two weeks. Keep the plant away from furnace vents or fireplaces. (Some gardeners move their conifers outdoors each evening to spend the night in

A
B
C
D
E
F
G
H

the bracing, often moist, winter air.)

After the holidays, the plant can move outdoors permanently, onto a patio or into a garden bed. Outdoors, most conifers need full sun (except in the hottest inland areas, where partial shade will protect them from sunburn) and a spot with good air circulation. Place a single potted plant to accent a path; two can flank an entry. Or, smack dab in the center of a patio or deck, potted conifers can act as anchors around which to arrange a cluster of pots or patio chairs.

Water potted conifers regularly during peak summer months. A lack of water, especially during hot dry spells, can damage or even kill them. Most are not heavy feeders; pines, especially, don't want to be fertilized.

Dwarf plants can live for years in containers. Every three years or so, it's a good idea to remove the plant from its pot and root-prune the rootballs. Add fresh potting soil when you do this. Early each spring, top-dress the container with fresh potting mix, then work it lightly into the soil.

Varieties that will reach timber-size when mature can be grown in pots for a few years as youngsters, but eventually they'll need to be planted out in the garden, with enough room to grow to full size.

Choice conifers for pots

The following conifers can live for years in containers.

Chamaecyparis obtusa (hinoki false cypress). Dozens of dwarf forms, such as *C. o.* 'Nana Gracilis', grow to about 4 feet tall. Foliage varies—some types are fern-leafed, some golden, others emerald green. Full sun or part shade. *Sunset* climate zones 4–6, 15–17.

***C. pisifera* 'Cyano-Viridis'** ('Boulevard'). A dense shrub or small tree with intense silvery blue-green foliage. Grows slowly to 8 feet tall, sometimes more, and half as wide. Full sun or part shade. Zones 4–6, 15–17.

***C. p.* 'Filifera Aurea'** (gold thread false cypress). Drooping threadlike branchlets are tipped with yellow. They can arch up to 8 feet, then plunge downward, creating a fountain-shaped plant. Full sun on coast, part shade inland. Zones 4–6, 15–17.

Cryptomeria japonica (Japanese cryptomeria). The species and several named varieties all make excellent and unusual Christmas greens. *C. j.* 'Vilmoriniana' is a slow-growing dwarf to 2 feet with fluffy gray-green summer foliage that turns purplish bronze in late fall and winter. Full sun. Zones 4–9, 14–24.

***Cupressus sempervirens* 'Swane's Golden'.** This classic Italian cypress is columnar. New growth is golden. It can eventually reach 60 feet. Full sun. Zones 4–24.

***Juniperus squamata* 'Blue Star'.** All the junipers make great (and exotically sculptural) Christmas greens. This one grows up to 2 feet, spreads out to 5 feet, and has brilliant blue foliage. Full sun on coast, partial shade inland. All zones.

***J. scopulorum* 'Gray Gleam'.** A perfect match for silver ornaments, this moderately slow-growing juniper will eventually reach 15 feet tall. Full sun. All zones (hardy to -30°F).

***Picea glauca* 'Conica'** (dwarf Alberta spruce). An elegant cone of green that grows slowly to 7 feet tall. Short, fine needles are soft to touch. Full sun or light shade; shelter from hot, reflected sun. Zones 1–6, 14–17.

***P. pungens* 'Glauca'** (Colorado blue spruce). This tree eventually reaches 80 to 100 feet but will grow happily in a pot for several years. Full sun or light shade. Zones 1–10, 14–17.

Pinus flexilis (limber pine). A classic Western pine. It grows slowly to 20 to 30 feet tall. The needles are slightly twisted and the branches droop artfully and irregularly. Tolerates aridity and thrives on hot dry slopes but needs well-drained soil. Full sun. All zones.

Pinus mugo mugo (dwarf mugho pine). Like its larger sibling, *Pinus mugo* (Swiss mountain pine), this dwarf form has a bushy shape that can be pruned into an open, sculptural form. Dark green needles turn branch ends into brushes. Growing to 4 feet tall with a nearly equal width, this is a great pine for pots. Full sun. All zones except desert, where it suffers in heat.

***Thuja occidentalis* 'Rheingold'** ('Rheingold' arborvitae). Of all the great arborvitaes, this one is exceptional for its golden, almost orange, winter foliage. Plants seldom exceed 6 feet tall. Summer shade in hot areas. Zones 2–9, 15–17, 21–24. ◆

Lime green dwarf golden arborvitae (*Thuja orientalis* 'Aurea Nana'), and blue-green chamaecyparis shown in summer; the former is underplanted with white-flowered bacopa.

Leaves of gold

Embellish gift pots with leaf prints

By Kathleen N. Brenzel
Design by Jill Slater

Tiny conifers, snowy paper white narcissus, cyclamens with petals flared like angels' wings—all make beautiful table decorations or holiday gifts. To enhance their presentation, drop them in tapered terra-cotta pots you've adorned with leaf prints.

The process is simple: Just coat the back of a leaf with patio paint (available at nurseries), then press it onto the surface of the pot. Leaves with complex shapes make the best impressions—ginkgo, liquidambar, and pin oak (if you can still find them on or around trees), or evergreens such as cedar, redwood, and juniper. Use a single-leaf motif or different leaves in different paint colors. Flat leaves work best: If necessary, press them between paper towels in a thick book a few days before using.

Choose your gift plants first (4- to 6-inch nursery containers are easiest to work with), then buy the pots to match. The ones pictured here are available in a range of sizes, from 3 to 6 inches in diameter and wider. Patio paint comes in many colors; gold and bronze create a rich sheen that glints softly when light hits them.

Leaf-print pots

TIME: About 30 minutes each, plus about 1 hour drying time

COST: $15 or less, depending on pot size

TOOLS AND MATERIALS

- Newspaper
- Tapered terra-cotta pot
- 2-ounce bottle gold patio paint (additional colors optional)
- Paper plate
- Paintbrush or sponge (1 to 2 in. wide)
- Leaves
- Plastic sandwich bag

DIRECTIONS

1. Spread out newspaper on a flat surface. Lay the pot gently on its side. Pour some paint onto paper plate. With the brush, paint the underside of a leaf, covering it thoroughly but not too thickly. (Also paint the stem, if attached.)

2. Lay painted side of the leaf gently against the pot. Slip your hand into sandwich bag; firmly and evenly press the leaf to the pot.

3. Peel away leaf; turn the pot upright and let dry about one hour. Repeat process, if you wish, to continue the design around the pot. Paint the pot rim. Once paint dries, drop in the plant. ◆

NORMAN A. PLATE (4)

Terra-cotta pots of various sizes contain miniature conifers; moist sphagnum moss covers the nursery pots inside. Leaf prints of gold, bronze, and teal dress up the pots for gift giving.

12 essential tools

An expert picks a dozen tools for the green thumbs on your gift list

By Sharon Cohoon

Photographs by James Carrier

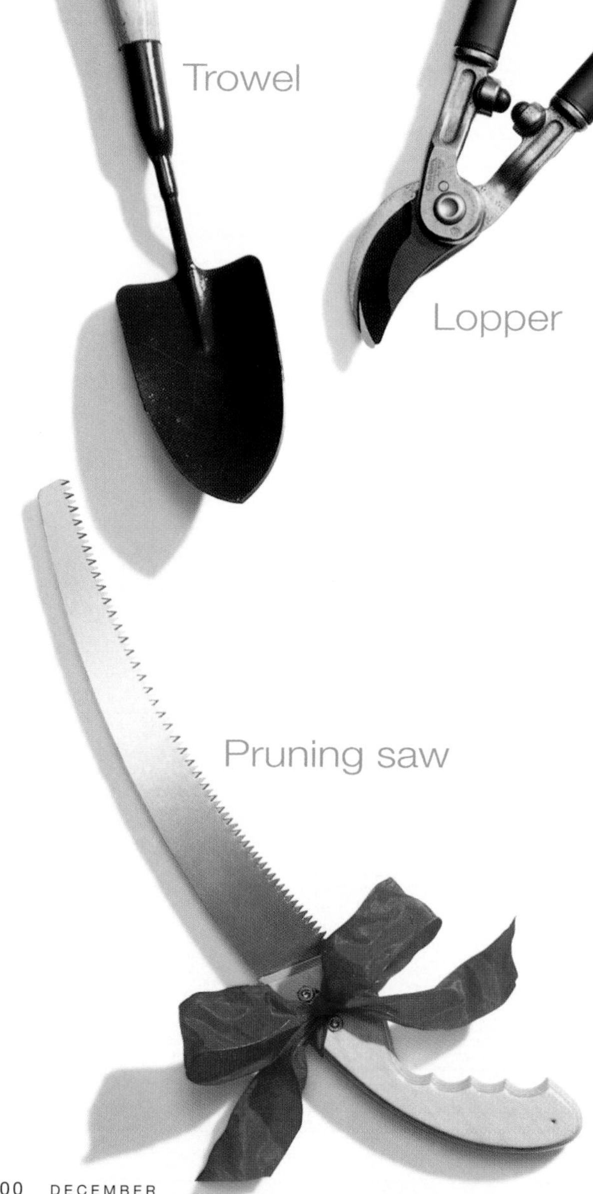

Which garden tools would you consider absolutely essential if you had close to 2,000 in your collection? Bob Denman has that many. Denman & Company, the store he runs with his wife, Rita, in Orange, California, sells nothing but garden tools, ranging from historic implements to the latest ergonomic designs.

To provide *Sunset* readers with sure-to-please ideas for the gardeners on their holiday gift lists, we asked Denman to narrow his choices down to a dozen tools. For each type of tool, a reliable brand and approximate retail price appear in parentheses.

Hand tools

■ TROWEL (Union Tools, $16). Essentially shovels with very short handles, trowels need little introduction. Most of us make do with inexpensive models and replace them regularly. Denman suggests investing in a fine-grade trowel instead. Using a high-quality tool makes a pleasurable task doubly so, he says.

■ LOPPER (Corona Clipper, $68). A lopper provides the leverage to cut branches that are thicker than $\frac{3}{4}$ inch. A heavy-duty model with $1\frac{3}{4}$-inch bypass blades and 26-inch-long handles suits most gardeners, says Denman.

■ PRUNING SAW (Fanno Saw Works, $29). When you exceed the capacity of your lopper—or your own strength—switch to a saw, says Denman. A saw with a 13-inch-long blade, which can handle up to 4-inch-thick branches, is the best size for most people, he says. He prefers a fixed saw to a folding model: "I don't use tools with sharp edges that can fold back against your hand." He likes the shock absorption of a wood handle and recommends Japanese triple-edge blades with razor-sharp teeth on three sides: "They're self-cleaning and twice as fast as conventional blades."

Long-handled tools

(pictured on page 402)

■ #2 SHOVEL (Union Tools, $52). Denman recommends a standard American round-point #2 shovel with an 8- by 12-inch blade. Get one with a solid forged-steel blade rather than a stamped-steel blade. "It's more expensive, but it's much stronger," says Denman. Also look for an ash handle with tight grain, and a forward-turned tread on the blade. "The British routinely garden in heavy boots, so they don't need that step to push against. But we garden in sneakers and sandals, so we do," explains Denman.

■ IRISH SPADE (Spear & Jackson, $66). If you want to loosen and turn soil, you can get by with a shovel, but the flat edge of a spade does the job better, says Denman. Also use a spade anytime you want to dig a straight-sided hole. He prefers the Irish spade, with its longer, narrower blade, to English and American models. "It takes smaller bites, but that allows you to work faster and for longer stretches, so you actually get the job done in a shorter amount of time." The Irish spade also performs beautifully in tight spaces or in heavy clay or rocky soils. One with a forged-steel blade, ash handle, and forward-turned tread is ideal, he says.

■ SPADING FORK (Clarington Forge, $58). After you've spaded your soil and shoveled in amendments, you need a fork to mix everything together—"like working shortening into flour when you make piecrust," says Denman. Forks are also useful for breaking up clods, dividing perennials, and digging up plants without slicing through roots. Buy a fork with flat tines, front and back. Since a spading fork is another serious digging tool, Denman again recommends forged-steel tines. (Note: Diamond-backed potato forks are not made for heavy-duty uses; they're designed for lifting root crops without damaging them.)

■ FLAT-HEAD RAKE (Union Tools, $52). To prepare a surface for planting, use a flat-head rake to clear away pebbles and other debris and to smooth out terrain. "If you turn up a missed clod with a flat-head rake, you can smash it with the tines or either end. And you can use the back to tamp down and firm the soil afterward," Denman says. Again, he opts for forged steel and ash handles.

■ CULTIVATOR (Spear & Jackson, $39). Once you've created nice, fluffy soil, you'll need a cultivator to keep it loose. A cultivator is also useful for working amendments such as compost or manure into the soil. Denman prefers a model with three prongs in a V pattern. "The front

Problem solvers

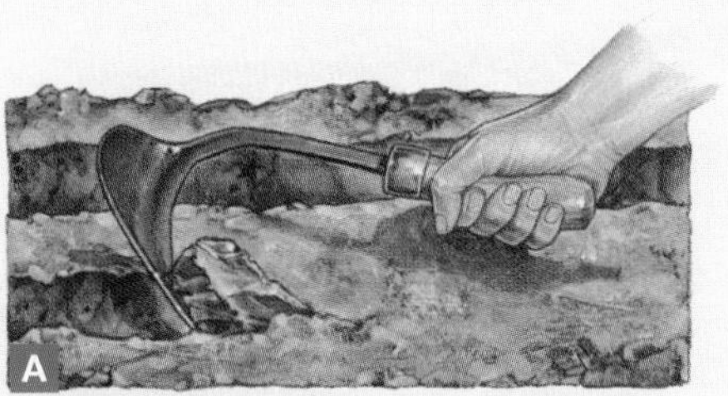

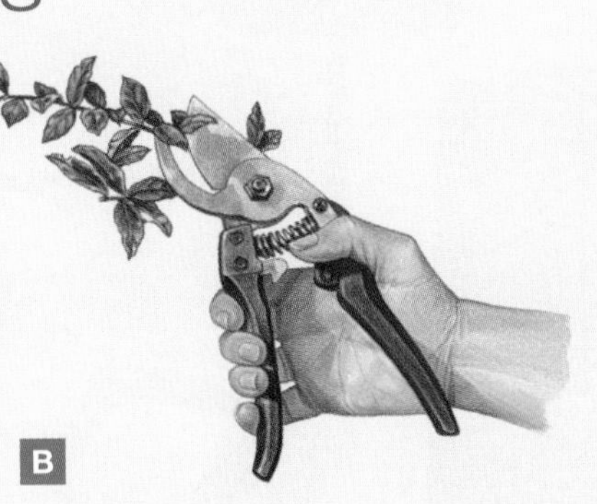

A. Korean hand plow (Denman & Co., $15). If Denman was forced to choose only one hand tool, the versatile Korean hand plow or *homi,* which dates back 2,000 years, would be his pick. "You can use it to cultivate, bust clods, make furrows, scuffle out weeds, and move dirt around when you plant. You adjust your grip as you change tasks," Denman says.

B. Pruner (Corona Clipper, $33). To keep woody plants in bounds, the first tool you need is a bypass pruner, or secateur, which has two blades that scissor slightly past each other, leaving a crisp, clean cut. This is the pruner to use anytime you cut live wood. (Anvil pruners, which have a single blade that closes against a flat anvil, are for cutting deadwood.) Start with the versatile ¾-inch-capacity blade, suggests Denman. His choice, from the Corona 6200 series, has some ergonomic features, including a 45° blade that "keeps your wrist level—in the power-grip position—which means you don't need nearly as much force to cut," he says.

C. Ball weeder (Denman & Co., $21). For weeds with deep taproots, like dandelions, which don't die when you slice off their heads, Denman uses a ball weeder, a common implement in the 1800s but now rare (Denman has the tool made exclusively for his store). The odd-looking wood ball acts as a fulcrum, transforming even a short handle into a powerful lever. "Tough weeds pop right out," he says.

LINDA HOLT AYRISS (3)

tine does the yeoman's job, and the back tines break up the soil even finer."

■ **HOE.** "To kill annual weeds, which is what 90 percent of weeds are, all you have to do is slice off the stem at ground level," he says. The best hoes for weeding have sharply angled blades which slide along or just under the soil surface. Some cut with the push stroke, some on the draw, and others, called scuffle hoes, in both directions. Denman's personal favorite, the diamond hoe (De Van Koek, $50), falls into this category.

With so many styles of hoes available, we asked for a second choice. Denman opted for the oscillating hoe (De Van Koek, $54). Also known as the Hula, or stirrup, hoe, it has a double-edged blade attached to the handle with a hinge, so the angle changes as you push forward and draw back. "The oscillating hoe tends to bounce off heavy weeds, but, if you weed regularly, it's very quick," he says.

Sources

Well-crafted tools can be difficult to find. Better nurseries and garden centers usually offer a limited selection. The following mail-order firms all carry serious tools, although not necessarily the same models listed here. Denman will be happy to fill requests (see listing at right).

The essential sharpening tool

According to Denman, most gardeners use dull tools and don't even know it. Shovels, spades, hoes, and trowels are usually sold with roughly beveled edges. That's for safety and also because tools get banged around in transit. Once upon a time, "when we all had relatives who still lived on farms, everyone knew you were supposed to sharpen them after you bought them," he explains. "Now people don't—and no one tells them to." So get a 12-inch mill bastard file and sharpen your blades, he says. "You'll be amazed at how much easier a sharp edge makes your work."

■ A.M. Leonard. *241 Fox Dr., Piqua, OH 45356; (800) 543-8955 or www.amleo.com.*

■ Denman & Co. *401 W. Chapman Ave., Orange, CA 92866; (714) 639-8106.*

■ Lee Valley Tools. *Box 1780, Ogdensburg, NY 13669; (800) 871-8158 or www.leevalley.com.*

■ Peaceful Valley Farm Supply. *Box 2209, Grass Valley, CA 95945; (888) 784-1722 or www.groworganic.com.*

■ Walt Nicke Company. *Box 433, Topsfield, MA 01983; (978) 887-3388 or www.gardentalk.com.* ◆

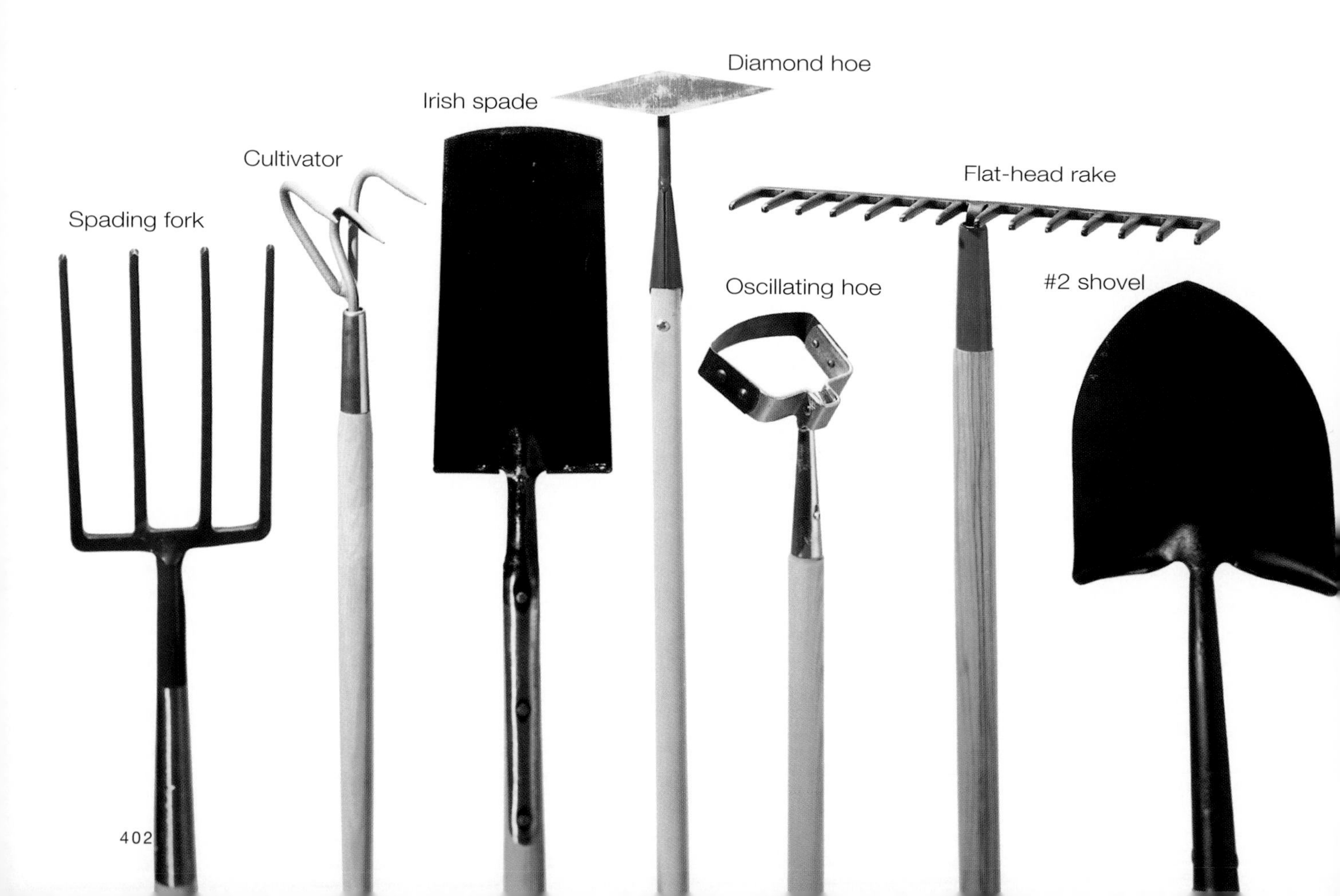

Article Titles Index

CROCOSMIA

ALL PHOTOS IN BOTH INDEXES BY NORMAN A. PLATE

HYACINTH

O

P

Q

R

S

T

U

V

W

Y

Z

DAFFODIL

General Subject Index

ORIENTAL AND ASIATIC LILIES WITH DAHLIAS

ACIDANTHERA

D

CALLA

H

I

DAHLIA

J

K

L

M

TUBEROSE

N

ORIENTAL LILY

O

P

GLADIOLUS, DAHLIAS, AND LILIES

Q

R

S

GLADIOLUS

T

LIATRIS

U

V

W

GRASSES AND WILDFLOWERS

Y

Z